The Costume Technician's Handbook

Third Edition

THE
Costume

Technician's
HANDBOOK

Third Edition

Rosemary Ingham
Liz Covey

HEINEMANN • PORTSMOUTH, NH

Photograph page ii: By Jay Westhauser, courtesy of the Milwaukee Repertory Theatre
Photograph page iii: By Carol Rosegg, courtesy of The Shakespeare Theatre
Photograph page xiii: Petticoat and bustle on actor Mitzi McKay portraying Queen Victoria
with cutter/draper Joan Mather. Photograph by Rosemary Ingham
Photograph page 435: Rehearsal of a scene from Tantalus *at the Denver Center*
Theatre Company. Photograph courtesy of Kevin Copenhaver

Heinemann
A division of Reed Elsevier Inc.
361 Hanover Street
Portsmouth, NH 03801–3912
www.heinemanndrama.com

Offices and agents throughout the world

Library of Congress Cataloging-in-Publication Data
Ingham, Rosemary.
   The costume technician's handbook / Rosemary Ingham, Liz Covey—3rd ed.
      p. cm.
   First ed. published 1980 under title: The costumer's handbook.
   Includes bibliographical references and index.
      ISBN 0-325-00477-3
      1. Costume design. 2. Costume. I. Covey, Liz. II. Ingham, Rosemary. Costumer's
handbook. III. Title.
   TT507.I47 2003
   646.4'78—dc21   2003007797

Editor: Lisa Barnett
Production: Lynne Reed
Cover design: Jenny Jensen Greenleaf
Cover photograph: Petronia Paley as Jocasta and Avery Brooks as Oedipus in *The Oedipus Plays*
at The Shakespeare Theatre. Costume design by Toni-Leslie James. Photograph by Carol
Rosegg, courtesy of The Shakespeare Theatre (see Plate 7).
Typesetter: The GTS Companies/York, PA Campus
Manufacturing: Steve Bernier

Printed in the United States of America on acid-free paper

07 06 05 04 03 RRD 1 2 3 4 5

Contents

Reference

Website of additional resources, including a Shopping Guide/Source List:
http://www.heinemanndrama.com/ingham-covey

Foreword

If the magical province of designers is that of seeing and dreaming, then the quintessential challenge belongs to the costume technicians who are the talented organizers who make those dreams take form. As dreamers and creators of images, we designers inhabit a world that can transcend time, space, and practical consideration for a while, but ultimately if we are to share our visions with anyone, we must come down to earth, talk with our technicians, and decide how we will make it all!

Our world is filled with disparate and wildly wonderful media: from feathers to fake mud, intricate beadwork to dental algenate, painted silk to melted plastic. What a grab bag of heady and hilarious things we find ourselves making! From the glove for a would-be king's deformed hand (Rosemary's and my first show together), or a ghostly specter who disrupts a meal, to just the right body padding that keeps an otherwise dignified and respectable soprano from bounding back into view after she has "leapt" to her death in *Tosca,* we create it all.

Dreams and reality come together in the costume shop—where hard work and the right technique can actually imbue a lump of clay and materials developed during America's space program into something that has its own spirit, an object that transcends its makers and in the most inspired of hands could be almost worthy of the priest-artisans of ancient Egypt.

It was in the old basement costume shop of the Milwaukee Rep that I first met Rosemary and Liz in the late 1970s. That tiny, concrete-floored shop with only two cutting tables generated not only wonderfully costumed shows but also lifelong friendships, and was in fact the seedbed where ideas for this book were first planted some twenty-plus years and three editions ago. Time has shown how valuable indeed *The Costume Technician's Handbook* has been to our business and its training programs.

Liz Covey and Rosemary Ingham have created what many professionals regard as one of the best handbooks in the business. *The Costume Technician's Handbook* possesses a wealth of information that is easily accessible, clear, precise, and well-supported with illustrations and photos. As times have changed, so has the content of each successive edition. Costuming becomes more sophisticated with each passing year, and new materials and technologies expand the world in which we work. Our authors—vital, inspired, and inspiring women who look at the world around them with questing spirit and wonder in their eyes—have updated this edition marvelously, most notably adding a detailed section on costume shop management and one that explores the present, and future, impact of computer technology on our work.

Since this book's first printing in 1980, I have not seen a shop without a copy of it, or heard a teacher who has not praised it as a valuable teaching tool. Both *The Costume Designer's Handbook* and *The Costume Technician's Handbook* are among the first books my undergraduate designers acquire for their own libraries, and veteran technicians in acclaimed shops across the country still find themselves accessing excellent material on which they can rely. (Personally, I still use the terrific bibliography at the back of the book as a resource today!)

I believe that teachers, parents, and authors who pass on their passions and knowledge share something in common: we are all indomitable optimists. We care about the future and can imagine it as being greater than the present. Future generations of costume technicians and costume lovers will have this fantastic updated helpmate at their sides as they set out to make those visions and dreams in the sketches into realities on the stage.

Thank you, Rosemary and Liz, for this wonderful gift!

—Susan Tsu
Costume Designer
Professor of Costume Design
Carnegie-Mellon University

Acknowledgments

Hundreds of colleagues, friends, and loved ones have contributed to this book. We thank you all.

The following is a partial list of people and organizations without whom, literally, *The Costume Technician's Handbook* would never have happened:

Janet Addis
Jon Aitchison
Frances Aronson
Susan Ashdown
Mark Avery
M. L. Baker
Keith Belli
Diane R. Berg
Frances Blau
Noel Borden
Rita Brown
Richard Bryant
Colleen Callahan
Pat Cavins
Laura Crow
Hillary Derby
Deborah M. Dryden
Suzanne Elder
Julie Engelbrecht
James Glavan
Susan Griffin
Susan Hilferty
Richard Ingham
Robert Ingham
Stephen Ingham
Nagle Jackson
Barbara Joyce
Nancy Julian
Jeffrey Lieder
Lynne Mackey
Colleen Muscha
Beth Novak
Sara O'Connor
Mary Ann Powell
John Saari
Mindy Simons
Jennifer Smith-Windsor
Deborah Trout
Susan Tsu
Carol Wells-Day
Randy Wimer
Arena Stage
Hartford Stage Company
McCarter Theatre
Milwaukee Repertory Theater
TheatreVirginia
Utah Shakespearean Festival
Valentine Museum

Additional Acknowledgments for Third Edition

Gordon DeVinney
David E. Draper
Susan Falk
Amanda French
Cynda Flores Galikin
Sara Gruber
Amy Horst
Sally Kessler
Marsha LeBoeuf
Donna Marie
Joanne Martin
Celestine Ranney-Howes
Nanalee Raphael
Monona Rossol
Pat Seyler
Stephanie Schoelzel
Christine Smith-McNamara
Ann Stephens
Gina Truelove

Virginia Vogel
Tom Watson
James Wolk
Actors Theatre of Louisville
American Conservatory Theater
Berkeley Repertory Theatre

Opera Theatre of Saint Louis
The Repertory Theatre of St. Louis
The Shakespeare Theatre
And a special thanks to everyone who responded to the questionnaire that helped us to focus this revision.

The Costume Technician's Handbook

Third Edition

COSTUMIING

1
The Costume Shop

Many changes have taken place in costume shops since the last revision of *The Costume Technician's Handbook* in 1992. Most of these have involved increased functionality in the design of work space, the widespread use of so-phisticated construction and craft equipment, and in the organization of shop personnel (see Chapter 10 for a discussion of costume shop management and staffing). It remains true that skilled technicians can produce beautiful, well-

FIGURE 1–1. A view of the costume shop at the American Conservatory Theater. *Photograph by Rosemary Ingham.*

1

FIGURE 1–2. The costume shop
at the Guthrie Theater.
Photograph by Maribeth Hite.

made theatrical costumes in less-than-efficient settings. However, even though top quality costume construction is not necessarily dependent on top quality work space, it's always a frustrating experience to work in an uncomfortable room without adequate light, electricity, machinery, or supplies. Costume technicians—professional, student, and amateur—deserve comfortable, functional space, and the best equipment their producing groups can supply.

Each year many new theatre facilities are built or adapted from existing structures. Unfortunately, there is no certainty that new theatres will have adequate costume shops. Costume shop requirements often receive low priority when budget and space cuts must be

made, and the costume construction area is often the victim. As a result, many recently built theatre complexes have inconveniently located, poorly lighted, badly ventilated costume shops, where mazes of electrical extension cords, in obvious violation of building safety codes, are necessary to operate machines.

On the other hand, many well-designed costume shops exist, some new and some old, some lavish and some done on a modest scale. These are the shops where costume designers and technicians work best, where they produce consistently good work, in a safe, pleasant, professional atmosphere. These are the shops that set a standard of excellence for the whole profession.

General Space

Only rarely does a costume designer or technician have a hand in laying out the actual space for a costume shop in a new building. If you do have this happy opportunity, make a careful estimate of how much space you need by listing

and measuring all the furnishings and machinery the shop will actually house. Draw a ground plan, place the furniture and machines in the space, then add a generous amount of room for traffic flow. Consider the advantages of having separate rooms or walled-off areas for cutting and stitching, crafts, dyeing, and laundry. Determine the amount of costume storage area you will need, in the present *and* in the future, and do not locate it too far from the shop. Make sure there is easy access from the shop to the dressing rooms and to the stage.

Costume shop walls should be built from materials that will support shelving and bulletin boards. Tile floors are the easiest to keep clean and, next to wood, provide the most forgiving surface for legs and feet. If concrete floors are unavoidable, see that they are adequately sealed, and make sure the budget allows for rubber mats to be placed in all the areas where people must stand a great deal.

Make safety a top priority from the first moment you begin to discuss plans for a new or renovated costume shop. Adequate ventilation is a prime concern, and your ventilating system will be more efficient and more economical if it's part of the original plan. For a detailed discussion of costume shop safety, see Chapter 2, "Health and Safety in the Costume Shop."

Before you begin to plan your new or renovated costume shop, visit other costume shops and talk to other costume designers and technicians. Even though each costume shop is unique, all shops share certain universal concerns, such as light, electricity, and machinery. As you see how other shops have solved common problems, you will be better able to find the best solutions for your own situation.

Light

It's unfortunate that natural light is such a rarity in costume shops. Far too many costume shops, in both professional and university theatres, are situated below ground level or in the interior of a building, without windows.

Aside from a multitude of aesthetic considerations, the presence of natural light has the same practical importance to a costume designer or technician as it has to a painter. Colors and textures must be matched, fabrics dyed, costumes painted and shaded. Architects, who would never consider planning a painter's studio without natural light, preferably a northern exposure, continue to locate costume shops in windowless areas. When costume technicians spend long, unrelieved hours working in artificial light, their enthusiasm for

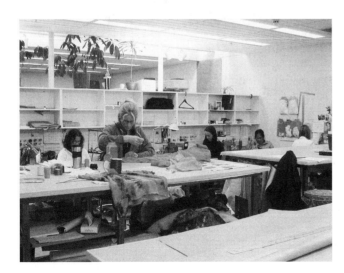

FIGURE 1–3. Natural and fluorescent light illuminate an area of the costume shop at the Oregon Shakespeare Festival. *Photograph by Rosemary Ingham.*

their work, and the quality of the work itself, are bound to suffer, particularly during the added stress of tech week.

A very good, commonly seen lighting situation for a costume shop is natural light, supplemented by a combination of fluorescent and incandescent lamps.

Ordinary fluorescent light creates good general illumination, and it's economical. Most fluorescent tubes, however, cast a chilly glow that can make a workplace seem harsh and institutional. Worst of all, most fluorescent light alters color, especially blues and reds, and flattens out texture. With or without natural light, ordinary fluorescent lighting, by itself, is not satisfactory in most costume shops.

Incandescent light allows you to see color and texture closer to the way they appear in natural light. However, incandescent lamps produce heat, and a shop lighted entirely with incandescent light soon becomes uncomfortably warm. Also, incandescent lamps are more expensive to operate than fluorescent tubes.

Adequate artificial light for costume shops, with or without natural light, is a combination of fluorescent light for general illumination and incandescent light in specific work areas. Simple track lighting, with incandescent lamps placed over the cutting table, in the craft and dye areas, and in the fitting rooms, is ideal. Make sure the fluorescent and incandescent lighting systems operate separately. For the greatest comfort and economy, install the incandescent lamps so they can be turned off and on separately or in clusters.

When you must rely entirely on artificial light in your costume shop, concentrate on creating warm work spaces, with specific light focused where it is most needed. Inexpensive architect's lamps, which fasten easily to the edges of tables, can greatly improve the quality of area work light.

If your shop doesn't have windows and fluorescent fixtures are your main light source, you might consider using color-corrected fluorescent tubes that produce light that "looks" like sunlight. Most of the companies that manufacture fluorescent tubes make a color-corrected variety. The price of color-corrected fluorescent tubes is higher than ordinary fluorescent tubes. However, most color-corrected fluorescent tubes have longer lives than ordinary tubes.

Electricity

Every costume shop needs an adequate amount of electrical current and a large number of outlets, conveniently placed. When the positions for electrical outlets are planned, remember that the arrangement of the shop space probably will not stay constant for all the years to come. Plan for the future as well as for the present.

Consider installing electrical outlet strips at the height of the machine tables rather than at floor level. With this arrangement, masses of electrical cords on the floor, catching dust, will be avoided. If strip outlets are planned, however, make sure it is known how many items can be plugged in before the circuits are overloaded. Irons, steamers, and hot glue guns all place heavy loads on the electrical capacity. Do not assume you have enough current; find out.

Electric clothes dryers and dye vats require more electrical current than the other machinery in the shop and 220-volt lines will be needed in the areas where these machines will be. Again, plan for the future. If you think you will add a second dryer in a couple of years, have two 220-volt outlets installed at the same time; it's cheaper.

Water

It's hard to work in any costume shop without a water source nearby. Even if you don't do laundry or dyeing in the shop, you still need to wash your hands at regular intervals when you are working with fabrics and craft materials.

In a large costume shop complex, adequate plumbing is a major consideration. Hot and cold running water must be available, with hook-ups for washing machines and dye vats, and good drainage.

Stainless steel sinks are preferable to any other type because they are easy to clean and impervious to most of the dyes and chemicals used in costume shops.

Setting Up Specific Work Spaces

Cutting and Draping Area

The center of every cutting and draping area is the cutting table. The ideal cutting table should be a flat, sturdy surface, wide enough to lay out a 45-inch wide piece of fabric, and between six and eight feet long. It should stand about waist high. (This is approximately 10 inches higher than a normal dining room table, which, if used for cutting, is guaranteed to produce a backache in anybody over 4'10" in height.)

You should be able to stick pins into the cutting table surface to hold your patterns and fabrics in place. In many shops the cutting tables are covered with ½-inch thick cork sheets. Cork makes a beautiful working surface, but it does have some disadvantages. It's expensive, hard to clean if something is accidentally spilled on it, and, after a couple of years of use, cork bits begin to chip away. A practical cutting table surface can be created with a sheet of homosote (also called wallboard, fiberboard, or building board) covered with muslin, brown paper, or plastic sheeting. Homosote is durable, the cover can be replaced whenever it gets dirty, and it's much less expensive than cork.

When you need to fashion temporary cutting tables, use folding banquet tables or ping-pong tables and set them up on wooden blocks, bricks, or cinderblocks. Cover a sheet of homosote, lay it on top, and you're in business.

Position cutting tables so they are accessible from all four sides. When cutting large capes or skirts with trains, it's helpful to be able to circle the whole table.

FIGURE 1–4. An improvised cutting table at the University of Maryland consisting of chests of drawers on a raised platform with a plywood and covered homosote top. *Photograph by Liz Covey.*

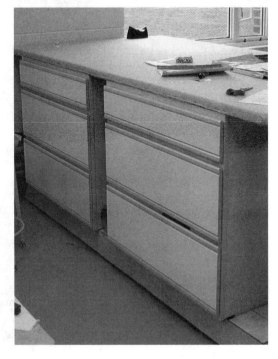

The space under the cutting table may be organized in many ways: shelves, drawers, bins, racks, and so on. The most efficient cutting tables have places for drafting tools, general supplies, brown paper, patterns, muslin, and cutting scraps.

The area around the cutting table should include adequate space for tailor's dummies and, ideally, a bulletin board to hang sketches, small pattern pieces, and bits of research material. A stool or chair that is the correct height for the cutting table should also be available. (See Figures 1–4 and 1–5 for examples of the above.)

Machine-Stitching Area

In some shops, sewing machines are all in a single area, often lined up along one wall. In others, two or three machines are grouped around each cutting area. In a great many shops, sewing machines end up wherever there are electrical outlets. Wherever the machines are placed, each one should have an adequate work light. The built-in light on a domestic sewing machine is not enough. An industrial sewing lamp or an architect's lamp fixed to each sewing table is ideal.

All sewing machines should sit on sturdy tables that do not shake when the machines are run. A wobbly table is not only distracting to the machine operator, the vibrations can actually cause machine parts to loosen up. Many of the tables and cabinets sold with domestic sewing machines are not sturdy enough for costume shop use. Be sure to try out a sewing table before you buy it. Consider building your own. Industrial sewing machines must be installed in appropriate industrial machine tables.

Most sewing machine tables have drawers for sewing supplies and notions. Some sort of

FIGURE 1–5. A custom-built cutting table with storage at the University of Cincinnati College-Conservatory of Music. *Photograph by Rosemary Ingham.*

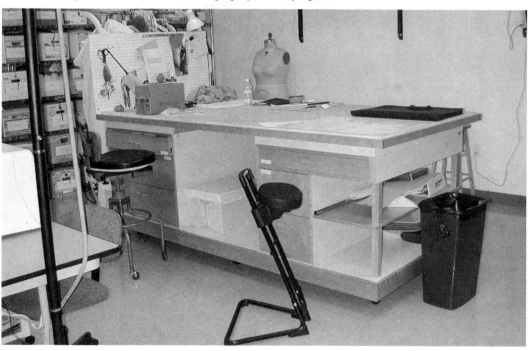

FIGURE 1–6. Bulletin board and patterns at the Oregon Shakespeare Festival. *Photograph by Rosemary Ingham.*

container for pins is handy to have, especially one that is fastened to the table to prevent spills. A magnetic pin catcher pad attached to the flat bed of a sewing machine is also useful. Do not, however, attach magnetic pin catchers to computerized sewing machines because the magnetic pad will interfere with the electronic controls.

Store threads near the machine sewing area. Wall racks for threads are particularly convenient and can be made easily by driving long nails into a board. Equip each machine with a multiple spool thread stand to allow use of large thread spools and cones, even with domestic machines. Thread is much cheaper when purchased in large quantities, and the stitching on all machines is more consistent when the thread feeds from a thread stand.

Equip each sewing machine with a pair of thread snipping scissors. Industrial thread nippers wear much better than the ones bought at the local fabric shop, and they cost about the same. Tie the nippers to the machine or tack them to the table with a ribbon short enough so the nippers will not hit the floor if they are dropped.

Each sewing machine should have a protective cover, cloth or plastic, to be put on when the machine is not in use.

Costume technicians sit at their sewing machines for many hours at a stretch. Make sure each machine operator has a chair that is the correct height and gives adequate back support. Adjustable, rolling, office-type chairs are comfortable and convenient, although threads will have to be snipped out of the wheels at regular intervals to keep them on the move.

Hand-Stitching Area

Plan a pleasant hand-stitching area somewhere in the shop. Make available good illumination—

FIGURE 1–7. Sewing machines at the University of Washington. *Photograph by Steve Cochran.*

FIGURE 1–8. An industrial Bernina. *Photograph by Liz Covey.*

next to a window if possible—comfortable seating, and a convenient surface to hold supplies and a cup of coffee or tea, if it's permitted.

Pressing Area

Locate the pressing area near the sewing machines. Make sure there is a shelf or a table near the ironing surface where pressing aids can be kept.

FIGURE 1–9. An industrial ironing board at the University of Maryland. *Photograph by Rosemary Ingham.*

FIGURE 1–9A. An industrial iron. *Photograph by Rosemary Ingham.*

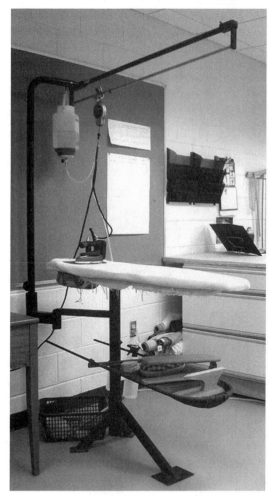

Purchase an industrial ironing board if at all possible. Domestic ironing boards are not sturdy enough for costume shop work; even the heaviest of them will tip over when pressing heavy capes and gowns. Most industrial ironing boards have baskets underneath that keep trains, floor length skirts, and long pieces of fabric from dragging on the floor.

Many costume shops use ironing tables instead of or in addition to ironing boards. Convert an ordinary wood table into an ironing table or have one built to your own specifications in the scene shop. Pad the surface of the table with something soft but firm, like a wool blanket, and cover it with muslin. Use pressing boards, tailor's hams, and other aids on top of the ironing table. (See Figures 1–9 and 1–10 for examples of an industrial ironing board and an ironing table.)

Craft and Dye Areas

Ideally, the craft and dye areas should be separated from the cutting and stitching area to minimize the opportunities for spilling accidents and to contain potentially hazardous chemicals. Even if separate rooms are not available, mask off the craft and dye areas with

9

FIGURE 1–10. An ironing table at the University of Washington. *Photograph by Steve Cochran.*

screens or stage flats. Hot and cold running water is essential in craft and dye areas, as are good lighting, sufficient electrical current, and adequate ventilation.

For more detailed discussions about craft and dye areas, see Chapter 2, "Health and Safety in the Costume Shop," Chapter 7, "Fabric Dyeing and Painting," and Chapter 9, "Costume Accessories and Properties."

Laundry Area

When a single area is used for doing laundry and for dyeing fabric, it is very difficult to prevent accidental dye staining unless every person who uses the machines and surfaces for dyeing purposes cleans up scrupulously after each task. Many theatre costume shop technicians are forced, because of space constraints or limited budgets, to work under these less-than-satisfactory conditions: dyeing fabric and laundering costumes in the same room and in the same machines. Ideally the theatre laundry area should be completely separate from the craft and dye areas and, if at all possible, convenient to the dressing rooms.

FIGURE 1–11. Small laundry area created from limited space at the Berkeley Repertory Theatre. *Photograph by Rosemary Ingham.*

10

FIGURE 1–12. Laundry facilities serving Opera Theatre of Saint Louis and The Repertory Theatre of St. Louis. *Photograph by James Wolk.*

Supply Storage

Locate stock supply storage as conveniently as possible to the general work area. Try not to put frequently used items on high shelves or behind less frequently used items. Medium-sized metal or wooden drawer units are excellent to store pins, needles, tracing papers, elastic, seam bindings, and so on, and they can usually be purchased reasonably from office

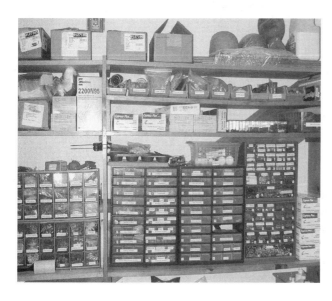

FIGURE 1–13. Some well-organized storage shelves at The Washington Opera costume shop. *Photograph by Rosemary Ingham.*

FIGURE 1–14. Stock fabric storage on a wall. *Photograph by Liz Covey.*

supply stores or at office liquidation sales. Old metal drawers will operate smoothly after they have been treated with a silicone lubricant.

Store currently used threads on thread racks; they will stay neater than if they are put on a shelf or in a drawer. Stock threads should remain covered in their boxes.

Frequently used fabrics, such as muslin, linings, and interlinings, and large quantities of stock trims are more accessible when stored on shelves or on racks than when tucked away in boxes or drawers. Take the time to roll stock fabrics on cardboard bolt boards or tubes before storing them; the fabrics won't get wrinkled and will be easier for the cutter to handle.

In the hand-stitching area, keep a supply of small containers to hold pins, thimbles, hooks and eyes, and buttons. If these items are in containers, they are less apt to end up on the floor and are much easier to return to the storage area once the work is complete. Cover bars of hard soap with scraps of fabric to make nee-dle storage cushions; the soap helps to keep the points sharp.

Stock Storage

Ideally, the stock storage area should be near but separate from the work area. If space permits, it's good to have one area for hanging stock and another for boxed stock. Both areas should be dry and protected from temperature extremes. Damp heat is particularly harmful to fabrics.

Very few theatres have enclosed ward-robes for hanging costumes. Banks of pipe racks are common. Racks for storing full-length period garments should be 6 feet tall, and even then trains will have to be looped up over another clothes hanger. Lower, double-tiered racks are suitable for storing men's suits, trousers, jackets, and contemporary daytime dresses. Make sure there are sturdy rolling racks available for moving costumes from place

FIGURE 1–15. Pipe rack costume storage at the Seattle Repertory Theatre.
Photograph by Liz Covey.

to place and rolling ladders that stop automatically when stepped on.

Shoes and boots are more accessible if they are stored on relatively shallow shelves rather than in deep boxes or bins. Sort shoes by size and fasten pairs together. Men's shoes should be in one area, women's shoes in another.

The box storage area should have shelves for small boxes and shelves for larger boxes. Adjustable metal shelving is ideal for this purpose. Never use storage boxes that are so large it is difficult to lift them when they are full. Thick cardboard boxes with close-fitting tops and hand holds are particularly good. Shoe boxes make suitable containers for small items, like handkerchiefs, gloves, and collars. When a box gets too full, separate the contents into two boxes.

Label each box clearly with its contents and be as detailed and specific as possible. Make a chart showing where specific boxes are located in the storage area and hang it in a prominent place.

Fitting Area

The fitting area is one of the most important spaces in the costume shop. It's next to impossible to conduct a careful, concentrated fitting in the open shop where there are far too many distractions, and where the actor, if he or she

13

FIGURE 1–16. A rolling ladder with "brakes" that are automatically applied when it is stepped on. *Photograph by Liz Covey.*

doesn't actively protest the lack of privacy, will find it impossible to relax under the gaze of the entire staff. If a separate room for fittings is not available, construct a private fitting space with curtains, screens, or flats.

The ideal costume fitting requires the presence of four people: the actor; the designer; the cutter, shop supervisor, or whoever is responsible for marking alterations on the garment; and another staff member who records fitting notes. Even if the staff is too small for the ideal, always try to have somebody on hand whose job it is to take notes. It's so easy to forget fitting details if they aren't written down immediately. The fitting area, therefore, must be large enough for several people to work in comfortably.

Outfit the fitting area with a full-length mirror, preferably three-way, one or two chairs, and a small table or cupboard for supplies, such as pins, marking chalk, tape measures, scissors, hairpins, wig caps, shoe horn, and so on. Provide a rack of some kind on which to hang the costumes and the actor's own clothing.

Atmosphere

Any place where costumes are being built is a busy place. Technicians—professional, student, or amateur—spend long hours at their various tasks, and it's important to make every costume construction space as comfortable and as attractive as possible.

Paint the walls a light color. Decorate with plants and posters and put sheets of covered homosote on the walls for bulletin boards. It's almost impossible to have too many bulletin boards in a costume shop. Everything, from designer's sketches to work schedules, machine threading diagrams, menus from local take-out restaurants, and the film program from the local movie theatre, inevitably turns up on costume shop bulletin boards.

Arrange work areas to allow conversation between staff members and to let the shop manager observe the whole range of shop activities without having to peer around corners.

FIGURE 1–17. A creative and colorful corner of the costume shop at Arena Stage. *Photograph by Liz Covey.*

Costume shops are little communities and it's important to arrange the space as creatively as possible.

Make sure the equipment for making coffee and tea is available and try to fit in a refrigerator to store perishable food and drinks, and a microwave oven for food preparation. If space is available, it is always a good idea to create a separate area for eating, relaxing, and, when the occasions arise, celebrating birthdays and other special events. Good work is always better in pleasant surroundings with congenial companions.

Machinery in the Costume Shop

Lock Stitch Sewing Machines

The first sewing machine was patented in 1790 by Thomas Saint, an Englishman. The machine was made of wood, executed a single-thread chain stitch, and was designed to sew leather. It never worked very well. In 1830, Barthélemy Thimonnier of France devised a machine to make soldiers' uniforms. It also carried a single thread, which was formed into a stitch by the backward and forward movement of a hooked needle. At one time, the French government had eighty of these machines in use. Unfortunately, inventor Thimonnier was almost killed when a mob of angry garment workers attacked him for inventing a machine that put men out of work.

Elias Howe invented the modern sewing machine. His model, patented in 1846, was the first practical sewing machine that could be manufactured in quantity and sold at a reasonable price. Howe's machine had a needle with an eye near the point. A shuttle carried thread below the cloth on a small bobbin, and the needle, carrying an upper thread, was fastened to an arm that vibrated on a pivot. The movement of the arm forced the needle through the cloth. The shuttle carried the under thread through the loop of the upper thread, forming a lock stitch. This is essentially the same mechanism used by the majority of domestic and industrial sewing machines manufactured today.

In 1851, the Singer Sewing Machine Company, under the enterprising leadership of Isaac Singer, developed the popular foot treadle machine, and, in 1889, Singer became the first manufacturer to put an electric motor on a sewing machine. By the turn of the century, Singer Company mechanics were busy converting old Singer treadle machines into electrically powered machines.

Today the manufacture of sewing machines and related equipment is a huge, highly competitive, international industry. Several companies produce domestic machines for the home sewing market, and others manufacture machinery for the garment and interior decorating industries. Some companies, such as Pfaff and Bernina, manufacture both domestic and industrial equipment.

The majority of sewing machines found in costume shops today are lock stitch machines, both domestic and industrial models. Most shops also have one or more sergers, also called overlock machines. Sergers are also available in both domestic and industrial models. Special use machines such as blindstitch machines widely used in the garment industry, are useful additions to many costume shops.

Industrial Sewing Machines

Industrial sewing machines are built for hard, constant use in the garment industry. Each individual industrial machine performs a limited number of operations, unlike domestic machines, many of which execute two or three dozen different stitches *and* make buttonholes automatically. Industrial sewing machines stitch with great precision at high speeds. Most are equipped with knee controls to raise and lower the presser foot, saving the operator many hand movements, and with bobbin winding devices that wind a bobbin from a separate spool of thread while the machine is in normal operation.

The majority of industrial sewing machines found in costume shops are straight stitch machines or machines that execute both a straight and zigzag stitch. Specialized industrial machines that do only a chain stitch or single- and double-needle decorative stitching, make bar tacks, or apply cording are invaluable in factories but have limited use in costume shops.

The busier the costume shop, the more important it is to have and use industrial sewing machines. They out-perform and out-last even top-of-the-line domestics. Train students and new employees to operate industrial equipment properly and the work rate in your

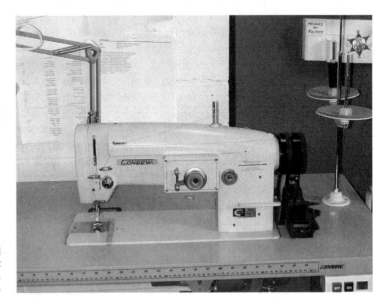

FIGURE 1–18. A sturdy industrial Consew which makes straight and zig-zag stitches. *Photograph by Liz Covey.*

shop will pick up. And the stitching will be more consistent.

How to Purchase Industrial Sewing Machines

Industrial sewing machines are expensive. When you purchase a new one, you must buy the machine head, motor, and table. Although some costume shops are able to fit a new industrial machine purchase into their budgets, many shops turn to the secondhand market with good results.

Manufacturers of industrial equipment are constantly upgrading their machinery, and garment factories, always anxious to increase their efficiency and performance, buy new and improved models, selling their old models at a fraction of their original cost. Also, because the garment industry is so volatile, firms frequently go out of business, putting scores of used machines on the market.

Even if there are no garment factories in your geographic area, you can buy a used industrial sewing machine through a garment industry supplier. If you purchase a used machine through a reputable supplier, you can be reasonably sure it's in good condition, and you can probably get a limited, three- to six-months warranty. The Internet is a good place to begin your search for such a company.

If you don't know anything about industrial sewing machines, be sure to talk with someone who does before making the purchase. Call a large costume shop, a garment factory, a tailor shop, or the alteration room of a department store or dress shop. Find out what kinds of industrial equipment they have and how they like them. Ask to visit and try out the machines yourself.

Industrial machine brands most often seen in costume shops in recent years include Bernina, Consew, Juki, Pfaff, and Singer, although you will find many more brands on the market when you set out to purchase one, as well as a bewildering array of model numbers to sort through. Although the vast majority of industrial machines manufactured throughout the twentieth century are wholly mechanical in operation, electronic components and programming features are beginning to appear and their use will certainly increase in the future. Along with its standard line of industrial machines, Bernina manufactures a versatile, multipurpose, lightweight industrial model that has been described as the "logical step up from a home machine." Its electronic components allow for a small number of built-in stitches as well as a buttonholer.

Industrial sewing machine model numbers refer only to the machine heads. Motors to power the machines, one-quarter- to one-half-horsepower, come separately, sometimes with tables. If you buy from a large supplier, however, you can usually purchase all the components from the same place. Secondhand machines most often come complete with table and motor. When you buy a secondhand industrial machine, be sure to find out whether the motor runs on 110-volt or 220-volt electricity.

Domestic Sewing Machines

At least half the sewing machines in most costume shops are domestic models. For costume technicians who have had limited experience with industrial equipment, domestic machines are much more familiar than industrial machines. And compared with new industrial machines, they are also much less expensive.

At the present time the most popular domestic sewing machine in American costume shops is manufactured by Bernina, a Swiss company. Technicians in professional shops report that they are sturdy and reliable; teachers of costume technology add that Berninas are particularly good choices in shops where students are learning to stitch, often for the first time. "They're simple to operate and the students learn quickly," one teacher reports. "And they manage to stand up under all the mistakes beginning students inevitably make." Bernina is one of the few manufacturers of high-quality domestic sewing machines that still makes an entirely mechanical model. Many costume technicians put great faith in machines, both old and new, that do not rely on electronic technology, and this mechanical Bernina is, at present, a great favorite; and it is modestly priced.

Other domestic sewing machine brands that are well represented in costume shops are Viking, Singer, Pfaff, Elna, and Kenmore, both the automatic stitch models that perform a wide variety of operations, and the older straight stitch or straight and zigzag combination stitch models.

Domestic sewing machines with electronic control boards and those with programmable features found their places in the American marketplace during the last quarter of the twentieth century. Although there are many brands of "computerized" machines, the most reliable (and most expensive) are manufactured by the Bernina, Huskvarna (Viking), and Pfaff companies. At the beginning of the twenty-first century, machines with electronic components that control a variety of sewing functions such as defining specific stitches, creating buttonholes, and allowing for variable up and down needle positions are found quite commonly in costume shops. Programmable machines—those that have memory capabilities and can execute more complex tasks, from making several buttonholes that are identical in size to creating, "remembering," and stitching elaborate embroidery patterns—are found less often. Many costume technicians feel that programmable machines are "too complicated," "too finicky," and "too troublesome" for the work they do. Indeed, many of these machines will perform a host of functions that few stitchers in any setting will ever use and it is always a good decision to choose a machine, for whatever purpose, that is as simple as possible but still meets the intended needs. Common sense tells us that

FIGURE 1–19. A versatile domestic Bernina. *Photograph by Liz Covey.*

fewer frills on costume shop sewing machines translate into fewer visits to the repair shop.

Sewing Machine Maintenance

In garment factories, where the sewing machine operators work on piece wage rates, each stitcher is responsible for routine cleaning of and minor adjustments to his or her machine. Naturally, it's to the operator's advantage to maintain the machine carefully so as not to lose valuable work time and income because of breakdowns. Costume technicians should develop the same habits, even without the piece wage incentive. Nothing is more frustrating than to have to stop working in the midst of a construction project because a machine is not functioning properly.

The majority of sewing machine breakdowns can be prevented by routine maintenance and by good operator habits.

Practice the following maintenance routine:

1. Brush lint away from the feed teeth and bobbin *at least* once a day, and two or three times a day if the machine is running steadily or if the material being stitched is especially linty.

Be sure you know if your machine is a self-oiling or a factory-oiled model. If it is *not* factory-oiled or self-oiling:

2. Clean thoroughly, and oil the machine once a week under normal use (approximately thirty hours per week) and more often when the use is heavier. Make sure both the top and bottom of the machine are cleaned and oiled.

3. Put a drop of oil on the bobbin casing, right under the hook, after *every five-hour sewing period.*

Many industrial sewing machines are self-oiling. They have enclosed oil reserves and a lubricating system that puts oil where it belongs when it's needed. The hook is usually lubricated when the machine is in operation. Self-oiling machines have a gauge indicating when the oil supply needs to be replenished.

Computerized sewing machines and some machines with electronic components are factory-oiled. Never put oil anywhere on a factory-oiled machine.

Even if the machine is self-oiling or factory-oiled, it still has to be cleaned, so don't forget to brush away the lint at regular intervals.

All sewing machines, industrial and domestic, benefit from routine yearly maintenance by a qualified repairperson.

Here are a few helpful hints for sewing machine operators:

1. Never use a screwdriver or other metal object to clean lint from your machine. You may scratch or damage parts. A wooden toothpick is an ideal instrument to remove lint from hard-to-reach places.

2. Never remove the bottom plate on a self-oiling, industrial sewing machine. This is where the oil pads are located.

3. Don't operate the machine if the needle is bent or defective. Change the needle immediately.

4. Never run the machine without the bobbin case in place or the sewing hook may become damaged.

5. Never wind the bobbin or run the machine with the presser foot down and no fabric under it. The feed teeth will scratch the bottom of the presser foot and may be damaged by it.

6. Always turn the machine wheel toward you.

7. When you're adjusting the bobbin tension, never turn the adjusting screw more than one quarter turn at a time.

8. Keep the outside of the machine clean and cover it when it's not in use.

In a shop where there are more stitchers than machines and several people use each machine, make sure that everyone knows how to operate and clean all the equipment. End each work period with time left for each operator to brush away the day's lint and oil the bobbin, if necessary. Rotate the weekly oiling schedule among the technicians.

In every shop there's always one staff member with a special knack for working with machinery. Encourage this person to learn more about the equipment, to observe when the repairperson is in the shop, and to perform simple adjustments and repairs.

Sewing Machine Needles

No part of the sewing machine takes greater punishment than the needle. So many stitching malfunctions are caused by bent, blunted, or incorrectly inserted needles that the first response to any stitching problem should be to change the needle. You may be using the wrong needle for the type of thread you're using or for the fabric you're stitching. More commonly, the needle may be slightly bent or blunted. A blunted needle may snag the cloth or refuse to penetrate the weave. A bent needle may not pick up the bobbin thread, and it may scratch the machine plate. If the needle is inserted incorrectly, so that the position of the long groove on the needle shank is not directly below the last thread guide, the machine simply will not stitch.

Purchase the best quality sewing machine needles you can afford, in bulk, from an industrial supply company. Keep a good supply on hand and do not practice false economy by continuing to use a machine needle after it's been damaged. Use the correct weight needle for the fabric being stitched; the needle used to stitch wool flannel will not do as good a job on batiste.

Most domestic sewing machine needles will work in most domestic machines, no matter what the brand. The Bernina company manufactures good needles and sells them in bulk. Schmetz needles, made in Germany, are also excellent. Cheap needles are never economical.

Industrial machines require a different kind of needle than domestic models, and the needles are not necessarily interchangeable between brands and models. If you don't know which needle styles your industrial machines require, call an industrial supplier and tell him the brand names and model numbers of the machines. With this information, he will be able to supply the correct needles in a variety of shank sizes.

Sewing machine needle sizes are standard and are expressed in American and/or European (metric) numbering. In both systems, larger numbers mean larger needles. Use the following chart as a guide:

Sewing Machine Needle Sizes

fabric weight	American	European (metric)
delicate	9 and 10	65 and 70
medium light	11	75
medium	12 and 14	80 and 90
medium heavy	16	100
heavy	18	110
extra heavy	19	120

Sewing machine needles come in three point styles: *universal,* which is a moderately sharp point suitable for most stitching; *ballpoint,* a rounded-end needle that will not cause picks in the fabric and that has been treated so as not to overheat when stitching on synthetic knit fabrics (there's no need to use ballpoint needles on natural fiber knits); and *sharp* or *jeans*, a very sharp, sturdy needle for stitching on dense fabrics such as denim. A standard nomenclature for machine needle point styles does not exist, and sometimes it's difficult to tell what kind of needle point you're buying. Fortunately, most of the needles on the market have universal points, and they are the ones used most.

Sergers

Sergers perform a single operation with variations. The most basic is the stretchable overcasting found on the seam edges of most factory-made clothing. The stitch is formed with three, four, or five threads, each coming off a separate spool from the top of the machine. There is no bobbin. Sergers also come equipped with a set of knives that, working in a scissor-like fashion, trim the seam edge just ahead of the overcasting.

Four- and five-thread sergers are sometimes used to stitch and overcast seams in a single operation, chiefly on garments made from knit fabrics. The four-thread serger has a mock safety stitch. On one side of the seam there appears to be a separate row of straight stitches alongside the overcast; on the other side, it looks like an extra-wide overcast. This not a true lockstitch and the seam will not be strong. The five-thread serger performs a true lockstitch, separate from the overcast stitch, and makes a very sturdy overcast seam.

Because stage costumes undergo hard wear and are laundered or cleaned often, most shops today routinely finish all exposed seam edges to discourage raveling and add stability to the costume. If you do not have a serger, you probably overcast seams with a zigzag stitch. When zigzagging seam edges on a domestic sewing machine, you're putting lots of extra wear on the machine, and, if it's an old one, overheating the motor. A serger will cer-

FIGURE 1–20. Michael Hammons operating an industrial serger at the Utah Shakespearean Festival. *Photograph by Rosemary Ingham.*

tainly be a time saver in your shop; it may also prove economical in the long run.

Industrial sergers have been used in the garment industry for more than a century and secondhand models are usually available from the same suppliers who sell industrial lock stitch machines and other sewing equipment. A common brand name in older sergers is Merrow, a machine no long manufactured but still available secondhand. Some old-timers in costume shops still refer to the serger as the "merrow machine" in the same way your grandmother called the refrigerator the "frigidaire." Common contemporary brands include Consew, Juki, Singer, and Brother.

By the early 1980s, most of the major domestic sewing machine companies were marketing sergers to home stitchers. The earliest domestic models did not hold up well under the demands of costume construction. Almost a quarter of a century later, however, domestic sergers have improved a great deal and are commonly seen in busy costume shops. Although they are not as speedy as industrial sergers, you can finish seams with a domestic serger four times as quickly as with a zigzag stitch. Manufacturers of excellent domestic sergers are the same companies—Bernina, Huskvarna (Viking), and Pfaff—that make high-quality lock stitch machines.

Blindstitch Machines

The blindstitch machine also performs one operation: it executes a single-thread chain stitch that tacks down a flat hem. The stitches are visible on the inside of the garment and virtually invisible on the outside. The machine operates much faster than the blindstitch function on automatic stitch domestic machines, and it always has a free arm that allows you to machine hem cuffs and pants legs.

The largest manufacturer of industrial blindstitch machines in the United States today is U.S. Blindstitch, and these machines are well

FIGURE 1–21. An industrial blindstitch machine with knee and foot controls. *Photograph by Rosemary Ingham.*

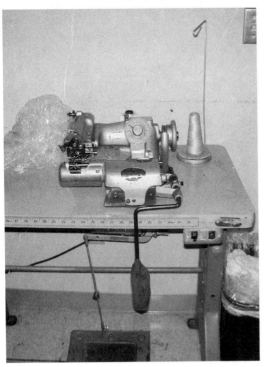

represented in costume shops. Other frequently seen brands are Consew, Tacsew, and Rex.

Secondhand blindstitch machines are harder to find than secondhand sergers or industrial lock stitch machines, and they tend to be expensive. If your shop can afford a blindstitch machine, however, you will save hours and have beautiful hems.

Laundry and Dry Cleaning Machines

Every costume shop, no matter how small, must have access to a washing machine and dryer. Not only are there costumes for the wardrobe staff to launder after actors have performed in them, there is always fabric to wash before it can be cut and stitched. Laundry machines designed for domestic use are most frequently seen in small and medium-sized shops. A large shop that handles two or three productions simultaneously might choose washers and dryers manufactured for industrial use because they are built for continuous use and have larger capacities than models intended for the home.

Variable water levels for loads of different sizes, and cold, warm, and hot water temperatures are the most important features to look for when buying a washing machine for a costume shop. Beware of washing machines that have too many settings or special features. The simpler the machine, the less apt it will be to break down.

The ideal clothes dryer for a costume shop has regular, permanent press, and air-fluff drying cycles. Place fabrics in the machine at the correct setting and leave them there for no longer than it takes for them to dry. Too much heat for too long a time shortens the life of any fabric, and sewing threads are particularly susceptible to being weakened by heat. Gas-operated clothes dryers are much less expensive to operate than electric dryers.

Very few theatres or educational theatre departments today still have commercial dry cleaning machines in their costume shops and the ones who do are well advised to remove them as soon as possible. The fluids used in the dry cleaning process are highly volatile, and the fumes are hazardous. Most states have stringent safety codes that regulate the installation and operation of dry cleaning equipment and very few, if any, costume shops can meet these regulations. If the safety codes in your state regarding dry cleaning machines aren't strict, they ought to be.

Because of stricter safety codes, the coin-operated dry cleaning machines that were once available in laundromats have all but disappeared in American cities. Many theatres have arrangements with dry cleaning establishments to have their costumes cleaned at a bulk rate that usually means the garments are cleaned but not pressed. Others promise to send all their cleaning and pressing to one friendly company in exchange for a discount.

Steam Irons

Every costume shop, large or small, should have an industrial steam iron. Given the amount of ironing that occurs daily in the costume construction process, an iron that is sturdy and substantial, has a continuous water supply, and produces steam pressure powerful enough to penetrate a variety of fabrics is very nearly essential. If the cost of an industrial iron appears prohibitive, you should take into account everything you expect a steam iron to do and then consider the average life span of a domestic iron in a busy shop. Costume technicians use the iron constantly. Domestic irons are not meant to stay turned on for hours at a time. Indeed, it is almost impossible today to find a new home iron without an automatic shut-off control, and for a busy stitcher this feature is not only nerve-racking, but also down-

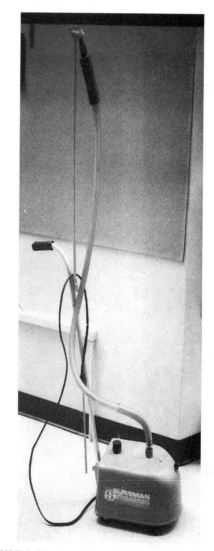

FIGURE 1–22. A portable steamer on wheels with steaming wand and flexible hose. *Photograph by Liz Covey.*

right inefficient. Also, because home irons are lightweight and must rest on end, many of them bite the dust after one, or several, falls to the floor, whereas an industrial iron weighs three to seven pounds and is constructed to sit flat on a heat-resistant pad. A broken domestic iron cannot, in most cases, be repaired. An

23

industrial iron will have a commercial warranty and necessary repairs are usually done by the company that sold you the iron. Many parts on an industrial iron can be replaced and, even when it is in constant use, the iron may have a life expectancy of up to ten years.

There are several types of steam iron systems on the market but the most popular in costume shops today are gravity-feed models. The steam is generated from a water supply tank suspended above the ironing surface. A demineralizing filter purifies the water in the tank and must be replaced when it changes color.

Dye Vats

A steam-jacketed kettle for fabric dyeing is a wise purchase for every costume shop with a place to put it and money for the original investment. Without a dye vat, technicians must dye and tint fabrics in washing machines or in pots on stoves or hot plates. Dyeing in a steam-jacketed kettle allows for even and permanent dyeing with a wide variety of dyestuffs and assists.

Steam-jacketed kettles are manufactured by companies that supply restaurants and other commercial food preparation companies. Steam-jacketing means that heat, carried by steam, comes into the kettle from all sides. This results in more uniform heating and simmering and is a more energy-efficient process than bringing a large quantity of water to boil only from the bottom.

Two major things to consider when shopping for a dye vat are size and energy source. Most shops opt for a 40- or 60-gallon

FIGURE 1–23. Commercial dye vat with pulley system at The Washington Opera. *Photograph by Rosemary Ingham.*

FIGURE 1–24. Dye vats at the University of Maryland. *Photograph by Liz Covey.*

kettle; some find the 80-gallon size more useful. Don't forget that you can heat a small amount of water in a large vat. Most dyers report that gas-powered kettles heat up much faster than those run by electricity.

Shears and Scissors

High-quality sharp shears and scissors are almost as important to costume shop technicians as reliable sewing machines. The best brands are relatively expensive, precision-made tools that should be treated with care.

Cutting shears usually measure 7 inches or more in length. The handles are bent, and the two blades are hinged with a screw. The bottom blade has a large handle that will accommodate two or three fingers for better control and leverage. Because of the bent handles, fabric remains flat on the table when it's being cut. Left-handed shears are available for left-handed cutter/drapers. Purchase one pair of extra-large shears, 12 to 14 inches long, for cutting especially heavy fabrics.

Scissors measure 6 inches or less in length. They have small, round handles that

FIGURE 1–25. Scissors, shears, and a rotary cutter. *Photograph by Liz Covey.*

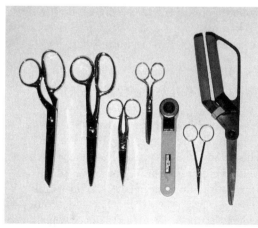

are not bent. Use scissors for trimming and delicate cutting. Do not use small scissors to trim extremely thick materials. If you have to force the scissors to cut through a fabric, you are in danger of damaging them.

Pinking and scalloping shears are intended to be used to finish the raw seam edges of fabrics that do not ravel easily. Since costume technicians overcast most seam edges in some manner, these specialty shears are not widely used in costume shops.

Always purchase the best shears and scissors you can afford. Shy away from unfamiliar brand names and do not expect bargain buys to cut cloth adequately. Never buy a pair that has a rivet attaching the blades instead of a screw; there is no way to adjust riveted blades. Scissors manufactured by Gingher have been favored in costume shops for many years.

Purchase several pairs of paper-cutting scissors for the shop and never cut paper with your good fabric shears. Moderately priced scissors with stainless steel blades are excellent for cutting paper and, when sharp, do an adequate job on fabric. Some brands seem able to go from paper to fabric without too much damage to the blades.

Protect your scissor blades by closing them when not in use and by storing them in protective covers. Few things damage a pair of shears or scissors more seriously than a fall to the floor, especially a concrete one. Hitting a pin when cutting always results in a nicked blade.

Most costume technicians find that they need to have their shears and scissors sharpened every two to three months, more often when silk or metallic fabrics are being cut. Since scissor sharpening is costly, you might want to consider purchasing a scissors-sharpening machine for your shop.

Some costume shop technicians use small, electrically powered industrial cutters for bulk cutting. These tools are moderately expensive and take some practice to operate.

Manually operated rotary cutting tools that come in several sizes are excellent for large garments, ruffles, bias strips, and so on, and can cut through several layers of cloth at a time.

Grommets, Eyelets, and Rivets

Grommets are the metal reinforcements for functional or decorative holes punched into leather or fabric. They come in a wide variety of sizes and may be purchased at leather supply stores and at craft shops. Large-size grommets are available from sail-makers and from compa-

FIGURE 1–26. A foot-pedal-operated, fully adjustable setting machine for applying grommets and other hardware at The Washington Opera. *Photograph by Liz Covey.*

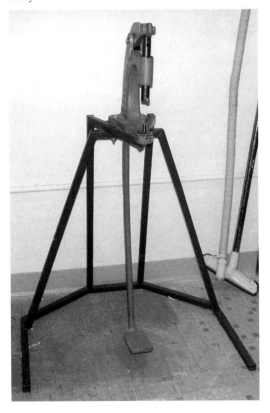

nies that make awnings. Grommets come in two pieces that are pounded or pressed together with a grommet setter. Each size grommet must be inserted with a setter, or die, of a corresponding size. Setters may either be simple, two-piece devices that hold the two grommet pieces in place while they are pounded into the material with a hammer or a more elaborate machine, operated with a hand or foot peddle. When hammering grommets in place, it's best to work on a hard surface, such as a stage weight.

Eyelets serve essentially the same purpose as grommets, but they are available only in small sizes, are made in a single piece, and are not as strong as grommets. The hand-operated eyelet-setting tool squeezes the eyelets into the cloth. Do not use eyelets in garments made from loose-weave fabrics or in areas where great stress will be put on the fabric edges. For example, eyelets are not the best choice to reinforce corset lacing holes. Sometimes, if the fabric layers are not too thick, a second eyelet can be inserted in the same hole in the opposite direction for reinforcement.

Pound rivets and pop rivets can be used to fasten leather straps to vacuum-formed plastic, fiberglass, or sized felt armor, to attach metal or plastic decorations to heavy garments and accessories, and to construct various belt arrangements and sword hangers. Pound rivets are hammered into place, and pop rivets must be set with a pop rivet gun or setter.

The Hot-Melt Glue Gun

It's hard to imagine how costume shops operated before hot-melt glue guns were available. This handy tool dispenses hot glue, which can be used either for binding materials together or for creating dimensional designs on armor, helmets, jewelry, and so on. The glue comes in pellets about the size of a fat crayon which feed into the gun. Liquid glue comes out of a small tip. In the simplest guns, the glue stick is pushed through the gun with a finger; other guns have triggers or levers that release liquid glue when pulled or depressed. When hot glue is used to bind two surfaces together, they can be separated by applying the heated tip of the gun to the glue that is already set. The glue will soften up immediately, and whatever is bound together will come apart. Hot glue is not water-proof, and it does not always hold up through dry cleaning.

Space Considerations, Machinery, and Supplies in a Fully Equipped Costume Shop

Very few costume shops start out "fully equipped." You add equipment over the years as it's needed and as the money becomes available. You should always grow with a plan, however. Assess your shop needs at regular intervals, giving priority to machines and tools that directly affect production costs, labor time, and costume quality. Be patient and persistent with management and administration. Purchase carefully and care for what you have.

A Checklist for Designing and Remodeling Costume Shops

GENERAL SPACE CONSIDERATIONS

- windows, if possible
- tile or wood floors; if floors are concrete, plan to put rubber mats in standing areas
- adequate ventilation (spray booth or dilution ventilation system)
- combination fluorescent and incandescent lighting with control flexibility
- adequate wiring
  strip outlets
  grounded outlets
  twist lock outlets for industrial equipment
  220-volt line for electric dryer and stove
  several heavy-duty extension cords for special uses
- plumbing, including drainage, for automatic washer and dye machine
- venting system for clothes dryer
- large, stainless steel sinks
- stainless steel counters beside laundry and dye machines
- shelving and cabinets with adjustable shelves
- bulletin boards

Equipment and Supply Lists, Organized by Areas

OFFICE AREA

- desk and desk chair
- file cabinets
- computer, printer, and fax
- costume research books, catalogs, and source materials
- paper, pens, pencils
- miscellaneous office supplies (paper clips, stapler, etc.)

- telephone
- telephone directories and telephone number file
- telephone message pads
- first-aid kit, including aspirin

PATTERN DEVELOPMENT, CUTTING, AND DRAPING AREA

- cutting table(s)
- rubber floor pad
- tall stools or chairs

- tailor's forms: male and female in a variety of sizes
- roll of brown craft paper
- roll of squared pattern paper
- pattern drafting tools:

  metal rulers: 6 inch, 12 inch, 18 inch, 36 inch, 45 inch

  tailor's square or right angle tailor's curve

  French curve

  18-inch C-Thru ruler

  flexible curve

FIGURE 1–27. An assortment of tailor's forms padded to individual actors' measurements at Arena Stage. *Photograph by Liz Covey.*

FIGURE 1–28. Male tailor's forms with legs. *Photograph by Rosemary Ingham.*

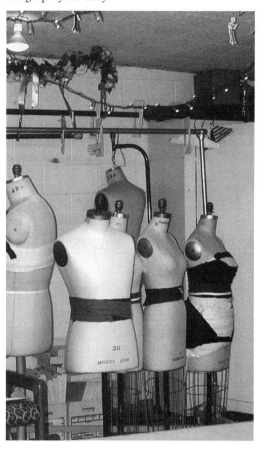

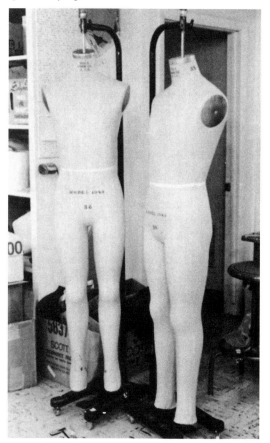

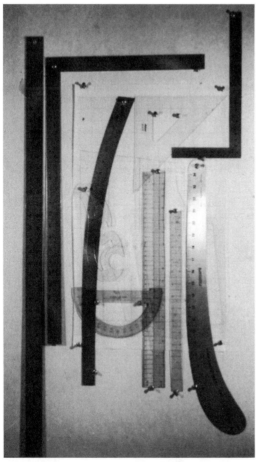

FIGURE 1–29. Pattern drafting tools. *Photograph by Susan Ashdown.*

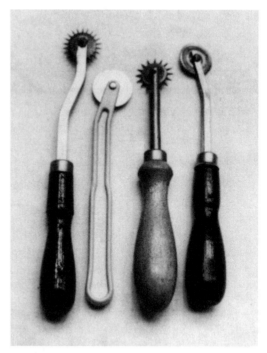

FIGURE 1–30. Tracing wheels. *Photograph by Liz Covey.*

- tape measures
- colored, indelible markers, assorted tips
- large sheets of tracing paper (red, yellow, blue, white) and tracing paper boards made by mounting tracing paper sheets on 20-inch by 30-inch boards
- tracing wheels: needle point, dull point, and smooth
- pushpins
- T-pins
- chalk: stone and wax in a variety of colors, chalk wheels

- marking or tailor's pencils
- tape dispensers and tape
- cutting shears
- paper-cutting scissors
- large envelopes or plastic bags for storing patterns
- cabinet or other container for storing patterns

MACHINE-STITCHING AREA

- industrial lock stitch machines
- automatic stitch domestic machines
- straight stitch and zigzag domestic machines
- sewing machine attachments:
  zipper foot
  roll hemmers
  ruffler
  buttonhole attachment, and so on.

- serger(s), industrial and/or domestic
- blindstitch machine
- stout sewing tables with lamps
- sturdy chairs with good back support
- thread stands for all machines
- thread nippers for all machines
- pin boxes or magnetic pin holders for all machines
- bobbins for all machines
- machine needles for all machines in a variety of sizes and point styles
- machine-cleaning equipment:
    machine oil: follow each manufacturer's suggestion for preferred oil
    weight, or use mineral oil, which is more expensive but will not stain most fabrics
    nylon bristle paint brushes for cleaning out lint
    toothpicks for cleaning feed teeth and bobbin casing
    long- and short-handled screwdrivers for removing parts
- muslin or plastic covers for all machines
- sewing thread on cardboard spools or cones
- straight pins, silk-type, sizes 18 and 20

FIGURE 1–31. Cutter/draper Alexander B. Tecoma hard at work at the Milwaukee Repertory Theater. *Photograph by Rosemary Ingham.*

HAND-STITCHING AREA

- table
- comfortable chairs
- hand-sewing needles of various sizes and types
- thimbles in several sizes
- seam gauges
- beeswax
- assorted fastenings:

  snap fasteners, black and silver, sizes 4 to 10

  hook and eye fasteners, loop and bar eyes, black and silver, sizes 4 to 10

  skirt hooks and eyes

  trouser hooks and eyes

  hook and eye tape

  snap tape

  zippers

  zipper tape, stops, and sliders

  Velcro

  buttons

FIGURE 1–32. Hand-stitching supplies. *Photograph by Susan Ashdown.*

- seam rippers
- razor blades
- scissors
- pincushions and containers for supplies
- heavy-duty thread
- nylon slip stitch thread

FITTING AREA

- three-way mirror
- additional clip-on light fixtures, if necessary
- chair
- rack for hanging
- rubber or carpet pad for actor to stand on
- supply cupboard containing:

  safety pins in various sizes

  colored, indelible markers

  marking or tailor's pencils

  chalk

  tape measures

  scissors

  wig cap

  bobby pins

  hair elastics

  shoe horn

  glove sizer

  ring sizer

  thin socks and footlets

PRESSING AREA

- industrial ironing board and/or ironing table
- industrial steam iron system, including metal and/or rubberized iron rest
- portable steamer
- sleeveboard
- press mitts
- tailor's hams

FIGURE 1–33. Pressing aids. *Photograph by Richard Bryant.*

- point presser
- needleboard for velvet
- pressing cloths
- spray starch and spray sizing
- clothes brushes and lint rollers
- iron cleaner

DYEING AREA

(See Chapter 7 for a discussion of equipping the dyeing area and a more extensive list of equipment and supplies.)

- respirator with appropriate filters
- protective gloves
- protective coverall or smock
- steam-jacketed kettle or dye vat
- washing machine and dryer
- hot plate
- stainless steel or enamelware pans, kettles, and buckets
- long-handled stirring spoons and sticks
- assorted glass jars with lids and plastic containers with covers
- bulk dye pigments
- fixing chemicals

- detergents
- stainless steel or glass measuring cups
- stainless steel measuring spoons
- gram scale
- fabric scale (baby scale)

CRAFTS AREA

- respirator with appropriate filters
- protective gloves, neoprene and latex
- protective coverall or smock
- worktable
- tall stool
- electric drill
- Dremyl with various bits
- grommet setters and grommets, several sizes
- eyelet setter and eyelets
- pound and pop rivets and pop rivet gun
- staple gun and staples
- hammer
- screwdrivers, regular and Phillips
- large pliers
- jewelry and needle nose pliers
- file
- hot-melt glue gun and glue pellets
- leather tools:
    awl
    leather punch
    thong stripper
    leather knife
    leather scissors
    glover's needles
    leather-stitching tool

STORAGE AREA

- racks, permanent and rolling
- shelving, various widths and depths

FIGURE 1–34. "Z" rolling racks at The Shakespeare Theatre. *Photograph by Rosemary Ingham.*

- boxes, assorted sizes, preferably with tops
- supply drawers, various sizes
- two-step ladders
- tall, rolling ladders with automatic stop mechanism

MAINTENANCE AREA

- washing machine
- dryer
- portable steamer for pressing
- detergent, softener, and stain removers
- enamelware pans for hand-washing
- lines or racks for drying hand-washables
- tackle box with emergency stitching supplies for backstage
- shoe polish, applicators, and brushes
- antistatic spray
- spray Lysol
- industrial vacuum cleaner
- mesh bag for delicate items
- broom and dustpan
- garbage cans

The Costume Shop Staff

A costume shop staff may consist of one person who does everything, or a dozen people, each with carefully defined responsibilities. In a college or university costume shop, jobs will be rotated among the students, under the direction of professional staff members and faculty. Each shop organization is unique. Job titles and job descriptions are not uniform. However, certain divisions of labor and some common titles exist in a majority of costume shops.

Costume Designer

- designs and sketches all costumes, including accessories, hairstyles, and specialty make-up, in collaboration with the director, the scenic designer, and the lighting designer.
- agrees to and works within a stated budget and accounts for all expenditures.

FIGURE 1–35. Head stitcher Maria Montoya in the costume shop at the American Conservatory Theater. *Photograph by Rosemary Ingham.*

- except when working with a custom costume shop is responsible for purchasing all fabrics and trims.
- consults with the cutter/draper about patterns and construction methods.
- attends fittings, production meetings, and dress rehearsals.

Assistant to the Costume Designer

- assists the designer with research.
- swatches and shops.

- often assembles accessories and works on costume props.
- attends fittings, production meetings, and dress rehearsals as required.

Costume Shop Supervisor or Manager

- is directly responsible for the day-to-day running of the shop.
- hires staff.
- supervises staff.
- orders supplies and equipment.

- keeps abreast of construction progress.
- conducts shop meetings.
- attends general theatre staff and production meetings.
- keeps track of budgets.
- remembers everything.

Cutter/Draper

- develops patterns and is responsible for cutting all fabric, including interlinings, facings, linings, bias strips, plackets, etc.
- plans the construction process for each garment.
- gives careful instructions to the first hand about cutting fabric and constructing each garment.
- attends fittings.
- supervises alterations.

First Hand

- serves as the cutter/draper's assistant.
- may develop some patterns or only cut fabric using patterns developed by the cutter/draper.
- supervises stitchers.

Stitcher

- assembles garments as instructed by the first hand
- may or may not do finishing.

Craftsperson

- plans the construction process for accessories and costume properties with the designer and carries the plans to completion.

Dyer

- dyes fabric before it is cut.
- dyes, paints, and distresses costumes after they are completed.

Some productions may require the more specialized skills of a milliner, a cobbler or bootmaker, an armorer, or a wigmaker. These craftspeople are not part of most costume shop staffs and may be jobbed in for a single production.

Wardrobe Maintenance Supervisor

- organizes and supervises costume changes during each performance and assists the actors as necessary.
- supervises dressers.
- is responsible for laundering, cleaning, and repairing the costumes during the run of the production.
- assumes complete responsibility for all the costumes in a production after opening night.

2

Health and Safety in the Costume Shop

In the 1970s, a few costume designers and technicians were beginning to suspect that certain art and craft supplies, combined with sloppy work habits, might constitute hazards to their health. Others, unable or unwilling to believe that those bottles, cans, and packets that were available at every corner hardware store could actually be dangerous, went on with their work as usual, continuing to blame recurring headaches, intermittent attacks of nausea, and occasional rashes on chronic fatigue, "flu bugs," and "allergies." And, even if you were one of the ones who suspected that the dyes, solvents, and sprays might be contributing to "the flu bug that won't go away," where could you turn for information? Who could tell you what was actually in a packet of dye powder that arrived in your shop in a plain brown paper parcel with no list of ingredients? And, who could identify and describe the incomprehensible names of chemicals when they did appear on the back of a solvent can? Somebody, somewhere knew these things but the information was buried in organic chemistry journals and reports written by congressional committees and industrial health and safety boards. Costume designers and technicians had neither the time nor the scientific background to dig out the information.

In 1979, Michael McCann, a chemist who specializes in the occupational health hazards of artists and craftspeople, published *Artist Beware—The Hazards and Precautions in Working with Art and Craft Materials.* For the first time, accurate information about the chemicals contained in ordinary art and craft materials, many of them used in costume shops on a daily basis, was between the covers of one book. Over the next few years, copies of *Artist Beware* were added to many costume shop libraries.

Throughout the 1980s, costume designers and technicians became more and more aware of health and safety problems in costume shops. Federal and state laws were passed that mandated safer workplaces, including costume shops. Articles and newsletters appeared on the scene. More books were published. Some were aimed at artists and craftspeople in general and some dealt specifically with theatre. (Monona

Rossol's *Health and Safety Guide for Film, TV and Theater* should be required reading for all theatre artists and craftspeople.) United Scenic Artists began to disseminate health and safety information to its members, and the United States Institute for Theatre Technology formed a Health and Safety Commission to organize workshops and contribute health and safety articles to USITT publications.

Today, almost a quarter of a century after Michael McCann's *Artist Beware* was first published, costume designers and technicians have no excuse for not *knowing* there are health and safety hazards lurking in many art and craft materials, and that sloppy work habits can result in illness and injury. As a result of all the shared information, of all the books, articles, workshops, lectures, and discussions, some costume shops have become safer workplaces, and many designers and technicians have developed safer work habits. On the other hand, too many costume shops remain as hazardous to your health as ever, and many designers and technicians refuse to change dangerous work habits.

The following is an excerpt from Chapter 1 in Monona Rossol's *The Artist's Complete Health and Safety Guide:*

One of the most humbling aspects of my first few years in industrial hygiene was observing how steadfastly both artists and administrators ignored my advice. I talked enthusiastically about health and safety programs, ventilation, respiratory protection, and so on. While I was talking, there would be interest, motivation, and good intentions. But before my vocal cords cooled, people would be back to business as usual.

It wasn't that people didn't want to be safer and healthier—they did. It wasn't that they didn't understand the technical information— they did. It wasn't even that the precautions would cost too much—they often didn't. The fail-

ure to institute proper health and safety procedures usually boiled down, in the main, to inertia and old habits.

These are formidable foes. We are all infected terminally with the desire to do the familiar—even if we know it is not in our best interest. There is an exquisite pain associated with the effort of hauling habits out of our spinal cord reflexes and putting them back into our brains to be thought through again. Confronting this resistance taught me that there is no industrial hygienist clever enough, no lecturer interesting enough, no argument convincing enough to make us change the way we make art. The lectures and training only make us feel a little more guilty as we routinely bet little bits of our life on risky familiar activities.

This chapter is intended to provide costume designers and technicians with introductory information about the most common hazards found in costume shops. Today there is considerably more concern about health and safety in costume shops than there was two and a half decades ago, but too much complacency and inattention still remain. Most theatre technicians agree with and intend to employ safe practices in the workplace. Unfortunately, many of them all too often ignore these practices when they are actually at work and under pressure to meet production deadlines. It is not enough to educate workers and encourage compliance with health and safety laws and regulations; there must be oversight. Although the laws and regulations have been enacted by federal, state and local governments, the first line of oversight in theatre organizations rests with production managers, costume shop managers, craft shop supervisors, and others who are responsible for employee welfare and can insist upon on-the-spot compliance with health and safety laws and regulations.

How Healthy Is Your Costume Shop?

A well-equipped, efficiently run costume shop can be a productive and happy workplace for costume technicians and designers. But, if the shop does not have adequate ventilation, safe wiring, and most important of all, firm, safety-minded regulations for working with hazardous art and craft materials, everyone who works there risks having his or her health seriously undermined. Chronic bronchitis, repeated bouts of flulike symptoms, headaches, and persistent dermatitis are only a few of the ailments commonly suffered by costume shop personnel. Many of these illnesses are caused by careless exposure to chemical solvents, dye powders, and irritating acids.

How many times have you seen a dye room in which cans of dye powders are left open all day while the dyer works with bare hands, splashing dye solution carelessly on counters and on the floor? How many times have you seen someone painting costume props with oil-based paints, while solvent vapors fill the space? How many times have you seen a costume designer "touch up" a costume with aerosol cans of leather dye in the dressing room or backstage? Each of these instances presents opportunities for an assault on health, not only the health of the person using the chemical carelessly, but also the well-being of other people in the area and of the actor who wears the newly "touched up" costume.

Spend a few days watching how the designers and technicians in your shop handle dyes, paints, and solvents. Then study the shop itself and its equipment. Are rubber gloves available and are they used? Is there a ventilation system? Where is it? Is it effective or can you smell the vapor even when it's running? Does the maze of extension cords on the floor constitute a fire hazard? Where is the fire extinguisher and when was it last checked? Are all paints and solvents properly labeled? Are flammable materials kept in a fireproof cabinet? With the door shut? Are emergency first-aid instructions posted where everybody can see them? Do you know what to do, and where to go, in case of fire?

Most important of all, are there people in your shop who are knowledgeable about potential health and safety hazards? Is there someone you can speak to about your concerns?

Now, what if you survey the health and safety situation in your costume shop and find it not so good? Less than perfect? Downright terrible? Suppose nobody is interested? What then?

"Free from Recognized Hazards"

All costume shop technicians who are compensated for their work are covered by state and/or federal regulations whose goals are to protect workers in the workplace. The general duty clause of The Occupational Safety and Health Act (OSHA), which was enacted in 1970, says, in part, that the "employer shall furnish . . . employment and a place of employment which are free from recognized hazards." That means you, your work, and your workplace. The person who is responsible for keeping your work and workplace "free from recognized hazards" is your employer, the person or entity who takes deductions from your paycheck.

Students working in college and university costume shops are usually protected by state health and safety regulations that may be even more stringent than the federal regulations. And teachers have a special obligation to maintain health and safety standards because they may be held liable for any harm classroom activities (which can be interpreted to include class assignments in the costume shop) may cause their students.

The only workers not covered by this complex of safe workplace regulations are self-employed artists, craftspeople, and teachers, in those instances when they work as independent contractors. However, the independent contractor employed in a costume shop is responsible for complying with all the regulations pertaining to that shop.

There is, as you can see, some degree of legal protection for everybody who works in costume shops. But what form does this protection take? Who enforces OSHA regulations? How can laws help make your costume shop a safer place?

Your Right To Know

It is unlikely that an OSHA inspector will visit your costume shop and threaten to close it down if somebody doesn't get rid of the extension cords and keep the dye tins closed. Quite frankly, the only way your costume shop might run afoul of OSHA regulations is if someone in the shop lodges a formal complaint. And, in the absence of flagrant disregard for human health or acute toxic reactions, most costume shop technicians would never think of "turning in" their colleagues or the management of their theatres simply to make the shop smell better or to get rid of extension cords.

Nevertheless, if you are seriously interested in helping to make your costume shop a safer place, it's worth your time to find out what these health and safety regulations are all about. What exactly can they protect you from, and how? The best place for a costume shop technician to begin is with those portions of state and federal occupational health and safety codes known as "right-to-know" laws. On the national level the "right-to-know" laws are in-cluded in the section of the Occupational Safety and Health Act called the *OSHA Hazard Communication Standard*. In Appendix IV, on page 454, you'll find the mailing address for OSHA as well as contact information, including telephone and fax numbers, and (in most cases) Web addresses, for state and territorial health and safety agencies.

The three most important requirements of "right-to-know" laws are:

1. Your employer must have a written protocol for dealing with health and safety matters and communicate this program to all employees.
2. Your employer must give you a complete inventory of all materials present in your workplace, *and* supply Material Safety Data Sheets (MSDSs), which are usually obtained from the manufacturer, for all potentially hazardous chemicals.
3. Your employer must require and make available formal training for employees

who are exposed to potentially toxic chemicals.

If you want to make your shop a safer place in which to work, your first step will be to contact the local department of labor in your city, town, or county and request copies of the state and federal right-to-know laws that apply to all the types of work done in costume shops. Read them, make sure you understand them, and set up a meeting with your coworkers and supervisors where you can discuss bringing your shop into compliance with national health and safety standards. The requirements are sensible and you should meet with little or no resistance to the idea of a safer, healthier workplace.

Many costume shops around the country have gone through the process of complying with the OSHA Hazard Communication Standard. They have inventoried workplace chemicals, identified hazardous products, and compiled loose-leaf notebooks full of MSDSs. They've applied proper labels to all containers, invited experts to present training sessions, and communicated all necessary materials to every costume technician in the shop. They may even have installed a more efficient ventilation system, made a glove box for mixing powdered dye pigments, and upgraded the costume shop wiring. These costume shops appear to have become model workplaces, potentially safe and healthy. What's left to do?

Old Habits Die Hard

Remember the old saying, "You can lead a horse to water but you can't make him drink"? Well, the same logic often seems to apply to the costume shop technician who knows about the dangers of using toxic chemicals and understands that sloppy work habits are unhealthy but just can't manage to substitute a safer product for the old familiar one, or bother to put on rubber gloves before fishing the fabric out of the dye pot. Safety protocol, accurate labeling, and current Material Safety Data Sheets can't make a workplace safe unless the human beings who work there learn to give up old habits and form new ones.

This is not to minimize the importance of complying with occupational health and safety standards. Every piece of improved equipment, every safety guideline, every discussion about making health-conscious material choices is a step toward making our costume shops better places in which to work. But, in the end, it's the everyday habits of each technician that make the difference.

As Monona Rossol pointed out in the passage quoted at the beginning of this chapter, just knowing is not enough. The next step, the hardest step, is taking what you know and putting it into everyday use. Don't just learn about health and safety regulations; follow them. Practice until you have formed new habits. Make a vow that you will not endanger others; insist that no one else endanger you. Be cheerful, pleasant, and positive and set a good example for your colleagues. Or, if those strategies don't work, lecture and nag until you force them to comply with safety rules in order to keep you quiet.

What Can Hazardous Chemicals Do to You?

Many chemicals interfere with the way your body works. Sometimes this interference is so slight you don't even notice it; sometimes the interference causes serious illness or even death. Chemicals commonly used in costume shops can affect your lungs, liver, heart, brain, or skin. One kind of exposure might give you a rash on your hands or arms; another might result in mental confusion, lack of coordination, and nausea; yet another will permanently damage your liver.

How Do Hazardous Chemicals Hurt Your Body?

Amount and Time

The toxicity of a substance is dependent upon the amount that enters the body and the length of time the body is exposed. For instance, a brief contact with lacquer thinner fumes might give you an annoying headache, while a concentrated dose for a longer period of time will produce severe headache, loss of coordination, nausea, and dizziness.

Chemicals that cause serious damage to the body in small doses are called *highly toxic. Moderately toxic* chemicals are destructive in higher doses. *Mildly toxic* chemicals may produce no damage at low doses but may become quite harmful if exposure is consistent and lasts for a long period of time.

Acute Reactions

The body's reaction to large doses of some chemicals over a brief period of time may be immediate, often dramatic, and is known as an *acute reaction*. If you spill acid on your skin, the damage occurs right away. If you breathe large quantities of turpentine vapor in a confined space, you may lose conscious-ness, and you may die. Acute physical reactions to chemicals are easy to diagnose since exposure and result are so close together in time.

Chronic Effects

The chronic effects of hazardous chemicals on the body are harder to isolate, and they are often very difficult to diagnose. Chronic effects are usually the result of repeated exposure to toxic materials over a long time. Chronic bronchitis, persistent dermatitis, and general feelings of weakness and malaise may all be chronic effects from the chemicals you encounter in your work.

Cancer is a special type of chronic effect from exposure to some hazardous chemicals. The chemicals that cause cancer are called carcinogens. Asbestos and benzidine dyes and dye pigments are known carcinogens; many other chemicals are suspected of being carcinogens. Cancers that result from contact with hazardous chemicals used in the workplace may take from ten to forty years to develop. It is very difficult to link these cancers with their causes.

Don't assume that, because you have already been exposed to toxic substances, you are destined to develop cancer or another serious illness, and, therefore, have no reason to avoid these chemicals. It's true that the longer you allow your body to be exposed to a dangerous chemical, the greater your chances are of becoming seriously ill. However, as soon as you end that exposure, your chances of becoming seriously ill begin to drop, quite quickly in many instances.

Allergies

In addition to the adverse effects many chemicals have on almost everyone who is exposed to them, some people develop individual allergic reactions to certain materials. Some substances are known to produce allergies in a large proportion of the people who encounter them. Poison ivy, for instance, causes allergic reactions in about 70 percent of the people exposed to it. Epoxy resins and hardeners, formaldehyde, turpentine, and photographic developers all produce allergic reactions in about 50 percent of the industrial workers who are regularly exposed to them. Many craftspeople also develop allergies to batik dyes and wood dust.

Allergic reactions, particularly skin allergies, often take many years to develop. Even if you have used a particular product for many years, you may suddenly become allergic to it.

Damage to the Next Generation

The effects hazardous chemicals have on the human egg and sperm and on fetal development is a controversial subject and one that's difficult to assess. Until there is more concrete information to go on, pregnant women are well advised to avoid unprotected contact with all hazardous chemicals for the duration of their pregnancy.

Chemicals may affect the next generation in three different ways:

Mutagens are chemicals that can alter the genetic blueprint (DNA) of cells. When mutagens affect the human reproductive cells (the egg or sperm), they may trigger inherited abnormalities.

Teratogens affect fetal organ development and cause birth defects. Two proven human teratogens are the drug Thalidomide and grain alcohol.

A *fetal toxin* is a chemical that can affect the growth and development of the fetus at any stage of development.

How Do the Chemicals Get In?

Toxic substances have to get into your body before they can harm you. The three avenues of entry for the chemicals you encounter in a costume shop are the respiratory system, the skin, and the mouth and digestive system. To safeguard your body from the toxic substances you encounter, you must provide barriers to keep them out.

Respiratory System

Dusts and vapors enter your body readily through your nose, carrying many kinds of chemicals that may hurt you. Some substances may irritate the mucous lining of your respiratory system, including your sinuses. Others may clog your lungs, interfere with air exchange, and eventually cause difficulty in breathing. Still others may pass through your lungs into your bloodstream, from which they may eventually end up harming your heart, liver, or other organs. The smaller the particle or mist you inhale, the more apt it is to penetrate deeply. *Sprays of all sorts are particularly hazardous.*

Skin

Your skin provides a stout barrier against many toxic substances, but it is not impervious to harm. Caustics, acids, solvents, peroxides, and bleaches can penetrate the skin barrier, damaging the skin itself, and possibly even enter the bloodstream. Some chemicals, such as benzene and wood alcohol, are able to penetrate the skin without damaging it and without your knowing it. A great many chemicals can enter your body through cuts and abrasions on your skin.

Mouth and Digestive System

Most toxic substances that enter the body through the mouth are brought into the mouth as a result of hand-to-mouth transfer, usually accidental. Another common way for a toxic substance to enter the digestive system is from dusts or vapors that have been trapped in upper respiratory mucus, coughed up, then swallowed.

Many of the poisons you ingest go almost immediately to your liver. One of the liver's main jobs is to detoxify harmful substances that have invaded your body. If, however, the onslaught is too great, your liver may suffer permanent damage.

How Can You Keep the Chemicals Out?

Don't Eat, Drink, or Smoke in the Presence of Chemicals

Whenever you eat, drink, or smoke in the area where you work with art and craft materials, you greatly increase your chances of being exposed to toxic substances. The particles in cigarette smoke can carry dusts and vapors deep into your lungs. You can ingest poisonous materials from the ends of your cigarettes, from off your fingers, and from the slice of cake or cup of coffee that has picked up particles from the air.

In addition, never point your paint brush with your lips or bite your nails while you are working.

Wear Protective Clothing

Protect your skin from chemical invasion by wearing long pants, a long-sleeved shirt or smock, and protective gloves. Never work with bare feet. If you inadvertently spill any chemical on your skin, flush it away immediately with large quantities of cool water, then clean the area thoroughly with hand soap and water. *Don't clean your skin with solvents.* Use baby oil to remove solvent-based paints and inks, followed by soap and water.

A pair of blue or yellow gloves from the grocery store will not protect you from most toxic chemicals, particularly from solvents. Find a protective glove supplier who can provide detailed information about the types of gloves needed to protect you from the chemicals you use. Many costume craftspeople are unaware that common solvents like acetone, glycol ether, and xylene require special glove protection.

Protecting Your Respiratory System

Taking the proper precautions against inhaling toxic chemicals is more complicated than protecting your skin or your digestive system from hazardous chemical entry. Do not be misled into believing that the presence of an odor signals toxicity while the absence of odor means safety. Every substance in any of its forms may, or may not, produce an odor. *There is no correlation whatsoever between the odor and the toxicity of the substance.* These are the different forms in which you can inhale toxic substances:

1. *Gases.* Gases are made up of lots of molecules moving rapidly and at random through space. They generally disperse throughout the air in a room, affecting everybody. Gases have various properties; for example, they may be mildly irritating or extremely poisonous. Welding produces toxic ozone and nitrogen oxide gases. Photographic developing solutions produce sulfur dioxide and acetic acid gases.

2. *Vapors.* A vapor is the gaseous form of a liquid. The most toxic forms of vapors usually found in costume shops are the organic chemical vapors from solvents such as turpentine, mineral spirits, and lacquer thinners.

3. *Mists.* Mists are tiny liquid droplets in the air, put there as a result of misting or spraying. Mist droplets may contain tiny particles of solid materials, such as paints. A mist of a substance is more toxic than the vapor of the same substance because it's more concentrated.

And, the finer the size of the droplet, the more deeply it can penetrate into the respiratory system.

4. *Fumes.* Fumes are very tiny particles usually created in high-heat operations such as welding or soldering. These particles are formed when the vapors cool and condense. Fume particles stay in the air for a long time.

5. *Dusts.* Dusts are small particles of solid materials. The finer the dust, the deeper it can be inhaled.

6. *Smoke.* Smoke is formed when organic matter is burned. It is a mixture of many gases, vapors, and fumes.

The Occupational Safety and Health Act (OSHA) regulates exposure to airborne chemicals in the workplace in a section called *OSHA Permissible Exposure Limits.* Airborne chemicals are evaluated and assigned a *Threshold Limit Value (TLV).* TLVs are included on Material Safety Data Sheets (MSDSs), which will be discussed later in this chapter.

Ventilation

When a label reads "use with adequate ventilation," this caution does not mean to open a window or to take your project outside. A breeze coming in a window may carry toxic vapors into the air breathed by everybody in the room. Although it is somewhat safer to work outdoors, a shifting wind may envelop you in a toxic mist.

"Adequate ventilation" means either removing the dangerous substance from the area where you're working or diluting the concentration of the toxic substance in the air to a harmless level. There are industrial ventilation systems that operate on both of these principles.

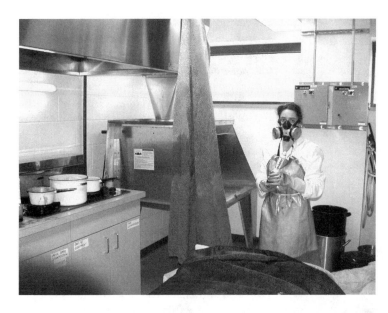

FIGURE 2–1. Dyer Julia Trimarco in respirator and gloves standing next to a spray booth at Opera Theatre of Saint Louis. *Photograph by James Wolk.*

FIGURE 2–2. Exhaust hood at the Berkeley Repertory Theatre. *Photograph by Rosemary Ingham.*

Local exhaust ventilation system. A local exhaust ventilation system traps toxic materials at the source, where you work with them, and takes them away. The system contains a *hood* that surrounds the workspace, *ductwork* to carry away contaminated air, an *aircleaner* to filter the air before it's released, and a *fan* to pull the air through the system. Spray booths, found in many scenic and theatre prop shops, are examples of local exhaust ventilation systems. (See Figures 2–1 to 2–3) This kind of system is preferable for dealing with moderate and highly toxic substances.

Dilution ventilation systems. This system does what it says it does: it dilutes or mixes air that has been contaminated with toxic airborne substances with large volumes of clean air to reduce the level of the contaminants to acceptable levels. The diluted air mixture is drawn out by fans while fresh air is drawn in.

Dilution ventilation systems, common in costume shops, are only adequate for removing mildly toxic substances or very small amounts of highly toxic substances. *A dilution*

FIGURE 2–3. A table unit that filters moderately toxic vapors from adhesives for use in making jewelry and other small items at The Washington Opera. *Photograph by Liz Covey.*

ventilation system is not adequate protection against mists created by aerosol cans, spray painting, or airbrush operations. It will not protect you against highly toxic or flammable solvent vapors, dye powders, or other dusts.

Best's Safety Directory, discussed at the end of this chapter on page 57, contains the names and addresses of companies that sell ventilating equipment. Study your own situation carefully and get professional advice before you decide on a specific ventilation system for your shop. Once it's installed, make sure you understand how to use, clean, and maintain it.

If you have the opportunity to help plan or renovate a theatre facility, make sure adequate shop ventilation is included in the original plans, and check to see that it does not get cut out later. Ventilation is not a "frill."

Substitute

In general, you can do a lot to help protect yourself against toxic chemical invasion by learning to substitute safe or safer products for unsafe products.

For instance, choose water-based or latex paints and inks over solvent-based products. Solvents are the most hazardous chemicals used by theatre artists and craftspeople. Acrylic and water colors are much safer to use than oils and enamels that have to be thinned with turpentine or paint thinner.

When you must use solvents, choose the ones that are the least toxic.

Choose products that do not create dusts and mists. Avoid, insofar as you can, products that come in powdered form or in aerosol cans.

Avoid all products that contain known cancer-producing chemicals (carcinogens) because these are unsafe even in minute quantities.

Evaluating Product Safety

How can you tell if one product is safer than another? First of all, make a habit of reading labels. Product labeling over the past two decades has improved dramatically, although labels still do not always give the complete safety information needed. If a product isn't adequately labeled, don't buy it.

Material Safety Data Sheets (MSDSs)

The best guide to finding out more about the hazards of a product is its Material Safety Data Sheet. By law, all manufacturers and importers must have Material Safety Data Sheets on all industrial products that contain potentially hazardous substances. The manufacturers and importers are required to provide MSDSs to all employers covered by the right-to-know laws. Federal regulations do not require manufacturers and importers to make MSDSs available to self-employed artists, theatre workers, or students, except in a few states that have state consumer right-to-know laws. Nevertheless, most manufacturers and importers will comply with requests for Material Safety Data Sheets, and, if they do not, you should refuse to purchase their products.

If you are self-employed, it isn't always easy to get the MSDS for products you use or are considering using, but they are the most valuable tool to evaluate product safety, so be persistent. First, ask the distributor to provide the MSDS. If you cannot obtain it from the distributor, write to the manufacturer, addressing the request to the manufacturer's technical service department.

When you use a purchase order to buy shop supplies, stipulate on it that no payment will be made until the Material Safety Data Sheets for all the products have been received. This is a particularly successful method of insuring your "right to know."

Once you have Material Safety Data Sheets in your hand, learn to read them to be able to evaluate the safety of the product, and compare the relative safety of competing products for the purpose of making intelligent substitutions. This is not always easy, even though your employer, if you have one, is required to train you.

There are places you can go to obtain instructions on how to read and use Material Safety Data Sheets. The Occupational Safety and Health Administration (OSHA) supports consultation services to answer questions although it is sometimes difficult to penetrate the dense language in which the answers are couched. The Health and Safety Commission of the United States Institute of Theatre Technology (USITT) offers advice to its members. United Scenic Artists (USA) provides consulting services as a courtesy to any union member of any theatrical, film, or TV union. Arts, Crafts and Theater Safety (ACTS), an independent organization founded in 1987, advises everyone who requests information. Monona Rossol is currently Health and Safety Officer of USA and President of ACTS.

Solvents and Dyestuffs

Due to their extreme toxicity, and because they are used regularly in costume shops, solvents (including solvent-based paints, varnishes, various craft materials, and adhesives) and dyestuffs present the most serious hazards to

the health of costume designers and technicians. The following section contains basic information that will help you use these substances as safely as possible. *It is only an overview.* Consult the Health and Safety section in the Bibliography for books that discuss these subjects in much greater depth.

Solvents

WHAT ARE SOLVENTS?

Solvents are liquid organic chemicals that dissolve solid materials such as oils, resins, waxes, plastics, varnishes, and paints. When solvent-based products are used, the solvents evaporate, allowing the product to dry or set. Most solvents evaporate quickly and cleanly. Solvents are also used to thin solvent-based products such as adhesives, oil paints, lacquers, inks (including the inks in many artists' pens and markers), varnishes, and so on, and to clean brushes, rollers, tools, and silkscreens.

ORGANIC CHEMICAL SOLVENTS

All organic chemical solvents are toxic. There is no such thing as a "safe" organic chemical solvent. Every single one presents the user with an array of potential health hazards. It is, however, possible to substitute products containing less toxic solvents for those containing the most toxic solvents and, by taking careful precautions, to protect yourself from health-threatening exposure.

SOLVENTS GET INTO YOUR BODY

Solvents can gain access to vital organs in your body through your skin, nose, and mouth. Breathing solvent vapor is particularly hazardous because the toxic materials may be carried deep into your lungs and directly into your bloodstream. A few solvents can enter your body directly through your skin; others gain entry through cuts and abrasions.

Barricade these accesses to your body with protective clothing, including proper gloves; adequate ventilation and/or a respirator; and good personal habits such as not eating, drinking, or smoking when using solvents and solvent-based substances.

"SOLVENT HIGHS"

Stop making jokes about "solvent highs." Many costume designers and technicians have experienced so-called solvent highs after using organic chemical solvents and solvent-based substances. The symptoms of this condition are slight disorientation, lack of coordination, and, subsequently, a headache. Solvent highs occur because these toxic chemicals depress your central nervous system, including the brain and spinal cord. Prolonged exposure can result in a severe depression of your central nervous system and may bring on coma and death. Although an isolated, mild solvent high probably won't do any permanent damage to your body, there's ample evidence that years of working with solvents can produce a kind of permanent brain damage whose symptoms include short-term memory loss, difficulties with hand-eye coordination, and depression.

As you can see, a solvent high is no joking matter.

INFORMED CHOICES

Learn to make informed choices. It would be nice to be able to make a chart that describes all organic chemical solvents in order, from most toxic to least toxic. Unfortunately, the subject is too complex for such a simple arrangement. Because many solvent-based products contain more than one solvent, you will have to consider the amount of the more toxic chemical or chemicals in the product and the amount of exposure you or your staff might be expected to sustain.

This section will focus on the solvents that are too dangerous to use under any conditions. Remember: no solvent is completely safe; precautions should be used to protect the body; and the less exposure to toxic substances, the better.

Because the solvents used in specific brand-name products do change from time to time, particularly now that there is pressure from purchasers for companies to develop safer products, no individual products are identified by their brand name in this section. Some up-to-date lists of brand-name products and the solvents they contain are available from the organizations mentioned earlier. Your best defense, however, is to read and to heed labels, to obtain and to learn to read Material Safety Data Sheets, and to make your own carefully considered choices and substitutions.

The Health and Safety Committee of United Scenic Artists has prepared a list of organic chemical solvents that are unarguably deadly and should be avoided. They are:

Methylene chloride, also called *dichloromethane, methylene dichloride, methylene bichloride*. Methylene chloride is used as a solvent for oil, waxes, cellulose acetate, and esters, as well as a paint remover.

This chemical is an animal carcinogen. Skin contact may cause burns as well as dermatitis. Both the liquid and the vapor can irritate the eyes and upper respiratory tract. Exposure can cause headache, giddiness, stupor, irritability, numbness, and tingling in limbs. Severe exposure has been seen to cause toxic brain dysfunction with hallucinations, pulmonary edema, coma, and death. Once in the bloodstream, methylene chloride forms carbon monoxide, which makes it particularly dangerous to smokers or to people with heart disease. Finally, when methylene chloride comes in contact with heat or flame, it will decompose to form highly toxic gases such as phosgene.

N-hexane is a chemical solvent used in many adhesives, including some of those used for leather bonding. N-hexane is an irritant to the mucous membranes and produces an anesthetic effect that may produce asphyxia (inability to breathe) in persons exposed to high concentrations of the chemical. Peripheral nerve damage and permanent central nervous system damage resulting in a disease similar to multiple sclerosis have also been documented from exposure to n-hexane.

Glycol ethers and their acetates are especially hard to identify in products because they have so many names. Some of these names are *ethoxyethanol, 2-ethoxyethanol, cellosolve, carbitol, Dowanol EE, Polysolve EE, Oxitol, ethylene glycol monoethyl ether*. These chemicals are used as solvents for resins, lacquers, paints, and varnishes. Because they mix easily with water, they are often found in products considered water-based such as spray cleaners and latex wall paints.

These solvents are particularly dangerous because they are easily absorbed through the skin. The most commonly used ones have caused atrophy of the testicles, miscarriages, and birth defects in four animal species. In humans, they have been found to cause anemia, brain and kidney damage, as well as skin, eye, and respiratory system irritation.

Toluene, which may also be called *toluol, methylbenzene, phenylmethane*, or *methylbenzol*, is used as a thinner for paint, varnishes, lacquers, and enamels, as a solvent for gums, fats, and resins, and as a paint remover.

Contact can cause irritation of eyes, skin, and the respiratory system. Acute exposure may cause severe central nervous system depression with symptoms including headache, dizziness, fatigue, muscular weakness, drowsiness, loss of coordination, numbness, collapse, and coma.

1-1-1-trichlorethane, also called *methyl chloroform*, is most often used as a stain remover. Upon exposure to hot metal (such as an iron), this chemical will decompose and form dangerous gases, such as hydrochloric acid gas, phosgene, and dichloroacetylene. Human exposure may result in depression of the central nervous system with symptoms such as: irritation, dizziness, loss of coordination, decreased reaction time, unconsciousness, and death.

Other solvents to avoid at all costs are:

methyl alcohol (methanol, wood alcohol)
gasoline
kerosene
benzene (benzol)
styrene (vinylbenzene, phenylethylene)
xylene (xylol, dimethylbenzene)
carbon tetrachloride
chloroform
perchloroethylene (tetrachloroethylene, perc)
methyl butyl ketone (MBK)
dimethyl formamide (DMF)
morpholine

For a comprehensive, readable, if not simple, chart of information about specific organic chemical solvents, divided into chemical classes, refer to Table 5, pages 95–103, in Monona Rossol's *The Artist's Complete Health and Safety Guide, 3rd edition.*

A WORD ABOUT SPRAYS

Solvent-based sprays are particularly hazardous. Aerosol sprays commonly used in costume shops are paints, leather dyes, finishes such as shellac, and hair spray. The paint, dye, or hair spray comes from the can as a fine mist, solvent droplets containing tiny bits of solid material. With a single breath you might inhale thousands of these dangerous droplets, bringing them deep into your lungs and dispersing toxic chemicals throughout your body by way of your bloodstream. In addition, aerosol sprays in pressure cans also contain chemical propellants that add even more ingredients to the toxic brew in the air.

To repeat: no method of spraying solvent-based substances is, in itself, safe. Water-based sprays are somewhat safer since the water is not a dangerous volatile solvent. Don't forget, however, that the color pigments carried by the water droplets may be toxic in themselves.

The *only* safe way to use sprays in a costume shop is in a spray booth where the mist can be removed from the general room air: a *local exhaust ventilation system.* A *dilution ventilation system* does *not* protect those in the room from spray mists. (See the brief description of ventilation systems on pages 44–45.)

Many technicians believe they can work safely with sprays in the absence of a spray booth when everyone in the room or area is wearing a respirator. Respirators, even when properly fitted and equipped (see page 57 for a discussion of respirators), do not offer complete protection from sprays. OSHA regulations, for instance, restrict the use of respirators for protection from airborne toxic substances on a regular basis. Also, don't forget that fine particles from sprays remain in the area for a long time, often several hours after respirators have been removed.

Do not ever spray if you can achieve a satisfactory effect with another process. It is much more dangerous to apply paints and dyes in spray form than it is to brush or sponge them on.

FIRES, SPILLS, AND DISPOSAL

Most solvents present fire hazards. When you study your Material Safety Data Sheets, pay particular attention to the *flashpoint* of the substance. The flashpoint is the lowest temperature at which the chemical gives off enough vapor to form an ignitable mixture. The lower the flashpoint, the greater the chance that the chemical will ignite. The MSDS will also give the *evaporation rate* of the solvent. Solvents that evaporate rapidly are more apt to be flammable than those that evaporate slowly.

To be on the safe side, treat all solvents as potential fire hazards. Store them in approved flammable storage cabinets. Do not allow smoking around solvents and keep heat and sparks away from them. Be sure fire extinguishers are approved for solvent and grease fires.

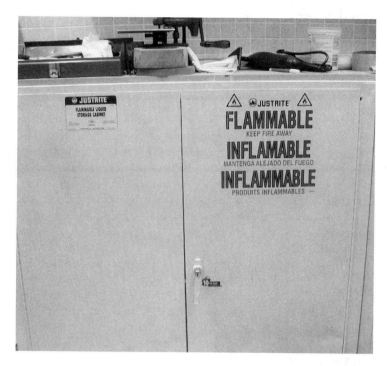

FIGURE 2–4. Storage cabinet at the University of Maryland. *Photograph by Liz Covey.*

Be prepared for spills. Be familiar enough with the solvents in stock to protect yourself and your staff from the acute effects of suddenly released solvent vapor. If large amounts of solvent are stored, keep a supply of chemical solvent absorber on hand to soak up accidental spills. (Kitty litter made of fired clay will work in a pinch.) Do not sweep large amounts of accidentally spilled solvent into a drain.

Dispose of chemicals in accordance with federal and local regulations. Theatre organizations, colleges, and universities should all have written disposal policies. If your organization has no such policy, contact the Environmental Protection Agency (EPA) for advice.

A FEW GOOD PRODUCTS
Finally, don't be daunted by the long lists of strange, hard-to-pronounce chemicals you must choose between. Your costume shop probably has no more than two dozen solvent-based products. Study the labels of what you have on hand. Separate out the products that seem excessively toxic and look for substitutes. Get Material Safety Data Sheets on every solvent and solvent-based product you purchase and use. Share all of this information with your staff, colleagues, or students, and, most important of all, set a good example by the way you make your choices and use these products.

Dyes and Dye Assists

Finding out about the hazards of fabric dyes is very complicated since each color in every type of dye is a discrete chemical with its own potentially hazardous properties. The companies that manufacture or import dyes are required by law to prepare a Material Safety Data Sheet for every color of every dye they make and sell.

51

However, some importers and many companies that repackage and sell these dyes in small quantities to costume shops do not provide proper MSDSs. Even when MSDSs are available, the health and safety information on dyes is in general incomplete. Only a few of the thousands of commercial dyes on the market have been studied for long-term or chronic effects and, even when the dye pigment appears to be relatively safe, the assistant chemicals necessary to make that pigment bond with the fabric may be toxic.

Therefore, given the facts that some dyes are known to be quite toxic, and the toxicity of many others is unknown, the best course of action is to treat all dyes with extreme caution.

KNOW WHAT YOU ARE USING

Before you purchase dyes, ask the supplier for the Color Index numbers and Material Safety Data Sheets for all the dyes, mordants, and other chemicals necessary to use them. Try hard not to accept products if this information is not available.

Color Index (CI) names and numbers are assigned to all commercial dyes by the British Society of Dyers and Colourists and the American Association of Textile Chemists and Colorists. The CI identifications are recognized internationally and make it possible to research the individual properties and hazards of that particular dye. Not all manufacturers and distributors use CI identifications. If they are not available, take your business elsewhere.

Along with the CI number, dyes are divided into "classes" that relate to their chemical structure, and you should know what "class" or kind of dye you're buying. Examples of these classes are "fiber-reactive dyes," "acid dyes," and "disperse dyes." Manufacturers often omit dye class information and may instead identify their dyes by the fabrics they will dye, or by the processes for which they can be used. Fiber-reactive dyes, for instance, may be called "silk dyes," "cold water dyes," or "batik dyes."

Most dyes used in costume shops are *synthetic*, as opposed to *natural*; natural dye colors are extracted from flowers, leaves, bark, nuts, and so on. Some manufacturers use the terms *aniline dye* and *synthetic dye* as if they were synonymous, although they are not; these terms simply mean that the dyes are chemically based. The first synthetic dyes were produced from aniline, a chemical produced from coal tar. Today most synthetic dyes are made from petrochemicals.

The common dyes you purchase in your local supermarket or pharmacy, such as Rit and Tintex, are called *union* or *all-purpose dyes*. Union dyes are mixtures of several classes of synthetic dyes, including acid dyes, direct dyes, and basic dyes, with assisting chemicals such as salt, all combined so the product will color as many kinds of fabric as possible. Just because a packet of union dye can be purchased from the supermarket shelf, do not treat it as a harmless product. It isn't. You must practice good hygiene and take proper precautions with all dyes.

Acid dyes are among the least hazardous of all dye classes, but they often require assisting chemicals such as sodium sulfate, sulfuric acid, or formic acid, which are hazardous.

Vat dyes are not recommended for use in costume shops because they require the addition of caustic compounds such as lye or caustic soda, and they must be oxidized with dichromate salts, which might be quite hazardous.

Azoic and naphthol dyes may cause severe allergic reactions. Use only with proper protection.

Fiber-reactive dyes ("cold water," "cold process," or "Procion dyes") are known to cause severe respiratory allergies, and may irritate the respiratory tract. Use only with proper protection.

FIGURE 2–5. Dye vat with drainage slide at the American Conservatory Theater. *Photograph by Rosemary Ingham.*

Disperse dyes may cause dermatitis in people who come in contact with the finished product after dyeing. It's safest to use disperse dyes on clothing that will be worn on top of another layer.

USE DYES SAFELY

Avoid inhalation. Dye powders are highly concentrated and easily inhaled. Once airborne, these powders can travel some distance, remaining in the air long enough to be inhaled by others in the room before they settle on clothing and personal items like your coffee cup.

Whenever it's possible to do so, purchase dyes in liquid rather than powdered form. Unfortunately, not all dyes are available in liquid form and when they are they tend to be more expensive.

To protect yourself from inhaling or ingesting airborne dye powder, work inside a

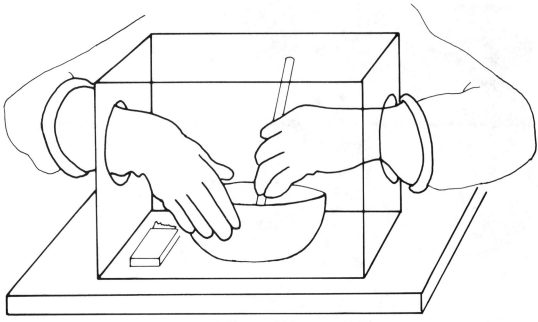

FIGURE 2–6. Glove box made of Plexiglas sheets glued together, which sits down over the work. (From *Stage Fright* by Monona Rossol.)

glove box. (See Figure 2–6 for a glove box you can make yourself.) Open the tin or package inside the glove box, measure out the dye powder, and "paste it up," mixing the powder with a small quantity of water. Be sure to close tins and packages before removing them from the glove box. Keep a toxic dust respirator available in case of accidental spillage of powder.

Also, while the dyepot is "cooking," refrain from inhaling steam and vapors that rise from it.

Protect your skin from contact with liquid dyes. Wear rubber gloves and a long-sleeved smock and if your hair is long cover it with a hat or a scarf. Clean up all spills immediately and be careful not to track dye out of the dye room on your shoes.

Protect yourself from ingesting dyes by *never* eating, drinking, or smoking in the dye area. Also, *never* cook or eat food with a pot or spoon that's been used for dyeing. Even though the item appears clean, most utensils are porous enough to hold hazardous amounts of residual dye.

Always work on cleanable surfaces. Never cover work tables with paper. Wet dye spills will return to a powdered state when they dry and the dye dust will escape into the air when the paper is rolled up to discard. Mop up liquid spills immediately and vacuum rather than sweep up dye powder spills.

Never use bleach or organic chemical solvents to clean dye stains off your skin. Wash with a mild cleanser and allow the remainder of the stain to wear off.

Create a Healthy, Safe Craft and Dye Area

1. All craft and dye areas should have conveniently located hot and cold running water.

FIGURE 2–7. Painter/dyer Carol E. Bonds at The Washington Opera opening a jar of dye in a glove box. *Photograph by Rosemary Ingham.*

2. All should have adequate ventilation. This is particularly difficult to accomplish in a basement, since to meet most local air pollution codes local exhausts must vent above the roof of the building. And it's an excellent reason for locating the costume shop on the top floor with windows!

3. Electrical wiring should be safe, with enough current and outlets to run all the equipment and to discourage the proliferation of extension cords. Keep electrical equipment away from wet areas as much as possible and install ground fault interrupters on all outlets. Provide adequate lighting, especially in storage areas where you must be able to read labels.

4. The area should be comfortably heated in cold weather and air-conditioned in hot

weather. If fans are necessary, make sure the blades have protective covers. No space heaters of any sort should be permitted; they present too many dangers.

5. Develop a protocol for evacuating the area in case of a fire or other emergency. Practice and review this protocol at regular intervals. Marked safety exits should be approved by the local fire codes, and the area should contain the following equipment to use in the event of a fire or other emergency:

- Fire extinguishers that are approved for A, B, and C types of fires. (Type A: ordinary combustibles; Type B: solvents and grease; Type C: electrical.) Make sure they are inspected regularly and that every person in the shop knows how to operate them.

FIGURE 2–8. Readily accessible first aid boxes at the University of Maryland. *Photograph by Liz Covey.*

- Sprinkler system, if possible.
- Smoke detector.
- A fire blanket.
- Chemical solvent absorbers.
- A first-aid kit, well stocked and well maintained.
- A list of emergency telephone numbers located by the telephone, up to date and easy to read.

MAKE THE CRAFT AND DYE STORAGE AREA SAFE

1. Store all materials in unbreakable containers and in the correct type of container that will not be corroded by the chemical inside.

2. Label all substances and include special safety instructions when necessary.

3. Keep all containers tightly closed.

4. Store all flammable materials in approved flammable storage cabinets and *keep the doors closed*.

5. Do not put hazardous materials on high shelves or in out of the way places where they could be dropped and spilled when you're getting them out.

FIGURE 2–9. OSHA-approved eyewash station at the University of Maryland. *Photograph by Liz Covey.*

6. Use a hand pump to dispense liquids kept in large cans or drums. This will help prevent spills.

7. Wear protective gloves, clothing, and goggles when you're transferring dangerous chemicals from one container to another.

SAFE DISPOSAL

1. Clean up all spills immediately.

2. Do not pour solvents and oils down the drain. Collect these liquids in an approved container and dispose of them according to the regulations in your area. If you do not know what the regulations are, consult the local water authority. (You are bound by the rules of the sewage treatment plant into which your waste discharges.) Rags and papers that have been soaked with art and craft materials should be collected in approved waste containers and emptied each day.

3. Some acid and alkali solutions can be disposed of by neutralizing or diluting them in large quantities of water and pouring them slowly down the drain, accompanied by more water. Before you do this, however, check with the water authority.

GENERAL HOUSEKEEPING AND PERSONAL HYGIENE

It's easier to clean up a well-designed craft area than one filled with a hodge-podge of old tables and pieces of cast-off stage furniture. Think safety when designing your work space.

1. Protect counter and floor surfaces with a sealer that will prevent dust from collecting in the cracks. Concrete floors create especially good hiding places for hazardous substances.

2. Wipe down all surfaces regularly with water and detergent.

3. Wash all containers and measuring tools at the end of each work day.

4. Launder protective clothing regularly.

5. *Never* eat, drink, or smoke in the craft and dye area.

6. Wash your hands a lot, but remember: *never clean them with bleach or with organic solvents.*

Safety Takes Longer

It takes longer to observe good safety procedures while you're working and to clean up properly at the end of every work period than it does to work haphazardly with art and craft materials, disregarding danger. To protect your health from careless exposure to dangerous chemicals, you must include safety time in your planning. Devise routine procedures for setting up work areas, gathering materials, protecting surfaces, and putting on protective clothing. Stop work in plenty of time to put everything away and dispose of wastes properly. Don't work with dangerous chemicals for protracted periods of time or when you're overly tired. Avoid all of the last-minute rushes that promote carelessness.

BEST'S SAFETY & SECURITY DIRECTORY
Best's Safety & Security Directory is a gold mine of information for costume shop supervisors with a commitment to making their shops safe and healthy places in which to work.

The publishers offer the following overview of what it contains:

This directory provides complete details on OSHA standards and regulations, checklists, training articles, and new product developments—everything needed to develop an effective safety program.

- *Buyers' Guides—a comprehensive product catalog grouped by region, product line, and brand name. The Guides include more than 6,800 product and service descriptions with all new products highlighted. Over 3,200 product manufacturers and distributors are represented.*
- *OSHA Summaries—contains completely revised and updated safety standards, allowing subscribers to determine their current OSHA responsibilities at a glance.*
- *Training Articles—discuss today's most vital safety and security concerns, assisting you with ongoing training ideas.*

Copies of *Best's Safety & Security Directory* may be ordered from:

A.M. Best Company, Inc.
Ambest Road
Oldwick, NJ 08858

Respirators

Respirators are not substitutes for adequate ventilation. According to OSHA regulations, respirators are "legal protection only": 1) when the hazardous process is used less than thirty times a year; 2) while ventilation systems are being installed, maintained, or repaired;

3) during emergencies; and 4) for entry into an atmosphere of unknown origin.

No costume shop should feel safe because respirators are in regular use. However, protection offered by a carefully chosen, properly fitted and maintained respirator—if it does not result in a false sense of security—is certainly better than no protection at all.

The responsibilities for purchasing, fitting, and caring for a respirator used by a costume technician who is employed by a theatre organization on a long-term basis should be undertaken jointly by the theatre administration and the technician. A technician, especially a dyer/painter or craftsperson who works on a freelance basis, must be responsible for his or her own respiratory safety, including health evaluations and the selection, fit, purchase, and maintenance of a respirator.

The following sections are taken in part from *The Artist's Complete Health and Safety Guide* by Monona Rossol, and a data sheet titled "Respiratory Protection: New Rules" written for United Scenic Artists, Local 829, IATSE, also by Monona Rossol in her role as USA Health and Safety Officer. The sources for the data sheet are the Occupational Safety and Health Administration (OSHA) rules for respiratory protection. These rules may be found in the OSHA code at 29 CFR 1910.134.

The Written Protocol

If your job requires you to wear a respirator on a regular basis (which, in a theatre costume shop, most often applies to dyers and craftspeople) the person who hired and supervises you is required to provide:

1. *A written program* explaining the protocol that is in place to protect your respiratory health. It should include all of the following requirements.

2. *A written hazard evaluation* to define and describe the hazards you will face on the job and why a particular respirator was chosen to protect you from these hazards.

3. *A medical evaluation* to determine your ability to wear the selected respirator and annual medical checks that may be done by a physician or a "licensed medical professional."

4. *Documented training* annually to ensure that you are familiar with the use and limitations of the equipment; know the procedures

FIGURE 2–10. Quarter-face respirator at The Shakespeare Theatre. *Photograph by Rosemary Ingham.*

for regular cleaning, disinfecting, and maintaining all respirators; and how to don, doff, and do a "seal check" before each use.

5. *Periodic program evaluation* to ensure that the respirator you are wearing continues to be effective.

Types of Respirators

There are three basic types of respirators: air-supplying, air-purifying, and powered air-purifying. Most costume technicians choose air-purifying respirators. They are affordable and, because they don't require additional equipment worn on other parts of the body, are the easiest to wear.

There are four types of air-purifying respirators: disposable, which look like dust masks and are discarded after use; quarter-face, which cover the mouth and nose; half-face, which cover mouth, nose, and chin; and full-face, which look a bit like gas masks.

Quarter-and half-face types have replaceable filters and cartridges; full-face types have a replaceable canister.

NIOSH

The acronym NIOSH should always be found on whatever type of respirator and supporting supplies you purchase. It stands for the National Institute for Occupational Safety and Health. NIOSH specifies the tests that all respirators and respirator products must pass. Make sure you never buy a respirator without this official seal of approval.

Fitting Respirators

A respirator is not something you can purchase casually at a hardware store in small, medium, and large sizes. One that does not fit your face is not only ineffective but may also prove to be

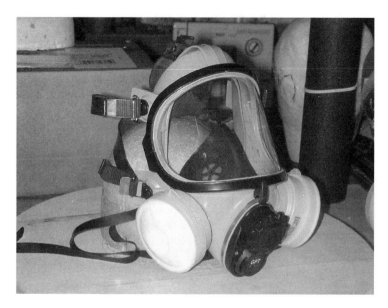

FIGURE 2–11. Full-face respirator at The Shakespeare Theatre. *Photograph by Rosemary Ingham.*

more dangerous, due to the possibility of concentrating toxic particles into the mask through leaks, than not wearing one at all.

A respirator must be fit tested by a "qualified person." Such qualified persons are rarely available from the companies that sell respirators. There are industrial hygienists or consultants in most areas of the country who are trained to fit test respirators but their services are expensive. The best solution for a theatre, professional or educational, is to have a staff or faculty member from one of the theatre shops (costumes, props, lights, or sets) specially trained to fit respirators and masks. This person can be called upon to help technicians select and purchase new respirators, and make periodic fit and maintenance checks on existing equipment.

Beards

Beards and respirators are not compatible. OSHA rules are quite explicit about this incompatibility: "The employer shall not permit respirators with tight-fitting facepieces to be worn by employees who have: facial hair. . . ." It is impossible to achieve a protective seal when a beard, mustache, sideburns, or even beard stubble is between the skin and the sealing surface of the facepiece.

Filters and Cartridges

Filters and cartridges provide the actual barriers between you and the toxic particles in your workplace. Filters are designed to trap particles, and cartridges containing chemical air-purifying materials trap vapors. When you draw in air, it passes through either a filter or a chemical material that traps the contaminant. Different cartridges and filters are designed to trap specific gases, vapors, fumes, dusts, and mists and you must be sure you have the correct type, or types, to protect you in your workplace.

No filter or cartridge can remove all the toxic substances in the air. A properly fitted respirator, however, with the appropriate filter or cartridge, can reduce the amount of a particular contaminant to an acceptable level as defined by NIOSH standards.

Be sure to change your filters and cartridges at the prescribed times. Filters clog progressively and you will find it increasingly difficult to draw breath through them. Forcing your breath through a partially clogged filter is dangerous because the pressure of breathing will cause more particles to come through.

Chemical cartridges stop working when they are spent. Approximately eight hours of use is their limit, or two weeks after exposure to air. Chemical cartridges also wear out with time and usually carry an expiration date.

Maintaining Respirators

One of the worst things you can do with your respirator is to leave it lying about on a table or shelf where it will collect dust and perhaps even be picked up by somebody else. The first rule in respirator maintenance is to keep track of your own while you are using it. (If a respirator is to be used by more than one person, it must be thoroughly cleaned and disinfected between users.) At the end of each work period, wipe all the surfaces of the respirator clean and put it into a sealable plastic bag. Store the bag away from sunlight. Cartridges that are left out will continue to capture contaminants from the air and should also be stored in sealable plastic bags. Never store respirators by hanging them on hooks out in the open.

3
Fabrics

Fabric history took a revolutionary turn during the two decades between 1940 and 1960 as an array of man-made, noncellulosic fabrics appeared on the market. These synthetic fabrics proved so successful that, by 1974, a high point year in synthetic fabric production, 70 percent of the materials consumed by United States' mills for yarn and fabric production were man-made, noncellulosic fiber. (Rayon is man-made *cellulosic* fiber, regenerated from natural products and is in a category all by itself.) At that time, in general, man-made fabrics were not only more available than natural fabrics, they also cost less.

During the last two decades of the twentieth century, man-made, noncellulosic fabrics made up about 50 percent of the total garment fabric market. The rises and falls in this percentage may be attributed, in large part, to the fluctuating price of petroleum products, as well as to fashion trends. No great changes are expected in the early years of the present century. Overall, synthetic fabrics remain less expensive than natural fabrics, although the differences in price are not as great as they once were.

The proliferation of synthetics throughout the textile and garment industries continues to pose problems for costume designers and technicians who are in the business of creating stage costumes for plays set in many historical periods, most of which fall before the invention of the wash-and-wear, crease resistant, nonsag "miracle" fabrics. Unfortunately, garments made from nylon, polyester, and acrylic fabrics do not look exactly like garments made from silk, wool, or cotton, especially in motion and under stage lights. But, because many synthetics are on the market and they are often cheaper, costume designers sometimes have to choose wholly man-made fabrics or blends of natural and synthetic yarns to create costumes that would have originally been made from cotton, wool, silk, or linen.

However, synthetic fabrics, intelligently chosen, don't necessarily detract from a period costume's success. They may, in fact, add their own good qualities and even help make the costume more durable and easier to wash or clean. To make wise fabric choices, however, costume designers and technicians must know

FIGURE 3–2. Alene Dawson, Libby Christophersen, Enid Graham, and Melissa Bowen in a production of *Love's Labours Lost* at The Shakespeare Theatre. The costumes, designed by Anita Stewart, use a variety of interesting textures and patterns. *Photograph by Carol Rosegg, courtesy of The Shakespeare Theatre.*

FIGURE 3–1. Caroline Lagerfelt as Elizabeth I and Marco Barricelli as Robert Dudley, Earl of Leicester, in a production of *Mary Stuart* at the American Conservatory Theater. Ms. Lagerfelt wears shimmering brocades with metallic trimmings, which reflect the sumptuous clothing of the sixteenth century, designed by Deborah Dryden. *Photograph courtesy of the American Conservatory Theater.*

some basic facts about natural and man-made fabrics: where they come from, how they are processed, and what behavior may be expected from the most common types of cloth.

Every time you purchase a piece of fabric, make sure you know exactly what you're buying. By law, each cloth bolt and roll must be tagged with the generic names of all the yarns used in its production and the percentage of each present. For example: 70 percent wool, 22 percent polyester, 8 percent silk. Generic names are assigned by the Federal

Trade Commission and always appear in lower-case letters, while brand names are capitalized. Textile manufacturing companies create brand names they hope will entice you to buy their product, not to inform you about it. Use generic names when you are researching fabric characteristics.

Clothing sold in the United States must also be tagged with fabric content and, in addition, with washing and/or dry cleaning information. Fabrics by the yard may or may not be accompanied by laundry instructions. Learn to guard against unwelcome surprises by reading all tags and labels before buying any fabric or wearing apparel.

FIGURE 3–3. Wallace Acton as Peer Gynt surrounded by desert maidens wearing an array of diaphanous and opaque fabrics with woven metallic patterns and borders. Paul Tazewell designed the costumes for this production of *Peer Gynt* at The Shakespeare Theatre. *Photograph by Carol Rosegg, courtesy of The Shakespeare Theatre.*

Fibers and Filaments

All fabrics begin as fibers or filaments. Cotton, linen, and wool begin as fibers. Most silk begins as a filament. All the man-made fabrics begin as filaments, although in many instances, the filaments are cut up and processed into fibers, sometimes called *staples,* before they are spun into yarn. The main differences between fibers and filaments are length and surface characteristics. Cotton fibers average 1¼ inches in length; wool fibers may be from 1 inch to 14 inches long, and flax (the fiber from which linen is made) from 15 inches to 25 inches long. A single silk filament is from 300 to 1600 yards in length and the man-made filaments may be any length the manufacturer chooses.

All fibers have uneven surfaces that allow them to adhere to one another when they are spun into yarn. Fiber surfaces absorb rather than reflect light and produce fabrics with natural matte finishes. Generally, filament surfaces are smooth and reflective. Most silk fabric is lustrous, and most made-made filaments produce shiny fabrics. "Raw" or "wild" silk has a duller surface than cultivated silk because the original filament contains irregularities. Man-made filaments may undergo various processes to reduce their reflective qualities.

The adherence property of fibers, plus an inherent "twistability," make it possible to spin fibers into yarns of many different sorts and strengths. Filaments do not have to be spun into yarn. However, in almost all cases, fila-ment yarns are made up of several filaments "thrown" or twisted together. The only common use today of monofilament yarn (a single, untwisted filament) is in nylon hosiery manufacture.

Try not to be confused by the fact that all manufactured cellulosic and noncellulosic textile materials are called "man-made fibers," even though they all begin their existence as filaments and may or may not have been cut and processed into actual fibers.

The Naturals

Cellulosic

COTTON

Even though the fashion industry's use of cotton has had tremendous ups and downs during the past several decades, cotton remains the leading clothing fabric worn worldwide. About eight million tons of cotton are produced annually.

Cotton is a vegetable seed fiber. Botanically, the fibers are the protective covering of the seeds in the cotton plant, a shrub that grows from four to six feet high. Dry cotton fiber is from 88 percent to 96 percent cellulose.

Before the discovery of the New World, Europe got its cotton from India. One of Columbus's most important discoveries in 1492 was cotton growing wild in the Americas. Ancient, beautifully woven cotton fabrics have been discovered in Mexico and in the southwestern United States, as well as in Peru where cotton was probably cultivated as early as 2500 B.C.

The first written account of cotton appears in 484 B.C. in Herodotus's account of his travels through India: "There are trees in which fleece grew surpassing that of sheep and from which the natives made cloth." In 1350, an English explorer, Sir John Mandeville, returned from his trip through India with a more fanciful description: ". . . there grew there a wonderful tree which bore tiny lambs on the ends of its branches."

Cotton cultivation and the process of turning the fleecy white bolls into fabric once required back-breaking labor and unremitting tedium. Over the years, mechanization has altered the early cotton industry almost beyond recognition. The effect of Eli Whitney's cotton gin is a case in point: In 1791, America shipped 400 bales of hand-harvested cotton to Europe. In 1792, Whitney introduced his cotton gin, and in 1800, America exported 30,000 bales of cotton; in 1810, 180,000 bales were exported.

China has long been the largest cotton grower in the world. In 2000, the Chinese produced approximately 20 million bales of cotton. The United States ranked second in that year with the production of 17.2 million bales.

Cotton fiber lengths range between ¾ inch and 2½ inches. American Upland cotton, which accounts for the bulk of the cotton grown worldwide, produces fibers that average

1 inch in length. Long staple cotton fibers come from varieties such as American Pima, Egyptian, and Sea Island. Naturally, the longest fibers produce the most luxurious yarns and the most expensive fabric.

Important Cotton Characteristics

1. Cotton fabrics are stronger wet than dry and can therefore withstand repeated vigorous washings.

2. Cotton has remarkable capacities to absorb moisture. Clean cotton fabric retains twenty-four to twenty-seven times its own weight in water. Because of this characteristic, cotton absorbs and releases perspiration quickly, bleaches well, and dyes easily.

3. Cotton can withstand high wet heat and can be sterilized without harm to the fabric. Because of this characteristic, cotton takes many dark-colored dye pigments that require high temperatures for setting.

4. Cotton fabric is quite strong and stands up well to abrasion tests.

5. The cotton fiber has very little elasticity, causing cotton fabric to wrinkle easily.

6. Cottons weaken and deteriorate when they are exposed to long periods of sunlight.

7. Pins and jewelry can cause holes in cotton fabric because they cut the fibers.

8. Cotton, stored in damp, warm conditions, will support mildew and mold and eventually rot away.

9. Cotton is resistant to moths and carpet beetles, but *not* to silverfish.

10. Properly stored and protected, cotton is not affected by age. Fabric conservators advise wrapping cotton fabric in acid-free tissue paper and storing it in boxes made from acid-free cardboard.

LINEN (FLAX)

Flax is a bast fiber taken from the stalk of a plant called *Linum usitatissimum*. Bast fibers comprise a large group—flax, ramie, jute, and hemp being the most common. Others are sunn, kenaf, and urena. All bast fibers are largely cellulose. Both the yarn and the fabric produced from flax are called *linen*.

Flax and wool are the two oldest textile fibers used by humankind. We know that the ancient peoples of Mesopotamia, Assyria, and Egypt had learned to cultivate flax and spin linen some 5,000 years ago.

Today, Russia is the world's largest producer of flax. Significant quantities are also grown in Belgium, Holland, Germany, France, and Ireland. Irish linen is particularly popular in the garment industry, and Belgium manufactures exceptionally beautiful table linens.

When shopping for linen fabric, pay careful attention to labels. A 100 percent linen fabric will be labeled "linen," "pure linen," or "pure flax." A blend that contains linen must be labeled with the percentage by weight of each fiber present in the fabric. Linen look-alike fabrics that are labeled simply "silk linen" are silk, those called "rayon linen" are rayon. A fabric that is labeled "linenlike" usually contains no linen at all.

Important Linen Characteristics

1. Flax is a long fiber, from 6 inches to 40 inches, with an average length of 15 inches to 25 inches.

2. The fibers are smooth and lint-free, with a high wax content that produces natural luster.

3. Flax fibers are creamy white to light tan in color.

4. Flax fibers are two to three times stronger than cotton fibers.

5. Linen is stronger wet than dry. It can be boiled without damage to the fibers.

6. Linen is highly absorbent and allows moisture to evaporate quickly. It has an excellent affinity for most dyes. Dark-colored dyes, such as black and navy blue, may rub off in areas of heavy wear or along crease lines.

7. Linen is an excellent conductor of heat.

8. Linen has poor elasticity. The flax fiber is smooth and has no natural crimp and, therefore, doesn't spring back readily after being creased. Linen wrinkles badly; crease resistant finishes help somewhat. Because flax fibers are so unresilient, they have a tendency to crack. Therefore, store linen on a roll rather than folded.

9. Linen yellows with age.

10. Linen resists moths and alkalies but is damaged by mold and silverfish.

RAMIE AND HEMP

Both ramie and hemp are bast fibers. Although they have been used to make clothing fabrics for hundreds of years, ramie and hemp fabrics became available by the yard and in the garment industry only during the last two decades of the twentieth century. Ramie is somewhat softer than linen, while hemp is a sturdy, rather dense fabric. Hemp is three times stronger than cotton and has good abrasion resistance. Both take dyes more readily than linen, and both wrinkle. They are often seen in blends with linen, cotton, rayon, silk, or polyester.

Protein

WOOL

Wool is probably the oldest fabric worn by humans. The Babylonians may have worn wool garments as early as 4000 B.C., and the Britons around 3000 B.C. A tablet from the ancient city of Ur, dated 2000 B.C., describes girls and women weaving wool.

Many ancient peoples herded sheep for wool, but it was the Romans who first introduced scientific breeding principles from which they developed the outstanding wool producing breed of all time, the Spanish Merino. Columbus carried sheep to America on the *Santa Maria,* and the Spanish conquistadors brought them to Mexico. In Colonial America, most households kept sheep, spun wool yarn, and wove woolen fabric for clothing. England's wool textile industry led the world from the seventeenth through the nineteenth centuries and still produces high-quality wool fabrics. Today, sheep are raised worldwide and many countries manufacture wool textiles.

Wool fibers are composed of a protein called *keratin,* and are in general composition similar to human hairs. The fibers have three parts, or layers: the *epidermis,* the *cortex,* and the *medulla.* The medulla is at the center of the wool fiber. Thick, stiff wool fibers have larger medullas; fine, flexible, easily spun wool fibers have almost invisible medullas.

The cortex layer is responsible for the natural crimp in wool fibers. It gives wool fabric elasticity and the ability to shed wrinkles.

The outermost layer of the wool fiber, the epidermis, is formed from scales that, under a high-powered microscope, look slightly like hooks. The epidermis helps make wool waterproof and resistant to abrasion. When the yarn is spun, the hooklike scales interlock with one another to create a strong yarn. These scales cause wool to feel "scratchy" and irritate some people's skin. Processes remove the scales from wool fibers before spinning. Woolens treated in this manner are not scratchy, and they are washable.

Standards in wool textile production are monitored today by The International Wool Secretariat, which pursues a policy of promoting and improving the performance of wool, irrespective of its country of origin. This organization created The Woolmark and The Woolblend Mark, used today by over 14,000 manufacturers as an international quality standard. Labels on wool products must also differentiate between "virgin," or "new," wool, which applies only to wool fibers taken directly from the fleece of sheep; "reprocessed" wool that has been recovered from wool products that have never been worn or used, such as the scraps from the ready-to-wear industry; and "reused" wool that is recovered from worn or used products and rarely used in garment fabrics. The International Wool Secretariat also sponsors scientific research within the wool industry and provides technical assistance to manufacturers.

Important Wool Characteristics

1. Wool fibers are strong and flexible. A fiber can be bent 20,000 times before it breaks.
2. Wool fibers are elastic. They can be stretched 25 percent to 30 percent of their lengths without breaking *and* return to their original length. The elasticity of wool fibers makes woolen fabrics naturally wrinkle resistant.
3. Wool absorbs moisture, up to 30 percent of its weight, without feeling damp. This is why wool feels warm: it absorbs and holds perspiration and does not allow the body to be cooled by evaporation.
4. Woolens have a natural insulation caused by the crimp in the fibers. This insulation helps make wool clothing, in different weights and weaves, warm in winter and cool in summer.
5. Wool felts when it's exposed to damp heat, agitation, and/or pressure. (This is what happens when your wool sweater finds its way into the washing machine on a hot water cycle.)
6. Wool is weaker wet than dry and should be handled carefully when wet.
7. Wool is the ultimate tailoring fabric. It eases well and can be shaped with steam.
8. Wool is water-repellent and flame-resistant.
9. Wool may be damaged by moths, carpet beetles, alkalies, chlorine bleach, prolonged exposure to sunlight, and a hot iron.

WORSTEDS AND WOOLENS

There are two distinct types of wool fabric: *worsteds* and *woolens*. Worsted yarns are made from the long wool fibers that have been both carded and combed, then spun into a tight, smooth, uniform yarn. On the whole, worsted fabrics are stronger, smoother, and more expensive than woolens. A popular worsted wool fabric is *gabardine*.

Woolen yarns are spun from shorter fibers that have been carded, but not combed, then twisted into a looser yarn with a fuzzy surface and, sometimes, large irregularities that create texture. Some woolen fabrics are firmly woven and some are loose. *Harris tweed* is a popular woolen with a firm weave.

Important Worsted Characteristics

(The term "worsted" was first associated with cloth produced in the parish of Worstead, in Norfolk, England.)

1. Smooth texture and firm surface.
2. Lustrous surface created by the tightly twisted yarns.
3. Holds a crease well, does not sag.
4. Greater tensile strength than woolen.
5. On the whole, uses a better grade of yarn.
6. Lighter and less bulky.
7. Tailors and drapes well.
8. Long wearing.

Important Woolen Characteristics

1. Soft feel and fuzzy surface.
2. Little shine or sheen.

3. Does not hold a crease well.

4. Relatively low tensile strength.

5. As a rule, less expensive than worsteds.

6. Generally heavier and bulkier than worsteds and may have a nap.

7. More suited to casual fashions.

SPECIALTY HAIR FIBERS

According to The International Wool Secretariat, wool may refer only to fabrics made from the fleece of sheep. Fibers from other animals, such as goats, rabbits, llamas, and so on, should be called *hair fibers*. The annual production of fabrics made from hair fibers is small. Nevertheless, these fabrics are important to the fashion industry. Many are blends of wool and hair fibers and, alone or in combination, hair fibers contribute to some of the most luxurious and expensive fabrics on the market.

These are some of the most common animals whose hair fibers are used in the production of fabric:

1. *Alpaca.* A small member of the South American camel family that produces a rich, silky, and lustrous fleece with hair length from 8 inches to 20 inches. Alpaca is used in lightweight fabrics, knitting yarns, and knitted garments.

2. *Angora goat.* Raised in the United States, Turkey, and South Africa. Produces a soft, silky hair fiber called *mohair,* generally used for suitings and novelty fabrics. Usually expensive.

3. *Angora rabbit.* Produces a long, silky, white hair that is clipped every three or four months. Raised in large quantities in France, Italy, and Japan. Angora is used primarily for knits, especially for children, and in soft felting.

4. *Camel.* The two-humped, or Bactrian, species is found all over Asia, but the animals producing the best quality hair come from Mongolia. Bactrian camel hair is reddish brown or tan and is usually left its natural color. The hair is obtained by shearing and by collecting hair that has been shed by the animals in the spring.

5. *Kashmir goat.* The animal whose hair produces a fabric called *cashmere.* Raised in Tibet, China, Iran, Afghanistan, and India. The hair, which is more like wool that any other hair fiber, sheds in the spring and is plucked from the animal or picked off bushes. Hair separation is tedious because they are so fine. Cashmere fabric is expensive.

6. *Llama.* The animals are indigenous to Peru and were first domesticated there, although raising them is beginning to spread to the United States and other countries. Llamas are sheared in early spring. The hair is brown or black, lustrous, very warm, and lightweight.

7. *Vicuna.* Members of the llama family, these animals live in Peru at elevations above 16,000 feet. They are small and very wild and are usually killed for their fleece. To protect them against extinction, the Peruvian government limits the number of vicunas that can be killed. Vicuna hair is the softest, lightest, and warmest of all the animal fibers. It ranges in color from reddish brown to white on the belly. One animal yields only about four ounces of yarn and vicuna is the most expensive fabric in the world.

SILK

Silk is a continuous protein filament produced by the silkworm to form its cocoon. The silkworm is the caterpillar of the silk moth (Bombyx Mori), and its cocoon is the shell it constructs to protect itself during its growth from caterpillar, to chrysalis, to moth. A single cocoon is made of a continuous filament that the silkworm extrudes from its body and throws about itself, layer within layer, into a thick, smooth, symmetrical ball larger than a robin's egg but smaller than a pigeon's.

Silk filaments were first turned into cloth in China about 4,000 years ago. For almost 3,000 years, the Chinese successfully guarded their silk secret and monopolized the highly lucrative silk trade. In the third century A.D., silk production began in Japan and in India, and in A.D. 550, two Nestorian monks, at the behest of the Emperor Justinian, smuggled silk-worm eggs and mulberry seeds out of China to Constantinople, opening the way for silk production in Europe. Today Japan produces the bulk of the world's raw silk, which is silk filament ready to be made into yarn. Japan, China, India, Thailand, and Korea weave most of the silk fabric used in clothing. Particularly fine silk fabrics come from France and Italy.

The care and feeding of silkworms from egg to cocoon is called *sericulture*. When silkworms hatch, they are about the size of small ants. They have finicky and insatiable appetites and demand the freshest of mulberry leaves every two or three hours. For five weeks they eat voraciously, day and night, and grow seventy times their original size. It takes 200 pounds of mulberry leaves to feed enough silkworms to produce one pound of silk.

After the silkworm has eaten its fill, it spins its cocoon. If nature were allowed to take its course, the worm inside the cocoon would develop into a chrysalis and the chrysalis into a moth. The mature moth would burst the cocoon and break the silk filament into many pieces. Because it is necessary to retrieve an unbroken silk filament, the silkworm is stifled by heat while still inside the cocoon, and the filament is unwound, a process called reeling, by hand or machine. Five to ten cocoons are usually reeled together and twisted into a single strand. Strands are then twisted into yarns, four or five strands for a fine yarn, ten or more for a thick yarn.

Short silk filaments, from damaged cocoons or from ends left after the main filament has been reeled, are retrieved and spun into yarn, much like cotton fibers. Spun silk fabric is not a firm or durable material, however, since the short filaments do not have the surface adherence properties of cotton fibers.

Tussah, or wild silk, is uncultivated. The silkworms that produce it grow wild and feed on many types of leaves, particularly on oak leaves. The filament that results from this mixed diet is not smooth and round, but flat, ribbonlike, and uneven. It's used extensively in making textured fabrics and is often blended with cultivated silk in fabrics such as shantung.

Important Silk Characteristics

1. Silk has a lower density than wool, cotton, or linen and is, therefore, lighter in weight.

2. Silk is a poor conductor of both electricity and heat. It feels warm next to the body and acts as insulation to protect the body from cold and from heat.

3. Silk can soak up 30 percent of its weight in moisture and still feel dry. This means it can absorb perspiration without becoming clammy and also accounts for its great affinity for dyestuffs at relatively low temperatures.

4. The silk filament is the strongest of all the natural fibers. A piece of silk filament is stronger than a steel filament of equal size.

5. Silk is weaker wet than dry and may shrink if washed in hot water; handle wet silk fabrics carefully and use warm water for washing and dyeing.

6. Silk will stretch as much as 20 percent of its length without breaking, but after a 2 percent stretch, it doesn't spring back.

7. Unstretched silk fabric is very resilient and has good wrinkle recovery.

8. Silk is resistant to mildew but susceptible to moths and insects.

9. Silk may be treated with hydrogen peroxide or sodium perborate-type bleaches but not with chlorine bleaches.

10. Light, heat, and age will cause silk fabric to become yellow.

11. Silk is damaged by strong soaps and detergents, acids, alkalies, perspiration, hot irons, and excessive sunlight.

The Man-Mades

In 1664, a British scientist, Dr. Robert Hooke, predicted the advent of man-made "artificial silk." More than 200 years elapsed before Dr. Hooke's prediction came to pass, and many scientists were responsible for the steps that led up to that first piece of "artificial silk" developed by Count Hilaire de Chardonnet in 1886. The man-made fabric was exhibited at the 1889 Paris Exhibition and by the early years of the twentieth century a new industry was underway.

There are two types of man-made fabrics: *cellulosic* and *noncellulosic*. The original "artificial silk," now known as rayon, and two subsequent varieties, acetate, triacetate, and lyocell, are cellulosic fabrics. They are derived from regenerated cellulose from natural sources, chiefly wood pulp and cotton linters, the tiny pieces of cotton fibers left behind after ginning. These materials are subjected to chemical processes that reduce them to a honeylike solution. This solution is forced through a spinneret, a device that looks much like a shower head with tiny holes, and comes out in slender, hairlike filaments. After the filaments solidify, they may be processed into different types of yarn. Differences in the chemical composition of the solutions and in the reduction processes account for the differences between the three cellulosic fabrics.

Noncellulosic man-made fabrics are based on a chemical reaction called polymerization and are derived mainly from the basic chemicals found in water, coal, and petroleum. The production of man-made noncellulosic fabrics is highly complex. As with man-made cellulosics, the first step is to liquify the basic chemical mixture, and the second is to force the resulting solution through the spinneret. The characteristics of the various noncellulosic materials—today twenty generic types are produced worldwide—are attributable to the different chemical structures of the solution and the different processes to which the extruded filament may be subjected.

Many people refer to the man-made cellulosic fabrics—rayon, acetate, triacetate, and lyocell—as *man-made,* and the man-made noncellulosic fabrics—nylon, polyester, acrylic—as *synthetic.* These are useful terms that may help you remember that, although man-made, rayon and acetate behave more like natural fabrics than do the synthetics, such as nylon and polyester.

Cellulosic Fabrics

RAYON

From 1886, when it was developed, until 1924, the fabric we call rayon was known as "artificial silk," a reminder of what textile chemists had been looking for. In 1924, the man-made fabric industry sponsored a contest to find a generic name for its product. Kenneth

Lord coined the word *rayon,* the first man-made word for the first man-made fabric.

Rayon began as an inexpensive substitute for silk and endured a long, slow climb up the ladder of respectability. For many years rayon was a limp fabric that sagged, stretched, wrinkled, and was anything but durable. Steadily, throughout the twentieth century, advances in manufacturing techniques have improved the quality and performance of rayon until it now plays a central role in the fashion industry. Rayon, also called viscose, is lightweight, soft, drapeable, and comfortable to wear.

Important Rayon Characteristics

1. Rayon is a relatively strong fabric when dry, but it weakens by 50 percent when wet. It should, therefore, be washed with care and not subjected to vigorous washing machine agitation or hand-twisting. (Older rayon garments, such as dresses from the 1930s and 1940s, may shrink a lot if they are washed; dry cleaning is safer.)

2. Rayon has very little resiliency, which causes it to wrinkle easily in its natural state.

3. Rayon is the most absorbent of all fabrics. This property makes it highly receptive to dyes, but it also causes it to dry more slowly than other man-made fabrics.

4. Rayon deteriorates when subjected to natural and artificial light for extended periods.

5. Rayon is susceptible to damage by mildew but is not harmed by moths or by most ordinary household chemicals.

6. Many rayons are flammable at high temperatures.

ACETATE

Introduced in 1924, acetate is related to rayon but is a different chemical compound with unique characteristics. Its name was taken from one of the important chemicals used in its production: acetic acid.

Acetate fabrics are lustrous, smooth to the touch, drape well, and are comfortable to wear. Acetate yarns are widely used to weave taffetas, satins, and brocades, often appearing in blends with cotton or silk.

Important Acetate Characteristics

1. Acetate does not absorb moisture readily. This means it dries quickly but it doesn't take dye well. To dye acetate, dyes must be used that are specially formulated for acetate fabrics.

2. Acetate is resilient and, therefore, resists wrinkling.

3. Acetate is thermoplastic. This means the fabric becomes more pliable when it is subjected to high heat and hardens into a set shape as it cools. Because of this characteristic, textile manufacturers can permanently imprint dimensional patterns and surface decorations into the cloth.

4. Acetate is resistant to moths, perspiration, mildew, and mold. It will dissolve in acetone or acetic acid (found in vinegar) and may melt under a hot iron.

TRIACETATE

Triacetate, a close relative of acetate, is no longer produced in the United States and does not play a large role in the fabric and garment industries.

LYOCELL

Lyocell, with its original trade name Tencel, is the newest fiber in the cellulosic family. It is similar to rayon in appearance but much stronger and more durable when wet. Lyocell fabrics are soft, lustrous, and wrinkle resistant.

Noncellulosic Fabrics

The following generic names for manufactured, noncellulosic fibers are recognized by the U.S. Federal Trade Commission:

acetate*	olefin*
acrylic*	PBI
anidex	PEN
aramid	PLA
azlon	polyester*
elastoester*	polypropylene*
glass	rayon*
lyocell*	saran
melamine	spandex*
metallic*	sulfar
modacrylic*	triacetate*
nylon*	vinal
nytril	vinyon

Whenever a new man-made noncellulosic fiber is invented with significantly different physical and chemical characteristics from the ones already in existence, the FTC assigns it a new generic name. However, if an existing generic fiber is only modified slightly, the modification becomes a variant of the original fiber. Therefore, there are many more types of man-made noncellulosic materials with many more different characteristics than is shown by the list above. Not all the fibers in the list are manufactured in the United States and only the starred ones have any likelihood of appearing in a costume shop.

NYLON

In 1927, the Du Pont Company initiated a research program in organic chemistry that led, twelve years later, to the first public showing of nylon hosiery at the Golden Gate International Exposition in San Francisco in 1939. On May 15, 1940, nylon hosiery went on sale in the United States, and a fabric revolution began.

Upon America's entry into the Second World War in 1941, all nylon was removed from the retail market and allocated for the production of war materials. Nylon replaced silk in parachutes and the new synthetic fiber was soon being used for tires, tents, ropes, ponchos, combat clothes, cargo riggings, and many other military supplies. After the war, a well-developed synthetic fiber industry turned its attention back to consumer goods.

Important Nylon Characteristics

1. Nylon is the strongest fiber used in wearing apparel.
2. Nylon is both elastic and resilient, stretches, and does not wrinkle.
3. Nylon resists absorption, causing the fabric to dry very quickly. However, poor absorption makes nylon difficult to dye and uncomfortably warm in hot weather or under stage lights. Nylon also retains dirt and stains because it does not absorb water and detergent solutions that could remove them.
4. Nylon collects static electricity that also helps attract dirt and lint.
5. Nylon yarns have a natural luster. Early nylon fabrics looked glassy and artificial but this has been significantly altered by various delustering processes.
6. Nylon fabrics pill, as a result of abrasion. Little balls of fuzz roll up on the surface but do not drop off as they do on wool or cotton.
7. Scissors, needles, and pins used on nylon fabrics become dull very quickly.
8. Nylon is impervious to attacks by moths, perspiration, and common household chemicals. Nylon is extremely sensitive to heat, however, and may melt if it comes in contact with a dry iron, even if the iron is set at a fairly low temperature.

POLYESTER

British textile chemists developed polyester between 1939 and 1941 and, after the end of the Second World War, began to market it under the name Terylene. In 1946, Du Pont secured exclusive rights to the fiber in the United States, called it Dacron, and began to produce it commercially in 1953. Du Pont introduced their new "miracle fabric" in a spectacular way: they exhibited a man's suit that had been worn for sixty-seven days, dunked twice into a swimming pool, and machine washed once, all without pressing. Polyester is the most popular of all the synthetic fibers but costume designers and technicians are usually less enthusiastic about it than the general public.

Important Polyester Characteristics

1. Polyester is extremely resilient and springy, wet or dry, and, therefore, in its natural state, virtually wrinkle free. The fabrics are smooth and crisp and garments made from them won't wilt or droop, even in muggy weather.

2. Ordinary polyester breathes somewhat better than nylon but still feels hot in summer or under stage lights and clammy in winter. Recent modified polyester fabrics are breathable and much more comfortable to wear. (See the section on microfibers, page 75.)

3. Polyester is virtually insensitive to moisture, therefore difficult to dye with ordinary dyestuffs. Also, when a polyester fabric picks up an oil-based stain or a perspiration stain, it's almost impossible to get enough detergent into the fabric to remove it.

4. It's thermoplastic.

5. It pills.

6. It's lightweight, strong, and resists abrasion.

7. Polyesters resist moths, mildew, most chemicals, sunlight, and weathering but may be damaged by a hot iron.

Cotton and polyester blends, in shirts, blouses, petticoats, and so on, often look exactly like cotton, are relatively pleasant to wear in hot weather and under stage lights, and are easier to maintain than 100 percent cotton garments because they require little, if any, ironing. If the amount of polyester yarn in the fabric is less than the amount of cotton yarn, a crease resistant finish is often added to help control wrinkling. You can destroy the crease resistant finish and damage the fabric if you wash the garment in hot rather than warm water or dry it in a too-hot dryer.

Polyester fiberfill is an excellent stuffing for body padding and soft-sculpted costume accessories. It's lightweight, resilient, and washable.

ACRYLICS

Du Pont developed acrylic fibers as part of its ongoing synthetic fiber research. They came into being in 1944 and the first fabric was distributed in 1950 under the trade name Orlon. The first acrylic fabrics were soft, warm, machine-washable substitutes for wools. Orlon sweaters were very popular in the 1950s. Now, acrylics may also duplicate the look and feel of cotton. They still find their widest use in knitwear, such as sweaters, socks, infantwear, and sportswear. Many fleece and pile fabrics are made up, all or in part, of acrylic fibers.

Important Acrylic Characteristics

1. Acrylic fibers are light and springy. Although they have a fluffy quality, they are strong and durable.

2. Like most synthetic fibers, acrylics have low moisture absorbency, which allows them to dry quickly but to resist ordinary

dyes and to retain stains and perspiration odor. However, even though they do not take up water readily, garments made from acrylics do have a tendency to pull moisture away from the body, an action called "wicking," which adds to wearing comfort.

3. Acrylics are thermoplastic, although not all clothing made from acrylic fabric is heat set. An acrylic garment that is not heat set may stretch out and not return to its original shape.

4. Acrylics are resistant to abrasion, moths, mildew, sun, and weather but are easily damaged by hot irons, hot dryers, steam, and vigorous spinning in the washing machine.

SPANDEX

Spandex was introduced in 1958 and found immediate use in foundation garments and swimwear. A fiber with extraordinary characteristics, spandex revolutionized fashion, especially sportswear. Today, small amounts of spandex are being added to many traditional fabrics to improve fit, comfort, and appearance.

The spandex fiber contains about 85 percent segmented polyurethane and is generally used as a monofilament yarn, a single strand, not twisted. Spandex yarn is lightweight and soft. It can be stretched more than 500 percent without breaking and always returns to its original length. Spandex adds stretch to any fabric, knitted or woven. It is used in small amounts, between 3 percent and 20 percent, to improve general stretch and recovery in casual clothing while dance costumes, skiwear, and swimsuits may contain as much as 50 percent spandex.

If you don't intend for the fabric to stretch, however, such as in a wool tailored suit, do not choose a wool and spandex blend.

Important Spandex Characteristics

1. Spandex is durable, lightweight, and very elastic.

2. Spandex is resistant to damage from abrasion, perspiration, body oils, and sunlight. And, although spandex in swimsuits is not damaged by chlorine in swimming pools, exposure to chlorine bleach and prolonged exposure to air will cause white spandex to yellow.

3. Very hot water, hot irons, and a too-hot dryer may damage spandex, causing the fiber to crack and lose its elasticity.

Spandex is frequently referred to as Lycra, which is one of its trade names.

ELASTOESTER

A spandex-like fiber that is sometimes used as a substitute for spandex and sometimes in combination with it. Elastoester is strong and durable. It withstands high heat when wet, retains dye well, and does not discolor when in contact with chlorine.

MODACRYLIC

Modacrylics are modified acrylic fibers used to make fleecy, furlike fabrics and synthetic hair for wigs. Almost all fake furs are made from modacrylic fibers. Modacrylic furs are warm and soft and resistant to damage by moths, mildew, and sunlight. Although they are easily damaged by heat, modacrylics are fire-resistant. Best of all, these fake furs, some of which are quite beautiful, can be machine washed in cool water and dried in a clothes dryer set on a low temperature, which makes them especially useful for children's stuffed animals.

METALLIC

Metallic is a manufactured fiber composed of metal, plastic-coated metal, metal-coated plastic, or a core completely covered by metal. Coated metallic filaments do not tarnish. They are used for many decorative purposes in wearing apparel: braids, laces, military decorations, and ribbons.

OLEFIN AND POLYPROPYLENE

Olefin and polypropylene are closely related fibers. Both are used in nonclothing products such as dishcloths, nets, upholstery, and batting. Because these fibers have a low specific gravity, which makes them lightweight, and excellent wicking qualities that allow body moisture to escape, they are popular components of winter sportswear and cold weather undergarments.

MICROFIBERS

Microfibers are not a class of fibers but a process for manufacturing both cellulosic and noncellulosic fibers, so far including acrylic, nylon, polyester, and rayon. The process produces a very slim fiber, slimmer even than a silk filament. The process was first developed in 1989 and the first microfibers were polyester. Fabrics made from microfibers are ultra fine and extremely drapeable. They are soft, with a luminous hand and a silken or suede touch. Waterproof microfibers are so tightly woven that water cannot penetrate them, yet they retain breathability.

Keeping Up with Man-Made Fabrics

The man-made fiber industry is constantly improving the performance of the fibers that are already in use and searching for new ones. Recent developments include: extremely lightweight bulletproof vests; flameproof fabrics with such diverse uses as ironing board covers and coveralls worn by firefighters, race car drivers, test pilots, and astronauts; and optical fibers that have revolutionized communication systems and certain kinds of surgery.

The development of new and improved synthetic fibers for wearing apparel textiles moves more slowly than the development of fibers for industrial and medical uses. Nevertheless, the next few years will certainly bring about enough new changes to warrant continuing interest. If you wish to obtain up-to-date information on the state of the synthetic fiber industry or acquire teaching materials, including videotapes, contact:

American Fiber Manufacturers Association, Inc.
1530 Wilson Boulevard, Suite 690
Arlington, VA 22209

The AFMA describes itself as "the trade association for U.S. companies that manufacture synthetic and cellulosic fibers. The industry employs 30 thousand people and produces over 9 billion pounds of fiber in the United States. Annual domestic sales exceed $10 billion. AFMA member companies produce more than 90 percent of the total U.S. output of these fibers. The membership is limited to U.S. producers that sell manufactured fiber in the open market. The Association maintains close ties to other manufactured fiber trade associations worldwide."

Leather and Synthetic Leather

Leather

Leather is the oldest material used by humans for clothing. Technically, leather is not a fabric because it is not woven, knitted, or felted. Nevertheless, leathers and imitation leathers are frequently used to construct costumes and it is important to know a few basic facts about these materials. (See Chapter 5, "Costume Construction," for *Stitching Leather, Suede, Synthetic Suede, and Vinyl.*)

Leather is the skin of an animal or a reptile usually with hair removed. A process called *tanning* that our prehistoric ancestors discovered during the Paleolithic Age, 30,000 to 40,000 years ago, preserves the leather, softens it, and makes it flexible. Tanning takes its name from tannin, an astringent substance found in certain leaves and tree barks, which was for many years the main ingredient used to preserve leather. Today, a number of different chemicals are used to tan skins, producing leathers with different characteristics.

When the outer side or hair side of a skin is the finished side, it is called *leather,* and the surface is smooth, firm, and somewhat lustrous. When the inner side or flesh side is finished, it is called *suede,* which has a soft, matte finish that appears to be slightly napped. If the hide is tanned with the hair left on, it is called *sherpa. Leather splits,* or *garment splits,* are thin layers of leather made from thick skins, usually sueded on both sides.

Skins for leather may come from many different animals: cowhide, pigskin, and sheepskin are common reasonably priced leathers. Buckskin and doeskin, from deer; cabretta, a lightweight goat skin; and various specialty leathers such as those from the ostrich, python, or other snakes may be much more expensive. *Always make sure the leathers you use come from legitimate sources; using skins from rare and endangered species is not only morally wrong, it is also a criminal offense.*

BUYING LEATHER

Leather is sold by the hide or skin. In general, skins refer to small animals, hides to large animals. Leather is measured in square feet, although it's often sold in square yards. Calculate how much leather will be needed for a garment by multiplying the ordinary yardage requirement by the number of square feet in a yard of fabric, adding 15 percent to account for flaws and irregularities.

- 1 yard of 36-inch wide fabric = 9 square feet
- 1 yard of 45-inch wide fabric = 11.25 square feet
- 1 yard of 54-inch wide fabric = 13.5 square feet
- 1 yard of 60-inch wide fabric = 15 square feet

Example: You need enough leather to make a jacket that requires 3 yards of 45-inch fabric. Looking at the equivalents above, calculate that you will need 33.75 square feet, plus 15 percent, or approximately 5 square feet, for a total of 38.75 square feet. If the available hides are 12 to 14 square feet each, you need three hides. If you are ordering leather from a catalog, you may also see that the skins and hides are described by weight. Leathers that weigh 1 to 1½ ounces per square foot are light and flexible, suitable for jackets and trousers; leathers that weigh 2½ to 3 ounces per square foot are heavier and more suited to outerwear.

Important Leather Characteristics

1. Tanned leathers are nonabsorbent, although they may pick up a variety of spots and stains.
2. Most leather is not washable and must be cleaned by a special leather dry cleaning process.
3. Leather dyes do not penetrate the material the way fabric dyes do and may rub off.
4. When you punch a hole in leather, it remains.
5. Leather has no grain, although, because of variations in thickness, some parts of a hide might stretch more than other parts.
6. Leather may be damaged by steam, a hot iron, and mildew.

Synthetic Suede

In 1972 the fashion designer Halston introduced a line of clothing made from a synthetic suede-like material called Ultrasuede, manufactured by Springs Mills and marketed by Skinner. Ultrasuede was an instant success. Today, along with several similar products such as Lamous, Belleseime, and Suedemark II, Ultrasuede remains important in the fabric and garment industries.

Ultrasuede is a nonwoven material composed of 60 percent polyester and 40 percent nonfibrous polyurethane, a thermoplastic resin. Ultrasuede does not shrink, crack, peel, or pill. The edges do not fray. It may be machine washed or dry cleaned.

Ultrasuede, and other synthetic suedes, are often used in costumes, sometimes to simulate real suede, and sometimes as a frankly synthetic fabric. Ultrasuede is much lighter weight than suede and more reflective; it doesn't hang or move like suede. Used creatively, however, for its own unique properties, synthetic suede can be an effective costume fabric. A good synthetic suede costs about the same as real suede, with the obvious advantage of being easy to wash and clean.

Synthetic Leather

Synthetic leathers, which are vinyl-like materials, are even less successful on the stage than synthetic suedes. They all have a tendency to stiffen, crack, and discolor. As they age, some become sticky. In addition, garments made from synthetic leather may acquire permanent creases from being folded or stored, and a synthetic leather jacket that doesn't let any air pass through the fabric is too uncomfortable for most actors to tolerate on stage under stage lights.

Identifying Fibers

Many times you find yourself faced with a piece of fabric that no longer has its Federal Trade Commission label. If you can't tell what the fiber content is by look and feel—which is growing more difficult to do as fabric contents become ever more complex—how do you find out what's in it? Your best bet is to burn a few yarns, twisted together, and observe their behavior. A simple burn test won't allow you to identify all of the fibers that are present in a fabric, but you can

Fiber	Approaching	Stationary	Withdrawing	Odor	Residue
cotton	ignites at first contact	burns rapidly	smolders, glows, smokes	burning paper or leaves	soft gray, not much
linen	ignites quickly	burns rapidly	burns actively	burning paper	soft gray, fine
wool	draws away from flame	melts, burns	self-extinguishing	burned feathers or hair	crushable, brittle, black
silk	draws away from flame	melts, burns	self-extinguishing	burned feathers or hair	crushable, brittle, black
rayon	ingnites on contact	burns	burns slowly	burning paper	little or no ash
acetate	melts before contact	melts, burns with yellow flame	melts	burning paper and vinegar	hard, dark bead
nylon	draws away and melts	melts, burns, drips	burns with difficulty	celery	hard bead, cream-colored or dark
polyester	melts before contact	melts, burns black smoke	burns for awhile; self-extinguishing	sweet chemical	hard bead, cream-colored or dark
acrylic	melts, burns before reaching flames	melts, burns	sputters, burns	broiled fish	hard, irregular bead

discover enough useful information to help you choose the correct fabric and care for it properly.

Several limitations are inherent in the burn test. First, certain properties of the fiber, such as smell and flammability, can be altered by the presence of a fabric finish, such as one applied for wrinkle control. Second, many fabrics are blends of several fibers, and it may be impossible to distinguish one from another. In these instances, it is sometimes helpful to unravel a bit of the fabric and burn warp yarns and weft, or filling, yarns separately. Third, some fibers such as cotton and rayon burn identically because they are both composed primarily of cellulose.

Take certain safety precautions when doing a burn test. Use a candle, which will give you a steady source of flame, in a candleholder placed on top of a piece of aluminum foil or fastened firmly in the middle of a tinfoil plate. Then, if the burning fiber drops, it will fall on a safe surface. Use tweezers to hold the twisted yarns. And have a container of water close by, just in case.

Examine the behavior of the yarn bundle as it approaches the flame, while it's in the flame, and after it's withdrawn from the flame. On the preceding chart, these three observations are labeled: *approaching, stationary,* and *withdrawing.* You will also observe the odor from the burning fibers and the residue left after the flame has been extinguished.

Once again, this is not an exacting test. A great many variables are present and sometimes the results are confusing. But, you can usually tell if there is polyester in the broadcloth or nylon in the flannel.

Producing Fabrics

The look and behavior of any piece of fabric is the combined result of its fiber content, the size and type of yarn from which it was produced, the manner in which the yarns were assembled, and the finishing processes that were applied to it. The three basic methods of creating fabrics are *weaving, knitting,* and *felting.* All three of these methods have been around for a long time; weaving and felting were invented well before the advent of written history.

Yarn

The first step in the production of fabrics is making yarn. Yarn is made from fibers or filaments, spun or twisted into a continuous strand.

Spun Yarn. Spun yarns are made from relatively short lengths of fiber that are twisted or spun to hold them together. The fibers in spun yarns may be the natural fibers, cotton, wool, and linen; short lengths of silk; or man-made staple fibers.

Carding and Combing. Before spinning, all fibers are carded to clean and untangle them. Some fibers are carded *and* combed. Combing helps produce a yarn that is smoother and more uniform than carded yarn. The fabrics produced from carded and combed yarn are soft, lustrous, and stronger than fabric made from carded yarn.

Filament Yarn. Filament yarns are made from continuous strands that may be several miles long. The only natural filament is silk; other filaments are man-made.

Multifilament Yarn. Most filament yarns are multifilament, several filaments twisted together to form a yarn. Because the twisting process in filament yarns is not done to keep the filaments together, as is the case with spun yarns made up of fibers, multifilament yarns have a much looser twist than spun yarns. The yarns tend to be smoother and more regular than spun yarns, and they generally have more luster.

Monofilament Yarn. Monofilament yarns are made from a single filament. In general, monofilament yarns tend to be stiffer than multifilament yarns. Nylon hosiery is made from monofilament yarn, and spandex is most often used as a single filament.

Yarn Twist. The amount of twist given to a yarn is expressed as *TPI, turns per inch. Soft twist yarns,* with two to twelve TPI, are soft, fluffy, and flexible. Knitting yarns are usually soft twist yarns. *Hard twist yarns,* with twenty to thirty TPI, are firmer, stronger, and sometimes kinkier. Filament yarns, as mentioned, usually have a lower TPI than spun yarns.

S Twist and Z Twist. Yarns are twisted to the right or to the left. A left twist yarn, in which the spirals run upward toward the left, is called an *S twist yarn;* and a right twist yarn, in which the spirals run upward toward the right, is called a *Z twist yarn.* There is no difference in quality between an S twist and a Z twist yarn. The direction of the twist may be important to fabric designers. For instance, crepe effects in fabric can be produced by alternating yarns with opposing twists in the weave. Yarns are usually unreeled, pulled off spools or cones in the direction of the twist.

Almost all sewing threads are left or S twist and come off their spools in the direction of the twist. This automatically causes you to thread your sewing machines *with* the yarn twist, rather than *against* it. When you thread

FIGURE 3–4. S twist yarn and Z twist yarn.

S & Z

a hand-sewing needle with the end of the thread that comes off the spool, you will have fewer knots and kinks than if you cut the thread first and put the cut end into the needle's eye.

Ply Yarns. The term *ply yarn* refers to yarns made up of two or more yarn strands twisted together. Most fabrics are woven from single yarns. Most of the ply yarns used to make fabrics are two-ply yarns. Because of the extra operation involved, ply yarn fabrics are more expensive than single yarn fabric.

All sewing threads are ply yarns, two-ply to four-ply.

Novelty Yarns. Novelty yarns are yarns fashioned by uneven twisting and by combining two yarn strands that are different in character. *Slubs* are bumpy, fuzzy, untwisted portions in certain yarns. Slubs create a great deal of surface interest in a fabric, but they also cause weak spots that are particularly susceptible to abrasion. Heavily textured fabrics look good on stage but do not always wear well. Choose with care.

Stretch Yarns. Stretch fabrics are getting better and better, a great boon to costume designers and technicians, particularly those who work with dance and sport costumes. Stretch fabrics fall into two general categories: *power stretch* and *comfort stretch.* Power stretch fabrics are made from *bare elastic yarns* and *covered elastic yarns;* comfort stretch fabrics are made from *core spun yarns* and *bicomponent and biconstituent stretch yarns.* Spandex and rubber are the stretch components of almost all stretch yarns. Rubber, which is less elastic than spandex and more susceptible to damage from perspiration, heat, moisture, and household chemicals, appears much less frequently than spandex.

Bare Elastic Yarn. This yarn is usually composed of monofilament spandex fiber and used in power stretch fabrics that provide softer, more gentle shape control than covered elastic yarn.

Covered Elastic Yarn. This yarn is composed of monofilaments of spandex or rubber completely wrapped or covered with a spun or a filament yarn. The power stretch fabrics tend to be heavier than those made from bare elastic yarn, providing firmer shape control. They are widely used in foundation garments.

Core Spun Yarn. This yarn has a central spandex filament core with staple fibers actually spun around the core. If the spun fibers are cotton, the fabric will look like cotton; if the spun fibers are acrylic, the fabric will look like acrylic, and so on. Core spun yarn can be spun very fine, providing elasticity without bulk. Core spun yarn has less recovery than covered elastic yarn and is used in comfort stretch fabrics.

Bicomponent and Biconstituent Stretch Yarn. This yarn is made from a process that creates a synthetic filament from two different synthetic materials, such as nylon and spandex, extruded parallel to each other. Bicomponent yarn is used in comfort stretch fabrics that have wide application in hosiery and panty hose manufacture.

Textured Yarn. Textured yarn is the name given to the whole group of synthetic yarns that are modified after they have been spun or twisted but before being woven or knitted. Texturing gives the yarn an entirely new surface texture and new behavior characteristics. Some textured yarns stretch, some have greater bulk, some breathe better and are better absorbent, some become softer and drier, and some become more wrinkle resistant.

Blends and Mixtures. A blend yarn has two or more different fibers mixed together. A mixture is a fabric made from two or more different types of yarns. More yarn mixture fabrics are on the market than fiber blend yarns. In the garment and fabric industries, yarn mixture fabrics are almost always referred to as "blends."

Yarn Size. Because industrial weavers purchase yarn by the pound, yarn sizes are expressed as a relationship between weight and length and are rather inexact methods of measuring actual yarn size. Filament yarn sizes are stated in the *denier system* and spun yarns in the *yarn count system.*

Denier System. The denier system is the simplest. The heavier and thicker the yarn, the higher the number. Sheer hosiery yarns are 10–15 denier and carpet yarns may be as much as 2,000 denier.

Yarn Count System. Yarn count numbers go in the opposite direction: the larger the number, the smaller the yarn. Yarn count sizes are determined by the relationship between a pound of fiber and a standard length of yarn drawn out from that pound. Standard lengths differ from fiber to fiber.

For example: The standard for cotton and cotton blend yarns is: one pound of cotton fiber drawn out to make 840 yards of yarn = #1. A #10 yarn count indicates that one pound of cotton fiber has been drawn out 10 × 840 yards, or 8,400 yards of yarn. Cotton yarns with a count of from #1–#20 are considered coarse; from #20–#60 are medium; above #60 are fine. The finest cotton yarn made in the United States was #160: one pound of cotton drawn out to a strand 134,000 yards long (over 76 miles!). Cotton yarns have been spun in England with counts of approximately #400.

Cotton and polyester sewing threads are most commonly #50 or #60. Heavy-duty hand-sewing threads, used for basting and quilting, contain yarns with a #40 yarn count.

Other standard lengths per pound of fiber are worsted, worsted blends, and 100 percent acrylic: 560 yards; woolen and woolen blends: 1,600 yards; linen: 300 yards.

Sewing Thread. Sewing threads are special kinds of yarns, processed specifically for the purpose of stitching seams together.

Sewing threads are, as stated, two-ply to four-ply yarns. They are strong and symmetrical and may be made from nylon, cotton, polyester, or cotton and polyester. Some nylon thread is twisted from filaments. The most common sewing thread is spun from either cotton fibers or polyester staple fibers. Another variety is core spun with cotton or polyester fibers spun around a polyester core.

Some sewing threads have no finish applied and are soft and a bit fuzzy; others are mercerized, which gives them a firm, smooth surface; still others have a waxed, or glacé, finish. Mercerized and glacé threads are stronger than unfinished threads.

For general stitching, most costume shops use long staple, spun polyester thread because it is strong and also has a bit of "give." Some technicians prefer mercerized spun cotton thread, in large part because if a stitched garment has to be dyed, cotton thread takes color better than polyester. Cotton thread does weaken over time, both on the spool and in the garment. The core spun thread, commonly called "cotton covered polyester" is the least satisfactory since it has the greatest tendency to shrink, cause puckered seams, and shred apart when used to stitch synthetic fabric seams.

Glacé thread is excellent for millinery work and for sewing buttons on heavy garments. Monofilament nylon thread is a good choice for slip stitching, some hemming, and for hand sewing trims.

Weaving

Weaving is the process of interlacing two sets of yarns on a loom. The original purpose of the loom was simply to hold the warp threads in position so the filling threads (also called the weft, woof, or picks) could be passed from one side to the other, over one warp thread, under the next, and so on. At first the warp threads were picked up manually; later they were separated by a stick or bar.

The development of the harness of heddles (or heddle-frame) paved the way for faster cloth production. The heddle is a wire with a hole in the middle, through which warp yarns are threaded. All of the heddles attached to one harness may be raised simultaneously with a single motion. The plain over-and-under weave can be carried out on a loom with only two harnesses, each harness raising an alternating set of warp threads. Additional harnesses accommodate more complicated patterns.

There are three distinct steps in the weaving process:

Shedding. Shedding is the formation of an opening, or shed, between the warp threads, through which the filling thread is passed. A shed is created by raising a harness.

Picking. When the shed is formed, the filling thread is carried through it and across the warp threads by a shuttle. One pass of the shuttle is called a pick.

Battening. Battening is the operation by which the filling thread or pick is beaten into the cloth by a batten or reed so the weave will be close and firm.

Accompanying the shedding, picking, and battening processes are the *taking up* and *letting off,* in which the newly woven cloth is rolled up on the cloth beam and the warp threads released from the warp beam.

FIGURE 3–5. A modern, four-harness loom manufactured by Norwood. *Photograph courtesy of Norwood Looms.*

Fabric Width

The width of a piece of fabric is determined by the width of the loom on which it was woven. Before the 1950s, most garment fabrics were 36 inches wide. Since then, there's been a move to weave wider fabrics so garment cutters can lay out their patterns to better advantage. Nowadays, cotton is usually 45 inches wide, wool fabrics are from 54 to 60 inches wide, and silk and silk-type synthetics are from 40 to 45 inches wide. Rayon and linen are usually from 45 to 60 inches in width. Fabrics made expressly for home decorating are generally wider than garment fabrics.

Fabric Grain

Warp and filling yarns are always at right angles to each other and differ from each other in their performance on the loom and in the fabric. Warp yarns are usually stronger, twisted tighter, and of a higher quality than filling yarns so they can withstand the tension exerted on them by the loom. Filling yarns can be weaker and of lesser quality because they aren't under tension in the weaving process. Sometimes filling yarns are unevenly twisted to give the finished cloth texture.

The differences between the warp and filling yarns make fabric grain considerations important when cutting garment pieces. *Lengthwise grain,* or *straight grain,* is the direction in which the warp threads run. *Crosswise grain,* or *cross grain,* is the direction of the filling yarn. The three major differences between the straight grain of the fabric and the cross grain of the fabric are:

1. Fabric is strongest lengthwise in the straight grain direction and usually stretches least.

2. Almost all fabrics shrink more in length than in width. This is because the warp threads are stretched on the loom and when washed, shrink back to their original length.

3. Fabrics are often stiffer in the crosswise grain direction than in the lengthwise grain direction. This causes the fabric to drape differently in the two directions. For example: a skirt cut with the cross grain running from waist to hem may be "rounder" than a skirt cut from the same fabric with the straight or lengthwise grain running from waist to hem.

If a pattern piece was developed to be on the straight grain of the fabric, don't switch it to the cross grain without thinking about the outcome. The two directions are not interchangeable.

The diagonal direction of woven fabric is called the *true bias.* This is the direction in which the fabric will stretch the most. Suspend a piece of fabric from its diagonal point, and it will achieve the deepest drape. If you substitute the true bias for the straight grain on parts of some women's garments, they will have a figure-molding drape. Dresses cut "on the bias" were particularly popular in the 1920s and 1930s.

Any direction on a piece of cloth between true bias and either lengthwise grain or crosswise grain is called a *garment bias.* A garment bias edge ravels more than a bias cut edge, a straight grain edge, or a cross grain edge. Most garment seams are garment bias edges and, therefore, require some seam finish to control raveling.

Selvage Edge

The selvage is a narrow edging, ¼ to ½ inch wide, that runs along both lengthwise edges of a fabric. The selvage edge is usually more tightly woven than the rest of the fabric, with warp threads closer together, and sometimes stronger. The purpose of the selvage edge is to keep the fabric from tearing. Sometimes, particularly after the fabric has been washed, the selvage edge is so tight that it distorts the straight and cross grains. You can usually release the grain by snipping the selvage at intervals; you may have to trim it away. No matter how flat the selvage edge of a fabric seems, beware of incorporating it into garment pieces.

Thread Count

The number of warp and filling threads in a square inch of fabric is called its thread count. This may be expressed with the warp count first, as 80×76 (eighty by seventy-six), or as a total of the two, as 156. Normally, the warp count is slightly higher than the filling count. The more balanced the thread count (a fabric with the same number of warp threads and filling threads is *balanced*), the stronger the cloth.

Muslin Thread Count Chart

Grade	Thread Count	Properties and Uses
back-filled muslin	less than 112 threads to the square inch	very loosely woven; contains excess starch; when washed it is too limp for most uses
lightweight muslin	not less than 112 threads to the square inch	too much starch to be used without washing; loose, soft drape when washed; wears moderately well; good for soft undergarments, peasant blouses, and the like
mediumweight muslin	not less than 128 threads to the square inch	strong, with very little filling; unwashed it is excellent for draping bodices, coats, and so on; washed it makes nice petticoats; widely used for costume underlining
heavyweight muslin	not less than 140 threads to the square inch	sturdiest, longest wearing muslin; used largely in hospitals, where durability is important; generally too expensive for costume shops

Unbleached cotton muslin, a fabric usually purchased in large quantities by costume shops, usually has a balanced thread count expressed in a single number. The higher the thread count, the better the quality of muslin. A good quality muslin with a high thread count will have a more stable grain, shrink less, ravel less, and be more durable. A low thread count muslin is likely to be impregnated with starch and sizing to firm up the loose woven surface. When you buy muslin, you should always rub the fabric between your fingers to check for a sticky, flaky residue. Use the above muslin thread count chart as a guide to muslin quality.

Fabric Weaves

There are three basic fabric weaves: *plain weave, twill weave,* and *satin weave.* All other weaves are variations or combinations of these. The weave of a fabric helps to determine many of its characteristics, such as luster, texture, strength, pattern, hand, color effect, and cost.

Plain Weave

The plain weave, sometimes called the *tabby,* is the simplest and most common weave. The regular over-and-under structure (see Figure 3–6) produces a sturdy, economical fabric.

Plain weave fabrics have no obvious right or wrong sides unless they have a woven design or a printed surface.

FIGURE 3–6. Plain weave.

Some widely used plain weave fabrics are muslin, batiste, calico, organdy, china silk, and osnaburg. Brocade and damask are plain weave fabrics with woven designs; gingham and madras are plain weave fabrics with woven checks and plaids. Challis, flannel, and melton are plain weave fabrics with brushed surfaces.

A common variation on the plain weave is the *rib*, which is produced by having warp threads heavier than filling threads *or* filling threads heavier than warp threads. In either case, the rib is an unbalanced weave, characterized by the presence of ridges. Broadcloth, for instance, has a very fine ridge, while faille, ben-galine, and grosgrain all have more prominent ridges. Rib weaves do not wear as well as other plain, balanced weaves. Abrasion marks may appear on the ridges and the fabric may split between the ridges. Consider this before you choose a rib weave for a pair of eighteenth-century knee breeches that will have to withstand the leaps and rolls of vigorous sword fighting. When the over-and-under alternation of the plain weave spans two or more threads at a time, the variation is called the *basket weave*. Basket weave fabrics tend to be softer and less stable than plain weave fabrics and the grain may slip on seam lines. Oxford cloth, monk's cloth, and hopsacking are all popular basket weaves.

Twill Weave

In the basic twill weave, the filling yarn interlaces, or "floats," over more than one warp yarn but seldom over more than four. On each successive line of the weave, the design moves one step to the right or to the left, forming diagonal wales that may vary in prominence, direction, and degree of angle but are always present in a twill weave. Twill weave fabrics all have right and wrong sides and because of the interesting surface pattern provided by the weave, twills are seldom printed with additional designs.

FIGURE 3–7. Hopsack or basket weave.

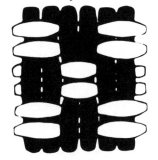

FIGURE 3–8. 2/2 twill weave.

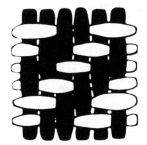

Shiny wear spots may appear on the elbows, knees, or seats of garments made out of soft twill weaves, such as wool gabardine. Steaming the fabric with a steam wand or by holding a steam iron close to the surface of the fabric may help raise the wales and reduce the shine. A stubborn shiny spot may also respond to gentle rubbing with a soft cloth that's been dipped in pure white vinegar diluted with water. Other common twill fabrics are denim, drill, serge, whipcord, and twill flannel. A popular twill weave variation is *herringbone,* in which the twill line is reversed at regular intervals to create a design that resembles a fish backbone.

weave *sateen,* which is usually a cotton or a cotton blend fabric.

FIGURE 3–10. Satin weave.

All satin weave fabrics have a right and a wrong side. If the yarn count is high and the weave is firm and tight, the fabric will be durable. A low yarn count satin ravels easily and is apt to snag becuse of the long, loose floats.

Firm, drapery-weight, cotton-backed satins are excellent choices for period stage garments. Crepe-backed satin, in which crepe yarns are used as filling yarns and low twist filament yarns for the warp, has a particularly smooth and lustrous surface, and the crepe yarns add softness and durability. Beautiful for contemporary gowns, they are often too shiny for pre-World War I costumes.

FIGURE 3–9. 2/2 twill-herringbone weave.

Satin Weave

Satin weave fabrics have a characteristic shine caused by *floats,* yarn passing over many yarns before being caught under one. The yarn that "floats" may be either the filling yarn or the warp yarn. The floats reflect light, produce a rich luster, and give the fabric a smooth, almost slippery feel. When warp yarns form the floats, the fabric is called a *true satin* and is usually woven from a filament yarn such as silk, acetate, or nylon. Filling yarn floats are used to

FIGURE 3–11. 5 thread sateen weave.

Specialty Weaves

Pile Weave

The pile weave fabrics, such as velvets and corduroys, are particularly popular with costume designers and technicians. To produce the fur-like surface, pile fabrics are made with three sets of yarns: warp yarns, filling yarns, and *pile yarns,* which may go in either the warp or the filling direction. Sometimes the yarns are cut, producing a cut pile fabric such as corduroy or velvet; sometimes they remain uncut, producing a fabric like terrycloth or uncut corduroy. The underlying weave in a pile fabric is usually a plain weave, although it may be a twill weave.

The higher the thread count of a pile weave fabric, the denser the pile will be and the stronger the base cloth. The closer the weave, the less likely the pile will be to snag or pull out. Before purchasing a pile weave fabric, hold a piece up to a light and examine the weave. If the base cloth is thin and irregular, beware.

Pile weave fabrics usually have an up and down direction called *nap.* Always cut garment pieces with nap running in the same direction, otherwise the costume will look as though it was made from two different materials.

Knitting

The forerunner of the modern knitting machine was invented in 1589 by the Rev. William Lee of St. John's College, Cambridge. In an age when mechanical inventions were a rarity, he contrived and constructed a machine that would knit stockings. Although Rev. Lee died broke and in obscurity, his brother carried on and became a successful manufacturer of knit garments. It was almost 200 years before any major improvements were made to Rev. Lee's machine.

Today's knitting machines are instruments of amazing ingenuity. A modern ribknitting machine can, for instance, produce over 1,000,000 stitches a minute and make fabric from two to five times faster than weaving looms.

Since the 1950s, knitted fabrics have been increasingly in demand. Technical advances in the knitting industry and in the production of synthetic fibers have contributed to a growing number of new knit fabrics. These fabrics stretch as the body moves and, depending on the fiber, may return smartly to their original shape. Most knit fabrics are washable and require little or no ironing.

Knit fabrics may be defined as: *fabric structures produced by the interlooping of yarns.* Loops are formed and new loops are drawn through previously formed loops. Each loop is called a *stitch.* The vertical column of stitches in a knitted fabric is called a *wale;* wales run lengthwise through the whole piece of fabric. Horizontal rows of stitches are called *courses;* courses run sideways, from edge to edge of the fabric. Industrial knitting is not the same as hand-knitting. In industrial knitting, each stitch or loop is on its own needle and each wale of the fabric is formed by one needle. For example, if there are 600 wales across a 40-inch piece of fabric, 600 needles have to be used.

Weft Knits and Warp Knits

There are two broad classifications of producing knit fabrics, weft knits and warp knits.

Weft Knits

The Rev. Lee's knitting machine, and all early knitting machines, were weft knit machines. Weft knits still make up the bulk of knit fabrics produced.

FIGURE 3–14. Purl knit—reverse and face sides are the same.

FIGURE 3–12. Plain knit—face side.

FIGURE 3–15. 1/1 rib knit.

FIGURE 3–13. Plain knit—reverse side.

Weft knits are formed side to side. All the stitches in one row, or course, are produced by one yarn. In a simple, single-color knit fabric, all of the courses in the fabric may be formed by a single yarn. Weft knit fabrics can be produced on either a flat or a circular knitting machine.

Fabrics may be jersey knit, rib knit, purl knit, or specialty knits that create color and surface designs. Most weft knit fabrics have significant sideways stretch and little lengthwise stretch.

Most fake furs are weft knit fabrics, usually a special type of jersey knit that incorporates staple fibers to produce the hairy or fuzzy surfaces. As stated earlier, modacrylic fibers are the most popular fibers used in fake furs.

Warp Knits

In warp knit fabrics, each wale is formed from a single yarn that moves in a zigzag fashion. The back sides of warp knit fabrics have characteristic, slightly angled, horizontal float patterns. There are two types of warp knits: *tricot* and *raschel*. Tricot jersey is the most common of all warp knits and is particularly popular for lingerie, sleepwear, and loungewear. Raschel knits are produced with a different kind of needle than tricot knits. Raschel knits often have intricate surface characteristics, from lace-like designs to the waffle weave in thermal underwear. Power stretch net fabrics knitted from spandex are also raschel knits.

Knit fabrics have dozens of uses in costume shops. A wool, or wool-like, double knit can be an excellent choice for eighteenth-century breeches. In *Designing and Making Stage Costumes,* Motley calls wool jersey ". . . the boon and solace of the harassed designer, the very *beau ideal* of fabrics." Corset wearing can be made more comfortable when a cotton knit undershirt is worn underneath. Nylon tricot is an excellent fabric to cover body padding.

Synthetic yarn knits have revolutionized dance costumes. Tights, leotards, and unitards cover bodies like second skins, permit completely free movement, and never sag.

Photographs of famous Shakespearean actors in the nineteenth and early twentieth centuries give graphic evidence to the difficulties they had maintaining heroic stances with cotton or wool tights sagging around their knees and ankles. Nylon and spandex have banished this bagginess forever. Modern, heavy-weight dance tights are a great boon to actors and to costume technicians. They can be dyed, painted, and laundered. And if they are handled with care, they have a relatively long life.

Felting

A fabric commonly used in costume shops, felt is neither woven nor knitted and is not fashioned from yarn. The best and most useful felt is made almost exclusively from wool noils (loose clumps of short wool fibers combed from longer fibers) matted together into fabric. This process, called felting, is made possible by the natural tendency of wool fibers to cling to one another in the presence of pressure, moisture, and heat. You have probably experienced the felting property of wool in the underarms of wool sweaters where heat and perspiration have stiffened and matted the yarns or when you have accidentally put a wool garment in the washing machine and had it come out a small, much more compact version of its original shape. Felt may also be made of acrylic fibers that produce a product that is not as strong or as malleable as wool felt.

Early man discovered how to make felt long before he invented weaving and used the process to create warm outer garments, tents, and groundcloths. Felt has many uses in costume shops. Thin, *decorator felt,* in bright, intense colors is popular for specialty costumes, especially animals and birds. Better grades of felt are used for hats; top quality hat felt is called *fur felt.* You can purchase hat felt flat, by the yard or in shapes. *Industrial felt* is the basic material for many costume properties and accessories, such as armor, helmets, crowns, belts, large medallions, and so on.

Industrial felt is not available in fabric shops. The material is manufactured for use in heavy industry, chiefly as shock-absorbing pads for machine parts. Industrial felt comes in a bewildering array of thicknesses and compositions. The most expensive is 100 percent wool.

Less expensive varieties contain rayon and miscellaneous mill wastes and are usually quite acceptable for costume items.

Because of its "pressed-together" construction, felt is not suitable for ordinary garments. There is little or no directional stretch to mold it around the figure. Felts tend to disintegrate if subjected to stretching and abrasion and to pull apart on folds and on stitching lines. Finally, it's virtually impossible to launder felt.

Nonwoven Fabrics

Nonwoven fabrics are modern cousins of felt. They are produced largely from man-made fibers that do not have the natural tendency of wool to mat together. Most are bonded with adhesives or by chemical reactions.

Nonwoven fabrics were first produced in the early 1940s, and their production has increased steadily as quality improved and more uses were discovered for them. These uses range from synthetic suedes and nonwoven interlinings to disposable cleaning cloths and tea bags.

Fabric Finishes

Directly off the loom or the knitting machine, most fabric is dull, limp, rough, and marred with blemishes. At this stage it is called *gray goods* or *greige goods*. Finishing processes convert the rough product into the wide variety of fabrics available today. The process of "finishing" a fabric is called *conversion,* and the companies that do the finishing are called *converters.*

There are approximately 200 possible fabric finishes to make fabrics look better, feel better, and give better service. Some of these have been in use for well over a hundred years, and some are brand new.

Finishes for Luster

The five main finishes that add luster to fabric are:

Mercerization. In mercerization, cotton and cotton blends are treated with caustic soda, under tension, which causes the fibers to swell, straighten, and present a smoother surface for light reflection. Mercerization makes fabric stronger and allows it to dye readily and more uniformly. (Mercerization of sewing threads is essentially the same process carried out in the yarn stage.)

Beetling. The beetling process involves pounding and flattening cotton and linen fabrics to produce a smoother and more light reflective surface.

Calendering. The calender is a huge, heavy ironing machine that exerts as much as 2,000 pounds of pressure per square inch. Fabric runs between its rollers and comes out smoother, flatter, and more lustrous.

Glazing. The shiny finishes on polished cottons and chintz are produced by glazing, a process in which resins, gums, starches, or sugars are added to fabric surfaces. Glazed surfaces on 100 percent cotton fabrics are long lasting but not permanent.

Sizing. The addition of sizing, starches, gums, or resins is one way of making inexpensive, loosely woven materials appear to be smoother, more lustrous, and to have a higher thread count than they actually have. Sizings fill in the open spaces in the weave and stiffen the fabric. Most sizings wash out; much of it may even be lost through handling. However, some fabric is permanently sized. Organdy, for instance, is made permanently smooth and crisp by the addition of an acid sizing.

Surface Design Finishes

Moiré Effect and Embossing

Moireé and embossed designs are created by variations on the calendering process. In both cases, the calender rollers have designs engraved on them; heat and pressure are used to transfer the designs to the fabrics. The designs are permanent on heat-sensitive synthetic fabrics, such as acetate or nylon, but are not permanent on silk. If the designs are not heat set, they may disappear entirely when the fabric is washed. If you're in doubt about the permanency of a moiré effect, wash a sample before you wash the whole piece.

The moiré, or watermarking, effect is a wavy, irregular design inspired by eighteenth-century taffeta that was actually patterned with water stains. Embossed designs can be of almost any nature.

In general, launder embossed fabrics with care and iron them between thick pile towels, using more steam than pressure.

Crinkle Effects

Sometimes crinkle effects, such as in seersucker, are woven into fabrics, but they may also be added as a finish. Chemicals are applied in strips to plain weave fabrics. The fabric is then given an overall chemical application that causes the treated strips to shrink and the untreated strips to crinkle. Be sure to iron chemically crinkled fabrics with a cool iron to avoid harming the finish.

Flocking

The flocking process involves painting designs on fabric with adhesive, then dusting short, fibrous particles over the painted areas. Flocked designs are more or less permanent, depending on the type and quality of the adhesive used. All flocking will eventually fall victim to abrasion.

Color Finishes

Dyeing

Industrial dyeing is done at different stages in fabric production. When fibers are dyed before they are transformed into yarn, the process is called *stock dyeing*. Stock dyeing affords excellent color penetration. The dyeing of wool fibers has given us the common expression, "dyed in the wool," to indicate constancy. Manmade fibers are sometimes dyed while still in solution in a process called *solution dyeing*. In *yarn dyeing*, hanks of yarn are treated with dye solutions. The most common industrial dyeing process is *piece dyeing*, which is done after the cloth is woven or knitted. Piece dyeing is the most economical method and the least permanent.

Printing

Colored designs decorate many fabrics. *Roller printing* is the common method used for long runs. The design is engraved on metal rollers and, after printing, the color is heat set. *Screen printing* is more expensive than roller printing because the process is more labor intensive. Screen printing allows for more flexibility than roller printing and for much larger repeats. *Photographic screen printing* is a popular variation. Always examine printed fabrics carefully to make sure the design has been printed on-grain, particularly if the design includes definite horizontal and vertical directions.

Performance Finishes

Shrinkage Control

Many factors affect shrinkage in fabrics: the original stability of the fiber, the amount of twist in the yarn, the type of weave, the yarn count, and other finishes the fabric has undergone. All shrinkage control processes subject the fabric to heat, both wet and dry; some are more effective than others. Since it is almost impossible to prevent some additional shrinkage, even in preshrunk cottons and cotton blends, the most trustworthy shrinkage control occurs under labels that promise the fabric won't shrink more than another one percent. A one percent shrinkage does not affect the fit of most garments. Labels that merely read, "preshrunk," promise nothing reliable with regard to the fabric's future behavior in the wash tub.

Some fabrics that have a crease resistant finish won't shrink noticeably until that finish has been damaged by hot water or by vigorous agitation. Once the finish has broken down, the fabric will shrink "overnight."

Crease Resistant and Drip Dry Finishes

Chemical crease resistant finishes are normally applied to linen, cotton, or rayon fabric. The cloth is treated with synthetic resins and gums, like phenol formaldehyde, urea formaldehyde, and acrylic resins, which increase the elasticity of the fibers and discourage wrinkles. The finishes are permanent if you don't use excessively hot wash water or agitate the garments too vigorously. Fabrics treated with crease resistant chemicals have a smoother, shinier surface than untreated fabric and, sometimes, a plasticlike sheen under stage lights. On stage, the discerning eye may prefer untreated cotton fabrics, but the easy care properties that accompany crease resistant finishes often outweigh pure aesthetic consideration.

Drip dry or permanent press finishes are much more permanent than crease resistant finishes because the fabric or the ready-made garment is heat cured after the chemical application. Trouser creases or skirt pleats can be set permanently. Permanent press garments are easy to launder and if properly dried never need ironing. Puckering in the seams is generally caused by faults in thread tension.

Permanent press finishes are only applied to cotton, linen, rayon, and some polyester and natural fiber blends. Synthetic fabrics have inherent permanent press properties.

Once permanent press, always permanent press, seems to be a good dictum. There's no use trying to iron a sharp crease into permanent press fabric, and absolutely no way of removing one once it's there, at least not with the equipment normally found in costume shops.

Stains, particularly oily stains, are difficult to remove from fabrics that have crease resistant or permanent press finishes. These finishes also tend to weaken cotton fabrics.

Napping

Napping affects both appearance and performance. Little wire brushes are used to pull up fibers on one or both sides of a napped fabric. These raised fibers form a downy surface, changing both the look and the hand of the fabric. Napped fabrics are more crease resistant because the napping process increases fiber elasticity. It is sometimes hard to distinguish between a pile fabric and a napped fabric without examining it closely.

Napping is only possible when the fabric weave contains some loosely twisted yarns. These loose yarns may weaken the fabric, but the napped surface hides the basic weave so well that it is difficult to determine quality. Always examine napped fabrics by holding them up to a light.

Flameproofing

Costume technicians must sometimes flameproof costumes. Each state has laws governing what must be flameproofed in public theatres. Stage scenery must usually be flameproof if it extends beyond the fire curtain line, or, on some open stages, when no fire curtain exists. Except in extraordinary circumstances, costumes are normally exempt from compulsory flameproofing. However, if an actor in a flowing garment must walk back and forth in front of or carry a torch on an outdoor stage with wind blowing, that garment ought to be flameproofed, whether or not the law demands it.

Use commercially available flameproofing chemicals and follow the directions carefully. Some high-luster fabrics will be somewhat dulled by the flameproofing finish, and some very light fabrics will be somewhat stiffened. Nevertheless, safety should come first. Furs, and other fabrics that might be harmed by water, should be sent to a professional dry cleaner for flameproofing.

Fabric Pricing

Fabric costs are second only to labor costs in the production of theatre costumes. Designers, design assistants, and shoppers spend hours searching for fabrics that fit their budgets. Knowing a bit about why some fabrics are more expensive than others won't necessarily help you balance your costume budget, but it might help you know where to look, how to look, *and* how to really appreciate a bargain when you find it. Most of you know that silk taffeta is more expensive than polyester taffeta, and that a Dan River gingham costs less than a Liberty lawn. Why? Why are fabric prices so different? These are the main factors that affect the cost of fabric:

Fiber Quality. Silk filament is more expensive than cotton fiber because the production of silk is more labor intensive and less is produced. Pima cotton fiber is more expensive than American Upland cotton fiber because Pima fibers are longer and of better quality. Polyester is more expensive than acetate because it costs more to produce.

Type of Yarn. A high-twist yarn is more expensive than a low-twist yarn, both because it demands a better fiber and because it is more difficult to produce. Novelty yarns are more expensive than regular yarns and, naturally, ply yarns cost more than single yarns.

Type of Weave. Some looms are more complex than others; some require more skilled operation than others. Fabrics woven on specialty looms are more expensive than those woven on plain looms. The number of yarns per inch also affects the price of fabric; more yarns equal bigger price tags.

Special Dyeing, Printing, and Finishing Process. Color, printed designs, and finishes always add to fabric cost. Some dye pigments actually cost more than others, and some dyes are more expensive to set than others. Intricate, precision prints require expensive machinery and attentive, well-paid labor.

4
Pattern Development

In most shops, costume garments are cut, stitched, trimmed, and finished by several costume technicians working in a group. The key member of this construction team is the technician responsible for creating the costume patterns and cutting the cloth. Called a *cutter,* a *draper,* or a combination of the two, *cutter/ draper,* this craftsperson works closely with the designer and is directly responsible for translating the silhouette, proportion, and drape of the costume garments from sketch to reality. In addition, the cutter/draper plans the construction steps, including fastenings and finishing, and supervises the first hand and the stitchers.

The importance of the cutter/draper's role in costume construction cannot be overemphasized. A beautiful design may become an ugly costume if it is poorly patterned, and no amount of trim can completely conceal awkward seam lines or cloth that's been cut with no regard for correct grain lines. A well-cut costume is balanced and graceful, fits the actor without sagging or binding (unless, of course, ill-fit has been "designed in"), and translates the proportions indicated in the sketch to the actual garment.

Good cutter/drapers are highly skilled craftspeople who have learned to use their hands and eyes in specific ways. They have complete command of a method or methods of pattern development, a keen eye for reading the reality in a costume sketch, and an affinity for solving problems. Whatever their backgrounds may be in education and experience, the best cutter/drapers have a unique ability to assimilate all the things they've learned about costumes and cloth and bring this knowledge to bear on every project.

It is neither possible nor desirable for a costume cutter/draper to memorize the patterns for every piece of historical clothing. Nor is it enough to collect basic patterns for each major period, and pull out the envelope marked 1888 when working on a play set in that year. Every stage garment is unique and, usually, one of a kind. Women today do not wear identical dresses made from the same pattern, and women in 1888 did not either. Besides, no one pattern will fit the style of every play set in 1888, the sensibility of every costume designer, or the body of every actor. A good cutter/draper is familiar with basic period shapes and has

FIGURE 4–1. Milwaukee Repertory Theater cutter/draper Louella Powell wielding tracing wheel and see-through ruler with pattern notcher at the ready. *Photograph by Rosemary Ingham.*

developed a process or way of working that pinpoints the variables in a given project: the play, the character, the design sketch, the historical period, the actor's measurements, the budget, the fabric, the number of stitchers and their skill level, the time allowed for construction, and so on. With these facts in hand, the cutter/draper can plan the patterning and construction steps that will result in a costume that fits well and looks the way the designer intended.

Cutter/drapers need to know a lot about their craft, and their effectiveness is enhanced by experience. It is probably true that most gifted cutter/drapers were born with certain innate abilities and talents. But it's equally true that basic cutting and draping skills are within the grasp of every serious costume student and that every working costume designer and technician ought to know how to create garment patterns. No book on costume construction or class in pattern drafting will produce cutter/drapers with artistry in their fingertips, but anyone who has a desire to learn and a willingness to practice can become an accurate cutter/draper whose garments fit and hang well.

Pattern Development Methods in the Costume Shop

The three main goals of drafting and/or draping a costume pattern are: (1) to manipulate a flat piece of cloth by cutting and shaping so it conforms to a specific three-dimensional body, while (2), at the same time, accurately translating a sketch prepared by a costume designer into reality, and (3) creating a costume that serves all the various needs of the script, the actor, and the production. This is a tall order and differs in several aspects from the goals of pattern-making in the fashion industry, where

most of the focus is on current styles and mass-produced, standard-sized garments. As mentioned earlier, cutter/drapers in costume shops may be asked to create patterns for clothing from any moment in history (including the future!) and for dramatic characters at every level of the socioeconomic scale (as well as the occasional animal, bird, angel, alien, or monster). Theatre costumes are usually built for a specific actor in a specific production and, although allowances are made for their use in other productions through alteration, patterning methods dependent upon standard sizes have limited use in costume shops. Perhaps the greatest differences between patterning in costume shops and in the fashion industry have to do with durability and freedom of movement. Theatre costumes are *built* rather than *made* and their ability to withstand repeated extreme activity must be part of the original patterning plan. After all, if a fifteenth-century doublet worn by a lead dancer falls to pieces midway through a tour, you can't purchase a replacement at the local shopping mall.

There are two basic patterning methods generally used in costume shops, with many variations of each. These are *flat pattern drafting* and *draping*. The *flat pattern drafting* method begins with a set of basic pattern blocks developed from the actor's measurements. Muslin proofs of the blocks may be fitted to the actor's body and pattern pieces for a specific costume design developed from them, first on paper, then "mocked-up" in muslin or some other suitable fabric for fitting. *Draping* involves manipulating fabric on a tailor's dress or suit form to create pattern pieces for a specific design. In order for the draped pieces to fit a particular actor, the tailor's form must have measurements very similar to the actor's.

Some pattern pieces are neither flat patterned nor draped but drafted directly from measurements, often using an established formula. These include stand-up collars (see page 150), cuffs, waistbands, and a variety of garments created from rectangles, such as kimonos.

Theatrical cutter/drapers use elements of flat pattern drafting, draping, and direct drafting interchangeably, depending upon the nature of the project. Students should learn both major patterning methods and how to draft certain pieces directly. Draping teaches you, through your hands and eyes, how flat shapes become three-dimensional. It is, for many cutter/drapers, an aesthetic and scuptural process. Flat pattern drafting, however, is an equally important learning tool that develops your ability to both see and create three-dimensional shapes through one-dimensional diagrams.

Practical considerations may determine which basic method is taught first in costume technology classes, and used most often as the initial step in creating costume patterns. Draping a pattern that will fit a specific actor requires a tailor's form that is at least close to the actor's measurements as it is, or through padding. Flat pattern drafting requires only a set of measurements, a wide piece of paper, and a few drawing tools. Many costume technology students who want to develop basic skills as quickly and as accurately as possible find that the flat pattern drafting approach is the easiest to learn and to apply.

Computer patterning programs are all based on flat pattern drafting, and are discussed in Chapter 11.

Flat Pattern Drafting

This flat pattern drafting method was devised in professional costume shops, and it has evolved as costume technicians and students all over the country have used and improved upon it.

Flat pattern drafting makes the assumption that, no matter what fashion silhouette the design requires, the basic goal—to manipulate flat cloth to conform to the contours of the human body—remains constant. What differs in each instance is the means of reaching the goal. For example: You can use many means of fabric manipulation to shape a garment over the female bust: darts, gathers, curved seams, tucks, shirring, a drawstring, or elastic—occurring singly or in combinations. Design and fashion dictate the choice of means.

In this flat pattern drafting method, the costume student learns how to solve the bust shaping problem by one means: a combination of bust and waist darts. The next step is learning how to execute variations on the original solution, employing other means. In the flat pattern drafting method, all the means by which cloth can be shaped over the female bust become extensions of the original solution rather than singular, unrelated problems.

The same is true for sleeves. A basic one-piece sleeve solves the initial problem of shap-

ing the fabric to fit the arm. A series of developments then allows you to change the style and design of the sleeve, into, for instance, a leg-o'-mutton sleeve, which still fits the same arm.

This book contains flat pattern drafting instructions for creating female bodices and blouses, male doublets, one- and two-piece sleeves, collars, skirts, and pants. Also included are examples of simple pattern development instructions and an illustrated draping essay. The procedures and exercises that follow will not begin to give you all the tools you need to pattern every costume you might encounter. They will, however, give you a foundation for your work to come, and a path on which you can begin your journey.

The Place of Period Patterns

Period pattern research is the study of how the people who cut and stitched clothes throughout history solved the dual problems of how to make the fabric fit the body and how to meet the fashion requirements of their day. Excellent books are available devoted to period patterns where you can find scale patterns of actual period garments and comments from contemporary dressmakers and tailors, fashion arbiters, and the people who wore the clothes. These patterns, and the contemporary comments, are invaluable research tools for working cutter/drapers and for costume students.

What period patterns cannot do, however, is help you fit your actor. If you draft up a full-scale version of a period pattern from

Norah Waugh's *The Cut of Women's Clothes,* for instance, you will have a beautiful example of accurate period line and style, but it probably won't fit any person in your cast.

A cutter/draper can, with experience, learn to draft up a period pattern and then alter its size to conform to the actor's measurements. But, since there is no step-by-step system for this kind of pattern alteration (instructions for grading modern patterns up or down in size do not work very well on patterns for Victorian bodices, frock coats, or an eighteenth-century sacque back gown), it is a difficult skill to learn and teach.

The practice of blowing up a period pattern with an opaque projector until it approximates the desired measurements is fraught with disaster. Which measurement do you choose as your guide? The period pattern may be for a coat that was created for a man with a barrel chest and narrow shoulders. If you blow it up until it is the size of your actor's chest measurement, it may still be too narrow for him in the shoulders. If you blow it up to his shoulder size, it will be much too large in the chest.

In an effort to minimize these difficulties, some period patterns are now available that have been adapted to modern bodies and standard sizes. Standard sizes may easily be graded up and down to other standard sizes by means of a simple formula. Unfortunately, standard sizing still does not solve the fitting problems for many period garments. A standard size 10 dress in a relatively simple, contemporary style will fit a great many women, even though they all have different measurements. This won't be true of a snug, boned, multipieced, seventeenth-century bodice. And, there is no such thing as a standard size 40-regular Elizabethan doublet. The more fitted and complex the fashion shape, the more individualized the garment must be.

The Basic Body Block

The pattern development method introduced here begins with a basic female body block drawn from a set of body measurements. (The body block may also be draped on a dummy that is very close to the actor's size; a brief discussion of this draping process begins on page 133.) Following the presentation of the basic female body block, you will find a series of developments explaining how to shift fullness and seam lines to create different bodice shapes.

Once you have mastered the theory behind these developments, you will be able to create many different bodice and blouse pattern shapes. If your original body block was accurate, and your subsequent developments were carried out carefully, you should never encounter serious fitting problems.

The male body block requires six measurements and the female version, eight measurements. The drafting and computing skills needed to draw the blocks are minimal. After you've drawn eight or ten blocks, and thoroughly understand how it's done, you will be able to produce one on paper in about twenty minutes. In another twenty minutes you can trace the stitching lines onto a piece of muslin and construct the body block mock-up. Twenty minutes' worth of fitting and pattern adjustment, and you're ready to move on to the actual garment pattern. If you work in a situation in which you will be cutting several different costumes for the same actor, the hour spent creating the body block will not have to be repeated, and you'll have a basic set of shapes from which much of the cutting for that actor can be done.

Remember that the body block is not a garment in itself; it is a representation of the body, drawn with a minimum of garment ease. It is the basic shape to which all the garment patterns you develop from it will return. It is the first step in developing a pattern.

Measuring the Actor

Most costume shops take many more than the six and eight measurements necessary for drawing up the male and female body blocks. These measurements will be recorded on specially designed forms and stored in a file or a folder where they are available to all the technicians. Some examples of measurement blanks follow on the next pages.

You cannot draw a successful body block without accurate body measurements. Many cutter/drapers prefer to take their own measurements to ensure accuracy and to note small physical details that may be too subtle to show up in recorded inches.

Try to have at least two people available for taking measurements, one to wield the tape measure and the other to fill in the form. To make sure that the person being measured is relaxed and at full dimension, assign a third person to chat with the actor while the other two are doing the work. A lively conversation will prevent the person being measured from inhaling and holding it just when you're measuring the waist.

The tools you need include a flexible tape measure, three lengths of narrow ribbon, cording or twill tape, a pencil, and the measurement form. Locate yourselves in a well-lighted fitting room or in a secluded part of the costume shop. Some people resent having their vital statistics shouted out in public.

You can take accurate measurements on an actor who is wearing a lightweight shirt or blouse, although the beginner will find it helpful and instructive to have the actor clad only in undergarments. Don't take measurements on anyone wearing a leotard or tights, since these garments distort the natural shape. Always have the actor remove bulky clothing and

empty all pockets. Make sure the person is standing firmly on both feet, head centered, arms hanging loosely to each side and is as relaxed as possible.

When measuring a woman for the basic body block, make sure she has on a brassiere that she is accustomed to wearing. If bustshaping undergarments will be part of the costume—a 1950s uplift bra, for instance, or a corset—you will either make necessary adjustments in the pattern developments or take another set of measurements of the actor wearing the costume undergarment and make another body block.

Prepare the actor for measurements by tying the waist and armscye markers in place. (See Figure 4–7 on page 107 for the correct placement of these markers.) The three markers are measurement guideposts.

Place the waist marker at the body's natural waist, no matter where the garment waistline will lie. The natural waist is approximately midway between the bottom of the rib cage and the top of the hipbone. It's where the body is the narrowest; above the natural waist the torso expands and below it the hips curve out. If a natural waistline is not apparent, ask the actor to place his or her hands on the hipbones. Place the waist marker around the body at the top of the hands.

The armscye markers serve to separate the torso from the arms and to keep you from drawing the body block too wide across the front and back. This is a particularly important fitting area since, if a tight-fitting bodice or doublet is cut too wide across the front, the seam that connects the bodice or doublet to the sleeve will sit out over the upper arm and prevent the actor from having full arm movement. Run the armscye markers under the arms

FIGURE 4–2. Measurement blank #1.

Name : _____ _____   Date Taken : _____
     Last   First

Height_____	Shirt_____	Tights_____
Weight_____	Trouser_____	Gloves_____
Shoe-USA_____	Bra_____	Allergies_____
Suit/Dress_____	Hat_____	L or R Hand_____

Head_____

Forehead to nape_____

Ear to ear over crown_____

Neck_____

Bust front_____

Point to point_____

Shoulder to point_____

PNT to PNT-halter_____

Overbust_____

Chest_____ Exp_____

Underbust/ribcage _____ Exp____

Waist_____

Fullest Hips at__" _____

Side waist to below knee_____

Side waist to floor_____

Inseam_____

Thigh_____

Below knee_____

Calf_____

Ankle_____

Half girth_____

Full girth_____

Armscye to armscye F_____ B_____

SH-SH F_____ B_____

Nape to waist F_____ B_____

Nape to floor F_____ B_____

Underarm to waist_____

Shoulder seam_____

Armscye_____

Bicep_____

Elbow(bent)_____

Forearm_____

Wrist_____

Shoulder to elbow_____

Elbow to wrist_____

Armpit to wrist_____

Shoulder to wrist_____

CB nape to wrist_____

Notes:
Measurements taken by:

FIGURE 4–3. Measurement blank #2.

Date_____

ACTOR: _____ CHARACTER: _____ PLAY: _____

Height: _____ Weight: _____ Blouse/Shirt: _____ Dress/Suit: _____

Skirt/Pants: _____ Bra: _____ Hat: _____ Tights: _____ Shoe: _____

Pierced Ears:　　yes　　no _____ Allergies: _____

TORSO

NECK: High _____ Low _____

    Center Neck Length _____

BUST/CHEST: _____

    Overbust _____

    Ribcage_____ Expanded _____

WAIST: _____

HIP: _____

SHOULDER SEAM: _____

ARMPIT TO WAIST: _____

ACROSS SHOULDERS: Front____ Back ____

YOKE: Front _____ Back _____

CENTER NECK-WAIST: Front____ Back ____

SHOULDER:　to bust pt: _____

           to below bust: _____

           to waist: _____

POINT TO POINT: _____

SLEEVE

OUTSIDE ARM LENGTH:

    center back to shoulder: _____

    to elbow: _____

    to wrist: _____

INSIDE ARM LENGTH:

    to wrist: _____

ARMSCYE: _____

BICEP: _____

ELBOW (90 degrees)_____

FOREARM: _____

WRIST: _____

HAND: _____

GLOVE: _____

HEAD

CIRCUMFERENCE: _____

FOREHEAD TO NAPE: _____

EAR TO EAR:　　top: _____

             back: _____

TEMPLE TO TEMPLE: back: _____

NAPE WIDTH: low: _____

NOTES:

BELOW WAIST

CENTER NECK-FLOOR: Front _____ Back ___

CENTER WAIST-FLOOR: Front _____ Back ___

WAIST to BELOW KNEE:_____

SHOULDER to BELOW KNEE: _____

INSEAM: _____

THIGH: _____

KNEE: above: _____ below: _____

CALF: _____

ANKLE: _____

GIRTH: Half _____ Full _____

CROTCH DEPTH: _____

FIGURE 4–4. Measurement blank #3.

MEASUREMENT FORM

Name _____ Phone _____ Date _____

Show _____ Character _____

HEIGHT _____ WEIGHT _____ SHOE _____ SUIT _____

SHIRT _____ PANTS _____ TIGHTS _____ HOSE _____

DRESS _____ BLOUSE _____ BRA _____ EARS PIERCED __

HEAD _____ F-NECK TO WAIST _____ to FLOOR _____

EAR to EAR _____ B-NECK TO WAIST _____ to FLOOR _____

NAPE to FRONT _____ SH TO WAIST-F _____ B _____

NECK BASE _____ SH TO BPT _____ SH SEAM _____

SHOULDER WIDTH F _____ B _____ SHOULDER to ELBOW BENT _____

ARMSCYE WIDTH F _____ B _____ SHOULDER to WRIST BENT _____

CHEST/BUST _____ BPT to BPT _____ SLEEVE LENGTH _____

UNDERBUST _____ UNDERARM TO ELBOW _____

WAIST _____ UNDERARM TO WRIST _____

HIPS _____ ARMSCYE _____

INSEAM _____ K __ A __ F __ BICEP _____

OUTSEAM _____ K __ A __ F __ FOREARM _____

THIGH _____ WRIST _____

KNEE ABOVE _____ BELOW _____ GLOVE _____

CALF _____ HALF GIRTH _____

ANKLE _____ FULL GIRTH _____

CROTCH DEPTH _____

NOTES:

MEASURED BY: _____

FIGURE 4–5. Measurement blank #4.

MALE MEASUREMENTS SHEET

NAME: _____   HEIGHT: _____   ALLERGIES: _____

DATE: _____   WEIGHT: _____   GLOVE: _____

PHONE/BOX: _____   HAT: _____   LT/RT HANDED: _____

ROLES: _____   SHIRT: _____   HAIR COLOR: _____

_____   PANTS: _____   PIERCED EARS: _____

_____   SUITS: _____

_____   TIGHTS: _____

_____   SHOE: _____

TORSO

1. NECK: BASE _____   6. FRONT NECK to WAIST: _____
   MID _____   to FLOOR: _____
2. ACR. SHOULDER: FRONT _____   7. BACK NECK to WAIST: _____
   BACK _____   to FLOOR: _____
3. ACR. CHEST: FRONT _____   8. SHOULDER to WAIST: _____
   BACK _____   9. UNDERARM to WAIST: _____
4. CHEST: REGULAR _____   10. SHOULDER LENGTH: _____
   EXPANDED _____   11. HIP: HIGH _____
5. WAIST: _____   LOW _____

ARM

12a. BICEP: _____   13. SHOULDER to WRIST: _____
  b. FOREARM: _____   to ELBOW: _____
  c. WRIST: _____   14. UNDERARM to WRIST: _____
                                                 to ELBOW: _____

LEG

15a. THIGH: _____   17a. WAIST TO FLOOR (SIDE): _____
  b. BELOW KNEE: _____   b. TO BELOW KNEE: _____
  c. CALF: _____   c. TO MID-CALF: _____
  d. ANKLE: _____   18. INSEAM TO FLOOR: _____
16. HALF GIRTH: _____   19. CROTCH DEPTH: _____

HEAD/WIG

1. _____ HEAD CIRCUMFERENCE
2. _____ HAIRLINE COMPLETELY AROUND HEAD
3. _____ OVER TOP OF HEAD-FOREHEAD TO NAPE
4. _____ TEMPLE TO TEMPLE ACROSS FOREHEAD
5. _____ EAR to EAR OVER TOP OF HEAD
6. _____ AROUND HEAD FROM TEMPLE TO TEMPLE

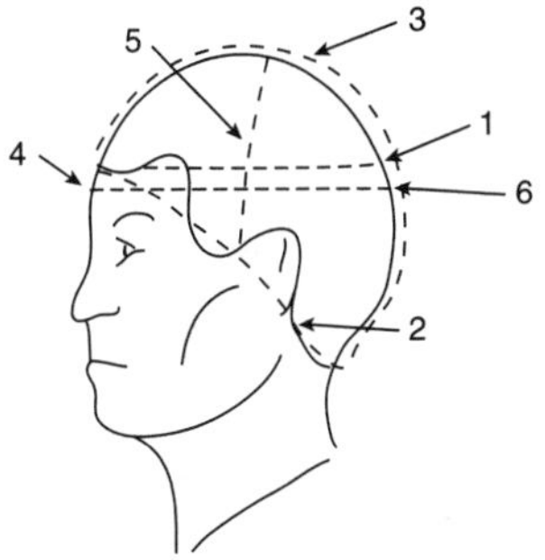

FIGURE 4–6. Measurement blank #5.

FEMALE MEASUREMENTS SHEET

Name _____ Date _____

Character(s) _____ Phone _____

Head _____ Shirt _____ Dress _____ Bra _____
Bust _____ Skirt/Pants _____ Tights _____ Ballet _____
Waist _____ Hat _____ Glove _____ Shoe _____
Hips _____ Piercings _____ Ring _____ Rt/Lt Handed ___
Sh. to W _____ Tattoos _____
W. to Floor _____ Hair Swatch Info: _____
Height _____ Other Hair Notes: _____
Weight _____ Posture: _____
Allergies: _____

HEAD

Around _____ Ear to Ear _____ Forehead to Nape _____ Hairline Note _____

TORSO

Around:

Neck: mid _____ lower _____ Above bust _____ Bust _____

Below bust _____ Waist: High (natural) _____

low _____ @ _____" down from H. Waist

Hips: fullest point _____ @ _____" down from H. Waist

Belly: _____ @ _____" down from H. Waist

Stride: _____ (around upper thighs with regular step taken)

Across:

Shoulder seam: _____

Shoulder F _____ B _____

Chest break: F _____ B _____

Bust SS to SS: F ___ B ___

B point to B point _____

Belly SS to SS: F ___ B ___

ARMS

Around:

Armscye _____ Bicep (flexed) _____

elbow (bent) _____ Forearm _____

wrist _____

hand (over hand w/thumb cupped in) _____

Length:

(bent) CB to sh. seam _____ elbow _____

to wrist _____

(straight) pit to wrist _____

to fingertip _____

LEGS

Around:

Thighs: upper _____ lower _____ above knee _____ below knee _____

Calf _____ ankle _____ Foot through instep _____

LENGTHWISE MEASUREMENTS

Mid-shoulder to bust point _____ h. waist, ctr. F ___ ctr. B ___; princess line F ___ B ___

Armpit to waist high _____ low _____

Waist to: mid-knee _____ mid-calf _____ ankle _____ floor F ___ ctr. B ___ *Heels?* _____

Inseam to: ankle _____ floor _____ *Crotch Depth* from h. waist _____ low waist _____

Girth: waist to waist _____ shoulder to shoulder _____ misc: _____

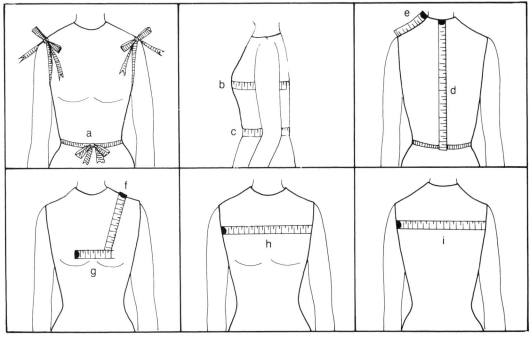

a. waist and armscye tapes
d. nape to waist
g. bust point to bust point

b. bust/chest
e. neck to shoulder
h. front width

c. waist
f. center of shoulder to bust point
i. back width

FIGURE 4–7. Body block measurements.

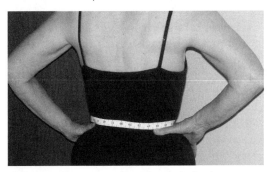

FIGURE 4–8. Hands on hips, thumbs indicating waistline.

and up over the shoulders so they rest in the small space created by the acromioclavicular joint (see Figure 4–9). This space is not always easy to find and will be in different relationships to the underarm, sometimes straight up, sometimes angling out, and sometimes angling

in. If the top of the armscye marker threatens to slip off a sloping or a narrow shoulder, pin it to the actor's clothing or secure it to the body with a piece of transparent tape.

Take snug measurements but don't draw the measurement tape so tightly that it makes an indentation in the actor's body. Believe your own eyes, not what is told to you. A waist measurement of 28 inches will never become 25 inches just because the person being measured assures you it will.

The following eight measurements are the ones you'll use to draft the female body block. Take them very carefully.

1. *Chest Measurement.* Take this measurement around the fullest part of the chest or bust. Make sure the tape comes straight around the back so the encircled area is parallel with the floor.

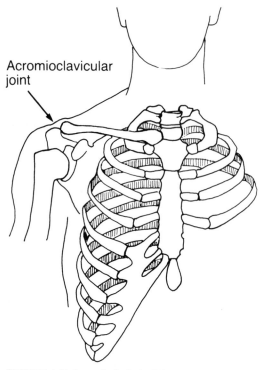

Acromioclavicular joint

FIGURE 4–9. Acromioclavicular joint.

2. *Waist Measurement.* Make certain the actor is breathing normally when you take this measurement. The tape should follow the waist marker and, like the bust measurement, be taken parallel to the floor.

3. *Back Nape to Waist Measurement.* Begin this measurement at the top of the most prominent cervical vertebra, where the neck begins to curve to the front. Be careful not to begin it too low. Extend the tape to the waist marker, following the back curve.

4. *Neck to Shoulder Measurement.* Begin this measurement where the neck joins the shoulder, at a point directly below the ear lobe. Extend the tape to the armscye marker. This measurement will average 4½ inches on women, 5 to 5½ inches on men, and includes only the torso portion of the shoulder, not the top of the arm. (See Figure 4–7.)

5. *Center of Shoulder to Bust Point Measurement.* Divide the distance between the neck and shoulder in half and begin the measurement at that point. Extend the tape down to the bust apex. The tape usually angles in for this measurement, but it may come straight down, or, in some cases, angle out.

6. *Bust Point to Bust Point Measurement.* Extend the tape from one bust apex to the other. If you have difficulty seeing the bust apex for this measurement, or for the center of shoulder to bust point measurement, ask the actor to point to her nipples. Both of the measurements involving the bust apex are extremely important in drawing accurate female body blocks. Neither measurement is taken on men.

7. *Front Width Measurement.* Use the armscye markers as your guides for the front width measurement. Place one end of the tape at the point where one armscye marker disappears under the arm and extend it straight across to where the opposite marker disappears. Don't run the tape under the arms. You want a front measurement only.

8. *Back Width Measurement.* Take this measurement in the same manner as the front width measurement, from where one armscye marker disappears to where the other disappears. The back width measurement is usually larger than the front width measurement but not always. On some people the two measurements are identical, and on some the front measurement will be larger.

Don't hurry when you take measurements. Read the tape measure carefully and take the measurement again if it doesn't seem right to you. Look at the body you're measuring and compare it to your own body and to others you've measured. Although no two bodies are exactly alike, there are certain types you'll learn to identify, and to account for, as you draw your body blocks.

Drawing the Basic Female Body Block

Read through all the instructions before you begin. Be sure you understand the two charts that you will use to determine the depth of the bust dart and the width of the waist dart.

Draw the body block on heavy brown craft paper or on squared pattern drafting paper. The first time you draw a body block, proceed slowly, checking each measurement. A majority of the mistakes that costume students make in their body blocks occur in the first couple of steps but don't show up until the block is complete.

Notice that the neckline and the bottom half of the armscye will be "eyeballed," that is, drawn in freehand. Refer to the illustrations for the shapes of these curves. Always draw these curves shallow rather than deep since it's easy to trim fabric away in a fitting but not easy to add it.

The paper pattern for the basic body block, once it's adjusted from the muslin mock-up fitting, will constitute a permanent record. In a shop where many costumes will be cut for the same actor, these paper blocks are often transferred to cardboard or tagboard.

Basic Female Body Block Drawn from Individual Measurements

The shapes of the body block pieces in the accompanying illustrations are based on one set of average measurements. Not every block will look the same (see examples below) so don't think you've made a mistake just because yours looks different or not like a "regular" pattern. Remember, the body block *is not* a garment pattern; it's a representation of an individual body.

FIGURE 4–10. Body block shape example #1.
1. bust–34; **2.** waist–26½; **3.** back neck to waist–16;
4. neck to shoulder–5; **5.** center shoulder to bust point–11; **6.** across front–12½; **7.** across back–13½;
8. bust point to bust point–7½.

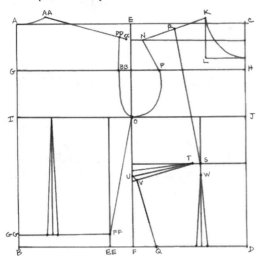

FIGURE 4–11. Body block shape example #2.
1. bust–45; **2.** waist–32½; **3.** back neck to waist–18½;
4. neck to shoulder–5½; **5.** center shoulder to bust point–11½; **6.** across front–16½; **7.** across back–15;
8. bust point to bust point–8½.

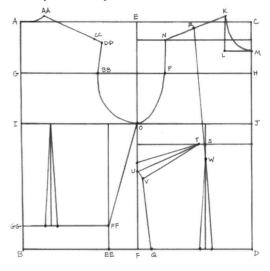

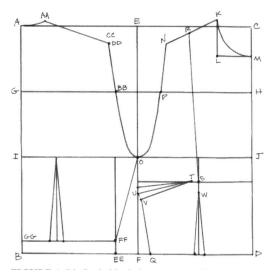

FIGURE 4–12. Body block shape example #3.
1. bust–32; **2.** waist–25; **3.** back neck to waist–15;
4. neck to shoulder–4; **5.** center shoulder to bust
point–9½; **6.** across front–13½; **7.** across back–13½;
8. bust point to bust point–8.

TOOLS NEEDED

> 24-inch ruler *or* yardstick
> right angle
> 18-inch plastic C-Thru
> ruler pencil
> craft or pattern paper

MEASUREMENTS REQUIRED

Note: In this step only, expand fractional measurements to the next ½ inch. For example: 33¼ inches becomes 33½ inches and 18¾ inches becomes 19 inches.

1. bust
2. waist
3. back nape to waist
4. neck to shoulder
5. center of shoulder to bust point
6. bust point to bust point
7. front width
8. back width

110

CHARTS FOR DETERMINING THE SIZES OF BODY DARTS

Chart 1: Depth of Bust Dart

Note: If the person is especially heavy busted, draw the dart deeper by ½ inch and make further adjustments in the fitting.

> 30½–32-inch bust measurement = ½ inch
>   deep bust dart
> 32½–34-inch bust = ¾ inch
> 34½–36-inch bust = 1 inch
> 36½–38-inch bust = 1½ inches
> 38½–40-inch bust = 1¾ inches
> 40½–42-inch bust = 2 inches
> 42½–44-inch bust = 2½ inches

Chart 2: Width of Waist Dart

The width of the waist dart is determined by the difference between the bust measurement and the waist measurement.

> 4–5½-inch difference = ½-inch wide waist
>   dart
> 6–7½-inch difference = ¾ inch
> 8–9½-inch difference = 1 inch
> 10–11½-inch difference = 1¼ inches
> 12–13½-inch difference = 1½ inches
> 14–15½-inch difference = 1¾ inches

Example:

bust measurement	36 inches
minus waist measurement	−31 inches
difference between bust and waist measurements	5 inches

Therefore, according to Chart 2, the width of the waist dart is ½ inch.

Before beginning with Step 1, make the following computations that you will need as you draw the body block:

a. depth of bust dart
b. width of waist dart
c. ½ total bust measurement

d. ¼ back nape to waist measurement

e. ½ front width

f. ¼ total waist measurement

g. ½ bust point to bust point measurement

h. ½ back width

The measurements and the computations used to draw the female body block in the following illustrations are:

1. bust—36 inches

2. waist—24 inches

3. back nape to waist—16 inches

4. neck to shoulder—4½ inches

5. center of shoulder to bust point—9 inches

6. bust point to bust point—7½ inches

7. front width—12 inches

8. back width—13 inches

a. depth of bust dart—1 inch

b. width of waist dart—1½ inches

c. ½ total bust measurement—18 inches

d. ¼ back nape to waist measurement—4 inches

e. ½ front width—6 inches

f. ¼ total waist measurement—6 inches

g. ½ bust point to bust point measurement—3¾ inches

h. ½ back width—6½ inches

Step 1: Draw a Rectangle

A–B and C–D equal the back nape to waist measurement, plus the depth of the bust dart.

Example:

nape to waist	16 inches
36-inch bust requires 1 inch deep bust dart (see Chart 1)	+ 1 inch
A–B and C–D	17 inches

A–C and B–D equal one-half the total bust measurement, plus ½ inch.

Example:

bust measurement is 36 inches

½ of 36		18 inches
		+ ½ inch
A–C and B–D		18½ inches

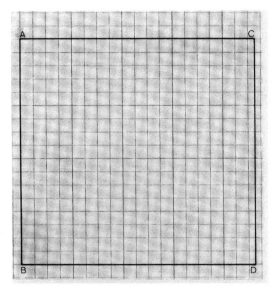

FIGURE 4–13. Female body block—Step 1.

Step 2: Add Construction Lines

Divide A–C and B–D in half and draw a vertical line, E–F.

From points A and C, measure down one-quarter of the back nape to waist measurement, creating points G and H. Connect points G and H, forming horizontal line, G–H. G–H is the front and back width line.

From points G and H, measure down the same distance again (one-quarter of the back nape to waist measurement), creating points I and J. Connect I and J, forming horizontal line, I–J. I–J is the chest line.

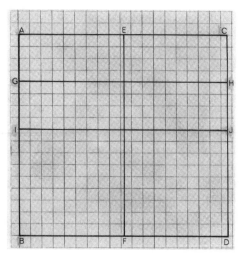

FIGURE 4–14. Female body block—Step 2.

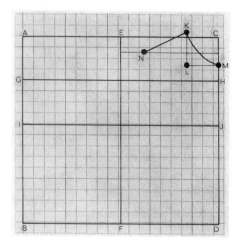

FIGURE 4–15. Female body block—Step 3.

BEGIN WITH THE FRONT SECTION

Front Section

Step 3: Front Neck and Shoulder

3 inches to the left, and ½ inch up from C, mark K.

3 inches down from K, mark L.

2½ inches down from C, mark M.

Connect K to L and L to M with straight lines, forming a right angle.

Draw in the neck curve from K to M as shown.

1⅜ inches below the A–C line, draw a horizontal line.

To determine the front shoulder line, place the small end of a ruler on K and angle it to hit the horizontal line you've just drawn, at exactly the neck to shoulder measurement on the ruler.

Mark N at this point and join K to N with a straight line.

Step 4: Front Armhole

Mark O on the I–J line at the point where it *crosses* the E–F line. O is the base of the armhole.

To the left of H, measure out half the front width measurement and mark P.

Connect N to P with a straight line.

Connect P to O with a curve, as shown, to complete the armhole.

FIGURE 4–16. Female body block—Step 4.

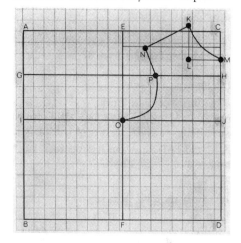

Step 5: Front Waist

To the left of D, measure out one quarter of the total waist measurement, plus the computed width of the front waist dart, *plus* ¼ inch, and mark Q.

Q is the base point for the side seam.

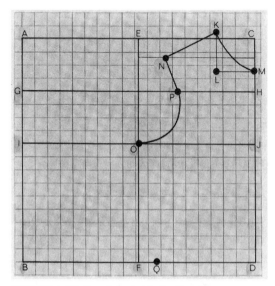

FIGURE 4–17. Female body block—Step 5.

Step 6: Bust Point and Bust Point Line

To the left of D, measure out half the total bust point to bust point measurement and draw a vertical line up to the I–J line. This line will be the center of the front waist dart.

Find the center of the shoulder line (K–N) and mark R.

Place a ruler with the small end on R and angle it so it hits the line just drawn at exactly the shoulder to bust point measurement on the ruler. Mark S. This is the bust point.

Draw a line through S, horizontal to I–J, out to lines E–F and C–D. This is the bust point line.

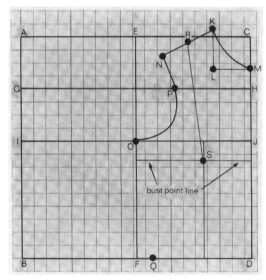

FIGURE 4–18. Female body block—Step 6.

Step 7: Bust Dart

To the left of S (the bust point), toward the E–F line, measure out ½ inch and mark T for the point of the bust dart.

FIGURE 4–19. Female body block—Step 7.

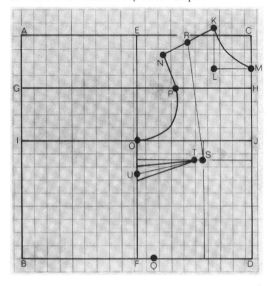

On the E–F line, measure down from the bust point line the *total* computed depth of the bust dart and mark U.

Connect T and U with a straight line. This is the center line of the bust dart.

On the E–F line, measure out one-half the total bust dart depth on each side of U, and mark.

Connect each of these marks with the bust dart point to form the dart.

Step 8: Side Seam

Measure the length of the top line of the bust dart.

From T, the point of the bust dart, measure out the same length on the bottom line of the bust dart, and mark V.

Connect V and Q with a straight line, completing the side seam.

Connect V to U, completing the bust dart.

FIGURE 4–20. Female body block—Step 8.

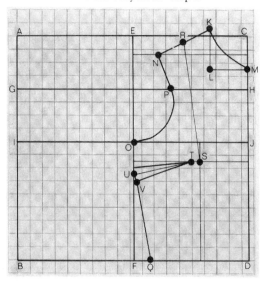

Step 9: Front Waist Dart

The center line for the waist dart has already been determined in Step 6.

On this line, measure down 1 inch from S, the bust point, toward the B–D line, and mark W for the point of the waist dart.

On the B–D line, on both sides of the spot where the waist dart center line falls, measure out half the total waist dart width, and mark.

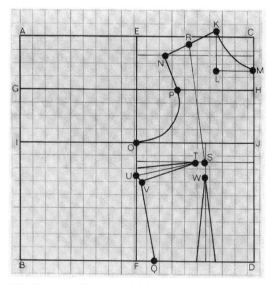

FIGURE 4–21. Female body block—Step 9.

Connect these marks with W, completing the waist dart.

Back Section

Step 10: Back Neck

2½ inches to the right of A, and ½ inch up, mark AA.

Connect A to AA with a slight curve, as shown. This is the back neck.

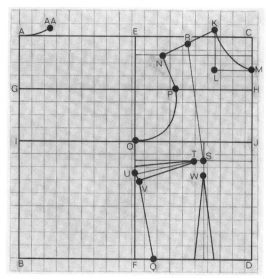

FIGURE 4–22. Female body block—Step 10.

3 inches up from BB, mark CC.

Place the small end of the ruler on AA and angle it so it passes through CC.

Draw a straight line from AA toward CC that is the length of the neck to shoulder measurement on the ruler, *plus* ½ inch. Mark the end of this line DD. AA–DD may be longer or shorter than the distance from AA to CC, depending on the neck to shoulder measurement.

Note: The back shoulder seam is ½ inch longer than the front shoulder seam. This extra ½ inch is eased into the seam when the muslin mock-up is stitched, to allow for shoulder movement.

Step 11: Back Shoulder

To the right of G, measure out half the total back width and mark BB.

Step 12: Back Armhole

Connect DD to BB with a straight line.

Connect BB to O with a slight curve, as shown, to complete the armhole.

FIGURE 4–23. Female body block—Step 11.

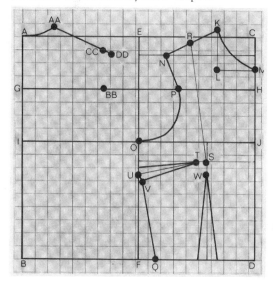

FIGURE 4–24. Female body block—Step 12.

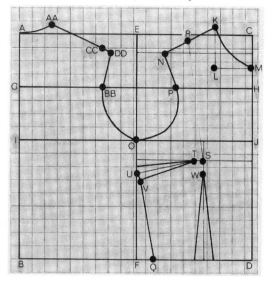

Step 13: Side Seam

To the right of B, measure out one quarter the total waist measurement, *plus* the width of the waist dart, *minus* ¼ inch. Mark EE.

Draw a vertical line up from EE to the I–J line.

Measure the length of the V–Q line on the front section of the block.

Place the ruler with the small end on the *top* of the bust dart, where it meets the E–F line, and angle it toward the vertical line just drawn on the back section, until the V–Q measurement on the ruler crosses the vertical line, and mark FF.

Connect FF and O with a straight line. This is the side seam.

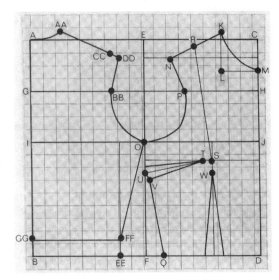

FIGURE 4–26. Female body block—Step 14.

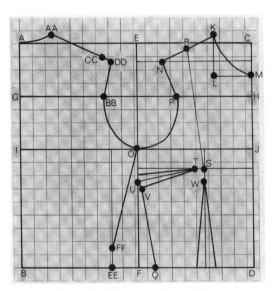

FIGURE 4–25. Female body block—Step 13.

Step 14: Back Waist

Draw a line to the left of FF toward the A–B line that is parallel to the B–D line. Where it intersects A–B, mark GG.

Step 15: Back Waist Dart

To the left of FF, measure out half the distance between FF and GG, *plus* ¾ inch. Mark.

Draw a vertical line from this mark up to the I–J line. This is the center line for the back waist dart.

FIGURE 4–27. Female body block—Step 15.

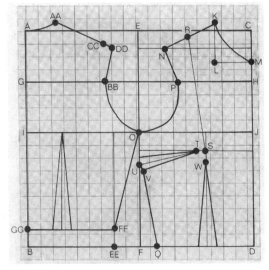

On the B–D line, to both sides of the back waist dart center line, measure out half the width of the waist dart, and mark.

Connect these marks with straight lines to the point of the waist dart, which rests on the I–J line.

Now you have finished drawing your body block. Take a good look at it and see if you can visualize where each part of the block will lie on the body. Make sure your straight lines are straight and your curves are smooth.

Check to see if you've drawn right angles at the intersections of the following lines:

1. center front at neck edge
2. center back at neck edge
3. shoulder at neck edge
4. shoulder at armscye edge
5. side front
6. side back

Correct these angles, as necessary, with your right angle or C-Thru ruler.

Transferring the Body Block from Paper to Muslin

Don't cut out the paper pieces now. You may have to make corrections, and these will be easier to draw in while the block is still together.

Use a large sheet of fabric tracing paper to transfer the stitching lines from the paper block to a length of unwashed, mediumweight muslin, which you have pressed and folded double. Make sure the muslin is on-grain and folded straight. Fold the tracing paper sheet in half, wrong sides together, and place it between the two layers of muslin. Secure the muslin, the tracing paper, and the brown paper pattern to the cutting table with T-pins or pushpins so they can't slip while you're tracing, or use masking tape if your table does not have

a surface that will accept pins. Trace the stitching lines and the dart center lines. Transfer the bust point marking; this is usually done with an X directly over the bust point.

After you've traced the front section, move the paper so the back section will be at least 1½ inches away from it. You need this space for drawing seam allowances.

You may place the center front of the body block on the fold, but always leave a *center back opening* with a 1-inch seam allowance.

Determining Seam Allowance

Determining the amount of seam allowance you want to leave around the edges of pattern pieces is a matter of individual preference. In some shops all stitching lines are traced very carefully on each piece of fabric cut, and the seam allowance is "eyeballed," that is, cut free-hand without measuring. When this method is used, the stitcher who sews the seams must match up the marked seam lines and secure them with pins, since the edges of the fabric do not line up.

Although it's always a good idea to trace stitching lines on fabric pieces as an accuracy check, it's helpful to measure the seam allowance so the stitcher can match up the edges of the cloth as well as the stitching lines. Measured seam allowances may vary from ½ to 1 inch in width. Commercial patterns are all drafted with ⅝-inch seam allowances, a width chosen both because it's wide enough to allow space for adjustments and not so wide that it's difficult to fit a curved seam.

If you choose to measure ⅝-inch seam allowances, use a seam gauge or the width of a tape measure, most of which are conveniently ⅝ inch wide. Simply move the gauge or tape around the edges of the pattern piece, marking the allowance with a pencil dot every two or three inches. Follow the dots as you cut. In some shops the measured seam allowance remains constant and in others it changes for different garments or for different parts of garments.

Constructing the Body Block Mock-up

Stitch the muslin mock-up together, with a long machine basting stitch, adding two or three back stitches at each end of each seam so the pieces won't come apart in the fitting. Follow the stitching lines precisely.

Remember that the back shoulder seam is ½ inch longer than the front shoulder seam. Ease this extra ½ inch into the seam. The ease is provided to allow for normal shoulder movement and is standard on many patterns. To distribute the extra length, pin each edge of the seam together, then stretch the front shoulder piece *slightly* over your knee or over a tailor's ham. Pin the seam together while the front shoulder piece is being stretched. Be careful to distribute the ease evenly. You should not end up with a tuck in the seam.

Fitting the Body Block Mock-up

Before putting the mock-up on the actor, clip the seam allowances around the neck, underarm, and waist, almost to the stitching lines. Gather the things you will need: scissors, safety pins, a felt-tipped pen for drawing on the muslin, and pencil and paper for taking notes. If possible, conduct the fitting in front of a full-length mirror in a well-lighted area.

The actor should be wearing only undergarments. Some cutter/drapers fit the mock-up with seams on the outside; others prefer to have seams on the inside. Fasten the center back seam with safety pins, placed 1 inch apart on the stitching lines. Pull the mock-up down into place on the body. Many cutter/drapers like to tie a ribbon or tape around the waist to hold the mock-up down during the fitting.

Stand away from the actor for a moment and look at the mock-up. Don't start making any adjustments until you've observed it from every angle.

If the mock-up is more than an inch too large around the fullest part of the bust, or across the front or back width, you've probably made a mistake in taking measurements or in computing some part of the body block. The same is true if it's more than an inch too small. Remeasure and check for mistakes. These three areas—around the bust, across the front, and across the back—should be nearly correct in all body blocks.

If you've made a mistake in measuring or in computing the body block, don't try to make the correction on the muslin mock-up. Redraw the body block and stitch another mock-up. The basic body block must be as accurate as possible so the patterns you develop from it will fit the actor.

The other important fitting area in the female body block is the position of the bust points and the correct relationship of the ends of the bust and waist darts to these points. The darts should end neither too close nor too far away from the bust points, and the cloth should fit smoothly over the bust without strain or puckers. If the bust points themselves are incorrectly located, you've made a mistake either in measuring or in computing and must redraw the block. If the darts end too close to the bust point, you may simply mark where they should end and make this alteration on your body block pattern.

Once you've seen that the upper chest area fits nicely, turn your attention to the areas where alterations are common, if not universal.

The straight front waist darts on the basic body block won't give a snug fit under most actor's busts, particularly on full-busted women. You can only achieve a close fit by pinning in and curving the waist darts. However, since the darts in the body block are only there for the purpose of developing patterns and won't be used, as they are, in a garment, don't make this alteration on the body block. If the waistline fits, the bust points are accurately positioned, and the ends of the waist and bust darts lie in good relationships to the bust points, the fit in the bust area is satisfactory.

The neck curve will almost always need redrawing. It was deliberately drawn high and usually has to be lowered by half an inch or so. If the neckline is so high that it makes the actor uncomfortable, clip it in a few places until it lies comfortably. Redraw your new neckline at the base of the neck. Be careful not to make the neckline too low because this is the edge that supports collars.

The lower armhole curves, both front and back, may also need adjustment. Be sure that the armholes lie close to the body but don't bind.

Check the position of the waistline. It will often ride too low in the back, particularly if the actor stands very straight. If the waistline is too low, redraw correct markings on the muslin.

The shoulder seams often need adjusting to account for different shoulder shapes and slants. Correct wrinkles at the center front by raising the shoulder seam at the shoulder edge and wrinkles under the arms by raising the shoulder seam at the neck edge. Use the cross grain of the fabric as your guide. The cross grain should be parallel to the floor in the area of the collarbone.

Sometimes there is too much fabric in the back shoulder section; eliminate this by pinning a tuck in the back shoulder seam.

The side seams may also need nipping in or letting out. The body block mock-up should fit closely but never skin tight. Don't upholster the body but don't allow the cloth to sag or wrinkle either. If the actor has unusually square shoulders, there may be a little fullness at the front of the armhole that is unavoidable and that will probably disappear when sleeves

FIGURE 4–28. The cross grain should be parallel with the floor in the area of the collarbone.

are set into the garment pattern you develop from the block.

If you do encounter an actor with a large discrepancy between the two sides of his or her

119

body, mark all adjustments carefully on both halves of the muslin, indicating which half is the right side and which is the left. Keep the muslin mock-up attached to the paper pattern. In most instances you won't cut a garment pattern to conform to an uneven body because then you have an unbalanced garment, which looks odd. What you do is add some sort of padding to the lower or smaller side so the body appears balanced. You must, however, have an accurate record of the actual body shape to plan your adjustments. The most common torso discrepancy is one shoulder lower than the other; a low shoulder is easy to correct with a shoulder pad.

Before you remove the mock-up from the actor, add two more important marks: lines indicating the top of the actor's shoulder, on both sides. These points may or may not occur on the shoulder seams; indeed, on this body block, they are generally ½ inch or so to the front of the shoulder seam. These marks will indicate the points from which all sleeves must hang. (See page 219, in Chapter 5, "Costume Construction," for a discussion of hanging sleeves that includes directions for finding top of shoulder points.) They're very important guideposts and should be transferred to all subsequent patterns.

Take one last look. Have you missed anything? Are your new lines clearly drawn and your alterations pinned in neatly and equally on each side? Does everything look okay? If so, close your safety pins and remove the body block from the actor.

Marking Adjustments on the Paper Pattern for the Body Block

Lay the muslin mock-up on the cutting table and with a felt-tipped pen mark all the new stitching lines you've pinned in, making sure to mark both sides of each seam. Remove the pins and take the muslin pieces apart. Press the pieces very lightly to remove wrinkles from the fitting, taking care not to stretch the pieces. Most of the time you will use only one-half of the mock-up to transfer corrections to the pattern. With a straight edge and/or a large French curve, draw new stitching lines from the pin marks. If you have made adjustments in the shoulder seam, make sure you retain the extra half inch for ease in the back shoulder seam. Check and correct all right angles.

Now, lay the muslin pieces on the paper pattern block, pin in place, and trace over the altered stitching lines with a needle-point tracing wheel. Remove the muslin and draw in the new lines, following the holes left by the tracing wheel.

Now you may cut out the paper pieces if you like, or you may leave the sheet intact. You will be making copies of the basic body block for your subsequent developments, and you may do this either by drawing around the original pieces or by tracing them onto fresh paper with a tracing wheel. Make sure the actor's name and the date are recorded on each pattern piece.

From Body Block to Garment Pattern

As you have seen, the basic female body block in this chapter is drawn with a waist dart and a bust dart. You will find other basic body blocks that control fabric fullness with other dart combinations or with a single dart. If you use a one-dart body block, you will not get as good a fit as you will with two darts, especially on fuller-busted women.

Very few costume patterns call for the particular arrangement of darts you've drawn into the basic body block. What you have achieved so far is a good fit, and what you will learn next is how to swing the fabric fullness, which is controlled by the waist and bust dart combination, into other dart combinations and into other means of control, such as curved seams, gathers, and tucks. Learning to manipulate fabric fullness control is the key to developing patterns from the body block.

Experiment with the five developments that follow, practice them, and then apply them to creating period patterns. Always check your results with a muslin mock-up. As you work with your paper patterns, try to visualize their final three-dimensional shape.

Adding Garment Ease

Garment ease is the additional length and width you add to your garment pattern pieces to allow for freedom of movement *and* to meet fashion and style requirements. Add garment ease to the appropriate pattern pieces *after* you have completed all steps of your pattern development. Add garment ease *before* you add seam allowances. Remember that most modern clothing has much more garment ease than most period clothing. Consult Figure 4–29 for a modern guide to garment ease. Note particularly the areas where ease *is not normally added.*

Add circumference ease at the widest part of the pattern piece and redraw the rest of the seam line. Make sure you have correctly divided the *total amount* of circumference ease into the number of body seams your garment has. For example: When you add 2 inches of garment ease to a bodice with

    side front seams (4 seam edges)
    side seams (4 seam edges)
    side back seams (4 seam edges)

divide the amount of ease (2 inches) by 12 (the total number of seam edges). (Normally, ease is not added to the center front or center back of a garment.) The amount added to each seam edge will be *slightly over ⅛ inch.*

A Guide to Garment Ease

bust — 2–3½"

waist — ½–1"

hips — 2–3"

CF length — ¼"

CB length — ¼–½"
shoulder to bust point — 0
bust point to bust point — 0
arm length (when measurement is taken
    with the arm bent)
        shoulder to elbow — 0
        shoulder to wrist — 0
cut waist circumference of skirt or pants ¾"
    larger than the waist circumference of
    bodice or waistband
correct ease for a fitted sleeve:
    underarm — from balance point to
        balance point, the sleeve and the
        armscye should be equal
    overarm — from balance point to balance
        point, the sleeve should be 1½" larger
        than the armscye, usually ¾" from
        balance point to top of shoulder in the
        back, and ¾" from balance point to top
        of shoulder in the front.

FIGURE 4–29. A guide to garment ease.

Measure garment ease additions carefully. Making each pattern piece "just a scooch bigger all the way around" is *not* the same thing as adding appropriate amounts of garment ease to your patterns.

If the garment you are patterning is designed to have shoulder pads, allow for them as you draw your pattern development. Raise the shoulder edge of the shoulder seam, front and back, the height of the shoulder pad, normally from ½ inch to 1½ inches, depending upon the design and the period. Redraw the shoulder seam from the raised edge to the neck edge.

Development 1

SWING FABRIC FULLNESS CONTROLLED
BY BUST AND WAIST DARTS INTO THE
WAIST DART ALONE

1. Trace adjusted front body block piece
   onto brown or pattern paper. Trace dart
   lines, including center lines, of both darts
   and bust point mark.

2. Close the bust dart with a straight pin or
   transparent tape. The pattern piece now
   has some bust shaping.

3. With paper scissors, cut up the center line
   of the waist dart to within ¼ inch of the
   bust point.

4. Flatten the paper pattern carefully on the
   table. Make sure the waist dart does not
   tear further. There will be some wrinkling in the area of the bust point; disregard this. The expanded waist dart is now
   sufficiently wide to control adequate fullness over the bust.

5. Draw a finished pattern piece by tracing
   around the construction pattern.

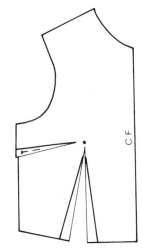

FIGURE 4–31. Development 1.

6. Transfer new dart: a. Drop dart point 1
   inch below bust point. b. Mark center of
   expanded dart at waistline and draw new
   dart center line up to the dart point. c.
   Draw stitching lines. The stitching lines
   on the new dart are the same as the ones
   on the original dart.

7. Correct the side seam as shown in Figure
   4–32.

FIGURE 4–30. Development 1.

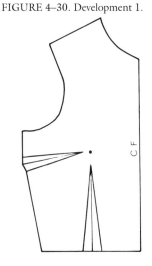

FIGURE 4–32. Development 1.

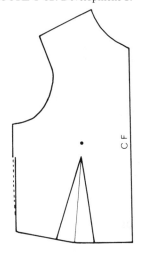

Development 2

LOCATE POSSIBLE DART POSITIONS

Figure 4–33 illustrates the nine locations where a bodice can be darted. One location or a combination of locations may be selected, according to period or design requirements.

1. Trace adjusted front block piece onto brown or pattern paper; include darts, dart center lines, and bust point mark.

2. Draw in desired dart line (or lines), always pointing the dart directly toward the bust point. A tailor's form may help you locate the dart positions on the pattern.

3. Close up the bust dart and the waist dart with straight pins or transparent tape.

4. Cut the center line of the new dart (or darts) to within ¼ inch of the bust point and flatten the paper construction pattern carefully on the table.

5. Adjust the seam edge of the new dart (or darts) for correct alignment, as follows:

   a. Tape a scrap of paper beneath the new dart space created on the construction pattern. Draw in the dart point 1 inch below the bust point, on the dart center line. Draw new dart stitching lines and score the lines with a tracing wheel.

   b. Fold the dart closed on the center line, matching the stitching lines carefully.

   c. Fold the dart flat in the direction you wish it to lie.

   d. Trim away the extra paper, following the seam line.

   e. Open the dart. The seam edge is now properly shaped for aligning the dart edges.

6. Follow instructions in Development 1 for drawing a clean finished pattern.

Development 3

CONTROLLING FABRIC FULLNESS WITH CURVED OR PRINCESS SEAMS

Seam Extends from Shoulder to Waist

1. Trace adjusted front block piece on brown or pattern paper; include darts, dart center lines, and bust point marks.

FIGURE 4–33. Development 2—Possible dart positions.

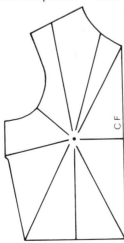

FIGURE 4–34. Development 3.

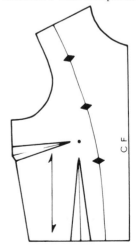

2. Draw in the desired seam line. (Placement of the seam line is determined by the design. Illustrations for two other princess seam line placements follow. Notice that the seam does *not* have to cross the bust point.)

FIGURE 4–35. Development 3.

3. Draw in straight grain line, parallel with CF, in the lower side section of the block as shown.

FIGURE 4–36. Development 3.

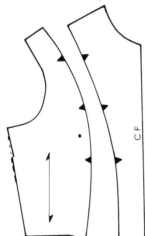

4. Draw in match-up marks as shown.

5. Close up the bust dart and the waist dart with straight pins or with transparent tape.

6. Cut the construction pattern in two pieces along the seam line and flatten the pieces carefully on the table. Can you see how the curved seams will control the fabric fullness necessary to fit the piece over the bust?

7. Trace clean pattern pieces and correct side and waist seams as shown in Figure 4–36.

Seam Extends into the Armhole

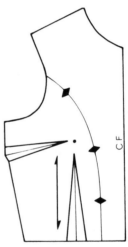

FIGURE 4–37. Princess seam extends into armhole.

FIGURE 4–38. Princess seam extends into armhole.

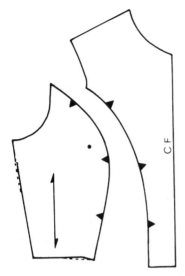

FIGURE 4–39. Princess seam extends into armhole.

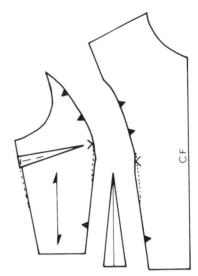

FIGURE 4–41. Princess seam extends into armhole and through the bust point.

Seam Extends into the Armhole and Through the Bust Point

FIGURE 4–40. Princess seam extends into armhole and through the bust point.

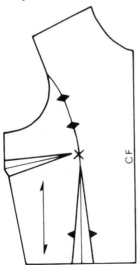

Development 4

CONTROLLING FABRIC FULLNESS WITH
WAISTLINE GATHERS OR TUCKS

1. Trace adjusted front block piece onto brown or pattern paper; include darts, dart center lines, and bust point marks.
2. Draw in cutting line as shown in Figure 4–42.
3. Close up the bust dart with a straight pin or a piece of transparent tape.
4. Cut along this line to within ¼ inch of the bust point; flatten out pattern carefully on the table.
5. Trace a clean pattern and correct side and waist seams as shown in Figure 4–43.
6. a. Indicate gathers as shown in Figure 4–44. When you construct the mock-up, gather this area until the piece equals one-quarter of the waist measurement.

125

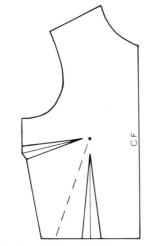

FIGURE 4–42. Development 4.

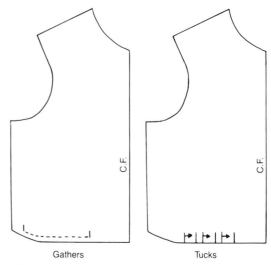

Gathers   Tucks

FIGURE 4–44. Development 4.

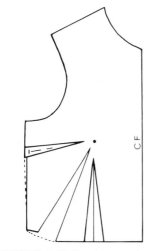

FIGURE 4–43. Development 4.

b. Indicate tucks as shown in Figure 4–44. To determine the width of the tucks, measure the width of the slashed pattern piece and subtract one-quarter of the waist measurement from it. Divide the remainder into two or three tucks. When the tucks are folded in, the waist meas-

urement of the pattern piece should equal one-quarter of the waist measurement.

Development 5

CONTROLLING FABRIC FULLNESS BY GATHERING INTO A YOKE

1. Trace adjusted front block piece onto brown or pattern paper; include darts, dart center lines, and bust point marks.
2. Draw in yoke line. (Yoke line position will be determined by the design.)
3. Draw in match-up marks.
4. Draw in cutting lines that extend to the bust point line, as shown in the illustration.
5. Cut construction pattern in two pieces along the yoke seam line.
6. Close up the bust dart and the waist dart with straight pins or transparent tape.

126

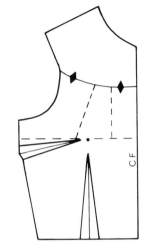

FIGURE 4–45. Development 5–Yoke.

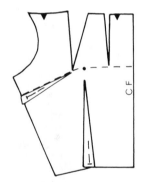

FIGURE 4–46. Development 5–Yoke.

FIGURE 4–47. Development 5–Yoke.

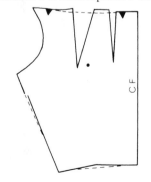

7. Cut along cutting lines to the bust point line and flatten pattern carefully on the table.

8. Trace a clean pattern piece and correct side and waist seams as shown in Figure 4–47.

9. Indicate gathering line as shown in Figure 4–48. N.B. The actual gathering line on the mock-up will be at the seam line.

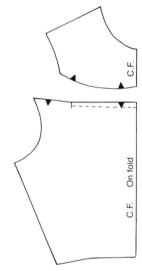

FIGURE 4–48. Development 5–Yoke.

When you cut the mock-up, place the CF on a fold. As you construct it, gather the top edge of this piece until it equals the bottom edge of the yoke.

Note: Development 5 gives you just enough fabric fullness to allow for the bust. If you wish to add additional fullness, slash the construction pattern to within ¼ inch of the waist edge and spread the pattern as wide as you like. With practice you will learn to determine how much spread to allow for fullness shown in a design. Don't forget that the CF remains on the straight of grain no matter how far you spread the pattern.

127

Drawing the Basic Male Body Block

Basic Male Body Block Drawn from Individual Measurements

The male body block is considerably simpler to draw than the female block because it has no bust dart. All the other steps are similar to those in the female block and there is only one illustration, a completed male body block.

TOOLS NEEDED

> 24-inch ruler *or* yardstick
> right angle
> 18-inch plastic C-Thru ruler
> pencil
> craft or pattern paper

MEASUREMENTS REQUIRED

Note: In this step only, expand fractional measurements to the next ½ inch. For example, 33¼ inches becomes 33½ inches, and 18¾ inches becomes 19 inches. The measurements below are those used to compute the following basic male body block.

1. chest–38 inches
2. waist–33 inches
3. back nape to waist–17 inches
4. neck to shoulder–5½ inches
5. front width–15 inches
6. back width–16 inches

CHART TO DETERMINE THE WIDTH OF THE WAIST DART

As in the female body block, waist dart width is determined by the difference between the chest and the waist measurements.

> 4–5½ inches difference = ½ inch
> 6–7½ inches difference = ¾ inch

8–9½ inches difference = 1
10–11½-inches differences = 1¼ inches

Before beginning with Step 1, make the following computations that you will need as you draw the body block:

a. width of waist dart
b. ½ total chest measurement
c. ¼ back nape to waist measurement
d. ½ front width
e. ½ total waist measurement
f. ½ back width

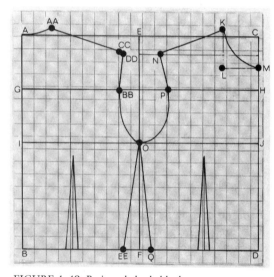

FIGURE 4–49. Basic male body block.

Step 1: Draw a Rectangle

A–B and C–D equal the back nape to waist measurement.

A–C and B–D equal one-half the total chest measurement, plus ½ inch.

Step 2: Add Construction Lines

Divide A–C and B–D in half and draw a vertical line, E–F.

From points A and C, measure down one-quarter of the back nape to waist measurement, creating points G and H. Connect points G and H, forming horizontal line, G–H. G–H is the front and back width line.

From points G and H, measure down the same distance again (one-quarter of the back nape to waist measurement), creating points I and J. Connect I and J, forming a horizontal line, I–J. I–J is the chest line.

You are ready to draw the front and back of the male body block.

BEGIN WITH THE FRONT SECTION

Front Section

Step 3: Front Neck and Shoulder

3 inches to the left, and ½ inch up from C, mark K.

3 inches down from K, mark L.

2½ inches down from C, mark M.

Connect K to L and L to M with straight lines, forming a right angle.

Draw in the neck curve from K to M as shown.

1⅜ inches below the A–C line, draw a horizontal line.

To determine the front shoulder line, place the small end of a ruler on K and angle it to hit the horizontal line you have just drawn, at exactly the neck to shoulder measurement on the ruler. Mark N at this point and join K to N with a straight line.

Step 4: Front Armhole

Mark O on the I–J line at the point where it *crosses* the E–F line. O is the base of the armhole.

To the left of H, measure out half the front width measurement and mark P.

Connect N to P with a straight line.

Connect P to O with a curve, as shown, to complete the armhole.

Step 5: Side Seam

To the left of D, measure out one-quarter of the total waist measurement, *plus* the computed width of the front waist dart, *plus* ¼ inch, and mark Q.

Connect O and Q with a straight line, completing the side seam.

Step 6: Waist Dart

From a point halfway between Q and D, draw a perpendicular line to a point 1 inch below the chest line. This is the center line for the waist dart.

On the B–D line, on both sides of the place where the waist dart center line falls, mark half the total dart width.

Connect these marks with the top of the waist dart center line, completing the waist dart.

Back Section

Step 7: Back Neck

2½ inches to the right of A, and ½ inch up, mark AA.

Connect A to AA with a slight curve. This is the back neck.

Step 8: Back Shoulder

To the right of G, measure out one-half the total back width and mark BB.

3 inches up from BB, mark CC.

Place the small end of the ruler on AA and angle it so it passes through CC.

Draw a straight line from AA toward CC that is the length of the neck to shoulder measurement, *plus* ½ inch. Mark the end of this line DD. AA–DD may be longer or shorter than the distance from AA to CC, depending on the neck to shoulder measurement.

Note: The back shoulder seam is ½ inch longer than the front shoulder seam. This extra ½ inch will be eased into the seam when the muslin mock-up is stitched, to allow for shoulder movement.

Step 9: Back Armhole

Connect DD to BB with a straight line.

Connect BB to O with a slight curve, as shown, to complete the armhole.

Step 10: Side Seam

To the right of B, measure out one-quarter the total waist measurement, *plus* the width of the waist dart, *minus* ¼ inch. Mark EE.

Connect O and EE with a straight line, completing the side seam.

Step 11: Back Waist Dart

From a point halfway between B and EE, draw a perpendicular line to a point 1 inch below the chest line. This is the center line for the waist dart.

On the B–D line, on both sides of the place where the waist dart center line falls, mark half the total dart width.

Connect these marks with the top of the waist dart center line, completing the waist dart.

Developing Patterns from the Male Body Block

The male body block will not normally be used to develop patterns for men's suits after the early 1800s. The major clothing styles for men in the nineteenth and twentieth centuries are tailored into shape and hang rather loosely on the body. Patterns for these garments are usually drafted from period tailoring instructions or developed from modern commercial patterns. Men's clothing worn before the early nineteenth century—gowns, tunics, jerkins, doublets, and a wide variety of form-fitting jackets and waistcoats—can be patterned from the basic block.

Developing a Doublet Pattern from the Male Body Block

1. Trace adjusted *front and back* block pieces onto brown or pattern paper; include waist darts and waist dart center lines.
2. Draw in desired seam lines. (Placement of seam lines is determined by the design.)
3. Draw match-up marks as shown.
4. Close up the waist darts with straight pins or transparent tape.

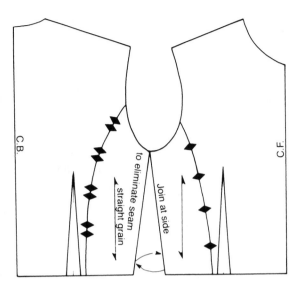

FIGURE 4–50. Doublet pattern.

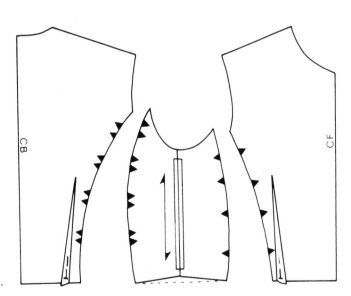

FIGURE 4–51. Doublet pattern.

5. Cut the construction pattern in two pieces along the seam line and flatten the pieces carefully on the table.

6. If you would like to eliminate the side seam, tape the small pieces together as shown and redraw the straight grain line parallel to the side seam position.

7. Trace clean pattern pieces and make any necessary corrections in the waistline seams.

131

Draping a Basic Body Block

To drape a basic body block, or other patterns, you must have a tailor's form that is close to the same size as the actor for whom the block or pattern is being done. The measurements that should as nearly as possible correspond to the actor's are front width, back width, back nape to waist, front neck to waist, around bust or chest, and waist. If the bust or waist of the tailor's form is smaller than the actor's, pad them out with polyester or cotton batting and secure the padding with muslin or a lightweight knit fabric.

The following photographic essay illustrates and explains the steps in draping a basic female body block. Once you have draped a basic block and can see where the straight grain and cross grain lines must be, practice draping the five bodice versions you have just completed in the flat pattern drafting method.

After you have draped your block or garment pattern in muslin and marked all the darts and seam lines, don't forget to lay it out on the table and correct all your stitching lines with a ruler, French curve, and right angle. Since muslin pieces stretch easily and lose their shapes, it's always a good idea to trace your final pattern on paper. You can make lots of mistakes when you cut directly from muslin pattern pieces.

1. Figure 4–52 shows a professional female tailor's form. It has collapsible shoulders so you can get clothing on and off it. The surface is soft enough for pins and there are prominent seams defining center lines and basic garment seam positions. The base is very sturdy and mounted on wheels.

2 and 3. In these photographs the draper is measuring the form before cutting a rectangle

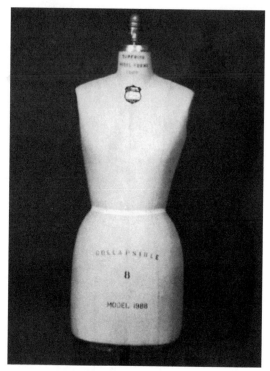

FIGURE 4–52. Draping a basic body block—#1. *This and all the following draping photographs are by Richard Ingham.*

of cloth for draping. Be sure to begin at the highest point of the shoulder for length. Cut the rectangle 3 or 4 inches bigger than necessary.

Notice the lengths of ¼-inch twill tape pinned to the form to add extra dimension to the center line and the bust point line. When draping garment patterns directly onto a tailor's form use twill tape to mark seams, darts, and garment edges.

4. The draper is using an all cotton, plainweave, striped fabric for this body block. The stripe helps define the straight grain of the

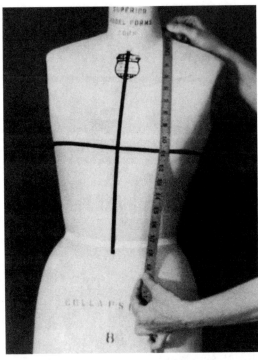

FIGURE 4–53. Draping a basic body block—#2.

FIGURE 4–54. Draping a basic body block—#3.

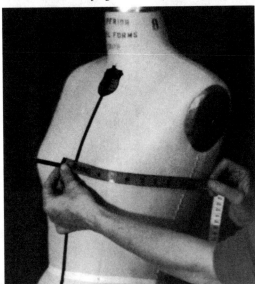

fabric. Notice the cross grain line drawn on the fabric with a black indelible pen. In this photograph, the draper is placing the fabric on the high point of the shoulder, making sure the cross grain is parallel to the floor. (Refer back to Figure 4–28.)

5. Using long quilting pins, the draper has fastened the fabric rectangle to the center front of the form. The pins follow the line of the twill tape. The fabric extends about 1½ inches beyond the center front.

6. Using the neckline seam on the form as a guide, the draper makes diagonal clips in the fabric to create the neckline curve.

7. The neckline curve is pinned in place, and the draper is pinning the armhole edge of the

FIGURE 4–55. Draping a basic body block—#4.

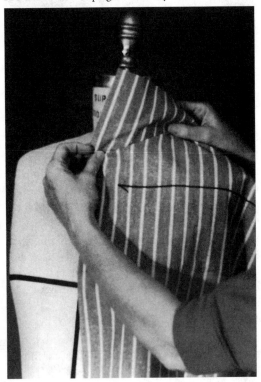

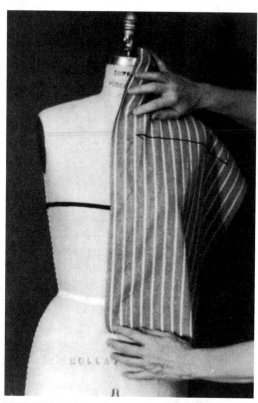

FIGURE 4–56. Draping a basic body block—#5.

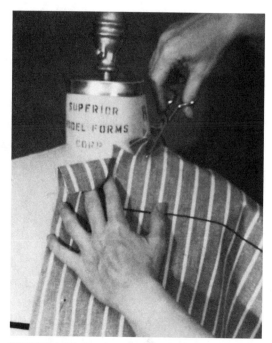

FIGURE 4–57. Draping a basic body block—#6.
FIGURE 4–58. Draping a basic body block—#7.

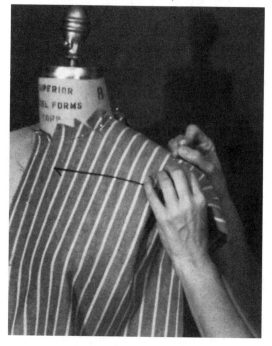

shoulder seam in place. This step secures the correct position of the cross grain.

8. Excess fabric length is gathered into the bust dart. The dart point is aimed directly at the bust apex, and the dart line is slightly angled.

9. The draper pins the waistline in place at the base of the side seam. Notice the clips made in the fabric that allow it to flare out over the hips. Notice that the draper is covering the tailor's form smoothly but not too tightly.

10. Here is the front portion of the drape with the waist dart pinned in place. Notice that neither the bust dart nor the waist dart extend all the way to the bust point.

134

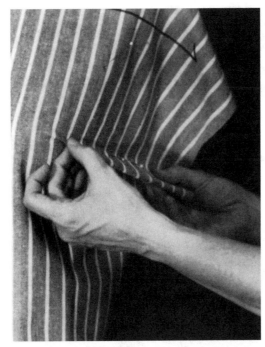

FIGURE 4–59. Draping a basic body block—#8.

FIGURE 4–60. Draping a basic body block—#9.

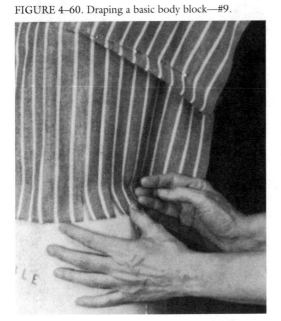

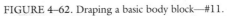

FIGURE 4–61. Draping a basic body block—#10.

FIGURE 4–62. Draping a basic body block—#11.

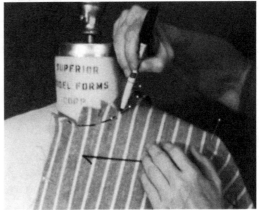

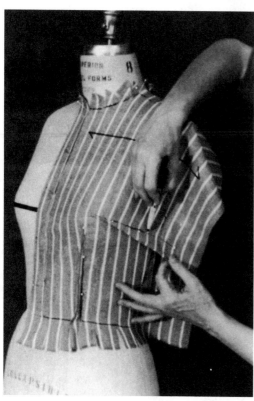

FIGURE 4–63. Draping a basic body block—#12.

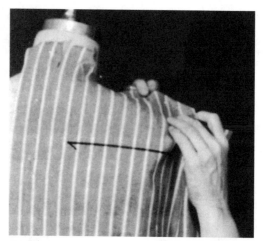

FIGURE 4–64. Draping a basic body block—#13.

FIGURE 4–65. Draping a basic body block—#14.

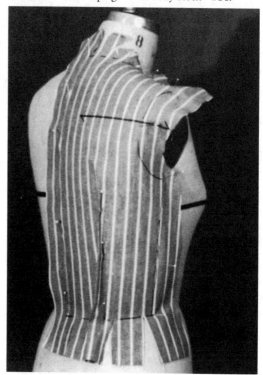

11. The draper uses an indelible black pen to draw in the stitching line around the neck.

12. Marking dart stitching lines. Draw side seam and armhole lines.

13. Draping the back is considerably easier than draping the front. Here the draper has fastened the fabric to the tailor's form and clipped the neck edge. She is pinning the armhole edge of the shoulder in place, adding a scant ½-inch ease across the back. (Do you recall the extra ½ inch added to the back shoulder seam of the drafted body block?)

14. Here is the completed back drape.

15 and 16. Here are the body block pieces off the form. Stitching lines have been redrawn and corrected.

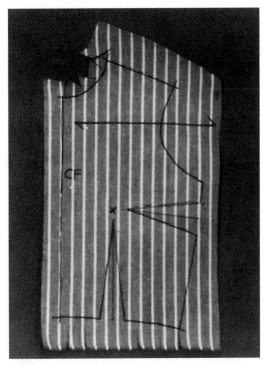

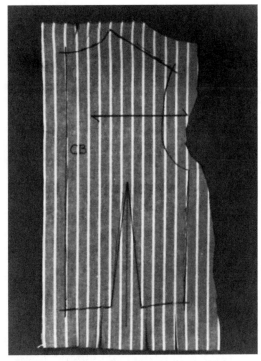

FIGURE 4–66. Draping a basic body block—#15.   FIGURE 4–67. Draping a basic body block—#16.

Sleeves

Basic One-Piece Sleeve Block Drawn from Individual Measurements

On most people, the basic one-piece sleeve block will fit into the basic body block armhole smoothly, with enough fullness to cover the top of the arm but without gathers or tucks.

TOOLS NEEDED

> 24-inch ruler *or* yardstick
> right angle
> 18-inch C-Thru ruler

pencil
craft or pattern paper

MEASUREMENTS REQUIRED

Note: Make sure the armscye marker (Figure 4–7) is in place and that all length measurements extend from that marker to below the wrist bone. Have the arm hanging straight down. Take the armscye measurement over the armscye marker and pull the tape snug.

1. shoulder to wrist
2. underarm to elbow
3. underarm to wrist

4. armscye

5. wrist

Step 1: Draw a Rectangle

A–B and C–D equal shoulder to wrist measurement.

A–C and B–D equal armscye measurement, minus 3 inches.

Example:

armscye =	16 inches
	− 3 inches
A–C and B–D =	13 inches

Step 2: Add Construction Lines

Locate E exactly halfway between A and C, and F exactly halfway between B and D. Connect points E and F with a straight line. (The section to the right of the E–F line is the back of the sleeve and the section to the left of the E–F line is the front of the sleeve.)

Locate G up from B at the underarm to wrist measurement and H up from D at the underarm to wrist measurement. Connect G and H with a straight line. Call this line the *bicep line.*

Locate I down from G at the underarm to elbow measurement and J down from H at the underarm to elbow measurement. Connect I and J with a straight line. Call this line the *elbow line.*

Step 3: Wrist Edge and Underarm Seams

Locate K 1½ inches to the right of B, and L 1½ inches to the left of D.

Connect G and K to form one underarm seam, and connect H and L to form the other.

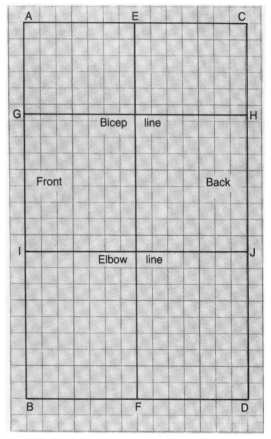

FIGURE 4–68. Basic one-piece sleeve—#1.

Step 4: Sleeve Cap

Divide lines A–C and G–H into six equal parts.

Note: A quick method for doing this is to cut a strip of paper the length of A–C (or G–H) and fold it into six parts. Use the fold marks on the paper strip as your drawing guide.

Draw vertical construction lines from G–H to A–C.

Connect G and E with a straight line and H and E with a straight line.

138

Working from left to right, beginning with the *first vertical construction line,* locate points M, N, O, and P on the vertical construction lines as shown in the illustration.

    a. Mark M ¾ inch *below* the G–E line.

    b. Mark N ¾ inch *above* the G–E line.

    c. Skip over center line, and mark O 1 inch *above* the E–H line.

    d. Mark P where the E–H line intersects the last vertical construction line.

Connect G, M, N, E, O, P, and H with curved line segments as illustrated to complete the sleeve cap.

Step 5: Sleeve Opening

Locate Q one-half the wrist measurement to the left of L.

Draw a line perpendicular to the wrist edge up from Q, 4 inches long. This is the position for a normal sleeve opening.

Step 6: Locate Sleeve Balance Points

The sleeve balance points are located at the points where the sleeve front curve intersects the E–H line. (The back sleeve balance point is the same as point P.) The sleeve balance points indicate where the sleeve cap ends and the underarm curve begins.

Always transfer the top of the sleeve mark, the underarm mark, and the balance points from your completed sleeve block to all the sleeve patterns you develop and the mock-ups you stitch.

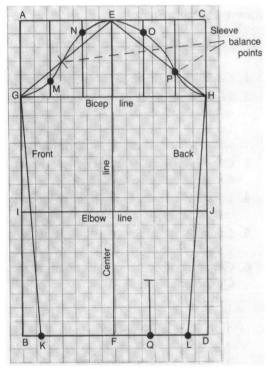

FIGURE 4–69. Basic one-piece sleeve—#2.

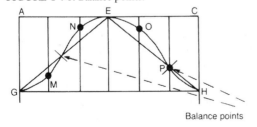

FIGURE 4–70. Balance points.

FIGURE 4–71. Important sleeve markings.

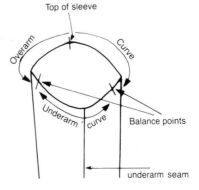

Sleeve Development 1

SIMPLE ONE-PIECE FITTED SLEEVE

1. Complete the basic one-piece sleeve block.
2. Locate I^1 ½ inch to the right of the point where the G–K and I–J lines intersect. Locate J^1 ½ inch to the left of the point where the H–L and I–J lines intersect.
3. Create new underarm seams as shown, curving them through I^1 and J^1.
4. Locate R ¾ inch to the right of the center line and elbow line intersection.
5. Locate S one-half wrist measurement *plus* 1 inch to the right of K.
6. Connect points R and S and points R and Q to create a forearm dart.

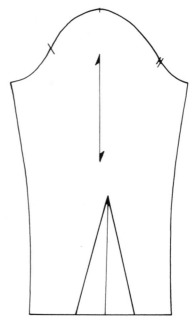

FIGURE 4–73. Sleeve development 1.

7. Trace clean pattern, as shown in Figure 4–73, and be sure to transfer the center of sleeve mark and balance points.

Sleeve Development 2

CHANGING WRIST EDGE OF BASIC ONE-PIECE SLEEVE BLOCK

1. Complete the basic one-piece sleeve block and trace a construction pattern from it. Include marks indicating top of shoulder, balance points, grain line, and sleeve opening.
2. Draw cut lines from balance points to wrist edge, perpendicular to wrist edge.
3. Cut from wrist edge to within ⅛ inch of the balance points.
4. To decrease width at the wrist edge, overlap cut edges as shown in Figure 4–75.

FIGURE 4–72. Sleeve development 1.

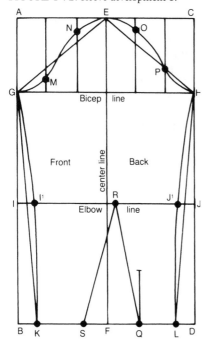

140

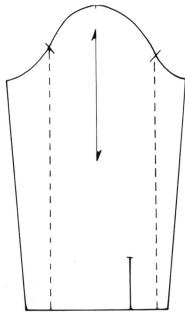

FIGURE 4–74. Sleeve development 2.

FIGURE 4–75. Sleeve development 2.

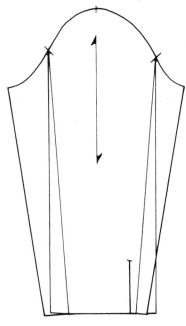

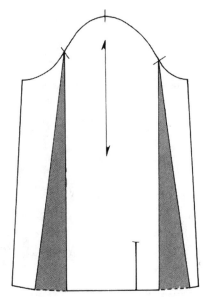

FIGURE 4–76. Sleeve development 2.

5. To increase width at the wrist edge, spread cut edges as shown in Figure 4–76.

Note: You have not changed the width of the sleeve at the armhole edge and have only made slight alterations in its shape.

Sleeve Development 3

CURVING WRIST EDGE OF SLEEVE
TO ACCOMMODATE THE NATURAL
HANG OF THE ARM

The curved wrist edge provides additional length at the back of the sleeve which, because the arm naturally hangs slightly bent and to the front of the body, is more graceful when it is longer than the front of the sleeve. The development may be carried out on many sleeve styles.

1. On the line from the front sleeve balance point perpendicular to the wrist line, locate a point ½ inch up from the wrist line.

141

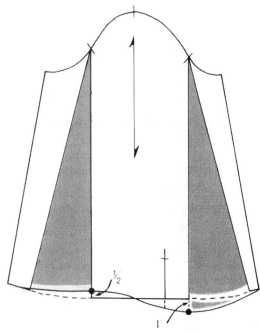

FIGURE 4–77. Sleeve development 3–curving wrist edge.

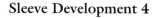

2. On the line from the back sleeve balance point perpendicular to the wrist line, locate a point 1 inch down from the wrist line.

3. Create a wrist line curve incorporating these two points as shown in Figure 4–77.

Sleeve Development 4

SHORT SLEEVE, BLOUSED AT
THE BOTTOM

1. Complete the basic one-piece sleeve block and trace a construction pattern from it. Include marks indicating top of sleeve, balance points, and grain line. Determine sleeve length on the underarm seam and shorten pattern.

2. Draw in cutting lines between sleeve balance points, as shown in Figure 4–79. *Do not cut on the underarm curve.*

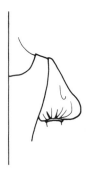

FIGURE 4–78. Sleeve development 4–short sleeve, bloused at bottom.

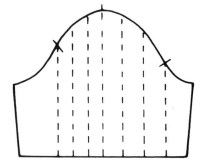

FIGURE 4–79. Sleeve development 4–short sleeve, bloused at bottom.

3. Cut and spread sleeve for additional fullness at the lower edge and curve this edge, as shown in Figure 4–80, as desired for blousing.

FIGURE 4–80. Sleeve development 4–short sleeve, bloused at bottom.

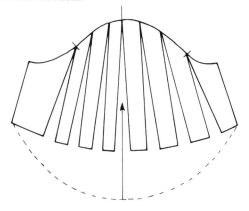

142

4. Draw a clean pattern. Transfer the important marks.

Sleeve Development 5

SHORT SLEEVE, PUFFED AT THE TOP

FIGURE 4–81. Sleeve development 5–short sleeve, puffed at top.

1. Complete the basic one-piece sleeve block and trace a construction pattern from it. Include marks indicating top of sleeve, balance points, and grain line. Determine sleeve length on the underarm seam and shorten pattern.

2. Draw in cutting lines between sleeve balance points, as shown in Figure 4–79. *Do not cut on the underarm curve.*

3. Cut and spread sleeve for puff at top edge and raise cap, as shown in Figure 4–82, as desired to increase height of puff.

FIGURE 4–82. Sleeve development 5–short sleeve, puffed at top.

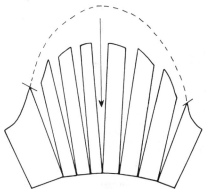

4. Draw a clean pattern. Retain important marks.

Sleeve Development 6

SHORT SLEEVE, BLOUSED AT THE BOTTOM AND PUFFED AT THE TOP

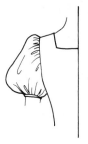

FIGURE 4–83. Sleeve development 6–short sleeve, bloused at the bottom and puffed at the top.

1. Complete the basic one-piece sleeve block and trace a construction pattern from it. Include marks indicating top of sleeve, balance points, and grain line. Determine sleeve length on the underarm seam and shorten pattern.

2. Draw in cutting lines between sleeve balance points, as shown in Figure 4–79. *Do not cut on the underarm curve.*

3. Cut pattern into pieces, as shown in Figure 4–84, and spread evenly for increased

FIGURE 4–84. Sleeve development 6–short sleeve, bloused at the bottom and puffed at the top.

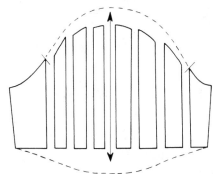

width at both upper and lower edges. Lower bottom edge and raise cap as desired.

4. Draw a clean pattern. Retain important marks.

Basic Two-Piece Sleeve Block Drawn from Individual Measurements

Follow the directions for drawing a basic one-piece sleeve block that begin on page 137. Omit Step 5: *Sleeve Opening*.

Step 7: Draw Cutting Lines

Locate point Q 3 inches to the right of point K.

Locate point R 3 inches to the left of point L.

Connect the front sleeve balance point with point Q.

Connect the back sleeve balance point with point R, as shown in Figure 4–85.

Step 8: Draw Match-up Marks

Draw match-up marks on the two cutting lines, as shown in Figure 4–85.

Step 9: Cut the Sleeve Block

Cut the sleeve block into three pieces along the cutting lines.

Step 10: Reassemble the Sleeve Block into Two Pieces

Tape the two under sleeve pieces together along the original underarm seam.

Mark grain lines as shown in Figure 4–87: upper sleeve perpendicular to top of sleeve and under sleeve following underarm seam.

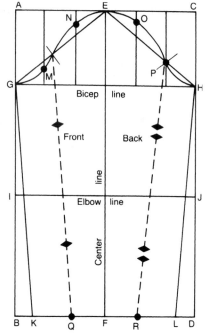

FIGURE 4–85. Two-piece sleeve.

FIGURE 4–86. Two-piece sleeve.

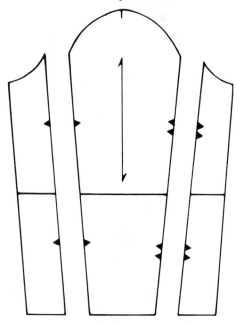

144

Lay the two pieces on the table so that the back sleeve seams are side by side.

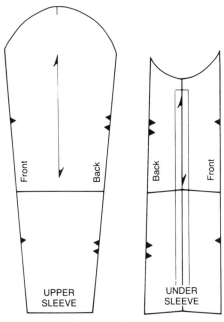

FIGURE 4–87. Two-piece sleeve.

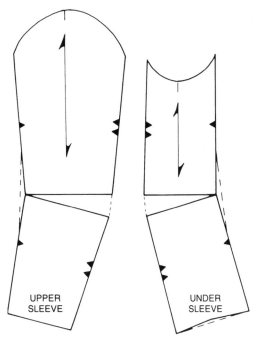

FIGURE 4–88. Two-piece sleeve.

FIGURE 4–89. Two-piece sleeve.

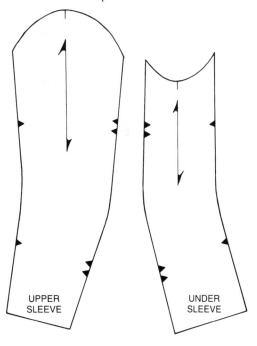

Step 11: Lengthen Back Seam and Curve Sleeve

Cut both pieces along elbow lines from back to front to within ⅛ inch of front seam.

Note: The back elbow line will angle down slightly to the right of the original underarm seam. Do not follow the angle; cut straight across from the back seam.

Spread the pieces open to 1½ inches on the back sleeve seams, as shown in Figure 4–88.

Step 12: Draw Clean Pattern Pieces

Draw around the cut and spread pieces. Correct curves and wrist edge as shown in Figure 4–88.

Transfer top of sleeve, underarm, and grain line, and match up marks to the clean pattern.

Collars

An Introduction to Terms

Neckline edge. The edge of the collar that is attached to the neckline of the garment.

Styleline. The outer edge of the collar, opposite the neckline edge.

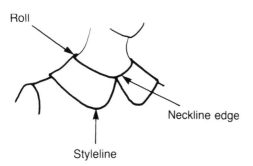

FIGURE 4–90. Collars—roll, neckline edge, styleline.

Stand. The portion of the collar that rises from the neckline to the roll.

Roll. The point at which the collar turns down or stops ascending and begins descending.

Breakline. The fold line of the lapel and the tailored collar.

FIGURE 4–91. Collars—breakline.

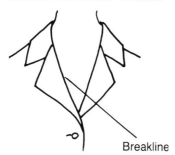

Breakline

A BRIEF EXPLANATION OF NECKLINE CURVES IN COLLARS

1. If the neckline edge of the collar has the same curve as the garment neckline, the collar lies flat and has little or no roll.

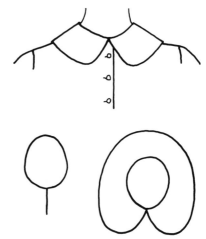

FIGURE 4–92. Collars—flat.

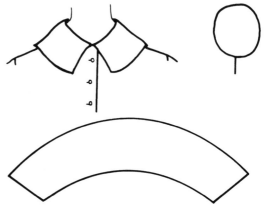

FIGURE 4–93. Collars—roll.

2. If the neckline edge of the collar is less curved than the garment neckline (even convex), the collar will have a roll.

3. If the neckline edge of the collar is more concave than the garment neckline (more inwardly curved), the styleline or outer edge of the collar will ripple.

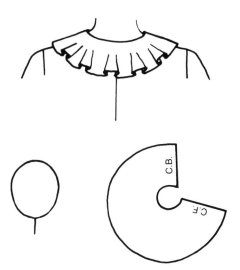

FIGURE 4–94. Collars—ripple.

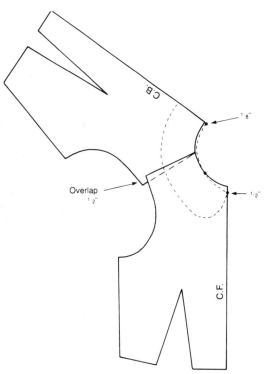

FIGURE 4–95. Collars—basic flat.

BASIC FLAT COLLAR, NOT WIDER THAN
3 INCHES AT THE SHOULDER

Note: Use your paper pattern pieces from the corrected body block. Cut out or trace construction pattern pieces.

Step 1: Align Shoulder Seams

Place shoulder seams of the front and back body block pieces together as shown in Figure 4–95. At the neck edge, the pieces should meet exactly. At the shoulder edge, overlap the pieces ½ inch.

Step 2: Draw Collar Neckline Edge

Draw a point ½ inch *down* from the top edge of the CF.

Draw a point on the neckline, *halfway* between the CF and the shoulder seam.

Draw a point ⅛ inch *above* the top edge of CB.

Connect these three points with a smooth curve to create the neckline edge of the collar.

Step 3: Draw Styleline

Measure desired collar width at CB and at the shoulder seam. Draw in desired collar styleline.

Step 4: Draw a Clean Pattern

Use tracing paper or a needle-point tracing wheel to transfer the collar pattern to a clean

147

sheet of paper. Mark where the collar neck edge meets the body block shoulder seam.

Collar Development 1

FLAT COLLAR WITH A ROLL (FOR EXAMPLE, A PETER PAN COLLAR)

1. Trace a construction pattern from the basic flat collar. Transfer the shoulder seam match-up mark.
2. Draw in cutting lines as shown in Figure 4–96.

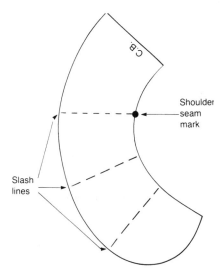

FIGURE 4–96. Flat collar with a roll.

3. Cut collar piece to within ⅛ inch of the neckline edge.
4. Overlap cut edges at the styleline edge about ½ inch. Note that you are changing the shape of the neckline curve but not its length.

5. Draw a clean pattern piece and include shoulder seam match-up mark. The CB of the collar lies on the straight grain of the fabric and may be cut on the fold.

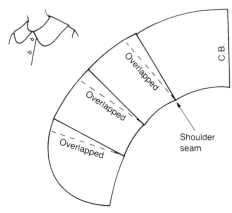

FIGURE 4–97. Flat collar with a roll.

Collar Development 2

FLAT COLLAR WITH FRONT RIPPLES

1. Trace a construction pattern from the basic collar. Transfer the shoulder seam match-up mark.
2. Draw in cutting lines as shown in Figure 4–96.
3. Cut collar piece to within ⅛ inch of the neckline edge.
4. Spread cut edges as shown in Figure 4–98.
5. Correct the neckline curve and the styleline edge if necessary.
6. Draw a clean pattern piece and include shoulder seam match-up mark. The CB of the collar lies on the straight grain of the fabric. The collar requires both CF and CB seams.

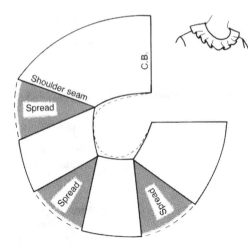

FIGURE 4–98. Flat collar with front ripples.

Note: If you wish to draw a collar that ripples evenly front and back, draw cutting lines in the back of the construction pattern as well as in the front. Spread all the cut edges but be sure you don't make your neckline curve so tight that you have no room left for seam allowances.

Collar Development 3

BASIC FLAT COLLAR THAT EXTENDS FROM NECKLINE TO SHOULDER

Step 1: Align Shoulder Seams

Place shoulder seams of the front and back body block pieces together as shown in Figure 4–99. The pieces should meet exactly and not overlap at the shoulder edge.

Step 2: Draw Collar Neckline Edge

Draw a point ½ inch *down* from the top edge of the CF.

Draw a point on the neckline, *halfway* between the CF and the shoulder seam.

Draw a point ⅛ inch *above* top edge of CB.

Connect these three points with a smooth curve to create the neckline edge of the collar.

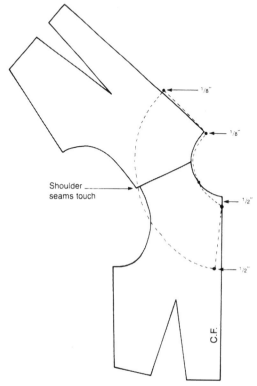

FIGURE 4–99. Basic flat collar that extends from neckline to shoulder.

Collar Development 4

DRAFT A QUICK-AND-EASY STAND-UP COLLAR

Measurements Required

1. *Base of neck*

    This measurement is taken at the thickest part of the neck where it goes into the body. It should be the same as the

149

neckline measurement of the corrected body block.

2. *Height of collar*

This will be determined by the design and by the length of the actor's neck. The collar used in Figure 4–100 is 1¼ inches.

Step 1: Draw a Rectangle

A–B and C–D equal one-half the base of neck measurement.

A–C and B–D equal height of collar *plus* 1 inch.

Step 2: Add Construction Points

Locate point E 1 inch up from point D.

Locate point F ¾ inch to the left of point B.

Locate point G the height of the collar measurement up from point C.

Step 3: Draw Collar

Connect C and E to create the neckline edge.

Connect G and F to create the top edge.

Connect E and F to create the CF.

STAND-AND-FALL SHIRT COLLAR

Using your stand-up collar draft, follow the drawings in Figures 4–101, 4–102, and 4–103 to turn it into a stand-and-fall shirt collar. You may want to reduce the height of the stand.

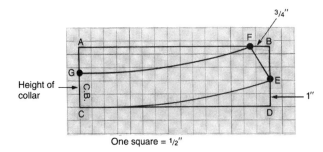

One square = ½"

FIGURE 4–100. Stand-up collar.

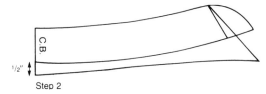

Step 1

FIGURE 4–101. Stand-and-fall shirt collar.

FIGURE 4–102. Stand-and-fall shirt collar.

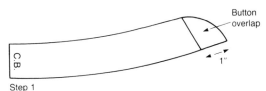

Step 2

FIGURE 4–103. Stand-and-fall shirt collar.

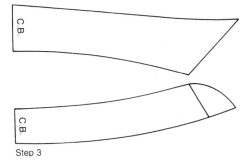

Step 3

Skirts

Basic Skirt Block

Compared to bodices, skirts are simple to pattern. The basic skirt block allows you to achieve a close fit from waist to hip and to maintain a stable cross-grain line, parallel to the ground, from the hip line to the skirt hem. The hip curve is controlled by two back darts and curved side seams. Remember that the basic skirt block is not a pattern in itself and has almost no walking room.

TOOLS NEEDED

> yardstick
> right angle
> 18-inch C-Thru ruler
> pencil
> craft or pattern paper

MEASUREMENTS REQUIRED

1. *Front waistline*
   Side seam placement to side seam placement across front.

2. *Back waistline*
   Side seam placement to side seam placement across back.

Note: If you don't have these measurements, use one-half the waist measurement for each and be prepared to adjust the side seam placement.

3. *Shoulder blade width*
   Distance between shoulder blades.

4. *Hip depth*
   Distance between the waist and the fullest part of the hips where the hip measurement will be taken.

Note: In the garment industry, the hip measurement is usually located 7 inches below the waist measurement. The true hip measurement, the fullest part of the hips, and the place from which the skirt will fall, may lie anywhere between 6 and 9 inches below the waist.

5. *Front hip*
   Side seam placement to side seam placement across front at the fullest part.

6. *Back hip*
   Side seam placement to side seam placement across back at fullest part.

Note: If you don't have these measurements, use one-half the hip measurement for each and be prepared to adjust the side seam placement.

7. *Waist to floor*
   Front.
   Side.
   Back.

Note: In the garment industry, skirts are usually cut ½ inch longer in the back than in the front.

Step 1: Draw a Rectangle

A–C and B–D equal the back skirt length. Determine the back skirt length by subtracting the distance from hem edge to floor from the back waist to floor measurement.

A–B and C–D equal one-half back hip measurement *plus* one-half front hip measurement.

Step 2: Add Construction Lines

From points A and B, measure down the hip depth (or 7 inches if the hip depth measurement is not available) and label E and F, as shown in Figure 4–104. Connect E and F with a straight line. This is the hip line.

Measure out one-half the back hip measurement to the right of points A and C and label G and H. Join G and H with a straight line.

Label the point where lines E–F and G–H intersect I.

Label the left portion of the construction rectangle "skirt block back" and the right portion "skirt block front."

Step 3: Draw Skirt Front

Locate point J on the B–D line at a distance below B determined by finding the difference between the front waist to floor measurement and the back waist to floor measurement.

Note: Some people have the same waist to floor measurement front and back. In those cases, eliminate point J.

To the left of B, locate point K at one-half the front waistline measurement.

Draw a curved line from K to J, as shown in Figure 4–105.

Draw a curved line from K to I completing the side waist to hip curve.

Step 4: Draw Skirt Back

To the right of point A, locate point L at a distance of one-half the back shoulder blade width measurement.

FIGURE 4–104. Skirt block—#1.

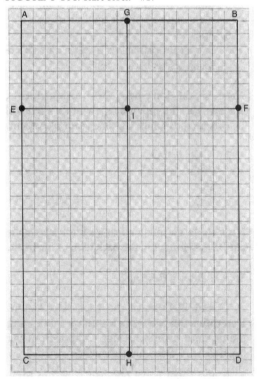

FIGURE 4–105. Skirt block—#2.

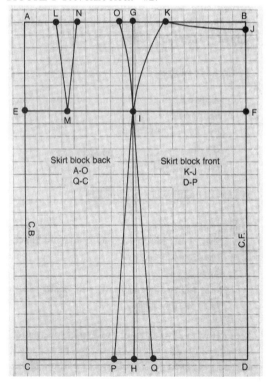

To the right of point E, locate point M at a distance of one-half the back shoulder blade width measurement, *plus one inch*.

To determine points N and O:

a. Subtract one-half the back waist measurement from one-half the back hip measurement. Cut a strip of paper this length and about ½ inch wide.

b. Fold the strip of paper into three equal parts.

c. Locate point N to the right of point L two-thirds of the length of the strip of paper you've just folded.

d. Connect L and M, and N and M to form the back hip dart.

e. To the left of point G, measure out one-third the length of the strip of paper and label O.

f. Draw a curved line from O to I, as shown in Figure 4–105. This is the back waist to hip curve.

Step 5: Complete Skirt Bottom

On line C–D, measure out 1½ inches on either side of point H, locating points P and Q, as shown on Figure 4–105. Draw lines I–P and I–Q, creating an equal amount of walking room on each skirt section.

Remember: *Skirt back section is A-O-Q-C.*
Skirt front section is K-J-D-P.

Skirt Development 1

CREATING FRONT SKIRT WAIST CONSTRUCTION DARTS

1. Trace front skirt block onto clean paper. Include hip depth line.

2. Measure length of front side curve and back side curve from waistline to hip depth line. Subtract the length of the back curve from the length of the front curve. The difference is usually around ¾ inch.

3. Locate point R 3½ inches from the CF, on the waistline.

4. Locate point S 3 inches from the CF, on the hip depth line.

5. Connect points T and S with a dotted cutting line.

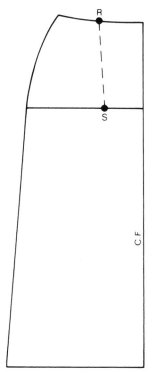

FIGURE 4–106. Skirt—waist construction darts—#1.

6. Cut the R–S line from waistline to hip depth line.

7. Fold up a dart on the hip depth line from the side seam to point S that equals the difference between the lengths of the back waist to hip curve and the front waist to hip curve, as determined in 2.

8. When the construction dart is folded up, the waist dart will open, transferring (swinging) the fullness control from the curved front side seam to the new vertical waistline dart.

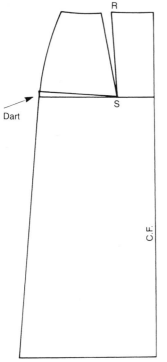

FIGURE 4–107. Skirt—waist construction darts—#2.

9. Draw a clean pattern, adjusting the side seam curve if necessary.

Skirt Development 2

CREATE THREE VERSIONS
OF A FOUR-GORE SKIRT

Using the skirt back piece from the basic skirt block and the front skirt piece with waist darts, develop the following three skirts as shown in the drawings.

Construction Pattern Showing Cutting Lines

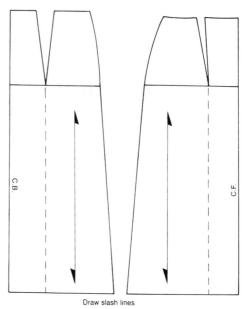

Draw slash lines

FIGURE 4–108. Skirt—development 2–construction pattern.

Four-gore Skirt with Slight Flare

Cut to hip line. Tape darts closed.

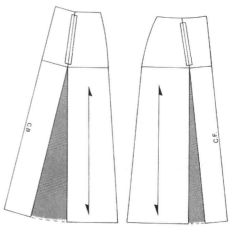

FIGURE 4–109. Skirt—development 2–four-gore skirt with slight flare.

Four-gore Skirt with Moderate Flare

Overlap darts.
Extend waist to hip curves at sides.

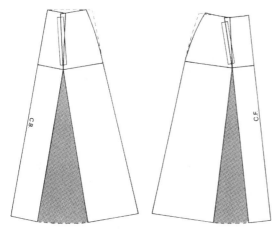

FIGURE 4–110. Skirt—development 2–four-gore skirt with moderate flare. #1

Locate straight grain lines down the center of each gore for even flare.

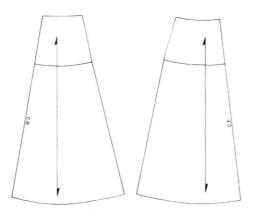

FIGURE 4–111. Skirt—development 2–four-gore skirt with moderate flare. #2

Four-gore Skirt with Additional Side Flare

Draw in additional flare from hip line to bottom of skirt.

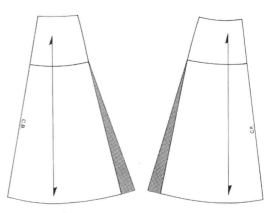

FIGURE 4–112. Skirt—development 2–four-gore skirt with additional side flare.

Skirt Development 3

CREATE A GATHERED SKIRT FROM THE BASIC SKIRT BLOCK

FIGURE 4–113. Skirt—development 3–gathered skirt #1.

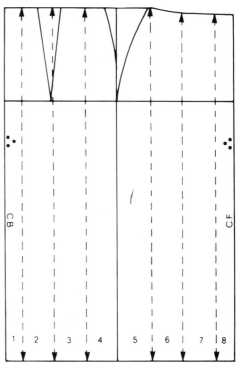

155

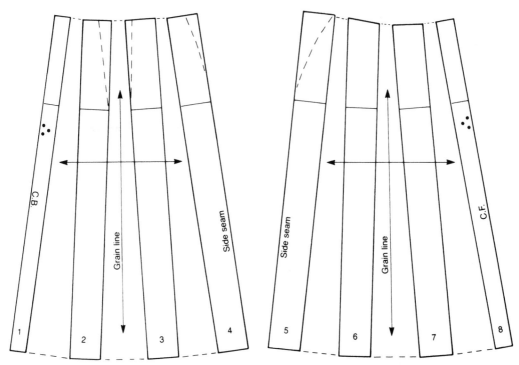

FIGURE 4–114. Skirt—development 3–gathered skirt #2.

DRAPE A BASIC GATHERED SKIRT

Also called a peasant skirt, or a dirndl, this skirt has seams on the straight grain of the fabric and the hip line on the fabric cross grain.

1. Cut two pieces of muslin 36 inches wide and the desired skirt length.
2. Stitch seams. Don't leave a skirt opening at this point.
3. Run two or three gathering threads at the waist edge.
4. Draw a hip line on the fabric, following the cross grain.
5. Draw a hemline on the fabric, following the cross grain.
6. Gather waist threads and place the drape on the tailor's form.
7. Pin the hip line parallel to the floor.

FIGURE 4–115. Skirt—development 3–draped gathered skirt.

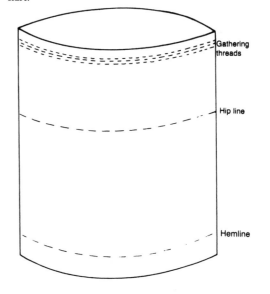

8. Arrange waist gathers so they lie smoothly above the hip line and are evenly distributed. Tie a piece of ¼-inch twill tape around the waistline. Draw the waistline on the fabric, using the twill tape as a guide.

9. Remove the drape from the tailor's form, pull out the gathers, and lay the fabric flat on the table. Adjust the waist curve you've drawn and make sure both sides of the skirt are symmetrical.

10. Trace a clean pattern and decide on skirt closing.

Skirt Development 4

DRAPE A PLEATED SKIRT

A skirt in which the pleats go all the way around and are set right next to each other requires fabric yardage that is three times the hip measurement, plus 1 inch for ease and whatever is necessary for seam allowances. Cut and stitch muslin pieces that will give you the correct circumference and whatever length is required by the style.

1. Draw the hip line on the fabric, following the cross grain.

2. Place the drape on the form, secure the waistline at front, back, and sides, and begin to pleat the fabric at the hip line. *Note:* It's a common mistake to begin to pleat skirts at the waistline. Don't. The hip is the take-off point for all hanging pleats. Adjust hip pleats first and waist pleats second.

3. When all pleats are pinned in at the hip line, baste them securely into place, following the cross-grain line you've drawn.

4. At the waistline, adjust each pleat into the smaller circumference. Pleats should

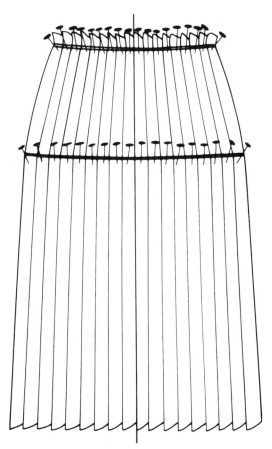

FIGURE 4–116. Pleated Skirt.

curve more on the sides than in the center front and center back.

5. Tie a piece of ¼-inch twill tape around the waist and draw in the waistline, using the tape as a guide.

6. Baste in the pleats at the waistline. Lightly steam the pleats in place from hip to waist.

7. Remove the drape from the form. Using a marking pencil, tracing paper, or running stitches, carefully mark in the pleat lines from hip to waist. Adjust the waist curve and make sure both sides are symmetrical.

8. Trace a clean pattern and plan closings and finishings.

157

Skirt Development 5

PATTERN FOR A FULL-CIRCLE SKIRT

A–B–C = one-half the waist measurement *minus* 1 inch.

A–D and C–F = desired side skirt length.

B–E = desired skirt front length.

B–G = desired skirt back length.

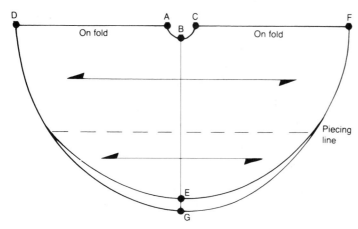

FIGURE 4–117. Full-circle skirt.

PATTERN FOR A HALF-CIRCLE SKIRT

A–E–B = one-half the waist measurement *minus* 1 inch.

A–C and B–D = side skirt length.

E–F = skirt front length.

Lay out skirt back sections the same way, with the skirt back length substituted for the skirt front length.

Notes:

1. These four skirt pieces may be cut with the CF of each piece placed on the true bias of the fabric. This is most successful using fabrics that do not sag excessively.

2. If your fabric is wide enough, the half-circle skirt can be cut without a CF or a CB seam.

Place CF and CB on the straight grain or on the true bias.

FIGURE 4–118. Half-circle skirt.

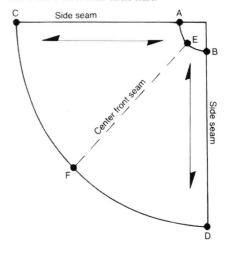

Pants

Basic Pants Block

This pants block is easy to draw and generalized enough to provide a starting point for pants patterns to fit both men and women. The back crotch seam will require considerable adjustment on individual bodies. For a more detailed discussion of adjusting back crotch seams, see the section "Pants Crotch Alterations" in Chapter 6, page 258.

TOOLS NEEDED

> yardstick
> right angle
> 18-inch C–Thru ruler
> pencil
> craft or pattern paper

MEASUREMENTS REQUIRED

1. *Waist*
   Taken exactly where the pants will be worn.
2. *Hip*
3. *Rise*
   Also called crotch depth.

Note: Take this measurement with the actor sitting on a firm surface. The measurement is from the surface on which the actor is sitting, straight up to where the waist measurement was taken. Some cutters like to take rise measurements with a large right angle or framing square.

If the rise measurement is not available and you have both inseam and outseam measurements on the actor, you may subtract the inseam from the outseam and use this figure for the rise

measurement. A standard rise measurement is 10 to 11 inches.

4. *Outseam*

PANTS BLOCK FRONT

Step 1: Draw Construction Lines

A–B = outseam.

A–C = rise.

Draw parallel lines squared out from points A, C, and B, as shown in Figure 4–119.

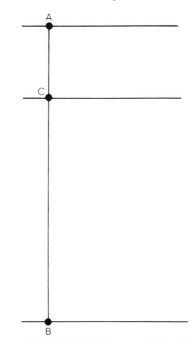

FIGURE 4–119. Basic pants block—#1

Step 2: Draw Front Waist Section

Locate point D one-quarter the waist measurement to the right of A.

Locate point E ½ inch up from point D.

Join points A and E with a curved line as shown in Figure 4–120.

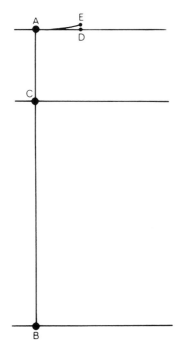

FIGURE 4–120. Basic pants block—#2.

Step 3: Draw Hip and Side Leg Section

Locate point F one-quarter the hip measurement to the right of C.

Locate point G halfway between point C and point F.

Locate point H directly below point G and connect these two points with a broken line.

Determine pants hem circumference, divide the circumference in half, and subtract ½ inch.

Example:

pants hem circumference = 18 inches
one-half 18 inches   = 9 inches
9 inches − ½ inch   = 8½ inches

Locate point I one-half of the measurement you computed, to the *left* of H.

Locate point J one-half the measurement you computed, to the *right* of H.

Connect points E and F with a curved line (use a hip curve if it's available).

Connect points F and J with a straight line.

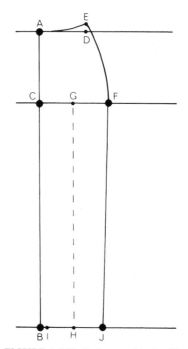

FIGURE 4–121. Basic pants block—#3.

Step 4: Draw Front Crotch Curve

If hip measurement is 32 to 35 inches, locate point K 1½ inches to the left of point C.

If hip measurement is 35½ to 37 inches, locate point K 1¾ inches to the left of point C.

If hip measurement is over 37 inches, locate point K 2 inches to the left of point C.

Locate point L halfway between C and B.

Connect point K to point L with a curved line.

Connect L and I with a straight line.

Measure the same distance above point C as point K is to the left of point C, and locate point M.

Connect points M and K with a shallow curve. (If the curve is drawn too deep, the crotch will be too low.)

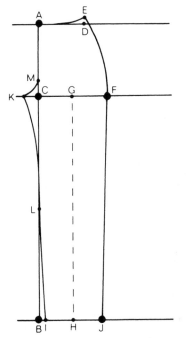

FIGURE 4–122. Basic pants block—#4.

PANTS BLOCK BACK

Step 5: Draw Construction Lines
1–2 = A–B from pants block front, *plus* ½ inch.
1–3 = A–C from pants block front, *plus* ½ inch.

Draw parallel lines squared out from points 1, 3, and 2, as shown in Figure 4–123.

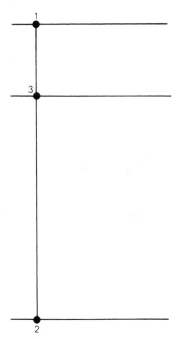

FIGURE 4–123. Pants block back—#5.

Step 6: Draw Waist, Hip, and Leg Section

Locate point 4 one-quarter waist measurement to the right of 1. (1–4 = A–D)

Locate point 5 one-quarter hip measurement, *plus* 1 inch to the right of point 3. (3–5 = C–F *plus* 1 inch)

Locate point 6 halfway between points 3 and 5.

Locate point 7 directly below point 6 and connect these two points with a broken line.

Locate points 8 and 9 to the left and right of point 7 as follows: 8–7 = I–H *plus* ½ inch and 7–9 = H–J *plus* ½ inch.

Connect point 3 to point 8 with a straight line.

Connect point 5 to point 4 with a broken straight line, and continue the line 2 inches above point 4 to create point 10.

Connect point 1 and point 10 with a straight line.

Connect points 5 and 9 with a broken straight line.

Locate point 11 *above* point 9, at a distance equal to the distance between I and L on the pants block front.

Locate point 12 one-eighth the hip measurement to the right of point 5.

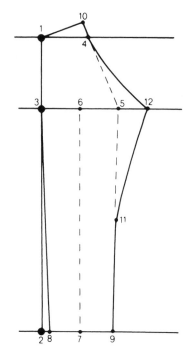

FIGURE 4–125. Pants block back—#7.

Step 8: Adjust Inseam Length

Measure L to K on the pants block front section and 11 to 12 on the pants block back section. As is usually the case, if 11–12 is longer than L–K, *drop* point 12 until 11–12 and L–K are equal. Draw adjusted crotch and inseam curves as shown in Figure 4–126.

Notes:
1. Straight grain lines parallel broken line G–H on pants front and broken line 6–7 on pants back.
2. Add ½ inch to ¾ inch on back and front side seams for ease.
3. Pin in darts and adjust side seams during mock-up fitting.
4. Frequent back crotch seam adjustments:
   a. High, prominent buttocks will require an even shallower crotch curve.

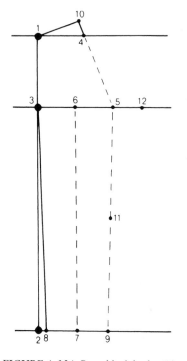

FIGURE 4–124. Pants block back—#6.

Step 7: Draw Crotch and Inseam Curves

Connect point 4 to point 12 with a shallow curve as shown in Figure 4–125.

Connect point 11 to point 12 with a shallow curve.

Note: The deeper this curve is drawn, the tighter the pants will fit in the legs.

b. Low, flat buttocks will require a deeper (and possibly lower) curve.

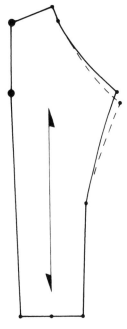

FIGURE 4–126. Pants block back—#8.

Commercial Paper Patterns

A theatrical cutter/draper is severely limited if he or she can only work with commercial paper patterns but so is a cutter/draper who refuses to use them. Commercial paper patterns are good places to begin, particularly for tailored suits and shirts. Be sure to make size adjustments on the pattern before cutting it and make a muslin mock-up unless the garment is very simple.

Patterns from past decades are excellent starting points for cutting garments from the twentieth century. Many cutter/drapers collect olds patterns that they find at rummage sales and in secondhand shops. Check pattern measurements carefully on older patterns; standard sizing has changed over the years.

Storing Patterns

Keep copies of the basic as well as the interesting and unique patterns you have developed. Even if they are not used again in their entirety, you may use them in part or for research. Store patterns in manila envelopes and file them in an orderly manner in metal drawers, crates, or cardboard boxes. Label each envelope with pertinent information such as: basic measurements of the actor for whom the pattern was developed; historical period; type of garment; name and date of the production; designer; and perhaps a simple sketch or photograph of the garment.

Cutting the Garment Pieces

Once the garment pattern has been developed, mocked-up, and adjusted for line and fit, it is ready to be transferred to the fabric chosen by the designer.

Washable fabrics should always be preshrunk before they are cut, and the length of fabric pressed carefully, with special attention paid to straightening the grain. Woolens may be preshrunk either by pressing with a stream iron and a damp cloth or by leaving the fabric rolled up in a damp sheet for two hours, removing it, and allowing it to dry on a flat surface. Never allow damp wool fabric to hang as it will stretch.

Lay out the fabric to be cut. If the pattern of the fabric is a plaid or a print that must be matched, the cutting is usually done on a single layer of fabric. Very stretchy or slippery fabrics should also be cut one layer at a time. A firmly woven, solid color or small print fabric can be folded in half, and identical fronts, backs, sleeves, and so on, can be cut two at a time. Some shops always insist upon single-layer cutting. When you are cutting on a single layer, it is imperative that identical pairs of pieces be cut. Take care not to let the pattern pieces slip.

It is a good idea to lay out all the pattern pieces for a garment on the fabric before cutting anything. This will help you make the most economical use of the fabric. If there is a directional nap, such as on corduroy or velvet, make sure the pattern pieces are all laid on the fabric in the same direction. Check with the designer before determining the direction of the nap. Although most street garments are cut with the nap lying smoothly from top to bottom, many costume garments are cut against the nap. This causes the fabric to appear deeper and richer under stage lights.

After the pieces have all been positioned on the fabric, check again for correct grain line, nap direction, and spacing. Pin the pieces to the fabric or use cutting weights; mark a seam allowance if necessary and cut around the pieces with sharp shears. Never raise the fabric up in the air to cut it. Always keep the base of the shears on the table. Do not remove the pattern pieces from the fabric until you have transferred all pertinent markings from the pattern to the fabric. Do this with tracing paper and a tracing wheel, a fabric marking pen, or, in the case of a soft, thick fabric, with tailor's tacks.

It's a good idea to cut all the pieces needed for a single garment at one time. This may include collars, facings, underlining, and lining. The construction process moves much more smoothly if all the pieces are cut and ready to stitch.

FIGURE 4–127. Muslin pattern on the dress form for Queen Victoria's costume in *The Pirates of Penzance* at the Utah Shakespearean Festival. *Photograph by Rosemary Ingham.*

FIGURE 4–128. Petticoat and bustle on actor Mitzi McKay portraying Queen Victoria with cutter/draper Joan Mather. *Photograph by Rosemary Ingham.*

FIGURE 4–129. The completed muslin fitting with alterations pinned and hem marked. First hand Shanaz Kahn records fitting notes. *Photograph by Rosemary Ingham.*

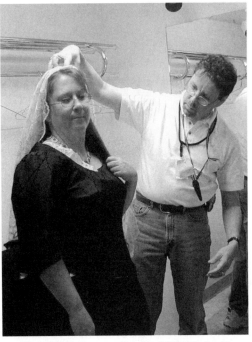

FIGURE 4–130. Costume designer Bill Black checking the headdress for "Queen Victoria" at a fabric fitting. See color plate # 12 for the final result. *Photograph by Rosemary Ingham.*

Costumes and Computers

The fashion and commercial pattern industries use computer technology almost exclusively for pattern making and grading. Many costume technicians, especially cutter/drapers, have been experimenting with the use of pattern development software in their work. Turn to Chapter 11, "Computers in the Costume Shop," for a discussion of computer technology in the twenty-first-century costume shop.

5
Costume Construction

Costume technicians speak of "building" or "constructing" stage costumes. The choice of words indicates an attitude toward the finished product. Like a modern building, a costume's foundation is as important as its facade, and its function on the stage determines the way it is made. A good stage costume is designed, planned, and built for beauty, strength, and utility, and no single aspect is more important than another.

Newcomers to the theatre are amazed at the wear and tear a costume takes, even in a production that runs only a few performances. Stage action is more focused than real-life action. Playwrights deliberately choose to write the most energetic rather than the most relaxed scenes in a character's stage life. Actors on stage are active and working all the time.

Even when stage movement is minimal, costumed actors are always in a state of heightened tension: they are turned on, engaged, ready to go. And, unless the costumes are stoutly built, they will also go—to pieces.

Costume technicians have to construct garments that can withstand the rigors of the play, even when the costume is made out of silk chiffon and must appear to be a fragile bit of nothing. You can simulate fragility on stage, but you must avoid actual fragility. Sturdy, functional costume construction results from always using the best cutting and stitching techniques available to you. Costume technicians often employ shortcuts and speed sewing techniques but carelessness and shoddy stitching waste time and have no place in good costume construction.

Steps in Constructing a Costume—An Outline

1. *Examine the design sketch with the designer.*

2. *Discuss fabrics and yardages with the designer.*

When calculating yardages, be sure to allow extra yardage for stripes, plaids, prints, napped fabrics, and for fabrics that will shrink when they are prewashed.

166

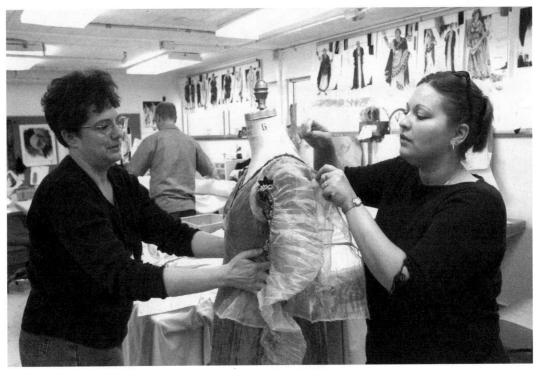

FIGURE 5–1. Dean Mogel's costume sketches for *Julius Caesar* adorn the walls in the background as cutter/draper Gina Truelove and her assistant, Jessica Smith, dress the tailor's form at the Utah Shakespearean Festival. *Photograph courtesy of the Utah Shakespearean Festival.*

3. *Choose appropriate interfacings, underlinings (often called flat linings), and linings.*

4. *Prepare fabrics.*

Shrink fabrics whenever necessary by washing, damp rolling, steaming, or dry cleaning. Straighten grain and press.

5. *Study, or review, period pattern research.*

You may not use the actual period pattern, but it will provide guidelines for your pattern development.

6. *Develop a pattern specifically for the actor who will wear the costume.*

While you are developing the pattern, be sure to work out closings and a construction sequence.

7. *Cut mock-up.*

Mock-ups or, as they are sometimes called, pattern proofs are usually made from muslin. If, however, the actual costume fabric is a knit or a lightweight fabric like chiffon, make the mock-up in an inexpensive fabric that will simulate, as closely as possible, the stretch or drape of the eventual costume. If you are using muslin, use the best muslin you can afford: soft, flexible, woven on grain, and without too much sizing.

Add seam allowances before cutting.

Transfer all important fitting identification and match-up marks onto the muslin mock-up: waistline, top of shoulder mark, center front and center back, cross grain on

FIGURE 5–2. Nicely detailed construction lines in a costume worn by Elizabeth Long as Julia in *The Duchess of Malfi* at The Shakespeare Theatre. Costume design by Robert Perdziola. *Photograph by Carol Rosegg, courtesy of The Shakespeare Theatre.*

sleeve caps, and, in most cases, all stitching lines.

8. *Assemble mock-up.*

Stitch accurately, with a medium-long machine stitch.

9. *Fit mock-up.*

The costume designer should be present at the mock-up fitting since this is when seam placements, proportion, and general garment silhouette will be okayed.

Draw corrections directly onto the mock-up fabric with *indelible* colored pens.

Make sure you have sufficient hem allowances.

Make sure the actor can perform all the movements he or she must do in the costume.

Take your time. Don't hurry the mock-up fitting. Alterations are easier at this stage than at any subsequent stage in the construction process.

10. *Transfer mock-up alterations to paper pattern. Use the corrected pattern pieces to calculate trim yardages.*

Don't use the mock-up pieces for pattern pieces. Fabric pieces stretch and shift, and your pattern shapes will lose their integrity. Use the markings on the mock-up pieces to correct your paper pattern. True the pattern pieces and use them to cut outer fabric, facings, linings, and so on.

Note: *When design or fitting alterations are extensive, you may want to alter your paper pattern pieces, or draw up a new pattern, and make a second mock-up. Although you might be reluctant to take the additional time to make another mock-up, you may actually be saving time by solving problems before you cut into the "real" fabric.*

11. *Cut fabric, underlinings, and interfacings.*

Don't cut facings and linings until *after* the first fabric fitting.

Transfer all necessary construction and match-up marks to the underlining or to the wrong side of the fabric if there is no underlining.

Write out the assembly sequence and make sure the technician who is stitching the pieces together understands it.

168

12. *Underline (flat line) pieces and finish edges.*

Many costumes are fully underlined. Underlining fabrics range from good quality cotton muslin to silk organza, depending upon the kind of outer fabric being used and the amount of drape or firmness desired. Some costumes are not underlined at all.

13. *Assemble the fabric shell.*

The fabric shell consists of all the major pieces of a garment, before collar, cuffs, or facings have been added. Some technicians baste both sleeves into a fabric shell before the fitting; some pin both sleeves in during the fabric shell fitting.

Some technicians use a basting stitch to assemble the fabric shell, but, if the muslin has been carefully fitted and the alterations done, it seems more sensible to use a regular stitch length so it's not necessary to restitch all the seams if the garment does fit.

14. *Fit the fabric shell.*

The actor should wear correct undergarments and shoes at this fitting.

Check again to make sure the actor's movement is not being restricted by the costume. Pay particular attention to armholes and sleeves.

Mark fitting adjustments.
Mark hems.

15. *Transfer additional alterations to paper pattern pieces.*

16. *Cut facings and linings.*

17. *Make alterations to garment shell.*

18. *Apply trim.*

At this stage of the construction, you can apply many kinds of trim by machine. Later on, after facings and linings go in, trim must go on by hand. Plan ahead to save time.

19. *Put in zippers or hook and eye tape.*

Always put zippers or hook and eye tape into the garment before facings, waistbands, or collars go on.

20. *Assemble and attach facings.*

21. *Baste up hems.*

22. *Fit the almost-complete costume.*

Have undergarments, shoes, and all other accessories present for this fitting.

Check carefully for:
correct garment balance
smooth seams
accurate, even hem lengths

Be sure the sleeves hit the actor at the same place on each arm. Most people's arms are different lengths, and most long sleeves have to be hemmed at different lengths to look even. Mark the hem on each sleeve separately, measuring up from each thumb. (See the photograph and detailed description of marking the hems on long sleeves on page 265.)

placement of shoulder pads
placement of buttons, pockets,
trims, and so on.

Mark final alterations.

One last time, make sure the actor's movement is not restricted by the costume.

23. *Carry out final alterations.*

24. *Assemble and put in linings.*

Make sure the linings are attached loosely, with a pleat at the center back and small tucks at hem edges so the outer fabric will hang freely.

25. *Put in hems, sew on buttons, apply final trim.*

26. *Press.*

27. *If possible, schedule a fourth and final fitting to see the completed costume on the actor before the dress parade, if one is scheduled, or before dress rehearsals begin.*

Basic Costume Construction Techniques

Cutting the Fabric

PREPARATION

Most natural fabrics, rayon, and some synthetics should be preshrunk before being cut. Preshrinking allows fabrics to relax and lose the extra length they acquired during the weaving or knitting process when the yarns were stretched and held under tension. Many fabrics shrink between 1 and 5 inches per yard in length and about half that much in a 45-inch width. If you don't preshrink a fabric before cutting, the costume may shrink dramatically the first time it is laundered; it may shrink in small increments as you work on the garment, and after the first wearing, even before laundering.

Washable Fabrics

If the fabric is washable, you should wash it before cutting. Measure the piece of fabric before it is washed so you will know exactly how much less you have after preshrinking and can make pattern adjustments if necessary. Wash and dry the fabric in exactly the same way the garment will be laundered once it's completed, using the appropriate water and dryer temperatures.

Preshrink washable fabrics even if they are to be used in a period costume that will be dry cleaned. Body heat, perspiration, and dry cleaning may all cause washable fabrics to shrink.

Some washable fabrics, such as rayon and linen, are labeled "dry clean only." Because these fabrics require washing with care, the manufacturers label them nonwashable, thereby clearing themselves of any legal responsibility if the fabrics are damaged by washing. Ignore the "dry clean only" label *but wash the fabric with care.* Rayons, because they are weak when wet, should be hand-washed or washed on a very gentle cycle. Both rayons and linen should be washed in lukewarm water and, ideally, line dried.

Use common sense and care but do prewash every fabric that can be prewashed.

Wools and Suitings

You may occasionally find good wool fabric on a bolt marked "scoured," "sponged," or "washable." The fibers in these fabrics, often obtained from the wool of merino sheep, have been "de-kinked" to prevent shrinkage. Any wool, or suiting, not so marked may shrink slightly during construction and after wearing and dry cleaning. All wools and suitings can be safely preshrunk in one of the following ways:

a. *Dry clean.* Be sure to tell your dry cleaner that you are having the fabric dry cleaned for preshrinking purposes and that you want it pressed carefully.

b. *Steam.* Steaming is easy if you have an industrial steam presser; it's harder and quite time-consuming if you are using a steam iron. Steam must penetrate every square inch of the fabric *and,* after steaming, the fabric must remain flat on the ironing table until it's cool and dry.

c. *Damp roll.* This is the most practical way of preshrinking wools and suitings. Dampen a piece of clean, lint-free, cotton fabric, such as a white bed sheet. (An easy way to dampen it just the right amount is to wet it and then spin the excess moisture out on the spin cycle in a washing machine.) Spread the damp sheet out in a single layer. Lay the fabric on top, folded in half lengthwise. Roll the damp sheet and the fabric up like a jellyroll and leave the roll for *1 hour.* Remove the fabric from the damp sheet and drape it over a drying rack, taking care that the fabric is supported at regular intervals. **Don't hang it on a clothesline or it will stretch rather than shrink.** If you preshrink a piece of fabric in this way, it will dry overnight.

Synthetics

Many synthetics do not shrink but some do and, since it's impossible to tell which will and which won't beforehand, you would be well advised to prewash everything. Also, virtually all synthetics are easier to stitch after they are washed.

Don't forget that most costumes have to be washed or dry cleaned. If a fabric will be destroyed by washing or by dry cleaning, you should know it before you build the costume, not after.

After the fabric has been washed, cleaned, or steamed, examine the weave and straighten the grain if necessary or possible. Pull a cross-wise thread from one end of the fabric and cut on the line that appears, or tear a strip if you can. Place the cut or torn edge against the edge of the table and pull the fabric diagonally until the cut or torn edge is at a right angle to the selvedge edges. You can straighten the grain in most natural fabrics and in rayon but not in most synthetics.

Choosing Underlining or Flat Lining, Interfacings, and Lining

UNDERLINING OR FLAT LINING

An underlining, or flat lining, is a layer of fabric placed under the outer fabric. It is cut from the same garment pattern pieces and, after the two layers are attached, they are treated as one layer. An underlining is not a lining.

The most common reason for underlining is to make the costume more durable. Underlinings may also add body and weight to the outer fabric and give the garment a more sculptured look. Tailors often underline jackets and coats in order to stitch interfacings, facings, and hems to the underlining and to keep the outer fabric smooth and stitch-free. If your outer fabric is loosely woven, textured, or slubbed, an underlining will help strengthen it and hold it together. Also, if portions of your garment, such as a front band, a collar, or a yoke, are to be cut on the bias, underline those areas with fabric cut on the conventional grain to prevent sagging.

Fabrics widely used for underlinings are a good quality muslin, batiste, china silk, marquisette, organdy, organza, and taffeta.

It is important to make sure the underlining pieces are not smaller than the outer pieces; if they are smaller the outer layer of fabric will pucker when it curves around the body. To assemble the two layers, lay the inner (underlining or flat lining) piece on a large brown paper roll or on a similarly curved surface with the side that will lie against the outer fabric facing up. Lay the outer fabric piece, right side up, on top. Make sure all edges are aligned. Pin or hand baste the underlining and the fabric pieces together with rows of pins or basting that follow the straight grain of the pieces. This allows you to assemble the layers and leave just enough "give" in the underlining to prevent puckering in the outer fabric. If you pin the layers together on a flat surface, take great care not to stretch the underlining.

Machine baste around the layered pieces, just inside the seam allowance so the stitching won't show when you stitch the seams. Don't baste across hem edges.

Finish seam edges with a serger or with a machine zigzag stitch. Don't finish hem edges or the edges of pieces that will be trimmed and turned, such as collars, cuffs, or waistbands.

INTERFACINGS

An interfacing is usually crisper than the garment fabric. It is used to add extra stability and shaping to collars, lapels, cuffs, garment edges, and larger areas such as coat and jacket fronts. *You should almost always attach the interfacing to the body of the garment, not to the facing, so the interfacing is between the outer fabric layer and the seam allowances.* Exceptions to this include lapels and some lightweight knits.

Interfacings in costumes are the rule rather than the exception. Always assume you will interface and make sure you have a good reason *not* to interface. Very sheer or soft fabrics and garments that are to be distressed are often not interfaced. In general, however, interfacing is an important part of good costume construction.

You can interface with commercial interfacings, muslin, organdy, organza, cotton batiste, or, particularly in sheers, a piece of the garment fabric. Commercial interfacings provide stability with a minimum of bulk.

Commercial interfacings may be *woven* or *nonwoven, sew-in* or *fusible*. You can have a woven sew-in or a woven fusible, a nonwoven sew-in or a nonwoven fusible. In general, nonwoven interfacings, fusible or sew-in, are less useful than woven interfacings, because nonwovens have no fabric grain and are difficult to shape. If you use a nonwoven interfacing in a collar, for instance, it may keep the collar from curving smoothly around the neck. Woven interfacings, fusible and sew-in, are preferable for general costume shop use; make sure the pieces are cut on the same grain as the fabric pieces they are to interface (unless stabilizing a bias piece).

Woven sew-in interfacings come in light, medium, and heavy weights. The most flexible interfacings are blends of rayon and polyester; the least flexible are 100 percent polyester. Heavyweight sew-in interfacings include several sorts of hair canvas used in tailoring and discussed on page 239. Attach a sew-in interfacing by stitching it to the seam edges of the fabric piece, just inside the seam allowance so the stitching will not show after the facing is applied. Trim the interfacing seam allowance back to the stitching line so it won't increase the bulk in the seam.

Some woven fusible interfacings are excellent and remain fused for the life of the garment; others tend to separate from the fabric after a single washing. Always try out a sample piece of a fusible interfacing before you purchase it in quantity.

Fusible interfacings are often advertised as time-saving products. But, if you fuse the interfacings properly, following the manufacturer's directions exactly, you may find that using fusible interfacings is just as time-consuming as using sew-in interfacings. Fuse all fusible interfacings with heat and steam. Use the heat setting required by the particular product and, if you don't have an industrial steam iron, use a damp press cloth. With the interfacing up, apply heat and steam for *ten seconds* without moving the iron around. Let the fabric dry and cool, turn it over with the fabric side up, and apply heat and steam for an additional *ten seconds*. Use a press cloth to protect delicate fabrics and those that might acquire a shine from direct heat.

If you need to take off a fused interfacing piece, press it lightly with a steam iron and remove it immediately. You cannot, however, reattach the interfacing piece you have removed.

Before you apply a fusible interfacing, make sure there is no seam allowance included. The edge of the fusible interfacing should come up to the stitching line but not extend beyond it.

Fusible knit interfacings are excellent for knit fabrics and also for adding soft stability to drapable woven fabrics such as wool or rayon challis, silk charmeuse, or china silk.

Preshrink woven interfacings when you preshrink your fabrics. Most can be machine washed and dried. Hair canvas should be dampened and allowed to air dry.

Most fusible interfacings do not shrink after they have been incorporated in a garment. A few do shrink and it is difficult to predict their behavior beforehand. If you wish to be absolutely safe, immerse the fusible interfacing in cool water and pat it gently. Do not agitate and do not wring. Allow the interfacing to drip dry.

There are many different brands and types of interfacings. Most costume shop technicians find a few interfacings they prefer and stock them in large quantities.

LININGS

Unlike underlinings, linings are not chosen to affect the characteristics of the outer fabric. Most linings are lighter in weight than the outer fabric but should not be so much lighter that they tend to bunch up.

Costumes are not always lined. Sometimes a lining can limit a costume's usefulness because it makes the garment more difficult to alter. However, some costumes must be lined because the inside of the garment will show or because it will be removed on stage. In general, a lining helps prolong the life of a garment by absorbing some of the strain from wear and by protecting the inside from abrasion. A lining also helps keep a costume from stretching and reduces wrinkles.

Lining fabrics are often slippery and allow the garment to slide easily on and off the body. Popular linings for costumes are Bemberg rayon, acetate taffeta, and sturdy silks. China silk is too weak a fabric for most linings, and polyester linings may be too hot for lining stage costumes.

Most lining fabrics stretch less than the outer fabric. Cut lining pieces slightly larger than the garment pieces. Add approximately ⅛ inch on all vertical seams, ¼ inch on horizontal seams, and 1 inch on hem edges. Cut jacket and coat linings with pleats in the center back.

Be sure the lining has the same laundry requirements as the rest of the costume. Bemberg rayon, acetate taffeta, and polyester linings seldom shrink. Always prewash silk linings.

Considerations of Nap and Directional Patterns

Velvet, corduroy, Ultrasuede, wool flannel, and fake fur are all fabrics that have a *nap*: when you brush the surface in one direction, lengthwise, it feels smooth; in the other direction it feels rough. Because light reflects differently on a down nap and on an up nap, normally, all fabric pieces are cut with the nap going in the same direction. Although most street garments are cut with the nap lying smoothly from top to bottom, many costumes are cut the opposite way, which, under stage lights, causes the fabric to appear deeper and richer.

Many other fabrics have subtly different directional differences and many cutter/drapers insist upon always cutting all fabric pieces in the same direction.

Some patterns are directional. Look carefully and lay all your pattern pieces in the same direction to avoid flowers growing upside down and birds flying with their feet over their wings.

RIGHT SIDE OR WRONG SIDE

You are as apt to make a costume with the "wrong" side of the fabric facing out as with the "right" side. In general, when fabric manufacturers fold fabric in half and wrap it around bolts, the "right," or "facing," side is folded in. The "right" side of fabric on rolls is usually face down on the roll. Even fabrics that don't appear to look different on the "right" side and on the "wrong" side may look different under stage lights. Make sure you know which side of the fabric the designer wants to use, then mark all the fabric pieces on the wrong side with chalk, tailor's pencil, or a small safety pin, so they won't get mixed up.

PLAIDS, STRIPES, AND SO ON

When you are matching plaids, stripes, or geometric designs, additional fabric will be needed. A reasonably accurate way of calculating the extra amount is to measure one complete repeat in the plaid or design and add one repeat to each yard of fabric purchased. **Example:** The pattern repeat is 4½ inches. The garment calls for 4 yards. 4 × 4½ inches = 18 inches. Buy an additional ½ yard, a total of 4½ yards.

Matching plaids is not difficult. But it takes thought, planning, checking, and careful cutting. Be sure to understand the plaid you are working with. A plaid can be balanced, which means the repeat is the same horizontally and vertically; it may be one-way directional, vertically; one-way directional, horizontally; or two-way directional in both directions. A balanced plaid is the easiest to match and a two-way directional is the most difficult.

The simplest and most reliable way to match plaids is to work out the actual plaid pattern on the paper pattern pieces, sketching in main design lines so the pattern pieces can be placed accurately on the fabric. Most plaids have to be cut in a single layer, one piece at a time. Be careful to cut identical pieces and either reverse pattern pieces for right and left sides or have separate pieces for each side. Remember that it is impossible to match plaids along every seam line in a garment, so concentrate on matching those that will be most visible.

CUTTING TIPS

No step in constructing a costume is more important to its success than cutting out each piece accurately and on the correct grain of the fabric. Lay the fabric carefully on the table, secure it with weights or pushpins, and place all pattern pieces with straight grain marks parallel to the selvage edge of the fabric. *Measure to make sure.*

Before you fasten down the pattern or begin to cut, lay out all the pieces to make sure you have enough fabric. Most cutter/drapers draw around all pattern pieces with a designer pencil, soft lead pencil, or chalk before cutting. Use weights, pushpins, or straight pins to hold the pattern pieces in place, draw in stitching lines, and/or add seam allowances. Cut out the pieces with sharp cutting shears. Never raise the fabric up in the air to cut it and always keep the base of the shears resting on the table. Never cut out pieces with pinking shears. Do

not remove the pattern pieces from the fabric until you have transferred all necessary construction and match-up marks.

Many fabrics can be cut double, right and left sides at the same time. Sheer and slippery fabrics, plaids, and prints may require single-layer cutting. When you are cutting one piece at a time, do not forget to reverse the pattern pieces so you will have a right side *and* a left side.

MARKING CONSTRUCTION AND MATCH-UP MARKS

Be very accurate when you transfer construction marks from the paper pattern to the mock-up and finally to the "real" fabric. You can transfer these marks with fabric-tracing paper and a tracing wheel or draw them on with chalk, a tailor's pencil, fabric-marking pen, or, in some instances, an ordinary drawing pencil. Occasionally, you will encounter a very spongy, textured fabric that must be marked with thread loops called tailor's tacks. Choose your method of marking carefully. Make sure the marks won't bleed through to the right side of the fabric. The waxy color from yellow fabric-tracing paper is particularly difficult to remove from anything.

Make edge-to-edge match-up marks with short lines drawn or traced perpendicular to the seam line. A slash or notch in a seam edge will get lost if you serge the edge of the piece before you assemble the garment.

Transfer construction and match-up marks to the wrong side of the outer fabric if there is no underlining. When there is an underlining, transfer marks only to that layer. If your underlined piece includes darts, hand baste or machine baste the fold line of the dart through both layers; this will prevent the layers from slipping when you stitch the dart.

ORGANIZING GARMENT PIECES

Most of the time, costumes are cut quicker than they are stitched. As you cut out the pieces for a particular costume, be sure to organize and label them carefully. Some cutter/drapers make a loosely tied bundle of all the pieces that belong to a particular costume; some shops provide plastic baskets for garment pieces.

Hand Stitching

Despite a heavy reliance on sewing machines in a costume shop, there is always hand stitching to do: hems to put up, facings to tack in place, buttons, snaps, hooks and eyes, and trim to attach. Costume technicians should be familiar with a few basic hand-stitches and know when to use them.

HAND-SEWING NEEDLES

Hand-sewing needles come in a variety of types and sizes. The finer or sheerer the fabric being stitched, the sharper and more slender the needle should be so it won't poke needlessly large holes into the fabric weave.

Sharps are medium-length needles with small, rounded eyes.

Betweens are shorter and also have small rounded eyes.

Milliner's needles are long, with small, rounded eyes.

Embroidery and *crewel* needles are of medium length and have longer, larger eyes.

Each needle type comes in a range of sizes, with smaller numbers indicating larger needles. Sizes five to nine are the most commonly used, although you should keep some larger sizes on hand for very bulky fabrics. Needles smaller than size nine will probably sit in a drawer, unused.

Glover's needles are used for sewing on leather. They have three sharp edges as well as a sharp point and should be handled with care. Glover's needles come in a much smaller range of sizes than ordinary hand-sewing needles and

are available from shops that sell leather supplies.

HAND-SEWING THREAD

Use a short length of thread for hand stitching; about twenty inches is ideal. When tempted to sew with a longer piece of thread, remember that it takes less time to rethread the needle with a new length of thread than it does to untangle the knots that spring up when sewing with a thread that is too long.

Always thread the needle with the thread as it comes off the spool, then cut the thread. Sewing threads are normally left twist and wound on the spools in the direction of the twist. When threading the needle directly from the spool, you stitch *with* the thread twist, rather than *against* it. If you cut a length of thread and thread the needle with the cut end, you will stitch *against* the thread twist, greatly increasing the potential for tangles and knots.

Rub beeswax on the end of the thread to make needle threading easier. For smoother sewing, run beeswax over the length of the thread and smooth it with your fingers before beginning to sew. For the smoothest of all threads, one that is very resistant to knotting and suitable for the finest hand stitching, rub beeswax over a length of thread, place the thread between two layers of muslin, and steam press.

Begin and end each row of hand stitching with a small knot or with several small stitches taken on top of each other. Try making a small, neat, *quilter's knot* by wrapping the long end of the thread two or three times around the needle, holding the loops in place with the right thumb and forefinger. Then with right thumb and forefinger, slip the loops down the length of the thread until they form a knot. It is very much the same as making a French knot in embroidery.

The running stitch, the slip stitch, and the blindstitch are usually formed with the hem edge parallel to you, and the needle moving from right to left. The stitches in the cross stitch are almost always worked from left to right, although the needle points to the left. The backstitch and the prick stitch may be worked from right to left, or diagonally, with the needle moving toward you. Try working the hemming stitch and the locked hemming stitch with the hem at a right angle, so you are stitching directly toward yourself. In general, work parallel, work toward yourself at a diagonal, or work toward yourself at a right angle. Your stitches will be more accurate when you find the best position for each stitch. Avoid sewing away from yourself because it is quite difficult to keep your stitches even and straight when you do.

Miscellaneous Hand Stitches

THE RUNNING STITCH

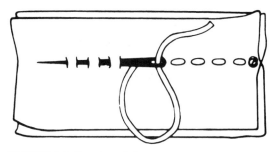

FIGURE 5–3. Running stitch.

The running stitch is the most basic of all hand stitches. It is used for basting, mending, easing, and gathering.

With the needle in one hand, take several small bites of the fabric, in and out, until you have from three to six stitches on the needle. Pull the needle through and don't draw the thread too tightly. Repeat the process until you arrive at your stitching destination.

THE BACKSTITCH

The backstitch is the strongest of all the hand stitches and was the stitch often used for seaming in the days before the invention of the

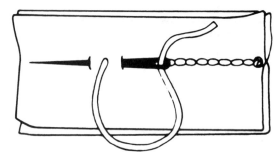

FIGURE 5–4. Backstitch.

sewing machine. It is especially useful for stitching seams unable to be reached with a sewing machine and for making hard-to-reach repairs. The backstitch has the appearance of a machine stitch on the right side but the stitches overlap on the wrong side.

To begin, bring the needle through the fabric layers to the upper side. First stitch: Insert the needle about ⅛ inch behind the place where you first put the needle in and bring it out about ⅛ inch in front of the place where you first put the needle in. Subsequent stitches: Insert the needle in the near end of the last stitch, and bring it out one stitch length ahead, as shown in Figure 5–4. The stitches on the underside will be twice as long as the stitches on the upper side. The shorter the stitch, the stronger the seam.

THE PRICK OR INVISIBLE STITCH

FIGURE 5–5. Prick stitch.

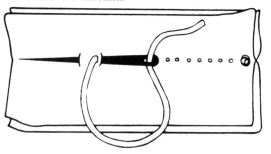

Use the prick stitch when you want a relatively strong, unobtrusive stitching line. It is an excellent choice for putting in zippers by hand.

The prick stitch is a variation on the back stitch. On the right side of the fabric, carry the needle back only one or two fabric threads, rather than all the way back to the last stitch you took. There will be tiny, almost invisible stitches on the surface of the fabric and a reinforced line of stitches underneath.

THE CROSS STITCH (HERRINGBONE STITCH, CATCH STITCH)

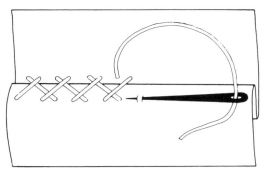

FIGURE 5–6. Cross stitch.

Use the cross stitch to attach facings and linings to the insides of garments, to tack down pleats or tucks, and in similar situations when you need to tack two fabric layers together and allow them to move apart as the body moves. *The cross stitch is not a suitable hem stitch.* The object in hemming is to keep the hem allowance firmly in place, not to let it move up and down.

Work the cross stitch from left to right. Make sure the stitching does not show on the right side of the garment.

Bring the needle up in the bottom left edge of the fabric. Take a small horizontal stitch, right to left, approximately ½ inch to the right, in the upper fabric. Then take a small horizontal stitch in the lower fabric, the same distance to the right, creating a diagonal cross stitch, as

shown in Figure 5–6. Repeat, making sure the needle always moves from right to left. *Be careful not to pull the thread too tight.*

Hemming Stitches

THE HEMMING STITCH

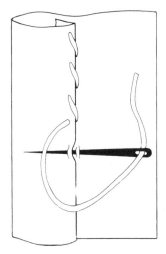

FIGURE 5–7. Hemming stitch.

FIGURE 5–8. Hemming stitch with needle perpendicular to hem edge. *Photograph by Rosemary Ingham.*

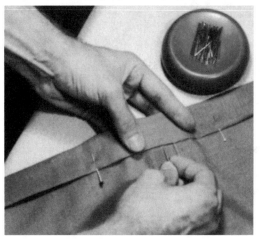

This hemming stitch is quite strong and suitable for hems on medium- or heavyweight fabrics. Prepare the edge of the hem allowance by serging, by folding back the fabric, or by attaching hem tape or bias tape. Position the garment so you are stitching toward yourself.

Begin by bringing the needle up through the hem allowance. Then take a tiny stitch in the garment and bring the needle straight up through the hem allowance edge. *Keep the needle perpendicular to the hem edge.* Continue in this manner, spacing stitches about ½ inch apart in mediumweight fabrics, and ½ to ¾ inch apart in heavyweight fabrics. Be careful not to pull the thread too tight.

THE LOCKED HEMMING STITCH

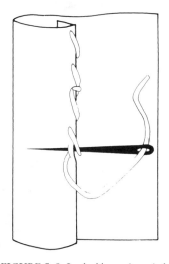

FIGURE 5–9. Locked hemming stitch.

The locked hemming stitch is especially strong and particularly suitable for gored or circular skirts and capes made from heavy fabric when the hem allowance has to be eased. Prepare the hem edge as you did for the hemming stitch.

Begin just as if you were doing the hemming stitch. *Remember to keep the needle perpendicular to the hem edge.* After coming up through the hem allowance, take another stitch, coming up from under the stitch you just made, but only through the hem allowance, as shown in Figure 5–9. This second stitch creates a lock. You can repeat this lock stitch every stitch, every other stitch, or every four or five stitches. With the locked hemming stitch, you can safely put the stitches a little further apart than with the plain hemming stitch.

THE SLIP STITCH

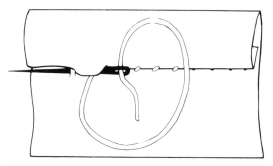

FIGURE 5–10. Slip stitch.

The slip stitch makes a sturdy, flat hem with hidden stitches. It is not the best hemming choice for a gored or circle garment when the hem allowance has to be eased into place. Prepare for the slip stitch by folding the edge of your hem allowance under.

Work the slip stitch from right to left with the folded edge of the hem allowance facing toward you and the folded edge of the garment facing away.

Bring the needle up through the hem allowance, then pick up a thread or two of the outer fabric with the needle. Insert the needle into the folded edge of the fabric, *a thread or two to the right of where the needle came out,* and slip it through for about ¼ inch. In one motion, bring the needle out from the folded edge and pick up another thread or two of the outer fabric. Repeat. Make four or five individual stitches, then draw up the thread firmly, taking care not to pull too tight. All the stitches should disappear.

THE BLINDSTITCH

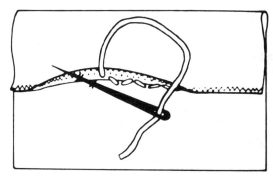

FIGURE 5–11. Blindstitch.

This hem stitch is hidden under the hem allowance. It does not produce a particularly strong hem and is only suitable for lightweight fabrics and knits. The edge of the hem allowance may be serged or zigzagged but must lie flat and cannot be folded under.

To begin, roll the finished edge of the hem back about ¼ inch. Take a small horizontal stitch through one thread of the hem allowance, then move the needle approximately ¼ inch to the left and pick up a thread of the outer fabric, creating a diagonal stitch. Keep the thread loose. Ideally, this stitch should be invisible on both sides of the garment.

Basting to Save Time

Basting is a temporary stitch used in various stages of garment construction and removed after the garment has been fitted and stitched permanently. You may associate hand basting with fine tailoring and dressmaking and believe that it's too time-consuming to do in a busy costume shop. There are, however, at least three specific stitching operations in which hand basting actually saves time. In each instance, use the running stitch, varying the stitch length so it is suitable for the job at hand.

SEAMING VELVET AND SOME OTHER NAPPED AND PILE FABRICS

Hand basting the seam lines in velvet and other napped fabrics before you machine stitch them may well save you time in the long run. Velvet, velveteen, velour, and some pile fabrics are particularly difficult to control under the presser foot. No matter how carefully you pin, the fabric layers tend to wander and to stretch. Since the marks made by the pressure of the sewing machine presser foot are difficult to remove from some rayon and silk velvets, you will not want to rip out an inaccurate seam and have to stitch it again. Baste first and avoid frustration later. Using a Teflon-coated presser foot to stitch the seam after basting may help you stitch velvet seams together more accurately.

SETTING HEMS

Hem lengths often change at final fittings. Hand baste the hem for the fitting and don't press the fold until after the hem is set and stitched.

FACED EDGES

To ensure that faced garment edges stay flat, machine understitch first (see Figure 5–32 on page 199), then hand baste with a diagonal basting stitch close to the folded edge before you tack the facing down or press it. Finger the facing just slightly to the inside of the garment and baste it in place, about ½ inch from the folded edge. The basting stitches will establish a clean edge and prevent the facing, and the seam line which attaches it, from being visible on the outside of the garment. Then tack the facings in place. Remove your basting stitches before you press because they may leave indentations in the fabric, especially in soft fabrics.

Hand-Stitched Closings

BUTTONS

Some buttons need to be stitched on with a thread shank and some do not. A thread shank connects the button and the garment and is long enough to permit the fabric around the buttonhole to lie smoothly beneath the button. You do not need a shank if the garment layers are quite thin, if the button is not practical, or if the button itself has a shank.

Figure 5–12 illustrates one method of creating a button shank. Bring a doubled, knotted thread up from underneath the fabric and through a hole in the button. Lay a toothpick across the button, between the two holes, and carry the thread across the toothpick and down into the other hole. Take six or eight stitches, then remove the toothpick and bring the needle up underneath the button. Wrap the needle threads firmly around the threads between the button and the garment fabric. Bring the thread to the underside of the fabric,

FIGURE 5–12. Sewing on a button with a thread shank.

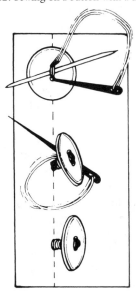

knot by creating a loop and pulling the thread through it, or take two or three end stitches, one on top of the other, and cut.

Another method is to insert the edge of your thumb under the button while you're stitching it on, which raises the button up from the garment surface, creating a space for a thread shank. Wrap and tie off as previously described.

When you sew buttons on heavy garments made from loosely woven wools or from leather or suede, reinforce the button on the underside so it won't tear out. Put a small shirt-size button on the underside, directly beneath the top button. Sew both top and botton buttons on at the same time. Only the top button needs a shank.

HOOK AND EYE FASTENERS

Hooks and eyes may well be the most popular of all costume closings. Individual hooks and eyes are usually hand stitched into waistbands, collars, cuffs, cape closings, and sometimes up the backs and fronts of period dresses and doublets. (Machine stitching hook and eye tape is described later in this chapter.)

Use large skirt- and trouser-type hook and eye fasteners for waistbands and heavy garments; use smaller ones, sizes three and four, for collars and cuffs. Stitch hooks and eyes firmly in place, making sure that at least one or two stitches go through *all layers of fabric*. Unless the fabric is very lightweight, use double strands of heavy-duty thread. Make sure you stitch skirt hooks extra firmly, leaving as little "give" as possible, because the sharp edges of these hooks tend to cut threads.

Use bar eyes when you want the closing to be tight and firm, and loop eyes when you want some flexibility. Do not forget to anchor down the end of the hook and the outer part of the hook eye, as illustrated in Figure 5–14.

SNAP FASTENERS

The large size, #10, snap fasteners, usually called "whopper-poppers," are particularly

FIGURE 5–13. Standard button sizes. Streamline Standard Button Gauge™, courtesy of Streamline Industries, Inc.

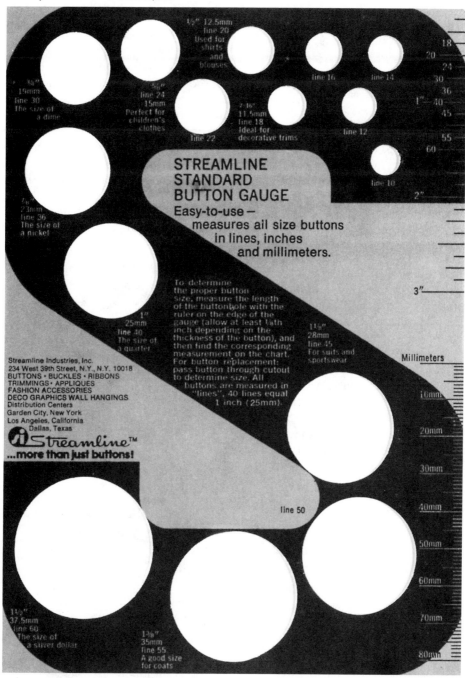

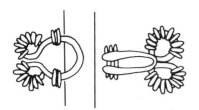

FIGURE 5–14. Hook and eye.

FIGURE 5–15. Whopper-popper.

popular in costume shops. These snaps are very strong, suitable for attaching costume props and accessories, such as bandoliers, uniform insignias, or bustle drapes, and closing bulky garments. Stitch whopper-poppers on with multiple strands of heavy-duty thread, making five or six stitches through each hole.

Place smaller snap fasteners in waistline and neck closings, sometimes combining them with hook and eye fasteners or with zippers. Snap fasteners may also be used to stabilize the underlap on a double-breasted jacket, coat, or dress.

Costumes without sleeves or with low necklines may need lingerie strap holders, with

FIGURE 5–16. Ribbon lingerie strap.

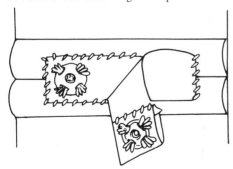

snap fasteners, on the inside of the shoulder seam. Make lingerie strap holders with either a bit of thread chain from the serger, or from chain you've made yourself, as shown in Figure 5–65. Stitch the ball part of a snap to one end of the chain and the other end to the garment. Stitch the socket part of the snap fastener to the garment. For heavyweight fabrics, substitute ribbon or tape for the thread chain. (Or, you can purchase ready-made, ready to stitch in, lingerie strap holders from your sewing notions supplier.)

If the fabric is very sheer and you don't want a bright metal snap fastener to show, cover both parts of the snap with a bit of the costume fabric before stitching the fastener to the garment. (See Figure 5–17.) A sheer covering won't interfere with the snap's performance.

FIGURE 5–17. Covering a snap with fabric.

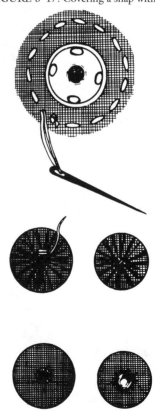

Hems

Every costume shop ought to have a procedure for marking, setting, and securing hems. Nothing ruins a handsome costume as surely as a lumpy uneven hem, and the best way to prevent unsightly hems is to establish a simple set of hemming steps that everyone can follow.

There are many different procedures. The following is one that has been used both in professional and educational costume shops.

PROCEDURE SHEET FOR MARKING
AND SETTING HEMS

Note: When you are setting the hem length of a costume, always bear in mind that stages are usually either lower or higher than audience eye level. If the stage is lower than audience eye level, the hemline will "look" longer; if it's higher, the hemline will "look" shorter. You may have to make appropriate compensations.

Marking

1. Do not mark hem lengths in a muslin fitting. However, do make certain that adequate length has been left for the garment length and the hem allowance.

2. Mark hem lengths in the first fabric fitting if there are not many fitting adjustments and in a subsequent fitting if there are. Make sure the actor is wearing the proper shoes and undergarments when marking the hem.

3. Fold up and pin part, or all, of the hem allowance so the designer can see the hem length but do not actually mark the length by folding up the hem.

4. The hem length is the distance between the bottom of the garment and the floor. Use a measuring tool to mark the hem length: yardstick, ruler, seam gauge, right angle, T-square, or a commercial chalk or pin hem marker.

5. Take special care with hems that are to be set at, or just above, floor length. Make sure that the actor is standing squarely on both feet, arms at his or her sides and eyes looking straight ahead. Explain that raising the arms, slumping, or looking down will all contribute to a hem that hangs longer in one place than in another.

The bottom of the garment will have been cut two or more inches longer than the floor. Arrange the fabric carefully and mark where the fabric hits the floor at six- to eight-inch intervals all the way around. Be very careful not to pull down while marking, especially if the fabric is heavy or the garment has a curved bottom edge. Most cutter/drapers prefer to use chalk for the initial marking, then put safety pins on the marks, preferably before removing the garment from the actor. The person doing the marking may either ask the actor to turn around slowly, or move around the actor.

Checking

1. Place the garment flat on a work table and turn up the hem as marked. Baste the hem up all the way around, about 1½ inches from the fold.

2. If the hem allowance is so deep that it will hang down below the fold, add a second row of basting higher up. **DO NOT PRESS!!!**

3. Check the hem length at the final fitting and/or the dress parade.

4. Adjust as necessary.

Setting

1. Determine what the proper hem allowance will be, and trim *evenly* all around. A normal hem allowance is 2 inches, but if you can leave more without adding too much weight or making ugly bulges, leave more. Gored and circle garments will need to have narrow hem allowances.

2. Finish the hem edge with an overlock stitch on the serger, a zigzag sewing machine stitch, a

turn-under, bias strips, or commercial hem tape.

3. Secure the hem with a blind hem stitch by machine whenever possible. If you hem by hand, the locked hemming stitch is the most secure.

4. After the hem is set, remove all basting stitches and, working from the outside, steam very lightly over a curved surface (a tailor's ham, for example, or a rolled-up towel), *never* resting the iron's full weight on the garment.

Special Hems

1. When you're marking a trained skirt, lay the train fabric out on the floor behind the actor and, with chalk, draw one-half of the train edge, from side to center back. When the garment is off the actor and back on the work table, use the marked half as a guide to mark the unmarked half.

2. Many trained and floor-length period skirts need to have weighted hems to hang correctly. Face the hem edge with a wide (4 inch to 6 inch) bias strip, or, in the case of a train, a wide-shaped facing piece, cut from fabric that is heavier than the garment fabric. You can also weight the hem with a wide bias or shaped interfacing and then face the hem with the garment fabric. Don't try to use wide bias around a train; it will pucker.

3. If the garment has a lining attached only at the shoulders or waistband, mark and set both layers separately.

Many people have difficulty setting and securing curved hems because there is so much fullness to control. Make sure the hem allowance is not too wide. Two inches is generally the maximum width for a curved hem and ½ inch if the curve approaches a circle. After trimming the hem allowance, run a row of machine gathering stitches around the unfinished hem edge. Pin up the hem allowance at the seams and wherever the skirt hangs on the straight of

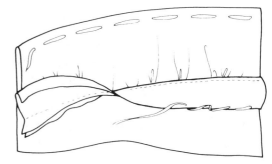

FIGURE 5–18. Stitching a curved hem.

grain. Between the pinned-up places, gather in the fullness and distribute it evenly. Baste the hem just above the fold. Attach bias tape to the hem edge (see Figure 5–18) and secure with a machine hemming stitch or with a locked hemming stitch by hand. Press lightly.

If using a serger with a differential feed mechanism, set it to gather, then overlock the hem edge.

There are several reasons why you may want to face rather than turn up a hem. Facings are indicated when the hem allowance is inadequate, when the hem edge is scalloped or dagged, or when it is sharply curved, as in a train. Once you've trimmed and faced a hem, you can never make that hem longer. Remember that and mark carefully.

Face a relatively straight and even hem with a plain bias strip, but if the hem is sharply curved as in a train or shaped as in scallops or dagging, you must cut a facing that is shaped just like the hem edge and placed on the same fabric grain. Stitch the bias strip or shaped facing to the hem edge, right sides of the fabrics together. Trim and grade the seam and understitch the facing if possible. Turn the facing to the inside, baste it down, and secure it with a machine hem stitch or with a locked hem stitch by hand.

A shirttail hem is done with a straight machine stitch. Fold the fabric edge under twice and top-stitch it on the machine. The shirttail hem is suitable for blouse and shirt bottoms and for some skirts. It is *not* suitable for steeply curved hems.

For a curved hem in lightweight or sheer fabrics, use a rolled hem put in with a rolled hemming foot. First run a line of straight machine stitching about ¼ inch from the raw hem edge, which helps to stabilize the fabric under the hemming foot. Machine rolled hems are quick and easy for many yards of ruffles, and you can dispense with the stitching line if the ruffles are cut on the straight.

Pressing

Pressing is an integral part of costume construction. Every costume technician should know when to press and when not to press—and why. It is particularly important to press as you go, with each pressing step done at the correct stage of construction. Press darts before assembling pieces. Open seams that run the length of the garment before stitching cross seams, and make sure all body seams are opened before attaching interfacings or facings. When you open seams, press them on the right as well as on the wrong side, and, if the fabric is soft, slip a piece of paper between the seam allowance and the outer fabric to avoid leaving a ridge on the outer fabric.

Pressing is not the same as ironing. When pressing, you move the iron very little and often use a curved surface, such as a tailor's ham, rather than the flat ironing table surface. *Always* press darts and curved bodice seams on the tailor's ham. Arrange the garment piece on the curved surface, place the iron lightly on it, and shoot steam through the fabric. Leave the garment piece in place for a few moments after removing the iron. If the cloth is not dry and cool before you move it, you might pull the piece out of shape.

Adjust the iron heat setting to suit the fabric. If you have any doubt about how much heat a certain fabric can withstand, test a scrap before going after the whole garment. If the fabric is very delicate or if it's apt to become shiny from heat and steam, place a pressing cloth between the surface of the iron and the surface of the fabric.

You can't press out stitching mistakes. If a garment is hanging badly because the layers of cloth slipped when the seams were being stitched, no amount of pressing will bring the garment back into balance. Many costume shop technicians harbor hopes that pressing will cure their mistakes. It won't.

Pressing Aids

Steam irons and ironing boards, or ironing tables, discussed in Chapter 1, are the major pressing equipment pieces. In addition to them, you should have several pressing aids.

1. *Sleeveboard.* This is a small ironing board that can be put on top of the ironing table. Use it to press sleeves, open seams, and touch up fine details. Some shops have two or three sleeveboards of varying sizes.

2. *Point Presser.* The point presser is a shaped board set on a base. It is flat on top and one end tapers to a point. The flat top and pointed end allow you to open seams in hard-to-get-at places like faced corners and collar points. The point presser base often doubles as a wooden pounding block, or clapper.

3. *Wooden Pounding Block, or Clapper.* The wooden pounding block is used, along with steam, to flatten the edges of lapels, collars, hems, pleats, and so on, particularly in tailored wool garments. Apply steam first, then slap the edge with the pounding block while the heat and moisture are still in the wool. Some people call this pressing aid a "spanking block," which is certainly descriptive of what you do with it.

4. *Tailor's Ham.* The tailor's ham is a fat, firmly stuffed item used for pressing curved shapes. Some are shaped vaguely like hams, others are kidney-shaped. Some are covered entirely in wool to not be slippery; others are wool on one side and canvas on the other. You can easily make one in the shop and fill it with sand or sawdust.

5. *Velvet Needleboard.* A needleboard is used to press velvet and other soft napped fabrics that might be crushed by pressing on a flat surface. Place the fabric on the board with the napped side down and steam lightly. Needleboards are expensive but worth the price. If you don't have one, make do with a piece of velvet or thick toweling and be careful never to rest the full weight of the iron on the fabric.

6. *Pressing Pads.* Use a pressing pad between the iron and the surface of the fabric when pressing over a zipper, pockets, bound button holes, or other decorative details. You can make a pressing pad from three or four layers of soft wool flannel stitched to a canvas backing. Press with the flannel side down against the garment.

7. *Pressing Cloths.* Keep a supply of clean, sizing-free pressing cloths near the pressing area. Soft, washed muslin is suitable for pressing many fabrics. White or off-white wool flannel makes an excellent pressing cloth for fabrics that tend to become shiny when pressed.

Pressing Tips

Always take out pins and basting stitches before pressing. Both may leave imprints on the fabric. Press from the widest part of the garment to the narrowest (the same direction in which you stitch). Before pressing the seam open, press both seam allowances together. Do not put the full weight of the iron down on the seam. Use the tip of the iron and steam. Press from the wrong side first, then turn to the right side. Always use a pressing cloth on the right side if there is any danger that the fabric might pick up a shine.

Press darts on the tailor's ham, moving from the widest part of the dart toward the point. When you press a dart, you're molding it into a curve. Use identical motions to press matching darts. If the dart is bulky and the edges might make an impression on the garment, place strips of brown paper between the dart and the outer fabric.

Many costume shops do not press sharp folds into skirt hems. If you press skirt hems lightly, there is less apt to be a mark left on the cloth, and the garment will be easier to adapt to another actor in another production. Press hems with a pressing cloth on the right side and rely more on steam than on pressure.

When you want to create flat sharp hems such as those on tailored jackets, combine lots of steam with sharp blows from the pounding block. Begin working on the wrong side of the garment and finish up on the right side. Always allow the garment edge to dry and cool before moving it.

Machine Stitching

All sewing machines have essentially the same working parts, although they may not always look the same. Figure 5–19 is a diagram of a very basic domestic sewing machine with all parts labeled. When you encounter a machine with which you aren't familiar, study its instruction book to identify the working parts. If an instruction book is not available, study the machine and practice sewing on a scrap of material. You can usually figure out how it works by comparing its operation with other machines you've operated.

There are three general types of domestic lock stitch sewing machines:

The *straight stitch machine* performs a forward and a backward straight stitch. (Some older models don't reverse.)

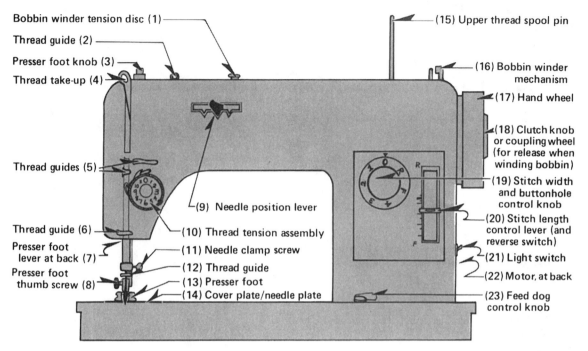

Bobbin winder tension disc (1)

Thread guide (2)

Presser foot knob (3)

Thread take-up (4)

Thread guides (5)

Thread guide (6)

Presser foot lever at back (7)

Presser foot thumb screw (8)

(9) Needle position lever

(10) Thread tension assembly

(11) Needle clamp screw

(12) Thread guide

(13) Presser foot

(14) Cover plate/needle plate

(15) Upper thread spool pin

(16) Bobbin winder mechanism

(17) Hand wheel

(18) Clutch knob or coupling wheel (for release when winding bobbin)

(19) Stitch width and buttonhole control knob

(20) Stitch length control lever (and reverse switch)

(21) Light switch

(22) Motor, at back

(23) Feed dog control knob

FIGURE 5–19. Parts of a domestic sewing machine.

The *zigzag machine* performs a straight stitch and a zigzag stitch, forward and backward. Straight stitch and zigzag machines are belt-driven, and, although very few machines of this sort are manufactured today, many secondhand models are available for reasonable prices.

The *automatic stitch machine* performs a variety of specialty and decorative stitches, in addition to the straight and zigzag stitches. Automatic stitch machines may be driven with gears, with a combination of gears and electronics, or they may be completely electronic and computerized. Prices for automatic stitch machines range from moderate to very, very expensive.

THREADING THE MACHINE

All domestic sewing machines have tension disks and a take-up lever. Once you've identified these two parts on a machine, you can figure out how to thread it. First, turn the hand-wheel toward you and bring the take-up lever to its highest position. If you are using the thread holder on the machine, position the spool so the thread comes off in a clockwise direction. Your first destination is the tension device, so pass the thread through the one or two thread guides that lead to the tension disks. Tension devices can be located at different places on different machines, but they always consist of a set of disks that exert pressure on the thread while stitches are being formed. From the tension disks, take the thread up, or over, to the take-up lever, then down to the needle. There may be one to three thread guides between the take-up lever and the needle. The last thread guide is located right above the needle, on the side of the shaft from which the thread should come. Virtually all new domestic sewing machines thread from front to back. Many older machines thread from right to left, some from left to right.

187

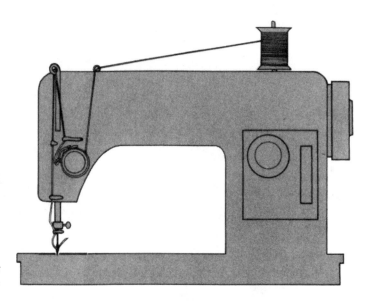

FIGURE 5–20. Top threading for domestic machine.

Industrial sewing machines are slightly more complicated to thread than domestic sewing machines, even though the threading sequence remains the same: tension disks, take-up lever, needle. In many shops it is common practice to tie on new threads and pull them through the machine, rather than rethread each time you need to change thread colors.

Figures 5–20, 5–21, and 5–22 are threading diagrams for a generic domestic sewing machine and a generic industrial sewing machine. These are only examples; each machine you operate will be slightly different.

Most domestic sewing machines have a bobbin winder on the right-hand side of the machine, near the handwheel. Before you wind a bobbin, you must take the machine out of gear, that is, disengage the needlebar so the needle won't continue to go up and down while the bobbin is being wound. On older machines loosen a coupling wheel on the hand wheel; on some newer machines there is a button to push, and on others the needlebar is automatically disengaged when the bobbin is slipped on the bobbin winder.

Get in the habit of winding bobbins at a moderate speed. If the machine is running too fast when you're winding a bobbin, you run the risk of stretching the thread that may then be the cause of puckered seams in your garment. Make sure the thread winds smoothly on the bobbin. Sometimes, on older machines, it helps to hold the thread lightly between the thumb and forefinger as it's being fed onto the bobbin. Always wind thread on an empty bobbin. When you wind one color thread on top of another color, you end up with a lumpy bobbin

FIGURE 5–21. Tension threading for domestic machine.

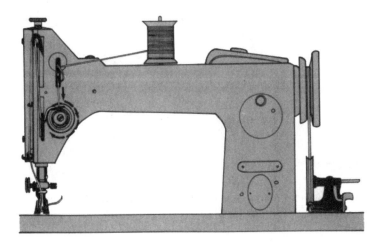

FIGURE 5–22. Top threading for industrial machine.

and uneven thread tension. Keep enough bobbins on hand for all the thread colors used.

Most industrial sewing machines have bobbin-winding mechanisms that operate while the machine stitches, feeding from a separate spool of thread. The winding process stops automatically when the bobbin is full. Most industrials do not have coupling wheels, so, if you have to wind a bobbin when you aren't stitching, make certain the presser foot is up so it won't get scratched by the moving feed teeth.

The thread inside the bobbin case may lead off in either a clockwise or counterclockwise direction. If you don't know how the bobbin threads on a particular machine, you'll have to experiment. If the thread is coming from the wrong direction, it will slip out of the threading notches and from under the tension spring. And the stitching line will be out of balance.

Once you have completed the upper threading and put in the bobbin case, draw the bobbin thread up through the needle hole in the throat plate. Hold the needle thread in your left hand, turn the handwheel toward you until the needle goes down and up again and the take-up lever is sitting at its highest point. Pull the needle thread. The bobbin thread should come up through the needle hole in a loop. Pull

the loop up until the free end appears. Place both the needle and bobbin threads under the presser foot and lay them off to the left side.

BALANCING THREAD TENSIONS

There are two thread tensions on a lock stitch sewing machine: upper tension, which is exerted on the top thread, and lower tension, which is exerted on the bottom thread. Control the upper tension by a dial on the machine face and the lower tension by a small screw on the bobbin casing.

Different fabrics require different thread tensions. If the tensions are much out of balance, loops appear on one side of the stitching line. If you suspect thread tensions are out of balance, check the machine to see that it is correctly threaded on top. Then look to see if the bobbin thread has slipped out from under the tension spring on the bobbin case.

If the machine is threaded correctly, you will have to adjust one or both thread tensions. Thread the machine with two different colors of thread, one on the top of the machine and the other on the bobbin. Make a line of stitching on the same fabric you've been using. If the bottom color shows on the top of the stitching, the upper tension is tighter than the bottom tension. If the top color shows on the bottom,

189

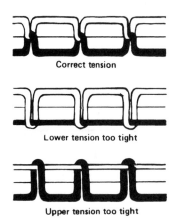

Correct tension

Lower tension too tight

Upper tension too tight

FIGURE 5–23. Machine stitch tension.

the upper tension is looser than the bottom tension. Figure 5–23 illustrates balanced and unbalanced thread tensions.

Make tension adjustments gradually, working first with the upper tension. When you alter the bottom tension—which you do only when you can't find a balance with top tension adjustments—never make more than a quarter turn of the small screw at a time. To make a rough tension check as you're adjusting, hold both top and bottom threads between your thumb and index finger and pull them to the back of the machine. As the tension is balanced, each thread offers equal resistance to your pull. Continue to adjust until your two-color stitching line shows only one color on the top and the other color on the bottom.

REGULATING STITCH LENGTH

Correct stitch length depends upon the type of seam being stitched and on the weight and texture of the fabric. In general, a fine fabric requires a shorter stitch than a heavy fabric. Stitches are generally shorter for curved seams than for straight seams. True bias and garment bias seams normally require shorter stitches than seams on the straight.

Different sewing machines mark their stitch lengths in different increments. Whatever the scale, "normal" will be approximately in the middle. Experiment until you find the correct stitch length for your stitching operation.

REGULATING PRESSER FOOT PRESSURE

On most sewing machines, the pressure of the presser foot on the fabric can be regulated by a presser foot knob, a thumb screw, or a dial on the top left-hand part of the machine head. When the pressure on the presser foot is too light, the machine feeds irregularly and the stitching line may be wobbly. If it's too heavy, the stitch length may be uneven, and the presser foot leaves marks on soft fabrics. If you think you're having problems with presser foot pressure, experiment on a small piece of the same fabric, adjusting the pressure until the problem is corrected.

Serger (Overlock) Stitching

Sergers are simpler than they look. Once you get past the initial shock of trying to follow the pathways of three or four (or five!) threads into one small piece of machinery, you'll discover that threading the serger is the hardest part of using this dandy little machine.

Sergers have been used in the garment industry since the 1890s, and many costume technicians have their first serger experiences with squat, square industrial sergers that are more than half a century old—and still operating perfectly. The first domestic serger, the Baby Lok, was manufactured in the mid-1950s, but it wasn't until the mid-1970s, and the growing popularity of knit fabrics for clothing, that a market for domestic sergers developed. Soon every major sewing machine company was making a line of sergers.

As stated in Chapter 1, sergers perform one sewing operation, an overcast stitch, with or without a "safety" stitch. And, at the same time, a set of knives operating in scissor-fashion trims off the excess fabric just ahead of the stitch mechanism.

The stitch is formed by one or two needles, an upper looper and a lower looper; there is no bobbin and no bottom thread. When you open the front panel on your serger, you can see the two loopers in operation. The upper looper carries a thread above the machine throat plate, and the lower looper carries a thread under the throat plate. The two looper threads, and the needle thread (or threads) "knit" together to form the overcast.

When you run your garment piece or pieces through the serger, the fabric on the right-hand side of the needle will be cut off by the knives or blades. Sergers overcast edges. You can't top-stitch a pocket with a serger, or make a buttonhole, or stitch a seam leaving a seam allowance. In most costume shops, sergers are used primarily to finish seam edges and to stitch and overcast seams in knit garments.

THREADING TIPS

Industrial sergers are more difficult to thread than domestic sergers. Domestic serger manufacturers compete with each other to make each new serger model easier to thread. All sergers thread a little differently, however, so you will almost always find a threading diagram painted on the inside of domestic sergers. For industrial serger threading, you will have to rely on instructions handed down from one costume technician to another, color-coded threading direction dots painted on the machine, or, best of all, a diagram of the machine, drawn by you or someone else in the shop, that shows correct threading and uses a different color for each thread.

The best serger threading advice is to avoid threading "from scratch" for as long as possible. When it's necessary to change thread colors, cut the threads that are being used and tie on the new ones. Always start with the far right thread (the lower looper), cut the thread

above the first thread guide, remove the spool or cone from the thread holder, put the new spool or cone in place, and tie on the new thread, using a *square knot*. It has to be a square knot that tightens as you pull on it; other knots come undone as they go through the tension disks and the loopers. Move to the left and tie on the upper looper thread, then continue left to the needle thread or threads. When you've tied on all three or four threads, hold the serger thread tail, make sure the presser foot is down, and run the new threads through the machine slowly and steadily. The looper threads will run through first, followed by the needle threads. If you're using a mid-sized serger needle, the small square knots will probably pass easily through the needle eyes. If the knot is too large for the needle eyes, stop the machine, snip off the knot, and thread the needles by hand.

Some technicians prefer to pull the threads gently through the machine rather than "sewing" them through. Before pulling the threads through, make sure the upper and lower looper threads are not crossed.

Some shops go along for days, even weeks, without anyone ever having to thread the serger "from scratch." However, because it's well known that serger threads always break the day before first dress, when the serger threading "expert" is in bed with the flu, all costume technicians should be able to do the job themselves.

Serger needles thread just like sewing machine needles: tension disk, take-up lever, needle. It's the loopers that are tricky, and the trickiest part is to make sure the looper threads aren't tangled; if they are tangled they will break again.

Thread the serger from right to left, beginning with the lower looper. Some lower looper threading includes a tube that the thread must pass through. If you have such a tube, you'll need a threading wire; any soft, lightweight, malleable wire will do. Because the lower looper operates under and to the left of the needle bar, it is usually partially concealed by the machine housing. Move the lower looper to the right to begin threading and then to the left to complete the threading. A pair of curved tweezers or forceps are helpful tools. Bring the thread through the eye of the lower looper, pull it out several inches, lay it under the presser foot and to the left, *and then move the threaded lower looper back to the left, out of the way of the upper looper.* Now thread the upper looper. This is easier to do because you can see where you're going. Make sure the upper looper thread doesn't go around the lower looper (which is why you moved the lower looper out of the way). Pull the upper looper thread up through the hole, under the presser foot and to the left. Make sure the presser foot is down and run the machine slowly. The three or four threads should begin to "chain" together.

If your looper threads break again after you've threaded the machine, it's probably because they are tangled. See Figure 5–24 for correct and incorrect looper thread positions. After you've threaded the serger, either by tying on new threads or "from scratch," check each thread tension mechanism to make sure

the thread is resting firmly between the disks. In general, thread tension disks on sergers are tighter than they are on sewing machines, and sometimes threads need a little extra tug to put them where they belong. If the thread is not firmly between the disks, the stitch tension will not be correct.

SERGER FEED

Once you have mastered the complexities of threading your serger, you can relax and enjoy the smooth, easy feeding mechanisms characteristic of these machines.

You've probably wondered about being instructed to run threads through the serger *with the presser foot down,* and no reminder to make sure to have fabric between the presser foot and the feed teeth. Because the serger doesn't have a bobbin or bobbin thread, its feeding mechanism is much simpler than the one on a sewing machine, and the feed teeth won't be damaged by running the machine without fabric. As a matter of fact, when you've finished a line of serging, you should always "chain off" for a couple of inches. When you begin a line of serging, you don't have to raise the presser foot; just place the fabric at the front edge of the foot and the long, narrow feed teeth will move it right along.

FIGURE 5–24. The most common serger threading mistake is incorrect threading of the upper and lower loopers. Drawing #1 shows correct looper threading. Drawings #2 and #3 show incorrect looper threading, which will result, in both cases, in tangled broken threads.

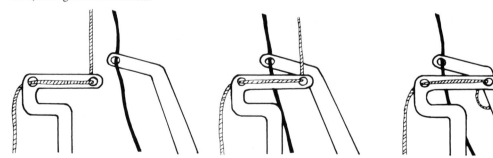

When you're stitching and overcasting two layers of fabric together on the serger, notice that the two layers feed evenly, without the tendency for the top layer to drag.

A serger with a single-feed mechanism will, however, work better on some types of fabrics than on others. Most sergers will do a great job with a wide range of mediumweight fabrics, but will tend to skip stitches on very heavyweight fabrics, and to gather or scrunch up very lightweight fabrics. To deal with this problem, some sergers are equipped with a *differential feed mechanism* that allows the operator to regulate the machine's feed to accommodate a wider range of fabrics. If you're purchasing a new serger, consider one that has a differential feed mechanism.

SERGER TENSION

Each serger thread passes through its own set of tension disks. Accurate stitch tension depends on the correct interaction of each individual thread. In an ordinary day of serging, on mostly mediumweight fabrics, serger tensions do not usually have to be changed. However, you may have to make adjustments for heavy- and lightweight fabrics, *and* you may have to make periodic tension adjustments on machines that are getting heavy use simply because some tension mechanisms tend to vibrate out of adjustment.

How do you know if your serger tension is correct or incorrect? Thread each needle and each looper on your serger with a different bright-colored thread. Make a line of overlock stitches on a piece of light-colored fabric and examine them. The upper looper thread should be on the top and the lower looper thread should be on the bottom, *and* they should interlock right at the cut edge of the fabric. The left needle thread should run straight down the left or inner edge of the overlock stitch, and the right needle thread, if there is one, should run parallel, usually to the right of the left needle thread. The stitches should all lie flat. Looping and loose stitches are the result of inaccurate tension, as are upper looper threads pulling to the bottom of the stitch or lower looper threads pulling to the top. *The first thing to do if you discover incorrect tension is to check to see if all the threads are sitting firmly under their respective tension disks.* If they are, identify which thread or threads need adjusting and *proceed cautiously.*

Most tension dials on sergers have numerical increments. If you have numbers on your tension dial, never increase or decrease the tension more than half a step at a time. Larger numbers mean more tension; smaller numbers mean less. Turning the tension knob with abandon will merely increase your problems. If the serger seems to be suffering from too much knob turning in too many directions, return all the knobs to a median position (if there are eight numerical increments, for instance, set all the knobs at four). Then stitch a bit on a piece of mediumweight fabric. Examine the stitch and, moving from right to left (lower looper to left needle), work out a new balance of the threads.

Most industrial sergers maintain relatively stable tensions, but some of the earlier domestic models can be troublesome indeed to regulate.

MISCELLANEOUS SERGER TIPS

Most sergers require special needles made for sergers. Serger needles are sized, however, just like sewing machine needles. A few domestic sergers use regular domestic sewing machine needles.

The handwheels on most sergers turn away from the operator, rather than toward the operator as sewing machines do. It is important to turn the handwheel in the correct direction to avoid damaging the gears.

Sergers stitch faster than sewing machines, in most cases about seven times faster. This speed is a real advantage in a busy costume shop. However, you will have fewer broken threads and tension problems if you begin stitching at a modest speed and work up to a high speed.

If the serger requires regular oiling—and most do—be sure to clean and oil it after every eight hours of operation. Sergers collect a great deal of lint, which you can brush away with a long-handled paintbrush. Use a good-quality machine oil and, if you don't have a manufacturer's oiling diagram, open all panels and place a drop of oil wherever two metal parts are moving against each other.

Seams

Whenever you stitch two pieces of fabric together, a seam is created. Seaming is the most frequently done machine-sewing operation. If you don't seam your garments accurately, on the correct stitching lines, they won't fit the actor for whom they've been patterned and cut. Accurate seaming is as important to a costume as a firm foundation is to a building.

STITCHING ACCURATELY

If your straight stitching has a tendency to wobble and your curved seams aren't absolutely smooth, perhaps you need to take the time to work on your machine-stitching skills. Figures 5–25 and 5–26 contain several stitching skill exercises that you can enlarge and reproduce on a photocopy machine. Unthread your machine, both top and bottom, and practice stitching on the exercise lines. Start stitching slowly and gradually increase your speed. Do not expect to master these exercises in one half-hour practice session. Spread the practice sessions over several days and give your hands a chance to learn machine-stitching control. When you can accomplish the exercises accurately on paper, draw a set of the diagrams on squares of unbleached muslin and stitch on the lines with bright-colored thread.

When you machine stitch a marked stitching line, do not look at the machine needle but at a point on the stitching line somewhat ahead of the needle. When the seam line is not marked, look at the outer edge of the seam allowance to keep it in line with the seam width indicator.

FIGURE 5–25. Straight and right angle stitching exercises.

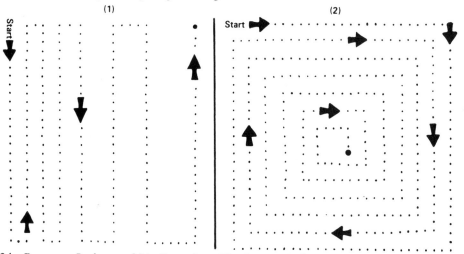

FIGURE 5–26. Curved and circular stitching exercises.

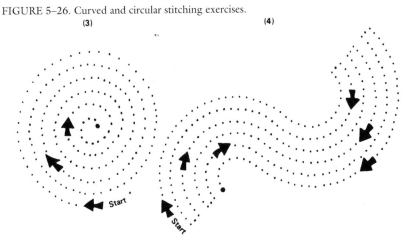

ALIGNING THE FABRIC

Cut two identical fabric rectangles, approximately 12 inches long on the straight grain and 5 inches wide. Seam them together along the 12-inch edge. Do not pin the seam before you stitch, and guide the layers very lightly under the presser foot, just enough to keep the seam line straight. Do not pull the fabric from behind the presser foot. When you reach the end of the seam, look at the layers. In almost all instances, the top layer will have stretched slightly over the bottom layer, and the edges of the fabric will be uneven at the bottom. This is called *presser foot drag*. Now open out the stitched piece and notice that the cross grains of the two pieces don't go straight across. Consider, for a moment, how easily you can throw a garment out of balance by seaming in such a way that the top layer of cloth stretches the whole length of the seam. One of the most important goals of accurate machine stitching is to maintain correct fabric alignment from one end of the seam to the other.

Presser foot drag is a universal problem with lock stitch sewing machines. It can be minimized by making careful presser foot pres-

sure adjustments, but it cannot be eliminated altogether unless the sewing machine is equipped with a dual feed mechanism, sometimes called a *walking foot*. Since most machines do not have dual feed mechanisms, it is important to learn to align two layers of fabric accurately with pins or with fingering techniques to prevent top-layer stretching.

The two pinning methods that seem to line up fabric layers best are:

1. Place pins every 1 to 1½ inches along the seam line, running them in the same direction as the seam. Place the pins so the pin heads will be toward you as you stitch. Remove each pin as you come to it. If you see that the top layer is beginning to stretch, take the pieces from beneath the presser foot, release the seam back a few inches, repin close together, and continue stitching.

2. Place a row of pins on each side of the seam line, leaving enough clearance for the presser foot to move between them. This method works best for more tightly woven fabrics.

Pinning across the seam line is not the most effective way to line up fabric pieces accurately since stretching tends to occur in the intervals between pins. And, if you stitch over your pins (a very dangerous thing to do!), you may end up with a series of tiny tucks along the seam line, which does nothing for the appearance of your garment.

Most sewing machine mechanics report that stitching over pins—even if the machine manual says it's possible—may throw off the machine's timing. Also, you run the risk of blunting or bending the machine needle, or of breaking off the end of the machine needle, which may then fly through the air and end up embedding itself in you.

The most efficient and most accurate method of aligning fabric pieces is to learn to manipulate the two layers with your hands, without using pins.

Rest your left hand firmly on both layers of fabric, to the side and in front of the needle. Separate the two layers with the fingers of your right hand and exert a slight pressure on the bottom piece of fabric. The amount of pressure will vary according to the stretchability of the fabric being stitched. Maintain this pressure as the two layers of cloth move beneath the presser foot. When stitching a long seam, pause every few inches to check the alignment. It may take you several practice sessions to learn to seam without using pins, but, because it's such a time-saving technique, learning it is worth the effort.

Although experienced industrial stitchers learn to stitch all seams without benefit of pins, most costume technicians find that they limit their "pinless seams" to straight, slightly biased, and gently curved seams, relying on pins or basting for armhole, neckline, and curvy "princess" seams.

DIRECTIONAL STITCHING

The general rule for deciding in which direction to stitch a seam is that you start at the widest part of the garment piece and stitch to the narrowest part. An **A**-line skirt, for example, should be stitched from hem edge to waist edge. The reason for choosing the widest to narrowest stitching direction becomes clear when you consider the fabric weave structure. If you stitch from narrow to wide, on a diagonal, you are opening up the weave, and this may result in ripples in the seam. If you stitch from wide to narrow, you are packing the weave and holding it firm.

Another way to determine correct stitching direction is to stroke the edge of the seam. If yarn ends scrape against your finger, you will be stitching against the weave; if the yarn ends lie down smoothly under your finger, you will be stitching with the weave. "Stitch," said one costume technician, "in the direction your cat prefers to be petted."

Most important of all, always make sure that you stitch identical seams on opposite sides of a garment in the same direction. If you stitch the left side front seam from top to bottom, and the right side front seam from bottom to top, chances are that the two seams won't be the same length when you finish.

ENDING THE SEAM

When you're stitching permanent seams in a garment, you will want to lock both the beginning and the end of the seam. The most common way of doing this is to make a few reverse stitches right on the seam line. Three or four stitches will do admirably. Be careful not to create a lump of threads. When you're using a machine that doesn't operate in reverse, sew forward a few stitches, make sure the take-up lever is in its highest position, raise the presser foot, and move the material toward you. Lower the presser foot and resume sewing directly over the first stitches. Another way of locking the beginning and end of seams is to put the stitch length regulator on zero and stitch three or four times in place.

FINISHING THE SEAM

Raw seam edges in costumes are usually finished in some manner to keep them from raveling during wear, in the wash, or at the dry cleaners. Sometimes the seam finish is applied before the garment is constructed, and sometimes after. If seam edges are finished before the garment is constructed, don't finish any edges that will be enclosed in a facing (you'll trim off any finishing you apply) or the hem edges of the garment.

A machine overlock produces the best all-round costume seam finish, although, as stated, some sergers do not perform well on extremely lightweight fabrics, such as chiffon, or on some soft, stretchy fabrics, such as milliskin.

If you don't have a serger, a machine zigzag stitch also makes a fine seam finish. Set the stitch width at its widest setting and make sure the zigzag encloses the outside edge of the seam allowance. A zigzagged edge is not as flexible as a serged edge, nor does it control an extremely loose weave fabric as efficiently; nevertheless, it does stop raveling. If edges are to be finished with a zigzag stitch before the pieces are assembled, be very careful not to stretch the pieces out of shape.

You may sometimes have to bind seam edges in garments made from very loose-weave fabrics. Apply binding only after the garment shell has been stitched, fitted, and altered but before the facings are applied. Use self-bias strips or commercial bias binding. Some sewing machines have a binding attachment that feeds folded bias binding directly over the seam edge. If possible, stitch the binding on with a zigzag stitch. If you do not have a binding attachment, open out commercial bias binding and stitch one edge of the binding to the seam allowance on the fold line. Turn the binding over to enclose the seam edge and stitch flat.

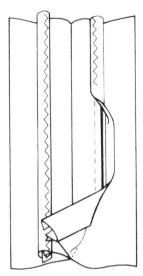

FIGURE 5–27. Seam finish: bias binding.

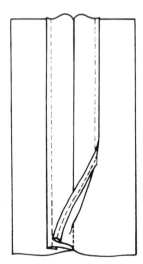

FIGURE 5–28. Seam finish: edge turned under and machine stitched.

A good-looking seam finish for unlined garments made from lightweight and medium-weight fabrics, especially if the seams will be visible as the garment moves or is removed, is to simply turn under each seam edge and stitch down with a row of straight machine stitches, as shown in Figure 5–28. A turned-under seam finish does not work well on steeply curved seams.

TRIMMING, GRADING, CLIPPING, AND NOTCHING SEAMS

It is very important that you know which garment seams to trim away and which to leave their full width, and that you understand the reasons for reducing seam bulk. Do not trim, clip, or notch seams in costumes unless you have to, that is to say, unless the full seam width will affect shape, hang, or fit of the garment. When you can leave full-width seams, you increase the possibility of altering the costume for another use. However, many sorts of seams must be trimmed, clipped, or notched, and if you try to leave the full seam width intact, the garment will be lumpy, wrinkled, or ill-fitting.

Most of the relatively straight seams used to construct the garment shell can be left full width unless the fabric is very bulky or very sheer. Curved garment construction seams, however, such as those up the side fronts of a princess-line garment, must be clipped and notched so you can press the seam open; you may also have to trim curved seams if the seam allowance is more than ½ or ⅝ inch wide.

Figures 5–29 and 5–30 illustrate trimming, grading, and clipping inside and notching outside curves. Trim the seam allowance layer that will rest against the outside garment fabric to approximately ¼ inch. Trim the seam allowance layer that will rest against the facing or lining to approximately ⅛ inch. Varying the seam allowance widths in this way is called grading.

Clip inside curves so the seam allowances will open up when the seam is opened or turned. On outside curves, cut small triangular notches out of the seam allowance so the curved seam can turn smoothly in on itself,

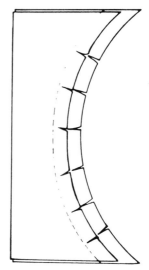

FIGURE 5–29. Grading and clipping an inside curve.

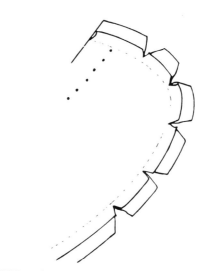

FIGURE 5–30. Grading and notching a Peter Pan collar.

without puckering. Notches or clips extend almost to the stitching line but not so close that fabric will unravel around the stitches.

An alternative to notching or clipping is to trim the entire seam allowance to within ¹⁄₁₆ inch of the seam line. Although this trimming looks dangerously close to the stitching line, some costume technicians feel that the seam remains stronger when trimmed close than when notched or clipped.

Always trim and grade facing seams. This includes all edge facings, collars, cuffs, double-layered pockets, peplums, and so on. If the faced piece includes a square corner or a point, trim as shown in Figure 5–31. Snip off the point quite close to the stitching line and then trim an additional piece from the seam allowance on each side of the point.

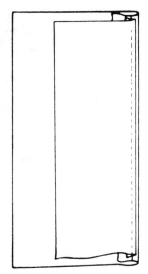

FIGURE 5–32. An understitched facing.

edge to turn in slightly. Secure the facing. Remove the basting. Press.

USEFUL SEAMS

Single Top-Stitched Seam

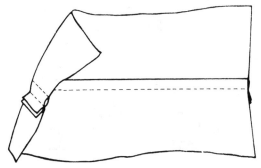

FIGURE 5–33. Single top-stitched seam.

The single top-stitched seam, or welt seam, is an excellent choice for places in the garment where there will be a great deal of strain on the seam: crotch, center back, snug two-piece sleeve, and so on.

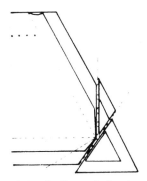

FIGURE 5–31. Grading and trimming a point.

UNDERSTITCHING

To secure edge facings inside a garment so they won't roll out and show, stitch the seam allowances to the facing on the underside. This is called *understitching*. Understitch only after you have fitted and altered the garment, stitched the facing in place, and trimmed and graded the seam. Open out the facing and all seam allowance layers; place these layers under the presser foot so your stitching line will be about ¹⁄₁₆ inch from the edge stitching line, on the facing side. *You will not be stitching on the outer fabric layer.* As you understitch, pull the facing and the seam allowances away from the garment.

After understitching, finger the facing to the inside of the garment and baste it down. You will notice that the edge seam automatically falls to the inside and causes the garment

Stitch the seam in the normal fashion. You may finish the edges separately at this point, or, after pressing both edges of the seam allowance to one side, finish the two edges together. Press the seam on the right side and, working from the right side, top-stitch through all three layers of cloth, ¼ to ⅜ inch from the seam line.

When you top-stitch identical seams on both sides of a garment, make sure you press the seam allowances of each in the same direction, in relationship to the body, both either toward the center of the body or both away from the center.

Double Top-Stitched Seam

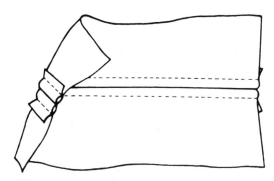

FIGURE 5–34. Double top-stitched seam.

The double top-stitched seam is purely decorative. Open the seam and press back the seam allowances. Top-stitch from the right side of the garment, on each side of and parallel to the seam line. Thread the top of the machine with silk twist thread for a particularly handsome top-stitching.

French Seam

A French seam is ideal for a very sheer fabric. It is actually a seam within a seam and is executed in two steps. The following directions assume a ⅝-inch seam allowance. First, place the *wrong*

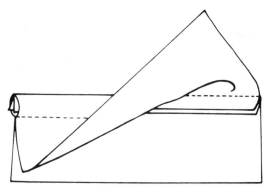

FIGURE 5–35. French seam.

sides of the fabric pieces together and stitch a seam ¼ inch from the edge. Trim about half the seam allowance away. Press the pieces open, both seam allowances going in the same direction. Now turn the right sides of the fabric together and press lightly, taking care that the fold line is smooth. Stitch a second seam ¼ inch from the folded edge, enclosing the original seam allowance. (¼-inch seam + ¼-inch seam + ⅛ inch for the fold = ⅝-inch seam allowance on all but very sheer fabrics.)

Flat-Felled Seam

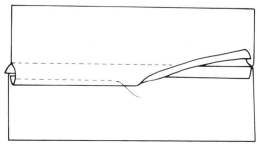

FIGURE 5–36. Flat-felled seam.

Many shirts and sports garments are made with flat-felled seams, which are both stout and decorative. Place the wrong sides of the fabric together and stitch the seam on the seam line.

The seam allowances will appear on the right side of the garment. Press both seam edges to one side. Trim the underneath edge. Fold the upper seam allowance under, enclosing the underneath seam allowance edge, and top-stitch close to the edge of the fold. Make sure that identical seams on both sides of a garment are flat felled in the same relationship to the body, either toward or away from the center. Flat-felled seams don't work well on steeply curved seams.

Basic Costume Construction Operations

1. Bias for facings, bindings, and covering cord
2. Continuous lap placket
3. Darts
4. Gathering
5. Gussets
6. Hook and eye tape
7. Point stitching
8. Scalloped, curved, and dagged edges
9. Setting in sleeves
10. Stitching knits
11. Stitching leather, suede, synthetic suede, and vinyl
12. Swing tacks
13. Trim
14. Waistbands
15. Zippers

Bias for Facings, Bindings, and Covering Cord

CUTTING BIAS STRIPS

To find the true bias of a fabric square, fold it diagonally so the lengthwise (warp) threads lie parallel to the crosswise (filling) threads. Crease or lightly press the fold and cut along the creased or folded line. You may also use a quilter's ruler to draw a line along the true bias. Determine the width of the bias strip you need, mark, and cut. (See Figure 5–37.) To join strips, place the right sides of the pieces together so the long edges of the strips match. One strip will be perpendicular to the other, and the pointed edges of the strips will protrude past the stitching line as shown in Figure 5–37. Stitch with a slightly shorter than normal stitch length and press the seam open.

If you need many yards of bias strips, use the tube cutting method. Begin with a rectangular piece of fabric. Fold it on the true bias at each corner, as shown in Figure 5–38. Using the fold as a guide, mark the desired width with a series of parallel lines, working from one fold to the other. Do not mark beyond the fold lines. Cut off and discard the triangular ends. Join the two shorter ends of the marked strip, which are on the straight grain, with one full bias width extending beyond each end of the tube. Stitch in place. Start cutting at either end of the tube and end up with one long, continuous bias strip.

BIAS YIELD CHART

The chart on page 203 will help calculate how much bias you can cut from given amounts of fabric. It is based on 1 yard of fabric in various

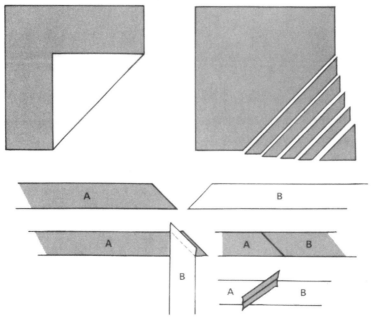

FIGURE 5–37. Cutting and joining bias strips.

FIGURE 5–38. Drawing, stitching, and cutting a continuous bias strip.

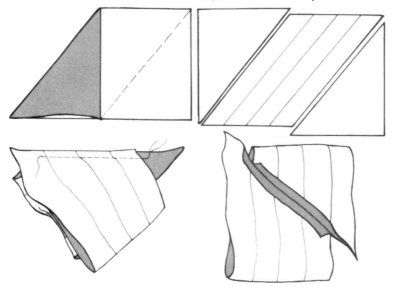

widths. Fabric widths run across the top of the chart and bias strip widths run down the left-hand side of the chart. Bias yield is given in yards.

Bias Strip	*Fabric Width*						
Width	*36"*	*39"*	*42"*	*45"*	*52"*	*54"*	*60"*
½"	62	68	74	80	92	96	108
¾"	38	41	44	48	56	59	68
1"	31	35	38	40	46	48	54
1¼"	26	27	29	31	37	39	45
1½"	21	22	24	26	31	32	35
1¾"	18	19	21	23	27	28	31
2"	16	17	18	20	23	24	27
2¼"	14	15	16	17	20	21	24
2½"	12	14	15	16	19	20	21
2¾"	11	12	14	14	17	17	19
3"	10	11	12	13	15	16	18

FINISHING WITH BIAS STRIPS

Costume garment edges that are not too deeply curved are often finished with bias strips used as facings. Use pieces of the garment fabric, or, if the garment fabric is too bulky to face with itself, use a lighter-weight fabric for the bias or commercially prepared bias tape.

Stitch the bias strip to the garment edge with the right sides of the garment and the bias strip facing. Trim the seam, clip or notch the seam allowance as necessary. Turn the bias facing to the inside, rolling the outer fabric over slightly to make sure the facing is inconspicuous. Understitching will give you an even sharper edge. Overlock the raw edge of the bias strip with a serger or turn the raw edge under and stitch the bias strip firmly in place. Do not use a bias facing on a deeply curved edge, such as a scooped neckline, where a shaped facing is needed to properly stabilize the curve.

BIAS BINDING AND COVERED CORDED EDGES

A bound or corded edge is often added to a costume for a decorative effect. Begin by cutting and assembling a bias strip that is approximately 2½ inches wide.

To bind the edge, stitch the bias strip to the garment edge, right sides facing. Trim and press the seam toward the bias. Fold the binding over until it is the correct width and tuck in the unfinished edge, trimming if necessary, and enclosing all the seam allowance. Stitch the binding in place by hand or by machine. Be careful not to stretch the binding as you turn it or you will cause wrinkles and a rippled edge.

For a corded edge, place a piece of cotton cord on the wrong side of the bias strip and fold the strip in half lengthwise, enclosing

FIGURE 5–39. Cording covered with bias strip.

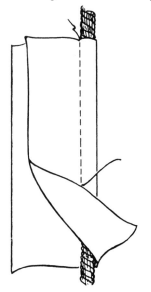

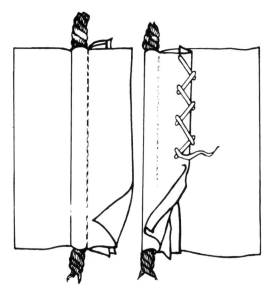

FIGURE 5–40. Applying cord to garment edge.

per foot and stitch about ⅛ inch from the cord. (If you stitch too close to the cord, you won't have room inside the tube to turn it.) To help prevent the stitches from breaking when turning the bias tube, either stitch with narrow zigzag or stretch the fabric gently. When you have finished stitching, one half of the cord will be covered. At the end of the bias tube, between the covered and the uncovered halves of the cord, stitch the fabric firmly to the cord. Trim the seam allowance to about ⅛ inch. Carefully work the bias tube back over the exposed cord, pulling out the cord that was in-

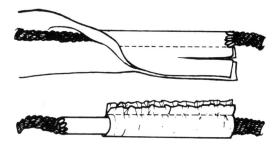

FIGURE 5–41. Cording covered with bias strip.

the cord. Using your sewing machine zipper foot, stitch through both layers of fabric, close to the cord. Lay the corded strip on the right side of the garment with all seam allowances going in the same direction. Stitch the strip to the garment along the same stitching line that you made to enclose the cord. Turn the seam allowances to the inside so the covered cord is on the garment edge. Trim the seam allowance of the garment and the bottom layer of the bias, close to the garment edge; clip or notch as necessary. Turn the raw edge of the remaining bias seam allowance under and stitch it down with a slip stitch, cross stitch, or machine stitch.

COVERED TUBULAR CORDING

The first step in constructing covered tubular cording is to cut a true bias strip three times the width of the cord, plus 1 inch. Choose a piece of cord that's *twice the length* of the piece of covered cord needed. Fold the bias strip with *right sides facing,* and insert the cord up against the fold. Use the sewing machine zip-

side the tube. Be careful not to twist the bias. Snip off the extra cord.

Use tubular cording for spaghetti straps, for braided belts, for trim appliques, and for making frogs. Another popular use for tubular cording or for plain bias tubing without a cord is to make button loops for ball-shaped buttons. Plan your garment with a separate facing and stitch button loops on before applying the facing. Determine the size of each loop and the spacing between them and mark your fabric. Place the loops on the right side of the garment, *facing away from the seam allowance.* Baste them in place, because pins are too apt to slip, and apply the facing, stitching the loops down at the same time. Turn the facing to the inside. The button loops will extend from the garment edge.

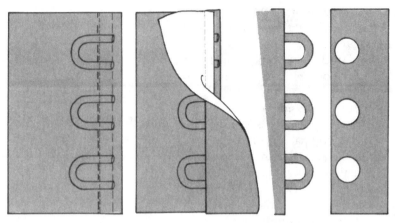

FIGURE 5–42. Button loops.

Continuous Lap Placket

A continuous lap placket or bound slash is a quick and relatively easy way to finish an opening in a sleeve, skirt, or neck edge, where no seam exists.

Cut the fabric to the desired depth. For the binding, cut a strip of garment fabric on the lengthwise grain, 1 inch to 1¾ inches wide (wider for heavyweight fabrics), twice as long as the opening, plus 1 inch. Open up the cut edges and place the right side of the strip against the wrong side of the garment, allowing an extra ½ inch of strip to extend at each end. Pin the strip in place or hold it firmly with your fingers. With the garment side up, machine stitch about ¼ inch from the edge. At the beginning, the two edges will be aligned; as you approach the point of the cut, the garment edge will have angled away from the edge of the strip, as shown in Figure 5–43.

FIGURE 5–43. Continuous lap.

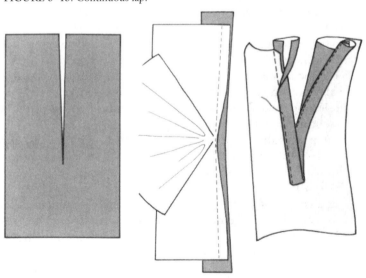

When you reach the point of the slash, put the needle into the fabric, raise the presser foot, make sure both layers of fabric are smooth, lower the pressure foot, and stitch up the other side of the slash, ending with both fabric edges once again aligned.

Fold the strip to the outside of the garment, turn the raw edge under, and stitch the strip in place over the original stitching line. The cut edges are now completely enclosed.

When attaching the cuff, waistband, collar, or facing, one-half of the continuous lap placket will form the underlap, and the other, folded back inside the garment, will form the overlap.

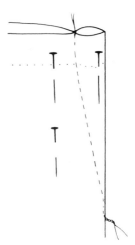

FIGURE 5–44. Plain dart.

Darts

Darts help shape fabric fullness over the bust, hips, shoulders, and elbows. Most darts occur in pairs, and it is important to stitch paired darts exactly the same so as not to end up with a lopsided garment.

When transferring dart markings from the paper pattern to the fabric, make sure you trace them accurately and include the dart center line. Some people like to draw a short line, perpendicular to the dart center line, that marks where the dart ends.

Fold the dart on the center line and secure the two layers of fabric with straight pins. Place one pin close to the fold line, inside the body of the dart, and two or three others to the left of the dart-stitching line, leaving room for the machine presser foot, as shown in Figure 5–44.

Stitch from the top or wide part of the dart to the point. Follow the stitching line carefully. When you reach the dart point, end by taking two or three stitches, close to the fold, then by running a couple of stitches off the fabric. Do not backstitch a dart point or you will create a lump. If the fabric is thick or springy, tie the two threads at the dart point to lock the stitching line.

Always press darts on a tailor's ham or on another curved surface. The ideal way to press a dart is in three steps. First, remove the pins and press the dart just as you've stitched it, right sides together. This will help "set" the stitches in the fabric. Then, from the wrong side of the fabric, press the dart to one side. Most body darts go toward the center and elbow darts go down. Finally, turn the fabric to the right side and lightly press again, still using the curved surface. If there's a chance that the dart will leave an impression on the outer fabric, such as with wool gabardine, slip a piece of brown paper between the dart and the outer layer before pressing. If the dart is particularly wide or bulky, split it down the center, open it out, and press both sides.

Contour darts or fish darts (see Figure 5–45) usually occur at the waistline and taper in two directions: up toward the bust and down toward the hips. Stitch contour darts in two operations, beginning each time at the waistline and stitching out to each point.

Before you press a contour dart, clip it at its widest point to within ⅛ inch of the stitching line. The dart will open up to give shape to

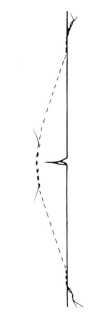

FIGURE 5–45. Contour dart.

the garment and flatten out for pressing. If the dart is bulky, clip it, and press it open.

Sometimes the darted area of your garment includes interfacing, such as in tailored jackets or bodices. Traditionally, to reduce excess bulk, interfacing darts are butted rather than folded. Cut the dart section out of the interfacing, pull the two edges of the interfacing together, and sew them together with a wide zigzag stitch.

Gathering

Gathering fabric is one of the most frequently done sewing operations in a busy costume shop, and it can take up a lot of time. The traditional method of gathering is to run three parallel lines of long stitches within the seam allowance and then pull up the threads. This method produces dense, even gathers, but it takes a long time *and* threads often break along the way.

To speed up the process, some stitchers wind heavy-duty thread on their machine bobbins, run one or two rows of long stitches within the seam allowance, and pull up the strong, heavy-duty thread. Unfortunately, most domestic sewing machines, and some industrials, don't make balanced stitches when there is heavy-duty thread on the bobbin. And, when using heavy-duty thread on the bobbin, you run the danger of damaging the tension spring on the bobbin casing.

A better alternative to the above is to secure a piece of heavy-duty thread at one end of the fabric you are gathering, then zigzag over it. Pull up the heavy-duty thread to gather the fabric.

An even more efficient way to gather (because you don't even have to get up from the machine to find a spool of heavy-duty thread!) is to pull the top and bottom threads on the sewing machine toward you until they are the length of the piece you need to gather. Then, zigzag over these two threads and use them to pull up the gathers. If the gathering doesn't begin at a fabric edge, bring both threads to the top of the fabric before you pull them toward you. You can control the fineness of the gathering by the length of the zigzag stitch; a shorter stitch will give you finer gathering.

PLEATER AND SHIRRING FOOT

When you have a large quantity of ruffles to gather, a sewing machine attachment known as a pleater or ruffler is a real time saver. Pleaters are available for both domestic and industrial sewing machines. The pleater operates by pushing small pleats into the fabric just before it moves under the needle. You can set the pleater for several different fullnesses. The tightest setting produces a fullness that is approximately three to one.

The shirring foot is slim and rectangular and has a hole in it. It is available for both domestic and industrial machines and produces

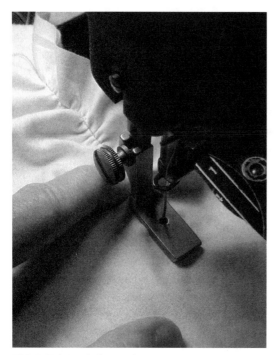

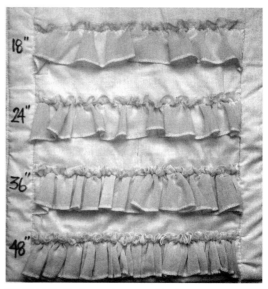

FIGURE 5–47. Cotton batiste ruffle chart. *Photograph by Liz Covey.*

FIGURE 5–46. A shirring foot in action. *Photograph by Liz Covey.*

soft gathers on light- and mediumweight fabrics. You can control the fullness of the gathering stitch both by tightening the upper thread tension on the sewing machine and by pressing your finger firmly on the fabric, directly behind the foot, as you stitch. The shirring foot is particularly good for gentle, consistent gathers.

A GATHERING FULLNESS CHART

"How full do you want that ruffle to be?" is one of the questions cutter/drapers often ask costume designers when they're examining sketches. Since this isn't an easy question to answer with words, some costume shop supervisors have found it helpful to prepare a chart of gathering samples, using two or three different fabric weights.

The charts in Figures 5–47, 5–48, and 5–49 were created with three fabrics: cotton batiste, cotton broadcloth, and cotton sateen.

Each sample began as 3-inch wide strips, serged on both long edges. The first example is 18 inches of fabric gathered into 1 foot; the second is 2 feet of fabric gathered into 1 foot; the third is 3 feet of fabric gathered into 1 foot; and the fourth is 4 feet of fabric gathered into 1 foot.

With this chart of examples to look at, it becomes a relatively easy matter for a designer to choose among them. (This is not to suggest that changes in the amount of fullness won't occur along the way, but the chart does help technicians and designers know where to begin.)

Gussets

A gusset is a piece of fabric added to the underarm part of a sleeve to provide extra movement room for the arm. Different kinds of sleeves require different kinds of gussets.

The simplest gusset is the one added to a relatively close-fitted, T-shaped garment. See

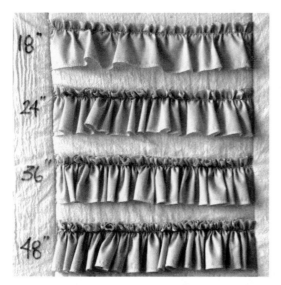

FIGURE 5–48. Cotton broadcloth ruffle chart. *Photograph by Liz Covey.*

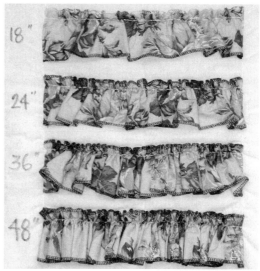

FIGURE 5–49. Cotton sateen ruffle chart. *Photograph by Liz Covey.*

Figure 5–50 for an example. Cut two triangular pieces so that the long side of the triangle is on the true bias. Stitch the cross grain side of one gusset piece to the front of sleeve, then stitch the other gusset piece to the back of the sleeve. With the body of the garment and the sleeve lying open, right sides facing, stitch the sleeve and the gussets to the body. Fold the sleeve and the body together at the shoulder, right sides facing, and stitch the underarm seam from the bottom of the garment to the wrist.

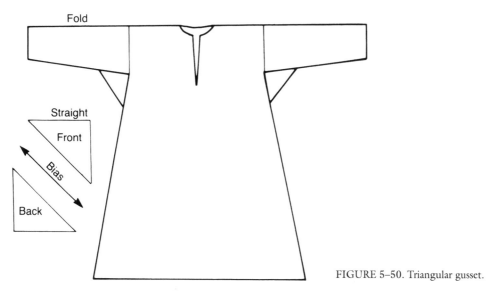

FIGURE 5–50. Triangular gusset.

209

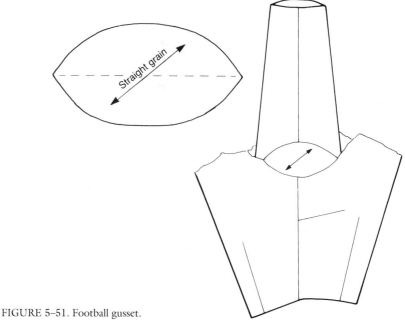

FIGURE 5–51. Football gusset.

The trickiest gusset is one added to the underarm of an already constructed costume with tight, set-in sleeves that are restricting the actor's movement. The problem is to create a gusset that gives the actor enough room to move but doesn't look ugly. Hopefully, you have pieces of the original fabric for the gussets; if not, match the fabric as closely as possible. Shape the gusset like a football with the points extending from front to back balance points in the armhole. (See page 139 in Chapter 4, "Pattern Development," for a discussion of sleeve balance points.) Be careful to measure accurately when the costume is on the actor and don't cut the gusset too short. The gusset may be from 2 to 4 inches wide at the widest point, width depending upon the size of the actor and the amount of room needed. Position the straight grain of the gusset fabric as indicated in Figure 5–51; notice that this positioning allows fabric bias to increase the amount of stretch at the underarm.

Be aware that this gusset works best with a sleeve that has a high, full cap and is set into an armhole seam that is well up on the shoulder and does not extend out over the top of the arm. If the shoulder seam extends too far out on the arm, there will be pulling between the balance point where the gusset begins and the top of the arm, sometimes creating as big a problem as the one you set out to solve.

If you can find a satisfactory fabric match, consider creating this sort of gusset from a knit fabric. You will get more stretch and much less bagging.

If you know in advance that you are going to have to add gussets to a costume, you can cut a gusset as part of the sleeve. See Figure 5–52 for an example. The gusset begins at the sleeve balance point. Notice that the underarm edges of the sleeve are extended so it will fit into the armhole of the garment.

A "circle" gusset in a dancer's costume helps permit the dancer to have a complete

210

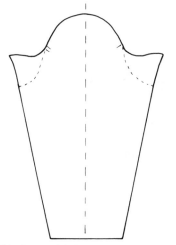

FIGURE 5–52. Gusset added to one-piece sleeve pattern.

(which is really shaped more like a very fat football) is to have the dancer put on the costume (or, better still, the costume mock-up), release the underarm seam from balance point to balance point, and then have the dancer put his or her arm up and over the head. The amount of underarm exposed equals the size of the gusset required. Keep the circle gusset as circular as possible for maximum room; you will have to taper it slightly at each end in order to fit it into the armhole seam. Position the fabric so that the true bias allows for maximum stretch when the arm is raised. When the dancer's arm is down, the circle gusset forms a pouch of fabric under the arm. If you can use a knit fabric, the pouch will be smaller.

range of arm movements. It works best when the bodice, doublet, or other upper body garment is cut with high, tight armholes and a snug sleeve, preferably cut on the bias. The best way to determine the size of the "circle"

Hook and Eye Tape

Hook and eye tape is a great time saver. Here is one method of putting it in that creates a strong, flat, and completely concealed closing.

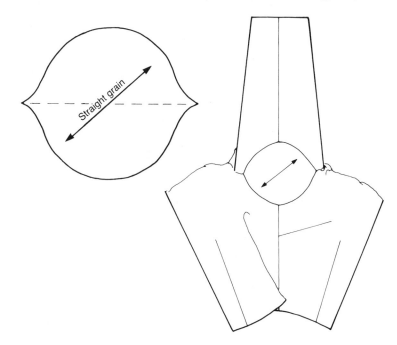

FIGURE 5–53. Circular gusset.

211

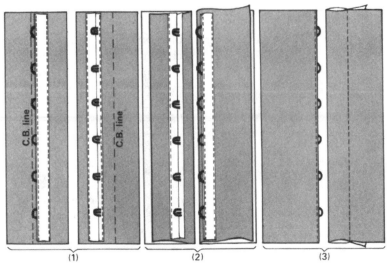

FIGURE 5–54. Setting hook and eye tape.

Cut both sides of the garment opening with a 2½-inch wide self-facing and be sure to mark the center, or closing, lines on each piece. On the overlap side of the opening, mark a fold line ½ inch from the center line, on the facing side.

Place the eye portion of the tape on the underlap side, with the eyes lying on the center line, facing away from the edge of the fabric. Stitch each side of the tape to the facing, then turn the facing and tape to the inside. Top-stitch close to the folded edge.

Matching up the hooks and eyes carefully, stitch the hook portion of the tape to the right self-facing, with the hooks facing up and away from the edge of the fabric, 1 inch from the center line. (See the first illustration in Figure 5–54.) Turn the overlap facing back on the fold line. The hooks should lie directly under the center line. Machine stitch the overlap facing down through all layers or, if you want a less obvious stitching line, use a row of prick stitches that are very close together and be sure to go through all the layers.

When you fasten the hook and eye tape, notice that the center lines of both sides have

FIGURE 5–55. Details on the wedding dress for a production of *Our Town* at the Cincinnati Playhouse in the Park, designed by Liz Covey. Decorative buttons cover a hook and eye fastening down the center back. *Costume draped and photographed by Mark Kabbes.*

come together and the overlap extends ½ inch over the closing, concealing it completely.

You may want to add 1-inch-wide placket on the underlap side of the closing to provide a cushion between the actor's body and the hooks and eyes.

Point Stitching

GUSSETS AND DECORATIVE DETAILS

When you insert godets and certain decorative details, you often have to stitch a pointed edge into a V-shaped edge. (See Figure 5–56.) The manner of stitching is similar to stitching a continuous lap placket, except that the seam allowance must remain constant on both pieces. (See page 205.)

FIGURE 5–56. Stitching a point: godet or decorative detail.

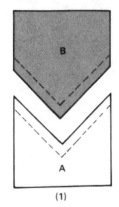

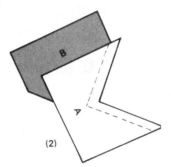

Mark the seam allowances carefully, as shown in the illustration. Lay the pieces with right sides together and stitch from one outside edge to the point. On the V-shaped side, clip the seam allowance almost to the stitching line. Pivot the piece, line up the remaining side of the seam, and continue stitching from the point to the other edge. Do not press the seam open; instead, press both seam allowances up. Top-stitch if the design requires it.

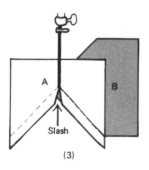

(3)

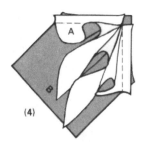

(4)

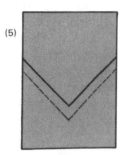

(5)

TURNED POINTS

There are turned points on collars, cuffs, belts, pocket flaps, tabs, and so on. All of these costume details deserve neat, flat points, and, in instances where there are two matching points, such as the two edges of a collar, the points should indeed match. Handsome turned points result from a combination of accurate stitching, careful trimming, and proper pressing.

When assembling an ordinary pointed collar such as a shirt collar, stitch the outside edge in two operations, beginning each time at the center back. This will prevent one side of the collar from stretching out more than the other. As you come to within 1 inch of the collar point, shorten the machine stitch by a couple of increments. Make sure the needle hits the stitching line right at the point, and stays in the fabric while you lift the presser foot and pivot the collar. Continue stitching with short stitches for 1 inch, then change back to a regular length for the remainder of the seam. These shorter stitches will help prevent raveling when you trim the seam close to the stitching line.

After the collar is assembled and trimmed, use the point presser to open the seam on all three sides. Make sure you get all the way up into the point. Then, put your thumbnail firmly into the point, on the wrong side, and turn it right side out. Using a needle threaded double with heavy-duty thread, take a stitch directly into the point on the right side and pull on the threads to bring the point completely out. (How many of you have poked the end of your scissors right through a point?) Press the collar over a curved surface, rolling the edge seam slightly to the inside. Use lots of steam and allow the collar to cool and dry before removing it.

Refer to these general directions for any kind of turned point you may be stitching.

Scalloped, Curved, and Dagged Edges

Many costume hems, sleeve edges, collars, and hats have decorative edges. Some may be as simple as enlarged scallops while others may be extremely intricate and fanciful. The process for finishing this sort of edge is the same, no matter how complex the design.

The first step is to translate the garment edge from the design, determining how deep and how wide the projections are, and how many individual projections each edge can contain. Draw a brown paper or light card-

FIGURE 5–57. Susan Shunk in cartridge pleated skirt and paned sleeves as Desdemona in the Utah Shakespearean Festival production of *Othello*. The design by Bill Black draws inspiration from nineteenth century stage costume. *Photograph by Karl Hugh, courtesy of the Utah Shakespearean Festival.*

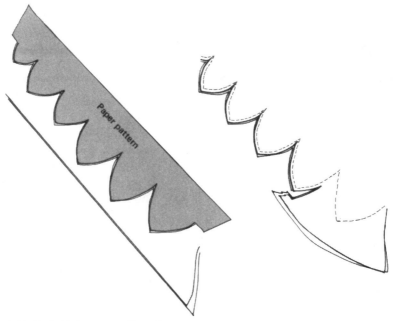

FIGURE 5–58. Facing a scalloped hem.

board pattern. If the pattern is simple and regular, you will only need a few repeats. If the projections are complicated and irregular, such as in a hanging sleeve that has gradually enlarging shapes running from wrist to floor, you will have to pattern the entire sleeve edge. Check your pattern with a mock-up and make sure the designer okays the shape and the scale.

Using the paper pattern, corrected if necessary, cut all layers: garment fabric, interfacing, facing.

Pin the layers together, right sides facing, and stitch around the projections, using a slightly shorter than normal stitch. Trim the seam allowance to ¼ inch or ⅛ inch; notch, clip, and trim points as necessary. Turn the fabrics back on themselves and work out the edges carefully, gently smoothing and rolling them until they lie flat. Press the edges over a curved surface.

Setting in Sleeves

Hanging a sleeve accurately in an armhole is not a difficult task. You will need match-up marks for the top of the shoulder and the underarm point, both on the body of the garment and on the sleeve. Transfer these marks from the pattern to the mock-up fabric, adjust them if necessary in the mock-up fitting, then transfer them to the actual garment pieces. Always mark the top of the shoulder on both sides of a garment since it may fall at a slightly different place on each.

PLAIN SLEEVES

A plain sleeve is one that does not have any obvious gathering across the cap once it's in place. The actual top curve of the sleeve, however, is about 1½ inches larger than the top curve of the armhole. The extra fabric in the

215

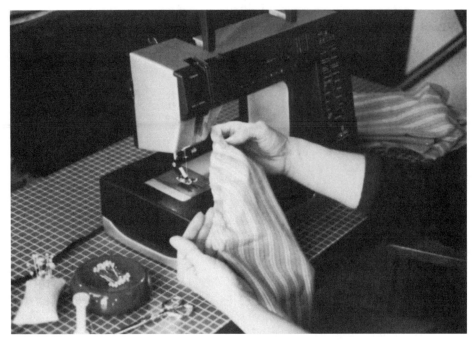

FIGURE 5–59. Turn the sleeve right side out. *Photograph by Richard Ingham.*

sleeve creates the cap that fits over the top of the shoulder and permits the upper arm to move. The underarm part of the sleeve and the underarm part of the garment body should be the same length.

Assemble the sleeve and either run a row of gathering across the top of the cap (see page 207 for gathering instructions), or ease the cap by stitching around it while you hold the fabric with your finger behind the presser foot.

Turn the sleeve right side out. Turn the garment to the inside with the armhole facing you. Make sure you are putting the sleeve into the correct side of the garment. Bring the sleeve up into the armhole, with the right sides of the fabric facing; pin the top of the sleeve to the top of the shoulder, from the inside. Match and pin the underarm points, also from the inside. Grasp the sleeve and the garment armhole and turn the armhole back

on itself, away from you, so the sleeve is curving around the armhole. (See Figure 5–60.) This position will allow you to distribute the sleeve cap fullness evenly. The underarm curves should fit smoothly together, without gathering or stretching. There should be fullness but no gathers around the sleeve cap. Pin on the seam line in the direction you will be stitching. When the sleeve is securely pinned into the armhole, return the armhole to its original position. Stitch from the inside of the armhole (garment layer on the bottom, sleeve layer on the top), beginning at the balance point above the underarm and stitching from underarm up to and around the sleeve cap, removing the pins as you go. If this is a final stitching operation, continue to stitch around the underarm a second time so this vulnerable area will be double-stitched.

216

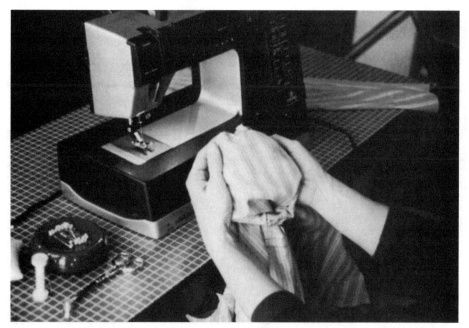

FIGURE 5–60. Grasp the sleeve and the garment armhole and turn the armhole back on itself, away from you, so the sleeve is curving around the armhole. *Photograph by Richard Ingham.*

FIGURE 5–61. Pin on the seam line, in the direction you will be stitching.
Photograph by Richard Ingham.

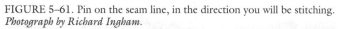

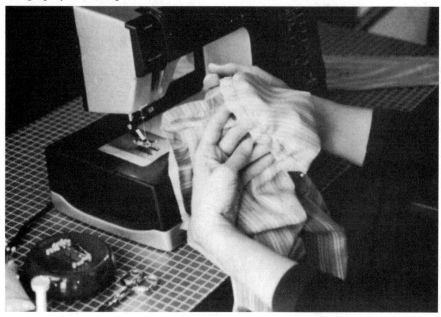

FIGURE 5–62. Stitch from the inside of the armhole (garment layer on the bottom, sleeve layer on the top). *Photograph by Richard Ingham.*

FIGURE 5–63. The set-in sleeve. *Photograph by Richard Ingham.*

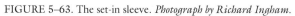

GATHERED OR PLEATED SLEEVES

The only difference between putting in a gathered or pleated sleeve and a plain sleeve is dealing with the fullness in the sleeve cap. Pull up the gathers or fold in the pleats before placing the sleeve in the armhole. Match up top of shoulder and underarm points, and pin in place. Turn the armhole back on itself, as described, and pin the underarm area. There should not be any fullness in the underarm part of the sleeve. Adjust the gathers, or pleats, across the top of the armhole, pulling them up tighter if necessary, making sure they are evenly distributed. Pin in place and stitch.

IMPORTANT SLEEVE NOTE

The most important thing to remember about setting a sleeve accurately in an armhole is that the *top of the sleeve cap* (which is, in most sleeves, on the straight grain) be aligned with the *top, or highest point, of the actor's shoulder.* Because human bodies are so different from each other, the point in the armhole from which the top of the sleeve cap should hang *will not necessarily be on the shoulder seam.* More often than not, the top of the sleeve will fall about ½ inch behind the shoulder seam, although sometimes, on a person who has extremely erect posture, the top of the sleeve will fall to the front of the shoulder seam. If it is important to the design that the top of the sleeve and the shoulder seam line up, alter the position of the shoulder seam. If the top of the sleeve cap is not falling directly from the top of the actor's shoulder, it will cause wrinkles to appear across the front of the garment; in extreme cases the sleeve will look like it's twisted in the armhole.

If you have trouble figuring out exactly where the top of the actor's armhole is (and it is often difficult to find on a man or woman with well-developed upper arm muscles), tie a pair of scissors onto the end of a piece of ribbon or twill tape. Ask the actor to let both arms hang naturally and place the end of the tape on his or her shoulder. Move the end of the tape backward and forward, ¼ an inch at a time, until the length of the tape drops straight down the actor's upper arm, from shoulder to elbow. Mark where the shoulder end of the tape is; that's the top of the actor's shoulder and the exact place from which the sleeve must fall to hang accurately. Don't forget that, on many people, the top of shoulder point is different on each shoulder.

Stitching Knits

Knit fabrics stretch. Ordinary straight sewing machine stitches do not stretch. And, as you know, if you stitch a knit shirt with a straight stitch, chances are some of those stitches will break when you put the shirt on. The main problem with sewing knit fabrics is to find a machine stitch that allows the fabric to stretch but doesn't cause unwanted stretching.

Four-thread and five-thread sergers will stitch knit fabrics together and overcast the seam at the same time. Seams stitched with a four-thread model are not as strong as those stitched with a five-thread.

However, most serged seams are not as tight and strong as some costumes require, particularly dance costumes. The strongest knit seams are made with a trimotion sewing machine knit stitch, a stitch that goes two stitches forward and one back, to allow for a moderate amount of stretch in the seam. Most automatic-stitch domestic machines include some form of this stitch in their repertoire.

You can also stitch knit fabrics together with a zigzag stitch set on a very narrow width so it looks like a wavy straight stitch. The "waves" allow for stretch.

If all you have available is a straight-stitch machine, loosen the top tension and the presser foot pressure slightly, shorten the stitch, and stretch the fabric *very slightly* as it goes under the presser foot. The short, loose stitch will allow for some stretch and your stretching will allow for more.

Always, before you begin to stitch knit garment pieces together, make test seams on scraps of the fabric.

MISCELLANEOUS TIPS FOR KNIT STITCHING

Long staple polyester thread has more inherent stretch than mercerized cotton thread and is somewhat preferable for stitching most knit fabrics.

When stitching knit fabrics, wind the bobbin on a very low speed so the thread will not stretch. Stretched bobbin thread is a major cause of puckered seams in all types of fabric.

Since the slightest defect in a needle can cause problems in a knit seam, put a new needle in the machine whenever you begin stitching a knit fabric costume. A machine needle with a universal point is fine for cotton and rayon knits; use a stretch knit, or ballpoint, needle for knit fabrics that contain nylon, polyester, or acrylic fibers. If you have trouble with skipped stitches along the seam line, change to a larger size needle and/or wipe the needle off with a needle lubricant.

Some knit fabrics tend to be heavy. Make sure the weight of the fabric is not stretching the seam you're sewing. Support the fabric on a wide table or over a chair and stop stitching every so often to rearrange the fabric.

If the edge of the knit fabric you're working with tends to roll in, spray it with fabric sizing and press, taking care not to move the iron around.

Most knits do not ravel. Consider the necessity of seam finishes and be particularly careful not to apply a bulky seam finish that may show on the outside of the costume.

If you need a crisp, sturdy edge on a knit garment, use a nonfusible, woven interfacing; for a softer edge, use a fusible knit interfacing. Stabilize zipper stitching lines, shoulder seams, armholes, and so on, with seam tape or twill tape.

Although it sounds silly, if you top-stitch a knit garment with a long, narrow zigzag stitch, it will look straighter than if you use a straight stitch.

Stitching Leather, Suede, Synthetic Suede, and Vinyl

LEATHER

You can stitch light- and mediumweight leather pieces on most domestic sewing machines; for heavyweight leathers, you will need an industrial machine or even a walking foot machine specifically designed to stitch leather.

An important thing to remember when stitching leather is to stitch as little as possible. Unlike either woven or knit fabrics, the hole a sewing machine needle makes in leather does not "fill in." As an example, take a scrap piece of leather and make a line of stitches. Stitch over the same line a second time. Notice that all the holes you made are still there; notice also that you may be able to tear the leather apart into two pieces along the line where the holes act as perforations. Needless to say, it is important to make accurate mock-ups of leather garments so you won't have to do much altering of leather seams.

When you stitch leather, set your stitch length a bit longer than normal. Universal point needles are suitable for stitching most leathers, although, for some heavier leathers, you may need machine needles specially made for sewing leather.

Cotton thread is not a good choice for sewing leather because the tannin in the leather may cause the thread to rot. Some leather workers recommend nylon thread and some recommend top-stitching weight, long staple polyester thread. Experiment and find out which works best for you.

Lapped seams (laying one edge of a piece over the edge of another piece and top-stitching) work better on leather than conventional seams.

If using a conventional seam, do not try to press open the seam allowances because they will not stay pressed. After the garment has been fitted, glue the seam allowances down. (All leather glues are toxic. Check the MSDS on the brand and kind of glue you are using and take all necessary precautions, including proper ventilation, gloves, and a respirator.)

"Baste" or "pin" leather seams together with dots of rubber cement that will hold the seam in place while you stitch it and which you can roll off later.

All leathers stretch, some quite a lot. To help control the stretching, lighten the pressure on the presser foot and/or use a roller foot on the machine or a foot with a Teflon bottom. If stitching leather to fabric, sew with the fabric side up.

SUEDE AND SYNTHETIC SUEDE

Never use leather needles to stitch suede or synthetic suede because they have sharp edges that will cut the material. Use a small universal point needle and a normal stitch length. Sew a test seam before you begin the garment, then hold the seam up to a light and check to make sure the holes made by the needle are barely visible. If the holes are too big and too close together, the material may tear along the stitching line.

Conventional seams are satisfactory in both suede and synthetic suede garments. You cannot, however, press the seams open and expect them to stay. Top-stitch suede and synthetic suede seams if the design allows for it. If not, use leather glue to fasten down suede seam allowances and a fusible fabric web, such as Stitch Witchery, for synthetic suede seam allowances. Lapped seams are preferable for suede and synthetic suede garments because they are stronger and less bulky, but they are not suitable for all types of costumes.

Use long staple polyester thread to stitch suede and synthetic suede.

Never press suede, especially with steam.

Always use a press cloth when pressing synthetic suede because it will pick up a shine from the iron and *always* use steam.

If you have trouble with skipped stitches when stitching synthetic suede, wash the material before sewing it. In general, synthetic suede is easier to handle after it has been washed.

HEMS IN LEATHER, SUEDE, AND SYNTHETIC SUEDE

Hems in leather, suede, and synthetic suede garments of all weights are usually either top-stitched or fastened down with glue or fusible fabric web. Make sure the seam allowance is not so wide that the hem will be bulky and wrinkled. For a top-stitched hem, use top-stitch-weight thread and a long machine stitch. Use leather glue for leather and suede hems and fusible web for synthetic suede.

Most leather glues are contact adhesives. That means you have to coat both sides of the materials being glued together, wait until the glue is *almost dry,* then press the pieces together. For the most secure bond, pound the layers together with a wooden or rubber mallet or with a conventional hammer whose head has been padded with several layers of thick fabric.

Be cautious when gluing lightweight leathers and suede because some glues will make these materials quite stiff. Experiment with different bonding agents and always run a test before you go to work on the actual costume. And don't forget to take proper safety precautions when using all leather adhesives.

VINYL

Vinyl is a particularly troublesome material to stitch because machine presser feet tend to drag on its surface, causing wrinkles and puckers. Use a rolling foot or a Teflon foot on the machine if either one is available. If you still have trouble with the fabric scrunching up, run a thin line of light machine oil in front of the presser foot as you sew, using the smallest possible squeeze bottle or needle-point oiling device. The oil will allow the presser foot to slide smoothly over the vinyl surface. Wipe the oil off after you've stitched the seam.

Swing Tacks

Swing tacks are used to hold two layers of fabric loosely together while leaving some room for movement. There are many practical uses for swing tacks: fastening linings to hems, overskirts to underskirts, wide collars to shoulders, wide cuffs to sleeves.

Use silk twist, top-stitch–weight thread, or button thread, doubled for strength. Stitch four or five times from one layer to the other, as shown in Figure 5–64, leaving thread lengths of approximately ½ to 1 inch between

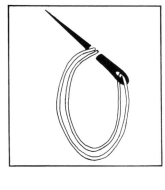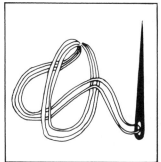

FIGURE 5–64. Swing tack with blanket stitch.

FIGURE 5–65. How to make a chained swing tack.

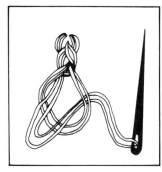

the two layers. Starting at one end of the threads, make a row of blanket or buttonhole stitches running the length of the threads to serve as reinforcement.

You can also make swing tacks with a chain stitch that you can form from thread, as shown in Figure 5–65, or from a length of serger "chain." Simply stitch the ends of the chains to each layer of fabric. However, swing tacks made from thread chains are never as strong as those shown in Figure 5–64.

Trim

Whenever it's possible to do so, work out trim placement early in the construction process so you can apply trim by machine, before the gar-

ment is lined or faced. If you have to wait until the garment is finished to place and apply trim, the work will probably have to be done by hand and will take more time. However, it's often difficult for designers to see exactly where the trim should go until after the garment is well along and they can judge its proportions accurately. In the long run, it's safer to wait until you are sure about where the trim is going before stitching it on. Removing and repositioning misplaced trim is one of the most time-consuming jobs of all.

Border trims such as braids and ribbons can almost always be machine stitched. Apply

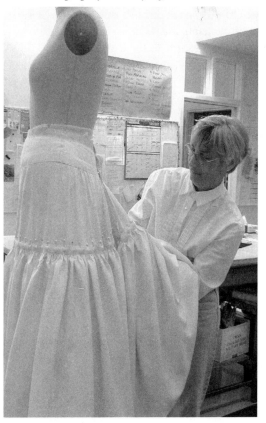

FIGURE 5–67. Cutter/draper Vivienne Friedman carefully pinning ruffles at the Oregon Shakespeare Festival. *Photograph by Rosemary Ingham.*

FIGURE 5–66. Roxanne Raja as Lily Bart in the American Conservatory Theater production of *The House of Mirth.* Fullness in the sleeves and skirt is controlled by rows of gauging. *Costume design by Anna Oliver. Photograph courtesy of the American Conservatory Theater.*

them just before the facings are attached. If the border trim is stitched on *after* the facings and linings are in place, you run the risk of having lumpy, wrinkled edges; in some cases the edge will be so thick the sewing machine will not be able to stitch through all the layers. For most border trims, use a fairly long, straight machine stitch, although some sorts will lie smoother if a zigzag stitch is used. Many border trims stretch as you stitch; pin carefully, running the pins in the same direction as the stitching line, and stop often to rearrange the garment edge and the trim. A lighter pressure on the presser foot may help control stretching.

Many appliqués, sequins, and beads have to be hand stitched. Be careful to place the trim pieces accurately and secure them with pins or hand basting. Some trims are easier to apply when the costume is on a tailor's form. Use an invisible hand stitch and strong, waxed thread. Be sure to secure all the thread ends and finish off with a drop of Fray-Check.

When you have a large, flat appliqué to apply to a costume, it's very helpful to use a fusible web to hold it in place while you stitch; otherwise, the edges of the appliqué will tend

to "creep" as you sew. You can purchase fusible web with a paper backing, iron it onto the underside of your appliqué fabric *before* you cut out the appliqué, then cut out the design and fuse it to the garment piece with a steam iron. After the appliqué is fused in place, you can stitch around it quickly and easily, with no "creeping." *Note*: You must always secure the appliqué with stitching; none of the fusible webs, or the fusible coatings that are found on the backs of some appliqués, will withstand repeated washings or dry cleanings.

Waistbands

Make sure your waistbands are adequately stiffened so they will support the skirts you hang from them. Use a good waistband interfacing that will not crumple and collapse as it's worn, washed, and/or dry cleaned.

For some reason, there is a great tendency for costume technicians to make waistbands too small. This problem probably begins because the original waist measurement was taken too snugly and is compounded by not

FIGURE 5–68. Waistband: two skirt layers attached to petersham belting.

leaving sufficient room for seam allowance layers and interfacings. Always cut waistbands 3 inches longer than the waist measure. This should leave sufficient room for seaming and for a comfortable overlap.

Waistbands that are more than 2 inches wide, finished, should be cut in such a way as to reflect the shape of the body.

When attaching a very heavy skirt to a waistband—and the waistband will be covered by another garment, such as a period bodice—consider setting the skirt flat on a sturdy waistband made from something like petersham belting. (See Figure 5–68.) Simply zigzag the skirt to the band, using two rows of stitching to flatten the gathers. If putting two or more layers of skirts on a single waistband, apply one below the other to reduce the bulk. If your favorite belting is too narrow to support two skirt layers (petersham belting is sometimes only available in a 1-inch width) simply stitch two pieces together with a small overlap and a zigzag stitch.

Zippers

In general, choose metal and heavy plastic zippers for costumes; they are the strongest and the least apt to pull apart. If the zipper must be very lightweight, choose one with nylon, rather than polyester, teeth.

Purchase zippers in quantity whenever possible. There is a shockingly large markup on individual zippers in cardboard packets. Buy long zippers, rather than short ones, since you can always cut the long ones to a shorter length. You may want to stock continuous zipper tape, stops, and pulls, from which you can assemble custom zippers.

SLOT (CENTERED) ZIPPER

The slot zipper usually goes into a center front or a center back seam. Decide how long the zipper needs to be and stitch the garment seam up to the bottom of the zipper. Press the seam open and press back the seam allowances along the opening where the zipper will go.

Choose a zipper at least 1 inch longer than the zipper opening and place it so the zipper pull is above the edge of the garment, as shown in Figure 5–69, page 226. With the zipper closed and the right side of the fabric up, pin or baste the zipper in place, working from bottom to top on each side. Push the folded edges closely together as you baste so the zipper will be adequately covered.

Use a zipper foot on the sewing machine and, beginning at the bottom of the zipper, right on the seam line, stitch across to the edge of the zipper tape. Put your needle down, pivot, and stitch up the length of the zipper. Repeat this process on the other side, making sure to overlap one or two stitches at the bottom of the zipper.

Open the zipper. Apply waistband, collar, facing, and stitch right across the protruding ends of the zipper tape. Slow down as you go over the zipper teeth. Trim the zipper tape when you trim the seam. Finish waistband, collar, or facing. By using a zipper longer than the zipper opening, you have saved yourself from having to stitch around the zipper pull when you stitched the zipper into the garment. And the zipper will fit snugly up against the waistband or collar. **Caution: Do not cut off the protruding ends of the zipper until after you have stitched on the waistband, collar, or facing.**

(Many stitchers are accustomed to machine basting the seam where the zipper will go, laying the zipper facedown on the seam, and then stitching it in place. This is a perfectly okay way to put in a zipper, *but* the fabric covering the zipper teeth will tend to roll back and reveal unsightly metal.)

LAPPED ZIPPER

A lapped zipper is usually the best choice for a side closing, lapping toward the back.

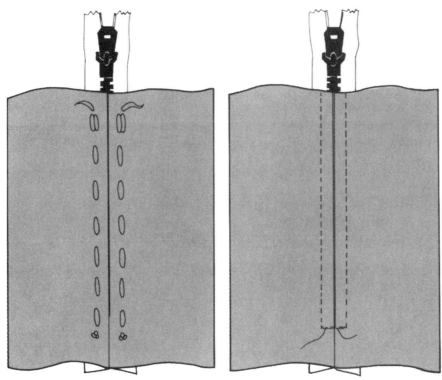

FIGURE 5–69. Slot or centered zipper.

Lapped zippers can be used in any other garment closing and are particularly good when you want the zipper completely hidden from view. It's easier to hide a zipper when you've left a 1-inch seam allowance on the zipper opening; plan ahead for this when making the pattern.

Stitch the garment seam with a regular stitch length up to the bottom of the zipper opening. Stop and take several stitches in place. Change the machine stitch to basting length and continue sewing to the top of the opening. Press the seam open.

Choose a zipper at least 1 inch longer than the zipper opening. Fold the underlap side of the seam allowance ⅛ to ⅜ inch back, as shown in Figure 5–70, and, with the right side of the zipper toward you, place the folded seam allowance close to the zipper teeth, allowing the extra length to protrude past the garment edge, and machine stitch in place.

Put the zipper facedown on the seam allowances, turn the garment to the right side and pin or baste the overlap side of the zipper in place. Starting on the seam line, at the bottom of the zipper, machine stitch or prick stitch the overlap side of the zipper. Remove the machine basting stitches carefully.

Open the zipper and attach waistband, collar, facing, and so on, as described for the slot zipper.

If you need to hide a zipper even deeper in, for example, a period doublet for a quick

226

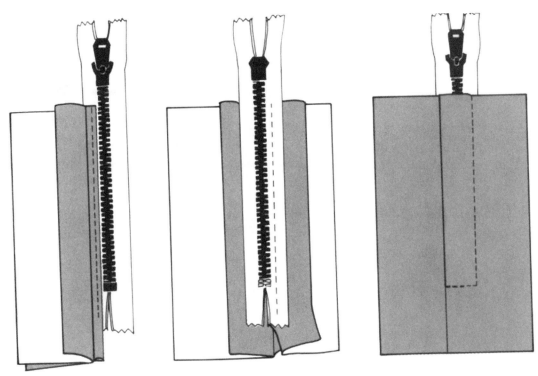

FIGURE 5–70. Lapped zipper.

change, cut wider seam allowances and create a wider overlap.

SEPARATING ZIPPERS

Separating zippers may be either centered or lapped and are set in exactly the same way as either of the above, without the line of stitching across the bottom. Make sure the bottom edge of the separating zipper is slightly above the bottom edge of the garment.

FLY ZIPPERS

Fly zippers are easy. There are several methods of putting in fly zippers, determined by the way the pants are cut. The method shown in Figure 5–71 uses three separate fly extension pieces to create the closing. Assemble the fly closing before stitching the front and back sections to-gether. Stitch the front crotch seam up to the bottom of the fly opening. Press open. Do *not* clip.

Sew one extension to the left trouser front, right sides of the fabric together. Press the extension out and place the zipper, right side down, on top of the extension, with the zipper tape along the side of the seam. On the left side of the zipper, stitch close to but not crowded against the zipper teeth; stitch again at the edge of the tape.

Turn the extension under, baste in place, then machine stitch down. Assemble the other two fly pieces, right sides meeting, and stitch along the curved side. Trim the seam to ⅛ inch, turn, and press. Overlock the raw edge or bind it with bias tape. This is the fly underlay.

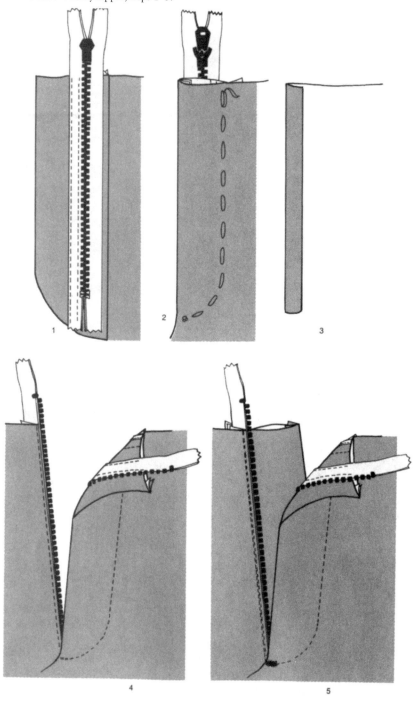

FIGURE 5–71. Fly zipper, steps 1–5.

On the right trouser front, turn the seam allowance under and press down. Open the zipper and stitch the free side to the right front so the fold is quite close to, although not crowding, the zipper teeth. Put in the fly underlay and stitch it in place, through all layers, close to the first stitching line. Lay the trouser fronts right side up and check the zipper for position. On the left front, top-stitch the fly facing through all layers. Be careful not to catch the fly underlay in the stitching line before reaching the bottom of the curve. Reinforce the bottom of the zipper closure with overcasting, a bar tack, or a tight zigzag stitch.

Special Costume Construction Techniques

1. Cartridge pleats
2. Corsets
3. Padding
4. Skirt understructures
5. Theatrical tailoring

Cartridge Pleats

Cartridge pleating has several important theatrical uses: for applying many seventeenth- and eighteenth-century skirts onto waistbands, for setting on some types of Renaissance, judicial,

FIGURE 5–72. Cartridge pleats on Italian Renaissance costumes worn by Danforth Comins and Christopher Marshall with Carrie Baker in the Utah Shakespearean Festival production of *The Two Gentlemen of Verona*, designed by Rosemary Ingham. *Photograph by Karl Hugh, courtesy of the Utah Shakespearean Festival.*

and academic sleeves, and for attaching stiffened materials to neckbands to form ruffs.

CARTRIDGE-PLEATED SKIRTS

In a cartridge-pleated skirt, the upper edge of the fabric is stiffened and folded into small, very precise pleats, which are then butted up against a waistband and tacked down, top and bottom, by hand. The skirt falls from the outer edge of the stiffened pleats, which are sometimes supported by a padded roll. Cartridge-pleated skirts are usually rectangular and have a characteristic bell shape.

First, determine the distance you want the pleats to extend before the skirt begins to fall. Measure this distance on the edge of the fabric to be pleated and fold down. Cut a strip of moderate to very stiff interfacing the width of the fold-down and insert it into the fold. Machine or hand baste through all three layers.

Calculate the depth of the pleats and make a cardboard template that is the width of the fold-down and 8 or 10 inches long. Make two rows of corresponding dots that represent the depth of the cartridge pleats, one row about ½ inch from the fold and the other about ½ inch above the fold-down edge. Punch out the holes with a hole punch and mark the dots on the wrong side of the garment.

On many cartridge-pleated skirts, the pleats are larger in the back and on the sides, growing smaller toward the front. Often, there's a completely flat panel in the center front. You will need a separate template, possibly a much longer one, for graduated sections. Always be sure that the second row of dots is directly beneath the first row.

Run a doubled, well-waxed button thread through the dots, in and out, as shown in Figure 5–73. Pull up the gathering threads tightly to form the pleats. Pull up and pleat the garment in several sections to make it more manageable.

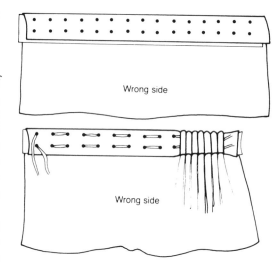

FIGURE 5–73. Cartridge pleating

Prepare a 2-inch- to 2½-inch-wide shaped waistband, firmly interfaced, that fits the body snugly. Butt the top edge of the pleats up against the middle of the waistband, as shown in Figure 5–74. Hand stitch the top and the bottom of each pleat to the waistband very securely, going through all layers; take care that

FIGURE 5–74. Attaching cartridge pleats to waistband.

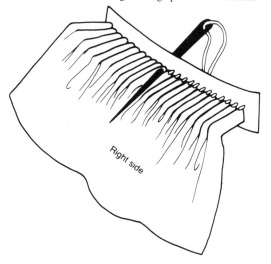

each pleat goes on straight, with top and bottom aligned.

CALCULATING YARDAGE FOR CARTRIDGE-PLEATED SKIRTS

Most cartridge-pleated skirts are cut on the cross grain so the skirt will have the most "belled" shape. If you plan to cut your cartridge-pleated skirt on the cross grain, make sure the width of the fabric is sufficient for the length of your skirt. Remember to allow for the fold-down at the top, the hem at the bottom, and the fact that a cartridge-pleated skirt goes out before it goes down. If the fabric is 60 inches wide, you probably have enough length; if it's 45 inches wide, measure carefully; if it's 36 inches wide, you will probably have to piece the skirt or cut the skirt on the straight grain.

By far the most accurate way to calculate the amount of fabric you will need to make the pleats in a cartridge-pleated skirt is to pleat up a sample section from fabric that is as close to the weight of the actual fabric as possible and attach it to a mock-up waistband. Measure the amount of fabric it takes to create pleats for a given number of inches on the waistband and multiply accordingly. Cartridge-pleated skirts require a great deal of fabric and it is very difficult to "make do" with less.

RUFFS

A ruff is a stiffened length of material, cartridge pleated onto a neckband. It may be lace-edged or made completely from lace and stiffened with nylon organdy or a heavyweight netting. Plastic horsehair, which comes in a variety of widths, makes handsome, durable ruffs that are very easy to keep clean.

Set ruffs on sturdy shaped neckbands that are firmly interfaced and fit comfortably around the actor's neck.

To make a rough estimate of the amount of fabric needed to make a particular ruff and

FIGURE 5–75. Cartridge-pleated ruffs designed by Susan Tsu for a production of *The Tempest* at the Oregon Shakespeare Festival. *Photograph by Susan Tsu.*

to check its width and the depth of the pleats, create a mock-up with brown craft paper and straight pins. For a more accurate fabric estimate, create a sample section as described above.

The length of material for the ruff should be finished on both edges and, if necessary, firmly interfaced. Transfer the two rows of pleating dots from the mock-up, or template, and pull up the pleats with waxed thread. Since the pull-up threads usually remain in the ruff to help keep it stable, make sure you use thread that is a compatible color. The pleats at the neck edge of the ruff will be quite tight, forming a small circle around the neckband; the pleats at the outer edge of the ruff will be much farther apart, enscribing a much larger circle. When stitching the pleats onto the neckband, make sure the bottom of each pleat is directly below the top and that the outer edge does not become twisted.

Corsets

CORSET RESEARCH

During most of the periods when corsets were a vital part of the female fashion silhouette, these rigid garments were put on young girls when their bones were still soft. As the girls became accustomed to wearing corsets, their bodies were actually molded by the stays.

Modern actors do not encounter corsets until they are grown up, and they cannot tolerate the extremely tight lacing some of our ancestors took for granted. The goal of most theatrical corseting is to create a shape for the actor that suggests the correct period shape and causes a minimum of discomfort. Therefore, the most important part of creating a theatrical corset is finding out exactly what shape it has been designed to create.

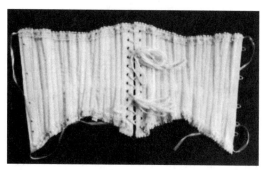

FIGURE 5–76. A boned corset with lacing and front busk. This corset pattern is available from *Past Patterns.* *Photograph by Liz Covey.*

Over the past couple of decades, the demand for well-made corsets has grown among theatre designers who insist upon correct silhouettes, and among independent designers who create eighteenth- and nineteenth-century costumes for historical reenactors. Corset patterns and custom-made corsets are readily available. Norah Waugh's groundbreaking *Corsets and Crinolines,* published in 1954, has been joined by several other excellent books on the subject and a host of journal articles. Some are dedicated to the precise reconstruction of actual period corsets; others address constructing practical corsets for the stage. Consult the Bibliography for titles.

Because a corset's purpose is to mold a three-dimensional figure, a picture of a flat corset without a body in it can never really show how the corset works. The very best way to find out about corsets is to visit a museum that has corsets in its clothing collection and see how these garments were actually made. Study the seams and shapes of the pieces, the bones and how they were angled, the finishing and the decoration. One corset in your hands is certainly worth a dozen pictures in a book.

DEVELOPING A CORSET PATTERN

After talking with the designer, studying the design, and reviewing your corset research, you should know exactly what the corset is going to look like. If you are using a corset just as it's pictured in one of the sources, photocopy it (enlarge it if you can) and sketch out the shape of each piece, paying careful attention to grain lines. If you have the time, and there's a scale pattern for the period corset you're copying, you might want to make a mock-up of it, realizing that a period corset seldom fits a modern body without a great deal of alteration.

The simplest way to develop a custom corset pattern is to create it from the actor's body block, using the pattern development method in Chapter 3. As you work, subtract a total of 2 inches from the circumference of the corset around the bust, the waist, and the hips if the corset extends to the hips, taking small equal amounts from each seam edge. The 2-inch discrepancy between the corset and the body measurements will allow for snug lacing and fabric stretch.

A corset redistributes the actor's flesh and, while altering the silhouette, *adds* to the body measurements. Be sure to measure the actor *with corset* before patterning the dress that will be worn over it.

Cut and stitch a corset mock-up from firm muslin. Using your research as a guide, draw in the bone placements. Pay careful attention to the way the bones are angled because these directions greatly affect the shape the corset will have on the body. Bones generally cross seam lines, which increases the strength of the corset.

Use plastic featherboning for your mockup corset. Featherboning is not as rigid as corset stays will be, but you will be able to get a fairly good idea of how the corset will eventually look and fit. Stitch a row of eyes from hook and eye tape on each side of the center back and thread shoelaces through the eyes to lace your mock-up. Fit the corset on the actor and mark adjustments.

Do not be too concerned if there's a gap of 1 inch to 1½ inches between the center back pieces. All corsets should be too small in the beginning. In the course of wearing the corset, the actor will grow more accustomed to being laced and will allow the garment to be made tighter. Heat and perspiration from the actor's body will also cause the corset to stretch.

CHOOSING CORSET FABRICS

Quoting from a French pamphlet published in 1769, which gives directions for making a set of "stays" or what we would call a corset, Norah Waugh, in *Corsets and Crinolines,* says: "Two layers of material are required, the top one of a closely woven linen or cotton and the bottom one of a stiff drill or tailor's canvas. . . ." In the nineteenth century, she continues: ". . . they are made of sattine or best French jean . . . and lined with calico between the doubles."

The best fabrics for corsets have always been tightly woven, sturdy, and *thin*. Since the purpose of a corset is to shape and slim the body, it is important that the corset itself not add any more bulk than necessary. Natural fiber fabrics are more satisfactory than blends because they shape better. Linen, such as rededged linen, coutil, and cotton drill cloth are all excellent choices. A corset can be constructed of a single layer of fabric with bone casings on the inside or outside. Or, it can be built with

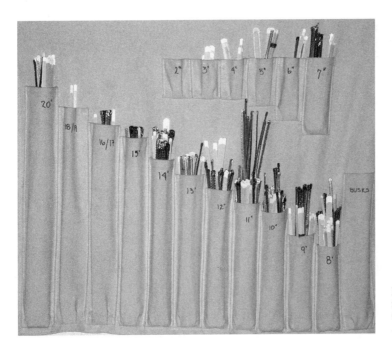

FIGURE 5–77. Hanging storage for assorted corset bones at the Cincinnati Playhouse in the Park. *Photograph by Liz Covey.*

two layers, an outer layer lined with itself, and the bone casings created by "tunneling."

BONING AND BONE CASINGS

Boning is no longer made out of bone and hasn't been since the mid-nineteenth century. Prior to that time, most corsets and skirt understructures derived their superstructures from whalebones that were taken either from whale fins or from the bony plates that line the mouths of certain species of whales. Whalebone appeared in women's undergarments as early as the fifteenth century. Around 1860, due to the collapse of the whaling industry and the development of new tempering processes for steel, new steel "bones" were developed for bustles and corsets. By the beginning of the twentieth century, most real whalebone bones had disappeared.

Although boned corsets are no longer fashionable, steel "stays" or "bones" continue to be manufactured for orthopedic corsets. Steel bones come in a variety of widths and lengths. Some are solid steel blades, shaped rather like tongue depressors or popsicle sticks. Others are made from twisted steel wire and are flexible. Flexible steel boning is used primarily in nineteenth-century corsets to allow them to curve over the hips.

Each corset stay in a boned garment must be the correct length for its casing. Two short bones cannot be pieced together. You can, however, cut long steel bones into shorter lengths using a pair of heavy-duty tinsnips. Round the ends as much as possible, file them smooth, and then coat them with corset bone tipping fluid or wrap them with cloth tape.

An alternative to steel bones is Rigilene polyester boning. Not to be confused with featherboning, Rigilene boning is rigid enough for successful period corsets and has the advantage of being very lightweight. Rigilene boning comes in a fabric casing that can be stitched directly to the corset.

There are two ways to attach steel bones to corsets. The simplest is to put two corset layers together and, with parallel stitching lines, create tunnels for the bones. Make sure the bones fit snugly into the tunnels. To be able to remove the bones easily, work a buttonhole at the top of each bone tunnel on the inside layer. Two-layer corsets tend to be excessively bulky, especially under lightweight dress fabrics.

The most common way of attaching bones to a corset is with a bone casing. Bone-casing tape is available in several widths. There is a pocket in the tape where the bone is placed and a narrow stitching allowance on each side. You can stitch bone-casing tape through all layers of fabric so the stitching shows on the outside or stitch the tape only through the inside layer so the stitching doesn't show on the outside.

If bone-casing tape is not available, use sturdy grosgrain ribbon or sturdy weave twill tape to make casings. Use a single layer of ribbon or tape if stitching the casing to all the corset layers and slip the bone between the ribbon or tape and the corset fabric. If stitching the bone casing to a single layer of fabric, use two layers of ribbon and put the bone between the ribbon layers.

When you need to add a corset stay to an already completed corset or garment and do not want to stitch a bone casing through all layers, attach the casing with a cross-stitch, as shown in Figure 5–78, catching only the underlining.

CORSET CONSTRUCTION TECHNIQUES

When working on the final version of a corset, stitch the seams firmly, press the seam allowances to one side and top-stitch. If the bone placement in the corset does not cross the side seams, leave the side seam allowances 1 inch or 1½ inches wide so the corset can be altered.

A good way to finish off the top edge of the corset is with a small, self-covered cord (see page 203 for bias-covered cording), which

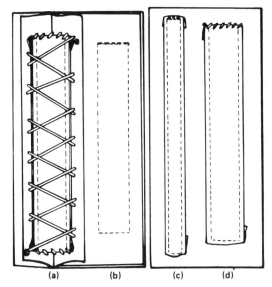

FIGURE 5–78. Bone casings: (a) Bone encased in two strips of twill tape and cross stitched over a seam. (b) Bone sandwiched between two layers of fabric. (c) Bone under a single strip of twill tape that has been stitched directly onto the fabric. (d) Bone slipped inside a special bone-casing tape that has been stitched directly onto the fabric.

looks nice and also helps to pull the top of the corset in around the body. Finish the bottom edge with a flat, narrow bias binding.

Insert the narrow bone on each edge of the back closing and set grommets just inside the bones. Make sure the grommets are close enough together to assure a firm alignment of both edges. Add a placket underneath the closing to protect the actor's body from being irritated by the lacings.

Consider putting a set of corset busks (available from corset supply companies) up the center front so the corset can be unhooked by the actor. It isn't usually possible to put on a corset with busk hooks, but they do make a convenient "quick out."

REHEARSING IN CORSETS

Actors who are going to wear corsets in a production should have ample time to rehearse in them. Make sure the actors and the director know exactly what movements will be restricted by the corset and be sure to provide rehearsal corsets until the actual corsets are complete.

Actors should not wear their corsets when they are lounging in the dressing room or the green room. The steel stays that support an erect body are very irritating to muscles and ligaments when the body is bent or twisted. Actors will adjust much easier to their corsets if they wear them only in the rehearsal hall, while they are rehearsing.

Extremely thin actors may find corsets particularly uncomfortable to wear because the corset stays rub against their unpadded ribs. Provide some padding, such as a thermal undershirt, for the actor to wear between corset and body.

MISCELLANEOUS CORSET TIPS

Nineteenth-century corsets, which go down over the hips, are best laced with two separate laces, both either beginning or ending at the waist. The bottom of the corset is laced much looser than the top.

Long corset laces are available from sources that sell corset supplies. Shoelaces work very well; you may have to tie two shoelaces together to get enough length.

A tank-top undershirt makes an excellent "chemise" to wear between body and corset.

Sometimes you can achieve a corseted effect by boning the costume itself and not using a separate corset. Stitch the bone casings directly onto the underlining of the garment or onto a separate canvas underbodice.

Padding

Costume technicians may be called upon to pad almost any part of an actor's body for the stage. Big bellies, shoulder humps, and expanded chests, both male and female, are most common.

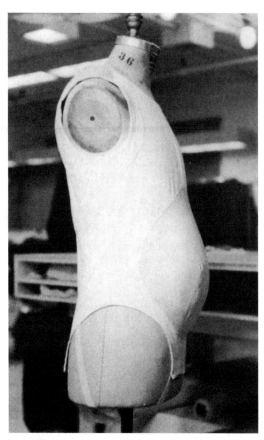

FIGURE 5–79. Tummy padding with crotch strap. *Photograph by Frances Aronson.*

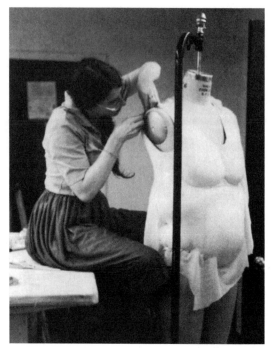

FIGURE 5–80. Costume technician stitching cover on body padding. *Photograph by Rosemary Ingham.*

Most padding is done in essentially the same way. All padding that involves the upper body, or the abdomen, requires a snug-fitting body garment to support it, with a crotch strap to hold the padding down. Construct this body garment from heavyweight muslin or lightweight canvas and the crotch strap from spandex or some other stretch fabric. Fasten it up the back with a stout, separating zipper or hooks and eyes placed close together.

When the body garment is fitted and complete, put it on a tailor's form and begin to sculpt the padded shape on it. The padding material may be polyester fiberfill, cotton bat-ting, or one of the several varieties of soft foam. Polyester fiberfill is preferable for most body-padding pieces, which, if they are properly con-structed, will keep their shape through numer-ous washings. Cotton batting tends to pack down and separate after it has been worn for a while or laundered a time or two, and it takes a long time to dry. High-density foam, air-conditioning foam, and others are often the materials of choice for extremes in padding, for animal and bird shapes and fantasy costumes. They sculpt beautifully and retain their shapes, but because foam is bulky and difficult to wash, it is not as appropriate for simple body padding.

Add the padding material in several lay-ers, trimming and arranging it to mold the cor-rect shape. Secure the layers with long T-pins (so they don't get lost in the stuffing and stick you or the actor later!). If your knowledge of muscle placement is vague, consult an anatomy book. When you've arrived at the proper shape and thickness, cross-stitch the padding material into place securely, using waxed, heavy-duty thread. Cover the whole piece with an outer layer of thin stretch fabric, such as nylon tricot or cotton spandex. Outline muscle groups with an in-and-out quilting stitch through all the layers.

If the required padding is only a simple thickening of the upper torso, stitch layers of fiberfill onto a cotton T-shirt and cover with a second T-shirt. Very loosely, cross-stitch all the layers together and create more subtle shaping with quilting.

Actors who will be wearing padding should have a good idea of how they will look as they rehearse, and they should have their padding for as much of the rehearsal period as possible. Fortunately, padding pieces are usually completed early because you can't make the costume until you've finished the body.

Skirt Understructures

PADDED HIP ROLLS

Some form of padded hip roll or pad was used by women (and occasionally by men) throughout several centuries to create fashionable silhouettes. As late as the 1890s, some women needed "hip improvers" to achieve the fashionable hourglass figure, and even today a woman who wants more hips or buttocks than she came into the world with can order additional curves from Frederick's of Hollywood.

Fat, sausagelike bum rolls, tapered hip rolls, bustle pads, and hip pads are all varieties of body padding and are made from the same materials: muslin or canvas and polyester fiberfill. Make sure you stuff the shape tightly and, in the case of a bustle pad or hip pads, cross-

stitch the padding into place so it won't "settle" to the bottom.

HOOPS, PANIERS, AND BUSTLES

Hoops, paniers, and bustles are all three-dimensional understructures for skirts. Hoops go all the way around the body, from the waist to the bottom of the skirt; the shape of the hoop varies with the period in which it was worn. Paniers belong largely to the eighteenth century; the structures extend out from each side of the waist to create wide skirts that are essentially flat in the front and back. Bustles appeared in the last decades of the nineteenth century, creating a skirt that is slim from the front view but which extends out in the back.

If constructing a hoop, panier, or bustle for the first time, be sure to study the pattern research carefully. Make mock-ups, using featherboning, so you can see exactly how these understructures make and keep their shapes.

Crinoline steel or steel hoop boning is the most common material used in costume shops to maintain the curved shapes in skirt understructures. It is thin, flexible steel, approximately ½-inch wide, plastic coated and usually available in 12-yard rolls. It can be cut into shorter lengths with a chisel and hammer; be sure to cover the sharp ends with cloth tape while you're working with crinoline steel. To make a hoop of crinoline steel, fasten the two ends together with connecting hardware or rivets.

Use very stout casings to attach crinoline steel to the fabric portion of the understructure, remembering that the shape of the garment is maintained by keeping the steel band under constant tension. In paniers and bustles especially, the crinoline steel ends are always trying to work themselves loose.

Lighter-weight alternatives to crinoline steel are various types of caning and banding steel, which is used in packaging.

Always consider the size and shape of the various skirt understructures in relation to the set design. If it's possible, when fitting the understructure mock-up, look at it on stage, preferably with the director and the scene designer in attendance. Check the width of paniers, bustle, or hoop against the width of chairs, sofas, doors, and staircases on the set and in relation to the overall size and arrangement of furniture pieces. If the skirt understructure is out of proportion with its setting, the costume won't be successful.

Theatrical Tailoring

WHAT IS GOOD TAILORING?

This description of a well-tailored jacket is from *Tailoring Suits the Professional Way* by Clarence Poulin.

Note, first, that the edges are thin *even where you would expect the seams to pile up thickly at their junctions. Thinness at the junction of seams is what all good tailors strive at. There are no bumps or slovenly, thick areas along the edges of a good coat.*

Note also that the edges all curl slightly inward, *never outward. This applies to the fronts, the sleeve vents, the pocket flaps, the revers, and the corners of the collar. Everything curls slightly inward; nothing sticks out.*

A good coat has straight seams and straight edges all over. There are no crooks or puckers. The front edge is smooth and not stretched at any point. All seams are well pressed open from the inside.

Linings are always loosely put in so that they do not interfere with the drape of the coat when worn.

Buttons are sewn with a "neck," and not too tightly, to avoid puckering about their bases. The buttonholes are handmade and are not hard.

The hand-sewing around the collar and elsewhere is even and inconspicuous.

In *Classic Tailoring Techniques,* author Roberto Cabrera describes a well-tailored garment in these words:

. . .The lapel was to roll gracefully open at the chest, without pulling the garment forward, away from the body. All edges of the jacket were to belie the existence of the several layers of fabric beneath, by being flat and sharp, without noticeable bulk. The collar and all curved edges of the garment were to incline ever so slightly inward toward the body, a graceful avoidance of the awkward, upward curl of collar tips and pocket flaps.

The goals of good tailoring are clear and these goals are as relevant to garments tailored for the stage as they are for street wear. The big difference between classic tailoring and theatrical tailoring is that costume tailors usually have a very limited amount of time to produce beautifully tailored costumes. A discussion of theatrical tailoring is largely a discussion of acceptable shortcuts.

Even with shortcuts, tailoring suits from all historical periods takes both time and skill. Building a tailored suit is not a project for a beginning stitcher, and any costume technician who embarks on a tailoring project should have studied tailoring techniques and, ideally, produced at least one tailored garment using traditional methods. Once you know exactly how a tailored jacket is assembled and finished, you are better equipped to make wise choices about shortcuts.

You can also learn a lot about how tailored garments achieve and maintain their shape by dissecting one. Take an old, well-tailored jacket apart (one you don't expect to have to reassemble!), layer by layer, and study the kind and character of facings, interfacings, pad stitching, taping, and so on, it contains.

The best way to learn tailoring is to take a hands-on class with a professional tailor or to work as an apprentice to a professional tailor. The second-best way is from a book. Two of the very best tailoring instruction books on the market are *Classic Tailoring Techniques: A Construction Guide for Men's Wear* and *Classic Tailoring Techniques: A Construction Guide for Women's Wear* by Roberto Cabrera and Patricia Flaherty Meyers. The instructions are clear and detailed and the illustrations are excellent.

CHOOSING FABRICS FOR TAILORED GARMENTS

Wool is the fiber of first choice for tailored garments. No other fabric takes and holds shaping as well as wool. A somewhat spongy woolen, such as Harris tweed, is the easiest wool to work with, and a hard-finish worsted wool, such as gabardine, is the most exacting. Wool flannel in all weights tailors beautifully. Wool crepe and loose-weave novelty wools are a bit harder to tailor successfully.

Suit-weight polyester fabrics are virtually impossible to tailor because they cannot be shaped. Wools mixed with polyester, nylon, or spandex (Lycra is a common brand name) also resist tailored shaping.

Tailored garments are often constructed from linen suiting fabrics and from silk suitings. Linen works best in loosely fitted tailored garments. With the proper underlining, silk suitings are almost as "shapable" as wools.

Costume tailors often find themselves tailoring suits, jackets, and coats from fabrics that would cause a nontheatrical tailor to throw up his or her hands in despair: velvet, velveteen, upholstery brocade, satin. These fabrics challenge tailoring techniques and the goals of good tailoring. Nevertheless, it's amazing what ingenuity, perseverance, and the skilled application of interfacings and underlinings can accomplish.

CHOOSING INTERFACINGS, UNDERLININGS, AND LININGS

Tailoring was "born" in the fourteenth century when men decided they would look better if they appeared to have somewhat larger chests than nature had given them, and so it became fashionable to add an underlayer of padding in the chest area of their doublets. The story of tailoring has always been about what's going on inside tailored garments.

Ordinary, untailored clothing relies solely on the human body for its shape. Tailored garments are, with varying degrees of rigidity, those that have been constructed to have inherent shapes. These shapes are created with various fabric layers, stitching, and steam.

The various roles played by underlinings (or flat linings), interfacings, and linings in general costume construction were discussed earlier in this chapter, on page 171. These layers play the same roles in a tailored garment, but the interfacing plays its part with added intensity.

The traditional tailoring interfacing material is *hair canvas*. Hair canvas is springy, resilient, and has a tendency to cling to other fabrics. Good-quality hair canvas shapes readily when steamed and/or stitched into place, and stands up under years of wear and repeated dry cleanings. Poor-quality hair canvas does none of the above and is not worth using. Purchase hair canvas made from wool and hair fibers (usually goat hair fibers); avoid hair canvas material that contains polyester. Unless you live and work in a metropolitan area, you will probably have to order hair canvas from a source that sells tailoring supplies. Hair canvas is used to shape the fronts of a tailored jacket, as well as the lapels, collar, vents, pocket flaps, and welts (see Figure 5–81). In the lapels and collar, the hair canvas is shaped with steam and pad stitching.

Preshrink hair canvas before using it. Soak the piece in cool water, allow it to drip dry, then press.

FIGURE 5–81. Interfacing for a tailored jacket.

There are two specialty tailoring interfacings that are particularly useful in theatrical tailoring: haircloth and prepadded collar melton.

Haircloth is a very stiff, thin material woven from cotton and hair fibers. It is used to add extra body in the chest and shoulder areas of a man's coat or jacket. Haircloth is not normally used in women's tailoring. Haircloth is invaluable when tailoring uniforms, frock coats, or other garments that must have firm but flat fronts. The little hairs that protrude from haircloth can make it quite prickly and it is normally padded with a piece of lightweight cotton flannel. Haircloth does not require preshrinking.

Prepadded collar melton is two fabrics—melton cloth and French linen—machine pad stitched together and used for undercollars. It is available in a variety of colors and if you can get a color that coordinates with the garment, you will save hours of pad stitching on the collar.

There is no perfect lining for a tailored costume coat or jacket. It must be slippery so it will slide off and on easily. It must be sturdy so it can absorb some of the wearing strain without ripping. Rayon and silk linings are among the best choices for tailored street wear but, since both rayon and silk are damaged by perspiration, they are not always suitable for costume linings. Polyester linings are strong and tough,

and they are not weakened by perspiration, but they breathe poorly and add to the heat the actor already feels wearing a wool jacket or coat on stage. Comfort or durability? It's up to you.

DEVELOPING PATTERNS FOR TAILORED GARMENTS

Most theatrical tailors do not develop their patterns from basic body blocks because the lack of direct relationship between the body and the tailored garment makes this a cumbersome way to work. Some draft their patterns and some start with basic tailored pattern blocks, grading them up or down until they fit. Look in the Bibliography for books in which you can find drafting directions and scale patterns for tailored garments from many different periods.

Do not hesitate to use a commercial pattern for a contemporary tailored suit or jacket. On the whole, men's patterns are quite well done. Ignore the sewing instruction sheet included in the pattern and turn instead to Roberto Cabrera's *Classic Tailoring Techniques*.

CLASSIC TAILORING DETAILS THAT SHOW

Proper Pressing

There really are no pressing shortcuts in tailoring. Pressing is an integral part of the tailoring

240

process; it must be done well and at the correct time.

To shape the garment properly, you will need heat, moisture, and pressure. Steam irons, even industrial models, do not supply enough overall steam for tailoring. When pressing seams and darts, keep both a dry and a damp press cloth handy. Place the dry cloth on the fabric and the damp cloth on top of the dry cloth. Press the iron down firmly without moving it around. Remove the iron and the cloths and *don't move the fabric until it is cool and dry.*

Don't forget to do your pressing over a curved surface.

Pad Stitching the Lapels and Taping the Roll Line

No matter what the period of the jacket or coat you are tailoring, the appearance of the lapels and the manner in which they roll back from the body of the garment are particularly important to the overall effect. Pad stitching the lapel by hand, while shaping it gently over a curved surface, and giving that little extra tug to the roll line tape which ensures a graceful roll are traditional techniques well worth the time spent doing them.

Diagonal Tacking

This is the stitch used to tack hair canvas to the underlining in a coat or jacket front: Take a tiny, horizontal stitch through the interfacing,

FIGURE 5–82. Diagonal tacking.

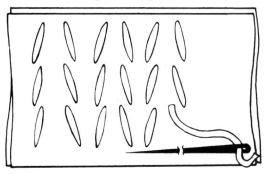

catching only a thread or two of the underlining. Repeat this stitch in a line directly below the first one, placing the stitches approximately ¾ inch to 1½ inches apart. A diagonal stitch will form on the interfacing side. Diagonal tacking adds additional firmness to the interfaced jacket front.

Do not tack down the hair canvas if there is no underlining. The stitches will go directly into the outer fabric and cause dimples. Instead, catch the edges of the hair canvas to the seam allowance. This method produces a softer look than the one described above.

Pad Stitching

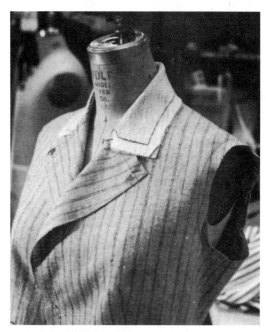

FIGURE 5–83. Pad stitching on undercollar. *Photograph by Susan Ashdown.*

Pad stitching shapes the collar and lapels, both creating the roll and holding the roll in place. Pad stitch whether or not there is an underlining and always stitch through to the outside cloth. Pad stitches are hidden under the collar and the lapels. The stitch is done exactly like diagonal tacking, but the stitches will be smaller and closer together.

Before pad stitching, shape the undercollar and lapels with steam, over the tailor's ham. Maintain the shape while stitching, rolling the undercollar over your index finger and laying the lapels over your knee or over a tailor's ham. Use small stitches on the stand-up portion of the undercollar, medium stitches on the collar fall, and large stitches on the lapels.

Pockets

No detail on a tailored garment shows up shoddy workmanship as obviously as poorly done pockets. A crooked welt with lumpy corners or a lopsided patch pocket can totally spoil a coat or jacket.

Making a proper welt pocket takes time and concentration and the first welt pocket you make will probably not be perfect. But, since there is no easy way to make a welt pocket, practice doing it the right way. Follow the directions in your tailoring textbook and make some samples. After four or five samples, you will be ready to construct a beautiful welt pocket on the real thing.

A patch pocket, on the other hand, is easy to make. Whether the patch has a rounded or a square bottom, it simply requires care in cutting, stabilizing, and stitching. Take your time, be sure you are cutting on grain and establish your stitching line accurately. A layer of fusible knit interfacing on the underside of the patch will help to get a firm, clean edge.

SOME SAFE THEATRICAL TAILORING SHORTCUTS

Fusible Interfacings

When time is of the essence, fusible interfacings may save the day. Choose a fusible knit interfacing or a weft insertion fusible interfacing with a brushed surface, both of which are somewhat shapable. Do not use any of the nonwoven fusible interfacings or crisp woven fusible interfacings that are not shapable. Trim the fusible interfacing very carefully so it does not protrude into the seam allowances and fuse it very carefully following the manufacturer's directions. As soon as the interfacing is fused, before it cools completely, turn the piece carefully to the right side, place it over a curved surface, and press the edges of the garment to encourage them to turn toward the body.

If you only need to save a little time, use hair canvas interfacing down the front of the jacket or coat and fusible interfacing everywhere else.

Sewing Machine Shaping

When you're using fusible interfacing in the coat or jacket front, you can shape the underside of the lapel with parallel rows of straight machine stitching, following the same lines you would have followed with hand-pad stitching. Stitch from the body side of the lapel underside to the front edge, each line of stitching going in the same direction. Set your stitch length a bit longer than normal and loosen the presser foot pressure so the foot does not drag on the fabric.

If you are not using prepadded collar melton for your undercollar, you can pad stitch your undercollar by machine. Use a straight stitch, follow the pad-stitching lines from your pattern, and begin every line of stitching at the center back of the collar.

Easy Buttonholes

Unless the edge of your jacket or coat is quite heavy, you should be able to make buttonholes on your automatic sewing machine. Many new machine models do a keyhole buttonhole that is particularly handsome on tailored garments. Add cording under the buttonhole stitching for extra strength.

If the fabric tends to catch on the feed teeth of the machine, place a small square of tear-away stabilizer, a stiff, paperlike backing such as Stitch and Tear, between the feed teeth and the fabric. The stabilizer should allow the buttonhole to work smoothly and you can tear it away as soon as you're finished.

Preparing for the Unexpected

Just when costume technicians feel that they have experienced most of the commonly done costume construction techniques, a new challenge always appears: a new play set in a seldom done period; an old play with highly stylized costumes; new fabrics; new craft materials; new techniques; and new machinery. As in all jobs, there is always routine work in a costume shop, but unlike most jobs, the unusual and unexpected requires much more time and involvement than the mere routine.

The Indispensable Costume Technician

The people who choose to work as costume technicians, who learn to expect the unexpected and solve problems on a daily basis, are remarkable people. In a world of automation, they work like Old World craftspeople, meticulously constructing one-of-a-kind items that will have brief careers on the stage before they end up in a box in storage. Costume technicians develop patterns, cut fabric, stitch seams, dye, and paint; they make shoes, jewelry, parasols, armor, hats, and gloves. As a group, they are overworked, underpaid, and underappreciated. Individually, they are cherished by a host of designers, actors, directors, playwrights, and other theatre artists who are dependent upon them. Costume technicians are simply those indispensable people who bring the costume designer's sketch to life, dress the actors, and do their considerable part to help put the playwright's words on stage.

FIGURE 5–84. Judith Light as Hedda Gabler and Dee Pelletier as Thea Elvsted in *Hedda Gabler,* wearing costumes designed by Murell Horton at The Shakespeare Theatre. *Photograph by Carol Rosegg, courtesy of The Shakespeare Theatre.*

6
Fitting and Alterations

For every hour you spend constructing garments in a costume shop, you will devote at least an equal amount of time to alterations. Hems go up and down; waistbands go in and out; pants must be cuffed, then uncuffed; buttons always need resetting. Major size, shape, and style alterations are common.

Most costume technicians would rather build a new costume than make substantial adjustments to an existing one. Alterations are not as interesting as making costumes from scratch. Altering is not considered fun.

Yet, many alterations are equally as challenging as constructing a new garment, and sometimes even more so. Many costume technicians discover that making a costume fit is just as interesting as stitching up a costume for the first time; now and again, it's even fun.

Until the appearance of inexpensive, ready-to-wear clothes, every home stitcher was adept at altering. A nineteenth-century ball gown was often worn by several women, and many wedding dresses saw more than one bride to the altar. Clothing was altered to keep up with changing fashion, as well as to fit different bodies. Clothing historians have to study the history of the alterations made in period garments, and often must undo a whole series of darts, tucks, and hems before arriving at the original shape of the dress or jacket.

Today, except for changing hem lengths, few people make alterations to their own clothes. Ready-to-wear clothing is available in so many different sizes that most people can find garments to fit, "after a fashion," with few if any size and shape adjustments. New fashion silhouettes merely send shoppers to the stores and dressmakers to their sewing machines.

Yet, the fine art of altering still lives in costume shops and is a vitally important part of every day's work. Two major reasons for altering costumes are to fit the garment to the actor's body and to change the look or style of an existing costume so it can be reused.

Every actor who goes on the stage in a costume deserves to be as comfortably fitted as the period of the garment allows. Besides causing discomfort to the actor, a poorly fitted costume destroys the effectiveness of even the most brilliant design.

FIGURE 6–1. First hand Kirsten Tucker at work in the costume shop at the American Conservatory Theater. *Photograph by Rosemary Ingham.*

Reusing costumes is simply good economics. Why spend money to build a new costume when an existing one can be altered to do the job equally as well? Good designers and costume shop technicians are always on the lookout for stock items that can be salvaged, reworked, and used again in another show.

The following discussion of alteration techniques touches on some of the most common procedures you will encounter, and will,
hopefully, provide a foundation for solving the most unique and complicated problems that will arise. Approach alterations methodically. Be patient. Don't hurry. Begin complicated alterations as though you were reversing the construction process so you will discover how the garment was built originally. As you uncover how it was done, you can plan your reconstruction, making the necessary changes along the way.

Fittings

The following discussion of the fitting process applies not only to making fitting or style changes to previously built or bought clothing, but also to fitting mock-ups and in-progress costume pieces being built in the shop.

What Is a Good Fit?

The two major elements to look for in a good fit are *balance* and *shape*. Each of these elements is dependent upon the other, and both are closely related to correct fabric grain line position.

A garment is properly balanced when it hangs equally on both sides of the body, whether from a front, a back, or a side view. The body should be in the middle of the skirt, the leg in the middle of the trouser leg, and the arm in the middle of the sleeve. Vertical seams should be perpendicular to the ground, and center front and center back seams should lie precisely at the center of the body.

A garment is properly shaped when the fabric lies smoothly around the body's curves without wrinkling or sagging.

FIGURE 6–2. Cutter/draper Gina Truelove and assistant, Kerri Miller, adjusting a hem during a fitting at The Washington Opera. *Photograph by Liz Covey.*

FIGURE 6–3. Paul DeBoy wearing a beautifully tailored frock suit as Dr. Finache in a production of *A Flea in Her Ear* at the Repertory Theatre of St. Louis. *Photograph by Liz Covey.*

A GOOD FITTING

The first step toward a good fit is a good fitting or, in most cases, a series of good fittings. No matter how beautifully a costume is designed or constructed, if it doesn't fit the actor who

FIGURE 6–4. Fitting room supplies hanging on the wall at the Berkeley Repertory Theatre include cushions with safety pins at the ready, clipboards with fitting sheets, boot hooks, tape measures, shoulder pads, pencils, marking pens, and a host of other things. *Photograph by Rosemary Ingham.*

wears it, it won't look good, and it won't work. Fittings give you the opportunity to adjust the costume to the actor, bringing the design and the character to life.

Fittings are too important to be haphazard events. Plan each fitting in advance, collect and organize everything you need, and, most important of all, allow plenty of time. The golden rule of fitting is: Don't hurry.

THE FITTING SPACE

Fittings should take place in a well-lighted space, before a large mirror (three-way, if possible), with the actor standing 4 to 6 feet back from the image. There should be enough room for the actor to move about, stretch, fall down, kneel, or do any of the actions the role demands. Equip your fitting space with a chair, a rack for hanging the costumes and the actor's street clothing, and a table, or chest, containing the supplies you will need for the fitting: pins, chalk, tape measure. Make sure you have some hairpins and a hair elastic handy, since you may need to tuck the actor's hair away from face and neck. *Always have the designer's costume sketch displayed prominently.*

THE FITTING TEAM

Ideally, there should be three people on a fitting team: the designer, who looks; the cutter/ draper, who pins and marks; and someone to write down fitting notes. Prior to the fitting, someone should be responsible for gathering up all the items needed for the fitting, and, at its conclusion, returning them to their proper places. These responsibilities often fall to the shop supervisor, the assistant to the designer, or to the first hand.

PREPARING THE ACTOR

Before the fitting begins, make sure the actor has seen the costume sketch, understands what all the garment pieces are, and knows which are being fitted. If the fitting is for a mock-up, make sure the actor knows the muslin or other mock-up fabric is *not* what the costume will ultimately be made from. A surprising number of shy young actors go through early rehearsals wondering why their costumes are being made from wrinkly, off-white material with lines drawn all over it! If there is no sketch, explain what items are being fitted, and for what purpose.

The actor should have on all the undergarments required by the costume and the correct shoes. Make sure the garments being fitted are properly adjusted and fastened, and that the actor is standing squarely on both feet, looking straight ahead, arms hanging loosely to the sides. The whole body should be relaxed but centered. Explain that looking down, raising the arms, and shifting the weight from leg to leg changes the way the garment hangs, causes hems to rise and to fall, and, in general, makes it difficult for the designer and the technicians to carry out a successful fitting. However, since standing in one position for long periods of time causes many people to feel faint, instruct the actor to bend his or her knees every few minutes, to take deep breaths occasionally, and, in case of dizziness, to sit down right away.

LOOKING

The first step is to look at the garment as a whole, paying particular attention to the mirror image in order to get the overall effect. Check general silhouette, balance, and shape. Notice what's correct, as well as which areas need adjusting. Make sure you're looking at the whole figure and not just at the clothing.

Now concentrate on the areas that need adjusting. Note the most obvious problems first, then move on to the more subtle alterations.

Remember that while the cutter/draper is checking fitting balance and shape, the designer is studying design elements, such as scale and proportion. If at all possible, try to deal with fitting problems first and design problems second. Many times, however, fitting problems and design problems are inseparable and must be attacked together.

MARKING

One person, and only one person, should actually mark alterations on a costume. No two pairs of hands handle fabric in exactly the same way, and it's important that consistency be maintained. Most cutter/drapers prefer to do the marking on their garments.

If you are marking alterations with pins, use safety pins. Once you've closed a safety pin, it cannot wound an actor who's getting out of a costume, and closed safety pins never fall out somewhere between the fitting room and the worktable.

Use pencils, colored pencils, or indelible marking pens when marking on muslin. When marking actual fabric, use chalk you can brush away or iron off. Be sure to sharpen the chalk or break it to produce a good line. Experiment on a scrap of the fabric before deciding what kind of chalk to use. The iron-off chalk discolors some fabrics. Stone chalk that brushes off has the maddening property of brushing off soft fabrics too easily, and, like straight pins, may vanish before the garment gets to the worktable. If chalk won't work for marking alteration lines, use a row of safety pins or even a line of basting stitches.

ONE LAST LOOK

Once all the alterations have been marked, take a few moments to look at the garment—the whole garment. Make sure the body is not overfitted, that the fabric is not straining over the chest, the back, or the abdomen. See that it is not underfitted, that it does not wrinkle or roll where it should not. Look at the sleeves. Do they hang straight from the top of the actor's shoulder, with the proper forward pitch? Is the neckline low enough? High enough? Is the waistline in the correct position for the style and period of the costume? Have you allowed adequate hem allowances?

When satisfied that the costume fits properly and is true to the design sketch, go over the fitting notes to make sure everything is written down, and then help the actor out of the costume.

Most designers admit that fittings are the most tiring part of the costume design process. Four or five fittings in a row exhaust everybody concerned. This is because fittings require such a high level of concentration and so much on-the-spot problem solving, while, at the same time, you're being cheerful and supportive to the actor, whose body is the main focus of everybody's attention.

Basic Fitting Alterations

Here is a set of basic alteration procedures you can apply to muslin fittings, fabric fittings, and to some fittings of already constructed, second-hand, or off-the-rack clothing. The alterations are illustrated on a female figure, but many of them are applicable to men as well. Each procedure tells you what to look for and suggests correction methods. If you're in the mock-up stage, make the alterations, then correct the pattern before cutting the garment fabric. If you are dealing with a finished or semifinished costume, you will have to figure out how to effect the alteration with the fabric you have in the garment or can add. Occasionally, you have to conclude that the alteration you would like to do is impossible.

Upper Body Garment Alterations

1. *Back neck too large*
   - Pin in the excess and distribute it in two small darts on either side of the center back. If possible, keep the center

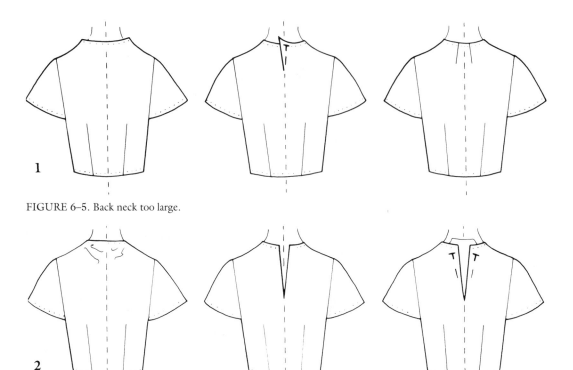

1

FIGURE 6–5. Back neck too large.

2

FIGURE 6–6. Back neck too tight.

back on the straight of grain. However, if the actor has a pronounced upper back curve, you may have to curve the upper portion of the center back seam if there is one, or create a center back neckline dart if there is not.

2. *Back neck too tight*

- Clip until the back lies smooth and fill in with fabric. In most instances, put the center back of the inserted piece on the straight grain.

3. *Front neckline too tight*

- This usually means the neckline is riding too high above the base of the neck.

- Draw a line around the neck base and clip the fabric down to that line. (Often the base of neck will be correct at the shoulders but too high around the front.)

4. *Front neckline too big or too wide*

- Fill in with shaped fabric.
- Raise the shoulder seam at the neck edge if necessary. Make sure the center front of the fabric insert is on the straight grain.

5. *Gaping V-shaped or scooped neckline*

- This is a common problem if the body being fitted has either a bulge or a hollow above the bust or chest line. There are two possible causes:

250

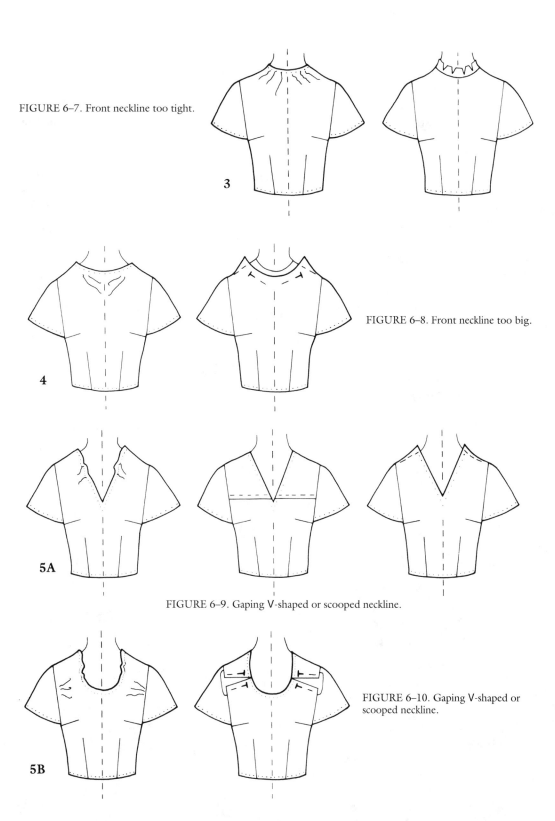

FIGURE 6–7. Front neckline too tight.

3

FIGURE 6–8. Front neckline too big.

4

5A

FIGURE 6–9. Gaping V-shaped or scooped neckline.

5B

FIGURE 6–10. Gaping V-shaped or scooped neckline.

There is too much fabric in the upper portion of the bodice.

A. If the armhole is also too low, pin in a tuck straight across the front, just above the base of the armhole.

If the armhole isn't too low, raise the shoulder seam at the neck edge.

The armhole is too small, which pulls and distorts the neckline.

B. Clip from neckline to armhole, as shown, and insert fabric. The center of the inserted piece should be on the cross grain of the fabric.

6. *Wrinkles at the underarm that point up toward the neckline and cause the cross grain across the upper bodice to tilt toward the arm*

- This problem is commonly caused by sloping shoulders.

- Raise the shoulder end of the front shoulder seam, as shown. *Note* that you will probably raise *only* the front shoulder seam, *not* the back shoulder seam.

- The accuracy of the alteration can be checked by making sure the cross grain across the upper bodice is parallel to the floor.

7. *Wrinkles that run from the outside edge of the shoulder toward the center front and cause the cross grain across the upper bodice to tilt toward the center front*

- This problem is commonly caused by square shoulders.

- Raise the neck end of the front shoulder seam, as shown. *Note* that you will probably raise *only* the front shoulder seam, *not* the back shoulder seam.

- The accuracy of the alteration can be checked by making sure the cross grain across the upper bodice is parallel to the floor.

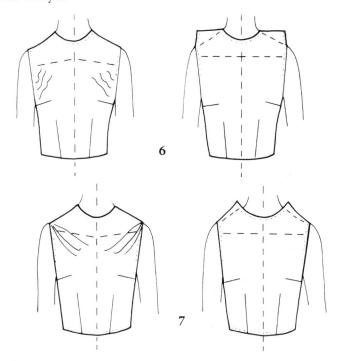

FIGURE 6–11. Wrinkles at the underarm that point up.

FIGURE 6–12. Wrinkles that run from the outside edge.

8. *Shoulders too wide, fabric drooping over the top of the arm*

- This problem and its solution can exist in the front and/or in the back of the garment.
- Create a dart perpendicular to the shoulder seam as shown.

9. *Waist sags at the sides, below the bust or chest line*

- This is a common fitting problem of people who have prominent busts or chests and short underarm to waist measurements.

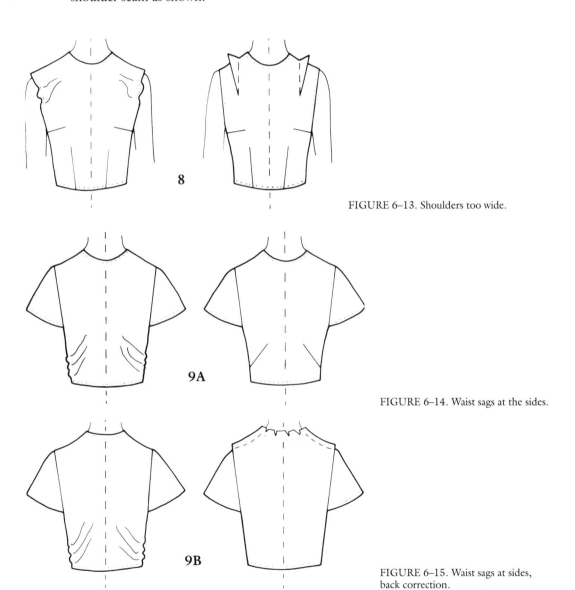

FIGURE 6–13. Shoulders too wide.

FIGURE 6–14. Waist sags at the sides.

FIGURE 6–15. Waist sags at sides, back correction.

A. *Front correction:*

Control the excess fabric with darts taken on the front side seams, angling up toward the bust point.

B. *Back correction:*

Lift the whole back of the garment at the shoulder seams. Be careful not to overcorrect. Lower the back armhole if necessary.

10. *Back too long, fabric sags in the middle but is correct at the sides*

A. If the sagging is above the armhole base, take a tuck across the shoulder blade line, as shown. Be careful not to shorten the armhole too much.

B. If the sagging is below the armhole base, take a tuck just above the waistline, and taper it to the side seams.

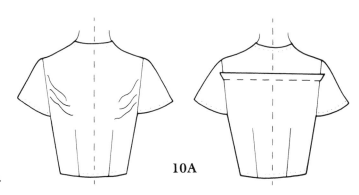

FIGURE 6–16. Back too long.

10A

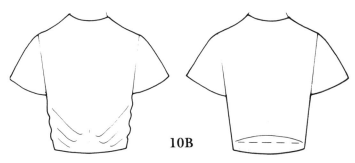

FIGURE 6–17. Back too long, sagging below armhole base.

10B

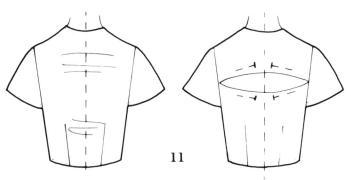

FIGURE 6–18. Back too short.

11

11. *Back too short, wrinkles around the upper armholes and stretched fabric across the back*
    - This is a common fitting problem on actors with high, rounded backs.
    - Clip as shown, across the back, between the armhole seams.
    - Insert a piece of fabric, making sure the center back of the insert is on the straight grain.

Sleeve Alterations

Don't fit a mock-up or a garment under construction with only one sleeve stitched in. You need to have both sleeves in place to balance the garment on the body and to make accurate fitting adjustments.

1. *Sleeve cap too short, causes the sleeve fabric to wrinkle up toward the shoulder*

    - Clip across the top of the sleeve cap, as shown, and insert a piece of fabric. Make sure the center of the insert is on the straight grain of the fabric.

2. *Sleeve cap too long, causes the sleeve fabric to droop on the outside of the arm*
    - Create a tuck across the top of the sleeve cap, as shown.

3. *Too much ease in the sleeve cap*
    - Release the armhole seam across the top. Create a dart at the top of the sleeve and slide the cap up under the garment shoulder until the fullness disappears.

    Note: Don't overcorrect; remember that there must be fabric for easing in the cap of a fitted sleeve.

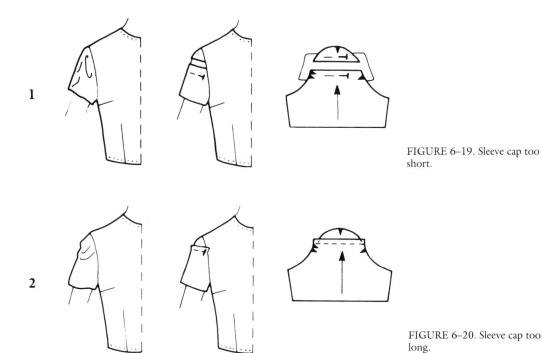

FIGURE 6–19. Sleeve cap too short.

FIGURE 6–20. Sleeve cap too long.

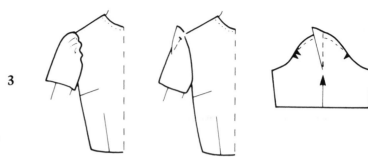

3

FIGURE 6–21. Too much ease in the sleeve cap.

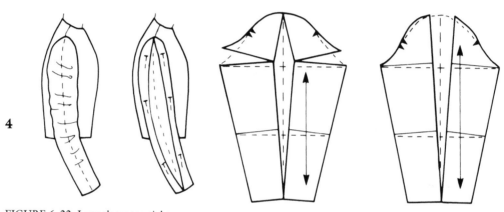

4

FIGURE 6–22. Long sleeve too tight.

FIGURE 6–23. Long sleeve too big around the arm.

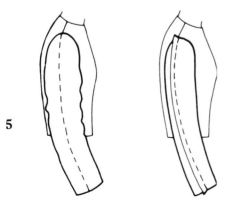

5

4. *Long sleeve too tight around the arm*
   - Clip the sleeve along the lengthwise grain and insert a piece of fabric, making sure the center of the insert is on the straight grain.
   - Your alteration may or may not include widening the sleeve cap. See Figure 6–22 for two different altered pattern shapes.

5. *Long sleeve too big around the arm*
   - Create a tuck down the sleeve, along the lengthwise grain.

Skirt Alterations

1. *Skirt wrinkles across the small of the back*
   - This fitting problem is commonly caused by an inner curved, or "swayed," lower back.
   - Lower back waistline, as shown.

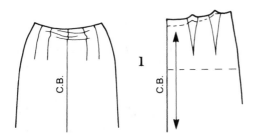

FIGURE 6–24. Skirt wrinkles across the back.

FIGURE 6–25. Skirt wrinkles from side seams.

2. *Skirt wrinkles from side seams, fabric drooping toward the center back*
   - This fitting problem is commonly caused by flat buttocks.

- Create tucks on either side of the center back, parallel to the center back. You may also have to raise the back waistline slightly.

3. *Skirt wrinkles above the hip line, all the way around the body*
   - Skirt is too tight across the hips.
   - Release side and center back seams. Insert fabric pieces as necessary, making sure that the grain lines on the inserts match the grain lines on the skirt pieces.

4. *Skirt wrinkles in the front, with fabric drooping from sides to center front*
   - Common fitting problem caused by a prominent abdomen.
   - Release skirt from waistband and allow the skirt to fall until the wrinkles disappear. Insert a fabric piece to raise the front waistline and "fill in" the skirt front, making sure the center front of the insert is on the straight grain.

   Note: Sometimes, when the abdomen is quite prominent, the front skirt waistline will curve slightly upward. This curve is necessary for the skirt to hang straight.

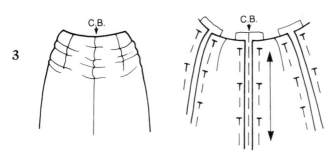

FIGURE 6–26. Skirt wrinkles above the hip line.

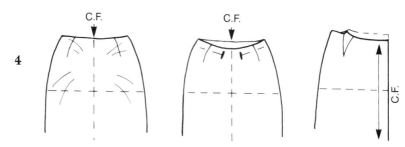

FIGURE 6–27. Skirt
wrinkles in front.

Pants Alterations

Alterations to the waist and hip portions of
pants are made just like the preceding skirt alterations.

Pants Crotch Alterations

1. *Wrinkles from crotch, pointing up toward
   the waistline*
   - These upcurving wrinkles, sometimes
     called "smile wrinkles," are the result
     of a crotch curve that is too short.

- Lengthen the crotch curve, as shown.

Note: If you are altering off-the-rack
pants and cannot extend the waistline
edge or the center front and center
back, you can still lengthen the crotch
curve as much as ¾ inch without
harming the way the pants legs hang.
Scoop out a very shallow curve at the
crotch intersection and don't extend
the curve into the center front and
center back of the pants.

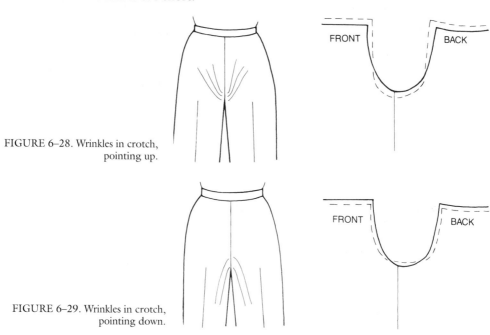

FIGURE 6–28. Wrinkles in crotch,
pointing up.

FIGURE 6–29. Wrinkles in crotch,
pointing down.

2. *Wrinkles from crotch, pointing down into the legs*

- These down curving wrinkles, sometimes called "frown wrinkles," indicate a crotch curve that is too long.
- Raise the crotch curve, as shown, and lower the waistline.

    Note: When altering off-the-rack pants, you will only be able to raise the waistline. As you raise the waistline, be sure to maintain the balance of the pants, making sure that the legs continue to hang straight down. You will probably *not* raise the waistline the same amount all the way around.

3. *Back crotch curve too short, from center back waistline down over the buttocks to the inseam*

- Clip pants back from lower third of center back seam straight across to the side seam.
- Raise top part of back as shown.
- Insert fabric piece, making sure the insert grain line is the same as the pants piece grain line.
- True center back and side seams.

4. *Back crotch curve too long, from center back waistline down over the buttocks to the inseam*

- Create dart from lower third of the center back seam straight out to the side seam, as shown.
- True center back and side seams.

5. *Front crotch curve too short, from center front waistline down over the abdomen to the inseam*

- Lengthen front crotch curve and upper part of inseam, as shown.

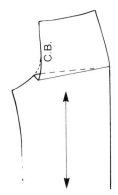

FIGURE 6–31. Back crotch curve too long.

FIGURE 6–30. Back crotch curve too short.

FIGURE 6–32. Front crotch curve too short.

6. *Front crotch curve too long, from center front waistline down over the abdomen to the inseam*

- Shorten front crotch curve by removing fabric from the inseam, as shown.

FIGURE 6–33. Front crotch curve too long.

Adjusting Sleeves That Hang Badly

Few fitting problems are more obvious to the audience or more uncomfortable to the actor than sleeves that do not hang smoothly from the armhole. A sleeve that is set in too far back will pull against the front of the arm and a sleeve that is set too far forward will pull across the back of the arm. In both instances, the sleeve will wrinkle in an unsightly manner across the upper arm. In a fitted, tailored sleeve, if the top of the sleeve is set only ½ inch to the front or the back of the top of the shoulder, the sleeve will not hang accurately.

Check sleeve positions carefully. Have the actor stand erect, looking straight ahead, with both arms hanging down loosely. Find the cross grain of the fabric across the upper arm; this cross grain should be parallel to the floor. Find the straight grain of the fabric that falls from the shoulder; mark it with pins if it isn't obvious.

FIGURE 6–34. Sleeve hanging correctly in armhole.

Using the same technique described on page 219, in Chapter 5, use a piece of ribbon or twill tape with a weight tied to the end of it, to check the position of the sleeve. Remember, the top of the sleeve cap does not necessarily have to fall from the shoulder seam of the garment, but *it must fall from the top, or highest point, of the shoulder.*

To make the alteration in the fitting, release the sleeve cap, from balance point to balance point, over the top of the bodice, blouse, or jacket armhole. Mark the top of the shoulder point on the armhole and pin the top of the sleeve cap (the top of the straight grain line), to it. Check to make sure the sleeve underarm point is lined up accurately with the garment

260

underarm. Pin or hand baste the sleeve into the armhole to check the hang.

Replace the sleeve, referring to detailed directions on page 215, in Chapter 5.

ARMHOLE ALTERATIONS

Approach all armhole alterations with caution. You can end up making matters worse.

If the garment armhole is too tight under the arm, but sits properly on the shoulder, carefully scoop out the underarm portion of the armhole, below the balance points. You can do this while the costume is on the actor, using a small pair of scissors, and taking away very little material at a time. Or, you can take an accurate armscye measurement and trim out the armhole after the garment is off the actor. Always be careful not to trim away too much fabric. You can't put it back.

If the armhole is too big, it's difficult to make it smaller.

1. You can raise the shoulder edge of the shoulder seam slightly but not so much as to throw off the cross grain of the bodice.

2. You can take in the side seam, but then you will usually have to trim out the front and back armhole curves, a tricky operation that may result in an armhole that's even bigger than it was before.

3. If the bodice is cut with a princess seam that extends into the armhole, you can take in the princess seam at the armhole edge, blending it carefully back into the bodice.

If your fitting problem is excess fabric across the front or the back of a garment, don't try to take it in by trimming away the armhole edge of the bodice. This always makes the armhole larger and compounds your problem. The sleeve will no longer fit properly into the armhole and, if you do get it in, the garment will have a tendency to bind the actor's upper arm.

Costumes from Stock

When a costume designer and the costume shop staff begin to make plans for a period production, one of the first considerations is: How many garments have to be built from scratch, and how many can be pulled from stock and altered? Pulling and adapting even one or two costumes from stock can add significantly to the money and time available for new costumes. All budget-conscious costume designers (which should mean *all* costume designers) develop a keen eye for reusable items.

Schedule early fittings to consider stock costumes. If there are several possibilities, have them all on hand. Place the actor well back from the mirror and give the designer plenty of time to decide whether the garment will fit into the production design scheme. If the stock item suits the designer, the shop supervisor or cutter/draper has to determine what alteration is necessary, and if it's possible. If the alterations are impossible to make, this is the time to say so.

Shopped Costumes

Plays set in the present, or near-present, are most often costumed with shopped rather than constructed garments, clothing bought new from clothing stores, or secondhand from thrift shops, consignment shops, or from antique clothing dealers. Before purchasing new clothes off the rack, make sure they are the correct size, and that they can be returned if they don't fit or aren't appropriate choices.

Keep off-the-rack costume alterations to a minimum because too many size and shape changes may spoil their "store-bought" look.

Whenever you buy old clothing to use on the stage, check it carefully to make sure the fabric is strong enough to last.

Old Clothing Alterations

NEW HEMLINES IN OLD GARMENTS

Lengthening hems in old skirts, pants, and dresses can be the most frustrating of all alterations. Even when the hem allowance contains a sufficient amount of fabric to let down, getting rid of the crease and discoloration around the original hemline often proves daunting. Here are a few suggestions:

1. Wools, silks, and some napped fabrics like velour or velvet may respond to steam and a lot of brushing.

2. You can sometimes remove hemline creases by using a press cloth that has been dipped in a solution of white vinegar and water.

3. Dry cleaning removes some creases. Be sure to let the hem allowance down before sending the garment to the cleaners.

4. Sometimes to remove a discolored line, you can brush a dye solution over the unsightly stripe, then redye the whole garment.

5. The designer may even come up with some appropriate trim that will conceal the discoloration.

All too often, however, a persistent crease, or an old, discolored hemline will render the entire garment unuseable.

Setting and stitching level hems in soft wool, silk, and rayon crepe dresses from the 1920s, 1930s, and early 1940s can be frustrating experiences. If the dresses have been packed flat, they will be in better shape than if they have been hanging on a hanger for several decades. In any case, you can be sure the hemlines will be uneven when you try them on actors.

Before beginning work on a dress or a skirt of this sort, let out the hem and send the garment to the cleaners. Fit the garment carefully and complete all other alterations before marking the hem. Press as little as possible while working on the garment.

Mark the hem at the final fitting, being very careful not to pull down on the skirt. Baste and stitch the hem according to the directions on page 183, in Chapter 5. Press *very lightly,* if at all. Steaming is preferable. Even with all of this careful treatment, the hem may still be uneven. But, take comfort, you've done your best.

Men's Shirt Alterations

Men's dress shirts are standard items of costume clothing, used over and over again under suits from many different decades. Even very small costume shops benefit from maintaining a stock of basic cotton and cotton blend dress shirts. Alter them carefully, maintain them well, and they will serve for many productions.

Common shirt alterations include changing the sleeve length, turning and refashioning shirt collars and cuffs, and adjusting the shirt body fit. However, the neck size in a man's dress shirt is virtually impossible to change. Always fit the actor in a shirt that fits correctly around the neck, especially when the costume calls for a necktie and/or a detachable collar.

A costume shirt is often worn under a suit, with only the collar, cuffs, and a bit of the front showing. When this is the case, you can lengthen a too-short sleeve by putting a fabric insert into the upper part of the sleeve, or shorten it by taking a tuck in the same place. Both of these alterations are visible and not suitable if the actor removes his coat on stage. If the shirt sleeves remain hidden by the coat, these alterations have the advantage of being very quick and easy.

When the shirt sleeves must show on stage, there is no way to make them longer. However, they can be shortened either at the shoulder or at the wrist edge, relatively time-consuming alterations that require ripping and restitching flat-felled seams.

Collars and cuffs are the first places on a shirt to show wear. If the shirt you want to use on stage is beginning to fray in these areas, you can easily refurbish it by turning the collar and the cuffs, a common mending trick in the first half of the twentieth century.

TURNING THE COLLAR

1. Remove the collar from the shirt by very carefully inserting the point of a single-edged razor blade under the stitches joining the collar and the band and gently cut the threads. Because the stitches are tiny and the shirt collar is usually starched, it is difficult to remove these stitches with a seam ripper or scissors.

2. When the collar is off, fold it in half and mark the center with a pin or with a pencil mark.

3. Mend the frayed area with a piece of iron-on mending fabric or with a machine darning stitch.

4. Reverse the collar so the mended side is down and the nonfrayed side is up. Replace the collar on the neckband.

TURNING CUFFS

1. If the frayed cuffs being mended are French cuffs, remove and mend them the same way as the collar. Reverse the cuffs so the mended part is hidden in the fold and restitch them to the sleeves.

2. Mend the frayed edges of button shirt cuffs by binding them with a bias binding that matches the shirt fabric. In most cases, you can take enough fabric from the shirttail to bind both cuffs.

Take in the body of dress shirts by shaping in the side seams, by creating fitting fish darts in the back of the shirt, or by a combination of seams and darts.

Tailoring Alterations

Before beginning to alter a tailored garment, hang it up or put it on a form and study it carefully. Remember: Your goal is to alter the garment in such a way that it will end up looking just as good as or better than it did before you began.

TAILORED JACKET AND COAT ALTERATIONS

The most common alterations to a tailored jacket are:

1. Shortening the jacket or coat. (Tailored jacket and coat hems are usually so narrow you cannot lengthen them.)
2. Raising and lowering sleeve lengths.
3. Adjusting body circumference.

SHORTENING THE JACKET OR COAT

For most of the twentieth century, the classic and most pleasing length for a man's suit jacket or sports jacket quite literally falls into the palm of the wearer's hand. A quick and easy way to check a jacket's length is to have the actor stand with his arms at his sides and grasp the bottom of his jacket, as shown in Figure 6–35.

There is a limit to how much you can shorten a tailored jacket without ruining its overall proportion. Pin up the amount you plan to remove from the jacket hem and check to see if this will cause the lapels or the pockets to sit too low and give the jacket an awkward, top-heavy appearance.

It takes a long time to shorten a tailored jacket. Each step has to be done with care, and it doesn't pay to rush. If the jacket fronts are squared off, you must make sure the newly

FIGURE 6–35. Grasping bottom of jacket to judge correct length. *Photograph by Liz Covey.*

Once the inner construction is loose and out of the way (here again, a razor blade is the best ripping tool because the stitches are small and hidden and difficult to get at with a seam ripper), turn the fabric up on the new hemline. Starting at the center back, hand baste the hem allowance in place, about ½ inch from the edge, basting first one half and then the other. Use fairly short basting stitches and be careful not to gather the fabric. End the basting about 2 inches away from the beginning of the front curve.

Making sure the canvas interfacing is out of the way, put the front facing and the front outer fabric together, right sides facing, and machine stitch them on the new curve line, following the basting stitches that mark the curve. Use a shorter than normal stitch length. Stop stitching at the edge of the facing. Trim the seam to approximately ⅛ inch, reinsert seam tape, and retack the interfacing. Turn the facing to the inside of the jacket, fingering the seam slightly to the inside and basting it in place. Steam press over a tailor's ham.

Trim the straight part of the hem allowance the same length as the original hem allowance. (Once you have shortened a tailored jacket, you cannot lengthen it again.) Stitch the hem in place, taking care that the stitches are invisible from the outside of the garment. Hand stitch the vent, the facings, and the lining back into place.

Many tailored overcoats are made from very bulky woolen fabrics. When you shorten a bulky wool coat, it is particularly important that you trim, stitch, and press carefully to make the hem edges as flat as possible.

RAISING AND LOWERING SLEEVE LENGTH

Changing the sleeve length of a jacket or coat is the most frequently done of all tailoring alterations. Although it is not a particularly time-consuming alteration, each step must be done carefully.

hemmed edges are smooth, flat, and *exactly the same length*. If the jacket fronts are curved, the two curves *must be identical.*

Before beginning to shorten a jacket with a curved hem, trace the existing curve onto a piece of cardboard to use as a pattern. Lay the cardboard pattern on the jacket at the desired height and mark the new curve with a line of basting stitches, in a contrasting thread, that goes only through the outer fabric layer.

Carefully, begin to take down the old hem, loosening the lining first and then the facing. Observe how the facing and interfacing are attached. Measure the depth of the finished hem allowance and take note of all the places where seams are clipped, trimmed, and taped. Remember that you want to return everything just as it was, only shorter.

Marking the correct sleeve lengths is the first step. *Always mark both sleeves.* A long-sleeved garment looks best when both sleeves end at the same place on the arms, usually just below the wrist bone. Since most people have one arm longer than the other, the two sleeves, while appearing to be the same length because they hit each arm at exactly the same place, will, in all probability, actually be different lengths.

Prepare to mark the sleeve lengths by having the actor stand with both arms relaxed and hanging straight down. Put the end of a tape measure at the tip of the actor's thumb and measure up to the sleeve, as shown in Figure 6–36; 4½ to 5½ inches up from the thumb tip is an average jacket sleeve length if you wish the shirt cuff to be visible below it. Nineteenth- and early twentieth-century tailoring research often gives you the precise sleeve length that was fashionable in a particular year. Measure up the desired amount and, if shortening the sleeve, place a safety pin to mark the correct length. If lengthening the sleeve, calculate the distance between the end of the tape and the end of the sleeve. Check to see if there is sufficient hem allowance in the sleeve, then make a note of how much the sleeve needs to be lengthened. To make correct sleeve length alterations on a jacket or coat, *it's entirely possible that you may find yourself shortening one sleeve and lengthening the other.*

Remove the jacket from the actor. Before you begin, baste sleeves and linings together just below the elbow line. This will help prevent the lining from twisting as you work. Then take out all the stitches holding the bottom of the lining and the sleeve hem in place. Remove sleeve buttons, thread them on a large safety pin, and fasten them to the jacket. Notice that you will not be able to lengthen the sleeve vent when you shorten a tailored sleeve, but, in most cases, this will not be noticeable. Examine the piece of interfacing at the bottom of the sleeve. This is usually a fabric called

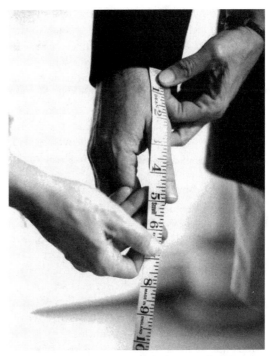

FIGURE 6–36. Sleeve length being measured up from the thumb. *Photograph by Rosemary Ingham.*

wigan, and it folds back on itself at the sleeve edge. Shake the lint out of the wigan, press the fabric lightly, and don't forget to put it back in the new hem edge. Press the hem and lining edges lightly; be careful not to stretch the fabric.

Mark the correct hem length with a line of hand-basting stitches, in contrasting thread. Since approximately 1830, tailored sleeve hems traditionally have been squared out from the back sleeve seam. This maintains most of the hem edge on the cross grain of the fabric and prevents it from rippling.

Turn the sleeve up on the new hemline, marked by basting stitches, put the sleeve interfacing back in place, and baste the hem up about ½ inch from the fold. Most tailored sleeve hem allowances are originally about 1½ to 2 inches deep. In a costume jacket, however, unless the fabric is very bulky, try to leave an additional inch or two of hem allowance so the jacket sleeves can be altered again. As you fold the new hem allowance inside, you will notice that it will not lie flat against the inside of the sleeve. This is because the sleeve is smaller around the hem than it is 3 or 4 inches up. Open the sleeve seams and spread the fabric until the turned-back hem allowance fits smoothly inside the sleeve and does not cause puckers on the outside.

Stitch the sleeve hem allowance to the interfacing using a plain hem stitch. Restitch the sleeve vent as necessary.

Before reattaching the sleeve linings, put the jacket on a tailor's form or hanger. The most common mistake made by technicians altering sleeve lengths is to hem the sleeve lining too short, which prevents the sleeve from hanging smoothly and causes unsightly wrinkles on the outside of the jacket sleeve. You are not as apt to make this mistake if the jacket is hanging.

There are several ways of attaching the sleeve lining to the sleeve. Here is a simple one: Turn the sleeve lining hem allowance up between the lining and the jacket sleeve until the folded edge of the lining is ¼ inch shorter than the sleeve hem edge. Baste the lining hem up about ½ inch from the folded edge. Move the lining hem edge ¾ inch up inside the sleeve and stitch the lining to the sleeve hem allowance, using the blindstitch (see page 179 in Chapter 5). Make sure the sleeve seams in the lining and in the jacket match up and be sure the blindstitches don't go through to the outside of the jacket or accidentally catch the outer layer of the lining. When the lining is in place, it will form a small pleat at the bottom of the sleeve, allowing the sleeve to hang freely.

When the hemming is complete, press the sleeves and replace the sleeve buttons. A normal placement for jacket sleeve buttons is: The first button, 1½ inches from the bottom

of the sleeve, and each button center ⅝ inch up from the one below it.

JACKET BODY ALTERATIONS

Most tailored jacket alterations are for the purpose of making the jacket smaller rather than larger. Tailored jacket seams are, for the most part, trimmed so closely that there is little or no room to make the jacket body larger.

A good general rule to follow when taking in a tailored jacket is that it normally cannot be adjusted more than 2 to 3 inches in circumference or about one standard size. If you take in the jacket body more than this, you may spoil the shape and proportion of the jacket as a whole. The best places to reduce the size in a jacket body are the center back seam and the two side back seams.

Mark the alteration on the actor. When the jacket is back on the worktable, carefully transfer the fitting marks to the inside, using pencil, chalk, or a line of basting stitches. If altering the two side back seams, make sure you take identical amounts from each seam.

Stitch the altered seam, being careful to blend the new stitches with the original seam line. Then remove the original stitches and press the altered seam open, using a press cloth and a maximum amount of steam. (Refer to directions for pressing on page 185 in Chapter 5.)

Avoid making center back seam alterations that would extend up into the back neck edge. It is virtually impossible to alter a tailored collar without spoiling it.

If the jacket is darted, you can either remove the darts to enlarge the jacket or deepen the darts to make the jacket more snug and shapely. *Body darts are often clipped in the middle to make them lie flat, so be sure to check them before you let them out.*

You can also take in a jacket along the side seams, if the alteration does not extend into the armhole. If the jacket has side front seams, you may be able to alter there as well.

However, the jacket front interfacing usually extends to the side seams, and it is often impossible to "get at" a side front seam to make a neat alteration.

Remember when fitting tailored jackets that most styles hang from the shoulders and are not form fitting. Study the design and the period research and be careful not to overfit.

ALTERING TAILORED TROUSERS

Trousers are easier to alter than jackets. In most costume shops, trouser hems go up and down constantly, determined not only by the length of the actor's legs but also by the trouser length common to the period for which the costumes are being altered.

HEMMING PLAIN TROUSERS

It is important to keep as much hem allowance as possible in trousers so they can be altered for different actors and for different productions. But, there is a limit to how much material can be folded up and stitched up inside trouser legs before they begin to look lumpy and hang badly. The width of a suitable hem allowance will vary according to the weight and character of the trouser fabric, but anything wider than 4 to 5 inches will give you trouble. As with sleeves, trouser legs are sometimes smaller around at the bottom edge than they are 3 or 4 inches up. If this is the case, the hem allowance won't lie smoothly inside the trouser legs. Let out the inseam or side seam from the edge of the hem allowance until it fits smoothly into the trouser legs.

Stitch the trouser hems up with a locked hem stitch or blindstitch, taking care that the stitches don't show on the outside of the trousers and that you do not pull the stitches too tight.

HEMMING CUFFED TROUSERS

When fitting cuffed trousers for length alterations, do not put pins or other marks on the fabric. Measure the amount the trousers need to be lengthened or shortened and record the measurement.

Bring the trousers back to the worktable and clip the tailor's tacks that support the cuffs at the side seam and at the inseam. Fold the cuff down and remove the hem stitches. Pull the whole leg out straight.

If shortening the trousers, measure up from the original inner fold line (the one highest up on the leg) the amount the trousers need to be shortened. Mark the new fold line with basting around the trouser legs. Press out all folds, using a press cloth and lots of steam. Then, measure down from the new fold line the depth of the cuff, usually 1½ to 1¾ inches, and mark with basting. This is the top cuff fold.

If the fabric is soft or lightweight, leave a hem allowance slightly less than twice the width of the cuff. Fold the hem allowance under on the top cuff fold line (the line of basting closest to the hem edge of the trousers) and secure with a locked hem stitch or blindstitch. Press the hem. Fold the cuff up on the new inner fold line. Fasten the cuff up loosely on the inseam and the side seam. Notice that the hemming line is *below* the top of the cuff.

If the trouser fabric is firm, you can leave a wider hem allowance, leaving more potential hem length for future alterations. With a wider hem allowance, the hemming line will be *above* the cuff and must, therefore, be invisible from the outside.

Reverse the above procedure to lengthen cuffed trousers.

FALSE CUFFS

When there isn't enough length in the trouser legs to lengthen a pair of cuffed trousers in the traditional way, you may be able to construct a false cuff.

Let all the hem out and measure the legs. If the measurement is the finished length of the trousers plus 1½ inches, you have enough fabric for a false cuff.

Stitch a strip of facing around the bottom of the trouser legs that is slightly less than twice the width of the cuff. Use a ½-inch seam.

From the facing seam, measure up the width of the cuff ½-inch deep and create a ½-inch deep tuck to simulate a cuff top. Press the tuck and slip stitch in place, making sure the stitches do not show.

Turn up the facing and secure with a locked hem stitch.

ALTERING TROUSERS AT THE CENTER BACK

Men's tailored trousers are usually constructed in such a way that center back seam alterations are relatively easy. There is often a 1½-inch wide seam allowance at the upper portion of the center back seam and the waistband may be constructed with an easy-to-alter center back seam.

As you remove belt loops, waistband, and center back seam stitching, remember to observe the way the pieces were originally constructed so you can reconstruct them the same way.

You can usually let out the center back seam all the way to the edges of the seam allowance without harming the way the pants hang. In situations when the trousers will always be worn on stage with a jacket, or, better yet, a tailcoat or frock coat, you can even add a triangular gusset to the center back seam for additional girth. If you can make the gusset out of a stretch fabric, the actor will be even more comfortable.

Unfortunately, you cannot take trousers in as much as you can let them out. A waist adjustment of more than 2 inches smaller means that the alteration line will have to extend well down into the crotch curve to blend with the original seam. When you do this, the crotch curve is flattened, and the trouser crotch be-gins to fall lower between the actor's legs, restricting movement and causing discomfort.

Also, when making trousers smaller at the center back, you risk bringing the back pockets too close together, creating what costume technicians often call "kissing pockets."

ALTERING TROUSER LEGS WIDTH

You can taper wide trouser legs and retain the correct front and back crease positions if you're careful to take in equal amounts in both inseam and outseam. Begin the tapering 2 or 3 inches below the side pockets and taper gradually.

You usually cannot turn bell-bottom trouser legs into straight legs without causing them to twist.

Period and Style Alterations

Period and style alterations often call for great ingenuity on the part of costume designers and technicians. Many changes can be made in a garment to integrate it into a particular production style or period, but the real trick is to recognize the potential for change in a garment that is, to the ordinary eye, quite unsuitable. Seeing this potential and figuring out how to realize it requires experience, skill, and a willingness to experiment.

The most important step in recognizing a garment that might meet a particular design need is to know exactly what you are looking for. Study the costume design sketch and the period research. Look carefully. Concentrate on silhouette. Stare at the materials until you can make a quick drawing, by memory, of the basic costume shapes.

Pay particular attention to lengths and widths. Note skirt, waist, sleeve, and jacket lengths. Also, notice the length of one garment in relationship to another: jacket to trousers, bodice to skirt, sleeve length to jacket length, and so on. In men's garments particularly, check length and width of trouser legs, shoulder width, lapel width, and chest prominence. For specific men's tailoring details, consult sources such as the Cunnington books and *Esquire's Encyclopedia of 20th Century Men's Fashions.*

Once you know exactly what you need, begin to look at your stock and at secondhand garments to discover which costumes can be created from things you already have.

You can always remove trim from fancy garments to make them more suitable for a somber production; you can add trim to plain garments for a richer look. Turn a sedate ball gown from the bustle period into a costume for a dance hall queen by raising the hem, lowering the neckline, and adding rows of thick fringe to the bustle folds and to the newly shortened skirt. Use gold braid, brass buttons, and fanciful ribbons to convert a modern white naval officer's jacket into a costume for a comic opera general.

Some chemise and sack dresses are adaptable to early 1920s styles. Collar trim added to a basic shirtwaist dress can turn it into a 1930s housedress. In the late 1960s, young women wore high-necked, puff-sleeved blouses that can pass for early twentieth-century shirtwaists when you release the front waist darts, gather and blouse out the front, and stabilize the shape with a waist tape. Create a skirt to go with the shirtwaist by redistributing the gathers on a long gathered skirt so that the front panel remains smooth and all the gathering moves toward the back.

The shape and height of necklines are particularly important to the period look of women's blouses and bodices, and they are relatively easy to change. Consider adding a dickey and collar to a scoop-necked bodice. Or, take the top part of one blouse and fill in the neck of another.

Look at men's suits with a sharp eye toward adaptation. Many "Ivy League" suits from the late 1950s and early 1960s can be altered into suits from the late nineteenth century and early twentieth century. Add a fourth button and buttonhole to the three-button jacket and create a new lapel fold line by stitching a piece of twill tape into the fold and shaping it with steam. "Ivy League" trousers were generally straight and slim so all you will have to do to them is remove the cuffs and lengthen the hems.

Collars and neckwear say a great deal about period in men's garments. When studying period research, take careful note of the shapes of shirt collars, the style and width of the neckwear, and the size of the tie knot. It is easy to change a shirt collar from one shape to another and even easier to take a collar off a shirt and add stud holes in the neckband so detachable collars can be used.

More Altering Information

As you can see by now, altering requires imagination, patience, and skill. The information in this chapter will give you a foundation on which you can begin to build your skills. For a detailed study of garment alterations, consult *Fitting and Pattern Alteration: A Multi-Method Approach,* by Elizabeth L. Liechty et al. (see the Patterns and Construction section of the Bibliography for the complete citation).

7
Fabric Dyeing and Painting

The first section in this chapter is an essay, "Fabric Dyeing and Painting—An Overview," written by Deborah M. Dryden, author of *Fabric Painting and Dyeing for the Theatre*.

Fabric Dyeing and Painting—An Overview
by Deborah M. Dryden

Dyeing and painting fabrics for theatrical costumes release the designer from the restrictions of using only commercially available fabric colors and patterns. Dyes and paints are used to change, or tint, the overall color of fabric, and also to print, pattern, texture, or age the fabric to suit the designer's needs.

Dyes and paints are distinguished from one another by a few simple factors.

Dyes are transparent; the color of the dyed fabric is affected or transmuted by the underlying color of the fabric. Dyes actually penetrate the fiber in the dye bath, thereby allowing the change of color to occur without changing the "hand" or feel of the finished goods. Dyes are also fiber-specific; it is necessary to know the fiber content of the fabric prior to choosing the appropriate dye for the dye bath. Most dyes require some form of "assistant" (frequently required assistants include salt, acetic acid, or washing soda) to allow the dye process to occur satisfactorily. The assistant required varies with the type or class of dye used. It is important to use only the appropriate assistant for the class of dye being used. Indiscriminate addition of salt or acid will often adversely affect the dye bath.

Dyes can also be thickened to create *dye pastes* which allow one to blockprint, silk-screen, or paint dye directly onto fabric. Fabrics printed or painted with dye pastes need to be steamed (in a steamer) upon completion to set the dye.

Fastness to washing and/or dry cleaning of dyed fabrics depends upon the type of dye used and the fiber content of the fabric.

270

FIGURE 7–1. Coronation robe for Richard III; designed by Deborah Dryden for a production at the Oregon Shakespeare Festival. The fabric is industrially textured, and trimmed with wide silk screened bands. See Figure 7–6 for an enlarged detail of the skull imagery. *Photograph by Deborah Dryden.*

Paints or pigments are translucent or opaque. They utilize a binder that adheres the color to the fabric. This binder invariably affects the hand of the fabric, although recently developed products have managed to reduce the resulting stiffness considerably. Paints are consequently less fiber-specific than dyes, allowing one to treat a larger cross section of the fiber types than is typical with dyes.

271

Paints are not usually recommended for vat dyeing, their use being more often employed for silk screening, blockprinting, direct painting, and aging and distressing.

Fabric painted with pigment mediums, such as textile paint, require little after-treatment—usually air drying or heat setting (*not* steam!). Specific setting instructions should be included with the directions for each product.

Dyes

Some confusion may arise for the beginning dyer as to what kind of dye to use for a given piece of fabric. The proliferation of brand names on the market can add to this confusion. It may be helpful to realize that there are fourteen classes of dyes, only a few of which are commonly used in the theatre.

Perhaps the most frequently used type of dye currently found in theatre costume shops is a type known as *union* or *household* dye. This dye has a number of familiar brand names: Rit, Tintex, Cushings, Deka L, and others. While not technically a dye class unto itself, union dyes are excellent core dyes for every shop as they consist of a combination of several other dye types. Although they don't possess the special characteristics (brilliance of color, for example) of each of their component dyes, they will dye a wider range of fabrics than the individual dye types. Simple to use, their only required chemical assistant is common uniodized salt for use on cellulosic fibers. (Some union dyes include salt in the purchased dye.)

As the number of mixed-fiber fabrics is high in theatrical costume shops, union dyes are a good "universal" dye to have on hand.

Acid and *basic* dyes are two types whose characteristics fall into the realm of those dyes that theatre artists have mistakenly been calling *aniline* dyes for many years. Aniline was a substance originally used in the creation of synthetic dyes, and while dye technology has all but eliminated its use in dyestuffs, the name has somehow continued to be used, particularly in theatre circles.

Acid and basic dyes are brilliant in color and are often used in scenic painting.

Acid dyes are so called because they require an acidic dye bath, one of the most common being the use of acetic acid (vinegar is a dilute solution of acetic acid) in the dye bath. Acid dyes provide brilliant color on silk, wool, and nylon. Fastness can be retained by dry cleaning, as many of these dyes are not fast to washing. Recent developments have resulted in acid dyes that provide better wash-fast results.

Basic dyes are similar to acid dyes in brilliance of color, fastness properties, and dyeability of silk, wool, and nylon. Basic dyes are notable in that they will dye acrylic fibers—something that is difficult with most other dye classes. Basic dyes are also used with shellac and alcohol to form FEV (French Enamel Varnish), discussed later under "Paint Mediums."

It is important to be aware that the dye particles of acid and basic dyestuffs are extremely fine and can be airborne easily and invisibly. Proper safety precautions should be strictly adhered to when mixing these dyes.

Fiber-reactive dyes were developed initially to dye rayon. Since then, this class has been developed to include a wide range of dye possibilities. Fiber-reactives work well on cotton, linen, rayon, reed, raffia—in short, cellulosic fibers. Some will also dye silk, although the colors will differ from the same dye bath on cotton or rayon. The advantage of these dyes is that they achieve high brilliance in cool to lukewarm dye bath temperatures. This makes them ideal for batik artists, where the temperature of the dye bath is critical to the preservation of the wax used in batiking. Known under various brand names (Procion MX, Hi-Dye, Cabacron F, Dylon, Fabdec, etc.), these dyes require common salt and washing soda as assistants. Note that washing soda available in grocery stores is often mixed with other substances. When you are using fiber-reactive dyes, it is important to add *pure* washing soda (soda ash), available from most dye suppliers. These dyes are most brilliant in color and remarkably colorfast on cotton, linen, and viscose rayon.

Direct dyes are inexpensive and easy to use. Direct dyes require only salt as an assistant; therefore, they are of great use for the theatrical dyer. Direct dyes are intended for use on cotton, linen, and viscose rayon, although some will also dye silk and wool. Wash-fastness of direct dyes is not high, although color loss can be minimized by cold water washes with a mild detergent or by dry cleaning. ProChem supplies an after-treatment for direct dyes that improves their wash-fastness.

Disperse dyes were developed specifically for synthetic fibers. They are simple to use and dye acetates and nylon to brilliant, intense colors. They are also used to dye polyester fibers, making them exceedingly useful to the theatrical dyer. Many disperse dyes require extremely high heat in the dye bath for the dye to work effectively. Once dyed, however, the color is extremely wash-fast.

There are many different kinds of disperse dye. Depending on the brand of disperse dye purchased, it may be necessary to use a carrier (purchased with the dye) to assist the dye penetration.

The fumes from the carrier in the dye bath can be extremely toxic and should not be used without proper ventilation and/or a respirator. Many dyers advocate seeking a disperse dye that does not require a carrier, to avoid the toxicity problem.

Some disperse dyes have also been reported to cause skin irritations in people wearing clothing that has been dyed with them. It might be prudent to use disperse dyes only for clothing that will be worn over other clothing.

Be sure to get the Material Safety Data Sheets (MSDSs) for the type of disperse dye and carrier available from your dye supplier.

DYEING FABRICS WITH
MIXED-FIBER CONTENT

Fabrics with mixed-fiber content—such as cotton and polyester, rayon and polyester, polyester and acrylic—are widely used in theatre. *Union* dyes, which color a variety of fibers, may be sufficient to achieve the appropriate color in a mixed-fiber fabric. If greater color intensity is desired, it may be necessary to go to a two-bath process. For example, if you have a fabric that consists of polyester and cotton, it may be necessary to dye the fabric once with disperse dyes for the polyester, and then overdye the fabric with fiber-reactive dyes, or direct dyes, for the cotton. *Do not mix different classes of dye in the same dye bath.*

COLOR REMOVAL

Removing color from dyed fabric, or "stripping," is an unpredictable process at best. Several products are commonly used to remove color from fabric.

Chlorine bleach can be used in dilute form on cellulosic fibers, but it is important to realize that the bleaching action continues after the initial application. This can ultimately destroy the fiber. To stop the action of the bleach, a solution of sodium bisulfite can be used. A long series of rinses can also help to diminish the ongoing action of the bleaching process. Bleach will destroy protein fibers, so it is definitely *not* recommended for use on silks and wools.

Spraying with diluted bleach is extremely hazardous. If spraying is required, for an aging or other discharge process, be sure to use proper ventilation, an appropriate respirator, and protective clothing.

Sodium hydrosulfite is the active ingredient most often found in household dye "color removers." It requires high heat to activate the bath and it has the distinct and foul-smelling odor of rotten eggs. A product preferable in terms of smell and effectiveness is *thiourea dioxide,* available from most dye suppliers. It has a longer shelf life and is stronger than sodium hydrosulfite, though it is used in the same manner. Adequate ventilation is required when using any color removal process in the vat or in a pot on the stove.

Be sure to wear a mask with a dust/mist filter when working with the powder form of sodium hydrosulfite or thiourea dioxide. It is dangerous to inhale either of these powders!

DYE SAFETY

Safety procedures are covered elsewhere in this book (Chapter 2—"Health and Safety in the Costume Shop"), and the reader is urged to re-view these practices before engaging in any dye or paint activity. A few additional cautions about dyeing:

1. Take the time to wear appropriate protec-tive garments. Theatre artists are notorious for foregoing this kind of discipline in the haste of deadline pressures. Such lapses, understand-able though they may be, are simply not worth it. Dyes can be absorbed into the body through the skin and lungs. Any theatre artist who prac-tices dyeing or painting regularly should have a respirator (capable of filtering vapors, fumes, airborne dusts, particles, and mists), protective smock, heat-resistant long gloves, and goggles. Theatre costume shops should be stocked with additional supplies of these items for the one-time or short-term user.

2. Dyes vary in terms of their potential harm-fulness to humans. MSDSs should be on hand for each product used in the dye room.

3. Dye particles can become airborne very easily. Make sure that all dye containers are covered when not in use, even when mixing

FIGURE 7–2. Dyer Chris Carpenter, wearing gloves and respirator, operating an airbrush in the crafts area at the Oregon Shakespeare Festival. *Photograph by Deborah Dryden.*

dyes. (See page 54 in Chapter 2 for an easy-to-make protective glove box for mixing dye powders.)

4. Check local hazardous waste removal com-panies in your area to determine how best to discard solvents, and paints.

5. Use flammables cabinets for all potentially flammable supplies in the dye shop.

6. Know the facts about adequate ventilation and encourage the production manager and managing director to make changes in the work space as necessary.

7. In mixing dye powders, make sure to always add *wet* to *dry,* not the other way around. In other words, dye powders should always be diluted with a small amount of water before

274

PLATE 1   Wallace Acton as Peer Gynt, Ted van Griethuysen as Old Man, and Kate Skinner as the Woman in Green in The Shakespeare Theatre's production of *Peer Gynt*. Costume design by Paul Tazewell. *Photograph by Carol Rosegg, courtesy of The Shakespeare Theatre.*

PLATE 2   A scene from *Play On* at Arena Stage. Costume design by Marianna Elliott. *Photograph courtesy of Arena Stage.*

PLATE 3   Actor Heidi Dippold as Priscilla in *Homebody/Kabul* at the Berkeley Repertory Theatre. Costume design by Lydia Tanjii. *Photograph by Kevin Berne, courtesy of the Berkeley Repertory Theatre.*

PLATE 4   Teri Hansen, George Hall, and John Christopher Jones in *Hans Christian Andersen* at the American Conservatory Theater. Costumes designed by Jane Greenwood. *Photograph courtesy of the American Conservatory Theater.*

PLATE 5   Tsidii le Loka as Cassandra in *Agamenon* at Arena Stage. Costume design by Lindsay W. Davis. *Photograph courtesy of Arena Stage.*

PLATE 6   Franchelle Stewart Dorn as Mistress Quickly and David Sabin as Falstaff in a scene from *The Merry Wives of Windsor* at The Shakespeare Theatre. Costume design by Kaye Voyce. *Photograph by Carol Rosegg, courtesy of The Shakespeare Theatre.*

PLATE 7 Petronia Paley as Jocasta and Avery Brooks as Oedipus in *The Oedipus Plays* at The Shakespeare Theatre. Costume design by Toni-Leslie James. *Photograph by Carol Rosegg, courtesy of The Shakespeare Theatre.*

PLATE 8 Aleah Windham as Young Ismene, Avery Brooks as Oedipus, and Mercedez Tasharmba Mitchell as Young Antigone in *The Oedipus Plays* at The Shakespeare Theatre. Costume design by Toni-Leslie James. *Photograph by Carol Rosegg, courtesy of The Shakespeare Theatre.*

PLATE 9 Martin Kildare as Iago and Jason Michael Spelbring as Rodrigo in the Utah Shakespearean Festival's production of *Othello*. Costume design by Bill Black. *Photograph by Karl Hugh, courtesy of the Utah Shakespearean Festival.*

PLATE 10 Andrew Long as Bosola and Elizabeth Long as Julia in The Shakespeare Theatre's production of *The Duchess of Malfi*. Costume design by Robert Perziola. *Photograph by Carol Rosegg, courtesy of The Shakespeare Theatre.*

PLATE 11   Period draping projects by students in Jim Glaven's class at the University of Texas. *Photograph by Jim Glaven.*

PLATE 12   Mitzi McKay portraying Queen Victoria in *The Pirates of Penzance* at the Utah Shakespearean Festival. Costume design by Bill Black. *Photograph by Karl Hugh, courtesy of the Utah Shakespearean Festival.*

PLATE 13   Judith Marie Bergen as Tamora and Ray Porter as Saturninus in *Titus Andronicus* at the Oregon Shakespeare Festival. Costume design by Susan Tsu. *Photograph by Susan Tsu.*

PLATE 14   Dancers Yvonne Cutaran and Jason Hartley in a scene from *Coyote Builds North America* at Arena Stage. Costume design by Bill C. Ray. *Photograph by Joan Marcus, courtesy of Arena Stage.*

PLATE 15   A scene from *The Women* at Arena Stage. Costume design by Paul Tazewell.
Photograph courtesy of Arena Stage.

PLATE 16   David Adkins as Alceste and Anthony Fusco as Oronte in *The Misanthrope* at the American Conservatory Theater. Costume design by Beaver Bauer. *Photograph courtesy of the American Conservatory Theater.*

PLATE 17   Kimberly King as Arsinoe and Rene Augesen as Celimene in *The Misanthrope* at the American Conservatory Theater. Costume design by Beaver Bauer. *Photograph courtesy of the American Conservatory Theater.*

PLATE 18   A scene from *Animal Crackers* at Arena Stage. Costume design by Zack Brown. *Photograph by Joan Marcus, courtesy of Arena Stage.*

adding them to the dye bath. Chemicals or salts should always be in solution before adding to the dye bath. This not only allows for more even dyeing but helps prevent splash-back of dye powders into the air. Add acid to water and not the reverse.

8. Contact lens wearers may experience eye irritation due to frequent exposure to dye particles and mists. Soft and gas-permeable lenses are especially susceptible to sprays and unprotected exposure to steam over a dye vat.

9. No food or drink or cooking utensils (coffeepots) should be allowed anywhere in the dye room. Make sure the dye/paint/spray area is separate from the rest of the costume shop. Be aware that children and pets have lower tolerance levels for toxicity than adults, so keep children and pets out of the dye/paint area at all times!

Direct Painting with Dyes

While every class of dye mentioned can be thickened into a dye paste (recipes vary per type of dye used) for direct painting on fabric, a few products exist that simplify this process and therefore deserve mentioning.

LIQUID FIBER-REACTIVE DYES (PROCION H)

These dyes are intended for *direct* application (not bath dyeing) on silk, wool, cotton, linen, and rayon. They are easy to use and have excellent wash-fastness properties when thoroughly steamed. They can be thickened for use in silk screening, stenciling, or block-printing.

Fabrics painted with dye pastes require *steaming* for fixation. (Page 285 has directions for making a simple steamer.) Dye pastes applied directly to fabric, properly steamed and rinsed, result in no change of hand of the fabric.

ALCOHOL-BASED LIQUID DYES

These *acid* dyes (Tinfix, Supertinfix, and others), in solution with water and alcohol, are very popular among fabric artists as they provide brilliant colors on silk and are easy to use. Once again, steam setting is required for adequate fixation and dry cleaning is recommended for colorfastness.

Paint Mediums

One of the most frequently used paint mediums for costumes is textile paint. Many types of textile paint can be purchased from silk-screen suppliers. Advance and Nazdar are two national companies with distributors in major cities across the country. Send for catalogs from both companies to add to your costume library.

Water-based textile paints are easier to apply and clean up than oil-based or lacquer-based textile paints. Many brands of water-based textile paints are available from dye suppliers and in art or craft stores. Common brand names include: Versatex, Wat-R-Tex, Aquaset, Profab Textile Inks, and others. A set of good water-based textile paints, regardless of the brand name, is a wise investment for any costume shop.

Water-based textile paints can be painted directly onto fabric, sprayed (if thinned with water), blockprinted, stenciled, or silk-screened. Most water-based paints are available with a clear extender that allows maximum quantity when diluting the consistency of the paint. These paints are generally translucent to opaque, although they may be thinned to increase their transparency.

The hand of the fabric is affected by the use of textile paints, but the resultant stiffness can be quite minimal, depending upon the consistency of the paint and the weight of the fabric used. Most water-based textile paints require heat setting to permanently fix the color on the fabric. Once the fabric has been painted and allowed to dry, it can then be ironed with a hot iron or tumbled in a hot dryer.

While water-based textile paints will adhere to a variety of fibers, it is always a good idea to test the fabric you wish to paint first and check its fastness to washing and dry cleaning.

Water-based textile paints are highly recommended for spraying in aging and distressing costumes.

Acrylic paints are also sometimes used to paint fabrics. Once dry, acrylic paints do not require heat setting for fastness. However, the resultant stiffness of hand is considerably greater than when the fabric is painted with water-based textile paints.

FEV (French Enamel Varnish) is a paint medium used in the theatre to create transparent glazes. FEV is made from combining transparent liquid leather dye (for color) and varying proportions of shellac and denatured alcohol (the shellac acts as a binder for the color; the alcohol is used to dilute the solution to retain softness of hand). While costumes painted with FEV are not particularly wash-fast or dry cleanable, the product is very useful in painting metal or plastic. The FEV base can also be used to adhere bronzing powders to leather, plastic, or metal. Adequate ventilation and/or a respirator should always be used with painting or spraying with FEV.

Leather dye sprays are used much too frequently by theatre artists to age and distress costumes. Leather sprays are good to color leather but their opacity makes them appear less believable on fabrics than other methods discussed above. Leather sprays are very expensive; they are not the most effective method of aging and distressing; and most important of all, the fumes of these aerosol sprays are very toxic and they should never be used without adequate ventilation and a proper respirator.

Digital Textile Printing

Increasingly in the textile industry, fabrics are being printed utilizing digital technology. For theatre artists that technology is becoming gradually more accessible. Small-scale printing using a standard printer is possible using prepared fabric (available from Dharma Trading Company and Rupert, Gibbon & Spider). Fabric printed in this manner generally requires steam setting following printing.

Images can be prepared utilizing Adobe Photoshop or other pattern-related software. Calibration of color between printer and scanner or computer monitor is essential to reduce large amounts of time spent in trial and error to achieve accurate color resolution.

Full-size textile printers are available to print a wide variety of fabrics in their full width. Types of inks vary and consequently, the need to steam the fabric after printing is related to the type of fabric and the inks employed, just as with more conventional printing methods. While these printers are currently beyond the means of most theatre costume shops, there are sources that offer custom textile printing for individual projects. While these services are not cheap, they may make it possible for theatres to utilize this form of digital textile printing for particular projects.

Summary

The dyeing and painting of theatre costumes can be an exciting addition to the designer's "tools." Since they simulate the painting techniques used by designers on costume sketches, dyeing and painting can successfully reproduce qualities of a costume idea or sketch that could not be reproduced in other ways.

The dyer-painter should not be overwhelmed by the enormous number of dye products on the market or by the ever-growing availability of safety information. Learn about unfamiliar products by requesting MSDSs; read and study them, and keep them on file. Practice the safety advice recommended in this book. Experiment with test samples and keep accurate records.

While time and money are the nemeses of most theatre productions, it is important to realize that many dye and paint techniques can be accomplished with a minimum of expense for supplies and equipment. Equipment that enhances safety in the dye room, however, should never be shortchanged.

Allowing sufficient time for dyeing or painting of costumes is a continual struggle in all costume shops. It is important to realize that each step of the dye-paint process must be scheduled into the construction time with care. Dyeing and painting are unpredictable art forms and sufficient time to conduct appropriate samples and experiments is a must.

Ms. Dryden is an Emeritus Professor of Design at the University of California at San Diego and a professional costume designer. She is currently the resident costume designer at the Oregon Shakespeare Festival.

Purchasing and Storing Dyestuffs

All costume shops that dye fabrics on a regular basis should make bulk purchases of the dyestuffs they use the most. The small packets or bottles of Rit or Tintex bought in the grocery store are very expensive, approximately five times more per ounce than union dye bought by the pound.

Bulk dyestuffs will usually come to you in containers made from metal, cardboard and metal, or opaque plastic. Inspect all containers before storing them. Make sure the cans are clearly marked with dye type, color, and all necessary instructions and precautions for their use. Collect the Material Safety Data Sheets and put them in a notebook or on a clipboard for easy referral. Keep all containers tightly closed when not in use, both to protect yourself from inhaling dye powders and because many dye pigments deteriorate under light.

You will probably purchase specialized types of dye in smaller quantities for specific projects. Be sure to store all leftover dyestuffs carefully. Tape paper packages closed and be sure to mark all packets and containers with

FIGURE 7–3. Harold Gould in the title role as *King Lear* at the Utah Shakespearean Festival. The motifs were done with a photo silk screen and textile paints with the addition of bronzing powder and hand-painted highlights. Costume design by Colleen Muscha. *Photograph by Colleen Muscha.*

their contents. Many costume shop cupboards contain tins, jars, and packets of unidentified substances that eventually will have to be disposed of because nobody knows what they are or how to use them.

Dye Vats, Pots, and Washing Machines

When you color fabric in an automatic washing machine, you are actually tinting the cloth rather than dyeing it. The water temperature in most automatic washing machines is not hot enough to set the dye permanently, and the colors will not become as deep and brilliant as they will at higher temperatures. Tinted fabrics lose their color after they have been washed repeatedly.

To do colorfast dyeing, you must either simmer the cloth in an open container or in a dye vat or set the dye with steam in a steamer. Most fabrics have to be simmered for forty-five minutes in a dye bath of union-type dye to achieve the most intense color possible and the most colorfast finish. A 190-degree temperature is optimum for silks, wools, and many blends, while cotton can withstand boiling.

Preparing Fabric for Tinting or Dyeing

Serge or zigzag each raw edge of the fabric being dyed. Weigh the fabric on a baby scale while it is still dry and record the weight to calculate the amount of dye solution needed. If a baby scale is not available, estimate that about two yards of a mediumweight fabric weighs about one pound.

Wash the fabric in a good, low-sudsing detergent and rinse well. Synthrapol is a particularly good detergent for preparing fabrics for dyeing. Synthrapol is available from most companies that sell bulk dyes. If the fabric is heavily sized, soak it in a 5 percent soda ash solution after it has been washed. Approximately ¼ cup, or 56.7 grams, of soda ash constitutes a 5 percent solution for 1½ pounds of fabric. Soda ash is caustic, so wear rubber gloves, eye protection, and dust/mist filter on respirator or dust/mist mask when working with it. The fabric should be both wet and warm when placed in the dye bath.

SAMPLE DYE SWATCHES

Before you set out to dye fabrics in your shop, make a dye swatch display that illustrates all the dye colors on hand. For the most effective and useful set of color swatches, use multifiber swatch fabric, available from Testfabrics, Inc. Multifiber swatch fabric is made up of strips of different fibers and fiber blends, woven in rows, on a single piece of fabric. One piece of multifiber swatch fabric, dipped in a single dye solution, will produce examples of the different color intensities you can expect to get on most of the common fibers and blends.

FIGURE 7–4. Dye samples on multifiber swatch fabric. *Photograph by Liz Covey.*

Study your sample swatches to determine which dye colors you should mix together to arrive at the color you want. Often, particularly when using union dyes, you will have to overdye the fabric to get the correct result, using two separate dye baths. Overdyeing may keep your colors from becoming muddy.

Snip several swatches from the washed, wet fabric to be dyed. Put a pot of water on to boil or let the hot water tap run until the water is as hot as possible.

Use extreme care when you measure out dye powders. Use a glove box, as shown on page 54 in Chapter 2, and wear an approved respirator. Don't forget to protect other people in the room who might also inhale airborne dye powder.

Measure the dye powders into a one-quart Pyrex measuring cup. Record the colors and the exact amount of each color used. Most people measure dye powders in teaspoons, but it is much more accurate to measure in grams. The average total amount of dye powder to add to 1 quart of water is ¼ to ½ gram.

Add a few drops of cold water to the dye powder and stir it carefully into a paste. When all the dye powder is "pasted," add the hot water to the paste, slowly filling the one-quart measure. Stir. Strain the dye solution through a nylon stocking or several layers of cheesecloth laid on the bottom of a plastic strainer, into a stainless steel or unchipped enamelware dyeing pan.

Place your swatch in the dye bath. If you're tinting the fabric in an automatic washing machine, stir the swatch around until it's a shade or two darker than desired, then remove it from the dye. If you're dyeing the fabric in a dye vat or in a pot, place the pan containing the swatch and the dye on the stove or hot plate and allow it to simmer for approximately twenty minutes. Don't forget that the wet dyed fabric is darker than it will be when it's dry.

Remove the swatch from the dye bath and rinse it until the water running through it is clear. Dry with a hair dryer. The direct application of heat, such as with an iron, can change the color.

Label the swatch with the amount of dye of each color used in the quart of water. If the color is not correct, prepare a new 1-quart dye bath and try a different dye color mixture.

DYEING THE FABRIC TO MATCH THE SWATCH

Once you have managed to produce an accurately colored swatch, you must proceed to color the whole piece of fabric to match. If tinting fabric in an automatic washing machine, you will need to know the number of quarts of water the machine holds. If dyeing in a vat or pot, calculate how many quarts of water you will need for the piece of fabric being dyed. Weigh the fabric on a baby scale and allow three to four gallons of water for each pound of fabric. Fill the vat, pot, or washing machine tub with hot water. Be sure to cut off the washing machine cycle as soon as the tub is full. (Don't forget that only top loading washing machines are suitable for dyeing.)

Multiply the amount of dye contained in the sample quart by the number of quarts of water contained in the vat, pot, or washing machine to find out how much dye will be needed. Measure this amount of dye powder into a deep-sided glass container. (Use a glove box and wear a respirator.) Add cold water to the dye powder and make a paste. Pour hot water into the container and stir carefully. Strain the dye solution into the vat, pot, or washing machine tub. Place any

FIGURE 7–5. Dye charts and color swatches in the dye room at The Washington Opera. *Photograph by Liz Covey.*

assistants, such as salt, into a container, add water, stir, and add to the dye solution. Stir the vat or tub carefully. (A kayak paddle makes a dandy stirring implement for a large dye vat!) Let the washing machine agitate for a few moments. Slowly add the warm, wet fabric to the dye solution. Return the washing machine to its automatic cycle; stir the vat or pot throughout the dyeing process. Once you've found a suitable recipe for the desired color, be sure to record the dye colors and amounts you used, including assistants, for future reference.

Many costume dyers do not measure as carefully as they should. Some resort to dipping the fabric over and over until they achieve the correct color. When tinting fabrics in an automatic washing machine, repeated dye cycles probably won't hurt the fibers. But, when simmering or boiling cloth to achieve a color-fast finish, you run the risk of harming the fibers if you repeat the process several times. Learn to weigh the fabric and to measure the dye accurately, and you will find that the fabric colors you create are more accurate and certainly more consistent than when you mix up a dye bath by tossing in colors until the solution looks right.

Don't be misled into thinking that costume dyeing is an exact art, however. There are so many variables in the process that it is virtually impossible to reproduce a color the second time. Even commercially done dye lots vary in intensity. Don't let the inevitable color variation frustrate you. Remember that there are times when the unexpected color turns out to be more perfect that the one you planned to get.

Equipment and Supplies for the Dyeing and Painting Area

Fabric dyeing and painting are messy activities. They need to be carried on in a protected area—preferably in a separate room—where there is little danger of damaging uninvolved garments with spills and sprays. Even when dyestuffs are handled most carefully, there is always the danger that tiny airborne dye particles will settle on another fabric, particularly a damp fabric, and spoil it completely.

Due to lack of space and because the activities have similar plumbing needs, many dye shops share quarters with costume maintenance. In these situations, great care must be taken to keep the dye area as clean as possible. Wardrobe personnel should always inspect the condition of the washing machines and dryers before putting laundry in them and be especially careful not to place damp laundry on a surface stained with dye. In the best of circumstances, laundry and dyeing should be done in separate rooms.

The following list of equipment and supplies for the dye area is a detailed one that includes most of the common items needed to stock the costume dyeing and painting area.

DYEING AND PAINTING AREA

dye vat—steam-jacketed soup kettle or small commercial dye vat

top loading automatic washing machine

automatic clothes dryer

nonautomatic washing machine with a wringer

hot plate or stove

gram scale for weighing dyes

infant scale for weighing fabric

plastic drying rack and/or clotheslines

stainless steel or unchipped enamelware pots—large and medium sizes

long-handled, stainless steel spoons

tongs—hospital sponge tongs are the best

long wooden stirring sticks—broomstick or 1" dowel

measuring spoons—several sets

plastic dishpans

quart-size Pyrex measuring cups

one-cup-size Pyrex measuring cups

widemouth jars and lids in assorted sizes

alarm clock or timer

ironing board

iron

hair dryer

tailor's form and/or display form

lightweight plastic to cover form

zigzag sewing machine or serger

measuring tapes and rulers

scissors

straight pins and T-pins

laundry marking pens

plastic laundry baskets

terry cloth towels

sponges

cheesecloth and a collection of old nylons—for straining dye solutions

plastic or stainless steel strainer—for straining dye solutions

roll of brown craft paper

scouring powder

hand soap

paper towels
protective gloves

DYESTUFFS AND ASSISTANTS

bulk dyes in an assortment of basic colors
common salt, uniodized
soda ash—for removing sizing
color removers
low-sudsing laundry detergent
other types of dyes and assistant chemicals, as
  necessary

SUPPLIES AND MATERIALS FOR
FABRIC PAINTING

textile paints, preferably water based, in an
  assortment of basic colors
colored inks
liquid leather dyes
shoe polish, liquid and paste
tempera paints
acrylic paints
spray gun, atomizer, and/or airbrush
assorted brushes: 2 inches, 1 inch, ½ inch,
  fine-tipped sable
stippling brushes
toothbrushes
sponges, natural and plastic
hot-melt glue gun and glue pellets

masking tape
stencil material
X-Acto handles and blades
single-edged razor blades
metallic powders
white shellac
denatured alcohol
flexible white glue
other adhesives, as necessary

TAKE CARE OF DYEING AND PAINTING
SUPPLIES AND EQUIPMENT

Throw out all old dye solutions promptly and scrub pans and other utensils with scouring powder. Check the filters on the automatic washing machine and clothes dryer *after each complete cycle* and keep them free of all lint. Remember to turn off electric hot plates and stoves when they are not in use. Keep your brushes clean. Remove dye pastes and water-based paints with cool water. Clean brushes that have been used to apply shoe polish, leather dyes, or FEV with denatured alcohol. When the brushes are free from dyes, paints, and polishes, wash them gently with mild soap and cool water, shake out excess water, smooth the hairs, and stand, brush end up, in a glass or jar to dry.

Costume Painting

Before beginning to work with any coloring material, make sure you are familiar with its properties and know what results you may expect. Always experiment by applying the paint or dye paste to sample pieces of the actual fabric before going to work on the actual costume.

If applying an overall pattern to the fabric, do the printing or painting on the fabric pieces before they are stitched together. It may be more convenient to work on the garment pieces after they have been chalked onto the fabric and before they have been cut out. You will probably use stencils, silkscreens, wood or linoleum blocks, or freehand painting for most overall patterns, with fabric paints or dye pastes as the color medium.

Borders and small pattern areas are often done after the garments are assembled. They may be done with stencils or blocks, or freehand with a brush or sponge. Permanent markers and liquid embroidery pens are also useful for decorating fabrics. Designs made with markers and embroidery pens must be heat set. Brands differ in permanence so read directions and experiment with heat setting methods. For a special effect, try dyeing lace and then painting it with bronzing powders and white glue.

FIGURE 7–6. Detail of the silk screening in Figure 7–1. Dyer/painter Lene Price was responsible for the screen printing. *Photograph by Deborah Dryden.*

FIGURE 7–7. Actor Lee E. Ernst wearing a painted Harlequin costume in a production of *Servant of Two Masters* at the Milwaukee Repertory Theater. Costume design by Santi Migneco. *Photograph by Jay Westhauser, courtesy of the Milwaukee Repertory Theater.*

FIGURE 7–8. A fabric steamer used for setting dyed and painted fabrics at the University of Cincinnati College-Conservatory of Music. *Photograph by Rosemary Ingham.*

Most fabric paints can be set with an iron or in an automatic clothes dryer. Some fabric paints "air dry" in thirty-six to forty-eight hours. Dye pastes require steam setting. See Figure 7–9 for instructions on how to assemble a simple steam container.

If your costume requires a raised pattern, lay it on with hot-melt glue, which you can paint with acrylics or FEV as soon as it dries, or with a flexible coating like Sculpt or Coat, which you can mix with paint. Hot-melt glue stiffens fabrics considerably and works best on heavy fabrics such as upholstery velvets and brocades. The flexible coatings stiffen less than hot glue. Fabrics decorated with raised patterns cannot be pressed.

Costume Shading

Costume shading is often done to give the garments more dimension and to increase their sculptured quality. You can shade so lightly and realistically that the garments look completely natural or more obviously to produce stronger contrasts and a stylized look.

Shade with dyes, dye pastes, and fabric paints. Choose your shading colors carefully. Black is rarely appropriate for shadows. Browns, grays, and purples are most effective, depending on costume, set, and light colors.

Apply shading colors with sponges and/or brushes whenever possible. Use sprays only if other methods of application are ineffective.

284

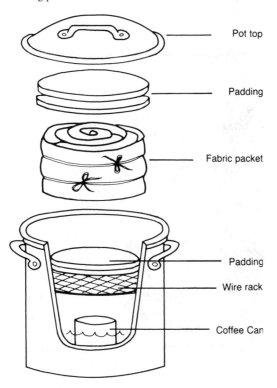

FIGURE 7–9. Steam container improvised from a large cooking pot.

Pot top

Padding

Fabric packet

Padding

Wire rack

Coffee Can

1. Put two inches of water in the bottom of the pot.
2. Remove both ends of a two-pound coffee can and place it in the bottom of the pot. Place a wire rack on top of the coffee can to act as a platform. Pad the wire rack platform with folded cloth, newsprint, or felt. The padding should not touch the sides of the pot.
3. Sandwich single-layer fabric between paper towels, roll in layers of clean newsprint or thin fabric. Tie in a loose bundle. Packet must not touch sides of pot.
4. Make more padding to put on top of the dyed fabric. Use folded cloth, newsprint, or felt.
5. Bring the water to a boil before putting the dyed fabric packet into the pot.
6. After all layers are assembled, put the lid on the pot and weight it down with bricks or boards to force the steam pressure up.
7. Steaming time varies from fifteen minutes to more than an hour.
8. When the dye is set, rinse the fabric in cold water until the rinse water runs off clear.

Don't forget to steam set shading done with dyes and dye pastes.

Painting with FEV

FEV, or French Enamel Varnish, is a versatile theatrical paint that dries with a bright, translucent shine, and can be used on many surfaces, including fabrics. FEV is a mixture of shellac, denatured alcohol, and dye. Different types of solvent-soluble dyes can be used: acid dyes, basic dyes, liquid leather dyes, and liquid shoe polish (except white). Bronzing powders may be suspended in FEV. A mixture of approximately one part shellac and five parts denatured alcohol is suitable for most fabric painting. Experiment with the proportions until you've achieved the surface effect you want. In general, more shellac will result in a stiffer surface. If the solution contains too little shellac, however, FEV has a tendency to rub off. Unlike most fabric paints, FEV penetrates the fabric. It produces a long-lasting effect but may fade after dry cleaning and should not be considered permanent.

Aging and Distressing

You can age a costume to give the garment a comfortable, lived-in appearance or you may virtually destroy its shape and the integrity of the fabric itself until the whole costume appears in shreds. In between these two extremes lie many different degrees of aging and distressing. Before beginning to age a costume, know exactly what final effect you're working toward. The aging process doesn't reverse easily. Proceed in logical steps. Do final touches only after you've seen the garment on the actor, on stage, under the stage lighting.

You can suggest simple wear by removing all sharp creases from the garment, by washing it several times, if it's washable, or by having it

285

FIGURE 7–10. Floyd King wearing suitably aged and crumpled clothes as Pandarus in a production of *Troilus and Cressida*, designed by Kit Surrey at The Shakespeare Theatre. *Photograph by Joan Marcus, courtesy of The Shakespeare Theatre.*

FIGURE 7–11. Floyd King as Lear's Fool in The Shakespeare Theatre's production of *King Lear*, in nicely tatty garb designed by Georgi Alexi-Meskhishvili. *Photograph by Carol Rosegg, courtesy of The Shakespeare Theatre.*

dry cleaned and not well pressed. To suggest a somewhat more advanced garment age, rub the elbows and knees with candlewax to give them a worn shine. Use a cheese grater or sandpaper to create subtly worn places at hems, cuffs, knees, and around buttonholes. Sponge the weakened areas lightly with shoe polish or paint to simulate ingrained soil. To make garments sag, place rocks, or other heavy objects in pockets and sleeves and steam the fabric to loosen the weave. Sand down shiny, new-looking buttons and paint them with dulling paint.

For more pronounced distressing, scrub the fabric with a wire brush and scrape it with a file or rasp. Holes created with a file or rasp look much more natural than those cut out with scissors. File garment edges vigorously for raggedness. Make slashes with a scissors blade or a knife but never make a straight cut. You can singe cut edges slightly with a torch but be careful not to set the whole garment on fire!

Apply dirt and food stains with leather dyes, acrylics, or enamel, or sponge them on with a paste made of tempera pigment, water, and flexible white glue. Paste shoe polishes are excellent for greasy looking stains. Simulate caked-on dirt with globs of flexible white glue, paint, and sawdust.

FIGURE 7–12. Wonderfully realistic aged and distressed clothes on actor Robert Hogan portraying Phil Hogan in a production of *A Moon for the Misbegotten* at Arena Stage. Costumes designed by Rosemary Pardee. *Photograph by Scott Suchman, courtesy of Arena Stage.*

Create faded areas on cotton and linen fabrics by sponging or spattering them with a solution of bleach and water. Do not use undiluted bleach, which will do too much damage to the fabric. Bleach is very destructive to wool and silk, so use it sparingly on these fabrics unless you want extreme disintegration. As soon as the bleach has created faded areas, rinse the garment in a solution of sodium bisulfite, or spray with a vinegar solution, to halt the bleach action.

Most polyester fabrics are extremely difficult to age. If you need the look of ragged cotton, make sure the garment you are to distress is cotton and not a cotton and polyester blend. Pure wool ages beautifully but a wool and nylon blend suit may resist all your attempts to make it saggy.

Remember that it takes years for a garment to age naturally, and you should never expect to age a costume in a single operation. Whenever possible, put the garment on a plastic-covered form while you are working on it. Examine your progress overall from time to time, standing well away from the garment to assess its total appearance.

8
Hair and Hats

A costume is more than clothing; it includes make-up, hairstyle, and all of the accessories or costume properties that are called for in the design. These may be items that can be purchased, borrowed, or found in your own stock, such as a nurse's cap, white shoes, and

FIGURE 8–1. Laurie Birmingham as Abby Brewster and and Leslie Brott as Martha Brewster wearing lace-fronted wigs in *Arsenic and Old Lace* at the Utah Shakespearean Festival. *Photograph by Karl Hugh, courtesy of Utah Shakespearean Festival.*

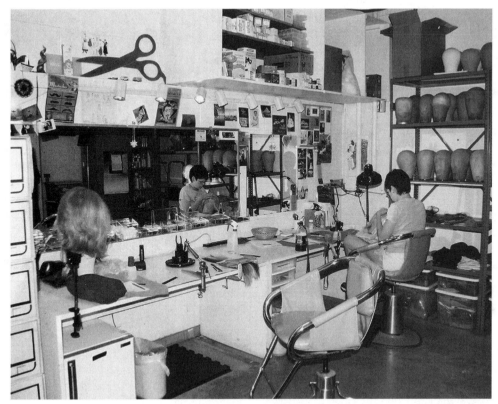

FIGURE 8–2. The wig shop at the Guthrie Theater. *Photograph by Maribeth Hite.*

stockings; or it may be something that must be fabricated, such as a crown, helmet, breast-plate, or mask.

This chapter focuses on the actor's head. The first part is a discussion of theatrical hair-styles; the second includes some basic instructions for making simple hats and tips for restyling and retrimming existing hats. The-atrical make-up is a large and complex subject that does not lend itself to overviews and help-ful hints, and, therefore, will not be discussed in this chapter. Please see the Bibliography for make-up books.

Theatrical Hairstyles

Almost all costumes require complementary hairstyles. In many instances the actor's own hair can be dressed into the appropriate style, but when this is not possible, hairpieces and wigs become necessary.

Many of the larger, resident theatre com-panies that produce half a dozen to a dozen plays in a season from a variety of periods, have a wig and hairstylist on staff, often installed in a separate, well-equipped wig room. Other

FIGURE 8–3. Wigmaker Jennifer Peterson-Alexander tying hair into a wig at the Utah Shakespearean Festival. *Photograph courtesy of Utah Shakespearean Festival.*

FIGURE 8–4. Wig master Jim McGough setting a wig for the American Players Theatre. *Photograph by Rosemary Ingham.*

producing groups hire freelance wig and hair-stylists only when they are doing a play that requires a significant amount of wig and hair-styling. In many costume shops, however, wig and hairstyling falls to the costume technician who has a "knack for doing hair." All costume technicians, whether or not they have a knack for doing hair, should have a basic knowledge of wig and hairstyling and maintenance.

A Look at Period Hairstyles

The height and width of fashionable hairstyles throughout fashion history has always had an interesting relationship to the width and length of clothing. Whenever ladies' hips widen, with paniers, hoops, or peplums, hairstyles rise up so the figure won't appear squat. When fashions are sleek and skinny, such as in the 1920s, hair is short and hugs the head. The same general principle applies to men. Closely trimmed hair

balanced the narrow lapels and shoulders of men's suits in the late 1950s and early 1960s. Longer and fuller hairstyles accompanied the wide lapels and ties and flaring shirt collars that followed.

The relationship between clothing shape and hairstyle operates only on the most generalized level, however, because each period includes many variations on what is fashionable. Besides, many people choose to ignore the prevailing fashion in hair and prefer to cut and arrange their hair in their own way. Others retain a favorite hairstyle from their youth, even though it is long out of fashion. When choosing a hairstyle for a dramatic character, consider the personality of that character carefully. Some characters, like some people, would never dye or tease their hair or change it from straight to curly, while others are eager to be in the fashion forefront.

Out of all the possible hairstyle variations within any fashion period, work with the costume designer to choose, if possible, a style that can be maintained without too much difficulty, and one that the audience won't find distracting. Avoid hairstyles that look as though they might be insecure and ones that are oddly proportioned, unless the characterization demands an unsteady upsweep or an exaggerated beehive.

Consider the Actor's Face

Within the range of styles appropriate for any period, you must take the shape of the actor's face into consideration when choosing a hairstyle. If the object is to make the actor as attractive as possible, complement the shape of the face with the shape of the hair.

A round face should not have too much fullness at the sides as this tends to accentuate round cheeks. Long, straight hair is not good for oblong faces, while medium-length hair is. A square face should have height on the top; but keep the hair on the sides away from the jaw line. Broaden the triangular face at the top with short bangs, while giving the heart-shaped face some fullness at the sides to widen the jaw. In general, tall people should avoid tall hairstyles, and both very large and very small people should stay away from flaring styles.

On the other hand, the object may not be to make the actor look as attractive as possible. A full, fluffy hairstyle that accentuates the roundness of a round-faced actor could be just right for Sister Woman in Tennessee Williams's *Cat on a Hot Tin Roof.* If the actor who requires a "lean and hungry look" already has an oblong face, strengthen the characterization with a long, straight hairstyle.

Haircuts

Haircuts should be done by licensed professionals. However, since barbers and hairstylists who do not specialize in theatrical work are only trained to create contemporary hairstyles,

be prepared to explain and illustrate the period style you want. Have the costume designer or a knowledgeable member of the costume shop staff accompany the actor to the shop or salon and be sure to have costume sketches and research pictures in hand.

Hair Color

Sometimes playwrights specify hair color for their characters. If the script reference cannot be changed to reflect the actor's own hair color and you cannot, for a variety of reasons, use a suitable wig, you may have to resort to hair dyes, tints, or sprays.

Permanent hair dyeing should always be done professionally, particularly if the color has to be lighter than the actor's own and requires a two-step dyeing process. Temporary hair colors, both rinses and sprays, are quite safe in the hands of a well-informed actor or costume technician. The sprays come in a wild assortment of colors and are readily available in local beauty supply shops and in large drugstores. Some temporary rinses will withstand several shampoos. Sprays, in general, come out with a single shampoo.

Actors often have to gray their hair to play older parts. There are several common ways to gray hair for the stage, some more successful than others. Avoid using white liquid shoe polish as a graying agent because it dries the hair and may cause a severe scalp rash in some people.

The major stage make-up manufacturing companies produce stick make-up, in a variety of colors, for graying hair. These do an especially good job of coloring small areas, such as the temples. They have a creamy consistency, are not harmful to most hair, and are easy to control.

When you need to turn a whole head of hair white or gray, it is most convenient to use hair-coloring sprays. Be sure to blend two or three colors. Do not just cover the whole head with a blizzard of white spray. Instead, combine both white and silver sprays and add a bit of blonde for toning. Develop a light touch on the nozzle when you spray. No one's hair is all one color or all one intensity.

Use hairsprays only with adequate ventilation and be sure to shield the actor's neck and face from the hairspray mist. You want to keep the hair color off the actor's skin, *and* you want to protect him or her from inhaling airborne spray droplets. Purchase a hairspray shield from a beauty supply shop or simply cut a cardboard frame that fits around the actor's hairline. Keep the shield in place for several minutes after you finish spraying.

If they are used in moderation, hair-coloring sprays won't harm most hair. Don't forget that most of them rub off and may even run if an actor perspires a great deal, causing definite problems in stage fights and love scenes! Hair coloring sprays may also stain hats.

Another very effective product to gray an actor's hair is Ben Nye's Silver Grey Hair Color. It comes in liquid form and is generally applied to the hair with a toothbrush. This process takes a little more time and patience than using sprays, but it looks more realistic, is less reflective, and doesn't flake. You can highlight with Ben Nye's Snow White Hair Color, also in liquid form. These products wash out with shampoo.

All of the coloring agents mentioned are suitable to use on human hair wigs and hairpieces. You can use certain hair-coloring sprays on synthetic wigs, but use fabric dyes when you want to dye synthetic wigs permanently.

DON'T FORGET TO GET PERMISSION
AND TO CALCULATE COST

Actors' Equity contracts require that a written agreement be made between the actor and the theatre if the actor is required to cut, perm, or change the color of his or her hair. Even if an actor is not protected by Actors' Equity rules and is an amateur or a student, it is only common courtesy to ask permission before assuming that he or she will happily agree to go from a long, straight blonde to a short, curly, flaming redhead.

Haircuts, perms, and hair coloring can be big items in the costume budget. Make sure to take these expenses into account from the beginning so you won't be shocked by unexpected costs just before dress rehearsal. And, don't forget that most Actors' Equity contracts and other types of performance contracts require the hiring theatre to pay not only for coloring an actor's hair for the role but also for restoring the hair to its original color, if the actor wishes.

Hairpieces

You can create many period hairstyles for the stage by making clever use of hairpieces such as falls, wiglets, switches, and cluster curls. In most cases, these need to be as close in color as possible to the actor's own hair.

A *fall* is a long hairpiece, often quite full. The hair is attached to a stiff net or buckram, is shaped to fit the crown of the head, and may have a built-in comb to use for attaching it to the actor's own hair. The hair hangs down the back of the head and may range in length from 7 or 8 inches to 35 or 36 inches.

Wiglets are small decorative hairpieces, usually curled, that can add height and shape to a style. They come in a variety of different sizes and lengths. Like a fall, the hair in a wiglet is attached to a piece of stiff net, buckram, or a flexible wire base.

Long *switches* are commonly used for braids or chignons and are among the most useful hairpieces for the stage. The hairs are

FIGURE 8–5. Sybil Lines wigged out in long tresses as Gertrude with Wallace Acton as Hamlet in The Shakespeare Theatre production of *Hamlet*. Costumes designed by Murell Horton. *Photograph by Carol Rosegg, courtesy of The Shakespeare Theatre.*

tied together at one end and are usually covered with a soft device through which you can fasten the piece to the actor's hair. Sometimes it is useful to use one or more switches as an under-structure to support the actor's own hair in one of the tall, upswept hairstyles.

Cluster curls are available as single curls or in clusters of two, three, or more. They can be pinned into many different hairstyles for a variety of effects.

Hairpieces must be firmly attached to the actor's real hair so the whole hairstyle is completely secure. Before attaching a fall, wiglet, switch, or curls, make two or three flat pin curls of the actor's own hair where the hairpiece will go. Secure each of them with two bobby pins, pinned to form an X. Slip the comb on the hairpiece into the pin curls under the bobby pins. Put a few long hairpins through the back-ing of the piece into the pin curls. If there is no comb on the hairpiece, stitch one in. Sometimes it is necessary to wrap or twist a section of the actor's own hair around the base of the hairpiece to hide the join. Ribbons and artificial flowers, when they are included in the costume design, are excellent coverups for hairpieces.

HAIRPIECES FOR BALDING ACTORS

Hairpieces for balding actors are costly, custommade items that are not usually provided for in costume budgets. However, many balding actors have their own hairpieces or a selection of hairpieces for stage use. If an actor is planning to wear his own hairpiece, be sure to ask him to wear it to all fittings—particularly hat fittings!—so you can see how it looks and fits with the costume. In most professional situations, Actors' Equity rules require the theatre to pay a rental fee for use of the actor's own hairpiece or wig in a production.

CREATING BALDNESS

Sometimes an actor with hair will have to simulate baldness, either to suggest age or character or to fulfill a script requirement. With the actor's permission, you can shave a bald spot, such as the one pictured in Figures 8–6 and 8–7. You can also suggest a receding hairline by shaving hair from the forehead.

There are a variety of products on the market that you can use to create a bald pate or a bald head. One such product is pictured in Figure 8–8. The edges of an artificial bald cap must be skillfully blended to the actor's skin for the effect to be believable. This is easier to accomplish on a large proscenium stage than when the playing space is smaller and more intimate. Ready-made bald pates may also be purchased from theatrical and make-up supply companies.

FIGURE 8–6. Actor Ted D'Arms having the top of his head shaved for the part of King in *The Adventures of Huckleberry Finn* at the Seattle Repertory Theatre. *Photograph by Liz Covey.*

FIGURE 8–7. Actor Ted D'Arms with partly shaved head. *Photograph by Joyce Degenfelder.*

FIGURE 8–8. Bald pate made with Kryolan's Glatzan L. *Photograph by Rosemary ingham.*

Wigs

SEVENTEENTH- AND EIGHTEENTH-CENTURY WIGS

Many plays set during the wig periods of the seventeenth and eighteenth centuries require rather elaborate wigs. Men wore wigs in France during most of the seventeenth century, while in England, wigs didn't catch on until after the restoration of the monarchy in 1660 when Charles II returned from his exile in France, bringing French fashion with him. Wigs were part of the well-dressed man's fashionable wardrobe throughout the Western world until the end of the eighteenth century.

In both the seventeenth and eighteenth centuries, fashionable women either added significant hairpieces to their own hair or wore full wigs. Women's wigs were generally dressed to simulate real hair. Men's wigs were less realistic and were often worn with such a casual attitude that a man was apt to raise his wig in public to scratch his head or to hang it on a fence post on a warm day while he chatted with friends.

Powdered wigs became fashionable around 1720. Powder was applied either with a large puff or with a bellows. In some houses a special room was given over to wig powdering. Some people began greasing their wigs before they were powdered, to make the powder stick. Wigs were most often powdered white or gray, but there were some colored powders: blue, violet, pink, and yellow being the most frequently used.

Wigs were "in" for nearly a century and a half. They disappeared entirely from general use after the French Revolution and the resulting association between wig wearing and the fate of the French aristocracy. However, clergymen, doctors, and lawyers continued to wear wigs as part of their professional uniforms into the early nineteenth century. The English judiciary adopted stylized wigs, some of which are still worn today. Also, footmen and liveried servants were outfitted in wigs for much of the nineteenth century.

Americans never took to wearing wigs as wholeheartedly as the English or the Europeans. Southern planters and fashionable Bostonians wore them, but as the country began to spread westward, wigs were largely abandoned. During the time of the American Revolution, most revolutionists refused to

FIGURE 8–9. David Adkins as Alceste in a natural style wig and Gregory Wallace as Philinte wearing a stylishly obvious seventeenth century wig for a production of *The Misanthrope* at the American Conservatory Theater. Costumes designed by Beaver Bauer. *Photograph courtesy of the American Conservatory Theater.*

FIGURE 8–10. Mary Dolson as Elaine Harper in a stylish 1940s wig with Brian Vaughn as Mortimer Brewster in the Utah Shakespearean Festival's production of *Arsenic and Old Lace. Photograph by Karl Hugh, courtesy of Utah Shakespearean Festival.*

wear wigs or wore ones made from naturally colored hair, not powdered. A man who wore an elaborately powdered wig was immediately suspected of royalist leanings.

WIGS FOR OTHER TIMES AND OTHER REASONS

Wigs are also frequently used on actors playing nineteenth- and early twentieth-century female characters because the hairstyles are complicated and may be difficult to create for each performance from the actor's own hair. An ac-

tor who is performing in two productions in a repertory season might wear his or her own short hair in one play and a long-hair wig for the other. Actors in plays with Asian settings, like *The Mikado,* will need appropriate wigs. Both male and female actors playing young characters in plays from the late 1960s and 1970s may need long-hair wigs. And, there is always the need for specialty wigs: a monk's fringe, a clown wig, wigs to accommodate quick changes, and a host of nonrealistic and fantasy wigs.

FIGURE 8–11. Enid Graham wearing a beautifully styled wig as Elizabeth of Valois in *Don Carlos* at The Shakespeare Theatre. Costumes designed by Robert Perdziola. *Photograph by Carol Rosegg, courtesy of The Shakespeare Theatre.*

BUY OR RENT?

You can rent or buy most wigs. A rented wig might be the best and least expensive solution for a production that runs only a few performances. If the production has a longer run, however, it might be more economical to purchase a good wig, which in the future, could be restyled and reused.

In general, the basic cost of a wig depends upon whether you are purchasing a stock wig or having one made up for the production. Naturally the stock wig is cheaper. Price for the made-to-order wig is determined by the length and color of the hair (long hair is more expensive than short hair; white hair is more costly than black hair), how much of the wig can be machine stitched and how much must be hand-tied, and whether or not the front of the wig has to be hand-tied (ventilated) into fine wig lace.

For a realistic look, wigs that are to be styled off the forehead, such as the Gibson girl pompadour, must have hand-tied fronts set on fine wig lace. When the actor puts on the wig, the wig lace is glued down to the forehead with spirit gum and make-up is applied on top. If the lace front is carefully made and the make-up skillfully applied, the wig lace is quite invisible, even in small, intimate theatres. A wig that has a fringe of hair hanging over the forehead to cover the hairline need not have a hand-tied front, and may, therefore, be much less expensive.

You can purchase inexpensive, frankly fake, synthetic-fiber period wigs from theatrical supply companies. They come heat set into specific styles, and you cannot restyle them. They may, however, be the suitable choice for liveried servants, comic characters, and the like. These prestyled wigs are not washable, but they can be dry cleaned with fair success.

WIGMAKERS AND WIGMAKING

Costume shop craftspeople often build frankly fake and stylized wigs from a wide variety of materials: yarn, fur, string, wood shavings, steel wool, and so on. Making wigs that fool the eye and appear to be real hair is usually a job for the experts who have special training, experience, and the proper tools. Wigmaking is meticulous and time-consuming work. If you would like to try your hand at human hair wigmaking, consult *Stage Make Up* (9th ed.) by Richard Corson and James Glaven for well-illustrated instructions.

FIGURE 8–12. Actors wearing intentionally obvious wigs in a production of *The Adding Machine* at Actors Theatre of Louisville. *Photograph by Richard Trigg, courtesy of Actors Theatre of Louisville.*

FIGURE 8–13. Wig styling with skinny rollers and drinking straws demonstrated by wig and make-up instructor Kelly Yurko, at the University of Cincinnati College-Conservatory of Music. *Photograph by Dean Mogel.*

FIGURE 8–14. Wig lace, ventilating needles, needle holder, and toupeé clip. *Photograph by Liz Covey.*

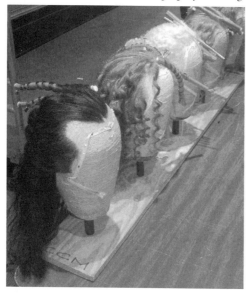

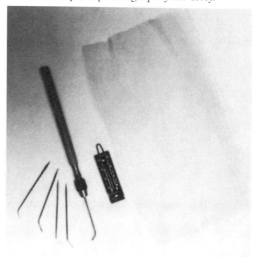

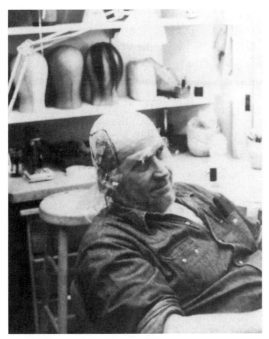

FIGURE 8–15. Actor Ted D'Arms in plastic wig-fitting cap with hairline drawn on. *Photograph by Joyce Degenfelder.*

WIG MEASUREMENTS

When you order a custom-made wig from a wigmaker, be sure to ask exactly which measurements you are to supply and precisely how you should take them. Normally, the measurements include:

1. *Head circumference,* taken around the forehead and fullest part of the back of the head, keeping the tape measure parallel to the ground.
2. *Center front hairline to nape of neck (or poll),* over the top of the head.
3. *Ear to ear,* over the top of the head.
4. *Temple to temple,* around the back of the head.
5. *Across back nape or hairline base.*
6. *Total hairline circumference.*

Many wigmakers also like to have a plastic wrap measurement cap formed directly on the actor's head. These caps convey particularly accurate information. See Figure 8–15 for an example.

To make a wig measurement cap, you will need thin plastic wrap, Scotch® Magic™ Tape, and two indelible markers in two different colors.

Place the actor in a comfortable chair while you are making the cap. If the actor has long hair, wrap it around the head and pin it down as close to the scalp as possible. Cover the actor's head with a layer of plastic wrap, over-lapping pieces as necessary. Make sure all the hair is completely covered and that the plastic wrap extends well below the hairline. Crisscross the entire head with Scotch Magic Tape, covering the plastic wrap entirely and molding it firmly to the head. Run long strips of tape all around the hairline.

Once the plastic cap is firmly taped in place, use one color marker to draw around the actor's own hairline. Be sure to outline the ears. With the other color, draw the hairline you want the wig to have and slip the cap off the actor's head.

Send the cap to the wigmaker, folded flat, in a manila envelope, along with measurements, drawings and description, and color. You can indicate color with a sample of the actor's own hair if the wig is to match. Or you can indicate the desired wig color on a ring of hair color samples available from most wigmakers and wig supply shops.

STOCK AND PURCHASED WIGS

The least expensive way to create a wig for your production is to style one from your own stock. You may also be able to purchase an inexpensive, ready-made wig at a local wig shop. They come in both human and synthetic hair versions, and may prove quite serviceable, especially for short-run productions. Examine the wigs in your stock or in the wig shop carefully and choose ones with enough length and full-ness to create the style called for in the design.

Don't begin to style a wig until you've tried it on the actor and know the foundation cap inside the wig fits. People's heads are very different in size, and the only way to be sure a wig fits is to put it on. Pay special attention to the length of the wig's foundation cap from the center front of the forehead to the nape of the neck. A wig that is too short from forehead to nape will invariably ride up on the actor's neck and look awkward, no matter how tightly you pin it down.

If the wig needs to be dyed a different color, do it or have it done before you begin styling. As mentioned earlier, use permanent hair dyes or temporary rinses, such as Fancifull Liquid hair rinse for human hair wigs and fabric dyes for synthetic wigs.

STYLING WIGS

When the wig is colored and dry, place it on a head block and set the block on a wig stand. A head block is made from soft wood covered with linen or canvas. Styrofoam head blocks, which can be useful for storing wigs, are not suitable for styling. They are too light, too slippery, and not the correct shape. You can purchase proper head blocks in a variety of head sizes from beauty supply shops.

The wig stand, also available from beauty supply shops, clamps onto the edge of your worktable. The head block fits down onto the stand's rod, which turns, tilts, and swivels so the wig can be worked on from all sides and angles.

Pin the wig to the head block with T-pins, but *never* put T-pins into fine wig lace. Brush the wig with a wire or a nylon brush and comb it with a wide-toothed comb. Always brush and comb down, which is the direction in which the hair has been tied or stitched. Work out tangles gently, without tugging at the hairs. Once wig hairs are pulled out, they won't grow back.

Be sure to have the costume sketch and research pictures in view while you work. You will probably be using rollers for the set, so decide whether you need to use small ones for a tight set or larger ones for a soft set. Figure out the correct directions for rolling the rollers and/or the pin curls. Start with the top of the head, then work on each side and finish up with the back. To research styling techniques for contemporary and period hairstyles, look for recent and vintage cosmetology books, salon magazines, and ladies' magazines in your public library and at yard and estate sales. Searches for "wigs" and "hairstyles" on the Internet will also bring up good information.

Human hair wigs. Use water or gel for setting human hair wigs. If time permits, let the wig dry naturally. If not, use a hair dryer, preferably one with a hood, set on moderate heat.

After removing the rollers from the thoroughly dried wig, comb, brush, and arrange the hair into the appropriate style, securing it with hairpins, bobby pins, barrettes, and so on. Use hairspray sparingly. Hold the spray bottle well above the wig and allow the spray to fall down evenly onto the wig. Choose a water-soluble spray, preferably one with a lanolin base.

Curling irons of various sizes are useful for setting curls and tendrils in a human hair wig, and for general style touch-ups. Make sure the heat setting is moderate and don't keep the curling iron in contact with the hair for long. Because wig hair doesn't contain the oils that are present in living human hair, the curling iron can do permanent damage to wig hair if it is overused.

Electric rollers are handy for quick wig settings but, for the same reason stated above, should not be overused.

Synthetic hair wigs. This is Colleen Muscha's method for setting synthetic wigs:

Roll up the wig dry, perhaps using a small amount of styling gel or hairspray to keep it under control. Using a portable maintenance steamer, a hat steamer, or an ordinary teakettle, steam the wig for ten minutes (twenty minutes if the hair is very long). Each curl should be completely saturated with steam. Let the wig dry completely, using a hair dryer if necessary. Make sure the wig is cool before unwinding. This is a quick method for setting synthetic wigs, and it results in a very tight curl.

To be on the safe side, don't use steam on a synthetic wig without first testing its effect on a hair sample. Some very inexpensive synthetic wigs will melt if you apply steam. Also, do not use curling irons on synthetic wigs. Hot rollers are okay but the curls they produce won't last long.

PUTTING ON A WIG

The actor's hair under the wig should be as flat as possible so the wig will sit close to the head. There are several ways to secure the actor's own hair, depending on its length and fullness. If the hair is short, simply use a headband to hold it off the forehead. Arrange medium-length hair in large pin curls secured with crossed bobby pins. Always point the bobby pins downward so they won't snag the wig. Wind long hair around the head and secure it with bobby pins.

Some wigs will rest more securely if the actor's own hair is covered by a wig cap, which can be purchased or made. Fashion a simple wig cap from the top of a queen-size stocking, from which the lower leg and foot have been cut. Simply stitch or knot the top closed. An Ace bandage wound around the head also makes an excellent wig cap but be sure not to wrap it too tightly or your actor will have a headache.

Sometimes it's helpful to stitch a strip of Velcro, the hook side, to the inside of the wig's foundation cap. The Velcro will grasp the hair or the wig cap and help prevent the wig from slipping.

To put on a full wig, grasp the lower back edge of the wig's foundation cap with both hands. Slide the wig over the forehead, leaving the hairline low on the forehead, and pull down snugly. With both hands on top of the wig, move it back until the front hairline is in the correct place. Secure the wig to the hair or wig cap with large bobby pins through the wig's foundation cap. *Don't put bobby pins through the wig lace.*

When there is wig lace around the front and/or sides of the wig, you may want to fasten it down with spirit gum. Be sure to loosen the spirit gum before removing the wig. Refer to the step-by-step directions on pages 303 and 304 for applying and removing spirit gum.

RUN-OF-THE-SHOW WIG CARE

Actors' Equity rules require that wig lace (and all facial hair lace) be cleaned and the wig touched up for every performance. This is a sensible practice that should be followed in all theatrical venues. Whether the wig receives its daily care from a wig specialist, a dresser, or from the actor who wears it, the person who maintains the wig must know how to care for it or be under the supervision of someone who does. Make sure actors wearing wigs understand the damage they can inflict on a wig by yanking it off by the hair or by pulling off the wig lace without first softening the spirit gum.

Clean wig lace as soon as possible after the wig is removed. Use spirit gum remover or 99 percent isopropyl alcohol. Avoid using acetone to clean wig lace. This is not a safe practice. Acetone use requires gloves, respirator, and adequate ventilation, none of which are normally present in dressing or hair and make-up rooms where wig maintenance is carried out.

After the wig lace is cleaned, place the wig on a head block for touching up. Almost all wigs need a touch-up before every performance. Some require recombing and rearranging every day and a few have to be restyled daily. The human body loses 78 percent of its heat through the head and when the actor wearing a wig is extremely active, the hair, no matter how carefully it's been set, will wilt.

END-OF-THE-RUN WIG CARE

Clean all wigs as soon as possible after striking the production. A handy first step in the wig cleaning process is to brush the hair gently but thoroughly with a wire brush to remove as much accumulated hairspray as possible. Do not use dry cleaning solvents to remove makeup that accumulates around the edges of human hair wigs. Even a small amount of a dry-cleaning solvent in an open pan produces a significant amount of harmful vapor, and it's flammable. If there is a great deal of make-up caked on the wig, you may have to presoak those areas before washing.

You can shampoo a human hair wig on or off a wig block. Make a mild detergent shampoo and warm water solution and place it in a shallow pan. Wet the wig thoroughly. Moving from the front of the wig to the back, work in the shampoo and water solution, taking care to go in the direction in which the hair is sewn or tied. When the wig is clean, replace the shampoo solution with warm water and rinse the wig thoroughly; this may require several changes of water. Add a wet hair conditioner to the final rinse.

Do not scrub or rub the hair or do anything to cause tangles. Lay the wig on a clean towel and blot gently. Pin it on a block to air dry. When the wig is completely dry, apply a good dry hair wig conditioner.

Wash synthetic hair wigs in household detergent, pure soap, or in special synthetic wig washes that are detergent based. Use lukewarm water. Rinse several times. You may be in the habit of using a liquid fabric softener in the final rinse to combat static electricity, but do be aware that many people are allergic to both household detergents and to fabric softeners, both of which tend to leave residue on dried wigs.

You do not have to put a synthetic wig on a wig block to dry. Allow it to dry naturally if time permits. If not, you can place it in a net lingerie bag and put it in an automatic dryer on the air fluff setting. Do not put any other items in the dryer with the wig.

STORING WIGS

The ideal storage for wigs is on correctly sized wig blocks in a dustproof cabinet. Since space is seldom available for the ideal, a good solu-

FIGURE 8–16. Wigs set to go at the Oregon Shakespeare Festival. *Photograph by Rosemary Ingham.*

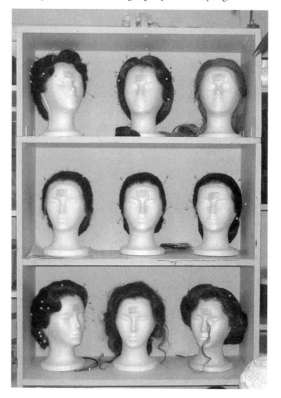

tion is to place the dry, clean wigs in a drawer or a box, separated from one another by tissue paper or muslin. Pack them loosely to leave room for air circulation. If it is more convenient to store wigs in plastic bags or boxes in order to see them better, be sure to make holes in the bags or containers so the wigs can breathe. Label carefully.

Separate and store wigs by color and length. Label each box carefully—"women's long blonde," "men's short gray,"—so you don't have to rummage through several boxes to find the wig you're looking for.

Beards, Mustaches, Sideburns

Beards and mustaches made out of crepe hair and latex are quite suitable for short-run productions, but long runs require sturdy, real hairpieces, hand-tied on wig lace. You can purchase beards, mustaches, sideburns, and eyebrows in a variety of styles and colors from theatrical supply houses, or you can order them custom-made from a theatrical wigmaker. If you want to try your own hand at making facial hairpieces, refer to Corson and Glaven's *Stage Makeup*. It goes almost without saying that custom-made facial hairpieces, fashioned to the contours of an individual face, will be much more successful than the ready-made variety and much more expensive.

Make sure the actors wearing lace foundation facial hairpieces know how to put them on, and how to take them off. Most facial hair is applied with spirit gum, although you can also use toupee tape for small facial hairpieces. Toupee tape is not as reliable as spirit gum, and it may shine through the hairpiece and be noticeable in a small theatre.

You might want to type up the following directions for applying facial hair with spirit gum and post them in the dressing rooms:

Applying Facial Hairpieces

1. Place the hairpiece on the face to see exactly where it should go.

2. Put a thin coat of spirit gum on dry, clean skin, on which there is no make-up. You can spirit gum a beard in place by adhering it just around the edges. Smaller pieces, such as mustaches and sideburns, should be stuck down completely. *Never apply spirit gum to the wig lace, and never use latex instead of spirit gum.* Allow the spirit gum to become tacky, which takes only a few minutes.

3. Press the lace into the spirit gum with a clean towel. Press straight into the face; don't let the lace slide. Use a clean section of the towel for each press.

4. When the spirit gum no longer looks shiny and the towel comes away without sticking, pat a damp cloth over the area.

5. Use a toothbrush or an eyebrow brush to lift up any hairs that have been stuck down by the spirit gum.

Removing Facial Hairpieces

1. Soften the spirit gum by applying spirit gum remover or 99 percent isopropyl alcohol directly to the areas that are glued down. *Never pull the hairpiece away from the face without using spirit gum remover* or you may damage the hairpiece and irritate the face. Spirit gum remover is available in both regular and hypoallergenic formulas.

2. When the spirit gum is soft, gently remove the hairpiece from the face. Remove all traces of spirit gum from the face and wash gently with mild soap and water. Rinse well.

In order to remove caked-on spirit gum and make-up, clean lace foundation facial hairpieces after each performance with spirit gum remover or 99 percent isopropyl alcohol. Pour a small amount of either liquid into a shallow glass or porcelain dish and put the piece into the liquid, lace side down. Allow it to soak until the spirit gum loosens. Use a soft toothbrush to remove all traces of spirit gum from the lace. Put the article onto a towel or soft absorbent cloth, lace side down, and gently pat it with the toothbrush so the cloth will absorb the remainder of the make-up and spirit gum.

Hats

A great many costume ensembles include hats: military uniforms, Victorian ladies' traveling suits, seventeenth-century Puritan dresses, mourning costumes from all fashion periods, and church outfits worn by all well-dressed women for the first sixty years of the twentieth century, to name only a few. In addition, playwrights seem to enjoy writing hat business into their plays. The hat-switching sequence in *Waiting for Godot* always draws a delighted audience response, and even the moody Hamlet pokes fun at foppish Osric's manner of wearing his "bonnet." Sight gags that involve a character donning the hat of another character have been common since the early days of comedy.

In most costume shops the time and effort spent on building, trimming, and refurbishing hats is second only to that expended on constructing costume garments.

The Two Biggest Hat Problems

There are two major problems that may afflict stage hats: the hat brim that shades or masks the actor's face and the large hat or headdress that is difficult to balance.

FIGURE 8–17. Joe Cronin, Leslie Brott, Philip Davidson, and Libby George dressed for a motoring trip in *Ah, Wilderness!* at the Utah Shakespearean Festival. *Photograph by Karl Hugh, courtesy of Utah Shakespearean Festival.*

FIGURE 8–18. Charles Metten as Smee and Jonathan Gillard Daly as Captain James Hook in *Peter Pan* at the Utah Shakespearean Festival. Costumes designed by Janet L. Swenson. *Photograph by Karl Hugh, courtesy of Utah Shakespearean Festival.*

FIGURE 8–19. Ellen Karas portraying Mary in the foreground, with Brigid Cleary as Edith, Martha Hackett as Sylvia, and Mary Fortuna as Peggy in a production of *The Women* at Arena Stage. Perfectly coifed in 1930s-style wigs with fashionable hats perched at jaunty angles. Costumes designed by Paul Tazewell. *Photograph courtesy of Arena Stage.*

Nobody wants a hat brim to shade an actor's face. Everybody knows there is a strong connection for the audience between being able to see an actor's face and hearing the words he or she says. But, it is not always easy to prevent brim shadows when, for example, the script specifically calls for a Stetson or for a Prussian helmet.

Brim shadows are more troublesome on open stages than on proscenium stages. On open stages most of the lighting instruments hang directly over the actors' heads, intensifying down shadowing. On a proscenium stage, front and side lights help to minimize the brim-shading problem.

A time-honored solution for eliminating hat brim shadows on the actor's face is to have the hat make only a token appearance. The actor wears the hat on stage, then removes it. Unfortunately, this ploy isn't always possible. When it's not, you must make the hat brim smaller, or turn it up, or ask the actor to wear the hat farther back on his or her head. A costume designer should always anticipate brim shadow problems early and take steps to solve them as quickly as possible. Most directors will eliminate a hat from a production rather

305

than allow the actor to walk and talk in shadow.

The weight and balance problem is usually limited to large hats, helmets, or elaborate headdresses. Dramatic characters seldom stand stock still while they are wearing their plumed helmets, or their mitres, or the 36-inch-tall fantasy headdress bristling with fiber optics. Instead they walk, skip, run, bend, jump, and dance. Always assume that characters wearing big hats will perform lively stage movements and be sure and check with the director to find out exactly what the hat will have to undergo before choosing materials and construction methods.

It is important to use lightweight materials for big hats and headdresses, but it is even more important to distribute the weight correctly. As a rule, a large hat or headdress has to be heavier in the front than in the back. The only way to check correct hat balance is to try it on at regular intervals while it is still under construction. Whenever you try on the hat or headdress, be sure to have the actor go through his or her full range of movements.

Milliners and Millinery Basics

Persons with millinery skills are particularly important in costume shops. Some shops keep a milliner on staff; others hire experienced, freelance milliners for specific productions. In many small shops, however, hatmaking falls to one or more general costume technicians who have shown evidence of the patience, the manual dexterity, and the deft and gentle touch with materials so important to fashioning theatrical hats.

This section on millinery basics is very general. For both broader and more detailed views of the craft, be sure to have copies of *From the Neck Up: An Illustrated Guide to*

Hatmaking by Denise Dreher and *Basic Millinery for the Stage* by Tim Dial in your shop library.

Hat Measurements

The basic hat measurement is taken with a tape measure around the head, just above the eyebrows. This measurement is called the head circumference, and it's the only measurement necessary for hats that simply sit on the head.

When constructing a hat from basic materials, such as buckram, willow, or felt, you have to turn the head circumference measurement into an oval, which is the basic head shape. Figure 8–20, taken, in part, from Denise Dreher's *From the Neck Up,* is a master oval pattern for a 22-inch head size, with directions for reducing and enlarging it. When you are using this master oval pattern, be sure to trace rather than photocopy it. A photocopied image is never quite the same size as the original.

Figure 8–21 is a conversion chart that converts head circumference measurements in inches and centimeters into standard hat sizes. Keep a copy of this information near the hat storage area to help you match actors to hats from stock.

Be sure to allow extra circumference if the actor you are measuring will wear a wig. Unfortunately, wigs are seldom ready when hat measurements are taken so you will have to estimate the additional circumference. If you are taking measurements for hats that will be worn in an opera or musical, be sure to ask if microphone packs might be placed in the hats as this will require extra room. When taking hat measurements, it's good practice to take forehead-to-nape and eartop-to-eartop measurements as well as the standard circumference. These additional measurements are

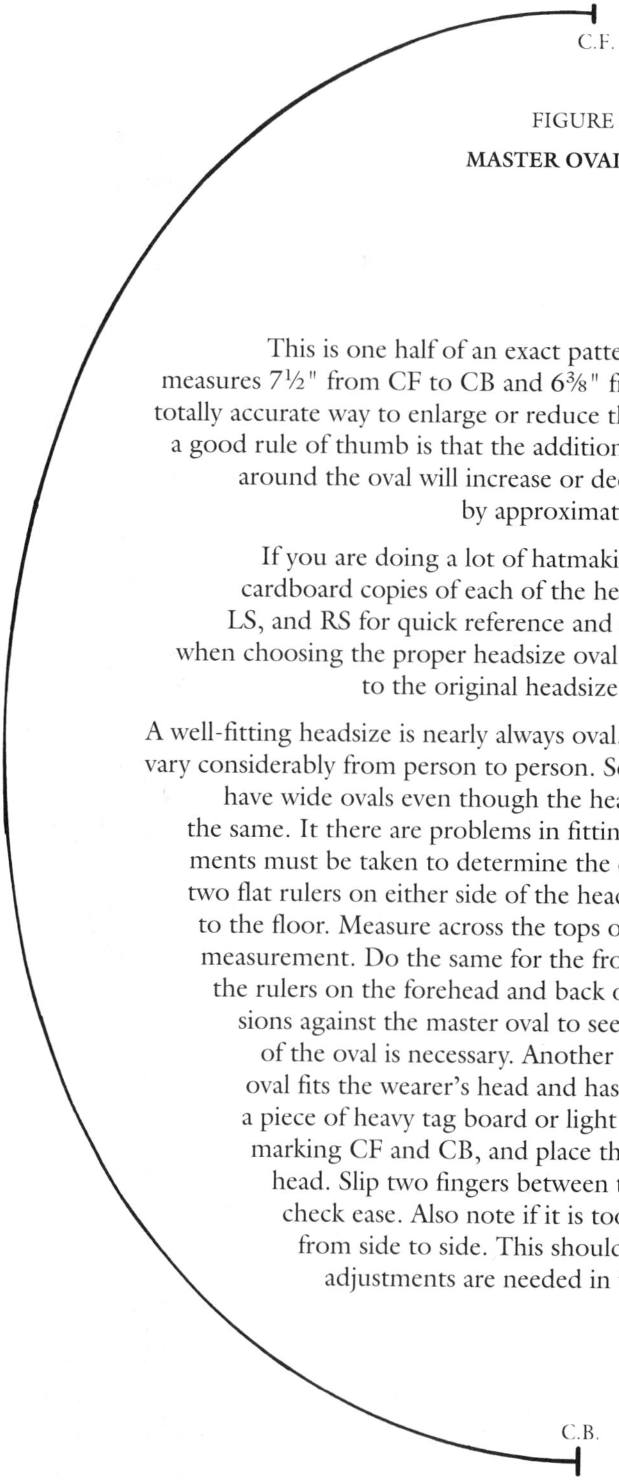

C.F.

FIGURE 8–20.

MASTER OVAL PATTERN

This is one half of an exact pattern of a 22" headsize oval. It measures 7½" from CF to CB and 6⅜" from side to side. Although there is no totally accurate way to enlarge or reduce the oval for larger or smaller head sizes, a good rule of thumb is that the addition or subtraction of ⅛ inch all the way around the oval will increase or decrease its overall circumference by approximately 1 inch.

If you are doing a lot of hatmaking, it is a good idea to make cardboard copies of each of the headsize ovals, marking CB, CF, LS, and RS for quick reference and easy pattern guides. Remember when choosing the proper headsize oval to add the necessary ease allowance to the original headsize measurement first.

A well-fitting headsize is nearly always oval, but the size and shape of the oval can vary considerably from person to person. Some people have long ovals and others have wide ovals even though the head measurement may be exactly the same. It there are problems in fitting the hat, two additional measurements must be taken to determine the dimensions of the head oval. Place two flat rulers on either side of the head above the ears and perpendicular to the floor. Measure across the tops of the rulers to get the side to side measurement. Do the same for the front to back measurement, placing the rulers on the forehead and back of the head. Check these dimensions against the master oval to see if an adjustment in the shape of the oval is necessary. Another way to check if your master oval fits the wearer's head and has enough ease is to trace it on a piece of heavy tag board or light cardboard. Cut out the oval, marking CF and CB, and place the cardboard on the person's head. Slip two fingers between the head and cardboard to check ease. Also note if it is too tight from CF to CB or from side to side. This should give a clue as to where adjustments are needed in the shape of the oval.

C.B.

307

Head Size		Standard
Inches	Centimeters	Hat Size
18¾	48	6
19⅛	49	6⅛
19½	50	6¼
19⅞	51	6⅜
20¼	52	6½
20¾	53	6⅝
21⅛	54	6¾
21½	55	6⅞
21⅞	56	7
22¼	57	7⅛
22⅝	58	7¼
23	59	7⅜
23¼	60	7½
23⅞	61	7⅝
24¼	62	7¾
24⅝	63	7⅞
25	64	8

FIGURE 8–21. Industry-standard hat-size chart.

necessary when building coifs, helmets, and other head-hugging hat styles.

Buckram

Rigid, fabric-covered hats are based on sturdy frames. Most hats of this sort that are built for the stage are constructed from buckram, a stiff, open-weave material sized with glue. Buckram is widely available and moderately priced. There are three weights: light, medium, and heavy. Medium and heavy weights are the most suitable for hat frames.

FIGURES 8–22 and 8–23. Two nicely done paper hat mock-ups. Notice the use of ethafoam rod and rope trim. *Photograph by Rosemary Ingham.*

Making a Buckram Hat Frame

Before you set out to make your first hat for the stage, try the simple, conical hat in Figure 8–24 for practice. Follow the directions carefully.

1. Make a paper pattern out of brown craft paper. Create the oval, following the instructions in Figure 8–20. Establish the width of the brim, remembering that any width over 3 inches can give you brim shadow problems.

The bottom curve of the crown piece and the angle of its sides determine how much slant the crown will have, and the circumference of the tip. (If, for example, the side angles are so steep that they go up to a point, you will have the shape for a witch's traditional hat.)

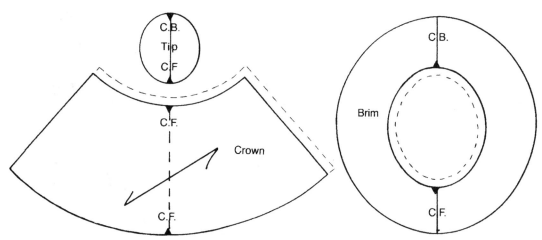

FIGURE 8-24. Pattern pieces for a simple conical hat.

2. Tape all the paper pieces together and try on the paper mock-up. Take care that the mock-up is roomy enough to allow for buckram, which is somewhat thicker than craft paper, and the fabric that will cover the frame. Make corrections in the paper pattern and try it on again. Don't cut the buckram until the paper pattern fits perfectly and is exactly the correct shape.

3. Lay your corrected pattern pieces on the buckram, paying particular attention to the marked grain lines. Draw around the pattern pieces, adding a ½-inch seam allowance to the inner edge of the brim and to one side and the top edge of the crown, as shown in Figure 8–24. Don't add seam allowance to any other edges.

4. Cut out the pieces. Clip the seam allowances on the inner edge of the brim and the top edge of the crown all the way to the edge of the actual pattern (stitching line), creating tabs ½ inch deep and about ½ inch wide. Fold the tabs on the brim up and the tabs on the crown down.

5. Curve the crown into a cone and overlap the seam allowance. Using heavy-duty thread and a firm backstitch, stitch the crown into a cone.

6. Assemble the brim, crown, and tip with tape and fit. Pay special attention to the brim's width. Correct the pieces if necessary.

7. Stitch hat wire to the outer edge of the brim, using either a hand blanket stitch or a machine zigzag. Cover the wire with bias tape and stitch in place.

8. Turn down the tabs on the top edge of the crown and put the tip in place. (If the tip doesn't fit exactly, make adjustments now.) Stitch the tip and crown together with an overcast stitch around the top edge. Use a small amount of nontoxic glue or plastic coating to fasten the crown tabs to the tip.

9. Turn up the tabs on the inner edge of the brim and place the crown piece of the hat form on the brim with the tabs inside. The overlapped crown seam will eventually become the center back of the hat. Stitch the brim to the crown at the base of the crown using a backstitch that catches all the brim tabs.

COVERING THE BUCKRAM FRAME
The following directions are for a stitched fabric cover. As a first step you may want to cover the buckram frame with a soft fabric, such as cotton flannel, in order to smooth the edges of the buckram and protect the outer fabric from rubbing directly against the buckram. The

steps in covering the buckram frame with a protective layer are the same as applying the final fabric cover.

1. Cut cover fabric pieces from the corrected paper pattern, leaving ½-inch seam allowances around each edge of each piece. Cut two cover pieces for the brim, one for the top and one for the bottom.

2. Cut lining fabric for the tip and the crown.

3. Cover the tip first. Backstitch the tip fabric to the crown, as shown in Figure 8–25. Trim seam allowance to ¼ inch and clip it so it will lie flat.

4. Machine stitch the side seam of the crown lining. Then machine stitch the tip lining to the crown lining.

5. Slip the lining up into the hat crown frame, seam allowances facing the buckram (right side out).

6. Stitch the lining tip to the crown, just below the row of stitches that hold the tip fabric to the crown. Stitch the bottom of the lining to the bottom of the crown.

7. Pin the fabric crown cover to the outside of the hat as shown in Figure 8–26. (*Do not* stitch the side crown cover seam beforehand.) Stitch the fabric crown cover to the top of the crown, as shown in Figure 8–26.

8. Trim wedges from the fabric crown cover seam allowance and pull the fabric down over the crown. Pull the cover smooth, straight, and tight around the crown. Pin, then hand blind stitch the side seam.

FIGURE 8–25. Backstitch top piece to crown.

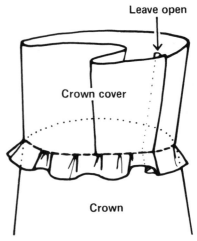

FIGURE 8–26. Covering the crown.

9. Clip the seam allowance at the bottom of the fabric crown cover so it will lie flat on the brim. Stitch the cover to the bottom of the crown, where the crown and the brim meet.

10. Attach the top brim cover as shown in Figure 8–27, stitching right at the base of the crown.

11. Smooth the cover fabric over the brim, turn it under the brim, and stitch it to the tape that binds the edge of the buckram frame.

12. Lay the bottom brim cover fabric in place, clipping as necessary to turn the seam allowance smoothly under. Pin, then blindstitch

FIGURES 8–27. Covering the brim.

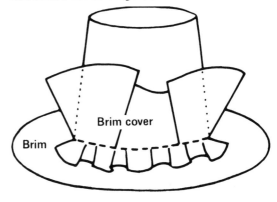

the outer brim edge. Pin, then blindstitch the inner brim edge.

13. Add a grosgrain or leather sweatband just inside the crown to stabilize the size.

Note: You may substitute machine stitching for several of these operations. However, you will learn more about the fundamentals of hat-making if you complete the project by hand at least once.

Shaping Hats on Blocks

You can use hat blocks to create a variety of rounded shapes that cannot be made by cutting and stitching a hat frame. Buckram, willow, and felt can all be shaped on a hat block.

Milliner's hat blocks are made from hardwood or balsa. Some have removable parts so you can remove the hat shape easily, and some have separate crown and brim blocks.

You can purchase some new blocks from millinery supply shops, although the mechanization of the hat industry, the limited importance of hats in the current fashion scene, and the shrinking number of independent milliners are lessening the demand for new blocks. Interesting secondhand blocks, however, are often available from milliners who are retiring or going out of business. Hat blocks may also turn up in antique shops, secondhand stores, and rummage sales.

If you do not have wooden hat blocks, there are workable substitutes. A sturdy, padded wig block makes a fine base on which to build hats. Create different sizes and shapes with layers of felt, foam, or modeling clay. Styrofoam wig blocks are less desirable because they are so light and crumbly, but even they will work in a pinch. Make a sturdy base by mounting the wig block on a piece of dowel and attaching the dowel to a wood base.

Some of the most successful of all hat block shapes are simple found objects. A very

FIGURE 8–28. An array of hat blocks at the Guthrie Theater. *Photograph by Maribeth Hite.*

FIGURE 8–29. A wooden hat stretcher. *Photograph by Liz Covey.*

small pail may be the perfect shape for a medieval page's hat; a basin may be the beginning of a helmet. When searching for a shape, look over the property shop storage area and your own kitchen shelves for objects that can be used alone or in combination for a hat block. Round off sharp edges with fabric or foam and hold everything together with strips of masking tape.

Whatever you use for a hat block, cover it before beginning to work. Buckram is impregnated with glue and will stick to any bare block after it has dried. The sizing used to stabilize molded felt shapes will also cling to a block that is not covered. Cover hat blocks with aluminum foil or a heavy duty, heat-resistant plastic wrap such as Saran Wrap. Make sure the surface of the covered block is as smooth as possible.

Shaped Buckram Frames

Cut a piece of buckram large enough to cover the entire block, with some to spare. Wet the buckram thoroughly and drape it over the block. Stretch and pin the buckram at the four straight grain points, as shown in Figure 8–30, keeping one hand firmly on top of the block so the buckram won't slip sideways.

Begin to work the buckram down between the four pins to eliminate the folds. This

FIGURE 8–31. Straw Salvation Army bonnets with machine embroidered ribbon and cardboard mock-up made by Cynda Flores Galikin for a production of *Major Barbara* at The Repertory Theatre of St. Louis. *Photograph by Liz Covey.*

is possible because the bias pull allows the loosely woven strands to pack closer together. Circles made of wire or taut elastic, with which you can force the buckram down over the block, are useful tools. For most hat shapes you will be aiming for a frame in which all the folds have been eliminated.

A special problem is presented by hat shapes that narrow from a bulbous crown to a narrow head opening. Remove as much fullness as possible, then arrange the excess buckram in evenly divided folds. When the frame is dry, snip the folds away and remove the frame from the block. Shape the bottom of the frame by bringing the cut edges together, forming butted darts. Cross stitch the edges together by hand or zigzag them by machine.

Always allow buckram frames to dry thoroughly before removing them from their

FIGURE 8–30. Shaping buckram on a hat block.

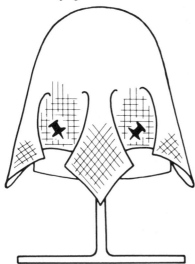

blocks. You can speed the drying by putting the block and the buckram under a hair dryer on a warm setting.

After the frame is dry and off the block, fit it on the actor, trim the edge as necessary, and wire and bind it.

Glue the cover fabric to the frame, choosing, if possible, a fabric with some stretch. Use lightweight fabrics to line rounded frames so you can take in folds without creating too much bulk. Don't pull any part of the fabric cover too tightly or the buckram frame might collapse.

Working with Shaped Felt Bodies

Shaped felt bodies have soft, rounded crowns and wide, floppy brims. They are used to create felt hats in many shapes: tricorns, bicorns, cowboy hats, rakish Cavalier hats, and so on. The felt bodies are shaped with moisture and heat, then, if necessary, firmed up with a layer of paint-on felt stiffener.

Felt bodies come in several sizes, different qualities, and many colors. Whenever possible, choose fur felt, which is more malleable

FIGURE 8–32. Felt body before steaming and shaping. *Photograph by Susan Ashdown.*

FIGURE 8–33. Wet the felt body and put it on a head block. *Photograph by Susan Ashdown.*

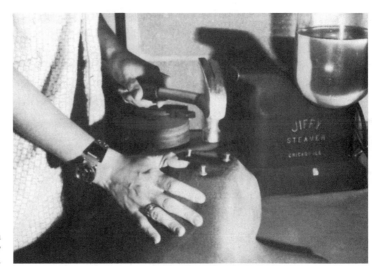

FIGURE 8-34. Secure the top with push pins. *Photograph by Susan Ashdown.*

FIGURE 8-35. Steam it. *Photograph by Susan Ashdown.*

and durable than wool felt. And, since it is virtually impossible to dye or color felt evenly, be sure you are working with an acceptable color to begin with. You can tone and shade felt with leather dyes or with liquid fabric dyes. Sponging and stippling are particularly effective painting techniques for felt hats.

The first step in shaping a felt body is to wet the felt thoroughly with hot water. Then drape it over the hat block. (See Figures 8–32 to 8–38.) Secure the top of the body to the block with pushpins, or hold it in place firmly with one hand while you are working. Progress in alternating steps: apply steam, stretch and mold the felt, apply more steam, stretch, and so on. For the steam source, use a hat steamer, a portable wardrobe steamer, a steam iron, or a steaming teakettle. Take care not to get your hands in the way of the steam.

314

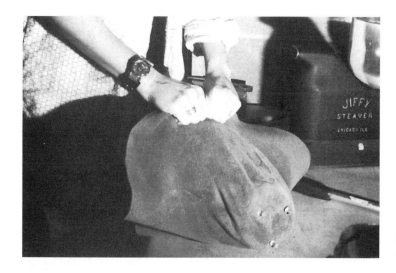

FIGURE 8–36. Stretch it.
Photograph by Susan Ashdown.

FIGURE 8–37. More steaming and stretching.
Photograph by Susan Ashdown.

FIGURE 8–38. The final shape. *Photograph by Susan Ashdown.*

If the felt is relatively thin, work it down over the block gently but firmly. Thicker felt can take more vigorous pulling and will stretch out a good deal. Many technicians, especially those with limited experience, find that molding felt takes more time than molding buckram. Both methods require persistence and patience; molding felt requires strong hands as well.

Leave the shaped hat on the block until it is completely dry. Apply lacquer or sizing to the felt and allow it to dry again. (See Appendix I, Hats—Stiff But Safe, page 437, for a discussion of hat lacquers and sizings.) Then remove it and fit it on the actor. Always add a leather or grosgrain sweatband inside the finished felt hat to control the size and to protect the hat from make-up and moisture.

If you are creating a hat without a brim or with a very small brim, you may want to begin with a *felt hood* rather than with a *felt body*. A felt hood hat is a soft, rounded crown without a brim. It responds to heat and moisture in exactly the same way as a felt body.

Ready-Made Frames and Bodies

You can purchase ready-made hat frames and felt hat bodies from millinery supply shops. Buckram frames, and a lighter weight sort made from sized lace-net, come in a wide assortment of shapes, many of which are adaptable to period styles. The edges are already bound and they are ready to cover.

Stiffened felt hat bodies come in a limited number of shapes suitable for blocking and styling. Using ready-made felt hat bodies, you can quickly create Cavalier hats, a whole array of cocked hats, ladies' eighteenth-century riding

FIGURE 8–39. Bonnet made by a student in Jim Glaven's class at the University of Texas. *Photograph by Jim Glaven.*

hats, American slouch hats, cowboy hats, and many others. Felt hat bodies come in different colors with either a smooth or a furry finish.

Recycling Old Hats

The least expensive and often the quickest way to produce a hat for the stage is to refurbish and/or restyle an old hat. Your costume stock probably includes a collection of as many old hats as you can conveniently store. They are easy to acquire from donations and at local secondhand shops. Many contemporary hat shapes adapt beautifully to period styles. Learn to look at old hats with a keen eye to what they can become.

In most cases, you will begin to restyle an old hat by stripping it down to its basic shape. Sometimes you can alter the basic shape with steam and sometimes you can't. Experiment gently. A soft, unsized felt hat may accept a new shape, while a stiff, sized felt will resist shaping and may even tear if it is manipulated too much.

Use steam to reshape straw hats, working gently to prevent cracking. Don't try to force a straw hat crown down over a hat block. Shape it with your hands and stuff it with tissue paper or muslin until it dries. Use millinery wire to stabilize straw hat brims.

Hat Trims

Down through the fashion centuries, an amazing array of objects, both real and artificial, have festooned hats. Embroidery, braid, precious stones and paste baubles, feathers, plumes, whole birds, fruit, leaves, and flowers are among the most common. Many designers and costume shop supervisors collect potential hat trims and tuck them away for future use. Keep them sorted and well marked so they can be found when you need them. Strip feathers, flowers, and leaves from old hats. Buy up trims at rummage sales and church bazaars. Save bits of ribbon, lace, and braid from costume construction. Experiment with unusual items and materials. Often the most successful hat trims are contrived from highly unlikely objects.

When setting up trim for a hat, assemble all the possibilities and try different arrangements and combinations. The hat trim must be in harmony with the hat shape or the trim will look like an afterthought. Don't use clunky bunches of trim unless you want a comic effect. Balance the trim and don't let the hat get top heavy. The actor's words should be more interesting to the audience than a towering bunch of daisies perched precariously on a hat.

FEATHERS

Many stage hats are trimmed with feathers or plumes. If they are taken care of, feathers can

FIGURE 8–40. Mock-up in buckram, brown paper, and wire with feathers for *Harlem Song,* designed by Paul Tazewell for the Apollo Theatre. Note the page with fabric swatches and the photocopied sketch. Courtesy of the Lynne Mackey Studio. *Photograph by Liz Covey.*

be reused many times. Always remove them from hats and costumes and store separately. Lay them flat so as not to damage the spines and never put them in plastic bags. Feathers and plumes need air, cool temperatures, and protection from dust.

Purchase feathers and especially plumes from reputable companies so you will be sure to get the best quality. Compare prices, since the cost of feathers fluctuates a good deal. You can purchase plumes and stiff feathers singly, but you will get a better price by the dozen. Small feathers are usually sold in bulk.

You can buy plumes already curled, but it's cheaper and sometimes more convenient to do your own curling. You can curl a plume by running a scissors blade *very gently* along each one of the fronds, in much the same way you curl decorative package ribbon. Or, you can steam the end of the plume for a few seconds and wrap the softened fronds around a broomstick until they dry. Most curling irons are too hot for curling feathers and will scorch the fronds. Unfortunately, old plumes with brittle spines won't curl.

You can dye feathers with either water-soluble or alcohol-soluble dyes. Don't be dismayed when the feather comes out of the dye bath looking naked and stringy; its fluff will return when it dries.

Feathers dry readily when they are secured in a net bag and put into an automatic dryer on a low setting. Another drying method is to shake off all excess moisture, then put two or three feathers into a brown paper bag that contains about half a cup of cornstarch. Shake gently. The cornstarch absorbs the moisture and the feathers come out dry.

You can create a thick plume by fastening two or more plumes together. Run a piece of mediumweight wire along the groove in the spine of the under plume. Place the upper plume on top, aligning the spines carefully to conceal the wire. Wrap the spines together with nylon thread. This technique will also allow you to repair broken feathers.

PEARLS, BEADS, AND SEQUINS

Pearls, beads, and sequins are often used as stage hat trims, sometimes in clusters, sometimes as an overall pattern. For the best result, stitch each pearl, bead, or sequin on separately. Although this is a time-consuming process, individual stitching will forestall the loss of many beads if a thread that holds a large number of them breaks.

RIBBONS

Bows, rosettes, and ties for hats can be made out of satin, velvet, taffeta, or grosgrain ribbons. The best choice for hatbands and the binding on brims, however, is grosgrain ribbon because the ribs in the ribbon fabric allow it to be shaped before it is applied to a hat. Rayon and cotton grosgrain ribbon shapes better than polyester grosgrain ribbon.

The first step in shaping a piece of grosgrain ribbon is to lay it on the ironing table and to place the iron on one end. Pull the ribbon into a curve and apply steam while you "iron in" the curve. As soon as the ribbon is dry and cool, hold it against the hat to see if the curve is correct. If it's not, return it to the ironing board and lay it in the correct curve. Apply heat and steam, using a "pressing" rather than an "ironing" motion. Be sure the ribbon is completely dry and cool before removing it from the ironing table.

Hoods

Hoods were particularly popular during the Middle Ages and were worn by people in all social and economic classes. Some hoods extended down over the shoulders in cowls, and some had long peaks, called *liripipes*, which

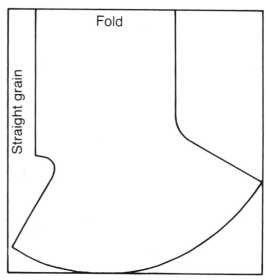

FIGURE 8–41. Simple hood.

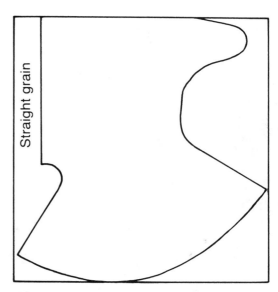

FIGURE 8–42. Monk's hood.

could be draped around the shoulders or wrapped around the head.

You can cut simple hoods in two basic pieces from a square or a rectangle of cloth. See Figures 8–41 and 8–42.

Chaperones

Although the original chaperone was a fancifully arranged hood, a stage chaperone should be constructed in three parts: the roundelet, the fabric cascade, and the liripipe. (See Figures 8–43 and 8–44.)

Make the base for the roundelet out of fat upholstery piping, an ethafoam rod glued into a circlet, or a fabric tube stuffed with fiberfill, shredded foam, or cotton batting. Cover the roundelet base with bias-cut fabric and add trim.

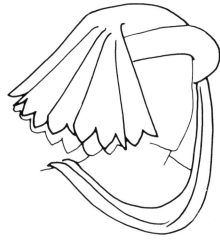

FIGURE 8–43. Chaperone.

FIGURE 8–44. Pattern for a chaperone.

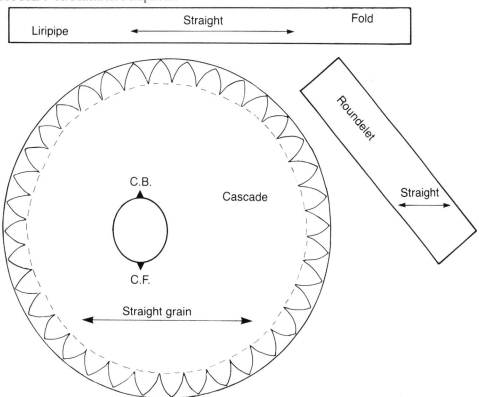

The fabric cascade is often lined with a contrasting color and may have a scalloped or dagged edge. Attach the cascade to the inside of the roundelet and stitch the lining in place.

The liripipe, which is essentially a fabric tube, may be graceful and elegant or overlong, skinny, and very comic. In either case you might want to fasten the draped liripipe to the costume at strategic points with snaps or dots of Velcro.

Chaperones appear in many paintings and statues and there are countless style variations. They are fun to create and most actors enjoy wearing these highly theatrical hats.

Wimple and Veil

The gentleman from the Middle Ages, wearing his chaperone, is often accompanied by his lady in wimple and veil. The wimple is a piece of soft fabric, usually white, that covers the chin and neck. It is drawn up on folds in either side of the face and is fastened just above the ears. Some are more closely fitted than others, and almost all are topped with a head veil and circlet or with a more elaborate headdress.

One stageworthy method of securing a wimple and veil is to fasten them to a chinband and a headband, as shown in Figure 8–45. Secure the chinband and headband with adjustable elastic pieces. Attach the wimple and veil to the chin-

band and headband with hooks and eyes or snaps.

Use the softest possible fabrics for the wimple so it will drape gracefully around the neck. Fine cotton and silk are best. Very lightweight jersey knits are particularly good if the wimple is close-fitting. Wearing a wimple takes some getting used to, so be sure to provide the actor with a rehearsal mock-up as early as possible.

Caps

No matter how many cloth caps there are in the hat stock, no theatre ever seems to have the perfect cap for any costume. Therefore, you end up making caps again and again.

Fortunately, caps are not difficult to make. A cap crown is basically a circle constructed from several shaped pieces, such as those in Figure 8–47. Cut your pattern out of brown paper and make a muslin mock-up. If you do not want equal fullness all around the cap crown, flatten the circle where you need to

FIGURE 8–46. Pattern shapes for a cap with eight sections.

FIGURE 8–45. Bands for securing wimple and veil.

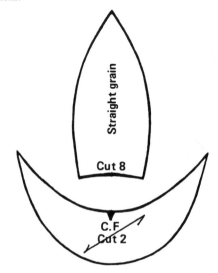

reduce fullness and take in the seam. Use the head circumference measurement to make a stabilizing band out of grosgrain ribbon, belting, or leather. Construct the cap brim from buckram or layers of stitched-together canvas, *cut on the bias* as shown in Figure 8–47. Cover the brim with matching or contrasting fabric *cut on the straight grain*.

Be sure to save all your cap patterns for future use.

Men's Nineteenth- and Twentieth-Century Hats

Men's top hats, derbies, soft felts, and straws make frequent appearances on stage. Since these are not easy styles to fabricate, you will normally pull them from your own stock, borrow, rent, or purchase them. Men's hats have changed gradually but decidedly during the

FIGURE 8–47. Top hat on John Glover playing the title role in the American Conservatory Theater's production of *Hans Christian Andersen*. Costume design by Jane Greenwood. *Photograph courtesy of The American Conservatory Theater.*

years, so be sure you know exactly what style you're looking for when you set out to find men's hats.

Top Hats and Opera Hats

Top hats were enormously popular during most of the nineteenth century. They were worn, in different colors and shapes, for both formal and informal occasions. By the end of the century, however, other hat styles had become more popular for informal wear, and the top hat, along with its close relative the opera hat, were reserved for formal occasions. This remains true today.

The top hat made its appearance as the "beaver" in the eighteenth century. The first beavers had slanted crowns, like the Pilgrim or Quaker hats, and flat, stiff brims. Gradually the slanted crown disappeared and, by 1830, the shape was much like a fat stovepipe. After the beaver supply in America was depleted around the middle of the nineteenth century, toppers were covered with grosgrain, merino cloth, shiny silk, or wool. Toppers were also made out of stiffened felt and the mechanical felting machine, developed in 1820, was a boon to hatmakers.

There are two major brim styles for the top hat: the flat brim and the rolled brim. By the end of the nineteenth century, the flat brim had all but disappeared, and the rolled brim appeared in many different shapes. Crowns were as high as 8 inches and as low as 5¾ inches. Some had straight sides, others had gently curved sides flaring into high crowns and large tops, and still others sported deeply curved sides and low, jaunty crowns. Only the most fashion-conscious gentlemen remained absolutely current in their choice of top hats. Many men wore a single formal top hat for a lifetime, caring little for the yearly fashion changes.

During the nineteenth century, black felt and rough beaver, as well as fawn, gray, and white top hats accompanied informal clothing. White was favored for the hunt. Brushed beaver, plush, and silk top hats graced formal dress.

The faille-covered, collapsible opera hat, or Gibus (the name of its inventor), appeared in Paris in the 1840s. The crown of the Gibus is supported by a spiral spring between the outer cloth and the lining. The spring can be collapsed and the hat folded quite flat for storage under the seats in well-appointed opera houses. The collapsible opera hat was worn interchangeably with the topper, although it was always much more suitable for formal dinners and the theatre, while fashionable weddings and state occasions required the more imposing silk top hat. Opera hats have relatively narrow brims, gracefully rolled, medium-low crowns, and deeply curved sides.

Opera hats were very popular with the young jet set during the 1920s and 1930s; one might be the perfect choice for a Noel Coward character who is on his way to dinner and a night on the town. Popping open a collapsible top hat often provides amusing stage business.

Always store opera hats in the expanded position. If stored collapsed, the silk covering will wear and crack.

Fortunately, there are a good many old formal top hats and opera hats still in existence. The men who owned them wore them infre-

quently and stored them carefully between wearings. Some of these hats eventually find their way into costume stocks. The informal toppers worn every day didn't survive in great numbers.

FIGURE 8–48. Top hat block and straw top hats. *Photograph by Joyce Degenfelder.*

FIGURE 8–49. Disassembled top hat block and straw top hats. *Photograph by Joyce Degenfelder.*

You can purchase new top hats, silk-covered and felt, and opera hats. The felt toppers generally come in black, gray, blue, brown, and white. Besides being rather expensive, the new models don't have the same style and flair as the hats produced a hundred years ago.

Some costume shops build their own top hats from shaped felt. See Figures 8–48 and 8–49 for photographs of a top hat block and straw top hats under construction.

Derbies

The first bowler hat appeared in England in 1850. It had a narrow, flat brim and a melon-shaped crown. Over the years the crown has varied in height and shape and the brim in width and amount of roll. Still called the bowler in England, after its inventor, William Bowler, it is known in America as the derby, from the Earl of Derby, who helped popularize the hat.

The derby is never worn with formal clothes. For several decades it was the most suitable hat to wear with a conservative business suit, particularly in gray or black. In America the brown derby became identified with the Democratic presidential candidate Al Smith and suffered a decided drop in popularity among men of opposing political persuasions.

Soft Felt Hats and Straw Hats

From the latter part of the nineteenth century until after World War II, most men wore hats for most occasions. Family photograph albums show straw skimmers or boaters with swimwear, toppers at weddings, caps on the golf course, and derbies or soft felts on the way to business. Even men lined up outside employment offices and soup kitchens at the height of the Depres-

sion retained the respectability of a covered head. By 1920, the soft felt hat was the most popular of all.

The fedora, the homburg, the snap brim, and the porkpie are all soft felt styles. The Stetson, which appeared in the 1870s, has been widely worn both on the ranch and in the city.

The most elegant of the soft felt hats is the homburg. In 1919, a *Men's Wear* feature writer called it the hat of choice of "the cultured, smartly turned-out men of the world who have social position, inherent good taste, and the means with which to satisfy it." The black homburg is quite suitable with a dinner jacket. Most popular in the darker colors, the homburg has a tapering crown and a medi-umwide rolled brim. Homburgs also come in straw.

Choosing and Fitting Men's Hats for the Stage

Most men's hats stay in style for a long time, with subtle shape changes occurring along the way. *Esquire's Encyclopedia of 20th Century Men's Fashions* by O. E. Shoeffler and William

FIGURE 8–50. Electric hat stretcher and steamer at The Washington Opera. *Photograph by Rosemary Ingham.*

Gale is an important research source for men's hats. If your character is fashion conscious, this book will tell you exactly what he should be wearing; if he's less than fashionable, you can determine what he might be wearing from the general survey material.

Finding the correct hat size to fit the actor is sometimes as difficult as finding the correct hat style for the character. Fortunately, you can alter hat sizes somewhat. If the hat is slightly too big, stuff the sweatband with pieces of foam or felt. You can stock strips of foam with adhesive backing that are very handy for hats. In a pinch, use tissues. Be sure to add the padding evenly on both sides of the hat or halfway around.

Stretching a hat takes a bit longer. Some dry cleaners will stretch hats at a modest price. You can do your own stretching, however, on a hat stretcher. Hat stretchers are expanding head shapes that come in wood or metal. Operate all hat stretchers with care; fabric, felt, straw, and leather will stretch only so far before tearing. A careful and judicious use of steam may aid the stretching process.

Storing Hats

The importance of having a hat stock to draw upon has already been mentioned several times in this chapter. Even the smallest theatre should allot some corner to a hat collection.

Be sure to cover all stored hats to protect them from dust. Store toppers and derbies in individual hat boxes. Plastic bags offer good protection for large women's hats. Stuff the crowns of soft felt hats with cloth or paper and store them one on top of the other, in deep boxes and storage barrels.

Organize the hats according to style and color and label all containers carefully. The less you have to rummage through the hat stock to find what you want, the better for your hats. During the run of a production, provide the actors with hat boxes to store their derbies and toppers and with head blocks to store their soft hats. (See page 447 in Appendix IV for additional hat storage ideas.)

Fine hats, well cared for, can have long and useful stage lives.

9
Costume Accessories and Properties

"Costume accessory" and "costume property" are terms often used interchangeably. In general, in this chapter, costume property refers to items fabricated from modern materials, using craft techniques. A costume accessory is more apt to begin with a contemporary item, bought or found, and not necessarily made from scratch from craft materials. There are times when the two terms will overlap.

Period stage accessories and properties usually suggest historical accuracy rather than reproduce it. Choices depend on such diverse factors as the production style, the distance of the stage from the audience, and what current fashions and fads look like.

Practical staging considerations also affect costume accessory and prop choice. Make sure you ask crucial questions early. Is there someplace for the actor to hang his hat and cane? Or someone to take it from him? Will the open parasol actually fit through the arch that leads into the garden scene? Is the sword suspended in such a way that it won't ensnare the lady's skirt when he passes her? Does his suit have a watch pocket and a place where he can conceal the letter? Whenever you can give the actors selected rehearsal props, you help prevent serious accessory and prop problems during dress rehearsals. Close cooperation between designer, actor, director, and the costume shop staff is the best assurance that you will have a handsomely attired production in which each costume element functions as it should.

How to Do It

No single book can tell you how to build, contrive, or find all the costume accessories and properties you will encounter in your career. Not only are there hundreds of items to produce but there are also dozens of different craft methods available for producing them, and these methods change rapidly as new and often safer materials appear on the market. This chapter is only an overview of the most common costume accessories and props. Instructions are basic and very simple.

Be sure to see Chapter 1, "The Costume Shop," and Chapter 2, "Health and Safety in the Costume Shop," for discussions about setting up and maintaining a safe and workable costume craft area.

FIGURE 9–1. June Kyoko Lu as Forgiveness From Heaven, Linda Gehringer as Wanda, and Pamela Nyberg as Victoria in *The Waiting Room* at Arena Stage. Wigs, headgear, and appropriate accessories help to transform the actors into three distinctly different characters. Costumes designed by David Woolard. *Photograph by Joan Marcus, courtesy of Arena Stage.*

Costume Accessories

Tights and Hosiery

Heavyweight knit tights, made from nylon or nylon and cotton and sometimes including spandex, are used today to represent most period tights and stockings. Be sure to buy a brand that has a reputation for being sturdy. Tights take dyes well. You can decorate tights with fabric paints and indelible magic markers.

Launder tights in warm water and air dry them or use the air fluff setting on an automatic dryer. Teach actors to put on tights carefully, beginning with the feet and working the tights gently up each leg. Pulling tights on by the waistband elastic is a sure way to cause holes and runs.

Some designs require that tights be made of woven cloth, often with patterns and textures that are impossible to produce with

FIGURE 9–2. Wayne Pretlow as Sweets and Julia Lema as Mary in *Play On* at Arena Stage make a delightful pair in stripes and polka dots with all the right accessories. Costumes designed by Marianna Eliott. *Photograph courtesy of Arena Stage.*

nylon knits. Cut cloth tights on the bias for a good fit. You can eliminate the need for gartering by stitching cloth tights onto a pair of cut-off tights, dance trunks, or bathing trunks. Cloth stockings will never fit the leg as smoothly as nylon tights, but the slightly wrinkled, rough look can, in certain cases, be very effective.

Modern, dark-colored socks are usually satisfactory for men's wear in nineteenth- and twentieth-century plays. Patterned knee socks, of the sort worn with knickers, are available at golf and ski shops.

Nineteenth- and early twentieth-century women's hosiery is more difficult to simulate. Nylon stockings didn't appear until after the

FIGURE 9–3. Wesley as Crab the dog and Michael Fitzpatrick in wrinkled and holey tights as Launce in the Utah Shakespearean Festival's production of *The Two Gentlemen of Verona*. Costume design by Rosemary Ingham. *Photograph by Karl Hugh, courtesy of the Utah Shakespearean Festival.*

FIGURE 9–4. Striped stockings and pointed shoes match her pointed hat and pointed nose on the Witch in the opera *Hansel and Gretel*, performed at the Lionel Hampton School of Music in Moscow, Idaho. Costume design by Joanne Martin. *Photograph by Joanne Martin.*

Second World War; before that, women wore cotton or silk stockings, or, after the First World War, cotton, silk, or rayon. All of these stockings were seamed up the back and silk stockings often had designs, called *clocking*, on the sides. (See Figure 9–5.)

Seamed stockings are sometimes available from contemporary lingerie shops, but these are usually too sheer for stage wear. Reproduction seamed stockings, made from denser fibers to simulate legwear from the 1920s through the 1940s, are available from a limited number of sources but are expensive.

Seamed stockings for the stage that suggest authenticity and are comfortable for actors at work can be created from lightweight, semi-opaque dance tights. Put the tights on the legs of a full-body tailor's form and draw a seam down the back with fabric paint. Or you can stitch a seam down the back of the tights' legs, using the rolled hem attachment on your serger. Clocking may be painted on with fabric paint or hand-embroidered with silk or pearl cotton embroidery floss.

Shoes

Shoes, on stage, have two purposes: they must make the actor comfortable, and they must

FIGURE 9–5. Clocking.

FIGURE 9–6. Actors in a production of *Twelfth Night* at the Idaho Repertory Theatre decked out in an array of argyle patterns. Costume design by Joanne Martin. *Photograph by Joanne Martin.*

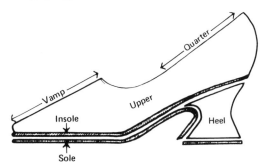

FIGURE 9–7. The principal parts of a shoe.

contribute to the total look of the costume. The first question many actors ask costume designers and technicians is: "What kind of shoes am I going to wear?" Take the actor's interest seriously. Record shoe sizes and foot problems and trace the feet at measurement time. Never expect an actor to wear shoes that don't fit.

It is equally important, however, for the shoes that fit correctly to also look right. Nothing can ruin the period look of a costume as quickly as the wrong shoe. This does not mean, however, that you have to reproduce a shoe of the period. All that is really necessary is that the shoe make a strong appearance of accuracy and complement the style of the whole production. In many cases, this means no more than the addition of period detail or a change of heels to make a modern shoe suitable.

THE PRINCIPAL PARTS OF A SHOE

A shoe is composed of an *upper* that covers the foot, a *sole* that rests on the ground, an *insole* that lies between the foot and the sole, a *heel*, and sometimes a *shank*. The shank is a piece of metal inserted between the sole and the insole, reinforcing the arch to help the shoe retain its shape and give support to the foot.

329

The upper part of the shoe is built on a *last,* which is a sort of mold made from wood or plastic. There is a different last for each shoe shape and size. The word *last* is sometimes, inaccurately, used to refer to the unique size and shape of a particular shoe.

The upper may be made from one piece of material, with a seam at the back, or it may be made in several pieces, as fashion dictates. The part of the upper that covers the front of the foot is called the *vamp,* while the back part is called the *quarter.* On some shoes there is also a *toe cap,* which may, as in the case of some work boots and military shoes, be reinforced with strong leather or metal. The portion of the quarter that fits around the heel almost always requires some form of stiffening.

You cannot change the basic shape of a shoe upper. This includes the height although not the shape of the heel. If you put a higher or a lower heel on a shoe, the sole may crack at the instep. However, you may be able to raise the heel and the sole at the same time, maintaining the original instep curve.

Flat Footwear

Although there are examples of raised or platform shoes and boots into antiquity, heels did not become common until about 1580. Before that, most feet rested firmly on the ground, in footwear that was generally soft and nonrestrictive and gave little support.

SANDALS

Sandals are simple to make. All you have to do is cut a sole from stiff leather or rubber, stitch or rivet straps to the sole, and glue an inner sole on top of this to protect the bottom of the actor's foot.

The biggest problem with sandals will occur in those styles that have an elaborate arrangement of straps extending up the wearer's leg. If the straps are too tight, they may cut off the actor's circulation, and, if they are too loose, they will fall down around his or her ankles. To help prevent these problems, make the straps from real rather than imitation leather. All imitation leathers stretch, and many are slippery. Prearrange the straps as much as you can, and stitch them together where they cross. If the costume includes tights, apply small pieces of the hook side of Velcro under the places where the straps cross; the tiny hooks will grab onto the tights and help keep the straps in place.

SOFT FLAT SHOES AND BOOTS

In plays set before the 1580s, costume designs often include soft leather shoes or boots without heels. For a simple version of such a shoe, see Figure 9–8. The uppers are cut in two pieces and stitched together at the center front and center back. This is then stitched to the sole, which may be cut from heavy leather or

FIGURE 9–8. A simple leather shoe with the upper cut in two pieces and stitched to the sole.

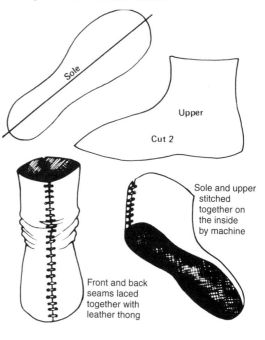

Sole

Upper

Cut 2

Sole and upper stitched together on the inside by machine

Front and back seams laced together with leather thong

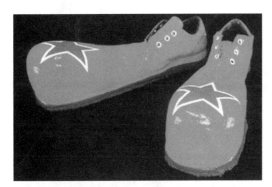

FIGURE 9–9. Clown shoes with Sculpt or Coat surface, created by artisan David Rawlins. *Photograph by John Saari.*

rubber. Glue an insole in place for comfort and add an arch support if the actor wants it.

Soft leather slippers are easily adapted to make medieval footwear. You might want to add rawhide lacings to make them look more interesting. Most of these slippers are made from cowhide, and the soles can be slippery as they accumulate dirt. You can help prevent this by stitching or gluing a piece of suede onto the sole.

Rhythm and gymnastic sandals are versatile soft suede shoes, available at dance supply shops. They blend well with a wide variety of

costumes in many periods, they are comfortable, and the soles have some traction.

Heeled Shoes

The fashion for heeled shoes and boots swept like wildfire through the Western world during the last quarter of the sixteenth century. Although the first heels were of modest height, about 1½ inches, they were not always placed properly and must have been wobbly and uncomfortable. Elizabethan diaries contain many references to swollen and painful calf muscles.

Since heel height will affect both the posture and the gait of its wearer, and it can be uncomfortable and awkward to wear a shoe with an unusual heel, actors should rehearse in the shoes they are going to wear in performance or in rehearsal shoes that are a close approximation of fit and heel. This can be as important for a woman wearing flat shoes when she's not used to wearing them as it is for a man making his first acquaintance with high heels.

From the late sixteenth through the eighteenth century, boots were extremely popular

FIGURE 9–10. Women's heel shapes from the Restoration.

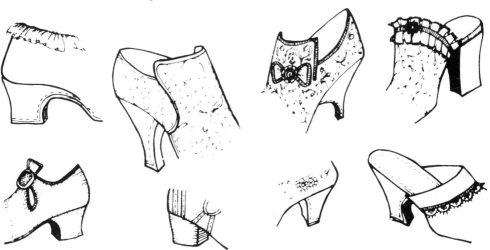

male fashion accessories. Until the 1630s, they were generally considered proper only for hunting, riding, and other outdoor activities. After that, they became acceptable for all occasions—boots and spurs being worn even at table.

In the early part of Elizabeth I's reign, boots continued to be close-fitting on the leg, as they had in earlier periods, but with the addition of folded-over tops, which in time became more and more elaborate. The fashionable man then began to wear boot hose to protect his stockings. These were almost always white and often very fancy, with embroidery or lace trimming at the tops, which were turned down over the turned-down boot tops.

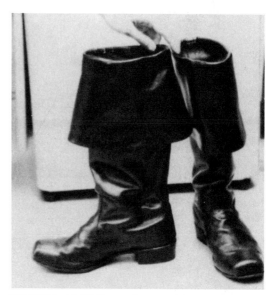

FIGURE 9–12. Wellington boots with leather cuffs added. *Photograph by Joyce Degenfelder.*

FIGURE 9–13. Custom-made over-the-knee leather boots in a production of *The Grand Duchess of Gerolstein* at the Opera Theatre of Saint Louis. Costume design by Liz Covey. *Photograph by Liz Covey.*

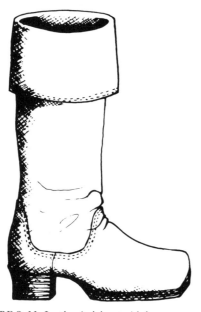

FIGURE 9–11. Leather jack boot with heavy top-stitching, similar to styles obtainable today.

Many modern styles can be adapted to boots of these periods. Choose a style that doesn't have extremely pointed toes and one that will accommodate a low to medium heel.

If the boot needs to be higher in the leg, stitch on a leather extension and turn down the top to cover the seam line.

FIGURE 9–14. Man's modern boot adapted for the seventeenth century with the addition of a leather cuff, boot hose, spur, and spur leather.

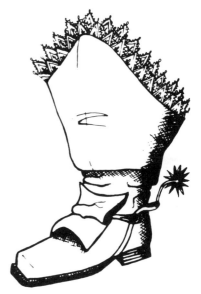

FIGURE 9–15. Bucket-top boot with spur.

You can construct boot hose like false cuffs, which fasten just inside the top of the boot. Glue one side of a strip of Velcro inside the boot and stitch the other side to the boot hose so you can remove them easily for laundering.

The Bucket-Top Boot

After James I became King of England, following the death of Elizabeth I in 1603, men's boot styles became extreme. Of these extremes, one of the most amusing, indeed one of the most amusing examples of fad footwear in *all* of fashion history, was the bucket-top boot. By 1630, the turned-down top of the boot had become so wide that it did look as if the wearer was standing in a bucket. These gaping tops were lined with drooping lace and linen, while the leather of the boot itself was so soft that the whole affair fell softly in folds around the ankle. The look was completed with elaborate spurs, held in place by equally elaborate spur leathers.

A modern Wellington, or short field boot, is a good base for a pair of bucket-tops. Cut the bucket-top from leather and stitch or glue it onto the boot. Use continuous hoop steel or metal bones to shape the bucket-top. Be sure not to make the bucket-tops so wide, particularly on the instep sides, that the actor can't walk.

Red Heels and Brass Buckles

In 1660, Louis XIV of France was given a pair of red-heeled shoes, and, as a result, they became an instant fad. Red heels remained popular with courtiers and dandies for more than a hundred years. They were, by and large, a masculine affectation, although some women also wore them.

The plain shoe with a buckle, first popular among English Puritans and other European Protestant groups, gained widespread acceptance during the last half of the seventeenth century. In his diary, Samuel Pepys notes the exact day in 1660 when he first put buckles on his shoes. By the middle of the eighteenth century, the town of Birmingham was producing some 2,500,000 buckles a year, and the rage continued, with the buckles becoming more and more ornate and expensive until the end of the century, when ribbon ties and rosettes replaced them in fashion.

FIGURE 9–17. Men's contemporary shoes with tongues and side leathers added to simulate eighteenth-century footwear. *Photograph by Liz Covey.*

FIGURE 9–16. Puritan shoe with buckle.

FIGURE 9–18. Custom-made period shoes at The Washington Opera. *Photograph by Rosemary Ingham.*

The fact that something is in fashion, however, does not mean that everyone wears it or wears it exclusively. During all this time, many people continued to wear laced shoes, usually with the laces threaded through a single eyelet.

As the eighteenth century progressed, shoe tongues grew in size, both wider and higher, sometimes sweeping out on either side of the ankle to produce a handsome line. Sometimes the tongues would be backed with a color that contrasted with the color of the shoe. Buckles or ties were fastened on top of the tongue, and there were many heel shapes.

Modern slip-on shoes, such as a plain-toe loafer with a medium heel, adapt easily to these styles. Change the heels, cut new tongues from leather and stitch or glue them to the inside of the shoe, and attach buckles you've found or fabricated.

The French Revolution and Flat Shoes

After the French Revolution, fashion literally collapsed. Clothing shrank, and shoes lost their heels. For about forty years, flat pumps were worn by most young women and by some young men. Women's pumps often had ribbon ties that crisscrossed up the calves. However, older women in many cases still wore plain shoes with small heels, and many men wore low-heeled boots, with a contrasting leather top, that hugged the leg.

Modern ballet slippers or simple, low-heeled pumps are suitable accessories for the thin, high-waisted dresses of this period. Create laces from narrow satin or grosgrain ribbon. Riding boots work well for men, with a band of contrasting leather around the top.

Nineteenth-Century Footwear

The short boot appeared early in the nineteenth century, worn by ladies and gentlemen alike. Some of them had stacked leather heels and elastic sides, others were laced or buttoned up the side.

Modern, elastic-sided boots with thin soles and 1-inch to 1½-inch heels are ideal for this period. The toes should be narrow and tapered and blunt rather than pointed.

There was a great gulf between the rich and the poor throughout the nineteenth century, and this is reflected in their clothing and shoes. The impoverished city dweller and the country peasant wore shapeless shoes, poorly made of inferior leather, with thick, clumsy soles, sometimes made from wood. The most broken-down, worn out pair of shoes you can find in stock or in a resale shop will make an excellent base for this kind of footwear.

By the 1850s, machines were developed to stitch leather, and shoes became less expensive. Rubber galoshes went on the market in 1844. Both men and women favored low boots: satin boots were popular for evening wear and soft kid for daytime. Some ladies' boots were fastened with buttons that matched the garment with which the boots were worn. Victorian ladies admired small feet, and many of them squeezed their feet into boots that were too short and too narrow and laced them up so tightly around the leg that one wonders how they managed to walk. This obsession with small feet is one of the reasons why existing shoes from this period are almost always too small, specifically too narrow, for modern feet.

Shoes with medium heels, broader toes, and center front laces, like modern "Granny shoes," were worn by those who favored comfort, while young girls favored flat-heeled dancing pumps that were rather like Mary Janes. Dancing pumps were often embroidered and decorated with bows.

FIGURE 9–19. Short, elastic-sided boot.

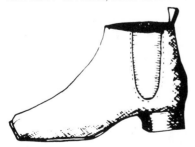

FIGURE 9–20. Woman's Victorian laced Oxford, similar to "Granny shoes" available today.

FIGURE 9–21. Two women's Victorian boots and three suggestions for spats to be worn over modern shoes with correct heel shapes.

High-buttoned and laced shoes are often fabricated in costume shops. If your budget is large, you can have high-topped shoes built by a specialty shoe and bootmaker. If not, you can construct a pair of uppers to be worn over a modern low-cut shoe. These uppers are cut rather like spats, from canvas fabric with a stiff underlining or leather. Like spats, the uppers can be worn over the shoes, held in place by the laces and by an elastic under the insteps.

For a smoother and more unified appearance, you can stitch or glue the high-topped upper to the low-cut shoe. Unless you have a cobbler on staff and proper shoemaking machinery, take the shoes to a shoe repair shop to be stitched.

FIGURE 9–22. Finished boot top ready to be attached to the shoe and become a lace-up boot. *Photograph by Liz Covey.*

FIGURE 9–23. Leather boot top taped to purchased shoe, ready to be stitched on. *Photograph by Liz Covey.*

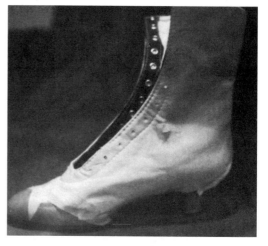

Before attaching the upper to the shoe, make sure to fit the two pieces carefully, asking the actor to go through his or her range of movements on stage. Use masking tape to position the two parts together.

Shoes, in General

If you cannot depict a period shoe accurately, use a shoe that doesn't look conspicuously "modern," even if it is no more than a "neutral style" straight from the shoe store. Rummage through attics, secondhand shops, and church bazaars to make a collection of as many different styles as you can. Collect heels of all kinds. Look especially for shoes with high vamps and such long-lasting styles as the sensible woman's lace-ups and the classic man's wingtip. Whenever you can't find a shoe that's absolutely right, opt for inconspicuous.

COLORING SHOES

Leather dyes, which come in both liquids and sprays, make it possible to change the color of shoes and coordinate footwear with garments.

Many costume shops rely on spray leather dyes for coloring shoes. Leather dyes in spray form are exceptionally toxic and should not be used without adequate ventilation. "Adequate ventilation" does not mean running outside to spray a pair of shoes. It means an approved spray booth and respirator protection for everyone who will come in contact with the spray mist. If you are properly equipped to use spray leather dyes, you can change the color on shoes or boots repeatedly without damaging the surface.

Be sure to remove old dye with a deglazing fluid. Then mask off the soles with masking tape and stuff the insides of the shoes with crumpled muslin or paper. Spray first with the color you want, then mist over that with one or

FIGURE 9–24. A glimpse into a corner of the spray booth room at the Cincinnati College-Conservatory of Music. *Photograph by Rosemary Ingham.*

two darker shades so the shoes will have depth under stage light. Be careful not to build up too thick a layer of dye, since this will crack or chip. When the shoes are completely dry, apply paste wax and buff lightly.

You can "mix" shoe coloring sprays by misting one color over another. On worn leather that has a scuffed surface and won't take the coloring spray, it sometimes helps to apply a thin undercoat of gold or silver spray. Apply the chosen color over the metallic. It will probably take two coats to cover.

Sprayed-on shoe color will scuff away eventually. During the run of a production, you can do little touch-ups. (Just be sure to bring the shoes to the spray booth; don't use sprays in the dressing room!) If, however, the shoes need to be redone, remove the old spray completely before applying the new coat.

At the end of the run, it is advisable to remove all of the spray and apply neat's-foot oil or mink oil to the shoes before returning them to stock. If the shoes are cared for in this way, they will last for years.

Liquid leather dyes give a flatter and more permanent color, but they are transluscent and can only be used to dye light-colored leather a darker color. After applying liquid leather dyes, allow the shoes to dry completely, rub them with a soft cloth to remove the excess dye, then polish them with paste wax. The surface can also be softened and deepened with a misting of spray color before waxing.

Experiment with different brands of opaque paint-on colors for leather shoes. Some dry with a chalky finish and tend to flake off. Others, however, produce excellent color and are long lasting. Once again, be sure to deglaze the surface of the shoes before applying the color.

Dyes used to color fabric-covered shoes are translucent, so you can only go from a light to a dark color, and you must also take the original color of the shoe into consideration. When dyeing, be careful not to get the fabric surface of the shoe too wet since excess moisture will loosen the adhesive that holds the fabric in place. Create your own fabric shoe dyes from water- or alcohol-soluble dyes. If you start with dye powders, be sure to strain the solution and take proper precautions when mixing, or use a liquid dye instead. You might also want to try permanent ink artist's markers on fabric-covered shoes, using the broad side of the tip to color in large areas and using the point for details. When considering a commercial product for dyeing fabric-covered shoes, Evangeline Slipper Dye is a good choice.

NONSKID SHOE SOLES

Since stage floors are often slippery, costume shoes may need to be half-soled and possibly heeled with rubber. This can be done at a shoe repair shop. But, since applying nonskid shoe soles can be expensive, many costume shop technicians do their own. You will need a metal shoe form, adhesives, and sheets of thin rubber from which to cut the half-soles and heels. Use a hand-held rasp to smooth off the edges of the soles and heels or an electric grinding tool such as a Dremyl, which is much more efficient.

Belts

SWORD AND DAGGER BELTS

For many centuries weapons, openly displayed, were important components of male clothing. Over the years different types of rigging developed, dictated by the size and shape of the sword and/or dagger and the fashion that prevailed in its wearing. Although there is an abundance of reference material available on historical weaponry, it is often difficult to find out exactly how swords were suspended. In portraits, the rigging is often concealed by a cloak or sash, or the figure is posed in such a way that the sword rigging is out of sight.

A dagger poses no particular problem because it is short. Sometimes a dagger was simply tucked into the belt next to the clothing; at other times a leather sheath, plain or decorated with gold, silver, and jewels, was threaded onto the belt to hold the dagger. Modern sheaths sold to hold hunting knives are easily adapted into period sheaths.

Sheathing and suspending swords, however, is more difficult. Swords must be suspended from more than a single point and the wearing angle adjusted to each actor individually. A sword that is not properly balanced in its rigging may swing about, tripping up the actor wearing it, or injuring other actors who happen to get in its way.

Figure 9–25 illustrates a stout rigging for a broadsword. The leather straps supporting the sword should be firm and not too narrow. If the broadsword tends to swing, move the straps farther apart on the belt. The sword itself must be moderately heavy and well balanced to hang properly.

Figure 9–26 illustrates one way of rigging a foil or an epee. Adjust the angle of the rigging until the foil stays at the correct angle. Check to see that it won't catch on the furniture and drapes or endanger passing actors. The portion of the rigging that controls the hanging angle should be a leather strap, a thong, or a piece of chain, and it should be as easy as possible to adjust.

BELTS WITH HANGING OBJECTS

Before there were pockets, men and women hung personal objects from their belts, often with amusing results. A lady's maid might appear with a whole arsenal of equipment to be used in repairing or maintaining her mistress's appearance: a brush, a box of powder, a puff, scissors, thread, a pincushion, a bodkin, a bottle of scent, a mirror, and so on, all hanging from her waist.

If you create such an accessory for the stage, take care that the scissors are dull and that the bottles and mirrors are unbreakable. Put grommets in the belt and tie the objects on with thongs or cords. Make sure that all items are securely fastened and that the thongs or cords from which they dangle are staggered in length so the items are less likely to become entangled. If the items are heavy, suspend them from a leather strap that can be riveted to the belt; if they are too light to hang properly, weight them with fishing weights or bits of hardware.

SASHES

Sashes are important costume items. They played an important decorative role on both men's and women's clothing in the middle and late 1600s. Throughout the sword-displaying centuries, men often wore sashes under and sometimes over their sword belts. Confederate officers in the War Between the States were especially fond of sashes, which in many cases had been hand-embroidered and decorated with fringes by their mothers, wives, or sweethearts.

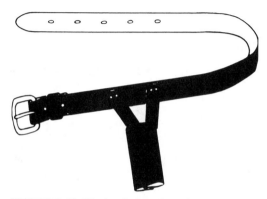

FIGURE 9–25. Rigging for broadsword.

FIGURE 9–26. Rigging for a foil or epee.

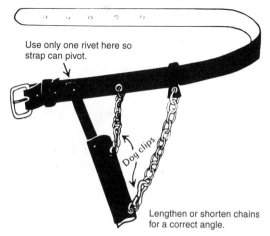

Use only one rivet here so strap can pivot.

Dog clips

Lengthen or shorten chains for a correct angle.

Modern military uniforms and ceremonial outfits still feature sashes.

If it is at all possible, prefix all stage sashes. Arrange the knot and the hanging ends and stitch them permanently to the sash. Fasten the sash with a combination of hooks and eyes and large snaps. A prefixed sash will always look the way you meant it to look and it won't ever sag or come untied.

CONSTRUCTING BELTS

Make simple belts by covering a strip of belting with an appropriate fabric. If the covering is thin, back it with muslin. Construct a tube of the covering fabric that is just wide enough to contain the belting snugly; turn the tube so the right side is out. Slide the belting into the fabric tube so the seam falls along the center of the wrong side of the belt. Press and top-stitch along each edge.

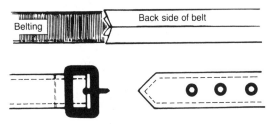

FIGURE 9–27. Making a fabric-covered belt.

Lightweight metal buckles, which come with instructions for covering them, are available in most fabric and notion shops. Keep an assortment of buckle kits on hand. Follow the directions carefully and always use a firm, lightweight backing, such as organdy, if the fabric is sheer.

Collect buckles. Remove them from worn-out belts and store them for future use.

Make holes for buckle prongs with grommets, with the eyelet attachment on your sewing machine, or simply make a hole and reinforce it with a hand-done blanket stitch.

When you use a slide buckle, which has no prong, secure the belt end to the belt with a snap or with a Velcro dot.

SUSPENDERS

In the 1890s, young and fashionable men began to wear leather belts to hold up their trousers. Older, less-fashionable men, and those with portly figures, continued to wear suspenders, and, before the First World War, tailors generally constructed trousers with both belt loops and suspender buttons. After many decades of being dull, utilitarian items, suspenders made a fashion comeback in the late 1980s, appearing in a wide array of colors and patterns.

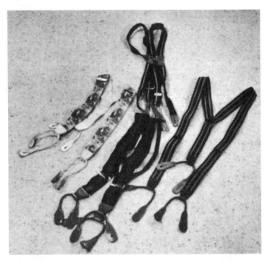

FIGURE 9–28. Assorted suspenders. *Photograph by Richard Bryant.*

Suspenders play an important part in many stage costumes. Tights, breeches, pantaloons, and trousers are all more secure when they are held up with suspenders. When the suspenders are worn for practical purposes only, they may remain out of sight beneath the costume. If the suspenders will be seen by the audience, make sure they are historically accurate and compatible with the costume. Button-on suspenders are preferable to the clip-on types because they are more dependable.

Stitch suspender buttons to the inside of the waistband: two sets of two buttons placed on either side of the center front, about 4 inches apart, and one button on either side of the center back, about 5 inches apart.

Wide elastic, stitched directly to the waistband crossed over in the back, and worn under the outer clothing, can be used instead of ready-made suspenders to hold up tights, breeches, and pantaloons.

Some male dancers hold up their tights with wide elastic suspenders, pulled very short and stitched onto the waistband. Others use adjustable webbing belts, available in military surplus stores. The belt is fastened over the tights, the tights are pulled up high and then rolled over the belt, concealing it completely.

Collars and Neckwear

THE RUFF

The shirt began as an undergarment to provide a soft layer next to the skin and, for a long time, it was completely concealed beneath the doublet. Then, in about 1530, little ruffles began to appear at the neck. This notion caught on, and the ruffles grew in size and complexity, developing in time into some of the most unique collars ever conceived. They are called *ruffs*.

Ruffs, originally made of linen or cambric, were extremely difficult to care for, since to hold their shape they had to be heavily starched and, because of their shape, they could not be ironed by any ordinary or easy means. The wet ruff was arranged on a setting stick made of bone or wood to form the pleats. Then wooden sticks were inserted to hold the pleats apart while the ruff was ironed into shape with a heated iron rod.

The Church, horrified to see so much labor expended on a secular task, branded starch, "the Devil's liquid" and condemned the ruff as wicked and sinful. Nevertheless, the fashion

FIGURE 9–29. Poking stick for ironing ruffs.

FIGURE 9–30. Neck and wrist ruffs on a costume in an exhibit of work by students at the University of Texas. *Photograph by Susan Tsu.*

persisted. Henry II of France, a particularly
meticulous dresser, scandalized his court by
applying the ironing rod personally, rather than
trusting this important step to a servant.
Queen Elizabeth I wore enormous ruffs made
of lace, embroidered with gold and silver
threads.

On page 231 in Chapter 5, "Costume
Construction," there are directions for constructing cartridge-pleated ruffs, called *wheel
ruffs*.

Another type of ruff often used on the
stage is the *standing ruff*. The standing ruff is a

FIGURE 9–32. Early seventeenth-century falling ruff.

FIGURE 9–31. Standing ruff.

large, stiff, fanned-out collar that frames the
head but does not meet in front.

A standing ruff can be made from fabrics
and lace and stiffened with buckram, cape netting, or miracle cloth. It can also be made from
fabrics and lace and permanently stiffened with
a flexible glue or coating (see page 367 for a
discussion of these craft materials). Bones may
be necessary to stabilize the standing ruff and
lightweight wire to shape its edge. The result
of all this careful construction should be a ruff
that appears delicate and airy but which is in
fact so sturdy and well supported that nothing
could make it fall.

THE FALLING BAND COLLAR

The ruff did fall, by stages and by design, until
by the middle of the seventeenth century, it
became the *falling band collar*.

FIGURE 9–33. Falling band (Cavalier) collar with band
strings.

FIGURE 9–34. Puritan collar.

FIGURE 9–35. Preacher's tabs.

A falling band collar, made for the stage, is usually detached from the shirt so it can be laundered separately. The collar is mounted on a neckband that sits against the neck, inside the high-standing doublet collar. The falling band collar falls from the top of the doublet collar and creates a sloping line to the shoulder.

At first, falling band collars were ruffled and soft. Then they became flat. The Cavalier collar spread all the way to the shoulders on either side and was relatively short in front. The Puritan collar was more like a stiff white bib. This bib became smaller, in time developing finally into the small tabs that persisted in Protestant ecclesiastical dress well into the nineteenth century.

BAND COLLARS, STAND COLLARS, AND STAND AND FALL COLLARS

The growing popularity of wigs in the late seventeenth and early eighteenth centuries hastened the demise of large collars. Since the wig hid most of the neck and shoulders, neckwear styles had to change.

FIGURE 9–36. Stanley Anderson as Corden in *The Piggy Bank* at Arena Stage. He is wearing a standing collar and striped cravat. Costume design by Martin Pakledinaz. *Photograph by Joan Marcus, courtesy of Arena Stage.*

First, shirts were gathered into collar-bands, which, in some portraits, are entirely hidden. Band collars themselves were unimportant, being entirely covered by neckwear: stocks and cravats.

Soon, however, the collar appeared again, this time as a standing collar, high enough to be turned down over the stock or cravat. By the end of the eighteenth century, wigs had passed from fashion and most standing collars rose steeply to the front, with collar points sometimes reaching as high as the cheekbones.

The high-standing collar of the early 1800s shrank down again, rising and falling on the tide of fashion throughout the century. In 1825, the collar was permanently detached from the shirt, to be fastened to the shirt neckband with studs. The most fashionable men wore the stiffest collars; men less concerned with such things wore softer ones. The standing collar stood straight up, was folded over, or had its points turned down, according to the mode of the moment or personal preference.

The wing collar, still worn today, made with points expressly designed to be turned down, was introduced for formal wear in 1860.

The two-part *stand and fall* collar, with a high stand and a fall that almost met in front, was popular by the end of the nineteenth century. At that time, both parts of the collar were very stiff.

Modern stand and fall collars sit close to the neck on a low stand, with style changes manifesting themselves for the most part in the spread and length of the points. Rounded and button-down points are important variations.

MAKING, FINDING, AND BUYING COLLARS

You can make the high-standing or the stand and fall collars of the nineteenth and early twentieth centuries with no great difficulty.

FIGURE 9–37. Actors wearing stand and wing collars in *Around the World in 80 Days* at the Utah Shakespearean Festival. Costume design by Margaret E. Weedon. *Photograph by Karl Hugh, courtesy of Utah Shakespearean Festival.*

See the collar pattern draft on page 150 in Chapter 4, "Pattern Development," for a way to begin.

The toughest problem to solve when making a collar from this period is to get enough starch in it to keep it stiff through a performance. A collar made from cotton and polyester-blend fabrics won't hold starch properly, and a collar treated with spray starch or sizing will wilt as soon as the actor begins to perspire. Choose a heavyweight handkerchief linen for the collar and interface it with a tightly woven cotton. When the collar is finished, wet it and dip it in boiled starch or undiluted liquid starch. Squeeze out all of the excess starch and let it dry. When it's dry, dampen the collar well and iron it between two pieces of soft cotton fabric to prevent scorching.

Look for old collars in antique clothing stores and at rummage sales. When you find them, measure carefully to make sure they will fit today's actors and snap them up for your collar stock.

Some theatres keep supplies of linen-finish paper collars on hand. For many years these disposable items were available from Gibson-Lee Collars and are still referred to as "Gibson collars." They are presently available from Amazon Drygoods in a variety of styles and a broad range of sizes. In most production situations, one Gibson collar can be used for several performances.

Stocks, Cravats, and Neckties

The bandstrings used to secure the center closing of the falling band collar were the forerunners of the necktie. At first, they were simply practical, plain, and often hidden from view. Later on they became decorative and were made from colored ribbons and had tasseled ends.

FIGURE 9–38. David Adkins as Alceste with Anthony Fusco as Oronte wearing a fancy seventeenth-century lace cravat in *The Misanthrope* at the American Conservatory Theater. Costume design by Beaver Bauer. *Photograph courtesy of the American Conservatory Theater.*

Around 1660, it became fashionable to wear a scarf or a piece of cloth around the neck, a fashion said to have been borrowed by the French from the dress of a regiment of Croatians who visited Paris in 1636. This neckscarf, or neckcloth, became quite popular, and from it developed both the stock and the cravat.

Stocks and cravats serve the same decorative purpose: they circle the neck on top of the collar stand. They may provide some ornamentation at the neck front, which may or may not

FIGURE 9–39. Late eighteenth-century cravat tied in bow showing shirt ruffles below.

FIGURE 9–40. Eighteenth-century stock with shirt ruffles below.

extend down onto the chest. At first, the distinction between the two was that the stock fastened in the back, while the cravat tied in front. However, this distinction blurred until, in the nineteenth century, it was possible to buy a ready-fixed cravat that, like the stock, fastened in the back.

Until 1715, the stock was pleated or folded, often with a bow or a knot stitched to the front, and was accompanied by a shirt frill, or jabot. Late in the eighteenth century, the stiff stock appeared. Most stocks were fastened in the back with buckles and straps. Most were white; some were black.

Stocks are the most characteristic neckwear of the eighteenth century, cravats of the nineteenth century. Both styles, however, were worn in both centuries. In time, the stock came to be considered the more conservative of the two.

Webster defines a cravat as "a wrapped neckcloth with ends knotted or tied." The term was known as early as 1636. Cravats were usually made of soft cotton or linen, liberally trimmed with lace. Louis XIV wore cravats made entirely of lace, which, among other

FIGURE 9–41. Early nineteenth-century black full-dress stiffened stock.

things, helped to encourage the development of the lace industry in France.

The folded, wrapped cravat appeared first in the 1790s. A large piece of fine white cloth folded diagonally, it was wrapped at least twice around the neck and tied in front, sometimes with a bow and sometimes with a knot. The knot was favored in France, the bow in Britain and America. Occasionally, a black cravat was worn on top of a white one.

Small bow ties, for formal occasions, and skinny cravats that were wrapped around the neck only once and tied with four-in-hand or Windsor knots began to appear in the late

FIGURE 9–42. Ties of different widths with assorted accessories. *Photograph by Richard Bryant.*

nineteenth century. Men no doubt had tired of having to pay so much attention to elaborate neckwear. Certainly the rising middle class, eager to improve its lot, was much too busy getting ahead to devote an hour or two each morning to the correct arrangement of a cravat.

The refinements of the cravat were left behind, and the term "necktie," which became popular late in the nineteenth century, correctly described the modern approach to neckwear.

Neckties in the twentieth century varied little except in width, size of knot, and color. Bow ties and knotted ties alternate in popularity, though neither goes completely out of fashion.

NECKTIES FOR THE STAGE

Almost all stage cravats should be pre-arranged, stitched in place, and rigged to close in the back. The closing can be con-

cealed by a strip of cloth that extends over the closing and snaps in front under the bow or knot.

Modern realistic plays, with their emphasis on the small actions of ordinary life, have given rise to many occasions on stage when an actor must tie a tie right in front of the audience. Every actor should be prepared to tie a bow, a Windsor knot, a four-in-hand knot, and an ascot, and every costume technician should be prepared to teach these methods. Figures 9–43 to 9–46 illustrate these methods of tying ties.

When you have to prearrange a contemporary necktie for a quick change, tie it on the actor and then slit it at the center back. Remove about a ½ inch from each end, and bind the ends with bias tape. Add a piece of elastic to each bound end so the tie will close snugly. Use a skirt hook and eye and/or large snaps for the closure.

FIGURE 9–43. Tying a four-in-hand. Pass the wide end, on the right, over and under the narrow end, then over again. Bring the wide end up through the center and slip it through the loop in front. Tighten the knot by pulling the wide end down and pushing the knot up.

FIGURE 9–44. Arranging an ascot. Start with both ends even and make a loop as shown to form a single knot. Pass the right end over and under the left end to make the second knot. Tighten the knot, then drape the left end over the right one and fasten with a stick pin.

FIGURE 9–46. Tying a Windsor knot. Start with the wide end on the right about 12 inches longer than the narrow end. Make a loop, then bring the wide end around and behind as shown. Pass the wide end over to the back, then bring it across the front, then under again. Finish by slipping the wide end through the loop in front. Tighten the knot and shape carefully.

FIGURE 9–45. Tying a bow tie. Start with the end crossed over to the left about 1½ inches longer than the other end. Make a loop as shown. Begin to form the bow with the shorter end and bring the longer end over it. Then push the long end through the knot to complete the bow. Even up the ends, tighten, and shape carefully.

Collar Pins, Tie Clasps, and Tie Tacks

Before the twentieth century, cravats and ascots were often decorated with stickpins, ranging from simple gold pins to pins decorated with precious stones. Sometimes, these pins were inserted through the neckwear into the shirt front, helping to hold the neckwear in place; sometimes, they were merely ornamental.

Collar buttons were used to hold collars in place. Although they were important accessories, often made of gold or gold and pearl, they were always concealed.

The collar pin came into use as men shifted from the high starched collar to the softer collar early in the twentieth century.

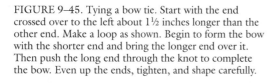

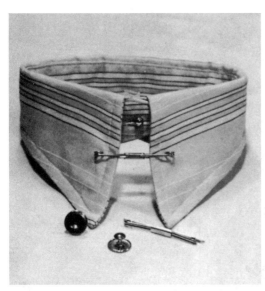

FIGURE 9–47. Collar with collar buttons and collar pins. *Photograph by Richard Bryant.*

Collar pins secure the points or rounded edges of soft collars and keep them from curling up.

The button-down collar appeared in the late 1920s, but the plain collar, worn with a collar pin, remained the most popular style through the 1930s.

Tie clasps became an important piece of male jewelry in the 1920s. In the 1930s, the most common decorative motif for tie clasps was sport: tennis racquets, dogs, guns, horses, golf clubs, and sailboats all appeared on them. In the 1940s, tie clasps were bigger and bolder than ever; in some cases they included a chain, through which the tie was slipped.

As ties became narrower in the 1950s, tie clasps correspondingly became shorter and smaller. The tie tack, which looked when in place much like the nineteenth-century cravat pin, became popular. These too were decorated with stones, animal heads, copies of ancient coins, and the like.

Eyeglasses

As is the case for all costume accessories, eyeglasses must conform both to the period of the production and the nature of the character who wears them.

Although the human race has been trying to solve the problems of poor eyesight since ancient times, corrective lenses were not widely worn until the sixteenth century. For a discussion of the delightful history of eyeglasses, refer to Richard Corson's *Fashions in Eyeglasses* and to other books whose titles are in the Bibliography.

MONOCLES, LORGNETTES, AND PINCE-NEZ

Period lenses most often called for on stage are *monocles, lorgnettes,* and *pince-nez.*

The monocle was developed from the eighteenth-century "quizzing glass," which was a lens mounted on a decorative handle. In time the handle was eliminated and the lens inserted directly into the eye socket. The monocle was popular with both men and women in the 1820s, but later in the century became an affectation.

The lorgnette, a female fashion, was a by-product of the early nineteenth-century fad for telescopes and opera glasses. It consisted of a set of framed lenses, variously shaped, attached to a metal, tortoise shell, or mother of pearl handle that folded, so the whole thing could be carried in the purse. Lorgnettes were so fashionable in the 1830s that women who had no vision problems whatsoever used them.

The pince-nez was the first widely used, truly middle-class style of eyeglasses. Its name describes the manner of its attachment: a spring mechanism that clamped the eyeglasses onto the nose. The pince-nez appeared in the 1840s and was widely worn, particularly in the last quarter of that century,

FIGURE 9–48. A bespectacled Charles Dean with Julie Eccles in *The House of Mirth* at the American Conservatory Theater. Costumes designed by Anna Oliver. *Photograph courtesy of the American Conservatory Theater.*

although it remained popular well into the twentieth century, especially with farsighted people who wore eyeglasses only for reading and close work. Its use is associated much more with old than with young characters.

One interesting variation of the pince-nez has a retractable chain that attached the lenses to a small, decorative pin worn on a lady's dress.

MODERN GLASSES

Until the developments of plastics, eyeglasses were framed with metal. Typically, the ear pieces were thin, and the frames gave limited protection to the lenses. Rimless styles, with the ear and nose pieces attached directly to the lenses, have been intermittently popular.

The advent of plastics greatly increased the possibilities for variety, both in color and

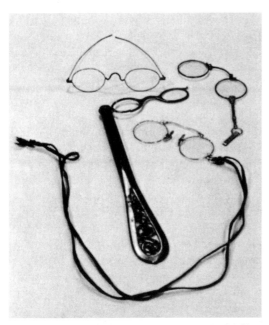

FIGURE 9–49. Assorted period spectacles. *Photograph by Richard Bryant.*

FIGURE 9–50. Fred C. Adams sporting a monocle as Major-General Stanley in the Utah Shakespearean Festival's production of *The Pirates of Penzance*. Costume design by Bill Black. *Photograph by Karl Hugh, courtesy of Utah Shakespearean Festival.*

frame shape, and some modern plastic frames are quite bizarre.

EYEGLASSES FOR THE STAGE

Many theatre costume shops acquire eyeglasses from donations, thrift shops, estate sales, and antique shops. Also, ask the owners of optical shops if they have old, out-of-date frames that they would be willing to sell for a reasonable price.

When planning to use a pair of second-hand glasses that have prescription lenses in them, be sure to remove the lenses since they will interfere with the actor's own vision. If the frames are sturdy, and the actor is working on a proscenium stage at some distance from the audience, you may be able to get by without lenses, but on an open stage or in a small house, you will have to substitute plain glass for the prescription lenses. This can be costly. Shop around and compare prices. See if you

FIGURE 9–51. Eyeglasses with plastic frames. *Photograph by Richard Bryant.*

can persuade an optician to change lenses in exchange for free tickets or for an advertisement in the program.

Make sure the actor has a sturdy case to protect his or her glasses when they are not being worn on stage. And make sure they are cleaned before you put them back into storage. Scrub the frames with a soft toothbrush. With proper care, stage eyeglasses can have a long life.

Fans

Fans have been a vital part of the ceremonial and cultural life of the Orient since before the tenth century B.C. The largest and most beau-

FIGURE 9–52. Assorted fans. *Photograph by Richard Bryant.*

tiful fans belonged to the Chinese emperors. Oriental fan display is practiced by men and women alike and plays a significant part in traditional Japanese and Chinese theatre. Great skill is required to execute the subtle gestures of these ancient dramas.

Portuguese sailors brought fans back from the Orient in the early fifteenth century, introducing to women of wealth and leisure a fashion that persisted for three centuries. The first imported fans were stiff and did not fold. They were made of feathers or of fabric and paper stretched over a lightweight frame.

The folding fan was brought to Paris in 1549 by Catherine de Medici, and it caught on quickly. It was much more graceful and offered more possibilities for subtle gesture than did the stiff fan.

Fan sticks, which form the frame of a folding fan, may be made of wood, ivory, ebony, or plastic. They may be embossed with gold and encrusted with gems, delicately carved or painted with exquisite miniatures. The two outer sticks called guards are always thicker than the inner sticks and often are decorated even more fancifully.

The fan leaf, which is glued to the sticks, can be made of paper, vellum, kid, silk, lace, or rayon. The decoupé fan made from paper, vellum, or kid was especially popular from the sixteenth through the eighteenth century. Intricate designs were cut into the leaf with tiny scissors to achieve the look of fine lace. The most beautiful eighteenth- and nineteenth-century fans were hand painted. In the hands of some fine artists, fan painting achieved the level of fine art.

Fan display reached a peak of frivolousness among the fashionable in eighteenth-century France. Specialty fans became popular. Some ladies had spectacles built into their fans so they could watch the opera on stage without anyone knowing they needed eyeglasses. The domino fan was cleverly designed to include eyeholes as part of an overall leaf design, so the lady could spy from behind her fan, undetected. The mask fan had a face painted on it, as unlike the face of the fan holder as possible, with eyeholes; ladies holding such fans could conceal their identities in public.

The fan became the instrument through which a complex courting conversation could be carried on. This practice is said to have begun in Spain, as a way of getting around the ever-present and sharp-eyed duenna. Pamphlets appeared, teaching fan language to

FIGURE 9–53. Tom Souhrada, Keith Weirich, and Scott Brush brandishing fans in *The Most Happy Fella* at The Repertory Theatre of St. Louis. Costume design by James Scott. *Photograph by Jerry Naunheim, Jr., courtesy of the Repertory Theatre of St. Louis.*

Spanish ladies, and they were quickly translated for use in other countries.

Here are some conventions of fan language, popular in the nineteenth century:

Placing the fan near the heart meant, "You have won my love."

Resting the shut fan on the right eye, "When may I be allowed to see you?"

The question, "At what hour?" was answered by the number of sticks shown.

Touching the unfolded fan in the act of waving meant, "I always long to be near you."

Threatening, with the shut fan, "Do not be so imprudent."

Pressing the half-opened fan to the lips, "You may kiss me."

Clasping the hands under the open fan, "Forgive me."

Covering the left ear with the open fan, "Do not betray our secret."

Hiding the eyes behind the open fan, "I love you."

To shut the open fan very slowly, "I promise to marry you."

Drawing the fan across the eyes, "I am sorry."

Touching the tip of the fan with the finger, "I wish to speak to you."

Resting the fan on the right check, "Yes."

On the left check, "No."

Opening and shutting the fan several times, "You are cruel."

Dropping the fan, "We will be friends."

To fan slowly, "I am married."

To fan quickly, "I am engaged."

To put the handle of the fan to the lips, "Kiss me."

To open the fan wide, "Wait for me."

To place the fan behind the head, "Do not forget me."

To do so with the little finger extended, "Good-bye."

Carrying the fan in front of the face with the right hand, "Follow me"; doing the same with the left hand meant, "I am desirous of your acquaintance."

Placing the fan on the left ear, "I wish to get rid of you."

Drawing the fan across the forehead, "You have changed."

Twirling the fan in the left hand, "We are watched."

Doing the same with the right hand, "I love another."

Carrying the fan, open, in the left hand, "You are too willing."

Carrying the fan, open, in the right hand, "Come and talk to me."

Drawing the fan through the hand, "I hate you."

Drawing the fan across the cheek, "I love you."

Presenting the fan shut, "Do you love me?"

In this day and age, the fan language seems a less-than-satisfactory method of conversing, with lots of room for misunderstood messages. One can only hope that the nineteenth-century lady and gentleman had both taken their codes from the same instruction book.

FANS FOR THE STAGE

Fanmaking is a specialized and difficult craft, and, if the fan must operate properly in a lady's hand, it probably should not be attempted in a costume craft shop. Even replacing a fabric cover on a period fan is an enormously painstaking task and very time-consuming.

Ask your local antique dealers to call you whenever they acquire sturdy fans. Don't ever purchase a fan sight unseen. Antique fans are usually costly and to be of any use on stage they must be in mint condition.

Elegant, expensive silk fans are available in most oriental import shops, as well as inexpensive paper fans. Both kinds are usually available in more than one size and can be adapted for many stage purposes.

A paper fan is stiff when you buy it and must be broken in with care. Open and close it slowly at first, then more rapidly; too quick a flick in the early stages may cause the paper leaf to rip. Do any painting, stenciling, or other ornamentation *after* you've broken in the fan. If the paper fan is much used, and the production runs more than half a dozen performances, be sure to have backups prepared.

Gloves

Gloves are important accessories for costumes from many historical periods. Fortunately, many styles can be fashioned from modern gloves available in department stores and formal wear shops. Use the Internet to shop for specialty gloves. Gloves with gauntlets, for example, are available from vendors who sell clothing and accessories to historical reenactors.

Gauntlets can be added to many kinds of gloves, including white cotton formal gloves, and leather, suede, and cotton work gloves. Figure 9–54 illustrates the steps involved in adding a gauntlet. The gauntlet should be stiffened with nylon cape netting or several layers of canvas. Use fabric or leather dyes to color the gloves and gauntlets.

Store formal gloves carefully, separated into pairs and protected by tissue paper or muslin. Hand wash fabric gloves and air dry on an absorbent towel.

FIGURE 9–54. Adding a gauntlet to a glove.

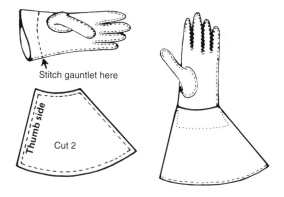

FIGURE 9–55. Leather gloves with leather gauntlets. *Photograph by Richard Bryant.*

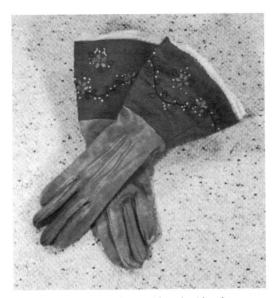

FIGURE 9–56. Cloth gloves with embroidered gauntlets. *Photograph by Richard Bryant.*

Fine kid gloves may also be hand-washed. Many people like to wash kid gloves by putting them on and gently swirling them

FIGURE 9–57. Actor James Farmer with a gloved and bejeweled Sevanne Martin in a production of *Olympia* at Actors Theatre of Louisville. *Photograph by Richard Trigg, courtesy of Actors Theatre of Louisville.*

in cool water and mild detergent. Rinse, press out as much water as possible, remove the gloves carefully, and air dry on an absorbent towel.

Kid gloves that are spotty or discolored with age may be dipped in a weak solution of tea or coffee, which will give them an overall buff or cream-colored look. Under most stage lights, buff or cream-colored gloves will appear quite white.

Purses

To avoid confusion in this section, *purse* will be the single term used to mean any container (smaller than a suitcase!) used by women and men to carry personal belongings. Handbag and pocketbook are roughly

FIGURE 9–58. Assorted purses. *Photograph by Richard Bryant.*

synonymous terms, but both seem inappropriate when referring to a dainty, lace-covered drawstring object or an elegant beaded creation from the 1920s. The word *purse* seems the most suitable for all styles.

Costume shops regularly construct drawstring, pouch, and clutch purses from a variety of materials. Figure 9–59 is a set of directions for a simple drawstring purse made from fabric. A different style drawstring purse is shown in Figure 9–60. It has a flat base stiffened with cardboard, buckram, or cape netting.

You can construct a flat pouch from three basic pieces, as shown in Figure 9–61, plus straps. For a handmade look, lace the pieces together with leather thongs; machine stitch the seams and turn them to the inside for a more finished look. Male characters often wear pouch purses on their belts, either suspended from two short strap loops or threaded through a strap loop stitched to the back of the purse.

Clutch purses, so called because they are usually constructed without straps or strings and have to be clutched in the hand or under the arm, are common twentieth-century accompaniments for a lady's evening costume. They were particularly popular from the 1930s through the 1950s and often matched the dress. They are constructed rather like an envelope over an understructure of canvas or buckram. Clutch purses can fasten with a button and loop, a large snap, or a simple clasp.

Contemporary purses are usually adapted from items you already have in stock or ones purchased new or used. There are so many different shapes and sizes around that it usually takes only patience to find a purse that will lend itself to being altered into whatever the designer wants.

Old trim can be removed and replaced with new trim. You can dye leather purses with leather dyes and color fabric purses with fabric dyes and paints. When you need to change the color of a plastic purse, be sure to use a coating made specifically for plastic surfaces. It may be necessary to use a primer coat under the color.

A stage purse becomes a challenge when it has to serve a practical as well as an accessory role. It is up to the costume staff member in charge of accessories to know exactly what items have to come out of the purse and to arrange the interior of the purse so the actor can find the required items with a minimum of digging. Be sure to work out these technicalities with the actor, the director, and the stage manager and make sure the actor has plenty of time to rehearse with the purse and its contents. It often helps to pad the bottom of the purse with shaped foam or batting to create a false bottom and eliminate corners into which compacts, combs, and lipstick cases get lost. Sometimes it's necessary to create side pockets or elastic loops inside the purse to hold small items.

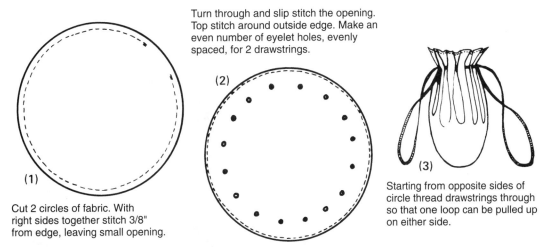

Turn through and slip stitch the opening. Top stitch around outside edge. Make an even number of eyelet holes, evenly spaced, for 2 drawstrings.

(1)

Cut 2 circles of fabric. With right sides together stitch 3/8" from edge, leaving small opening.

(2)

(3)

Starting from opposite sides of circle thread drawstrings through so that one loop can be pulled up on either side.

FIGURE 9–59. Directions for constructing a simple drawstring purse made from fabric.

FIGURE 9–60. Directions for constructing a drawstring purse with a stiffened base.

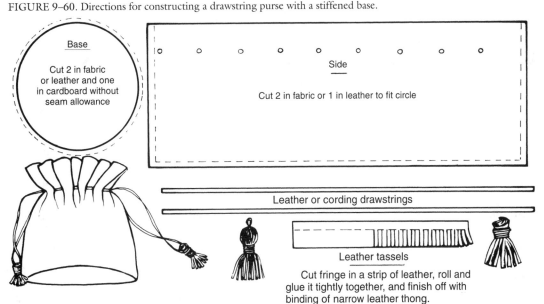

Base

Cut 2 in fabric or leather and one in cardboard without seam allowance

Side

Cut 2 in fabric or 1 in leather to fit circle

Leather or cording drawstrings

Leather tassels

Cut fringe in a strip of leather, roll and glue it tightly together, and finish off with binding of narrow leather thong.

Seam side edges together to form tube. Slip one tube inside the other with right sides together and stitch 3/8" from top edge, turn through, and top stitch.

Working from the inside, join side piece to one circle. Glue cardboard on top of circle, then hand stitch the second fabric circle to cover it and form lining, or simply glue the second leather circle to the cardboard. Turn purse to right side and insert drawstrings. Finish drawstrings with small tassels.

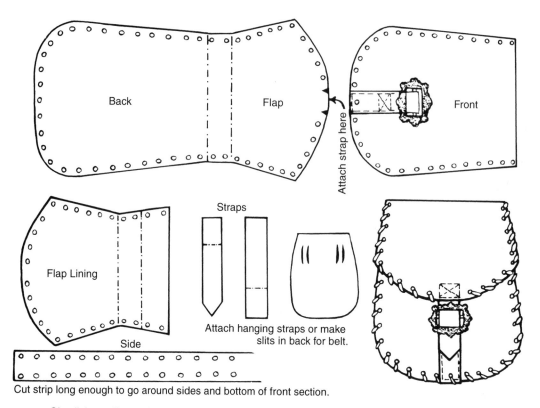

Back

Flap

Attach strap here

Front

Flap Lining

Straps

Side

Attach hanging straps or make slits in back for belt.

Cut strip long enough to go around sides and bottom of front section.

Glue lining to flap and attach strap and buckle with machine stitch. Punch holes and join together with leather thong. Be careful to space the holes evenly and match them up to corresponding pattern pieces.

FIGURE 9–61. Directions for constructing a flat pouch.

Umbrellas and Parasols

Umbrellas are, for the most part, practical items designed to protect their bearers from rain. Stage umbrellas usually come from stock or are purchased new or secondhand. A collection of plain black umbrellas is a valuable holding for all costume stocks.

Occasionally it's necessary to make an umbrella appear to look wet. Real water has a frustrating way of not looking wet on stage, and it dries very quickly under stage lights. Add a "wet look" to the umbrella by spattering it with glycerin or a flexible glue or coating that

dries clear. Plan ahead if you use glycerin as it takes several hours to dry.

The major differences between a parasol and an umbrella, for all practical purposes, are length of handle and sometimes the size of the top. A parasol handle is usually longer than an umbrella handle and the top smaller.

Parasol frames can be purchased from theatrical supply companies. Be sure to buy the sturdiest ones available; they are well worth the extra cost.

To cover a parasol or umbrella frame that has no cover on it, begin by draping the main pattern piece. Open up the frame and drape muslin between two spokes. Place the straight grain of the fabric in the middle of the section and don't stretch it too tight. Leave adequate seam allowances. Count the number of pieces the parasol cover requires, cut them from muslin, and stitch them together. Fit the mock-up. Make sure each seam passes directly over a spoke in the frame and that each piece tapers smoothly toward the center. Don't cut the cover fabric until the muslin is perfect.

When recovering a parasol or umbrella that has an original cover, you can separate one of the pieces, press it carefully, and use it for a pattern. Or you can open it and drape a pattern as just described. The cover pieces on some antique parasols may not be completely accurate.

Once the fabric cover is assembled, secure it tightly to the top and bottom of each spoke. The spokes on many frames have holes in them through which you can stitch on the cover. Add ruffles, fringe, and other edge decorations to the cover after it has been put on the frame. Machine stitch trim between the spokes and stitch it by hand over the spokes. As you work on the frame, open and close it frequently to make sure the cover isn't interfering with the parasol's action.

FIGURE 9–62. Shirley Knight as Ranevskaya in *The Cherry Orchard* at Arena Stage. She carries a lace parasol that complements her lace dress, lace fan, and embroidered net gloves. Costume design by Miruna Boruzescu. *Photograph by Joan Marcus and courtesy of Arena Stage.*

Most parasols have wooden handles, which you can paint to complement the cover fabrics and the overall costumes. Be sure to use an enamel paint that won't rub off on costume pieces or on the actor's hands.

Canes and Walking Sticks

In ancient times, the walking stick or staff was reserved for gods and heroes. From its mythic beginnings, it was a symbol of its bearer's power, a significance epitomized in a king's sceptre. Popes, bishops, judges, and generals throughout history have carried staffs. In the twentieth century, military officers often display a baton, a swagger stick, or a riding crop to indicate their importance.

Except for three periods, late in the fifteenth century, briefly in the eighteenth, and for a time in the nineteenth, the walking stick has not been popular with women. Even during these times, women preferred a long, slender stick, too delicate to suggest power.

In the fourteenth and fifteenth centuries, the walking stick was accessory to acts of violence. It was often made with a hollow compartment, in which its owner could conceal a knife or poison.

In trained hands, the quarterstaff could be a deadly weapon, as could the large oak sticks the Puritans often carried.

The walking stick lost some of its combative nature in the late sixteenth and seventeenth centuries. The use of bamboo and other forms of cane gave rise to a new term, *cane,* which soon became synonymous with "walking stick." Short canes were very popular with mid-seventeenth-century French gentlemen; they were made of ivory, ebony, whalebone, and lovely woods.

In the eighteenth century, the walking stick grew to 4 feet in length. Gentlemen used it to support elegant poses. Around 1780, an elegant lady was out of fashion unless she affected a shepherdess' crook.

In the nineteenth century, both men and women carried canes, the female version often being a walking stick–parasol combination. At the end of the nineteenth century, men's canes were again hollowed out, but this time to conceal items such as telescopes, camera tripods, folded toilet tables, and footstools.

Canes have fallen out of favor in our time, except for those who need them as an aid to walking.

FIGURE 9–63. Canes and a stick for the stage. *Photograph by Richard Bryant.*

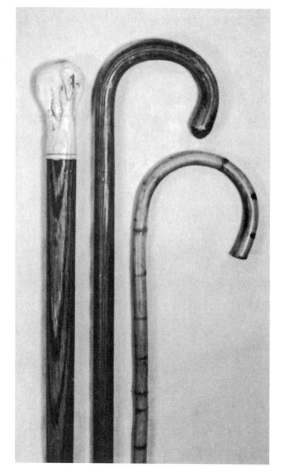

Many people collect antique walking sticks. Fine ones are often hard to find, and, when you do, they are expensive. Some collectors will be happy to loan a stick for use on stage. If you don't know a collector, advertise your need in a local paper. Needless to say, don't borrow an antique stick if it's going to be used as a weapon!

The hardest thing about making sticks and canes in the shop is making them as strong as the real thing. Hardwoods are difficult to shape without a woodworker's skills and a lathe, and soft wood doweling will crack when the actor puts his or her weight on it. Billiard cues make excellent eighteenth-century walking sticks, and you can fashion shorter nineteenth-century versions from bannister rods. To keep

the sticks from slipping, use rubber tips of the sort used on crutches.

Jewelry

FOUND JEWELRY

The term *found jewelry* means those pieces of stage jewelry that are bought, borrowed, rented, or adapted from modern pieces. In most cases, it is best to keep jewelry to a minimum on stage, but some costumes need jewelry to look properly finished. Use jewelry where its use is indicated, make certain it's evocative of the period, and avoid distracting pieces or pieces chosen simply for show unless a particular characterization calls for them.

FIGURE 9–64. Martin Kildare as Iago and Carrie Baker as Emilia with the "strawberry handkerchief," a vital accessory to the plot of *Othello*. Costumes designed by Bill Black for the Utah Shakespearean Festival. *Photograph by Karl Hugh, courtesy of the Utah Shakespearean Festival.*

FIGURE 9–65. Actress Enid Graham wears pearl drop earrings with her jewel-encrusted costume as Elizabeth of Valois in The Shakespeare Theatre's production of *Don Carlos*. Costume design by Robert Perdziola. *Photograph by Carol Rosegg, courtesy of The Shakespeare Theatre.*

EARRINGS

Earrings were commonly worn by women in the ancient world. They fell out of fashion during the Middle Ages when women covered their heads or wore veiled headdresses but reappeared late in the fourteenth century and continued to be popular throughout the centuries.

Until modern times, all jewelry, including earrings, was expensive and worn only by the rich. Gold, silver, precious and semiprecious stones were the materials from which they were made, and pieces were handcrafted.

The size and shape of earrings have changed through the years. For instance, in the 1870s, large hanging earrings of gold or enamel with gold fringe were popular but by the end of the century a single diamond stud in each ear was preferred.

Inexpensive costume jewelry became available during the early years of the twentieth century and women of all classes began to suspend things from their ears. The screw-back earring was invented in 1900, making it possible for women to wear earrings without having to submit themselves to ear piercing.

362

Throughout the twentieth century, earrings have been an important part of female dress. The screw-back and clip-back types were favored until the 1960s, when some women began to pierce their ears again. Earrings for both pierced and nonpierced ears are readily available today.

There are so many earrings on the market, and so many of them are copies of old designs, that it's often possible, with patient shopping, to find something suitable for almost any period costume. There are also a great many craftspeople who make earrings. Indeed, you may find a jewelry maker among your costume technicians.

Beautiful earrings for the stage can be created with a few tools and bits and pieces of old jewelry of the sort that collects in most costume shops. When you run short of usable pieces, visit secondhand shops and yard sales to replenish the stock. Craft suppliers sell ear wires, posts, screw backs, and clip backs.

Consider adding a book such as *Design and Creation of Jewelry* by Robert von Neumann to your costume shop library.

PINS

Ornamental pins were first used to hold draped garments in place and are particularly important for Greek and Roman costumes. These pins are usually large and ornate and, when constructed for the stage, it's usually by one of the "made jewelry" techniques found later in this chapter.

From 1500 to 1700, a great many ornamental pins were worn by both sexes. Men particularly fancied pins on their hats. The early nineteenth century saw a great rage among women for cameos, which were either worn at the throat or used to stabilize a shawl. At the end of the nineteenth century, when the machine manufacture of jewelry began, costume jewelry pins in a vast array of shapes and sizes became available to women of modest means.

FIGURE 9–66. Joe Cronin as Julius Caesar and Katy Elizabeth Mixon as Calpurnia in *Julius Caesar* at the Utah Shakespearean Festival. Costume design by Dean Mogel. *Photograph by Karl Hugh, courtesy of the Utah Shakespearean Festival.*

Costume jewelry pins are an important part of every costume shop's jewelry collection. Collect and save broken pins and pieces; you never know what you can incorporate into an entirely new creation.

It is usually a good idea to stitch a costume pin onto the garment so there is no chance of it falling off on stage.

BEADS AND NECKLACES

Beads are the most ancient of all ornaments. Anything a person could poke a hole in was strung on a thong and hung around the neck: nuts, animal claws, bones, shells, and beads formed from clay. Civilization brought more sophisticated tastes. The Egyptians were particularly fond of necklaces, preferring deep collars consisting of many rows of strung beads, often created from precious and semiprecious stones. Great hanging chains and long ropes of pearls were popular throughout the Renaissance.

Any string of beads used on the stage must be very securely strung. Not only will a broken bead strand interrupt the action of the play, it may also create hazardous walking conditions for all the actors on stage. String stage beads on dental floss, fishing line, or jewelry wire. For added precaution, place a knot between each bead and put a dot of flexible white glue on each knot. Long strings of beads, such as those worn by ladies in Queen Elizabeth's day, might be stitched to the bodice front to prevent them from swinging loose and ensnaring fans, props, or even other actors.

BRACELETS

Bracelets are worn less often on the stage than they are in everyday life. Unless the script calls specifically for them, bracelets are usually avoided because they can be so distracting when the actor gestures. Particularly avoid a

FIGURE 9–67. Craftsperson Lee Harper making a jeweled crown at the Utah Shakespearean Festival. *Photograph courtesy of the Utah Shakespearean Festival.*

collection of bracelets that make clanking noises. When choosing bracelets for the stage, make sure they are appropriate, fit the actor well, and have secure clasps.

RINGS

Rings are perhaps the most symbolic of all accessories. First, there is the ring as a symbol

FIGURE 9–68. Assorted stage rings. *Photograph by Richard Bryant.*

364

of power and authority. Included in this group are royal seal rings, popes' and bishops' rings, and the wearing of ostentatious rings by the wealthy and powerful. Rings may also signify agreement, dependence, and protection. Fraternity and sorority rings, marriage rings, and rings that are worn as charms against disease and disaster come under this heading.

Long tradition lies behind the symbolic wearing of rings. The signet ring, or seal, was common to the Egyptians, the Assyrians, Hebrews, Greeks, and Romans and was adopted by all the kings in Western Europe. The ring as a symbol of agreement may well be rooted in the ancient myth of Prometheus. After Prometheus was released from the rock to which he had been chained, Zeus instructed him to wear a ring on his finger by which he would remember his former bondage and the understanding under which he had been released.

The marriage ring, worn by women, dates back to ancient days. It was used by the Egyptians and by both Greeks and Romans. It was placed on the left hand because that was considered to be the hand of submission, while the right hand was the hand of power. Ancient Egyptian writings explain its placement on the third finger of the left hand because they believed this finger was connected directly to the heart by a single artery. Early Christians considered the marriage ring a pagan custom but were persuaded to adopt it by A.D. 860. During the period of the British Commonwealth, 1649–1660, the marriage ring was outlawed as heathenish, and some fundamentalist Christian sects still do not accept it. The wearing of marriage rings by men is a very recent custom that only became popular in the twentieth century.

Unlike bracelets, which may detract from the gestures made by an actor, rings seem to be inherently dramatic and often enhance a performance. Most actors enjoy wearing rings.

When planning rings for a period production, look at paintings and at whatever other visual sources are available for the time to discover on which fingers rings were worn. Rings have been and are worn on all fingers, including the thumb. The forefinger is a particularly good spot for a ring that symbolizes power.

You can build many handsome rings from odds and ends of costume jewelry glued to adjustable finger bands. You can add swirls of hot glue and gold or silver leaf to bring your creation together, and touch up the whole piece with bronzing powders suspended in French Enamel Varnish.

Many inexpensive rings look great on stage. Discount department stores and jewelry outlets carry wedding bands in many sizes, and may have a variety of other rings, some with adjustable bands. Use your imagination to find and create costume rings. They are worth the effort.

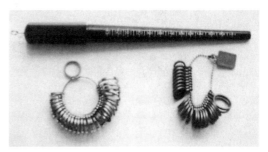

FIGURE 9–69. Ring sizers, available through your local jeweler. Find the correct ring for the actor's finger and determine the size on the gauge. *Photograph by Liz Covey.*

WATCHES

A few men began to carry watches in the late sixteenth century. These were not especially accurate timepieces, but they were set in small, handsomely wrought cases and served as expensive affectations for the wealthy. A century later, men's watches were much more dependable and, in the eighteenth century, they played a decidedly decorative role in male costume. The timepiece was concealed in a watch pocket in the trousers, while a large fancy fob hung outside, a sort of handle for pulling out the watch. Paintings from the period picture some men wearing two watches in two watch pockets, each with a fob.

Nineteenth-century watchcases were generally quite plain. Midway through the century, the machine-made watch was born and, by the century's end, you could buy a watch for a dollar, and almost every man carried one. The watch was usually worn in the vest pocket and often fastened to a gold chain stretched across the body, or sometimes carried through a special buttonhole on the vest and secured inside the opposite vest pocket. A small watch fob, usually gold, might dangle outside the pocket.

Nineteenth-century women wore dainty watches suspended from chains around their necks. Beginning in 1900, and for a dozen years after, many women wore small watches made up as pins and fastened to their shirtwaists.

The wristwatch, for both sexes, was introduced just prior to World War I and gained immediate popularity.

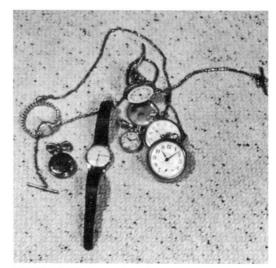

FIGURE 9–70. Assorted watches. *Photograph by Richard Bryant.*

Stage watches don't need to keep time. Old timepieces that are past repair are often available from watchmakers for a nominal price. Many of these are beautiful and perfect for stage wear. Collect watches and take good care of them. Watches are important stage accessories and cannot be easily fabricated.

Costume Properties

The following sections will introduce you to some of the most common "made-for-the-stage" costume properties: jewelry, crowns, armor, and masks. The focus is on choosing simple techniques that do not require lots of specialized equipment, using the safest craft materials available in the safest possible ways, and training your visual imagination to see the creative potential in everything from beads and buttons to bits of plumbing hardware.

The shared tips and experiences of a great many costume property artists and designers have made the following pages possible. Special acknowledgment goes to Deborah Dryden, Lynne Mackey, Colleen Muscha, Julia Powell, John Saari, and Deborah Trout for their descriptions and photographs of specific costume craft techniques.

Adhesives, Coatings, and Molding Materials

Some of the most important ingredients in making costume props are substances that allow you to:

1. Stiffen materials such as industrial felt and lace.
2. Glue many different items and surfaces to one another.
3. Apply a primer coat surface to almost anything so it will accept a variety of paints.
4. Create a permanently shaped and molded item that is strong, relatively lightweight and will accept various paints and adhesives.

There are many "white" glues on the market. Almost all of them dry clear, but there the similarity ends. "White" glues vary widely in the surfaces and materials to which they will adhere and in their flexibility. Some dry hard and brittle, some hard and not brittle; some dry moderately flexible and some extremely flexible. Some dried surfaces will accept paint and some won't. All of the "white" glues probably have some use in a costume craft shop, but it is extremely important to know exactly what you can expect from each type. Read labels carefully, ask for detailed directions for using the products, and don't use any of them until you have a Materials Safety Data Sheet in hand.

Sculpt or Coat is a popular product that combines both coating and adhesive properties. John Saari, one of the developers of the product, describes it as a "nontoxic, water base cream," which has the following properties:

- Dries to a translucent plastic coating.
- Acts as a weave filler that allows fabric to be molded and sculpted to near rigid forms.
- Is a great texturing agent.
- Creates a protective, nonreactive coating for polystyrene and foam rubber.
- Adheres to practically anything, including metal, wood, fabric, plexiglass, PVC.

Figure 9–71 is a photograph from a production of Edward Albee's *Seascape,* produced by the Ensemble Theatre of Cincinnati and directed by Mr. Albee. The lizard costumes, designed by Rebecca Senske, have hands, feet,

FIGURE 9–71. Actor Gordon Greene with a couple of lizards, portrayed by Keith Brush in front and Dale Hodges in the background, in a production of *Seascape* at the Ensemble Theatre of Cincinnati. Costumes designed by Rebecca Senske. *Photograph by Sandy Underwood, courtesy of John Saari.*

knees, and scales reinforced and textured with Sculpt or Coat. The product was also used to attach sand to the carpeted dune structures and to create the rocks.

Low-temperature thermoplastics, a class of rigid plastics originally developed for the space and medical industries, are excellent materials for creating shaped and molded items such as crowns and masks. Unlike the plastics used in making vacuum-formed items where the process requires a great deal of heat, low-temperature thermoplastics become malleable in hot water or with the use of a hair dryer or hot air gun. Once shaped, the plastic "sets" in minutes. Most of the thermoplastics are reusable: just apply hot water or heat and you can reshape or return the piece to its original flat shape to store.

Thermoplastics are reported to be safe and nontoxic. The surfaces can be painted, gold leafed, sprayed, tinted, and dyed. They come in various forms: open mesh, solid or perforated sheets, modeling pellets, and impregnated fabrics. Some of the brand names are Friendly Plastic, Vara-Form, Adapt-It, and Protoplast. Although thermoplastic materials are expensive, they are all extremely strong and durable.

New and improved thermoplastic products will undoubtedly appear on the market. Check your local craft store shelves regularly and discuss various uses of thermoplastics with your colleagues. Many distributors will sell small quantities of these products to theatre craftspeople for the purpose of experimenting.

"Made" Jewelry

Most prop jewelry made for the stage accompanies costumes from the ancient world up through the sixteenth or seventeenth centuries. Rough, prosiac materials and simple methods often produce striking pieces of prop jewelry, whether it's a shoulder ornament for Julius Caesar or a crown for Richard III. In general, prop jewelry is usually built on a slightly larger than real-life scale, with simple, bold designs. Jewelry from all ages is well represented in paintings, on statues, on carvings, and in collections of actual antique pieces in museums, so there should be no lack of research materials for ideas and inspiration.

Industrial felt, sized with flexible white glue, is an excellent material on which to base many prop jewelry pieces. The felt is lightweight and easy to cut and shape. It accepts a great many adhesives and paints, and you can easily stitch a sturdy kilt pin to the back of the "jeweled" piece, *before* you size the felt.

For prop jewelry that must represent fairly intricate gold work, stiffen bits of lace with flexible white glue and, when the glue dries, spray with gold paint or brush with bronzing powders suspended in FEV. You can build a necklace from individual lace links, stiffened and sprayed and attached to a chain. Lace can also simulate gold filigree work when it is glued over a piece of colored glass or an imitation pearl.

As an alternative to gold or silver paint, you may want to cover pieces of prop jewelry with metallic foil papers, available in art and craft supply shops. Apply the foil to the object and rub it firmly in place with a wooden clay modeling tool. Use a chopstick or wooden toothpick for small areas. Be careful not to rip the foil. Foil papers create a hard, shiny finish that you may want to tone down with FEV.

Another widely used method for decorating costume prop jewelry makes use of the hot glue gun and imitation gold or silver leaf. Apply the design to the piece with hot glue and allow it to cool slightly. Lay the metallic leaf on top and pat gently into place with a large *soft* paintbrush. After the glue has cooled and hardened completely, brush away the excess leaf with a *stiff* paintbrush.

With a little practice, you can make all sorts of intricate raised designs with glue and leaf. The metallic leaf adheres only to the glue and, after it is firmly set, you can shade it with permanent markers or FEV. Be sure to allow the glue to cool slightly before you apply the leaf, which tends to wrinkle and get dull if the glue is too hot.

MOLDED JEWELRY PIECES

When you have to produce identical decorative items for large pieces of jewelry or many matching pieces, such as cape pins, buckles, or ornaments for armor or helmets, the most efficient way to create the pieces is in molds. The following photographs are from a process for making molded decorative items used by

Mackey and Trout. Deb Trout describes the process:

We started with clay sculpts and RTV Silicone Rubber molds. RTV affords excellent detail and makes it easy to deal with undercuts in the sculpt. It is, of course, much more expensive than plaster.

We have photos of two types of finished pieces: 1. Clear line molds made from polyester resin, which is very toxic; and 2. EZ plastic, which dries white and very hard and is great for jewelry. (See page 370.) It doesn't require any kind of backing, but is a good deal heavier than sized felt or poured latex pieces.

Both polyester resin and EZ plastic are two-part materials and both require the use of a respirator.

FIGURE 9–73. Michael Genét as Creon in The Shakespeare Theatre's production of *The Oedipus Plays.* Costume design by Toni-Leslie James. *Photograph by Carol Rosegg, courtesy of The Shakespeare Theatre.*

FIGURE 9–72. Naomi Jacobson as Artemis in a production of *Agamemnon* at Arena Stage. Costume design by Lindsay W. Davis. *Photograph courtesy of Arena Stage.*

FIGURE 9–74. Clay sculpt for decorative item. Notice designer's sketch. *Photograph by Deb Trout.*

FIGURE 9–75. Pouring silicone rubber for mold. *Photograph by Deb Trout.*

FIGURE 9–76. Releasing decorative item from silicone rubber mold. Round item is EZ plastic; square item is polyester resin. *Photograph by Deb Trout.*

FIGURE 9–77. Drilling holes into a decorative item made from EZ plastic. *Photograph by Deb Trout.*

FIGURE 9–78. Finished belt with molded decorative items. *Photograph by Deb Trout.*

FIGURE 9–79. Finished necklace with molded decorative items. *Photograph by Deb Trout.*

REDUCING THE SHINE ON JEWELRY SURFACES

In general, avoid too much glitter on the stage. Stage lights often pick up shiny surfaces and reflect them in distracting ways. You can often buff away shiny spots or tone them down with a layer of soap. For shiny surfaces that resist simpler methods, apply a layer of one of the dulling materials used by model airplane hobbyists for removing the shine from plastic model surfaces. It's available in most hobby shops.

You can age stage jewelry with a wash of brown, khaki, or gray paint. Rub and Buff, a paint used in antiquing furniture, is also good for aging and dulling too-new surfaces. Apply it, in tiny amounts, with your finger so it reduces the shine without killing it altogether. Paste shoe polish will do essentially the same thing, but it kills more shine and tends to rub off on clothing.

FIGURE 9–80. Malcolm Gets wearing his crown in the title role as *Edward II* at the American Conservatory Theater. Costume design by Beaver Bauer. *Photograph courtesy of the American Conservatory Theater.*

CHAINS

Experiment with different materials when making gold or silver chains for the stage. Bamboo chains, painted with metallic paints, make excellent lightweight stage chains. You can also use strips of flexible rubber tubing or curtain rings. Create a roughly forged chain from strips of cardboard, put together in much the same way you make paper chains for Christmas trees, and coat the links with a flexible adhesive into which you've mixed paint and a texturing material such as sawdust.

Crowns

A great many plays feature kings and queens, often wearing their crowns, and sometimes seizing them from less fortunate monarchs. Unless the play is farcical or there is some specific reason why the crown should look a bit foolish, crowns should look rich and weighty enough to represent the power and position of the king or queen who wears it. Pay particular attention to the size of the crown in relation to the actor's head. The crown should neither be so small that it looks silly, nor so large that it overpowers the actor. Always make a paper mock-up of the crown (see page 308 in Chapter 8, "Hair and Hats," for a discussion of paper mock-ups for hats) that you can fit on the actor's head and study from all angles.

Once you've fitted and approved the crown mock-up, create the crown itself from sized felt or a low-heat thermoplastic and decorate it in a variety of ways with hot glue, flexible glues and coatings, and a variety of "found" objects.

For a somewhat different look in stage crowns, try using tooling metals with torched edges. Tooling metal sheets can be purchased in many craft supply shops. They normally come in 36-gauge (.005") thickness, in 12-inch wide sheets that are 5, 10, and 25 feet long. Copper,

brass, and aluminum are all available. In addition, colored aluminum comes in coppertone, goldtone, redtone, bluetone, and greentone.

Use heavy scissors or tinsnips to cut tooling metals and back the pieces with industrial felt or leather to ensure sturdiness. Before applying the backing, touch the edges of the crown with a propane torch to give the metal depth. After the backing is in place, be sure to turn under, bind, or cover any sharp edges. Add additional strips of industrial felt or foam rubber to the inside of the crown for comfort and a good fit.

Armor

Many plays from many periods require actors to be suited up for battle. In some plays, *Macbeth,* for example, or *Richard III,* battles are actually fought on the stage. Most battles be-

FIGURE 9–81. Wallace Action as Richard II, Bill Hamlin as the Abbot of Westminster, and Andrew Long as Bolingbroke in *Richard II* at The Shakespeare Theatre. Costume design by Lawrence Casey. *Photograph by Carol Rosegg, courtesy of The Shakespeare Theatre.*

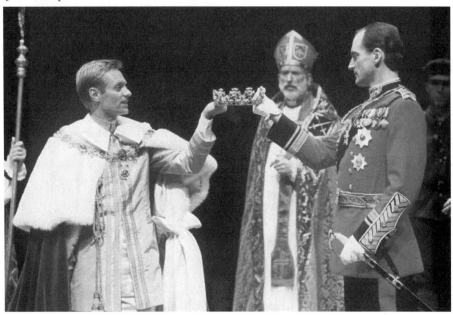

FIGURE 9–82. William Metzo wearing chain mail as Philip, King of France, in *King John* at the Utah Shakespearean Festival. Costume design by Rosemary Ingham. *Photograph by Julia Powell.*

fore the end of the seventeenth century were fought by soldiers wearing some type of armor. Since the dawn of civilization, men have dressed themselves in various heavy shells to protect their bodies from attacks by other men. Animal skins and leather were the first protective coverings, followed in time by bronze and iron. Early armor protected the vulnerable areas: chest, back, and head. Beginning in the twelfth century, men covered their arms, legs, and necks with chain mail, and the rest of their bodies with metal plates. From the fifteenth through the seventeenth century, complete suits of metal plate armor were

worn, even over the face, hands, and feet. After the seventeenth century, weapons became so powerful that armor could no longer protect a man from bullets and shells. The character of war changed, and soldiers no longer wore individual armor suits.

Like other costume properties, costume armor may be either stylized or realistic. It is sometimes fiercely real, as in a production of *Saint Joan,* or funny, as in *Lysistrata.* Whatever its nature, stage armor only appears to be impenetrable; in actuality it must be both lightweight and comfortable and not create an undue burden for the actor who wears it.

There are several common methods for making stage armor. The choice of the method depends on the material being simulated, the style of the production, and the size of the costume budget.

LEATHER ARMOR

Leather armor can range in complexity from a rough leather jerkin-type chest and back covering, to molded leather armor plates made from boiled leather and shaped to the human form. Leather is an expensive material but its impact on the stage is well worth the cost. When you plan to use a large quantity of leather for armor, plan well ahead and compare a lot of prices. If possible, buy the leather from a tannery or jobber rather than from a retailer. Bargain for the best price and don't forget that you can make stage armor from imperfect and oddly colored skins that very few other customers will buy.

Imitation leather and synthetic suede are not acceptable substitutes for leather stage armor.

DIRECTIONS FOR MAKING JERKIN-TYPE LEATHER ARMOR

1. Develop a muslin pattern from the actor's body block, leaving ample ease room for garments that will be worn underneath and allow for thickness of felt.

FIGURE 9–83. Metallic foil being heat set onto knitted chain mail at the Utah Shakespearean Festival. *Photograph by Julia Powell.*

FIGURE 9–84. Back view of armor made of industrial felt, treated and painted to simulate leather. *Photograph by Julia Powell.*

2. Fit the muslin to the actor and make adjustments.

3. Cut the armor pieces from industrial felt without seam allowances. Remember that felt has no fabric grain and the pieces can lie in any direction on the felt. Stitch shoulder seams and side seams by butting the two pieces of felt together and joining them with a wide zigzag machine stitch. You can strengthen the seam by adding a strip of canvas on the underside. Leave the center back open. Fit the felt pieces on the actor and make adjustments.

4. Use the corrected pattern pieces to cut the leather, adding a 1-inch seam allowance around each piece. This will be trimmed or turned under later.

5. Cover a male tailor's form with plastic and place the felt armor backing on the form. Pin it firmly in place.

6. Use an appropriate flexible white adhesive to glue the leather to the felt. (Avoid using solvent-based leather glues as much as possible, particularly in large quantities.) If the glue you use makes a contact-bond, spread a thin layer of it on both surfaces. Don't glue down the edges of the leather pieces, which you can fold under and lace. If your glue makes a simple bond, spread it only on the felt layer.

Before the glue sets completely, remove the jerkin from the tailor's form, place it on a table and pound the surface with a rubber or rawhide mallet. This will assure you of a firm bond and will improve the look of the leather surface.

7. At each seam line, trim the leather away, leaving just enough for a ¼-inch turnback. At the edges of the armor—bottom, around the armholes, around the neck, and down the center back—trim the leather to ½ inch from the

FIGURE 9–85. Wallace Acton buckled up in leather as Richard in *Henry VI* at The Shakespeare Theatre. Costume design by Tom Broecker. *Photograph by Carol Rosegg, courtesy of The Shakespeare Theatre.*

edge of the felt. At each seam line, glue the ¼-inch turnbacks to the inside. Make sure the turned-back leather edges meet over the seam lines. Pound for firmness.

8. Make slits or holes for the seam line laces. These seams will not actually receive any stress so you don't have to reinforce the holes. Use a leather bodkin to carry laces through the holes.

9. Create reinforced holes for lacing up the center back. These holes go through both the felt and the leather layers and will receive lots of stress. Reinforce them with flexible glue, eyelets, or grommets.

10. Bevel the edges of the felt all around the armor edges: bottom, neck, and arm edges, and up the center back. Fold the ½-inch turnback over the beveled edge and glue it down. Pound with the mallet for firmness.

The armor piece is ready for aging, toning, and so on.

FAKING LEATHER

If leather is prohibitively expensive, a relatively realistic-looking simulated leather finish can be applied to plain industrial felt. Construct the felt armor body from the previous directions and place it on a plastic-covered tailor's form. Put a thick bed of newspaper or a plastic drop cloth underneath the form, because this is a messy process.

Mix about a pint of flexible white glue with the same quantity of water. In another container, mix the same amount of FEV solution, using dye that will give you whatever leather color you want.

Apply a coat of the glue and water solution. Make sure this layer soaks into the felt. Allow this layer to dry overnight, but it need not dry completely. Now begin to alternate layers of the FEV solution and the glue solution, without allowing the layers to dry. Be sure to extend each layer of glue and FEV all the way to the edge of the armor piece. Repeat these layers until a leather texture begins to form. As soon as the whole surface looks sufficiently "leathery," allow the piece to dry. This may take up to two days.

When the armor piece is dry, remove it from the tailor's form. You can use it as it is, with the seams sewn, or you can rip the seams apart, trim the edges, and lace the pieces together.

This technique gives you a mottled, uneven surface that requires very little aging or toning. If there are shiny spots, paint them with dulling coat or rub them with soap, Rub and Buff, or paste shoe polish.

MOLDED ARMOR

Stage armor that simulates leather or metal plates is constructed from a variety of materials that can be molded into firm shapes. These materials must be lightweight and they must accept glues and paints. You can create credible armor pieces from papier-mâché, but they are completely inflexible and crack easily. Fiberglass armor is lightweight and practically indestructible, but it's much too hazardous a material for most costume shops to work with. The most commonly used stage armor materials are thermoplastic forms molded in a vacuum-forming machine, low-temperature thermoplastics, and sized felt. The following general directions are for body armor pieces, but armor pieces can be made for legs, arms, and heads, using the same methods.

VACUFORM ARMOR

Most costume shops purchase vacuform armor pieces. There is a large selection available, including most breast and back plate styles, greaves, helmets, decorative plaques, and insignia, as well as complete suits of body armor.

Choose the armor pieces that most nearly conform to the design you're creating. Fit the pieces on the actor and trim them if necessary. Most breast and back plates will be fastened at the shoulders and at the sides with straps and buckles. Determine where the straps will go and mark their placements.

Most vacuform armor pieces are white or light gray. Apply a base coat of black or brown paint. Plan out your decorative steps. Add raised areas first. If you are using individual vacuform plaques or insignias, glue them on. You can also create designs directly on the armor with rope, felt, string, or yarn and white glue. Or, use the hot glue gun to make raised designs. For raised elements, use split cork balls, buttons, or wooden disks.

Once the surface is complete, paint over everything with an adhesive coating like Sculpt

FIGURE 9–86. Kathleen McCall as Joan la Pucelle (also know as Joan of Arc) in vacuform armor over knitted chain mail in *The War of the Roses* at the Utah Shakespearean Festival. Costume design by McKay Coble. *Photograph by Julia Powell.*

or Coat mixed with paint: brown paint if the surface simulates leather or bronze, black if it looks like silver or iron. If you want a rough surface, put a bit of sand or sawdust in the glue and paint mixture.

There are as many methods of aging, toning, and finishing a piece of armor as there are costume craftspeople. Use these instructions as a way to get started and develop your own set of decorative materials and painting techniques for each project.

FIGURE 9–87. A group of soldiers in chain mail surround Rick Hamilton as Richard Plantaganet wearing a suit of vacuform armor in a scene from *The War of the Roses* at the Utah Shakespearean Festival. Costume design by McKay Coble. *Photograph by Julia Powell.*

FIGURE 9–88. A close-up view of the vacuform armor in Figure 9–87, which was fabricated with applied felt details and belting leather, then painted with metallic paints by craftsperson Julia Powell. *Photograph by Julia Powell.*

MOLDED FELT ARMOR

Molded felt armor is particularly good when a bulky look is wanted. The breastplate in Figure 9–89 was created from felt using this technique.

The first step in making molded armor is to create a mold on which to shape it. The simplest mold is the body of a male tailor's form, padded

FIGURE 9–89. Textured, sized felt breastplate. *Photograph by Susan Ashdown.*

out to correspond to the actor's measurements, making sure to add extra room for clothing. If you don't have a tailor's form you can use, see if you can acquire a discarded shirt display form at your local department store or men's shop. These don't usually have much shape but they can be built up with clay, foam, or other padding materials. Cover the mold with plastic.

Always use industrial felt with a high percentage of wool in it. Cut the felt to fit the clothed actor and make some allowance for shrinkage that will occur during the process.

Soak the piece thoroughly with a mixture of two parts white flexible glue to one part water. Place the piece on the mold and work it firmly into place, pushing and stretching until it is smooth. Pin the felt to the mold with long T-pins. Allow the piece to dry, which may take several days. When it's completely dry, remove

it from the mold and apply a thin layer of shellac to the inside and outside of the pieces.

Decorations on sized felt armor are usually larger and simpler than those used on the other two types. After the raised decorations are applied, lay on a base coat of paint and proceed with texturing and finishing. Sized felt is the thickest of the three armor materials discussed, and if straps and buckles are being riveted onto the armor pieces, be sure to purchase long shanked rivets and reinforce them from behind.

CHAIN MAIL

You can knit very effective chain mail from string worked on large size knitting needles. Purchase colored string, in gray, dark green, or black so you won't have to dye it before applying a final coat of bronzing powder mixture or metallic paints.

FIGURE 9–90. Chain-mail suits from the Utah Shakespearean Festival. *Photograph courtesy of the Utah Shakespearean Festival.*

FIGURE 9–91. Helmet research for a production of *Troilus and Cressida* at the Utah Shakespearean Festival. *Photograph by Julia Powell.*

FIGURE 9–93. The finished helmet after a base coat of metallic paint and gold and silver highlights have been added. *Photograph by Julia Powell.*

FIGURE 9–92. The vacuform helmet in the first stage with relief decoration applied by craftsperson Julia Powell. *Photograph by Julia Powell.*

HELMETS

The visible parts of helmets can be made from the same materials and decorated in the same ways as body armor pieces. The challenge in creating helmets for the stage is to make them fit securely, particularly if they are to be worn in actual fight scenes.

Base all "fighting" helmets on construction workers' hard-hat liners. These liners can be adjusted to the heads of the actors and, because the outer hat is suspended on an inner fitting ring, they are comfortable to wear. After the helmet is made, it can be riveted permanently to the liner.

Vacuform helmet shells are available in a wide variety of styles. You can paint, texture, and apply decorative elements to the shell just as you decorated the armor plates. If the helmet will come off on stage, don't forget to paint the inside.

Molded felt is suitable for constructing simple helmets. The steps are the same as those

379

FIGURE 9–94. The same helmet, distressed and repainted for reuse in a production of *Julius Caesar,* designed by Dean Mogel, in a subsequent season at the Utah Shakespearean Festival. *Photograph by Julia Powell.*

FIGURE 9–96. Molded felt armor gauntleted glove with flexible fingers. *Photograph by Susan Ashdown.*

FIGURE 9–95. Another vacuform helmet from *Troilus and Cressida* with additions, applied decoration, and metallic finish. *Photograph by Julia Powell.*

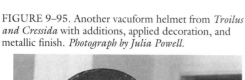

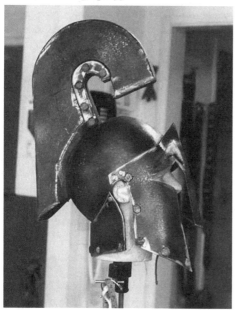

for molded armor pieces. Be particularly careful to allow room in the original felt shape for shrinkage and use a sturdy mold based on a wooden head or hat block.

Masks

It is impossible to discuss theatrical masks in any detail without devoting an entire book to the subject. The mask has had a long and fascinating history in the theatre, and it continues to have a lively presence. Both ancient plays and modern plays may require masked actors. The effect of a mask may be frightening, funny, or alienating. The mask may be a realistic representation of a human face or an imaginary monster. It may be an animal, a bird, or a fish. In fact, it may be anything.

More than with any other costume property, maskmaking requires an artist's touch and

FIGURE 9–97. Leather armor for the title character in a production of *Titus Andronicus,* designed by Susan Tsu, for the Oregon Shakespeare Festival. The shoulder wings pivot for movement and Chinese coins make the decorative closures. *Photograph by Rosemary Ingham.*

FIGURE 9–98. Randy Redd as Sugar Mecklin and Spike McClure as the Red Rooster wearing costumes designed by Clyde Ruffin for a production of *Mississippi Sugar* at The Repertory Theatre of St. Louis. *Photograph by Judy Andrews, courtesy of The Repertory Theatre of St. Louis.*

FIGURE 9–99. Harpy mask for *The Tempest* at Utah Shakespearean Festival. Created by Wendy Juren. *Photograph by Rosemary Ingham.*

a sculptor's eye. The methods are simple, but the outcome depends on more than the skillful application of technique. Not everyone will excel at maskmaking, but all costume technicians should give it a try.

MAKING A LIFE MASK

The first step in making most theatrical masks is to create a plaster mold of the actor's face, on which to mold the mask. Although this is not a particularly complicated task, it is time-consuming. Some maskmakers prefer to model the actor's face directly in clay, using measurements of the head and face, but for those who do not have sculpting skills, it's best to make a life mask.

The life mask is made in two steps. First, a negative mold is taken from the face, then a plaster positive is made from this negative.

FIGURE 9–100. Judith Marie Bergen portraying Tamora in *Titus Andronicus* at the Oregon Shakespeare Festival. The costume, designed by Susan Tsu, includes a leather-covered breastplate, fabric-wrapped bamboo wings, gold-leafed leather headdress, and a blindfold. *Photograph by Susan Tsu.*

These two steps should be done consecutively, although the actor's presence is required only for the first step.

Schedule an hour for step one. It may not take quite this long, but some actors, especially those who have not had this process done before, may be nervous. Explain the steps carefully and offer reassurance that the experience will be neither dangerous nor uncomfortable. The actor's most important task in this process is to remain still and not move the facial muscles. If the actor should smile or raise an eyebrow while the negative is being taken, the mold will be destroyed. Therefore,

a comfortable, relaxed, informed actor is an essential ingredient in making a life mask.

If you have access to a barber's or dentist's chair, place the actor in a semireclining position. If not, have the actor lie on a table with the upper body raised slightly on a firm pillow. Cover the actor's clothing with plastic sheeting and construct a cardboard collar that will fit around the neck to catch any drops from the molding material. Tuck the hair into a bathing cap or cover it with plastic wrap secured with tape. Rub a small amount of silicone hand lotion into the face. *Do not use cold cream.* The molding material is not usually irritating to the skin.

Dental moulage is the material most commonly used for negative face molds. Dentists use it to make impressions of teeth, and it can be obtained from dental supply companies. Follow the directions on the package for making up the moulage, but use half again more water than the instructions call for, to slow down the set-up time. Even so, you must work quickly, for dental moulage sets up in a matter of minutes. As soon as the mixture is smooth, apply it to the face, starting with the forehead and working down. The layer should be about ¾ inch thick. Make certain the actor keeps his or her eyes closed. Cover the entire face except the nostrils; some technicians place straws in the actor's nostrils and cover the entire nose with moulage. Continue to work quickly because once the moulage has dried, wet moulage won't stick to it.

When you are finished and the moulage is dry, moisten several strips of plaster-impregnated bandage with water and apply them on top of the moulage, to give the mold additional strength. If you use the new low-temperature thermoplastic-impregnated bandages, you will need to use hot water. Pay particular attention to strengthening the protruding portions of the mold: the nose, the forehead, and the chin. As soon as the plaster sets up, which should only be a few minutes, ask the actor to sit up, bend over, and wiggle the facial muscles to loosen the moulage. Catch the mold as it falls from the actor's face and place it, inside up, in a box containing several inches of sawdust. Push the mold down into the sawdust, which will support it while you pour the plaster positive.

Go on to the second step right away, since moulage tends to shrink as it loses moisture. Pour about two pints of water into an enameled or stainless-steel pan. Slowly sprinkle the plaster into the water until some plaster begins to float on the surface. Carefully knead the plaster with your hands to smooth out all the lumps; never stir plaster vigorously. The mix-

ture should have the consistency of heavy cream. Bang the bottom of the pan several times to release air bubbles, then pour the plaster into the negative mold, filling it to the top. As the plaster sets up, it grows warm, and when it has finished setting, it will turn cool. When it's cool and set, turn the mold over and remove the moulage.

Allow the positive plaster mold to dry thoroughly, for at least twenty-four hours. When it's dry, give it a coat or two of shellac to protect it, since otherwise it will chip easily. It is always a good idea to mark the back of the mold with the actor's name and the date of casting.

FIGURE 9–101. Wallace Acton in the title role with Matthew Walsh and Christopher Bagg as players in *Hamlet* at The Shakespeare Theatre. Costumes designed by Murell Horton. *Photograph by Carol Rosegg, courtesy of The Shakespeare Theatre.*

FORMING THE MASK MOLD ON THE LIFE MASK

A mask mold is made on the actor's life mask so the inner surface will conform to the actor's

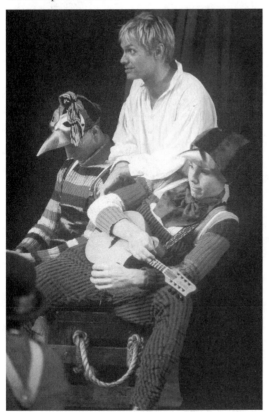

FIGURE 9–102. A golden-horned Ray Porter as Saturninus in *Titus Andronicus* at the Oregon Shakespeare Festival. Costume design by Susan Tsu. *Photograph by Susan Tsu.*

features, and thus be comfortable to wear. If you can sculpt the mask mold so the mask will still fit the actor's face, then you can make the mold and create the mask directly on the life mask. A hawk nose, an overhanging brow, a protruding chin can all be sculpted onto the life mask without completely reshaping the face. Keep in mind that every place you put modeling clay is a place where the inside of the mask *will not* touch the actor's face.

On the other hand, if the mask mold has to be much wider, much longer, or much more protruding than the life mask, the mask that is created on it will no longer fit the actor's face. In these cases, you should create a plain mask on the life mask to serve as a base that will fit the actor's face before you begin to sculpt the

FIGURE 9–103. Craftsperson Sylvia Burton making antlers at the Utah Shakespearean Festival. *Photograph courtesy of the Utah Shakespearean Festival.*

exaggerated mask mold. Eventually the mask itself will be constructed in two parts: a basic mask that fits the face and the exaggerated mask that covers it. Sometimes the exaggerated mask is built directly on the fitted mask base.

MASKMAKING MATERIALS

Over the years, masks have been made from many things: most commonly wood, leather,

FIGURE 9–104. Masked actors in a production of *Tantalus* performed by the Denver Center Theatre Company. *Photograph by P. Switzer, courtesy of Kevin Copenhaver.*

FIGURE 9–105. *Aimee Boatman* mask formed from pieces of corrugated cardboard applied to a plain mask base with plaster tape. Shadows created with FEV; bronze paint highlights. From the craft design class at Florida State University. *Photograph by Colleen Muscha.*

clay, metal, cardboard, papier-mâché, and molded buckram and felt. Highly theatrical masks have been formed from willow caning and large animal heads with wire frames covered with layers of foam and fake fur. Modern maskmakers tend to combine traditional maskmaking techniques with space-age materials, such as low-temperature thermoplastics and fabrics impregnated with flexible glues and coatings.

Theatrical masks need to be light in weight, very durable, and somewhat flexible. Modern materials allow the maskmaker to meet all of these needs at once.

FIGURE 9–106. Wallace Acton as Peer Gynt, Ted van Griethuysen as Old Man, and Kate Skinner as the Woman in Green in *Peer Gynt* at The Shakespeare Theatre. Costume design by Paul Tazewell. *Photograph by Carol Rosegg, courtesy of The Shakespeare Theatre.*

Whatever material you choose, follow the product directions scrupulously and give yourself plenty of time to experiment. Make sure you have a very clear idea of what the designer wants the mask to look like, keep the sketches and all other visual information close at hand, and don't wait until the mask is finished before you fit it on the actor.

Odd and Unusual Costume Props

Many costume craftspeople have come to the conclusion that odd and unusual is synonymous with costume prop. There appears to be no end to the kinds of costume props and accessories playwrights, directors, and designers can think up to put on the stage. A play like

FIGURE 9–107. Huge Elizabethan puppets designed by Susan Tsu portray the Goddesses in a production of *The Tempest* at the Oregon Shakespeare Festival. One actor from the cast held the main body while two other actors operated the hands. *Photograph by Susan Tsu.*

FIGURE 9–108. Actors "in the clouds" surround the happy couple in a scene from *Animal Crackers* at Arena Stage. *Photograph courtesy of Arena Stage.*

On the Verge offers one kind of challenge while a postmodern design for *Twelfth Night* offers another.

The costume craftspeople who create these odd and unusual items are themselves an unusual lot. They work in New York and Los Angeles, at regional theatres, at Shakespeare festivals, in children's theatre, and at colleges and universities all over the country. Wherever they work, they share an unusual position in this era of mass production: costume craftspeople spend their lives fabricating things that have never been made before. They are seldom, if ever, asked to make the same thing twice.

10

Managing, Supervising, or Directing the Costume Shop

In the 1970s, the person who organized and "ran" a costume shop in an educational or professional theatre anywhere in the United States was likely to have stumbled into the job simply because he or she had been cutting and stitching and/or designing costumes for several years and had become interested in (or had been talked into becoming interested in) bringing a sense of order and direction to an often chaotic process. The job title was generally "costume shop manager" and the job descriptions, in the beginning, were more than a little vague. During the last quarter of the twentieth century, costume shop managers became increasingly central to the costume design and construction process. In addition, they now serve as vital members of administrative teams responsible for the technical infrastructure that makes it possible for scripts and the work of directors, actors, and designers to become integrated theatrical events. Today, as before, costume shop managers are expected to possess a strong general background in theatre with specific costume design and construction training or experience. More and more, however, there is also the expectation that cos-

tume shop managers have additional experience or training in management, budgeting, negotiation, conflict resolution and mediation, workplace safety, as well as in a variety of other related areas.

Many of the most effective costume shop managers working today stumbled into their management positions and, after the fact, discovered they possessed the necessary organizational and "people" skills to get the job done. Today, however, it is not unusual to find young costume technicians just entering the field whose professional goals include becoming a costume shop manager. Many theatre departments teach and encourage the development of practical theatre management skills, including stage management and technical direction as well as costume shop management. A large number of professional theatre companies offer apprenticeships and internships in all these areas. The information in this section is intended to provide a snapshot of what constitutes current costume shop management in a variety of settings across the United States. What do costume shop managers do? For what are they responsible? How do they fit into the overall

FIGURE 10–1. Costume Shop Manager Christine Smith-McNamara in her office at the Oregon Shakespeare Festival. At the height of the season in Ashland, Oregon, Ms. Smith-McNamara directs a costume staff of fifty-five to sixty technicians. *Photograph by Rosemary Ingham.*

management scheme of their organizations? How do they learn what they need to know? What do all the different job titles mean? And what are some of the joys, as well as the frustrations, of being a costume shop manager?

What's in a Name?

Once upon a time the person who did everything in a costume shop, from designing to cutting and stitching, was known as a *costumer*. Today, in an age of increasing specialization, this title is no longer widely used, although it has not disappeared completely. There is, quite commonly, a clear division between the *costume designer* and the *costume technician*. The distinctions are obvious: the designer is responsible for creating the look of the costume; the technician is responsible for creating some part of the actual costume as described or specified by the designer.

Under the general title *costume technician,* there are a number of more specific positions. These are briefly outlined in Chapter 1, "The Costume Shop," on pages 32–35, and discussed in more detail in this chapter. In a large costume shop there will be a person to fill each of the these positions. In a smaller shop, the same person may switch hats many times in order to do all the jobs costume construction demands.

Since the last revision of *The Costume Technician's Handbook,* most of these job titles and the responsibilities delegated to them have remained relatively constant. The most significant changes have taken place in the title and the responsibilities of the *costume shop supervisor* or *manager.*

In a business or organizational structure, titles are significant. A title speaks to what the person does and how much responsibility he or she has. It defines the position held within the larger organization and may reflect the education and training background and, potentially, the worth (salary range) of the person who holds it. People take pride in their professional and academic titles; the evolution of what title best fits the people who are responsible for making costume shops run effectively reflects both personal and professional concerns.

Costume shop manager appears to have been the earliest title given to the people who rose up to direct the work in costume shops; it was followed by *costume shop supervisor.* In some places, largely as an attempt to define the work of costume craftspeople and artisans with more clarity, and to give them greater stature, the *costume shop* became the *costume studio.* These rival designations have created a mildly contentious issue within the profession: those who prefer *costume shop* consider *costume studio* an unnecessary and pretentious label, while the *costume studio* advocates point out that studio is the correct name for a place where works of art and craft are created (e.g., theatre costumes) while a costume shop may be mistaken for a place that sells manufactured Halloween outfits. At the moment, those who prefer *costume shop* are in the majority but there are signs that the *costume studio* fans are increasing. The titles *costume studio manager* and *costume studio supervisor* do exist but are not common. It appears that when a costume shop becomes a costume studio, the one who heads it becomes the *costume studio director* or, more often, simply the *costume director.*

The journey from a *costume shop* to a *costume studio* and from *costume shop manager* to *costume director* is significant. As the title suggests, the costume director's responsibilities have now expanded beyond the confines of the actual space in which costumes are constructed. (Indeed, this expansion of responsibility has occurred whether there has been a change in title or not.) Costume directors/supervisors/managers in some of the country's largest producing organizations report that they are increasingly involved in the work of the theatre as a whole. "I represent the impact of costumes throughout this organization," one costume director commented. "I'm involved from the moment we begin to choose a new season of plays, which, by the way, starts while we're still getting the current season up and running. I have responsibilities for planning, budgeting and accounting, staffing, publicity, educational outreach, and workplace safety. There are a lot of meetings to attend and a good deal of paperwork. At the same time, even if I'm not actually cutting or stitching, I'm in the shop every day and I always know what's going on with each show. I'm constantly moving from the big picture back to the details. I like that. I feel valued. It works for me and I believe it works for the theatre."

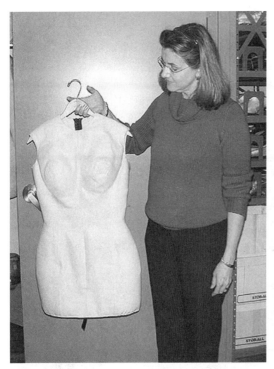

FIGURE 10–2. Costume Director Marsha M. LeBoeuf displays body padding built for a specific performer at The Washington Opera. A closet full of individualized hanging "bodies" helps to fulfill one of Ms. LeBoeuf's major responsibilities: facilitating the work of the cutter/drapers in a shop where lead performers are not always available for fittings until quite late in the building process. *Photograph by Rosemary Ingham.*

FIGURE 10–3. Body padding from Figure 10–2 zipped onto a size 12 tailor's form. *Photograph by Rosemary Ingham.*

Costume staff and faculty members in academic theatre programs, particularly those who work as costume shop managers and teach courses in costume technology, also report that they are increasingly involved in and responsible for departmental issues such as planning and implementing production schedules and developing curricula.

There is no single pattern of job responsibility for costume shop managers in the United States at this time. There is no agreement on what the title for this position should be. The following discussion is not an attempt to define exactly what a costume shop manager should do or what he or she should be called. It is a reflection of what is actually being done by costume shop managers, costume shop supervisors, and costume directors in a variety of not-for-profit theatres (large, medium, and small) and educational theatre programs (undergraduate and graduate; liberal arts–based and professional training programs) all across the country. Simply because it has the longest track record, costume shop manager will be the most frequently used title.

The Team

Costume Shop Manager

"My first responsibility is to the sixty-two people who make up my costume shop staff," said one costume director. Then she went on to explain that there is no way she can personally, on a day-to-day basis, supervise that many costume technicians: cutters, first hands, stitchers, milliners, dyers and painters, and so on. "I'm dependent upon a structure in which

FIGURE 10–4. Kandis Chappell as Queen Elizabeth in *The Beard of Avon* at the American Conservatory Theater. Costumes designed by Beaver Bauer. *Photograph courtesy of the American Conservatory Theater.*

some people, the team leaders, are directly responsible for the people they supervise. And it's very important that each person on every team has the necessary skills to do the job. And," she added with emphasis, "a good work ethic."

One of the biggest differences between a costume shop that is part of a professional theatre and a costume shop in a college or university is the degree of specialization among the costume technicians. Undergraduate theatre students are expected to study and work in all areas of theatre and to gain the broadest possible experience. Graduate students in costume design and/or costume technology programs

FIGURE 10–5. The workroom at The Washington Opera. A combination of natural light from the tall windows and a mixture of fluorescent and incandescent light inside makes for a pleasant and well-lit work space. *Photograph by Rosemary Ingham.*

learn as many approaches, methods, and skills as their instructors are able to cram into the two or three years they spend in school. The faculty and staff members who teach these students must also maintain a broad range of skills and experiences in order to meet the needs of their students.

Most costume shops in professional theatres, particularly the larger organizations, hire technicians to fill well-defined positions. When, for instance, one of the summer Shakespeare festivals advertises costume shop positions for the coming season, the ad may read: "Needed: first hands, stitchers, milliner, wardrobe assistants." Recently graduated students, whose educational theatre experience has encouraged—indeed, required—them to engage in a variety of costume construction and craft projects in a single term, are now faced with applying for, and accepting, a job in which they may be working in a single area for several months. Lucky is the costume technology student who has been fortunate enough to discover a knack, and a liking, for making hats, stitching seams, or working with actors backstage. This is not to say that being hired as a stitcher as one's first professional job after graduation means being pegged as a stitcher forever. Most costume technicians, particularly in the early years of their careers, work in a number of different areas. Before becoming a full-fledged draper, for instance, it is necessary to gain experience as a stitcher and as a first hand.

There are many steps in the costume construction process. Whether these steps are shared by a costume shop staff of five (as in a small college or a small professional theatre) or carried out individually by "specialists," each step is a necessary part of the process. The costume shop manager is responsible for hiring or assigning staff, supervising or teaching the person(s) who will carry out each step, and for making sure the end product is satisfactory.

FIGURE 10–6. A view of the costume shop at Santa Clara University. The undergraduate students at this liberal arts institution are working on the costumes for a theatre department production. *Photograph by Rosemary Ingham.*

Naturally, not every theatre costume will require every step listed below. If, however, the shop were creating an historically accurate costume for Queen Elizabeth I (see Figure 10–4), every area of technical expertise from cutter/draper through make-up supervisor would be required.

Assistant to the Costume Shop Manager

Many, but not all, fully staffed costume shops include this staff position. The responsibilities differ considerably from one place to another. In one shop, for instance, the assistant costume shop manager schedules fittings and supervises the wardrobe staff.

In another this person acts as a floor manager, directly supervising the drapers and keeping the costume director informed about the status of the overall construction process. In yet another, the assistant to the shop manager orders supplies and shops for costume designers. The increasing need for assistants has paralleled the broadening of responsibilities for many shop managers.

In educational theatre, the faculty or staff member who manages the shop may assign a student to be his or her assistant for a single production period in order to provide the student with a management opportunity. This can be a rich and eye-opening experience for costume students who are interested in costume technology as a career.

Assistant to the Designer

In some theatres it is the assistant to the costume shop manager who serves as the assistant to guest or resident costume designers. In others it is a separate staff position. In a large theatre where the costume shop is building costumes for two or three productions at the same time, with a different costume designer for each, the theatre company may provide individual design assistants. A good many theatres do not have design assistants on staff, and some costume designers work only with their own assistants.

Working as a design assistant has long been a recognized path by which young costume designers can "learn the ropes" and make their way into the field. This experience also provides excellent preparation for costume technicians, particularly those whose professional goals include shop management. Some theatre departments include experience as a design assistant, either to a faculty member or a fellow student, as a required part of the design and technology education process.

What does an assistant to the costume designer actually do? Understandably, these duties will vary with the nature of the play, the size and skill level of the costume shop, and the needs of the costume designer. In the best of situations, the design assistant will enter the process early enough to observe (although not necessarily participate in) the development of ideas that will lead to design decisions. The assistant may contribute to period and style research for the production; swatch fabrics; shop; scan the Internet for clothing, accessories, or specialty items; make endless telephone calls; jot down notes at meetings; and, in general, do whatever needs to be done. In some cases, when the designer is not available, the design assistant attends fittings as the designer's "eye" and, in the same capacity, may also sit in on production meetings. Working as an assistant to several different costume designers in a busy costume shop over a period of months cannot help but give any costume technician the best possible understanding of the design and construction process in its entirety.

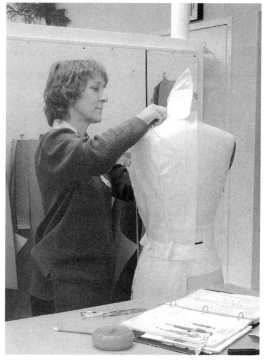

FIGURE 10–7. Cutter/draper Elaine McBennett draping a bodice and collar on a tailor's form at the Oregon Shakespeare Festival. Note the loose-leaf notebook containing sketches and research. *Photograph by Rosemary Ingham.*

Cutter/Draper

In some theatres this staff member is called a **cutter,** in some a **draper,** and in still others, a **cutter/draper.** Whichever title is attached to the position, the person who does this work has the vital responsibility of creating patterns for every sort of costume that might be required by any script or imagined by any designer. These could range from an historically accurate Queen Elizabeth I in *Mary Stuart* to the Yeti in *On the Verge,* with an infinite number of challenging projects in between. In addition to creating the pattern itself, this very important costume technician also oversees the step-by-step construction of the costume and, with the help of a first hand, supervises the stitchers who are assigned to the project.

The "cutter" part of the title usually refers to a pattern development process known as *flat pattern drafting* (see Chapter 4, "Flat Pattern Drafting," page 99) in which patterns are drafted on paper from measurements. The "draper" part refers to a more three-dimensional approach to pattern creation called *draping* (see page 133 in the same chapter) in which fabric is arranged (draped) directly onto a tailor's form. Both methods are now part of the training process for costume technicians and most cutter/drapers drape or draft depending upon the nature of the project.

Cutter/drapers are team leaders. They are responsible for the entire process that begins with a group of designer's sketches and instructions and ends on opening night when the production is complete. Within a five- to six-week period, for example, a cutter/draper may translate a dozen or more designs into their component parts (pattern pieces); plan the construction process, including all finishing techniques; oversee, and/or participate in, the cutting of fabric; conduct fittings at several stages throughout the work period and make alteration decisions in consultation with the designer; keep track of the progress on all the costumes for which he or she is responsible and report to the shop manager at regular intervals; attend dress rehearsals and see that last-minute changes and alterations are made. Throughout the process, cutter/drapers create and maintain a close working relationship with the first hand and stitchers who cut and assemble the costumes. The most effective cutter/drapers give clear directions, encourage questions, and answer them with patience and clarity; they recognize good work and provide constructive criticism when necessary; they set a standard of excellence and inspire a sense of group responsibility in their team members. The work done by cutter/drapers is always challenging and no

FIGURE 10–8. Tailor Jeffrey Park pounds a collar at The Shakespeare Theatre. *Photograph by Rosemary Ingham.*

costume shop, professional or educational, can work effectively without a well-trained, experienced person (or persons) in this position.

Some theatre costume shops have a **tailor** on staff. A tailor has unique skills that relate to cutting, assembling, fitting, and finishing tailored garments such as men's and women's suits, overcoats, and uniforms. A tailor in a costume shop operates as a specialized cutter/draper, with a team that also includes a first hand and a stitcher or stitchers. Theatrical tailors, unlike "civilian" tailors who work primarily on contemporary garments, must be able to create tailored suits, coats, and uniforms from every period since the birth of tailoring.

First Hand

This is one of the most interestingly descriptive titles for a costume shop position. The first hand might also be referred to as the cutter/draper's "right hand" because the work itself is a direct extension of the patterning process. The main responsibilities of the person filling this position are cutting fabric pieces from the pattern pieces developed by the cutter/draper, marking them appropriately, and telling the stitchers how to assemble each costume. This very often occurs in two stages because most garments are cut first out of muslin or some other suitable fabric for a fitting mock-up, then cut out of the costume fabric itself. Needless to say, cutting the cloth is not as simple as it sounds.

In order to lay out, mark, and cut the pattern pieces from fabric, the first hand must understand how the pieces will ultimately fit together and by what series of steps. In order to carry out the next part of his or her responsibility—effectively passing this information on to the stitchers—it is essential that the first hand not only understand all parts of the process, but also be able to give directions in a clear and concise manner.

Out of necessity, the first hand not only supervises the work of the stitchers who assemble the costumes, but may also be a sewing teacher. A stitching position is often given to a novice who may require considerable tutoring. Even when stitchers come to their jobs with training and experience, they

FIGURE 10–9. Kitty Muntzel operates an industrial sewing machine at Berkeley Repertory Theatre. *Photograph by Rosemary Ingham.*

must often learn new or different stitching techniques required by the nature of the costume design or the desires of the designer or cutter/draper. Encouraging an experienced stitcher to adopt and apply a sewing operation with which he or she is unfamiliar may be a challenging task and require considerable tact.

First hands must bring knowledge and experience in pattern development with them to the job. In some shops the first hand may be asked to pattern and cut facing pieces regularly and, if time and the workload allow for it, the cutter/draper might share more demanding patterning projects with the first hand. Working for a season or two as a first hand is excellent preparation for future work as a cutter/draper.

Stitcher

Stitchers stitch seams together. They also carry out a variety of other sewing operations, both by machine and by hand, that include: gathering, setting in zippers, applying trim, making buttonholes, cartridge pleating, hemming, and more. Although the stitcher position is often considered a "beginning" job in a costume shop, it takes many years to develop all the skills needed to assemble and finish complex period costumes. No matter how beautifully a costume is designed and patterned, a sloppy, careless stitcher can ruin the garment.

Commercial costume shops in New York and elsewhere hire professional machine stitchers who assemble costumes quickly and with great accuracy. Finishers are responsible for all the hand-stitched hems, buttons, and other details that complete the costume. These machine and hand stitchers are specialists, professionals who take pride in the work they do.

FIGURE 10–10. Justin Buton puts hand-stitched finishing touches on a costume at The Shakespeare Theatre. *Photograph by Rosemary Ingham.*

Unfortunately, in not-for-profit theatres all across the United States, and in educational theatre departments, the art and craft of the stitcher is neither as highly regarded, nor as well compensated, as it might be and too many young technicians do not consider it a career in itself. Perhaps the managers in these shops might begin to recognize and support the technicians who find particular satisfaction in a perfectly constructed bodice or an invisible hem. Encourage them to develop their skills to a professional level and then convince management to recognize their worth with higher salaries.

FIGURE 10–11. Sarah Havens, craftsperson at the Cincinnati Playhouse in the Park, works on a lightweight cardboard hat mock-up. *Photograph by Rosemary Ingham.*

Costume Craftsperson

Costume crafts (also called costume properties or "props") include hats, jewelry, armor, shoes, belts, assorted leather goods, masks, and a host of less-common items such as wings, horns, haloes, and a variety of delivery systems for stage blood. Many of the people who work in the costume crafts area come to theatre with backgrounds in studio art. Others begin with fabric and sewing machines, then find that their true skills lie in creating three-dimensional objects, experimenting with different materials, and finding ways of fabricating items such as armor, crowns, and masks from the most unlikely objects. Costume craftspeople are faced with daily challenges from costume designers and their work is seldom repetitive. Although books exist and classes are offered to aid in training people interested in this area, true expertise results from experience and experimentation. Apprenticeships in the crafts area of a costume shop that does many different kinds of productions are especially valuable for people interested in costume crafts.

Millinery is a distinct branch of costume crafts and the people (milliners) who are particularly skilled in this specialty may find jobs in large theatre organizations that allow them to work primarily on hats. In most costume shops, however, making hats is one of the responsibilities of the general craftsperson.

Dyer/Painter

"The thing I want most in a dyer/painter," explains a costume director, "is a kind of chemist's outlook, the ability, and the desire, to measure and mix with precision and take the time to record every step. There are lots of technicians out there who brag about tossing a bunch of dye pigments into a pot until the color looks right. Well, it may look all right in the beginning but that doesn't help me a month into my season when I have to replace a pair of tights and have no idea what amounts of which colors went into that pot."

Although, in some theatres the costume craftsperson is also the dyer/painter, there is no doubt that dyeing and painting processes require special knowledge and, as this costume director noted, a meticulous approach to the work. An increasing number of larger theatres have added a dyer/painter position on the staff; others hire a freelance dyer/painter for specific projects.

FIGURE 10–12. Dyer/painter
Chris Carpenter distresses a
primitive pleated gown at the
Oregon Shakespeare Festival.
Photograph by Rosemary Ingham.

A dyer/painter works closely with costume designers. The most straightforward, although hardly simple, part of the day's work is to dye fabrics the specific colors chosen by the designer. Accessory pieces and entire garments may require a color change as well. The dyer/painter may also be asked to interpret surface designs from a costume sketch and create full-size patterns for silkscreen, stencil, or other printing process.

"Distressing" is the term used to describe the process of turning newly made or bought garments into old clothes: sometimes lightly worn, sometimes dirty and sweaty, and sometimes in tatters. (See page 285 in Chapter 7, "Fabric Dyeing and Painting," for a discussion of distressing.) This is a job for the dyer/painter and one that requires a good eye for the reality of wear and the willingness to experiment with a variety of techniques on a host of fabrics with many different fiber contents.

Health and safety practices are important throughout the costume shop (see Chapter 2, "Health and Safety in the Costume Shop") but nowhere more so than in the area where fabric dyes and paints, all complex chemicals, are in use. Dyer/painters must take personal responsibility for educating themselves about the chemicals they use and how to use them safely. And they must keep up with health and safety issues that affect all artists and craftspeople.

Hairstylist/Wigmaker

Creating a hairstyle that complements and is appropriate for a period costume, either with the actor's own hair or with a wig, is central to the success of that costume. Working with hair and wigs is a specialized art and craft that's taught, as a specialty, in only in a few university theatre departments. Many of the people working in this area received their training in beautician schools or in technical programs geared toward the film and television industries. Wigmaking, however, is a specialty within a specialty and is usually taught in courses and workshops outside the regular stylist program, and through an apprenticeship with a professional wigmaker. Larger theatres may have a stylist/wigmaker on staff, full- or part-time; others bring in this specialist when needed.

Make-Up Supervisor

The make-up supervisor may also be the hairstylist/wigmaker. Make-up supervision varies widely in different theatres. In many instances it involves only giving advice to actors who do their own make-up. In other theatrical situations—opera, for instance—the make-up supervisor (often referred to in opera and film as the make-up artist) may design make-up for the production and supervise its application at every performance. In all types of theatre when there are roles that require unusual face and/or body appearances, the make-up supervisor may create prosthetic pieces and apply them to the actor. In most educational theatre departments make-up is taught to both acting and costume students. In the professional world there is always a close collaboration between actors and make-up supervisors.

Wardrobe Maintenance Supervisor

The group or "crew" of technicians who takes care of theatre costumes from the time the production goes into performance until it closes are the unsung, and often underpaid, heroes and heroines of the theatre company.

They are responsible for helping the actors into and out of their costumes (often in mere seconds!), checking to see that each actor is properly dressed before going onstage, and, at the end of every performance, doing the laundry and making repairs. Costume laundry presents more challenges than home laundry because of the fabrics chosen, the trims and hardware applied, the dyes and paints used, and the complex construction techniques that often include built-in layers and sometimes padding. Repairs to costumes are inevitable and ongoing and occasionally involve total replacement of a destroyed garment. Playwrights seldom write plays about relaxed and peaceful events, and actors at work are always in a state of physical tension. One wardrobe supervisor pointed out that, in his experience, a costume worn onstage for eight weekly performances takes as much wear in a month as a professional uniform worn daily in the "outside" world takes in a year.

The wardrobe supervisor, in close collaboration with the costume designer and the shop manager, creates both a *dressing list* that includes every item worn by every actor in the production, and a *care instruction list* that notes which costume pieces can be washed (by hand or by machine; in cold, warm, or hot water) and which must be dry cleaned. Items such as shoes, gloves, and wigs present special cleaning problems, as does stage blood, thrown food, and other messes thought up by playwrights, and sometimes by directors, which must be removed from costumes between performances. When the acting company is made up of or includes Actors' Equity Association members, there are certain laundry standards agreed upon by contract. Wardrobe supervisors are often involved in decisions that lead to building or purchasing duplicate costume pieces to use on performance days when both afternoon and evening performances are given.

Season Planning and Reading Scripts

A season of plays may run anywhere from ten summer weeks to an almost year-round forty- to forty-two weeks. College and university production schedules are constrained by academic terms and outdoor theatres by the season. No matter how long or how short the season will be, choosing the best plays for a company to perform and its audience to see and hear constitutes perhaps the most important set of choices a theatre organization makes. Costume shop managers often do, and always should, have a role to play in this process.

From an entirely practical standpoint, the shop manager can offer informed information about how much it *might* cost and how much time it *might* take to produce costumes for a specific play. Such estimates are always "ballpark figures" since many plays can be dressed in a wide variety of periods and styles, and the number of actors involved may also vary. "Ballpark figures" do, however, provide valuable guidelines for making choices.

The costume shop manager is also concerned with the production sequence. If a play with a large cast and, presumably, elaborate costumes, such as *Tartuffe* or *The Skin of Our Teeth,* is being considered, the shop manager might well suggest that it be followed by a less-demanding script with a smaller cast, rather than with another costume blockbuster.

The involvement of the costume shop manager in choosing and scheduling plays is not, however, limited to practicalities. Most people in this position are well-educated, seasoned theatre professionals who are deeply interested in seeing their theatres produce strong, interesting scripts that will entertain and challenge audiences. Although final decisions about play choice almost always rest with artistic directors, in the best of situations the critical responses of costume shop managers to plays that are being proposed for production should not be overlooked.

One of the great complaints shop managers have about reading prospective scripts is finding time to read plays that may be handed to them only a day or two before their reply is required. This problem is made more acute when the script is new or not widely available, and there are a limited number of copies to go around.

It is important, therefore, added to their other expanding responsibilities, that costume shop managers become perceptive script readers who have developed a clear understanding of dramatic structure, can "fill in the blanks" left by dialogue-only constructs, and respond articulately, and in some detail, to what they read. "I had to work hard to learn to read scripts efficiently," one shop manager said. "Novels are easy, relaxing. But I sure did have to practice plowing through all that dialogue to figure out what was happening. And now I sometimes have to do it overnight."

"I believe," said another shop manager, "that the most important thing I do every season is get everybody who's working in the shop together during the first day or two and talk to them about the plays we're going to work on. I encourage all of them to read the plays themselves but I know not everybody does. I concentrate on what I know, from talking to directors and designers, about why certain plays have been chosen and how the productions are being planned. I'm a sort of cheerleader for the work we're going to do. I believe it makes us all feel like we're more a part of the process."

Hiring a Staff

Most producing groups, whether in the professional or academic world, know months, and sometimes a year ahead what plays they will produce in the coming season. Indeed, as one shop manager has already mentioned, the next season is usually chosen while the costume shop is busy turning out costumes for the present one. Planning ahead may require extra script reading and going to more meetings but, in the long run, it allows all the department heads within the organization to plan ahead for the work to come.

Some costume shops are blessed with staff members who have remained in their jobs for many years and are able to provide important continuity to each season's work. Others, particularly those shops associated with companies that perform only during summers, experience a large annual turnover in personnel and the costume shop manager may face the prospect of hiring two to three dozen technicians in a relatively short time to fill key positions. Experienced cutter/drapers are in highest demand and, because the manager knows which plays are on the schedule, he or she will try to hire people known to have expertise in the particular periods and styles required by the plays being done, or prior experience working with specific designers. Obviously, this is not always, or even usually, possible. Hiring a large costume shop staff can be a frustrating experience. It means reading piles of resumes, calling dozens of references, conducting telephone interviews and traveling to a variety of venues where costume technicians come, portfolios and resumes in hand, looking for work.

Costume shops that have significant annual turnovers provide jobs for a great many beginning technicians: those still in school, just out of school, or people from allied fields who are making new career decisions. Having these entry-level positions is important for the profession even though it adds great pressure to the responsibilities of those shop managers who must foster teamwork in a new group of people in a very short period of time, every year. One seasonal hiring veteran concludes: "Sometimes I find a great bunch, a really special team. Other times, it's . . . just okay."

In shops where the basic staff remains fairly constant, with only occasional personnel changes in the established positions, hiring the right people for the coming season often means overhire: an additional cutter/draper for *Peer Gynt;* a milliner to work with the on-staff craftsperson on *The Misanthrope;* or an armor specialist brought in for *Henry V*. Overhire is expensive, more so in theatres outside major metropolitan areas where transportation and living expenses have to be included along with salary. An effective shop manager knows how much and what quality work his or her regular staff is capable of doing and makes well-calculated, judicious decisions about bringing in additional technicians, always well in advance of a crisis.

A few shops, both professional and educational, overhire certain positions on a regular basis. There is an economic advantage to the theatre or department's budget in doing this. Salaried employees "cost" the employers more than their salary. Contributions must be made to Social Security and unemployement compensation; health insurance and retirement benefits are often part of the salary package. People working for a short period of time—overhire—may be hired as contract workers and paid a one-time fee, from which the employer may not be required to withhold federal or state taxes. Even if the compensation is paid as salary, the part-time employee is seldom included in health insurance and retirement plans. Thus, a theatre may decide to hire only a given number of costume technicians on the permanent staff, a sample group being, for example: shop manager, cutter/draper(s), craftsperson, wardrobe supervisor. Stitchers and wardrobe running crew members may then be brought in for limited periods of time as overhire positions.

Costume shop managers seldom set salaries. They supervise staff members, but in matters of compensation, they occupy a typical "middle management" space between a financial officer who budgets and pays the bills, and the income needs, desires, and sometimes demands, of the people on whom they depend to get the work done in the shop. However, no matter how large or small, how permanent or temporary the costume staff is, the shop manager knows, and always feels some degree of responsibility for, what the technicians are paid. And when a financial conflict arises, for example, between the best cutter/draper in the shop and the person who determines wages, the costume shop manager may well be the person to whom this technician comes for advice and support. Overall, raises and increased benefits for members of the costume shop staff often depend upon the manager's willingness to be an advocate for an individual or for the entire staff.

Budgets

Costume shop managers spend and account for a great deal of money in a variety of budget categories: equipment purchases, equipment maintenance, basic shop supplies, day-to-day operating expenses, production budgets. For most theatres, these separate budgets begin as a lump sum, allocated by a business manager and based on past expenditures, production estimates for the upcoming season, donations and grants, and advance subscription sales. Out of this lump sum the shop manager, in consultation with directors and designers, the production manager, the artistic director and others, eventually assigns budgets to each expense category, and to each production that has been scheduled for the coming season.

According to several shop managers, the most underbudgeted item in most costume budgets is equipment maintenance. "When we were finally able to buy that industrial machine everybody said was the best, I expected it to go on running forever," remarked a stitcher. "It did for three years. But then the timing got messed up and it cost a lot to fix it." Every piece of equipment in a costume shop will need attention at one time or another. Parts wear out, adjustments are necessary, and some machines require routine professional maintenance for peak performance. It's not an easy matter to predict how much repair and maintenance costs will be in a season but it is probably a good idea to allow more than is expected.

The budget line for stock supplies includes the basic items without which the shop cannot run, such as sewing machine oil and laundry detergent, and sewing supplies that will be used by all the productions: thread, flat lining fabrics, snaps, hooks and eyes, tailor's chalk, elastic, bias tape, and so on. Purchasing basic supplies in bulk is always less expensive than running to the local fabric shop for yet another package of twill tape. (And there are, of course, theatres in isolated locations where the local fabric shop is not at all local.)

Purchasing can take up an enormous part of a shop manager's ordinary day, but the amount of time spent purchasing stock supplies at the beginning of each season never ceases to amaze even those who have been doing it for many years. "If there was just one place where I could buy everything!" is the repeated cry of costume shop managers all over the country. Competition, however, is what makes the modern economic world go round and it is the duty of the shop manager to find the best possible merchandise at the lowest possible price. This may translate into a hundred Internet visits and as many follow-up telephone calls to find out if what was on the screen is really in stock; thumbing through a thigh-high stack of catalogues; filling out countless purchase orders; receiving and opening mountains of packages and scrambling to grab the invoices before they disappear into the trash; and, inevitably, negotiating returns because somebody somewhere always makes a mistake. At the end of this gigantic shopping spree, however, is a well-stocked costume shop ready to welcome the technical staff and designers and get a new season underway.

This is not to say that shopping for and ordering supplies ends for the shop manager when building costumes begins. Shopping and buying take another turn at this point and are largely driven by the individual needs of the designer, or designers, for the upcoming productions.

Production budgets come next. These are particularly difficult decisions to make in situations when costume designers and directors haven't yet been hired and it's impossible to know what the period or style of the production might be. Nevertheless, shop managers can rely on experience and intuition to make estimates. Many decide not to allocate *all* of the remaining budget to individual productions, but instead put aside a slush fund that can be used as needed. Other shop managers automatically withdraw a percentage from each budget to put toward both shop supplies and unforeseen purchases. "I might tell the designer the show has an overall budget of, say, $4,000, but he has only $3,500 to spend," one shop manager explained. "Or, I might not tell him."

What about those the stock supplies that were purchased at the beginning of the season? Can the designers use them freely? Or are they charged against individual shows? Often it is a combination of both. Supplies such as thread, elastic, bias tape, hooks and eyes, and snaps are there for the using, a permanent part of shop overhead. Many of the specific construction supplies that designers would have to purchase for their productions, such as silk, rayon and acetate linings, various underlinings and interfacings, coutil for corsets, corset bones, and shoulder pads and understructures for tailored

garments, can be taken from stock and charged to the shows. This is advantageous to the designer, who will pay less for these items because they were bought in bulk. Not only does this make good budget sense but it also saves the designer shopping time. Some organizations, including university programs where several student designers may be working at the same time, provide designers with a list of available supplies, perhaps including fabric swatches for linings and interfacings, the cost to the production of each one, and a sheet on which to record in-shop "purchases."

Keeping Records

No budget of any sort works if the person who's spending the money doesn't keep a record of expenditures. Shop managers depend upon designers and, sometimes, designer's assistants to keep all receipts and a record of everything they purchase, in order to know how much they've spent and how much they have left. If a designer has spent his or her own money to purchase fabrics and trims, the receipts must be turned in and recorded before a reimbursement check can be issued. If the organization has advanced the designer a sum of money with which to purchase fabrics and clothing for the show, the receipts must also go to the business office to confirm what was spent. Some theatres maintain blanket purchase orders with specific suppliers so the designer can shop and not have to carry large sums of money or put the purchases on his or her own credit card. A few theatres issue temporary credit cards to designers for shopping. Blanket purchase orders and organizational credit card bills must both be reconciled with receipts. Each and every costume designer needs to develop a good method of accounting for everything he or she buys, and a foolproof method of collecting and protecting their proofs of purchase. All shop managers have to keep tabs on every designer's shopping progress and collect receipts on a regular basis.

Today, virtually all shop managers and many designers keep purchase records on a computer. Some keep their expenses organized on a commercial software program such as Quicken; others use adaptable spreadsheet programs such as Excel. (Look for more about computer use in costume shops in Chapter 11.)

An excellent piece of advice offered by one longtime shop manager is to never to allow an invoice, receipt, purchase order, or bill to leave the costume shop without making a copy of it. Something always gets lost in transit.

The Costume Shop Manager and the Costume Designer

A good working relationship between a costume shop manager and a designer is essential to a successful collaboration between the designer and the costume shop staff as a whole. This relationship often begins at an early production meeting when ideas are still being discussed and the designs are far from complete. It continues through informal telephone calls

FIGURE 10–13. A composite costume sketch by Susan Tsu for the characters Tamora, Chiron, and Demetrius in Shakespeare's *Titus Andronicus* and the realized costume for Chiron (page 407), played by Christopher Jean. The production was directed by James Edmundson at the Oregon Shakespeare Festival. *Photographs by Susan Tsu.*

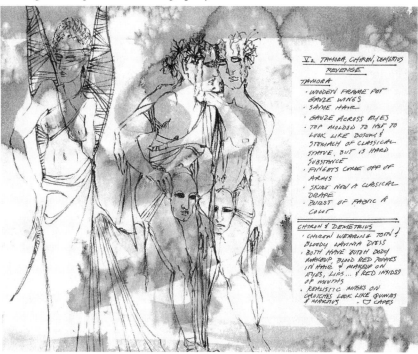

and e-mails, or over coffee if the designer and shop manager are working in the same organization. The first important peak is reached when the designs are finalized and the shop manager (with the cutter/draper and, perhaps, the dyer/painter and/or craftsperson) and designer meet to discuss each sketch and to make detailed plans for the construction process.

Here are Susan Tsu's comments on the ideas that inspired the costume for Chiron, the middle character in the sketch on page 406, and the shopping and building process that became the realized costume. Although these comments were made after the production had opened, the explanations of why the costume was designed in this particular way and what went into its creation provide a window into the conversations that occur between designers and technicians on their journeys from sketch to reality.

FIGURE 10–13. (*continued*)

In the Oregon Shakespeare Festival production of Titus Andronicus, *a violent play that decries the revenge cycle, Chiron was conceived as a vain and sexual creature, a Goth who, unlike the Roman Andronicus family, has wild hair, bare skin, and clothing of leather and home-spun in cool colors. This is the costume he wears late in the play after he and his brother, Demetrius, seeking revenge for the death of their brother, have raped and mutilated Titus' daughter, Lavinia, and murdered two of her brothers. Both Chiron and Demetrius are, by this point in the play, utterly depraved. With their equally monstrous mother, Tamora, they visit Titus in disguise. Chiron wears Bacchanalian grapes in his hair and a loincloth to which the skinned face of Lavinia's murdered brother is gruesomely applied.*

The costume for Chiron was made of many disparate materials, some costly, some not, all transformed by the expert cutter/drapers, stitchers, dyers, craftpersons, and wigmakers of the Oregon Shakespeare Festival.

Wig: *Synthetic and moderately priced, enhanced with hair braids, twine, bones, beads, and a bracelet from stock as the topknot.*

Headdress: *Wire base covered with a sweatband; the grapes came from a craft store.*

407

Dress: Made from an expensive silk designer fabric purchased at an off-price shop in New York, already ombre dyed at the hem with painted streaks throughout. This dress is a distressed version of Lavinia's first dress so a double amount of fabric was necessary. The fabric for both dresses was primitive pleated by the OSF draper. The distressed version was then torn and painted with blood and body stains by the OSF dyer. Costume jewelry bracelets, covered with net, are at the shoulders; brass beads on edges of overlayer are from stock; and brass weights at overlayer tips are also from stock.

Loincloth: Constructed on a dance belt with twisted and stitched cotton gauze (chincha). The mask, needing to be flexible, was made of latex foam rubber over a face cast of the actor who played Livinia's murdered brother.

Drape: Fashioned from a rectangle of black fabric found in stock.

Titus Andronicus *was truly a labor of love by the costume shop. The expertise, invention and creative genius of the team members, and their tightly integrated working relationship resulted in one of the happiest collaborations of my career.*

Getting off on the right foot is vital, particularly if the shop manager is working with a designer for the first time. The two most important things the shop manager can do to facilitate the initial meeting are to have read the script and to exhibit genuine enthusiasm for the project on which the two of them are about to collaborate. This is not always the easiest thing to pull off when a shop manager has to talk to several different designers about several different productions in the space of a week, or when this is the fourth student designer the shop manager has met with in a challenging academic term that began three months ago. It is, however, ultimately worth the effort.

If the shop manager is able to meet the designer while the design process is still ongoing, there is the advantage of spotting a potential problem early on. "At our very first meeting," the costume director at a Shakespeare festival theatre recalls, "it became obvious that, whatever the costumes ended up looking like, there was one scene when they would be pretty well soaked in blood. Knowing about the blood that far ahead gave me time to work with the designer on finding fabric the blood would wash out of and planning the costume change out of the bloody stuff in such a way that the blood wouldn't get on everything else." Designers and directors should understand that the shop manager who enters the collaboration at an early stage is not attempting to influence the design process itself; but only to facilitate the designer's work within the budget, schedule, and "possibility parameters" of his or her own shop.

There may be many weeks, or even several months between the beginning of a costume designer's work on a production and the deadline for finished sketches. The deadline for sketches is always stated in the written contract between a theatre organization and a designer. In an educational theatre department, it is determined by a previously agreed-upon production schedule. There may be other deadlines as well: for a costume plot, rough sketches or "thumbnails," fabric purchases, and so on. It is part of the costume shop manager's responsibility to see that these deadlines are kept. (In some theatres the costume shop manager sets these deadlines.) Meeting the deadline for finished sketches is particularly important when the costumes are scheduled to "go into the shop" at the same time. The best way to keep track of the designer's progress is to stay in touch. E-mail is an easy way of doing so.

During the weeks or months between the time the design ideas for a production are finalized and the date the final sketches are due, the shop manager might want to ask the designer to recommend research material the cutter/draper and craftsperson can use for advance preparation. This may also be the time to pull costumes from stock that could be used, either as samples for patterning or as possible costumes for the show. Assemble measurements. If an actor is not in residence and has never worked at the theatre before, his or her measurements may be available from another theatre where he or she has worked; they can come by mail, e-mail, or fax. Good planning and organization on the part of the shop manager assures that the whole shop will be as prepared as possible for the beginning of the "build period."

What happens if the costume designer doesn't meet the deadline for final sketches? This is a relatively common occurrence and, in some cases, is the result of a popular and busy designer working on too many projects at once. Another reason for the delay may be that the director and designer are still making decisions and the designs are simply not done. If the shop manager knows ahead of time that the sketches will be a day or two late, it is well to be calm and understanding. If they're a week or more late, however, the entire staff stands to lose several important workdays. The shop manager must point this out to the designer. Make sure the director and the production manager, or department chair, know about the delay. (This is not being a "tattletale." A situation may well arise in which in the shop manager has to request overtime hours or an additional pair of hands in order to finish the costumes on schedule and the groundwork needs to be laid for this request.) Designers can usually give the shop something on which to start: undergarments, pulling shoes and accessories, fitting pulled costumes on actors who are available. If the designer is in another city or state, digital or Polaroid photos of the fittings can be sent. It's important that the shop manager remain calm and never "bad-mouth"

the designer to the staff. That will only get the building period off to a poor start at precisely the time when everybody needs to work at the highest level of efficiency.

More times than not, the sketches will arrive on the expected date, preferably in the hands of a designer who is prepared to discuss each one with the shop manager, cutter/draper, and other technicians who will be involved in realizing various portions of each design. This may involve a single meeting with several technicians present, or a series of individual meetings. One or several, these conversations are crucial to successful work whether they are taking place in one of the largest and most affluent professional theatres in the country or in a small college theatre department where a student is presenting sketches for the first show he or she has ever designed. It is the role of a shop manager to see that a sufficient amount of time is scheduled for the meeting, or meetings, and that there is enough space and light in which to look at the sketches comfortably. The staff should be told, preferably in the designer's hearing, that this is their time to ask questions, and even the shyest one should be encouraged to do so. It is an indisputable fact that five people can all look at exactly the same costume drawing and see five very different images. The major purpose of studying each sketch individually, and the design as a whole, is for everyone to end up seeing what the designer sees.

At what point, or points, in this process is the costume shop manager likely to suspect that the costumes as designed may cost more than the budget allocated or take more human hours than the combined staff members can expend? The more experienced the shop manager is, the earlier this will occur. The choice of a particularly lavish period in which to place the production, which is often one of the first considerations when doing one of Shakespeare's plays, might send up alarm signals. The director's asking for a larger-than-expected cast of townspeople; a decision to use full face masks on principal characters; or costumes designed to incorporate elaborate dyeing and painting techniques—each is a potential money and time inflator that was not foreseen when the original budget estimates were made. The "insufficient budget" card should not be raised too soon, because many early design ideas disappear completely in subsequent discussions. However, when there is a real and serious discrepancy between the time and materials budgets and the potential demands of the design, the shop manager must speak up. The most tactful approach might be to talk privately with the designer rather than to bring the issue up in a general meeting. It's important to state concerns clearly and then listen to whatever the designer has to say. He or she may have already come up with some cost-saving ideas for realizing the costumes. The shop manager and other technicians may also have some suggestions; as the issues are discussed, compromises will often occur and a solution be found without further hassle. Occasionally it will be necessary for the designer to go back to the drawing board. Expect the director to become involved in the discussions if significant design changes become necessary. New sketches may have to be drawn, painted, and approved. The most important thing is to keep talking.

A costume crafts director, speaking to a group of student technicians, began her talk by saying: "There are at least two key elements always present in a successful collaboration between the head of any costume area and a designer: professionalism and communication." Professionalism in a costume shop is founded upon mutual respect between theatre artists and craftspeople and a common commitment to the work at hand. Communication, which includes talking *and* listening, makes it possible for the work to happen. Most of the time.

Inevitably, in the course of a career supervising a costume shop, a manager will encounter a "no compromise" situation, with a show that's too expensive and too big for the available resources, and a designer who insists that everything be built exactly as he or she has imagined and sketched it. When these rare occasions arise, it is well for the manager to know at the outset that the probable outcome of such an impasse is that the designer will more than likely get exactly what he or she has designed, without compromise. The only recourse a shop manager may have is to mitigate the pressures and frustrations on the staff as much as possible, and keep the inevitable overtime hours to a minimum. Once again, it is important that the shop manager speak up. And this time make sure to speak with those who have influence: production manager, artistic director, managing director, and so on. Nothing is helped by merely griping to the staff. Costume shop technicians often repeat inevitability adages, such as: "When the ox is in the ditch, somebody has to pull him out." However, while it's true that no one is willing to see half-clothed actors on stage in front of an opening night audience, it also falls to the costume shop manager to try and keep that ox from marching toward a ditch the next time—and all the times to come.

The Nature of Compromise

Every person who manages a costume shop needs to have a sizeable bag of ideas from which to bring out compromise suggestions to offer designers. Make sure the ideas don't violate the designer's vision but simply present an alternate way of achieving it.

Build, Pull, or Rent

In their heart of hearts, most costume designers would like to build every costume they design "from scratch" in order for it to look exactly the way it does in their sketches. (Some even dream of weaving, dyeing, and printing perfect fabrics, presently unavailable at any fabric store in the world!) Although there are some occasions when a set of costumes is so specific and detailed that every piece must be built to order, most productions in regional and educational theatres are costumed with a combination of new and previously worn items. A few shop managers, particularly those working in theatres that produce musicals and other large-cast shows, may even greet new designers with a ready-made "build vs. find" formula. "I tell them up front," said one experienced shop manager. "We can build a third, you can rent a third, and the other third has to be pulled from stock. You're welcome to decide which third is which."

Even in the absence of such a formulaic approach, one of the first things many shop managers look for in the earliest and roughest of sketch is a costume, or costume piece, that might be pulled from stock. Many designers, especially those who respect and adhere to established costume budgets, will ask the shop manager about the availability of certain items in the theatre's stock even before beginning to draw. Digital photos of possibilities may be e-mailed to the designer early in the process. Pulling from stock shouldn't mean that the designer doesn't get the costume that's been designed. Indeed one of the definitions of *design* is "the successful bringing together of disparate objects or ideas." A costume shop manager may be the person who contributes to the design by finding precisely the right skirt or vest.

Renting one or more costumes for a production doesn't necessarily save money, but it does save time. Rental prices vary greatly. The lowest price usually comes from another theatre or theatre department, a good many of which rent costumes on a regular basis; some even have one or more staff members or stu-

dents dedicated to servicing rentals. The Costume Collection, an organization in New York, maintains a costume stock that is available for rent to not-for-profit groups at reasonable rates. Full-service commercial costume renters and companies that specialize in renting military uniforms and men's formal wear are the most expensive. Renting agencies of all sorts often maintain websites that display some of the items they have to rent, and your ability to fax or e-mail the company an image of what you're looking for makes the process much easier than it once was. Do not, however, forget to add round-trip shipping expenses to the price of renting.

"Outsourcing"

The last decade of the twentieth century saw "outsourcing" become a common, if grammatically controversial, phrase as more and more organizations found it both easier and more cost-effective to have certain portions of their work done by outside groups. College and university bookstores, for example, are now almost all operated by big chain booksellers and many theatres hire commercial services to run their subscription campaigns. Although outsourcing as a general way of doing business is largely absent from theatre costume shops at present, there are times when a costume shop manager, in collaboration with a designer, finds it wise to "job out" one or more costumes to another costume shop, or to an independent technician, although making sure the jobbed-out costume will fit the actor for whom it is being built is always a concern. Sometimes the outside contractor will be brought to the theatre to take his or her own measurements and at other times it may be necessary to fit the costume on site at least once before it is completely finished. Shared photographs between the off-site shop or technician and the designer are helpful. Whenever work is done off site, there are many organizational issues that the shop manager will have to oversee carefully.

Jobbed-out items might range from a set of chorus costumes for a musical to a man's period suit. Outsourcing a costume, or a small number of costumes, does not usually save money but it is yet another way, if the budget permits, for a shop manager to facilitate the designer's needs without overburdening the shop.

Alternatives

Could I try another way of patterning the sleeve that will be less complicated for the stitchers? Can the corset be built into the bodice? Have you ever thought about using Friendly Plastic for the crown? Suppose we adapt a pair of contemporary boots rather than have them made? Don't you think that starting with a vacuform breastplate would make it stronger?

These are the kinds of questions that the costume shop manager and other technicians ask as they study the designer's sketches, suggesting alternatives that may save time or money, or result in a better product. The shop manager will ask some of them but must always encourage the cutter/draper, craftsperson, and other area heads to express themselves as well. No one should hesitate to speak up because the designer might be irritated or insulted by questions coming from the costume shop staff. Most designers accept questions and comments as indications that the technicians are interested in and prepared to be involved in the project. Every technician's input, if it's thoughtful and well-stated, is important to the collaborative process and should be welcomed. There's no risk that you will adversely affect

the design; if the designer wants to have the boots built, you'll work together to find a way to afford it.

The Bible

It is customary for a costume shop manager to assemble a complete record of the costume construction process for every production; this record is called the costume bible. The bible is a sort of super scrapbook. It contains a great deal of information used by the technicians who build the costumes and by the wardrobe staff that maintains them while the show is running. At the end of the run, the bible helps the staff return all costumes to their proper places in the stock area and/or to places from which they have been borrowed or rented. If the production is revived, the costume bible is an invaluable record for a costume shop staff that may not have worked on the original production. Most theatres keep costume bibles as part of their production history.

A costume bible will contain most, but not necessarily all, of the following:

- A production calendar
- Production meeting notes
- Photographs of each actor:
    head shot
    front full-length view
    side full-length view
- A completed measurement blank for each actor
- Costume plot
- Fabric swatches, including:
    yardage
    fiber content
    source
    price,
    where used

- Photocopy or scanned print of each costume sketch
- Research images
- Swatches of dyed fabric, before and after, including dye recipes
- Craft notes with list of materials used for each object
- A list of all borrowed and/or rented costumes with an explanation of how the item from each source is marked or tagged
- Dressing list
- Costume care list
- After the production opens, add:
  production program
  individual record photos of each costume
  archive production photographs

Fittings

Although not every costume shop manager attends every fitting, it is the manager's responsibility to see that fitting requests are made in the approved manner, that actors arrive on time, and that all fittings are carried out in a timely manner. In theatres where most or all of the actors are Actors' Equity Association members, a fitting is scheduled into the actor's workday by a stage manager. Protocols differ from theatre to theatre but there is always a correct procedure to follow. The costume shop requests a fitting in a certain way (by sending the stage manager an actual request form or, more often these days, by way of an e-mail request) and before an agreed-upon time (usually late in the afternoon on the previous day). A cutter/draper or craftsperson will initiate the fitting request but it is usually transmitted to stage management by the shop manager. From the view-

point of many directors, a fitting, particularly when it involves a leading actor, is time taken out of rehearsal; an unwelcome annoyance. In order to protect the continuity of rehearsals; to keep directors, actors, and stage managers happy; and to avoid paying an actor overtime, fittings have to be well-organized and efficient.

Longer fitting times are necessary in educational theater programs so student designers and technicians can learn the fitting process without having too much time pressure. These are, in fact, teaching sessions and the shop manager is the primary instructor.

FIGURE 10–14. A fitting room at the Guthrie Theatre. Notice the three-way mirror, adjustable track lighting, and rolling cart filled with fitting supplies. *Photograph by Maribeth Hite.*

FIGURE 10–15. Four views of Michelle Shupe's muslin fitting for the lady-in-waiting costume she wears in The Shakespeare Theatre's production of *The Duchess of Malfi*. Notice the attention paid to fit and detail. Costume design by Robert Perdziola. *Photographs courtesy of The Shakespeare Theatre costume shop.*

Fitting Notes

Actor   Role   Show   Date

Garment Item	Notes	Muslin Fit	First Fit	Final Fit

Items to Pull or Buy

FIGURE 10–16. Many costume shops use a form on which to record fitting notes. Notetaking is often done by the first hand. This is a sample fitting notes form.

FIGURE 10–17. Another sample fitting notes form.

FITTING NOTES

Actor _____   Character _____

Show _____   Attending _____   ☐ Mock Up
                                                                            ☐ 1st Fabric
Date _____   ☐ Final

ITEM	NOTES	
PULL	BUY	DYE

Nevertheless, it is always a good idea to plan fittings carefully and make some limits on their duration.

A shop manager will often generate a form used for notes taken at all fittings. These notes are usually written down by the first hand from verbal notes given by the cutter/draper, whose hands are full of pins. In some theatres the fitting notes are photocopied so that one copy can be stored in the measurement book (separate from the bible and usually the property of the cutter/draper) and the others given to the various technicians who will work on the notes. One shop manager daydreams about the day when fitting notes are recorded on a handheld mini-computer right in the fitting room, are quickly transferred to the costume shop network, and are then immediately visible on each technician's personal computer screen. Someday.

Dress Rehearsals

Many costume shop managers attend all dress rehearsals. It's merely customary in some theatres and part of the manager's job description in others. There is an important role for the shop manager to play. When present, he or she provides support for the designer and another trained eye to study the costumes for problems. "You look for the sewing stuff," one designer says to the shop manager. "Tonight I'm concentrating on art." Not a bad division of labor when you think about it.

There are times when the costumes for a production are completely finished for the first dress rehearsal but this is a relatively rare occurrence. Even when all the garments are complete before the actors put them on, there are almost always small fitting adjustments to make: a too-tight collar, a hem that is not quite level. And because costumes seldom look the same on the properly lit stage with the house lights extinguished as they did in the fitting room or at a preliminary dress parade, color and style changes also come into play: a different tie, black shoes instead of gray. "Whatever made us think that pink purse would work?"

When the shop manager regularly attends dress rehearsals, he or she is much better equipped to encourage the shop staff as they set about their altering and changing tasks. It's not nearly as pleasant to take a blouse apart in order to adjust a collar and reset a sleeve as it was to assemble it in the first place. If the shop manager can explain why the alteration is necessary and suggest that it may even help the actor give a better performance, the work may be more appealing.

Dress rehearsals, any number from two to five, inevitably lead to the first performance with an audience. This is the time when everyone who has worked on the costumes, from costume designer and shop manager to the youngest and least experienced stitcher, sees what they have all had a hand in creating: costumes for actors; appropriate clothing for characters; an integral part of the theatrical event.

Day by Day

The average time required to build (pull, borrow, rent, alter, etc.) the costumes for a single, medium-sized professional or educational theatre production is from four to six weeks. In theatres that produce a full season of plays, the normal work week is five days; in costume shops connected with summer-only producing groups, a six-day work week may be normal. In some states, overtime pay is regulated by state law and automatically goes into effect at the end of the hourly work week limit set by that state. Other states do not regulate work hours at all. When state laws permit, some theatres "pay" overtime by way

FIGURE 10–18. Rehearsal of a scene from *Tantalus* at the Denver Center Theater Company. Notice that the actors are wearing both rehearsal costumes and rehearsal masks. *Photograph courtesy of Kevin Copenhaver.*

of compensatory time: employees are compensated for overtime hours by taking time off later.

Managers and technicians in college and university costume shops, who are not faculty members, work under guidelines set by the institution. These vary widely. Costume faculty members are not normally included in institutional work week regulations and are free to remain on the job for as long as they choose. Student employees in costume shops are usually hired for a specific number of hours each week while graduate students, whose costume shop work is considered part of their academic program, may work an unregulated number of hours.

Every costume designer and technician working in theatre today is well aware that it takes many hours and a great deal of concentration to build beautiful costumes. The technicians who do the hands-on construction work are craftspeople who have developed, or are in the process of developing, very special skills. Those who are successful are committed to their craft and take pride in what they create. Costume construction, like most other craft processes, is not a nine-to-five process because the steps necessary to complete projects are often unpredictable. A cutter/draper may have to execute two or three mock-ups before the pattern is perfect. A maskmaker often experiments for many days before creating a shape that allows the actor to see and speak effectively. Stitchers have to rip out and redo seams. Designers alter trim placements, sleeve lengths, and the amount of fullness in a ruffle in order to increase the effectiveness of the design. Every completed costume is a unique creation. The process of building theatre costumes is the opposite of an assembly-line production process.

However, there has been increasing pressure from severely overworked costume technicians, and the organizations for which they work, to lessen the pressure on and limit the work hours of the people who cut, stitch, and create theatre costumes. At the same time, there has been an equal amount of pressure from costume technicians for better pay and increased benefits. The basic problem in regulating work hours and, at the same time, increasing salaries and benefits for costume technicians is rooted in the nature of financing not-for-profit theatre in the United States. No matter how enlightened theatre organizations become to the needs of costume technicians, live professional theatres all across the country depend on private philanthropy, the backing of business organizations, and a modest amount of state and federal government funding to subsidize production costs. These subsidies make it possible for theatres to produce plays and sell tickets at affordable prices, although many theatre artists believe ticket prices have already risen so high that far too many people cannot afford to attend. In general, it is not easy to balance a theatre budget and, although salaries and working conditions for costume technicians have improved considerably over the past two decades, all theatre artists and craftspeople sense a limit. Building beautiful stage costumes means hard work and modest remuneration, and the number of craftspeople willing and eager to work in theatre costume shops may be growing smaller.

Costume shop managers all over the country are deeply concerned about filling the positions in their costume shops with trained, experienced people who are, or may become, personally and professionally committed to the work. The most optimistic of the managers see partial solutions in better and more productive ways of organizing the day-to-day work in their shops. These efforts might include everything from a more efficient arrangement of the work space to the conscious fostering of more effective interpersonal relationships among the staff members.

The wise investment of funds, particularly when money becomes available outside the regular budget, is crucial: Technology that allows a costume painter to create surface designs on the computer screen and print them out full scale on a length of fabric will ultimately save time and add to the technician's creative potential. Redesigning the storage facility so that stock costumes are maintained in a dust-free, humidity-controlled environment will ensure that they can be reused in future productions. Adding a staff member to organize and operate a rental service to other theatres may pay off in generating funds to purchase a piece of equipment that previously appeared too expensive to consider.

A costume shop manager is also very responsible for day-to-day issues that make the costume shop a safe and pleasant place in which to work. Good lighting, supportive chairs, effective health and safety policies, and well-maintained equipment all facilitate good work. Also, innovative costume shop managers must pick up on small issues as well as large ones. One costume supervisor pointed out a library-style book holder she had installed in a central location to be the "home" for the measurement book used jointly by several technicians. "Now it's not nearly as apt to end up on somebody's cutting table hidden under piles of fabric. Most people have gotten used to returning it to its home as soon as they finish using it. If somebody doesn't, everybody else yells."

People in costume shops work in close proximity to one another. There is conversation. Technicians form friendships. Or not. Whatever personal relationships develop within the shop—friendly, tense, or even adversarial—it is the combined responsibility of the shop manager and the area heads to maintain a professional working atmosphere that transcends the individual and promotes the group effort. Surprisingly enough, theories on effective business management report that tension between employees is often dissipated when the manager pays particular attention to each employee as an individual. "Policies that aim toward treating everybody just alike," remarked an arts administration teacher, "are not only impossible to enforce; they are ultimately unfair. No two people have exactly the same needs and it's unfair to treat them as though they do." Costume shop managers should get to know everybody who works in the shop and be interested in and receptive to each staff member's needs and concerns on a professional level. That doesn't mean prying or invading a person's privacy but it might mean recognizing the need for and giving an extra nod of approval to a young technician who obviously needs encouragement.

Every costume shop manager is well advised to: Remember everybody's birthday and celebrate each one in a uniform fashion. Encourage wedding, anniversary, and new baby gifts without allowing these events to become overly elaborate or expensive. Do something for opening nights, even if it's only an arrangement of garden flowers or a bowl of candy kisses. Plan an occasional treat for no reason at all. Very few of these amenities are possible in an assembly-line shop where interrupting the regulated work flow is next to impossible and breaks can only be taken at appointed times. Costume shop technicians work very hard and in very long stretches—even when shop breaks are scheduled into the workday, many technicians are too absorbed in what they are doing to take them. Unregulated birthday breaks and the occasional midafternoon surprise ice cream bar treat add immeasurably to the quality of daily life in costume shops.

Regular costume shop staff meetings are often held to discuss the overall progress on the current project and to plan for what comes next. This is particularly important in a large costume shop with many technicians working in a variety of places, but no shop is too small to benefit from weekly, biweekly, or monthly meetings. The shop manager should announce the amount of time set aside for the meeting, prepare a flexible agenda, and see that the conversation remains focused on the subjects at hand.

Given all the larger issues discussed in this section, what are the routine daily tasks of a costume shop manager? Allowing for differences in size and scale of production and the professional or educational focus of the shop, most shop managers undertake the following tasks regularly, if not every day:

1. Check the fitting schedule and make sure all garments that need to be tried on are ready. Make sure the fitting rooms are supplied and in order.

FIGURE 10–19. Production meeting at The Repertory Theatre of St. Louis. *Photograph by Marla Fisher.*

2. Check in with the designer whose show is in the shop. The check-in may be in person, by telephone, or via e-mail.

3. Order supplies that staff members have requested. This may entail research into vendors and product availability. (Pay attention to time zones!)

4. Prepare for and attend the day's meeting. (There's always a meeting.)

5. Enter receipts turned in by designers and arrange for reimbursement if necessary. Update show budgets.

6. Receive a donation of clothing and send a letter of acceptance and thanks.

7. Make sure the coffee and tea supplies are adequate and the microwave and refrigerator are clean.

8. Check personally with your draper (or drapers), craftsperson, and painter/dyer to make sure they are on schedule and not experiencing panic.

9. Respond to a request from a local elementary school teacher who has asked you to visit her classroom with examples of costumes from Elizabethan England. If your reply is in the affirmative, schedule a block of time for your visit.

10. Read the proofs for the upcoming program and make sure the names of all the costume technicians are in place and correctly spelled.

11. If at all possible, attend all or part of the run-through rehearsal of the play that's being worked on in the shop. This is not required, but it makes you more comfortable to know exactly what the actors will be doing in their costumes.

12. If the play has a long run, check in on the performance at regular intervals to make sure the costumes look as good as they did at the beginning of the run.

13. Begin to read a new play that is being considered for the coming season.

11
Computers in the Costume Shop

At the beginning of the last decade in the twentieth century, fewer than half the costume shops in the United States had computers on site. Even in professional theatres and educational theatre departments where computer technology was being used every day in administrative offices and to sell tickets, the costume shop was often the last place in the building to enter the computer age. Several shop managers recall that the first computers to arrive on their desks were rejects "from upstairs" that had been replaced by newer models. Now, in the early years of the twenty-first century, it's hard to find a costume shop that doesn't have at least one computer, usually located on the shop manager's desk. In larger professional theatres, and in almost all educational theatre departments, the costume shop computer is connected to an electronic network that allows access to other computers in other departments within the organization and to the Internet.

As in the rest of our daily lives, computers in costume shops have come to stay, and, most of the time, they're in daily use. But how are they being used, and for what? The follow-ing discussion is not a how-to-do-it manual on operating a computer. There are more than enough of those already on bookstore shelves. It will instead focus on how various members of the costume staff are relating to the presence of computers in the hands-on, craft-centered world of the costume shop, and the various uses that have been and are being found for computer technology in this setting.

Change

Technological innovation has been a part of human life throughout history: the wheel, the printing press, the compass, the automobile—just to name a few—and now the computer. In every instance, when new technology appeared, some people always protested that a vital element in the human condition was being lost. There is no written record of a person expressing concern that the advent of the wheel would surely result in weaker muscles (although it's probable someone did), but there are accounts predicting that the printed word, widely distributed, would adversely affect

FIGURE 11–1. Joan Raymond, Assistant Shop Manager; Cynthia Quiroga, Design Assistant; and David F. Draper, Shop Manager pause for a chat in the administrative section of the American Conservatory Theatre costume shop. *Photograph by Rosemary Ingham.*

human memory (and it probably did). Since the introduction of the personal computer in the 1980s, and subsequently the Internet, many people have expressed fears about the potential negative effects of everything from automatically corrected spelling and reconciled bank accounts ("Nobody will be able to spell or add a column of figures anymore!") to the availability of too-easy communication ("Nobody will ever write a letter again!"). Many are also horrified by the deluge of advertising, the massive amounts of conflicting product information, and the endless number of posted thoughts by every person with online access, no matter how "far-out" or hate-filled those thoughts might be. A negative initial reaction to the computer is normal. The automobile brought air pollution, expensive and difficult-to-maintain highways, a politically charged dependence on oil, and yet another cause of accidental death. Few people, however, demand abandoning the car and returning to feet and horses; and very few people who possess computer technology that is well integrated into their lives would consider giving it up.

So, what does it mean to integrate computer technology into your personal and/or professional life? The simplest answer is: to use it. Almost no one owns a car merely to look at it, but a surprising number of computer owners buy one and either never get around to turning it on or, more often, use only one or two functions and ignore the rest. The first people in the theatre to integrate computers into their working lives were those whose routine daily tasks were made easier, quicker, and more accurate by the operations computer technology is good at: keeping track of financial transactions; recording ticket sales and subscriptions; and composing newsletters, brochures, and programs. When computerized stage lighting systems came on the market, the lighting designer, master electrician, and everyone else working in that production area quickly integrated digital technology into their working lives. Computer aided design (CAD) programs crossed over from architecture and engineering and entered the workday of scene designers, technical directors, and property artisans, providing them with onscreen tools for producing both technical and illustrative drawings. Costume shops were the last places in most theatre complexes to integrate digital technology into what they do and how they do it. This was, in large part, because computers are expensive—and were much more so in the early 1990s—and for a long time there was no perceived need.

All that has changed. Costume shops have computers and many technicians have welcomed the time-saving, money-saving, and additional creative advantages offered by digital technology. In one way or another, computers are being integrated into the everyday work life of the costume shop staff, individually and as a group.

Managers First

The costume shop manager was often the first person in the shop to perceive the need for a computer and, usually after a good many requests and considerable negotiation, the first to have one installed on his or her desk. Because need first appeared limited to a modest amount of word processing, generating forms and procedure lists, and keeping track of production accounts (online shopping and research came later), the first computers in most costume shops had limited capabilities. In many cases, it took quite a while for administrators to recognize the advantages of extending wires far enough to connect the costume shop with the rest of the organizational network.

However, even with hard drives measured in megabytes rather than gigabytes and severely limited random access memory (RAM), many costume shop managers found their work lives changed overnight by the computers on their desks. As costume shop computers were upgraded to more powerful machines and their users became more skillful, the potential for change, particularly innovative change, increased.

It is not that a costume shop manager today is doing different administrative tasks than in those days before the first computer landed on his or her desk. Most of the activities remain the same: entering production purchases and routine expenditures somewhere, reconciling financial records, filing records of actors' measurements, and keeping up with routine correspondence. Now, however, with a little help from digital technology, these jobs can be done quicker, more efficiently, and, remarked one costume supervisor, "in ways that are lots more interesting."

The managers in almost all costume shops record and reconcile accounts on their computers. Some use financial management software and other create their own account profiles on a spreadsheet program. Since most shop managers are responsible for several different budgets simultaneously, this is an area where digital technology always saves time and increases accuracy. Once the accounts are defined, any new expense can be posted in the correct place and the account balance will adjust automatically. On reconciling the total account for one production, a shop manager explained: "I confess I use a commercial software program because it does so much of the work for me. In this case the designer, the craft supervisor, and I entered all the purchases. When the show closed I went through the purchase orders, the petty cash receipts, and the credit card statement. I checked off each item, added several receipts that hadn't been recorded, corrected a couple of mistakes we'd made in entering, and watched the math happen. We balanced out. In about twenty minutes."

Database programs are also useful for costume shop managers. "I collect information all the time," one costume supervisor explained. "Sure, I could keep all that stuff in a file folder, or on three-by-five cards. But when I turn that information into a computer database, I can set it up so it organizes the stuff in

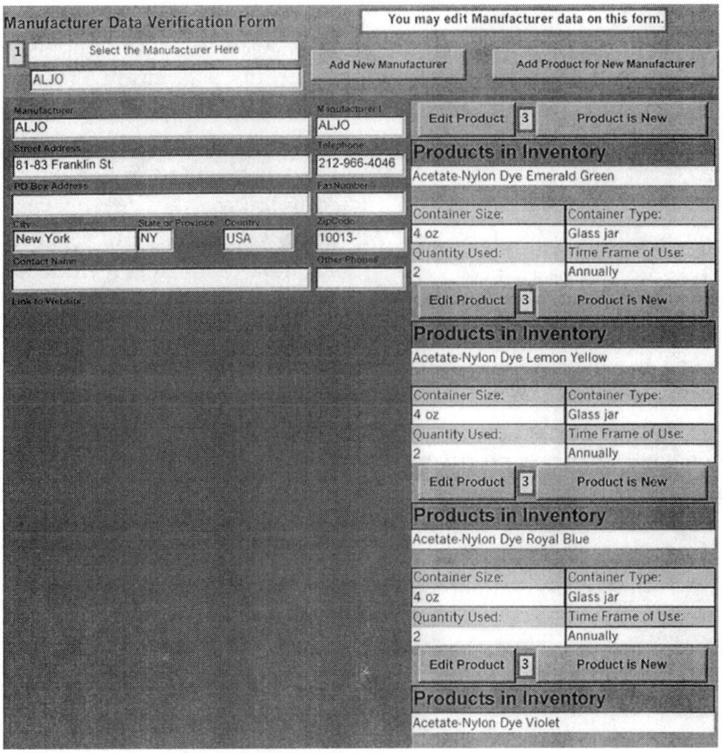

FIGURE 11–2. The product inventory view of the MSDS database written by costume director Gordon DeVinney at the Cincinnati Playhouse in the Park. The window defines several colors of acetate-nylon dye distributed by Aljo and used in the costume shop.

FIGURE 11–3. Another view in the same database as 11-2. This window features emergency instructions for treating someone who has come into accidental contact with the dye. The MSDS database can be accessed from every computer on the Cincinnati Playhouse in the Park network, making it easy to find in the event of an accident involving any product in the database. The database was compiled on Microsoft Access. *Forms courtesy of Gordon DeVinney.*

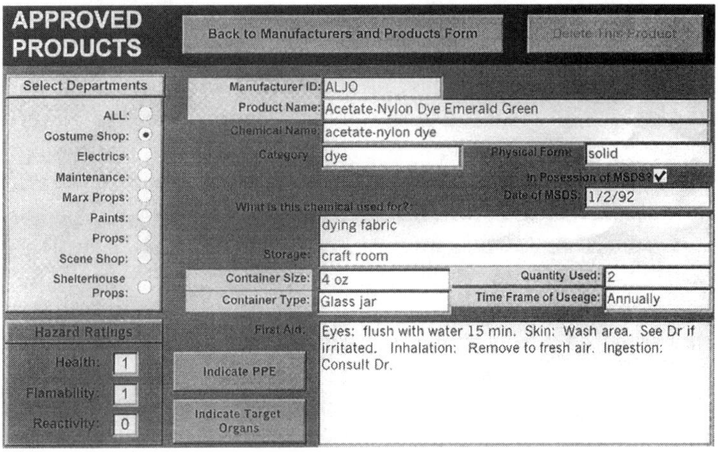

a whole bunch of different ways." He likes to exhibit the database he created to store and organize actors' measurements. It contains measurements of all the actors who've performed at his theatre for the past eight years. Within the database each actor's "vital physical statistics" are entered in such a way that his or her information can be retrieved in several different configurations. "I can pull up a group consisting of all men or all women," the shop manager explains. "Or the actors in a specific production. Or a particular season. I can also make a selection of individual actors and create a group "cheat sheet" that has all the basic measurements the shopper needs when she hits the streets." He pointed to the measurement form displayed on the computer screen. "And if somebody in Alaska needs this actor's measurements for a show she's rehearsing in up there, it's only an e-mail or a fax away."

In another costume shop, a similar database program contains records of all the clothing donations that have been made to the costume stock. After each donation is recorded, a mouse click instructs the program to generate a form letter expressing thanks for the donation and explaining the theatre's policy regarding the assessed value of whatever was donated. Another mouse click activates the printer and the letter appears, followed (after click number three) by a properly addressed envelope.

Peripherals and Posture

The central processing unit (CPU), enclosed in its plastic shell, is the main piece of hardware in all computer systems and, all by itself, it does a great many things. Without additional pieces of hardware, however, the CPU alone cannot perform all the operations that fully integrate digital technology into costume shops. These other items, referred to as peripherals, are the auxiliary units that extend, and sometimes complete, the work of the CPU. The peripherals attached to most costume shop computers include a scanner, a printer and, in some places, a wide-bed printer and/or a plotter.

In addition, if the computer system is a few years old, there may be an external modem connecting the computer to the Internet and an external Zip drive for backups and storage. A newer CPU will more than likely include an internal modem and a CD-ROM drive. By the beginning of the twenty-first century, CDs (compact discs) were rapidly replacing all other kinds of disks for backing up and storing files. Who knows what new and improved forms of information storage will soon be on the market?

Whatever computer system a costume shop has, or is planning to have, it will include a number of separate but connected pieces of equipment and require a sturdy desk or table, comfortably accessible to users. Because health and safety concerns now include protection against repetitive motion injuries and related physical strain, it's important to position all parts of the computer system so that the back, neck, and wrists of anyone using the computer can be in the most optimum position relative to the screen and keyboard.

A standard desk is almost always too high for good computer posture when a person is working at the keyboard. Ideally, elbows should maintain a ninety-degree angle so wrists don't break downward as the fingers move over the keys. The thighs should also be at a ninety-degree angle to lower legs. For many technicians, this means raising the chair height until the elbows are at the correct angle, then adding a footrest. Tall people may now find that their thighs are bumping the underside of the desk or table. An adjustable computer workstation is a good investment if it fits into the budget and into the available space. A less-expensive alternative is a keyboard holder that can be attached to the underside of a desk or table. This has the double advantage of lowering the keyboard to the correct height and freeing up more desk space.

Make sure the computer screen (monitor) is also at the proper height to protect the cervical spine from compression. Experts say that the monitor should be at a fifteen-degree angle below the sight line. Most technicians can recognize this angle without actually measuring it. It means that the eyes are focused slightly down and the head is neither tipping forward nor leaning backward. This position allows the person working at the computer to sit up straight, with shoulders relaxed. Maintaining correct posture while working at the computer will prevent a great many aches and pains caused by physical stress, and protect all technicians from more serious repetitive motion injuries.

People whose vision is corrected by glasses or contacts may suffer considerable eyestrain after spending many hours working in front of a computer screen. They may have to visit their eye doctors to have the focal point of their corrective lenses adjusted for the distance between the lens and the screen. Some people who wear glasses, particularly bifocals, have a pair they use only when working at the computer.

Last, but not least, take breaks. It's important for people working in any job that requires them to be in the same position for many hours to get up, walk around, stretch, and look out into the distance for several minutes during every work hour. A shop manager who is spending most of a day at the computer should take scheduled breaks. Out on the shop floor, stitchers should stand up and leave their sewing machines at regular intervals while cutter/drapers should step away from their tables and do the same.

Everybody Online

The frequency of computer use in a costume shop speeds up considerably when an Internet connection is introduced. E-mail and access to the World Wide Web can affect everyone's work positively when computer use is integrated into the total process of building costumes.

The first thing the staff will notice when the costume shop goes online is that communication becomes easier and the telephone doesn't ring as much as it did before. "I love the fact that you never get a busy signal when you send an e-mail," one technician remarked. "Or get put on hold."

E-mail connects the costume shop staff with designers who are out of town. One of the remarkable things about e-mail is that it has opened the door for asking little spur-of-the-moment questions that very few people would think deserving of a long-distance telephone call. Unable to figure out a detail in the costume sketch, a cutter/draper finds it easy to pose her question on the computer screen and send it off to the distant designer with a single mouse click: "Is the belt on her first act dress separate or built-in?" If the designer has a scanner or a drawing tablet, the e-mailed answer may contain a drawing as well as a written answer.

E-mailing within a theatre organization is a highly efficient means of sending messages to groups of people or departments without having to print out copies and distribute them by hand. Many theatres have shops and rehearsal halls located blocks or miles away from administrative offices. E-mail bridges the distance, especially when it's a quick question that requires only a brief response. "Can I send a stage manager to pick up Joe's shoes so he can rehearse in them tomorrow?" "Yes." Or "No. They won't be back from the repair shop until Thursday."

The World Wide Web opens many different doors for costume shop technicians. During one workday:

- A shop manager spends forty-five minutes examining the features of several different industrial ironing systems on

FIGURE 11–4. Cincinnati Playhouse in the Park buyer John Saunders ordering shop supplies online. *Photograph by Rosemary Ingham.*

illustrated websites before selecting and putting in a purchase request for one.

- A costume designer and her assistant search for a supplier who sells lederhosen. (They find one.)

- An assistant shop manager looks for the manufacturer of a new thermoplastic product she recently read about in a theatre journal article.

- Before ordering a new brand of fabric paint, a painter/dyer goes to one of several independent MSDS database sites to check on its toxicity, because, he says, "It's almost impossible to get an MSDS from a supplier before you purchase the stuff."

- A craftsperson, searching for help on a current project, enters a descriptive phrase into a search engine and is rewarded with a website on which another costume technician has posted tips for covering Victorian parasols.

Every technician in the costume shop will eventually integrate the World Wide Web into his or her workday.

Digital Cameras

A digital camera records an image that can be transferred directly into a computer. In minutes the image can be examined on the screen, printed, and saved in a file. Even more important for costume technicians, that image can also be e-mailed, posted on a website, or written to a CD and sent by mail.

It's difficult to find a costume shop today, or indeed a costume designer, that doesn't have a digital camera. Most technicians and designers use them regularly in a variety of situations:

- An assistant travels to a nearby theatre to "pull" and borrow men's suits for an upcoming production. Rather than selecting a dozen possible suits from the racks and hauling them back for the designer to see, the assistant puts each of the suit jackets on a tailor's form and snaps digital photos from which the designer can choose the suits she likes and wants to try on the actor.

- A theatre that has agreed to rent a costume to another theatre e-mails digital images of items that might fill the request. From these the designer can narrow the choice. With already high shipping costs going nowhere but up, it makes sense to pack and send only those costumes that stand a good chance of being used.

A costume director sums up one of the most important uses of a digital camera in her shop: "A digital camera keeps the design communication going, particularly if you have a designer who is in and out of the shop a lot during the build of their show. Preliminary mock-ups can be photographed, then e-mailed; or I can print them out and send them by fax. Follow-up discussions by phone result in clearer responses and quicker decisions."

Computer Aided Design

Costume technicians have been slow, however, to accept digital technology into the design and craft aspects of their work. This is understandable because the impact of computers has not directly affected the costume shop as much as the areas of scenery and lighting. As noted, there have been no technological leaps in costume shop hardware (comparable to computerized stage lighting systems) that would have forced costume technicians to use computers in order to operate their equipment. Very little costume-specific software has appeared (like the drafting and rendering programs widely used by scene designers and technical directors) that might have lured costume technicians to integrate digital technology directly into the planning and realization of costume garments and accessories. This status quo, however, may be changing.

Digital Textile Printing

On page 276, Deborah Dryden concluded her fabric dyeing and painting essay with a paragraph about the exciting possibilities of digital textile printing in the costume shop. The first part of the process, creating a design on the computer or importing one from another source, is relatively straightforward once the technician has learned to use an appropriate software program such as Adobe Photoshop or ProCreate's Corel Painter. Printing a color design on a piece of fabric larger than a letter- or legal-size sheet of paper (8½ × 11 or 8½ × 14 inches), however, is more complicated and requires a far more expensive piece of equipment.

As Ms. Dryden points out, designs generated from or scanned into the computer can readily be printed from the screen onto fabric pieces, using an ordinary inkjet printer, *if those pieces are no larger than the sheets of paper that fit into your printer tray.* Pretreated fabrics firm enough to move through the printer are available commercially or you can prepare your own. (See Figure 11–5 for directions on one method of preparing a fabric piece for use in an inkjet printer.) Once they are steam-set for permanence, computer-generated designs printed on fabric can be used in many ways to trim and decorate small areas in costumes: collars, cuffs, bodice insets, sashes, and so on.

But what about printing a large, computer-generated design onto all four sides of a shawl? Or as borders on several skirt lengths? Or a repeatable design printed on two yards of fabric that can then be cut and stitched into a blouse? For any of those operations you will need a *wide-bed,* or *wide-format,* textile printer. (See Figure 11–6 for a photograph of a wide-bed textile printer.) These printers are in use throughout the fabric and fashion industries but very few theatres or college and university theatre departments have one or have access to one. There are different brands and models but all of

1. Precut the fabric to the size of the printer tray.
2. Soak the fabric in a commercial setting liquid, available at craft stores. Allow the fabric to drip dry, then iron.
3. Cut a piece of freezer paper (Reynolds brand is widely recommended) the same size as, or slightly larger than, the dry, ironed fabric.
4. Place the wrong side of the fabric on the shiny side of the freezer paper; cover with a piece of thin craft paper and iron. In a few seconds the shiny side of the freezer paper melts just enough to bind paper to cloth.
5. Trim the stiffened fabric to *exactly* the same size as a piece of paper that fits into the printer tray.
6. Check to see that there is a small stack of regular printer paper in the tray. Place the fabric on top of the paper with the fabric side facing in the direction on which the printer will print. Make sure the fabric is straight in the tray.
7. Check printer setting. Choose the "special paper," "highest quality," and "darkest print level" settings.
8. Print and allow the fabric to dry completely. Peel off the freezer paper.

FIGURE 11–5. Direct printing on fabric using a desktop inkjet printer.

them share similar features. Each model is wide enough for a standard fabric width, starting with 36 inches. (The wider the print bed, the more expensive the printer.)

When working with large pieces or several yards of cloth, most dyer/painters choose to begin with fabric that has already been prepared for the printer with a stiffening layer. Pre-prepared fabrics by the yard are available commercially. The ink supply comes from color sets that can be changed from one type to another for use on fabrics with different fiber contents. After printing, the fabric is steam-set in a commercial steamer.

A wide-bed digital textile printer, such as the one in Figure 11–7, that is manufactured and targeted toward small fabric or fashion design businesses, is an excellent choice for a costume shop. It requires only a moderate amount of space, is simpler to use than the massive digital textile printers found in major industries, and costs far less.

At the time of this writing, the digital hardware that will allow costume shops to generate computer aided designs and print them on large pieces of fabric seems well beyond the means of most theatre budgets. But remember,

FIGURE 11–6. Wide-bed textile printer at the Oregon Shakespeare Festival. *Photograph by Deborah Dryden.*

430

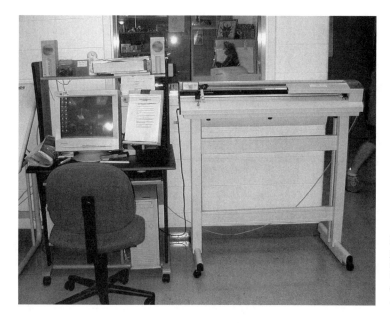

FIGURE 11–7. Computer and plotter arrangement in the costume shop at the University of Cincinnati College-Conservatory of Music. *Photograph by Rosemary Ingham.*

computers themselves were considered too expensive for costume shops in the early 1990s. Since then, because of improved technology and the volume of sales, every piece of digital equipment on the market has come steadily down in price. As this trend continues and sophisticated computer systems become increasingly integral to the work done in costume shops, the more desirable, and affordable, this equipment will become.

What are the major advantages of being able to create digital images and print them on fabric in your costume shop? There are two: The process takes much less time than silkscreening, stenciling, or block printing, the methods most commonly used by dyer/painters to transfer images to fabric. More important, however, is the presence of another tool to stretch and broaden creative potential, for costume designers and for costume technicians.

Computer Pattern Drafting

A faculty member in a university theatre department who has been using a commercial computer drafting program for several years, both in her classes and in the costume shop, describes her experiences:

The benefits of computer use in the costume shop for pattern drafting have far outweighed the in-

evitable challenges and frustrations inherent in building and maintaining a computer lab for students and staff. As a tool, computer pattern drafting has reduced our overall cutting and fitting time by forty to fifty percent. What made this possible was finding a program for pattern drafting that "thinks" in the same way I was trained to think about the process when I

431

had only paper, pencil, ruler, tape, and scissors for tools.

As a teacher of costume design and technology, it is important to me that my students have a working knowledge of efficient problem-solving methods that will enhance the accuracy of their work and protect the precious commodity of time. I have reached a point where I cannot live without the computer as a drafting tool. I see this tool as a positive addition in any shop and to every cutter/draper's bag of tricks.

While discussing the pros and cons of using digital pattern drafting in a professional theatre costume shop, another costume director commented: "I'd be all for it if I thought it would save on fitting time. I mean, I figure about half of every fitting is taken up with making things fit the actor's body, not with scale and proportion or the style and period of the costume. If we could mostly eliminate fitting problems . . . well, wouldn't that be great?"

There are a host of commercial software programs for generating garment patterns on your personal computer. Most are based on garment industry methods and focus on standard sizing and grading pattern pieces from one size to another. Many come with previously defined contemporary pattern shapes and do not allow for much in the way of design alteration. These programs are not particularly useful to cutter/drapers working in the theatre who have to create pattern shapes for all historical periods, as well as for all the "way-out" costumes that might emanate from a designer's overactive imagination. What is needed is a program that "thinks" the way theatre-trained cutter/drapers think. The program used by the costume design and technology teacher whose comments opened this section is called Custom Pattern Maker; its strength lies in the freedom users have to "draw" one-of-a-kind pattern shapes on a defined body block, much like the flat pattern drafting methods described in

Chapter 4. The developer of Custom Pattern Maker is still refining the program, and in all probability, there are other software developers at work on similar projects.

To print out a full-scale pattern generated on a computer, you will need a plotter to draw the shapes you've created onscreen. Plotters are expensive but a great many scene shops already have one on site and you might be able to share it with a cooperative technical director, particularly when you're still experimenting with the program. One shop manager said she was able to get an architectural firm to donate a plotter to the costume shop when the firm was upgrading its equipment. "It's an old one," she says, "but it works perfectly."

No single tool can do every job and digital pattern drafting is only a tool. If it is well integrated into the costume shop, however, it can save time and allow the cutter/draper ever more flexibility in his or her ways of working.

The Learning Curve

No sane person expects to get behind the wheel of a car for the first time, drive directly onto the highway, proceed into the city, and parallel park on a narrow side street. And yet, this very same sane person often expects to sit down at a new computer, open a powerful software application, and negotiate it immediately. This is, in part, because the advertising for computers and computer software all too often leads users to expect instant mastery. "User friendly." "Draw like a professional!" "Take easy control of the basics." "Create one-of-a-kind custom designs easily!" This is nonsense.

A graduate student in costume technology holds up a paper pattern piece to show her classmates. She explains, "I made this on the computer. It took a week out of my vacation, forty or fifty hours just to get there." She holds

FIGURE 11–8. A corner of the computer design lab used by all theatre design and technology students at the University of Cincinnati College-Conservatory of Music. *Photograph by Rosemary Ingham.*

up another. "I did this one earlier today. Same computer. Fifteen minutes."

Fewer people would give up on using digital technology, particularly computer aided design programs, if they knew and had accepted from the outset that the learning curve is quite steep and it will take many hours to achieve competence (additional hours if the person has limited computer skills at the outset). Costume technicians already know it takes a considerable amount of time and practice to use a sewing machine skillfully and even more time to become proficient as a cutter/draper using traditional methods. Understanding and using a digital pattern drafting program is like doing both of the above at once. The technician must learn to operate the machine itself, and then to negotiate the program, to "think" in the appropriate steps. Like driving a car, however, once the "apprentice" has learned to drive and has put in a sufficient number of practice hours behind the wheel, many parts of the process become automatic and the driver is then free to take that car anywhere a person might want to go.

A Note to Teachers of Costume Design and Technology

In the twenty-first century, freshman students come into costume technology classes with more computer skills than many of their teachers have managed to acquire in ten to fifteen years of struggling with and learning to integrate digital technology into their professional lives. These students are more than ready to accept the computer as an additional tool (along with books and lectures, sewing machines and dye vats, life drawing and drafting classes) for learning about theatre and building costumes. As these young costume technicians leave school and move out into the future world of theatre, their computers will already be fully integrated into their personal lives. It's up to today's theatre teachers to see that they will also bring the potential of digital technology into their professional lives as well—into costume shops.

Conclusion

More than two decades have passed since the first edition of *The Costume Technician's Handbook* (originally titled *The Costumer's Handbook*) was published in 1980. It is the hope of the authors that this third edition will continue to reflect the always changing practical aspects of creating costumes for the stage. In conclusion, as in previous editions, it seems appropriate to speak briefly about art: the art of the theatre, the costume designer's art, and the role of visual production elements in the theatre.

Theatre is called one of the lively arts, and it is certainly true that producing a play on the stage is a lively activity, requiring a great deal of human energy. (It is also fervently hoped by everybody associated with a production that the audience attending the play should have a lively experience in the theatre.) Many artists work together to produce a play: playwright, actors, director, designers, technicians. Theatre happens because this group of artists decides to enter into a lively collaboration with one another. A significant difference between theatre artists and artists who work alone, such as sculptors, painters, and poets, is not only that theatre artists are willing to enter into a creative collaboration but also that the collaboration is central to their work.

Theatre artists cannot create alone. The playwright's words are without life until they are spoken; the playwright's world is unseen until it appears on the stage. The task of revealing, performing, exploring, and exploding a piece of dramatic writing is shared equally by all members of this unique community of artists. All are intent upon the same goal, but each approaches that goal from a different vantage point. Their responsibilities are at the same time separate and interdependent. Although actors do not generally design their own costumes and scenic artists do not tell actors where to move onstage, both the actors and the designers working together on a production want their work to produce the same thing: a coherent work of art, accessible in every facet to the sensibilities of the audience for whom it is performed. The technician who creates an appropriate piece of stage jewelry serves this coherence just as faithfully as the director who is responsible for keeping track of the play's meaning and the total production design.

The success of a theatrical production depends very much on each artist's knowing his or her job and doing it well. Talent is never enough. Theatre artists must also be trained and disciplined to participate effectively in the creative collaboration.

All theatre artists learn from one another. Ideas and information are shared whenever and wherever theatre people assemble. This book is a result of sharing. A great many costume designers, technicians, scenic and lighting designers, directors, actors, and playwrights contributed to its contents. But, it remains only a beginning. For every method of garment construction, every craft technique, every suggestion for economical restyling and creative making-do, there are a dozen others that could not be fitted in. And, there is still a lot we don't know. Since 1980, many excellent costume design and construction books have been written and welcomed. It continues to be our hope that more theatre artists and craftspeople will be inspired to fill in the gaps that still exist in the design and technical literature.

Look for the regularly updated Shopping Guide/Source list for *The Costume Technician's Handbook* on our web site: http://www.heinemanndrama.com/inghamcovey

434

REFERENCE

Appendix I   Hats—Stiff But Safe

Although the term "mad hatter" is most often connected with the character in Lewis Carroll's classic 1895 children's book, *Alice's Adventures in Wonderland,* it actually describes a common disease suffered by hatmakers in the nineteenth century. At that time mercury was used in the manufacturing process of turning wool into felt for hats. The combination of mercury fumes and long days spent in poorly ventilated workshops caused many of the workers to accumulate mercury in their bodies, resulting in mercury poisoning. The symptoms included trembling, stumbling, slurred speech, memory loss, depression, irritability, and anxiety. The poisoned hatters were frequently pronounced mad.

Mercury is no longer used in the manufacture of hats. However, milliners may still face health hazards when they stiffen felt or straw hats with hat lacquer while working in less-than-safe conditions. Most hat lacquers, especially in spray form, are among the most toxic materials used by costume technicians.

The particularly dangerous ingredients in the most popular brand of hat lacquer used in costume shops are toluene, ethyl acetate, n-butyl acetate, and i-propl alcohol. The MSDS that accompanies this product has the following to say about "Potential Health Effects":

Acute Effects

> Inhalation: May cause central nervous system depression.
> Eye: May cause severe irritation and/or injury.
> Skin: May cause moderate skin irritation.

In addition, overexposure to toluene "has been suggested as a cause of liver abnormalities." On the "Other Information" section of the MSDS is the statement, "This product contains the following substance(s) known to the state of California to cause reproductive harm or cancer—Benzene, Toluene."

The MSDS advises the following protective equipment when using this product: an approved ventilation system and, only in its absence, a NIOSH-approved air-supplied respirator. Because toluene can enter the body through the skin, OSHA also recommends wearing "wear resistant" gloves, chemical splash goggles, and "impervious clothing and boots."

Alternatives to hat lacquer are available, and, given the increasing concern about using toxic substances in costume shops, more may be on the way.

Leko Gelatin Sizing

Water-soluble stiffening substance for straw and felt hats available from Hats by Leko, is advertised as "non-hazardous." It comes in a powder form that must be mixed in water before using. The mixed sizing has a gelatin-like consistency and may be brushed or sprayed onto a dry, blocked hat. Store any leftover mixture in a refrigerator for two to three days or in a freezer for up to six months.

Leko Felt Hat Stiffener

Also available from Hats by Leko, this stiffener is described by the distributor as follows: "Nobody in the women's hat industry has had a felt hat stiffener in decades that penetrates felt without leaving a residue, until now." And, remarking on its safety: "This product, before being mixed with alcohol, is used in candy as confectioner's glaze and on fruit to make them shine." Leko Felt Hat Stiffener is sold pre-mixed with alcohol. The solution can be applied with a brush. Many milliners like to put on several light coats, leaving time in between for each one to dry. This product can be used to restore shape and body to old hats as well as to stiffen newly blocked ones.

Considering the dangers inherent in using hat lacquer, these far safer products are worth a try.

Fosshape

Another very different approach to safer millinery is to use a thermoplastic material such

FIGURE A I–1. Top hat constructed from Fosshape by James Albrecht at the American Players Theatre. Worn by Kerby Joe Grubb. *Photograph courtesy of Michael Broh at the American Players Theatre.*

as Fosshape. Fosshape is a product of the Foss Manufacturing Company and is available through most theatrical suppliers. One of its greatest advantages is that, unlike buckram, it will not soften or wilt on an actor's sweaty head under stage lights or on an outdoor stage in hot, humid, or rainy weather conditions. Costume designer and technician Nanalee Raphael offers the following user's report:

In my shop we've made men's top hats, bowlers, kepi, mitres, a Mad-Hatter-type hat, bicornes, and tricornes. The product shapes into lovely rounded crowns and curvaceous brims. You can shape it by blocking a large piece like felt, or by cutting, seaming, and/or darting and then pressing heavily with a steam iron. There's no need to use glue. Setting time is only as long as it takes for the steam to dissipate from the hat. After the various parts have been molded, you can cover and assemble the hat, and wire the brim, using traditional millinery techniques. Machine stitching is okay.

Fosshape is about the weight of double crown buckram. It's really wonderful stuff, especially since it's nontoxic and your hands don't get dirty or sticky from working with it. It is a good idea, however, to use a press cloth to protect your iron.

There are at least two weights of Fosshape. We use the lighter weight for hats and a heavier weight for costume props such as crowns and armor pieces.

Appendix II   Lace-Covered Buttons

The photograph in Figure AII–1 is worth any thousand words that might describe the beautiful lace-covered buttons pictured there.

These are the work of cutter/draper Heidi Hafer from the Repertory Theatre of St. Louis.

FIGURE A II–1. Buttons on right covered by circles of lace shown at left. Made by Heidi Hafer at the Repertory Theatre of St. Louis. *Photograph by Liz Covey.*

Appendix III   Mathematics for Costume Technicians

Mathematics for Costume Technicians
common equations used in constructing costumes © 2000

by Susan I. Davis, Kaufman-Davis Studio
USITT Denver March 2000

Math Basics Review

A) The diameter of a circle is equal to twice the radius (d = 2r).
B) Pi (π) = 3.1415926 . . . but 3.14 is adequate for our calculations.
C) The circumference of a circle is equal to the diameter multiplied by pi (c = πd).
D) Begin with the insides of the parentheses when solving an equation.
E) The area of a square is equal to the length times the width (a = l × w).
F) Use only one unit of measure in each equation (inches, centimeters, etc.) and convert the final answer to yards or meters as needed.

ESTIMATING YARDAGE FOR STRAIGHT RUFFLES

L = length of ruffle needed, after gathering
R = fullness of ruffle
LR = total length of ruffle
D = depth of ruffle including all seam and hem allowances
F = fabric width
Y = amount of fabric needed

Determine the total length of the ruffle (LR) by multiplying the length of ruffle after gathering (L) by the fullness of the ruffle (R).

THEN

Determine the amount of fabric needed by multiplying the depth of ruffle (D) by the total ruffle length (LR) divided by the fabric width (F).

Total length of ruffle = length of ruffle after gathering × fullness of the ruffle

THEN

amount of fabric needed = depth of ruffle × (total length of ruffle / fabric width)

LR = L × R THEN Y = D × (LR/F)

Example: A 60" skirt hem (L) needs a 10" ruffle (D) that is gathered 3:1 (R). The fabric is 42" wide (W). What amount of fabric is needed to cut this ruffle?

LR = L × R	Y = D × (LR/F)
LR = 60 × 3	Y = 10 × (180/42)
LR = 180	Y = 10 × 4.29*
	THEN Y = 10 × 5
	Y = 50

This ruffle takes 50" of fabric.

*NOTE: LR/F, the number of strips of ruffles needed, must be rounded up to the next whole number.

CREATING PROPORTIONATE CIRCULAR RUFFLES

To pattern circular ruffles of a specific length with a specific fullness, i.e., 3:1 from hem to top, the radiuses of the concentric circles must have the same relationship.

PART ONE

R = radius of inner circle
L = length of ruffle
F = fullness of ruffle from hem to top

ESTIMATING YARDAGE FOR BIAS BINDING OR PIPING

L = length of bias needed
W = width of bias to be cut
A = area of bias
F = fabric width
Y = amount of fabric needed

Determine the area of bias (A) needed by multiplying the length (L) by the width (W).

THEN

Divide the area (A) by the fabric width (F) to determine the amount of fabric needed (Y).

area of bias = length of bias × width of bias   THEN
amount of fabric needed = area of bias / fabric width

A = L × W THEN Y = A/F

Example: a gown needs 540" of piping (L), the piping needs to be 2" wide (W), the fabric available to make the piping is 20" wide (F). How much fabric is needed for this piping?

A = L × W	Y = A/F
A = 540 × 2	Y = 1080 / 20
A = 1080	Y = 54

This piping requires 54" of fabric.

PATTERNS FOR FULL CIRCLE SKIRTS

C = circumference of the circle (top of skirt)
R = radius of the circle

Determine the radius of the circle (R) by dividing the circumference of the circle (top of skirt) (C) by pi (π). The circumference of the circle should include any additions for seam allowance, ease, or fullness.

Two times the radius of the circle = circumference of the circle / π

$$2R = C / \pi$$

Example: a skirt needs to be cut 27" at the waist, plus 1" of ease, for a total of 28". What radius is needed to draft this pattern?

$$2R = C / \pi$$
$$2R = 28 / 3.14$$
$$2R = 8.92$$
$$R = 4.46$$

The radius of the circle is 4.46".

Create the pattern using 4.46" as the radius of the circle. Draw a concentric circle based on the desired skirt length.

PROPORTIONS FOR DRAFTING MEN'S WEAR

Vest Length = 1/4 height plus 1/4 chest
Vest length is measured from the nape of neck, over shoulder to center front hem.
(chest size 46 or greater add 3/4" to 1" in length)

Pants Rise = 1/4 of 1/2 hip plus 1/8 of 1/2 hip plus 2".

Inseam = 1/2 height minus 2"
(height 5' 6" or less reduce the inseam by 1/2" to 3/4")

CONVERTING BETWEEN IMPERIAL AND METRIC MEASUREMENT SYSTEMS

Multiply inches by 2.54 to convert to centimeters.

inches × 2.54 = centimeters

Multiply centimeters by .4 to convert to inches.

centimeters × .4 = inches

Determine the radius of the inner circle (R) by dividing the ruffle length (L) by the fullness (F) minus 1.

Radius of the inner circle = ruffle length / (fullness−1)

$$R = L / (F-1)$$

Example: a robe requires circular ruffles on the hem that are 4" long (L) and have 3:1 fullness from hem to top. What is the radius of the inner circle?

$$R = L / (F-1)$$
$$R = 4 / (3-1)$$
$$R = 4 / 2$$
$$R = 2$$

The radius of the inner circle is 2".

Create the pattern by drawing the inner circle with radius 2". The outer circle will have the same axis, and be the length of the ruffle from the inner circle.

PART TWO

C = circumference of inner circle
R = radius of inner circle (see part one)
T = total length needed
N = number of circles needed

Find the circumference of the inner circle (C) by multiplying 2pi and the radius (R).

Determine the number of circles needed (N) by dividing the total length needed (T), by the circumference of the inner circle (C).

Circumference of inner circle = radius multiplied by 2 pi.

THEN

Number of circles = total length needed / circumference of inner circle

$$C = 2\pi R \quad THEN \quad N = T/C$$

Example: the dressing gown, mentioned above, needs ruffles on 140" of hem. How many circles are needed?

$C = 2\pi R$	THEN	$N = T/C$
$C = 2(3.14)(2)$		$N = 140 / 12.56$
$C = 6.28(2)$		$N = 11.15$
$C = 12.56$		

The dressing gown needs 11.15 circles*.

*NOTE: seam allowances are not included; add additional circles to account for seam allowances.

FIGURE A III–1. All the math you'll ever need to know in the costume shop!

Appendix IV Preserving and Reusing Costume Stock

A costume shop manager explains why it's not a good idea to use *costume storage* as the name for the place where costumes go after the show is struck. "Storage means warehousing to most people, and that's not what we do with our costumes. We don't just store them; we preserve our costumes in order to use them in future productions. Without integrating items from our stock into virtually every production, we could never afford to do the shows we do."

In most theatres, costume stock consists of all the costume pieces that were built for specific productions, clothing and accessories that have been donated from shops or individuals, items that are bought and used in quantity such as t-shirts and men's black socks, and, occasionally, costumes purchased from other theatre productions, touring shows, and so on, that have closed. It doesn't take many years of stock building for the collection to become far more valuable to the production process than most theatre administrators are aware. It is not unusual to find a theatre's costume stock housed in off-site storage units and temporarily vacant buildings that are dirty and lack any climate control. The stock itself is seldom adequately insured.

When searching for a better way of preserving costume stock in order to keep it more useable, and accessible, keep track of all the stock items used in the productions for a season or academic year. Figure out how much it would have cost to purchase or build those items and present these figures to whomever is responsible for the budget in the theatre or department. Begin to refer to the costume stock as *inventory*. As a result, plans for preserving and housing that valuable inventory may well jump to a much more prominent place on the list of future theatre projects.

Many theatres have found spaces in which to preserve and maintain their costume stocks and are organizing them in a variety of excellent, innovative ways. Only a very few shop managers, however, will admit to having "enough" space for their stock. Where are theatres putting their valuable costume inventories? What are some of the things that are most important to the preservation of costume garments and accessories? And what can be done to make these items easily accessible to designers and technicians? Whenever a theatre complex is being built or renovated, it is imperative that a representative of the costume area—ideally the costume shop manager—be involved in the planning process from day one. The safest and most convenient place for the costume stock is within the theatre complex itself, as near as possible to the shop. Housing costume stock, however, will not be foremost in the minds of theatre planners and architects and it is up to the costume staff to be sure they make a strong case for including an appropriate area within the building, backing it up with facts and figures. According to costume technicians who have been through this process, it will not be enough to make an initial proposal for costume housing. Plans for public buildings go through many steps and stages and it is necessary for the costume shop representative, or representatives, to attend every meeting to make sure the space that was allocated to costumes isn't being turned into an additional parking garage!

"If I can't have a storage area across the hall and it has to be across town, at least I want it to be big enough and spread out enough so designers can see what's here," says one shop manager, indicating a broad expanse of former warehouse space with sturdy Uni-Strut pipe racks and a good deal of walking room in between. The biggest problem with many of the places provided for costume stock, either off site or in some makeshift place within the building, is that there's not enough floor space. Costumes take up much more room than most organizations plan for. "The going advice," says a costume director who's currently working with architects and administrators on plans for a new theatre, "is to calculate how much space you think you'll need for all those costumes, and then double it."

A few things to consider—other than amount of floor space—when searching for space in which to house costumes:

1. *Heating and/or cooling systems.* In a humid climate, mold is a big problem. Not only does it destroy fabrics, but it can also make people sick. Also, designers and technicians find it very difficult to make sensible and aesthetic costume choices when the temperature is below 50 or above 90 degrees.

2. *Dust and dirt.* One of the big problems with many commercial storage units is that they are not adequately sealed. Dirt blows in around the door and settles on costumes. Old buildings often have flaking plaster and beams or ledges that have been collecting dust for half a century. Not at all good for fabrics.

3. *Too many windows.* Sunlight causes color to fade. If natural light is important, cover the windows with Plexiglas treated to filter out harmful rays; if not, block it out with sheets of wood or black plastic.

4. *Access.* Don't forget that costumes will constantly be going into and coming out of the space. Can a car or truck get close to the building? Are the doors (or halls) wide enough for boxes and racks? If the space is not on the ground floor, is there an elevator? Stairs can be treacherous when a technician is negotiating them, arms loaded with costumes.

5. *Lighting.* Is there enough lighting? If not, will the wiring in the building permit adding more fixtures safely?

6. *Windows and roof.* Are there any signs of leaking around windows or from places in the roof? Any sort of dampness damages fabric and encourages mold.

7. *Fire protection.* Is there a sprinkler system? Are there up-to-date fire extinguishers in handy locations?

8. *Location.* Is the building located in a safe area where break-ins are not frequent occurrences and where it's safe for technicians to come and go at many different times of the day and evening?

Once the space for housing your costume stock is built, remodeled, rented, donated, or purchased, what are some of the things to consider in organizing the space and putting it to use? Many of the following ideas, observations, and suggestions came from conversations with the staff and faculty members who provided access to their costume stock spaces at the American Conservatory Theatre in San Francisco; the Cincinnati Conservatory of Music at the University of Cincinnati; the Cincinnati Playhouse in the Park; the University of Maryland, and The Washington Opera in the District of Columbia. Other costume technicians from colleges, universities, and professional theatres added more excellent comments.

Put it where you can find it. It's just like a library. If the book, or the costume, isn't where it's supposed to be, it's of no use to anybody. Take the library as an example and *label everything:* rooms, doors, hallways, racks, boxes, individual costume pieces. Set up a system for labeling (it doesn't have to be as complicated as the Library of Congress system for shelving books!) that works for you, that you can explain to everyone else, and that everyone concerned can follow. *No more handwritten labels and no*

FIGURE A IV–1. Costumes come to you with this motorized, circulating storage rack for hanging garments. This one is located at the University of Maryland. *Photograph by Liz Covey.*

FIGURE A IV–2. Traditional double-hung pipe rack storage at the Guthrie Theatre. Notice the easy-to-see tags containing measurements that hang from each garment. *Photograph by Maribeth Hite.*

more writing directly on boxes. Use the computer to print out labels in big, bold letters.

Hanging storage takes up most of the floor space in every area that houses costumes, and pipe racks are commonly used. (However, at least two university theatre departments store their hanging costumes on electrically operated circulating racks like those found in dry cleaning establishments. See Figure A IV–1.) Some technicians prefer permanent pipe racks that are bolted to the floor. Others opt for rack arrangements that can be moved without a great deal of difficulty when the need arises. Make sure the racks are strong and braced at regular intervals; several dozen men's suits can be surprisingly heavy. And, if at all possible, keep the spaces between the racks of clothing wide enough for walking and looking. If the room is large, you can arrange the racks on a single level, taking care to position some higher than others to hold long gowns and period dresses. In an arrangement of this sort, all garments are accessible from floor level. When floor space is limited, racks must be higher and the costumes may be double or even triple hung, with perhaps a row on top for blouses, short jackets, and other garments that are relatively short. Be-

cause accessibility is important to making good use of costume stock pieces, if your costume stock is double or triple hung, be sure you have good sturdy ladders that move easily. (See Figure 1–16 on page 14 for an example.)

Most technicians agree that, when organizing costumes hanging on a rack, the divider on which the identifying label is placed should go in front of the group being identified. "Don't know why it is," a wardrobe supervisor explained, "but it seems more natural to put hangers behind the labels."

How to organize? There are as many answers to this question as there are costume technicians doing the organizing. Some plan of separation by historical period is common, but the actual divisions differ; men's clothing is separated from women's clothing; children's from adults'. Uniforms may be in one section, with men's business suits in another. Day dresses are usually in a different location from dinner dresses and evening wear. Some theatres keep certain, if not all, costumes from specific productions together; a few organize entirely by show. Within the sections themselves, the costumes may be subdivided by size, or by color. One set of costume stock guidelines states:

FIGURE A IV–3. A tennis ball covering the end of a pipe in the costume stock area at the Berkeley Repertory Theatre. *Photograph by Rosemary Ingham.*

FIGURE A IV–4. Box storage at the University of Maryland. The boxes have lids and are uniform in shape. The shelving has been assembled to fit the boxes. *Photograph by Rosemary Ingham.*

"Racked costumes are arranged left to right (facing the pipe) by color. White, Red, Yellow, Green, Blue, Violet, Gray, Black. And within each color section from lightest to darkest."

In order to keep your stock room as safe as possible, take care to pad the ends of hanging pipes, particularly when the they protrude at different heights. One shop managers mentioned an incident in which a technician working in hanging storage sustained a head injury requiring stitches from an encounter with an unprotected pipe end. A common means of protection is a tennis ball, cut open and slipped onto the end of the pipe. (See Figure A IV–3.)

Which items go into boxes and how the boxes are arranged on shelves also depend a great deal on the personal opinions of the technicians in charge. It is generally agreed, however, that shelves should be fitted to boxes so that boxes are never piled one on top of another. Easily adjustable shelving is highly recommended. A box should not be so big that a person of medium size cannot get his or her arms securely around it, and boxes with lids, cardboard or plastic, are favored by all. "And when one box is full," a technician advised,

FIGURE A IV–5. The stock storage area at The Washington Opera has very high, built-in shelving. Boxes fit the shelves and are accessible by way of a library ladder that slides from side to side. *Photo by Rosemary Ingham.*

FIGURE A IV–6. At the Cincinnati Playhouse in the Park, shoes are stored on narrow metal shelf units purchased at a government surplus sale. Notice that the shelves are installed upside down and angled up at the back. Shoes are prevented from falling off by the lip on the underside of the shelf, and are more visible than if they were sitting flat. *Photograph by Rosemary Ingham.*

"start another box. Don't cram." Perhaps the most interesting method of organizing boxes comes from the same costume stock guidelines just quoted. "Accessories stock is arranged from head to foot, meaning that the top shelf is headwear and the lowest shelf is footwear. Collars, ties, gloves, etc., are in between."

Hats and shoes are particularly difficult items to store. There are always so many, and they never fit comfortably into boxes. Hats, in particular, are easily damaged. In one large costume stock space, the shop manager installed enough narrow metal shelving for the theatre's entire collection of useable shoes, side by side, in a single layer. In order to make the shelving more shoe friendly and visually accessible to designers and technicians, the shop manager

turned each length of shelf upside down and attached it to the side pieces at a slight angle in order to raise the back of the shoe. (See Figure A IV–6.) Boots may be hung from pipe racks (see Figure A IV–7); as can hats (see Figures A IV–8 and A IV–9).

In many costume shops the "skin parts" of costumes (bras, dance belts, camisoles, bodysuits, hose, etc.) are not kept with the rest of the costume stock. Because they're used so frequently in fittings, these items may be kept in the costume shop or, if there's enough room, in or near the fitting rooms.

Consider different methods of moving costumes from one place to another. Rolling

FIGURE A IV–7. Hanging boots at The Washington Opera. *Photograph by Rosemary Ingham.*

racks are a necessity and the "Z" type rack is particularly noted for its stability and easy turning. (See Figure 1–34.) Various types of rolling carts are in regular use: grocery carts, domestic laundry carts, large industrial laundry carts with canvas bodies, and rolling shelf units. Label all carts with who it belongs to and where it should be stored when not in use.

Once the costume stock is housed and organized, it must be adequately maintained.

FIGURE A IV–9. Rack upon rack of hanging hats at the Guthrie Theatre. *Photograph by Maribeth Hite.*

FIGURE A IV–8. Hats hanging above dresses in the stock area at the American Conservatory Theatre. *Photograph by Rosemary Ingham.*

FIGURE A IV–10. Small accessory storage drawers at the American Conservatory Theater. *Photograph by Rosemary Ingham.*

FIGURE A IV–11. Hanging tie unit at the Berkeley Repertory Theatre. *Photograph by Rosemary Ingham.*

Some theatres hire, or appoint, a specific technician to make sure pieces are clean and returned to their proper places. In other places, the whole staff participates in restocking. Once every season or academic term, costume stock usually needs to be reorganized. A final point made by several shop managers is a reminder that maintaining the costume stock in the most efficient way possible is a process of ongoing reorganization. "It's okay today," one shop manager commented. "But there are still several things I mean to do to make it better. Maybe at the beginning of next season."

FIGURE A IV–12. Hanging belts at the American Conservatory Theater. *Photograph by Rosemary Ingham.*

Appendix V   Story of a Wig

A photographic essay of a wig designed and created by Amanda French.

FIGURE A V–1. 16–18" synthetic wig. The wig was thinned only enough to front it and to provide hair for the kiss curl (added last) and the baby/ribbon curls (also added last).

FIGURE A V–2. Wig is blocked and setting has begun. No length was removed. Curls have been steamed with a commercial clothes steamer (hand-held travel steamers don't get hot enough).

FIGURE A V–3. Back view of front roller set. Back of the wig was divided into 3 layers and braided (rope braid–it was easiest). Only purpose was to get the hair out of the way and prevent tangles. The back was *not* steamed.

FIGURE A V–4. Side view of in-progress set.

FIGURE A V–5. Back set in-progress. Again, waves held in place by Aquanet and hairdryer. The hair is pinned with silver bobby pins at the top behind the front style set.

FIGURE A V–6. Side view of finished set.

FIGURE A V–8. Final view of completed style and make-up (photo taken around opening night). Actress is wearing false lashes; patches were made by coloring in natural freckles with liquid eye liner. Moon patch was either black felt cut out *or* a pre-fab sequin. I don't remember which we used for her. Entire project (the wig) took approximately 8–10 hours to front, and 8 hours to set and style. *Notes and photograph by Amanda French.*

FIGURE A V–7. Final back style. The ends were allowed to curl over on themselves and pinned and sprayed into place.

Appendix VI   Stage Blood

Whenever the prospect appears of bloody wounds, bloody bodies, weapons that drip blood, or, most challenging of all, physical attacks that result in actors actually spilling blood on stage, many costume technicians cringe, cross their fingers, and hope the director will change his or her mind and opt for symbolic blood—a length of red silk, for example. Sometimes that happens. Often it does not. The most prudent response a costume technician can have to the probability of stage blood being required in a production is to begin planning immediately.

Things to consider:

1. The location of the blood on the character's body. If the wound (or wounds) has been inflicted off stage, it's important to know exactly where it will be and what sorts of bloodstains and additional bleeding, if any, might be expected. Should the wound be inflicted on stage, its location will be an important factor in planning how the blood will be delivered.

2. The location of the blood source on the actor's body. Stage blood delivery systems can be as simple as a blood-soaked sponge or a plastic baggie fastened with a twist tie. Or, the action of the play might require something as complicated as an intravenous bag with plastic tubing and a conveniently placed stopcock, connecting the blood in the bag to the place where it will appear. Whatever the method, all blood delivery systems must be considered in relationship to costumes and, even in theatres where blood is the responsibility of Stage Properties, planning should include the costume designer and the costume shop manager. And because actors usually control the actual flow of stage blood (by squeezing the sponge, breaking the plastic bag, or releasing the stop-

cock), it's important that they also be included in the conversations as early as possible.

3. The amount of blood. It's important to know how much blood the director wants the audience to perceive. The actual amount of stage blood it will take to create this perception may not be known until tech rehearsals. However, an early statement about "how much" can help the costume technicians prepare for the amount of potential bleeding on the costumes.

4. The length of time the bloody or bleeding actor will remain on stage. This can be a crucial piece of information because it will help to plan for cleaning. Most kinds of stage blood are harder to remove once they've dried and may require a prewashing treatment.

5. Blood that comes from the actor's mouth. Only certain kinds of stage blood can be safely used in the mouth. None, for example, containing liquid detergent.

6. The fiber content and weave of the fabrics that will be used in the costume of the bloody or bleeding actor as well as the costumes of other actors who may also come in contact with blood. Raise this question as soon as stage blood is mentioned. Suggest early tests with blood and fabrics, well before the costumes are built.

7. Allergies. Two of the ingredients frequently used in stage blood—peanut butter and liquid detergent—are also associated with common allergies. Make sure the actors involved do not have allergic reactions to these substances.

Although stage blood is available commercially, many technicians prefer to make their own. Here are three recipes selected from many.

FIGURE A VI–1. The bloody murder of Julius Caesar, played by Joe Cronin, in the Utah Shakespearean Festival production of *Julius Caesar.* Costume design by Dean Mogel. *Photograph courtesy of the Utah Shakespearean Festival.*

FIGURE A VI–2. All the Roman senators dip their hands into Caesar's blood after the murder, and wipe their bloody hands on their costumes! Utah Shakespearean Festival production; costume design by Dean Mogel. *Photograph courtesy of the Utah Shakespearean Festival.*

Recipe 1.

> 1 cup creamy peanut butter
> 1 quart white corn syrup
> ½ cup non-suds soap
> 1 ounce red food coloring
> 15–17 drops blue food coloring

Mix the peanut butter with enough corn syrup to make it runny. Add soap and food colors and mix well. Add remaining corn syrup and shake until a good solution is obtained.

Recipe 2.

> 4 ounces petroleum jelly
> 8 teaspoons warm water
> 1 teaspoon red food coloring
> 2 drops blue food coloring

Use a clean spoon or a whisk to combine the ingredients. If the color is too bright to be visible under stage lights, add one or two more drops of blue coloring. Experiment with other colors and the amount of water to create fresh blood, dried blood, dripping blood, and so on.

Recipe 3.

> 2 level teaspoons flour
> 1 cup water
> 1 ounce red food coloring
> ⅛ teaspoon green food coloring

Mix the flour and water, stirring vigorously until there are no lumps. Bring to a boil and simmer for ½ hour. Cool completely. Stir well, then add the red and green food colorings. (Adding a little dishwashing soap will make this "blood" easier to wash out of costumes.)

FIGURE A VI–3. A bloody Lavinia, played by Judith Marie Bergen in the Oregon Shakespeare Festival production of *Titus Andronicus*. Costume design by Susan Tsu. *Photograph by Susan Tsu.*

Appendix VII   Where to Write for National and State Health and Safety Standards

Office of Federal and State Operations
U.S. Department of Labor
Occupational Safety and
Health Administration
200 Constitution Avenue, NW
Washington, D.C. 20210

ALABAMA
Alabama Department of Labor
P.O. Box 303500
Montgomery, AL 36130-3500
Ph: 334-242-3460
Fax: 334-240-3417
Internet: www.dir.state.al.us

Department of Industrial Relations
Industrial Relations Bldg.
649 Monroe Street, Room 204
Montgomery, AL 36130
Ph: 334-242-8990
Fax: 334-242-3961

ALASKA
Department of Labor
P.O. Box 21149
Juneau, AK 99802-1149
Ph: 907-465-2700
Fax: 907-465-2784
Internet: www.labor.state.ak.us

ARIZONA
Industrial Commission
P.O. Box 19070
Phoenix, AZ 85005-9070
Ph: 602-542-4411
Fax: 602-542-8097

State Labor Department
P.O. Box 19070
Phoenix, AZ 85005-9070
Ph: 602-542-4515
Fax: 602-542-8097
Internet: www.az.gov

ARKANSAS
Department of Labor
10421 West Markham
Little Rock, AR 72205
Ph: 501-682-4541
Fax: 501-682-4535
Internet: www.state.ar.us/labor

CALIFORNIA
Department of Industrial Relations
455 Golden Gate Ave., 10th Floor
San Francisco, CA 94102
Ph: 415-703-5050
Fax: 415-703-5059

Division of Labor Standards Enforcement
Department of Industrial Relations
455 Golden Gate Ave., 9th Floor
San Francisco, CA 94102
Ph: 415-703-4810
Fax: 415-703-4807
Internet: www.dir.ca.gov

COLORADO
Department of Labor and Employment
1515 Arapahoe Street, Tower 2, Suite 400
Denver, CO 80202-2117
Ph: 303-318-8000
Fax: 303-318-8048

Labor Standards Office
1515 Arapahoe Street, Suite 375
Denver, CO 80202-2117
Ph: 303-318-8468
Fax: 303-318-8400
Internet: http://cdle.state.co.us

CONNECTICUT
Labor Department
200 Folly Brook Boulevard
Wethersfield, CT 06109-1114
Ph: 860-263-6505
Fax: 860-263-6529
Internet: www.ctdol.state.ct.us

DELAWARE
Department of Labor
4425 N. Market Street,
4th Floor
Wilmington, DE 19802
Ph: 302-761-8000
Fax: 302-761-6621
Internet: www.delawareworks.com

DISTRICT OF COLUMBIA
Department of Employment Services
Employment Security Building
77 P St. NE, Suite 3007
Washington, D.C. 20002
Ph: 202-671-1900
Fax: 202-673-6993
Internet: does.ci.washington.dc.us

FLORIDA
Department of Labor and
Employment Security
2012 Capitol Circle, S.E.
Hartman Building, Suite 303
Tallahassee, FL 32399-2152
Ph: 850-922-7021
Fax: 904-488-8930

Internet: www.state.fl.us/dles/ or
www.MyFlorida.com

GEORGIA
Department of Labor
Sussex Place, Room 600
148 International Blvd., N.E.
Atlanta, GA 30303
Ph: 404-656-3011
Fax: 404-656-2683
Internet: www.dol.state.ga.us

HAWAII
Department of Labor and Industrial Relations
830 Punchbowl Street, Room 321
Honolulu, HI 96813
Ph: 808-586-8844
Fax: 808-586-9099
Internet: www.dlir.state.hi.us

IDAHO
Department of Labor
317 W. Main Street
Boise, ID 83735-0001
Ph: 208-334-6112
Fax: 208-334-6430
Internet: www.labor.state.id.us

ILLINOIS
Department of Labor
160 N. LaSalle Street
13th Floor, Suite C-1300
Chicago, IL 60601
Ph: 312-793-1808
Fax: 312-793-5257
Internet: www.state.il.us/agency/idol

INDIANA
Department of Labor
402 West Washington Street

Room W195
Indianapolis, IN 46204-2739
Ph: 317-232-2378
Fax: 317-233-5381
Internet: www.state.in.us/labor or
teenworker.org

IOWA

Iowa Workforce Development
1000 East Grand Avenue
Des Moines, IA 50319-0209
Ph: 515-281-5365
Fax: 515-281-4698

Division of Labor Services
1000 East Grand Avenue
Des Moines, IA 50319
Ph: 515-281-3447
Fax: 515-281-4698
Internet: www.state.ia.us/iwd

KANSAS

Department of Human Resources
401 S.W. Topeka Boulevard
Topeka, KS 66603
Ph: 785-296-7474
Fax: 785-368-6294
Internet: www.hr.state.ks.us

KENTUCKY

Kentucky Labor Cabinet
1047 U.S. Hwy. 127 South, Suite 4
Frankfort, KY 40601
Ph: 502-564-3070
Fax: 502-564-5387
Internet: www.kylabor.net

LOUISIANA

Department of Labor
P.O. Box 94094
Baton Rouge, LA 70804-9094

Ph: 225-342-3011
Fax: 225-342-2717
Internet: www.ldol.state.la.us

MAINE

Department of Labor
20 Union Street
P.O. Box 259
Augusta, ME 04332-0259
Ph: 207-287-3788
Fax: 207-287-5292

Bureau of Labor Standards
Department of Labor
State House Station #45
Augusta, ME 04333-0045
Ph: 207-624-6400
Fax: 207-624-6449
Internet: http://www.state.me.us/labor

MARYLAND

Department of Labor, Licensing
and Regulation
500 N. Calvert Street, Suite 401
Baltimore, MD 21202
Ph: 410-230-6020 ext. 1393
Fax: 410-333-0853 or 410-333-1229

Division of Labor and Industry
1100 Eutaw St., 6th Floor
Baltimore, MD 21201
Ph: 410-767-2999
Fax: 410-767-2986
Internet: www.dllr.state.md.us

MASSACHUSETTS

Department of Labor and Work
Force Development
1 Ashburton Place, Rm 2112
Boston, MA 02108
Ph: 617-727-6573
Fax: 617-727-1090

Internet: www.detma.org/index.htm or
www.state.ma.us

MICHIGAN
Department of Consumer and
Industry Services
P.O. Box 30004
Lansing, MI 48909
Ph: 517-373-3034
Fax: 517-373-2129
Internet: www.cis.state.mi.us/bsr/
divisions/whd/home.htm

MINNESOTA
Department of Labor and Industry
443 Lafayette Road
St. Paul, MN 55155
Ph: 651-296-2342
Fax: 651-282-5405
Internet: www.doli.state.mn.us

MISSISSIPPI
Employment Security Commission
P.O. Box 1699
Jackson, MS 39215-1699
Ph: 601-961-7400
Fax: 601-961-7406
Internet: www.mesc.state.ms.us

Workers' Compensation Commission
1428 Lakeland Drive
P.O. Box 5300
Jackson, MS 39296-5300
Ph: 601-987-4258
Fax: 601-987-4233
Internet: www.mwcc.state.ms.us

MISSOURI
Labor and Industrial Relations Commission
P.O. Box 599
3315 W. Truman Boulevard

Jefferson City, MO 65102-0599
Ph: 573-751-2461
Fax: 573-751-7806

Department of Labor and Industrial Relations
P.O. Box 504
Jefferson City, MO 65102-0504
Ph: 573-751-9691
Fax: 573-751-4135
Internet: www.dolir.state.mo.us

MONTANA
Department of Labor and Industry
P.O. Box 1728
Helena, MT 59624-1728
Ph: 406-444-9091
Fax: 406-444-1394
Internet: http://dli.state.mt.us

NEBRASKA
Department of Labor
550 South 16th Street
Box 94600
Lincoln, NE 68509-4600
Ph: 402-471-9792
Fax: 402-471-2318
Internet: www.dol.state.ne.us/

NEVADA
Business and Industry
555 E. Washington Avenue
Suite 4100
Las Vegas, NV 89101-1050
Ph: 702-486-2650
Fax: 702-486-2660
Internet: www.nv.gov

NEW HAMPSHIRE
Department of Labor
95 Pleasant Street
Concord, NH 03301

Ph: 603-271-3171
Fax: 603-271-6852
Internet: www.state.nh.us/dol

NEW JERSEY
New Jersey Department of Labor
John Fitch Plaza
13th Floor, Suite D
P.O. Box CN 110
Trenton, NJ 08625-0110
Ph: 609-292-2323
Fax: 609-633-9271
Internet: www.state.nj.us/labor

NEW MEXICO
Department of Labor
P.O. Box 1928
401 Broadway, N.E.
Albuquerque, NM 87103-1928
Ph: 505-841-8409
Fax: 505-841-8491
Internet: www3.state.nm.us/dol

NEW YORK
Department of Labor
State Campus, Building 12, Room 500
Albany, NY 12240-0003
Ph: 518-457-2741
Fax: 518-457-6908

or

345 Hudson Street
New York, NY 10014-0675
Ph: 212-352-6000
Internet: www.labor.state.ny.us

NORTH CAROLINA
Department of Labor
4 West Edenton Street
Raleigh, NC 27601-1092

Ph: 919-733-0360
Fax: 919-733-6197
Internet: www.dol.state.nc.us

NORTH DAKOTA
Commissioner
Department of Labor
State Capitol Building
600 East Boulevard, Dept. 406
Bismarck, ND 58505-0340
Ph: 701-328-2660
Fax: 701-328-2031
Internet: www.state.nd.us/labor

OHIO
Department of Commerce
77 South High St., 23rd Floor
Columbus, OH 43266
Ph: 614-644-7053
Fax: 614-466-5650

Division of Labor and Worker Safety
50 West Broad St., 28th Floor
Columbus, OH 43216
Ph: 614-644-2239
Fax: 614-728-8639-5650
Internet: http://www.state.oh.us/ohio/agency.htm

OKLAHOMA
Department of Labor
4001 N. Lincoln Blvd.
Oklahoma City, OK 73105-5212
Ph: 405-528-1500, ext. 200
Fax: 405-528-5751
Internet: www.state.ok.us/~okdol

OREGON
Bureau of Labor and Industries
800 NE Oregon Street #32
Portland, OR 97232

Ph: 503-731-4070
Fax: 503-731-4103
Internet: www.boli.state.or.us

PENNSYLVANIA
Department of Labor and Industry
1700 Labor and Industry Building
7th and Forster Streets
Harrisburg, PA 17120
Ph: 717-787-3756
Fax: 717-787-8826
Internet: www.dli.state.pa.us

PUERTO RICO
Department of Labor and Human Resources
Edificio Prudencio Rivera Martinez
505 Munoz Rivera Avenue
G.P.O. Box 3088
Hato Rey, PR 00918
Ph: 787-754-2119 or 2120
Fax: 787-753-9550

RHODE ISLAND
Department of Labor and Training
1511 Pontiac Avenue
Cranston, RI 02920
Ph: 401-462-8870
Fax: 401-462-8872
Internet: www.det.state.ri.us

SOUTH CAROLINA
Department of Labor, Licensing
and Regulations
Synergy Center—King St. Building
110 Center View Drive
P.O. Box 11329
Columbia, SC 29211-1329
Ph: 803-896-4300
Fax: 803-896-4393
Internet: www.llr.state.sc.us

SOUTH DAKOTA
Department of Labor
700 Governors Drive
Pierre, SD 57501-2291
Ph: 605-773-3101
Fax: 605-773-4211
Internet: www.state.sd.us/dol/dol.htm

TENNESSEE
Department of Labor
Andrew Johnson Tower
710 James Robertson Parkway, 8th Floor
Nashville, TN 37243-0655
Ph: 615-741-6642
Fax: 615-741-5078
Internet: www.state.tn.us

TEXAS
Texas Workforce Commission
101 East 15th Street
Austin, TX 78778
Ph: 512-463-2829
Fax: 512-475-2152
Internet: www.twc.state.tx.us

UTAH
Utah Labor Commission
P.O. Box 146600
Salt Lake City, UT 84111-2316
Ph: 801-530-6880
Fax: 801-530-6390
Internet: www.labor.state.ut.us

VERMONT
Department of Labor and Industry
National Life Building
Drawer #20
Montpelier, VT 05620-3401
Ph: 802-828-2288
Fax: 802-828-0408
Internet: www.state.vt.us/labind

VIRGIN ISLANDS
Department of Labor
2303 Church St., Christiansted
St. Croix, U.S. VI 00820-4612
Ph: 340-773-1994, ext. 230
Fax: 340-773-0094
Internet: www.vidol.org

VIRGINIA
Department of Labor and Industry
Powers-Taylor Building
13 S. 13th Street
Richmond, VA 23219
Ph: 804-786-2377
Fax: 804-371-6524
Internet: www.dli.state.va.us

WASHINGTON
Department of Labor and Industries
P.O. Box 44001
Olympia, WA 98504-4001
Ph: 360-902-4203
Fax: 360-902-4202
Internet: www.lni.wa.gov

WEST VIRGINIA
Division of Labor
Bureau of Commerce
State Capitol Complex
Building #6, Room B 749
Charleston, WV 25305
Ph: 304-558-7890
Fax: 304-558-3797
Internet: www.state.wv.us/labor

WISCONSIN
Department of Workforce Development
P.O. Box 7946
Madison, WI 53707-7946
Ph: 608-266-7552
Fax: 608-266-1784
Internet: www.dwd.state.wi.us

WYOMING
Department of Employment
Herschler Building, 2-East
122 W. 25th Street
Cheyenne, WY 82002
Ph: 307-777-7672
Fax: 307-777-5805

Labor Standards
Department of Employment
U.S. West Building, Room 259C
6101 Yellowstone Road
Cheyenne, WY 82002
Ph: 307-777-7261
Fax: 307-777-5633
Internet: http://wydoe.state.wy.us/

Annotated Bibliography

Categories

General Costume History

Ashdown, Mrs. Charles H. *British Costume from Earliest Times to 1820: With 468 Illustrations.* New York: Dover Publications, Inc., 2002. Paperbound reprint.

Ashelford, Jane. *The Art of Dress: Clothes and Society 1500–1914.* New York: Laura Ashley/National Trust. Distributed by Harry N. Abrams, Inc., 1996. Beautiful color illustrations include extant clothing, paintings, engravings, and photographs.

Bailey, Adrian. *The Passion for Fashion: Three Centuries of Changing Styles.* Limpsfield, Surrey, England: Dragon's World, 1988. Monochrome and color photographs and illustrations of men's and women's fashions, including some extant garments, hats, and accessories.

Barton, Lucy. *Historic Costume for the Stage.* Boston: Walter H. Baker Company, 1935. New material added, 1961 in renewal, 1963. Illustrated with line drawings. Useful for research information.

Barwick, Sandra. *A Century of Style.* London, Boston, and Sydney: George Allen & Unwin, 1984. Illustrated with 80 black-and-white photographs of women in England from the 1860s to the 1980s who set their own individual styles, including princesses, fashion designers, and actresses.

Batterberry, Michael, and Ariane Batterberry. *Mirror, Mirror: A Social History of Fashion.* New York: Holt, Rinehart and Winston, 1977. Monochrome and color illustrations and photographs from primary sources. Antiquity to 1970s.

van den Beukel, Dorine. *A Pictorial History of Costume.* A Pepin Press Design Book. New York: Costume and Fashion Press. 1998. An Imprint of Quite Specific Media Group Ltd. Paperbound reprint. 500 color plates illustrating costume from antiquity to nineteenth century. Includes ethnic, religious, military, and civilian costume from all over the world at various periods throughout history.

Black, J. Anderson, and Madge Garland. *A History of Fashion.* New York: William Morrow and Company, Inc., 1975. Monochrome and color illustrations from primary sources. Antiquity to 1970s.

von Boehn, Max. *Modes and Manners.* 4 vols. in 2. Joan Joshua, trans. New York: Benjamin Blom, Inc., 1971. Reprint of 1932 edition. Covers ancient world to eighteenth century.

Boucher, François. *20,000 Years of Fashion: The History of Costume and Personal Adornment.* New York: Harry N. Abrams, Inc. Monochrome and color illustrations from primary sources. One of the best general surveys available.

Bradfield, Nancy. *Historic Costumes of England 1066–1968.* New York: Costume and Fashion Press, an Imprint of Quite Specific Media Group Ltd. Paperbound reprint. Line illustrations with brief explanatory text.

Bradley, Carolyn G. *Western World Costume: An Outline History.* New York: Dover Publications, Inc., 2002. Paperbound reprint of 1954 edition. Prehistory to mid-twentieth century. Line illustrations are not great but each chapter lists artists and books for costume reference as well as a glossary.

Braun and Schneider. *Historic Costume in Pictures.* New York: Dover Publications, Inc., 1975. Reprint of a 1907 German publication. 125 monochrome plates. Countries of the world from ancient times to late nineteenth century.

Broby-Johansen, R. *Body and Clothes: An Illustrated History of Costume.* New York: Reinhold Book Corp., 1968. Translated from Danish. Line drawings, monochrome and some color illustrations from primary sources. Includes chapters on primitive peoples, the Arab haik and the Indian sari.

Contini, Mila. *Fashion From Ancient Egypt to the Present Day.* New York: The Odyssey Press, 1965. Monochrome and color illustrations from primary sources.

Ribeiro, Aileen, and Valerie Cumming. *The Visual History of Costume: Seven Centuries of Costume*

History in One Volume. New York: Costume and Fashion Press. An Imprint of Quite Specific Media Group Ltd. Paperbound. Comprehensive history from fourteenth to twentieth centuries. Monochrome and color illustrations from primary sources.

Davenport, Millia. *The Book of Costume.* New York: Crown Publishers, Inc., 1948. 2 volumes. Monochrome illustrations from primary sources. Ancient times to 1860s. Invaluable information on American and European clothing, accessories, armor, and ecclesiastical vestments.

Dorner, Jane. *Fashion: The Changing Shape of Fashion Through the Years.* London: Octopus Books, 1974. Monochrome and color illustrations from primary sources.

Dunlevy, Mairead. *Dress in Ireland.* London: B. T. Batsford, Ltd., 1989. Comprehensive scholarly survey, Bronze Age to twentieth century. Illustrations from primary sources.

Earnshaw, Pat. *Lace in Fashion: From the Sixteenth to the Twentieth Centuries.* New York: Drama Book Publishers, 1985. 200 monochrome illustrations, 4 color plates.

Ewing, Elizabeth. *Fur in Dress.* London: B. T. Batsford Ltd., 1981. Monochrome and some color illustrations from primary sources. Early times to 1970s.

Fox, Celina. *Londoners.* New York: Thames and Hudson, 1987. All walks of life, seventeenth to early twentieth century. Valuable source for genre costume.

Ginsburg, Madeleine. *An Introduction to Fashion Illustration.* London: Victoria and Albert Museum/Owings Mills, MD: Stemmer House Publishers, Inc., 1980. Fashion illustrations from sixteenth to twentieth century.

Hall, Lee. *Common Threads: A Parade of American Clothing.* Boston, Toronto, and London: A Bullfinch Press Book, Little, Brown and Company, 1992. Black-and-white photographs and illustrations ranging from Native Americans and seventeenth-century settlers to Nancy Reagan and Elvis.

Hansen, Henny Harald. *Costume Cavalcade: 689 Examples of Historic Costume in Color.* London: Eyre Methuen, Ltd., 1972. 2nd edition. Originally published in Copenhagen, 1954. The color illustrations, redrawn from primary sources, are useful for quick reference.

Klepper, Erhard. *Costume Through the Ages.* London: Thames and Hudson, 1963. Line drawings taken from primary sources. Ancient times to 1930.

———. *Costume Through the Ages: Over 1400 illustrations.* New York: Dover Publications, Inc. Paperbound reprint of the above.

Laver, James. *Costume and Fashion: A Concise History.* New York: Thames and Hudson, 1985. Revised edition.

Lechevallier-Chevignard, Edmond. *European Costumes of the Sixteenth Through Eighteenth Centuries in Full Color.* New York: Dover Publications, Inc., 1995. Paperbound. 150 illustrations redrawn from primary sources.

Levi-Pisetzky, Rosita. *Storia del Costume in Italia.* 5 vols. Milan: Istituto Editoriale Italiano, 1964. Early times to nineteenth century. Primary source illustrations.

Levey, Santina M. *Lace: A History.* New York: Costume and Fashion Press. An Imprint of Quite Specific Media Group Ltd., 2002. 500 black-and-white photographs.

Mackrell, Alice. *An Illustrated History of Fashion: 500 Years of Fashion Illustration.* New York: Costume and Fashion Press. An Imprint of Quite Specific Media Group Ltd. London: B. T. Batsford. Monochrome and color illustrations.

deMarly, Diana. *The History of Haute Couture 1850–1950.* New York: Holmes and Meier Publishers, Inc., 1980. An interesting selection of monochrome and some color illustrations.

McClellan, Elizabeth. *Historic Dress in America 1607–1870.* New York: Arno Press, 1977. 2

vols. in 1. Monochrome illustrations, photographs, and line drawings.

Municipal Museum of The Hague. Text by Ietse Meij. *Haute Couture & Pret-a-Porter: Mode 1750–2000*. A choice from the costume collection of the Municipal Museum of The Hague. The Hague: Waanders Publishers, Zwolle Gemeentemuseum Den Haag, 1998. Paperbound. Monochrome and color clothing and fashion illustrations.

Payne, Blanche. *History of Costume: From the Ancient Egyptians to the Twentieth Century.* New York: Harper and Row, 1965. Line drawings, monochrome illustrations from primary sources, and some scale patterns.

Poli, Doretta Davanzo. *Maternity Fashion.* The Twentieth Century Histories of Fashion Series. Modena, Italy: Zanfi Editori, 1988. Distributed in the U.S. by Costume and Fashion Press. An Imprint of Quite Specific Media Group Ltd. Monochrome and color line drawings, photographs, fashion illustrations, etc. fourteenth century to 1980s.

Racinet, Albert. *The Historical Encyclopedia of Costumes.* London: Studio Editions, 1988. New York: Checkmark/Facts on File, 1988. Originally published in the nineteenth century in 6 volumes as *Le Costume Historique.* Byzantium to 1880s.

Racinet, Auguste. *Racinet's Full-Color Pictorial History of Western Costume.* New York: Dover Publications, Inc., 1987. Paperbound reprint from the nineteenth century. Color plates redrawn from primary sources. Middle Ages to 1800, includes some armor, military uniforms, and ecclesiastical clothing.

Robinson, Julian. *The Fine Art of Fashion: An Illustrated History.* New York/London: Bartley & Jensen Publishers, 1986. Monochrome and color illustrations, line drawings, and photographs. Seventeenth to twentieth century.

Rothstein, Natalie, ed. *Four Hundred Years of Fashion.* London: Victoria and Albert Museum in association with William Collins, 1984. Revised edition, 1992. Paperbound. Monochrome and color photographs of men's and women's costumes and accessories from the museum's collection. Sixteenth to twentieth century.

Squire, Geoffrey. *Dress and Society 1560–1970.* New York: A Studio Book. Viking Press, 1974. Monochrome and some color illustrations from primary sources.

Stibbert, Frederick. *European Civil and Military Clothing: From the First to the Eighteenth Century.* New York: Dover Publications, Inc., 2001. Paperbound reprint. 217 plates of wonderful line engravings with captions but no text.

Tortora, Phyllis, and Keith Eubank. *A Survey of Historic Costume.* New York: Fairchild Publications, 1998. 3rd edition. Comprehensive, well-organized text—constantly updated. Monochrome illustrations and color photographs of primary sources.

Period Catalogues, Chronological Order

Bryk, Nancy Villa, ed. *American Dress Pattern Catalogs 1873–1909.* Four complete reprints. New York: Dover Publications, Inc., 1988.

The Butterick Publishing Company. *Metropolitan Fashions of the 1880s from the 1885 Butterick Catalog.* New York: Dover Publications, Inc., 1997. Women's and children's clothing.

Bloomingdale Brothers. *Bloomingdale's Illustrated 1886 Catalogue: Fashions, Dry Goods and Housewares.* New York: Dover Publications, Inc., 1988.

Adburgham, Alison, intr. *Victorian Shopping: Harrod's Catalogue 1895.* Reprint. Newton Abbot, Devon, England: David and Charles, 1972.

Emmet, Boris, Intr. *Montgomery Ward and Company's Catalogue, Spring and Summer 1895.* Paperbound. Reprint. New York: Dover Publications, Inc., 1969.

The Butterick Publishing Company. *Butterick's 1892 Metropolitan Fashions.* New York: Dover Publications, Inc., 1994. Paperbound. Reprint from an original catalog of 1892–93, with over 1,000 illustrations of women's and children's garments for Butterick patterns.

Israel, Fred L., ed. 1897 *Sears Roebuck Catalogue.* Paperbound reprint. New York: Chelsea House Publishers, 1968.

Langbridge, R. H., comp. *Edwardian Shopping: A Selection from the Army and Navy Stores Catalogues 1898–1913.* North Pomfret, VT: David and Charles, 1975.

Amory, Cleveland, intr. *The 1902 Edition of the Sears, Roebuck Catalogue.* Paperbound reprint. New York: Bounty Books, a Division of Crown Publishers, Inc., 1969.

Elite Styles Company. *Elite Fashions Catalog, 1904.* New York: Dover Publications, Inc., 1996. Paperbound. Line illustrations of women's and children's fashions.

Sears, Roebuck and Co. *The 1906 Edition of the Sears, Roebuck Catalogue.* Paperbound reprint. Secaucus, NJ: Castle Books, a Division of Book Sales, Inc., n.d.

Schroeder, Joseph J., Jr., ed. *Sears, Roebuck & Co. 1908.* Paperbound reprint. Northfield, IL: Digest Books, Inc., 1971.

National Cloak & Suit Co. *Women's Fashions of the Early 1900s: An Unabridged Republication of New York Fashions, 1909.* New York: Dover Publications, Inc., 1992. Paperbound.

Olian, JoAnne, ed. *Everyday Fashions 1909–1920: As Pictured in Sears Catalogs.* New York: Dover Publications, Inc., 1995. Paperbound. Monochrome illustrations.

The Home Pattern Company. *The Home Pattern Company 1914 Fashions Catalog.* New York: Dover Publications, Inc., 1995. Paperbound. Over 625 black-and-white illustrations. Republication of Home Book of Fashions, Vol. 1, No. 2, Winter 1914, published by the Home Pattern Company, New York.

B. Altman & Co. *Altman's Spring and Summer Fashions Catalog, 1915.* New York: Dover Publications, Inc., 1995. Paperbound. Monochrome illustrations.

Gimbel Brothers. *Gimbel's Illustrated 1915 Fashion Catalog.* New York: Dover Publications, Inc., 1994. Paperbound. Over 2,000 black-and-white illustrations.

Livoni, Phillip, ed. *Russell's Standard Fashions 1915–1919.* New York: Dover Publications, Inc., 1996. Paperbound. Over 1,000 black-and-white illustrations of women's and children's clothing.

Perry, Dame & Co. *Women's and Children's Fashions of 1917: The Complete Perry, Dame & Co. Catalog.* New York: Dover Publications Inc., 1992. Paperbound. Monochrome illustrations.

Philipsborn's. *Fashions of the Early Twenties: The 1921 Philipsborn's Catalog.* New York: Dover Publications, Inc., 1996. Paperbound. Over 1,600 black-and-white illustrations. Republication of the spring and summer catalog published by Philipsborn's, Chicago, IL, 1921.

B. Altman & Co. *1920s Fashions from B. Altman & Company.* New York: Dover Publications, Inc., 1999. Paperbound with monochrome illustrations.

Blum, Stella, ed. *Everyday Fashions of the Twenties: As Pictured in Sears and Other Catalogs.* New York: Dover Publications, Inc., 1981. Paperbound with monochrome illustrations.

Franklin Simon & Co. *Franklin Simon Fashion Catalog for 1923.* New York: Dover Publications, Inc., 1993. Paperbound. Fashion illustrations and photographs.

Mirken, Alan, ed. *The 1927 Edition of the Sears, Roebuck Catalogue: The Roaring Twenties.* Paperbound reprint. New York: Bounty Books, a Division of Crown Publishers, Inc., 1970.

Sears Roebuck. *Sears, Roebuck Catalogues of the 1930s.* Paperbound. New York: Nostalgia Press Inc., 1978. Selections from the decade.

Blum, Stella. *Everyday Fashions of the Thirties: As Pictured in Sears Catalogs.* New York: Dover Publications, Inc., 1986. Paperbound. Monochrome illustrations and photographs.

Olian, JoAnne, ed. *Everyday Fashions of the Forties: As Pictured in Sears Catalogs.* New York: Dover Publications, Inc., 1992. Paperbound. Monochrome illustrations and photographs.

Gottwald, Laura, and Janusz Gottwald, eds. *Frederick's of Hollywood 1947–1973: 26 Years of Mail Order Seduction.* New York, NY: Castle/Drake Publishers, Inc., 1973. A collection of monochrome illustrations from the catalogs. No text.

Olian, JoAnne, ed. *Everyday Fashions of the Sixties: As Pictured in Sears Catalogs.* New York: Dover Publications, Inc., 1999. Paperbound. Hundreds of black-and-white illustrations from the 1960s Sears catalogs.

Shih, Joy. *Fashionable Clothing from the Sears Catalogs: Late 1950s.* Atglen, PA: Schiffer Publishing Ltd., 1997. Paperbound. Illustrated throughout with monochrome and color illustrations of men's, women's, and children's clothing and accessories from Sears catalogs.

———. *Fashionable Clothing from the Sears Catalogs: Mid 1960s: With Current Values.* Atglen, PA: Schiffer Publishing Ltd., 1997. Paperbound. Color illustrations of men's, women's, and children's clothing and accessories from Sears catalogs.

Smith, Desire. *Fashionable Clothing from the Sears Catalogs: Late 1960s: With Price Guide.* Atglen, PA: Schiffer Publishing Ltd., 1998. Paperbound. Color illustrations of men's and women's clothing and accessories from Sears catalogs.

———. *Fashionable Clothing from the Sears Catalogs: Early 1970s: With Price Guide.* Atglen, PA: Schiffer Publishing Ltd., 1998. Paperbound. Color illustrations of men's and women's clothing and accessories from Sears catalogs.

Antiquity

Houston, Mary G. *Ancient Egyptian, Mesopotamian & Persian Costume and Decoration.* London: Adam and Charles Black, 1954. 2nd edition. Line drawings. Includes draping illustrations and scale diagrams of cut.

———. *Ancient Greek, Roman and Byzantine Costume and Decoration.* London: Adam and Charles Black, 1947. 2nd edition. Line drawings and color plates. Diagrams show how garments were cut and draped, including several styles of the toga. Covers 2,100 B.C. to twelfth century.

Hope, Thomas. *Costumes of the Greeks and Romans.* New York: Dover Publications, Inc., 1962. Reprint from 1812. Engravings of costumes, accessories, furniture, etc.

Laver, James, and Erhardt Klepper. *Costumes in Antiquity.* London: Thames and Hudson, 1964. Monochrome plates redrawn from primary sources. Covers 3,000 B.C. to sixth century A.D.

Norris, Herbert. *Ancient European Costume and Fashion.* New York: Dover Publications, Inc. 2000. Paperbound reprint. Prehistory to 1066, Black-and-white and color illustrations.

Middle Ages and Renaissance

Anderson, Ruth Matilda. *Hispanic Costume 1480–1530.* New York: The Hispanic Society of America, 1979. Comprehensive, well-documented work on the costume of the Iberian peninsula, with monochrome and color illustrations.

Ashelford, Jane. *Dress in the Age of Elizabeth I.* London: B. T. Batsford Ltd., 1988. New York: Drama Book Publishers, 1988. Excellent monochrome illustrations from primary sources throughout the text with color insert.

———. *A Visual History of Costume: The Sixteenth Century.* London: B. T. Batsford Ltd., 1983.

New York: Drama Book Publishers, 1983. Paperbound edition published 1993. Monochrome and some color illustrations from primary sources.

Bentivegna, Ferruccia Cappi, ed. *Abbligiamento e Costume nella Pittura Italiana.* 2 vols. Vol. 1, Rinascimento (fifteenth and sixteenth century). Rome: Carlo Bestetti, Edizioni d'Arte, 1962–64. Monochrome and some color illustrations from Italian paintings, all showing costume.

Birbari, Elizabeth. *Dress in Italian Painting 1460–1500.* London: John Murray, 1975. Monochrome illustrations from primary sources. Line drawings of reconstructed patterns to scale.

Cunnington, C. Willett, and Phyllis Cunnington. *Handbook of English Mediaeval Costume.* Boston: Plays, Inc., 1969. Revised edition. Line illustrations redrawn from contemporary sources. Men, women, and children. Ninth to fifteenth century.

———. *Handbook of English Costume in the Sixteenth Century.* Boston: Plays, Inc., 1970. Revised edition. Line illustrations redrawn from contemporary sources. Men, women, and children.

Herald, Jacqueline. *Renaissance Dress in Italy, 1400–1500.* History of Dress Series. Atlantic Highlands, NJ: Humanities Press, 1981. Monochrome and color illustrations from contemporary sources.

Houston, Mary G. *Medieval Costume in England and France: The 13th, 14th and 15th Centuries.* London: Adam & Charles Black, 1939. Reprinted 1965. Line illustrations, monochrome, and some color illustrations. Covers armor, ornament, religious and academic dress and includes diagrams of cut.

———. *Medieval Costume in England and France: The 13th, 14th and 15th Centuries.* New York: Dover Publications, Inc. Paperbound reprint of the above.

Lawner, Lynne. *Lives of the Courtesans: Portraits of the Renaissance.* New York: Rizzoli International Publications, 1987. Monochrome and color illustrations from primary sources covering Italy, France, Germany, and the Netherlands.

Morse, H. K. *Elizabethan Pageantry: A Pictorial Survey of Costume and its Commentators from c. 1560–1620.* London: The Art Book Co., 1980. Reprint of 1930 edition. Monochrome plates and useful contemporary descriptions.

Newton, Stella Mary. *Fashion in the Age of the Black Prince: A Study of the Years 1340–1363.* Totowa, NJ: Rowman and Littlefield, 1980. Monochrome illustrations from primary sources. Scholarly.

Norris, Herbert. *Medieval Costume and Fashion.* New York: Dover Publications, Inc. 1999. Paperbound reprint.

———. *Tudor Costume and Fashion.* New York: Dover Publications, Inc. 1997. Paperbound reprint. 1485–1603. Black-and-white and color illustrations.

Scott, Margaret. *A Visual History of Costume: The Fourteenth and Fifteenth Centuries.* London: B. T. Batsford Ltd., 1986. New York: Drama Book Publishers, 1986. Monochrome and some color illustrations from primary sources.

———. *Late Gothic Europe, 1450–1500.* History of Dress Series. Atlantic Highlands, NJ: Humanities Press, 1980. Comprehensive text, well illustrated with monochrome and color illustrations from primary sources.

Vecellio, Cesare. *Vecellio's Renaissance Costume Book: All 500 Woodcut Illustrations from the Famous Sixteenth-Century Compendium of World Costume.* New York: Dover Publications, Inc., 1977. Paperbound reprint, originally published in 1598.

Seventeenth and Eighteenth Centuries

Baumgarten, Linda. *Eighteenth Century Clothing at Williamsburg.* Williamsburg, VA: The Colonial Williamsburg Foundation, 1986. Beautifully illustrated with monochrome and color photographs of clothing, accessories, prints, and paintings.

Baumgarten, Linda, and John Watson with Florin Carr. *Costume Close-up: Clothing Construction and Pattern 1750–1790.* Williamsburg, VA: The Colonial Williamsburg Foundation in Association with Fashion Press. An Imprint of Quite Specific Media Group Ltd. New York and Hollywood, 1999. Paperbound. Patterns for eighteenth-century clothing taken from extant garments. Beautifully illustrated with monochrome and color photographs.

Bentivegna, Ferruccia Cappi, ed. *Abbligiamento e Costume nella Pittura Italiana.* 2 vols. Vol. 2, Barocco-Impero (seventeenth and eighteenth century). Rome: Carlo Bestetti, Edizioni d'Arte, 1962–64. Monochrome and some color illustrations from Italian paintings, all show costume.

Bernier, Olivier. *The Eighteenth-Century Woman.* Garden City, NY: Doubleday and Company, Inc. The Metropolitan Museum of Art, 1981. Published in conjunction with an exhibit at the museum. Monochrome and color illustrations and photographs from primary sources.

Blum, Stella, ed. *Eighteenth-Century French Fashion Plates in Full Color: 64 Engravings from "Galeries des Modes," 1778–1787.* New York: Dover Publications, Inc., 1982. Paperbound.

Buck, Ann. *Dress in 18th Century England.* New York: Holmes and Meier Publishers, Inc., 1979. Monochrome and some color illustrations from contemporary sources.

Cumming, Valerie. *A Visual History of Costume: The Seventeenth Century.* New York: Drama Book Publishers, 1985. Monochrome and some color illustrations.

Burnston, Sharon Ann. *Fitting & Proper: 18th Century Clothing from the Collection of the Chester County Historical Society.* Texarkana, TX: Scurlock Publishing Co., Inc., 1998. Monochrome photographs and patterns of extant clothing and accessories for men, women, and children from the museum in Pennsylvania. An excellent source for plain and simple everyday clothing as well as some fancier garments.

Cunnington, C. Willett, and Phyllis Cunnington. *Handbook of English Costume in the Seventeenth Century.* Boston: Plays, Inc., 1973. Revised edition. Line illustrations redrawn from contemporary sources. Men, women, and children. Many contemporary quotations. Good reference work.

———. *Handbook of English Costume in the Eighteenth Century.* Boston: Plays, Inc., 1972. Revised edition. Line illustrations redrawn from contemporary sources. Men and women's clothing and accessories. Many contemporary quotations. An excellent reference work.

Daniel, Howard, ed. *Callot's Etchings.* New York: Dover Publications, Inc., 1974. 338 prints of seventeenth-century French life.

Earle, Alice Morse. *Two Centuries of Costume in America 1620–1820.* 2 vols. Rutland, VT: Charles E. Tuttle Company, 1971. Reprint from 1903 edition. Monochrome illustrations from primary sources.

The Gallery of English Costume. Picture Book number 2: *Women's Costume: The Eighteenth Century.* Manchester, England: Art Galleries Committee of the Corporation of Manchester, 1954. Monochrome photographs of clothing, underwear, and accessories from the Gallery of English Costume, Platt Hall.

Gehret, Ellen J. *Rural Pennsylvania Clothing: Being a Study of the Wearing Apparel of the German and English Inhabitants in the Late Eighteenth and Early Nineteenth Century.* York, PA: George R. D. Shumway, 1973. Excellent source of information.

Hart, Avril, and Susan North. *Fashion in Detail from the 17th and 18th Centuries.* New York, NY: Rizzoli International Publications Inc., 1998. London, England: V & A Publications, 1998. Beautiful detailed color photographs and line drawings of men's and women's extant garments and accessories in the Victoria and Albert Museum collection.

The Kyoto Costume Institute. *Revolution in Fashion: European Clothing 1715–1815.* New York: Abbeville Press, 1989. Beautiful color photographs of men's and women's extant costumes and accessories. Published in conjunction with a joint exhibition held at the Fashion Institute of Technology in New York and the Kyoto Costume Institute, Japan.

Laver, James, intr. *17th and 18th Century Costume.* London: His Majesty's Stationery Office, 1951. Paperbound. Monochrome fashion illustrations from the Victoria and Albert Museum, London.

le Bourhis, Katell. *The Age of Napoleon: Costume from Revolution to Empire 1789–1815.* New York: The Metropolitan Museum of Art/Harry N. Abrams, Inc., 1989. Color and monochrome illustrations and photographs. Published in conjunction with an exhibition at the museum.

Maeder, Edward, ed. *An Elegant Art: Fashion and Fantasy in the Eighteenth Century.* New York: Harry N. Abrams, Inc., in association with the Los Angeles County Museum of Art, 1983. Published in conjunction with an exhibit at the museum. Beautiful monochrome and color illustrations and photographs of extant costumes, textiles, and accessories.

de Marly, Diana. *Costume and Civilization: Louis XIV & Versailles.* London: B. T. Batsford, Ltd., 1987. Monochrome and some color illustrations.

McClellan, Elisabeth. *Historic Dress in America 1607–1870.* New York: Arno Press, 1977. Reissue. 2 vols. in 1. Originally published 1904–1910, reissued 1937 and 1968 as *History of American Costume.* Monochrome illustrations and line drawings.

Ribeiro, Aileen. *The Art of Dress: Fashion in England and France 1750–1820.* London and New Haven, CT: Yale University Press, 1995. An in-depth study of fashion through the

artists of the period, with beautiful color and monochrome illustrations.

———. *Dress in Eighteenth Century Europe 1715–1789.* London: B. T. Batsford Ltd., 1984. Monochrome and some color illustrations from primary sources.

———. *Fashion in the French Revolution.* London: B. T. Batsford, Ltd., 1988. Monochrome and some color illustrations from primary sources, 1789–1799.

———. *A Visual History of Costume: The Eighteenth Century.* New York: Drama Book Publishers, 1983. Monochrome and some color illustrations from primary sources.

Shep, R. L. *Federalist & Regency Costume: 1790–1819.* Mendocino, CA: R. L. Shep, 1998. Reprint from contemporary sources on tailoring, fashion, embroidery, etc. Monochrome illustrations of tailoring patterns; embroidery; men's, women's, and children's fashions.

Shesgreen, Sean, ed. *Engravings by Hogarth.* New York: Dover Publications, Inc., 1973. 101 plates with commentary. Wonderful details of eighteenth-century everyday clothing.

Tozer, Jane, and Sarah Levitt. *Fabric of Society: A Century of People and their Clothes 1770–1870.* Carno, Powys, Wales: Laura Ashley Ltd., 1983. Monochrome and color photographs and illustrations of men's and women's clothing and accessories.

Warwick, Edward, Henry C. Pitz, and Alexander Wyckoff. *Early American Dress: The Colonial and Revolutionary Periods.* New York: Bonanza Books, 1965. Monochrome plates and line drawings.

Nineteenth Century

Alland, Alexander, Sr. *Heinrich Tonnies: Cartes-de-Visite. Photographer Extraordinaire.* New York: Camera/Graphic Press Ltd., 1978. Paperbound. Monochrome photographs throughout—no captions or page numbers. German photographer's pictures of German and Danish people from all walks of life c. 1860s to 1890s.

Beam, Phillip. *Winslow Homer's Magazine Engravings.* New York: Harper and Row, Publishers, 1979. Covers 1857–1875. Useful for costume.

Bentley, Nicholas. *The Victorian Scene: A Picture Book of the Period 1837–1901.* New York: Spring Books, 1968. Monochrome and color illustrations of occupational and working clothes as well as fashionable dress.

van den Beukel, Dorine, ed. *Fashion Design 1850–1895.* New York: Design Press, 1997. An Imprint of Quite Specific Media Group Ltd. Paperbound. Illustrations from contemporary sources of the era. Excellent source, *but* nothing is dated and illustrations are grouped together by subject—e.g., day skirts, sleeves, outdoor wear, dresses, fans, purses, etc.

Blum, Stella, ed. *Fashions and Costumes from Godey's Lady's Book: Including 8 Plates in Full Color.* New York: Dover Publications, Inc. 1985. Paperbound. 1837–1869.

———. *Ackermann's Costume Plates: Women's Fashions in England, 1818–1828.* New York: Dover Publications, Inc., 1978. Paperbound. Monochrome and some color illustrations.

———. *Victorian Fashions & Costumes from Harper's Bazaar: 1867–1898.* New York: Dover Publications, Inc., 1974. Paperbound. Original fashion plates and engravings includes underwear, hairstyles, accessories, and children's fashions.

———. *Paris Fashions of the 1890s: A Picture Source Book with 350 Designs, Including 24 in Full Color.* New York: Dover Publications, Inc., 1984. Paperbound. Prints of French fashions that originally appeared in *The Young Ladies Journal.* Brief descriptions, no text.

von Boehn, Max, and Max Fischel. *Modes and Manners of the Nineteenth Century as Represented in the Pictures and Engravings of the Time.*

New York: Benjamin Blom, Inc., 1970. Reprint of 1927 edition. 4 vols. in 2. Covers 1790–1914. Illustrations from primary sources.

Bott, Alan. *Our Fathers (1870–1900). Manners and Customs of the Ancient Victorians: A Survey in Pictures and Text of Their History, Morals, Wars, Sports, Inventions & Politics.* New York: Benjamin Blom, Inc., 1972. Reprint of 1931 edition. Monochrome illustrations and engravings from primary sources.

Bott, Alan, and Irene Clephane. *Our Mothers: A Cavalcade in Pictures, Quotation and Description of Late Victorian Women 1870–1900.* Benjamin Blom, 1969. Reprint of 1932 edition. Monochrome illustrations and engravings from primary sources, many showing clothing.

Buck, Ann. *Victorian Costume and Costume Accessories.* Carlton, Bedford, England: Ruth Bean, 1984. 2nd revised edition of original 1961 publication. Paperbound edition distributed in the U.S. by Costume and Fashion Press. An Imprint of Quite Specific Media Group Ltd. Monochrome photographs and line illustrations.

Butterick Publishing Co. *Butterick's 1892 Metropolitan Fashions.* New York: Dover Publications, Inc., 1994. Paperbound. Black-and-white illustrations of Butterick patterns.

Byrde, Penelope. *Nineteenth Century Fashion.* London: B. T. Batsford, Ltd., 1992. Monochrome illustrations from primary sources throughout with color insert.

Coleman, Elizabeth Ann. *The Opulent Era: Fashions of Worth, Doucet and Pingat.* New York: The Brooklyn Museum in association with Thames and Hudson, 1989. Published in conjunction with an exhibit at the Brooklyn Museum. Beautifully illustrated in monochrome and color.

Cunnington, C. Willett. *English Women's Clothing in the Nineteenth Century.* New York: Dover Publications, Inc., 1990. Reprint of the 1937 edition. Line illustrations from contemporary sources. More extensive coverage of women's clothing and accessories by decade than the *Handbook* below. Monochrome illustrations and line drawings. Excellent reference.

Cunnington, C. Willett, and Phyllis Cunnington. *Handbook of English Costume in the Nineteenth Century.* Boston: Plays, Inc., 1970. Line illustrations redrawn from contemporary sources. Men, women, and children. Clothing and accessories with many contemporary quotations. Excellent reference.

Dalrymple, Priscilla Harris. *American Victorian Costume in Early Photographs.* New York: Dover Publications, Inc., 1991. Paperbound. Over 280 photographs of men, women, and children from the 1840s to the turn of the century.

Daniel, Pete, and Raymond Smock. *A Talent for Detail: The Photographs of Miss Frances Benjamin Johnston 1889–1910.* New York: Harmony Books, 1974. Monochrome photographs.

Earle, Alice Morse. *Two Centuries of Costume in America 1620–1820.* 2 vols. Rutland, VT: Charles E. Tuttle Company, 1971. Reprint from 1903 edition. Monochrome illustrations from primary sources.

Ford, Colin, ed. *An Early Victorian Album: The Photographic Masterpieces (1843–1847) of David Octavius Hill and Robert Adamson.* New York: Alfred A. Knopf, 1976. Monochrome photographs.

Foster, Vanda. *A Visual History of Costume: The Nineteenth Century.* New York: Drama Book Publishers, 1984. Monochrome and some color illustrations from primary sources.

The Gallery of English Costume. Picture Book Number Three: *Women's Costume 1800–1835.* Manchester, England: Art Galleries Committee of the Corporation of Manchester, 1952. Monochrome photographs of clothing, underwear, and accessories from the Gallery of English Costume, Platt Hall.

———. Picture Book Number Four: *Women's Costume 1835–1870.* Manchester, England: Art Galleries Committee of the Corporation of Manchester, 1951. Monochrome photographs of clothing, underwear, and accessories from the Gallery of English Costume, Platt Hall.

———. Picture Book Number Five: *Women's Dress 1870–1900.* Manchester, England: Art Galleries Committee of the Corporation of Manchester, 1953. Monochrome photographs of clothing, underwear, and accessories from the Gallery of English Costume, Platt Hall.

Gelman, Woody. *The Best of Charles Dana Gibson.* New York: Bounty Books, 1969. The famous "Gibson Girl" illustrations, many showing clothing and hairstyles.

Gernsheim, Alison. *Victorian and Edwardian Fashion: A Photographic Survey.* New York: Dover Publications, Inc., 1981. Paperbound. Originally published as *Fashion and Reality (1840–1914).* Monochrome photographs of men, women, and children.

Gibbs-Smith, Charles H. *The Fashionable Lady in the 19th Century.* London: Her Majesty's Stationery Office, 1960. Monochrome fashion illustrations from the Victoria and Albert Museum, London, 1800–1900.

Ginsburg, Madeleine. *Victorian Dress in Photographs.* London: B. T. Batsford Ltd., 1982. New York: Holmes and Meier, Publishers Inc., 1983. Men's, women's, and children's occupational and regional clothing. 1840s–1980s.

Goldthorpe, Caroline. *From Queen to Empress: Victorian Dress 1837–1877.* New York: The Metropolitan Museum of Art, 1988. Distributed by Harry N. Abrams, Inc. Published in conjunction with an exhibit at The Costume Institute of the museum.

Harris, Kristina. *Victorian & Edwardian Fashions for Women 1840–1919.* Atglen, PA: Schiffer Publishing Ltd., 1995. Illustrations, monochrome and color photographs throughout, many showing models wearing extant clothing. Brief text.

Harris, Kristina, ed. *American Victorian Fashions in Vintage Photographs.* New York: Dover Publications, Inc., 2001. Paperbound.

———. *Victorian Fashions in America: 264 Vintage Photographs.* New York: Dover Publications, Inc., 2002. Paperbound. Monochrome photographs of men, women, and children, 1850s–1910.

Jensen, Oliver. *America's Yesterdays: Images of Our Lost Past Discovered in the Photographic Archives of the Library of Congress.* New York: American Heritage Publishing Co., Inc., 1978. Many monochrome photographs.

———. *A College Album or Rah Rah, Yesterday.* New York: American Heritage Publishing Co., Inc., 1974. Monochrome photographs.

Johnson, Judy M., ed. *French Fashion Plates of the Romantic Era in Full Color: 120 Plates from the "Petit Courrier des Dames," 1830–34.* New York: Dover Publications, Inc., 1991. Paperbound.

Kunciov, Robert, ed. *Mr. Godey's Ladies: Being a Mosaic of Fashions and Fancies.* New York: Bonanza Book, 1971. Engravings and color fashion plates from *Godey's Lady's Book* 1830s–1870s.

Kunhardt, Dorothy Meserve, and Philip B. Kundhardt, Jr. *Matthew Brady and His World.* Alexandria, VA: Time-Life Books, 1977. Monochrome photographs 1840s–1870s.

The Kyoto Costume Institute. *Revolution in Fashion: European Clothing 1715–1815.* New York: Abbeville Press, 1989. Beautiful color photographs of men's and women's extant costumes and accessories. Published in conjunction with a joint exhibition held at the Fashion Institute of Technology in New York and the Kyoto Costume Institute, Japan.

———. *The Evolution of Fashion 1835–1895: Clothing That Captured the Imagination of Japan.* Kyoto, Japan: Kyoto Costume Institute, 1980. From an exhibit at the National Museum of Modern Art, Kyoto, Japan. Color and monochrome photographs with English and Japanese captions.

Lambert, Miles. *Fashion in Photographs 1860–1880.* London: B. T. Batsford Ltd., 1991. Black-and-white photographs of men, women, and children from the National Portrait Gallery, London, with explanatory text.

Laver, James, intr. *19th Century Costume.* London: The Ministry of Education, 1947. Paperbound. Monochrome men's and women's fashion illustrations from contemporary sources from the Victoria and Albert Museum, London.

le Bourhis, Katell. *The Age of Napoleon: Costume from Revolution to Empire 1789–1815.* New York: The Metropolitan Museum of Art/Harry N. Abrams, Inc., 1989. Color and monochrome illustrations and photographs. Published in conjunction with an exhibition at the museum.

Levitt, Sara. *Victorians Unbuttoned: Registered Designs for Clothing, Their Makers and Wearers, 1830–1900.* London: George Allen and Unwin, 1986. Monochrome illustrations.

———. *Fashion in Photographs 1880–1900.* London: B. T. Batsford Ltd., 1991. Black-and-white photographs of men, women, and children from the National Portrait Gallery, London, with explanatory text.

Lucie-Smith, Edward, and Celestine Dars. *How the Rich Lived: The Painter as Witness 1870–1914.* New York: Paddington Press, Ltd., 1976. Monochrome and some color illustrations of paintings, all show clothing.

Mankowitz, Wolf. *Dickens of London.* New York: Macmillan Publishing Co., Inc., 1976. Monochrome and color illustrations from contemporary sources. 1830s–1870s.

McClellan, Elisabeth. *Historic Dress in America 1607–1870.* New York: Arno Press, 1977. Reissue. 2 vols. in 1. Originally published 1904–1910, reissued 1937 and 1968 as *History of American Costume.* Monochrome illustrations and line drawings.

The Metropolitan Museum of Art. *The Imperial Style: Fashions of the Hapsburg Era.* New York: Metropolitan Museum of Art/Rizzoli, 1979. Published in conjunction with an exhibit at the museum.

Milbank, Caroline Rennolds. *New York Fashion: The Evolution of American Style.* New York: Harry N. Abrams, Inc., Publishers 1989. Beautifully illustrated with monochrome and color photographs and fashion illustrations. Covers nineteenth century to 1980s, but concentrates mostly on twentieth century.

———. *Couture: The Great Designers.* New York: Stewart, Tabori & Chang, Inc., 1985. Monochrome and color photographs and illustrations. Covers couture designers including Worth, Chanel, Dior, Schiaparelli, Vionnet, Poiret, Armani, Valentino, Hartnell, McCardell, Issey Miyake, and more. 1840s–1980s.

Museum of the City of New York. *The House of Worth: The Gilded Age in New York.* New York: Museum of the City of New York, 1982. From an exhibit at the museum.

Norris, Herbert, and Oswald Curtis. *Nineteenth-Century Costume and Fashion.* New York: Dover Publications, Inc. 1999. Paperbound reprint. Black-and-white and color illustrations.

Olian, JoAnne, ed. *Full-Color Victorian Fashions: 1870–1893.* New York: Dover Publications, Inc. 1999. Paperbound.

de Osma, Guillermo. *Fortuny: The Life and Work of Mariano Fortuny.* New York: Rizzoli International Publications Inc., 1980. First paperbound edition, 1985. 2nd paperbound edition, 1994. Monochrome and some color illustrations. Covers the multifaceted career of Fortuny as artist, stage designer, inventor, textile artist, and couturier.

Quennell, Peter. *The Day Before Yesterday: A Photographic Album of Daily Life in Victorian and Edwardian Britain.* New York: Charles Scribner's Sons, 1978. Monochrome photographs showing people from all walks of life, including tradespeople, laborers, etc. Useful for costume.

Ribeiro, Aileen. *Ingres in Fashion: Representations of Dress and Appearance in Ingres's Images of Women.* New Haven and London: Yale University Press, 1999. Beautifully illustrated analysis of clothing depicted in the artist's work covering more than 50 years. Over 150 monochrome and color illustrations include extant clothing and contemporary fashion illustrations as well as the artist's portraits.

———. *The Art of Dress: Fashion in England and France 1750–1820.* London and New Haven, CT: Yale University Press, 1995. An in-depth study of fashion through the artists of the period, with beautiful color and monochrome illustrations throughout.

Rinhart, Floyd, and Marion Rinhart. *Summertime: Photographs of America at Play 1850–1900.* New York: Clarkson N. Potter, Inc., 1978. Monochrome photographs.

Setnik, Linda. *Victorian Costumes for Ladies 1860–1900.* With price guide. A Schiffer Book for Designers and Collectors. Atglen, PA: Schiffer Publishing Ltd., 2000. Paperbound. Monochrome photographs of the era with explanatory captions and some informative text.

Severa, Joan. *Dressed for the Photographer: Ordinary Americans & Fashion, 1840–1900.* Kent, Ohio, and London, England: The Kent State University Press, 1995. Full of great monochrome photographs with explanatory text. An invaluable source of visual and written information.

Shep, R. L. *Federalist & Regency Costume: 1790–1819.* Mendocino, CA: R. L. Shep, 1998. Reprint from contemporary sources on tailoring, fashion, embroidery, etc. Monochrome illustrations of tailoring patterns; embroidery; men's, women's, and children's fashions; etc.

Simon, Marie. *Fashion in Art: The Second Empire and Impressionism.* London: Zwemmer, 1995. Beautiful color and monochrome illustrations. "The dialogue between fashion and art" illustrated by paintings and photographs.

Tinterow, Gary, and Philip Consibee, eds. *Portraits by Ingres: Image of an Epoch.* New York: The Metropolitan Museum of Art, 1999. Distributed by Harry N. Abrams, Inc. Beautifully illustrated with drawings and paintings in monochrome and color. Published in conjunction with an exhibit at the National Gallery, London; The National Gallery of Art, Washington, D.C., and the Metropolitan Museum of Art, New York. A definitive work.

Time-Life Books. *Our American Century: Prelude to the Century.* Alexandria, VA: Time-Life Books, 1999. Monochrome and some color illustrations and photographs of American life. A revised edition of *This Fabulous Century 1870–1900.* A useful source.

Tozer, Jane, and Sarah Levitt. *Fabric of Society: A Century of People and their Clothes 1770–1870.* Carno, Powys, Wales: Laura Ashley Ltd., 1983. Monochrome and color photographs and illustrations showing men's and women's clothing and accessories.

Wilson, Angus. *The World of Charles Dickens.* New York: The Viking Press, Inc., 1972. Paperbound. Monochrome and color illustrations from contemporary sources c. 1820–1870.

Wood, Christopher. *Victorian Panorama: Paintings of Victorian Life.* London: Faber and Faber, Ltd., 1976. Monochrome and some color illustrations of all walks of life from contemporary sources. Useful for costume.

Twentieth Century, General History

Baudot, Francois, *Fashion: The Twentieth Century.* New York: Universe Publishing. A Division of Rizzoli International Publications, Inc. London: Thames and Hudson, 1999. Paperbound with monochrome and color photographs of high fashion.

Benton, Barbara. *Ellis Island: A Pictorial History.* New York and Oxford, England: Facts on File Publications, 1985. Monochrome photographs. Good for ethnic costumes.

Blum, Stella. *Designs by Erte: Fashion Drawings & Illustrations from Harper's Bazaar.* New York: Dover Publications, Inc., 1976. Line illustrations and some color plates. 1915–1930s.

von Boehn, Max, and Max Fischel. *Modes and Manners of the Nineteenth Century as Represented in the Pictures and Engravings of the Time.* New York: Benjamin Blom, Inc., 1970. Reprint of 1927 edition, 4 vols. in 2. Covers 1790–1914. Illustrations from primary sources.

Byrde, Penelope. *A Visual History of Costume: The Twentieth Century.* New York: Drama Book Publishers, 1986. Monochrome and some color illustrations from primary sources.

Carter, Ernestine. *20th Century Fashions: A Scrapbook—1900 to Today.* London: Eyre Methuen, 1975. Monochrome fashion illustrations and photographs.

Cawthorne, Nigel. *The New Look: The Dior Revolution.* Edison, NJ: Wellfleet Press (a Division of Book Sales), 1996. Originally published by Hamlyn, an imprint of Reed Consumer Books Ltd., London, 1996. Monochrome and color photographs throughout. Covers 1920s–1950s. Useful source—well illustrated, entertaining reading.

Clancy, Dierdre. *Costume Since 1945: Couture, Street Style and Anti-fashion.* New York: Drama Publishers, 1996. Paperbound. Line illustrations throughout—all redrawn from other sources— with explanatory text. Some useful information.

Clephane, Irene. *Ourselves 1900–1930.* London: John Lane, The Bodley Head Ltd., 1933. Monochrome illustrations covering all walks of life.

Coleman, Elizabeth Ann. *The Genius of Charles James.* New York: The Brooklyn Museum/ Holt, Rinehart and Winston, 1982. Published in conjunction with an exhibit held at the Brooklyn Museum. Monochrome and color photographs and sketches of high fashion. Late 1920s–1950s.

Cunnington, C. Willett. *English Women's Clothing in the Present Century.* London: Faber and Faber, Ltd., 1952. Line drawings, monochrome and some color illustrations and photographs from contemporary sources. Covers 1900–1950 in great detail. An excellent reference.

Dars, Celestine. *A Fashion Parade: The Seeberger Collection*. London: Blond and Briggs, 1979. Monochrome photographs taken between 1909 and 1950. French photographer's studio collection showing women (and some men) wearing fashionable clothing.

Erte. *Erte Fashions*. New York: St. Martin's Press, Inc., 1973. Monochrome and some color illustrations of clothing, jewelry, and accessories.

Ewing, Elizabeth. *History of 20th Century Fashion*. New York: Costume and Fashion Press. An Imprint of Quite Specific Media Group Ltd., 4th revised edition, 2002. Paperbound. Monochrome illustrations and photographs from contemporary sources reviewing women's fashion, including couture and mass production. 1900–2000.

The Gallery of English Costume. Picture Book Number Six: *Women's Costume 1900–1930*. Manchester, England: Art Galleries Committee of the Corporation of Manchester, 1956. Monochrome photographs of clothing, underwear, and accessories in the Gallery of English Costume, Platt Hall.

Glynne, Prudence, with Madeleine Ginsburg. *In Fashion: Dress in the Twentieth Century*. London: George Allen and Unwin, 1978. Monochrome and some color illustrations and photographs of men's and women's fashions, 1900–1970s.

Harris, Kristina. *Victorian & Edwardian Fashions for Women 1840–1919*. Atglen, PA: Schiffer Publishing Ltd., 1995. Paperbound. Illustrations, monochrome and color photographs throughout, many showing models wearing extant clothing. Brief text.

———. *Vintage Fashions for Women 1920s–1940s*. Atglen, PA: Schiffer Publishing Ltd., 1996. Paperbound. Color and monochrome photographs and line illustrations throughout of vintage clothing, accessories, and fashion

illustrations. Actual vintage clothing photographed on various models does not look as wonderful as it might!

Howell, Georgina. *In Vogue: Sixty Years of Celebrities and Fashion from British Vogue*. New York: Penguin Books, 1978. Paperbound. Black-and-white photographs and fashion illustrations with color insert. Covers fashion trends, celebrities, entertainment, etc. from 1916–1975.

Jensen, Oliver. *America's Yesterdays: Images of Our Lost Past Discovered in the Photographic Archives of the Library of Congress*. New York: American Heritage Publishing Co., Inc., 1978. Many monochrome photographs.

———. *A College Album or Rah Rah, Yesterday*. New York: American Heritage Publishing Co., Inc., 1974. Monochrome photographs.

Life. *The Best of Life*. New York: Avon Books, 1973. Monochrome and color photographs from *Life* magazine from 1936–1972, covering fashion, war, political events, sports, etc.

Mansfield, Alan, and Phyllis Cunnington. *Handbook of English Costume in the Twentieth Century, 1900–1950*. Boston: Plays, Inc., 1973. Line illustrations redrawn from contemporary sources are not as clear as those in the earlier handbooks, but still an excellent reference for men's and women's clothing.

Mendes, Valerie, and Amy de la Haye. *20th Century Fashion*. London and New York: Thames and Hudson, 1999. Paperbound. Monochrome and color photographs.

Metropolitan Museum of Art. *Fabulous Fashion 1907–1967*. New York: Costume Institute, Metropolitan Museum of Art, n.d. Published in conjunction with an exhibit in Australia of costumes from the Metropolitan Museum. Monochrome and color photographs.

Milbank, Caroline Rennolds. *Couture: The Great Designers*, New York: Stewart, Tabori & Chang, Inc., 1985. Monochrome and color photographs and illustrations. Covers couture designers including Worth, Chanel, Dior, Schiaparelli, Vionnet, Poiret, Armani, Valentino, Hartnell, McCardell, Issey Miyake, and more. 1840s–1980s.

———. *New York Fashion: The Evolution of American Style*. New York: Harry N. Abrams, Inc., 1989. Beautifully illustrated with monochrome and color photographs and fashion illustrations. Covers nineteenth century–1980s, but concentrates mostly on twentieth century, by decade.

Mulvagh, Jane. *Vogue History of 20th Century Fashion*. London: Bloomsbury Books, 1988. Black-and-white photographs and fashion illustrations. Covers 1909–1986.

O'Donnol, Shirley Miles. *American Costume, 1915–1970: A Source Book for the Stage Costumer*. Bloomington, IN: Indiana University Press, 1982. Small line drawings and monochrome photographs of clothing.

de Osma, Guillermo. *Fortuny: The Life and Work of Mariano Fortuny*. New York: Rizzoli International Publications Inc., 1980. First paperbound edition, 1985. 2nd paperbound edition, 1994. Monochrome and some color illustrations. Covers the multifaceted career of Fortuny as artist, stage designer, inventor, textile artist, and couturier.

Owen, Elizabeth. *Fashion in Photographs 1920–1940*. London: B. T. Batsford Ltd., 1993. Black-and-white photographs of men, women, and children from the National Portrait Gallery, London, with explanatory text.

Robinson, Julian. *The Golden Age of Style*. New York and London: Harcourt Brace Jovanovich, 1976. Art Deco fashion. Color illustrations, monochrome plates, and fashion photographs. 1901–1939.

Rolley, Katrina, and Caroline Aish. *Fashion in Photographs 1900–1920*. London: B. T. Batsford Ltd., 1992. Black-and-white photographs of men, women, and children from the National Portrait Gallery, London, with explanatory text.

Steele, Valerie. *Women of Fashion: Twentieth-Century Designers*. New York: Rizzoli International Publications, Inc., 1991. Monochrome and color photographs. European, Japanese, American designers including Chanel, Vionnet, Schiaparelli, Sonia Rykiel, Betsey Johnson, and many more.

———. *Fifty Years of Fashion: New Look to Now*. New Haven, CT, and London: Yale University Press, 1997. Monochrome and color photographs. Includes haute couture and pop fashions.

Time-Life Books. *Our American Century: Century of Flight*. Alexandria, VA: Time-Life Books, 1999. Monochrome and color illustrations and photographs. Useful source for information on air and space travel in peacetime and war.

———. *Our American Century: Events That Shaped the Century*. Alexandria, VA: Time-Life Books, 1998. Monochrome and color illustrations and photographs. Useful source for people and major events of the century.

———. *Our American Century: Immigrants: The New Americans*. Alexandria, VA: Time-Life Books, 1999. Monochrome and color illustrations and photographs.

———. *Our American Century: People Who Shaped the Century*. Alexandria, VA: Time-Life Books, 1999. Monochrome and some color illustrations of prominent people from all walks of life, some from other countries. A useful reference.

Torrens, Deborah. *Fashion Illustrated: A Review of Women's Dress 1920–1950*. New York: Hawthorn Books Inc., 1975. Monochrome and color fashion illustrations and photographs from contemporary fashion magazines.

Tosa, Marco. *Evening Dresses 1900–1940*. The Twentieth Century Histories of Fashion Series. Modena, Italy: Zanfi Editori, 1988. Distributed in the U.S. by Costume and Fashion Press. An Imprint of Quite Specific Media Group Ltd., New York. Nicely illustrated with monochrome and color illustrations of women's evening clothes from primary sources. Includes a chapter on pre-1900 fashions.

Worsley, Harriet. *Decades of Fashion. The Hulton Getty Picture Collection.* Cologne, Germany: Konemann, 2000. Paperbound. Useful assortment of monochrome (and a few color) photographs with explanatory captions. Covers all walks of life throughout the twentieth century.

Twentieth Century, Chronological Order

See also listings in Period Catalogues

Daniel, Pete, and Raymond Smock. *A Talent for Detail: The Photographs of Miss Frances Benjamin Johnston 1889–1910.* New York: Harmony Books, 1974. Monochrome photographs.

Bentley, Nicolas. *Edwardian Album: A Photographic Excursion into a Lost Age of Innocence.* New York: A Studio Book. The Viking Press, 1974. Monochrome photographs showing Edwardians at work and play.

Gordon, Colin. *A Richer Dust: Echoes from an Edwardian Album.* Philadelphia and New York: J. B. Lippincott Company, 1978. Monochrome photographs.

Gernsheim, Alison. *Victorian and Edwardian Fashion: A Photographic Survey.* New York: Dover Publications, Inc., 1981. Paperbound. Originally published as *Fashion and Reality (1840–1914).* Monochrome photographs of men, women, and children.

Deslandres, Yvonne. *Poiret.* New York: Rizzoli International Publications, Inc., 1987. Beautiful monochrome and color photographs and illustrations throughout. C. 1900 to mid-1920s.

Harris, Kristina. *Victorian & Edwardian Fashions for Women 1840–1919.* Atglen, PA: Schiffer Publishing Ltd., 1995. Paperbound. Illustrations, monochrome and color photographs throughout, many showing models wearing actual period clothing. Brief text.

Priestley, J. B. *The Edwardians.* London: Heinemann, 1970. Monochrome and color illustrations and photographs.

Quennell, Peter. *The Day Before Yesterday: A Photographic Album of Daily Life in Victorian and Edwardian Britain.* New York: Charles Scribner's Sons, 1978. Monochrome photographs showing people from all walks of life including tradespeople, laborers, etc. Useful for costume.

Stevenson, Pauline. *Edwardian Fashion.* London: Ian Allan, Ltd., 1980. Line drawings, monochrome and some color illustrations and photographs. Clothing and accessories for men, women, and children.

Thompson, Paul, and Gina Harkell. *The Edwardians in Photographs.* London: B. T. Batsford, Ltd., 1979. Monochrome photographs showing the rich and poor at work and play.

Time-Life Books. *Our American Century: Dawn of the Century 1900–1910.* Alexandria, VA: Time-Life Books, 1998. Monochrome and some color illustrations. A revised edition of *This Fabulous Century 1900–1910.* A useful source.

———. *Our American Century: End of Innocence 1910–1920.* Alexandria, VA: Time-Life Books, 1998. Monochrome and some color illustrations. A revised edition of *This Fabulous Century: 1910–1920.* A useful source.

Ishsiyama, Akira. *French Fashion Plates in Art Deco.* Tokyo, Japan: Graphic-Sha Publishing Co., Ltd., 1988. Ninety-six fashion illustrations in color 1908–1924. Captions in English and Japanese.

Ridley, Pauline. *Fashion Illustration.* London: Academy Editions, 1979. Forty-eight French fashion plates in color. 1908–1925.

Olian, JoAnne, ed. *Parisian Fashions of the Teens: 352 Elegant Costumes from "L'Art et la Mode."* New York: Dover Publications, Inc. Paperbound. Black-and-white illustrations.

Barbiere, Georges, et al. *Parisian Costume Plates in Full Color (1912–1914).* New York: Dover Publications, Inc., 1982. Sixty plates reproduced from *Journal des Dames et des Modes.*

Nuzzi, Cristina. *Fashions in Paris from* Journal des Dames et des Modes *1912–1913.* London: Thames and Hudson, 1980. Color fashion plates including accessories.

———. *Parisian Fashion.* New York: Rizzoli International Publications, Inc., 1979. Color fashion plates from *Journal des Dames et des Modes.* 1912–1914.

Battersby, Martin. *Art Deco Fashion: French Designers 1908–1925.* London: Academy Editions, 1974. New York: St. Martin's Press, 1974. Monochrome and color fashion illustrations.

LePape, Georges, George Barbiere, et al. *French Fashion Plates in Full Color from "Gazette de Bob Tom" (1912–1925). 58 Illustrations of Styles by Paul Poiret, Worth, Paquin and Others. As Rendered by Georges LePape, Georges Barbiere, et al.* New York: Dover Publications, Inc., 1979.

Laubner, Ellie. *Fashions of the Roaring 1920s.* Atglen, PA: Schiffer Publishing Ltd., 1996. Paperbound. Monochrome and color illustrations of actual garments, fashion plates, and period photographs. Covers fashions and accessories for men, women, and children.

Holscher, Joost, ed. *1920s Fashion Design.* A Pepin Press Design Book. New York: Costume and Fashion Press. An Imprint of Quite Specific Media Group Ltd., 1998. Paperbound. A collection of monochrome and color fashion illustrations of clothing and accessories for men, women, and children. No text or dates, but loads of good and useful stuff.

Sann, Paul. *The Lawless Decade: A Pictorial History of a Great American Transition: From the World War 1 Armistice and Prohibition to Repeal and the New Deal.* New York: Bonanza Books, 1957. Monochrome photographs and illustrations from contemporary sources. 1920–1929.

Eckardt, Wolf Von, and Sander I. Gilman. *Bertolt Brecht's Berlin: A Scrapbook of the Twenties.* Garden City, New York: Anchor Press/Doubleday, 1975. Monochrome photographs of German life.

Ginsberg, Madeleine. *Paris Fashions: The Art Deco Style of the 1920s.* New York: Gallery Books, 1989. Fashion illustrations in color from *Art-Gout-Beauté,* include clothing, accessories, jewelry, children's wear, and textiles.

Grafton, Carol Berlanger, ed. *French Fashion Illustrations of the Twenties: 634 Cuts from "La Vie Parisienne."* New York: Dover Publications, Inc., 1987.

Hall, Caroline. *The Twenties in Vogue.* New York: Harmony Books, 1983. Monochrome and some color photographs and illustrations from *Vogue.* Fashions, social events, the arts, etc.

Herald, Jaqueline. *Fashions of a Decade: The 1920s.* London: B. T. Batsford Ltd., 1991. Part of a series covering each decade from 1920s–1990s.

Jenkins, Alan. *The Twenties.* New York: Universe Books Inc., 1974. Monochrome and color illustrations and photographs of events, fashions, the arts, etc.

Laver, James. *Women's Dress in the Jazz Age.* London: Hamish Hamilton, 1964. Monochrome photographs and illustrations from contemporary sources. 1920s.

Olian, JoAnne, ed. *Authentic French Fashions of the Twenties: 413 Costume Designs from "L'Art et la Mode."* New York: Dover Publications, Inc., 1990. Monochrome fashion illustrations.

Time-Life Books. *Our American Century: The Jazz Age: The 20s.* Alexandria, VA: Time-Life Books, 1998. A revised edition of *This Fabulous Century: 1920–1930.* Monochrome and some color illustrations and photographs. Useful source for events and personalities of the decade. Includes entertainment, sports, etc.

Yapp, Nick. *The Hulton Getty Picture Collection: 1920s.* Cologne Germany: Konemann 1998.

Small paperback. Monochrome photographs with captions in English, French, and German. Useful source.

Amory, Cleveland, and Frederic Bradlee, eds. *Vanity Fair: Selections from America's Most Memorable Magazine. A Cavalcade of the 1920s and 1930s*. New York: The Viking Press, 1960. Numerous monochrome illustrations and photographs. Useful for costume.

Dorner, Jane. *Fashion in the Twenties & Thirties*. London: Ian Allan, 1973. Black-and-white photographs and illustrations of fashions and accessories.

Harris, Kristina. *Vintage Fashions for Women 1920s–1940s*. Atglen, PA: Schiffer Publishing Ltd., 1996. Paperbound. Monochrome and color photographs, fashion illustrations and line drawings. Actual vintage clothing photographed on various models does not look as wonderful as it might!

Brassai. *The Secret Paris of the 30s*. New York: Pantheon Books, 1976. Monochrome photographs of Parisian nightlife.

Hall, Carolyn. *The Thirties in Vogue*. New York: Harmony Books, 1985. Monochrome and some color photographs and illustrations from *Vogue*. Fashions, social events, the arts, etc.

Horan, James D. *The Desperate Years: A Pictorial History of the Thirties*. New York: Bonanza Books, 1962. Monochrome photographs of events from the stock market crash to World War Two.

Jenkins, Alan. *The Thirties*. New York: Stein and Day, 1976. Monochrome and color illustrations and photographs from contemporary sources. Literature, the arts, sports, etc.

Costantino, Maria. *Fashions of a Decade: The 1930s*. London: B. T. Batsford Ltd., 1991. Part of a series covering each decade from 1920s–1990s.

Robinson, Julian. *Fashions in the 30s*. London: Oresko Books, Ltd., 1978. Paperbound. Monochrome and some color fashion illustrations from contemporary sources.

Gutterman, John. *The Restless Decade: John Gutterman's Photographs of the Thirties*. New York: Harry N. Abrams, Inc., 1984. Paperback edition 1996. Black-and-white photographs—all walks of life—mostly of U.S.

Rothstein, Arthur. *The Depression Years: As Photographed by Arthur Rothstein*. New York: Dover Publications, Inc., 1978. Monochrome photographs.

Time-Life Books. *Our American Century: Hard Times: The 30s*. Alexandria, VA: Time-Life Books, 1998. Monochrome and color illustrations and photographs throughout. A revised edition of *This Fabulous Century: 1930–1940*. A useful source.

Yapp, Nick *The Hulton Getty Picture Collection: 1930s*. Cologne, Germany: Konemann, 1998. Small paperback. Monochrome photographs with captions in English, French, and German. Useful source.

Baker, Patricia. *Fashions of a Decade: The 1940s*. London: B. T. Batsford Ltd., 1991. Part of a series covering each decade from 1920s–1990s.

Feininger, Andreas. *New York in the Forties*. New York: Dover Publications, Inc., 1978. Monochrome photographs of New York life.

Hall, Carolyn. *The Forties in Vogue*. New York: Harmony Books, 1985. Monochrome and color illustrations from *Vogue*. The war, the arts, celebrities, etc.

Jenkins, Alan. *The Forties*. New York: Universe Books, 1985. Monochrome and some color illustrations and photographs of people, events, the arts, sports, fashion, etc.

Laboissonniere, Wade. *Blueprints of Fashion: Home Sewing Patterns of the 1940s*. Atglen, PA: Schiffer Publishing Ltd., 1997. Paperbound. The book consists mostly of color photographs of cover envelopes of 1940s paper patterns.

McDowell, Colin. *Forties Fashion: and the New Look*. London: Bloomsbury Publishing Plc, 1997. Published in conjunction with an exhibit at the Imperial War Museum, London.

Beautifully illustrated with monochrome and color photographs.

Robinson, Julian. *Fashions in the 40s*. New York: St. Martin's Press, 1976. Small paperbound book. Monochrome and a few color fashion illustrations and photographs.

Time-Life Books. *Our American Century: Decade of Triumph: The 40s*. Alexandria, VA: Time-Life Books, 1999. Monochrome and color illustrations and photographs. Useful source for people and major events of the century.

Yapp, Nick. *The Hulton Getty Picture Collection: 1940s*. Cologne, Germany: Konemann 1998. Small paperback. Monochrome photographs with captions in English, French, and German. Useful source.

Dorner, Jane. *Fashion in the Forties & Fifties*. London: Ian Allan Ltd., 1975. Paperbound. Monochrome and some color photographs and fashion illustrations. Some men's but mostly women's clothing.

Baker, Patricia. *Fashions of a Decade: The 1950s*. London: B. T. Batsford, 1991. Part of a series covering each decade from 1920s–1990s.

Chancellor, John. *The Fifties*. New York: Pantheon Books, 1985. Monochrome photographs by well-known American photographers.

Drake, Nicholas. *The Fifties in Vogue*. New York: Henry Holt and Company, 1987. Monochrome and color illustrations from *Vogue*. The arts, fashion, movies, etc.

Horsley, Edith. *The 1950s*. London: A Bison/Domus Book, 1978. Illustrated with monochrome and some color photographs of events, fashion, the arts, politics, etc. of the decade.

Laboissonniere, Wade. *Blueprints of Fashion: Home Sewing Patterns of the 1950s*. Atglen, PA: Schiffer Publishing Ltd., 1999. Paperbound. Cover envelopes of 1950s paper patterns.

Lewis, Peter. *The 50s*. London: Heinemann, 1978. Monochrome photographs covering events, fashion, entertainment, and news items of the decade.

Time-Life Books. *Our American Century: The American Dream: The 50s*. Alexandria, VA: Time-Life Books, 1998. Monochrome and color illustrations and photographs. Useful source for events and personalities of the decade. Includes arts and entertainment, sports and lifestyles, etc.

Yapp, Nick. *The Hulton Getty Picture Collection: 1950s*. Cologne, Germany: Konemann, 1998. Small paperback. Monochrome photographs with captions in English, French, and German. Useful source.

Jones, Mablen. *Getting it on: The Clothing of Rock and Roll*. New York: Abbeville Press, Inc., 1987. Monochrome and color photographs of performers, musicians, costume sketches, etc. 1950s–1980s.

Polhemus, Ted, and Lynne Procter. *Pop Styles: An A-Z Guide to the World Where Fashion Meets Rock 'N' Roll*. London, Melbourne, Sydney, Auckland, Johannesburg: Vermillion and Company, 1984. Monochrome and color illustrations.

Bernard, Barbara. *Fashion in the 60s*. New York: St. Martin's Press, 1978. Small paperbound book. Monochrome photographs and fashion illustrations.

Connikie, Yvonne. *Fashions of a Decade: The 1960s*. London: B. T. Batsford, 1990. Part of a series covering each decade from 1920s–1990s.

Drake, Nicholas, ed. *The Sixties: A Decade in Vogue*. New York, London, Toronto, Sydney, and Tokyo: Prentice-Hall Press, n.d. Monochrome and color photographs from *Vogue*.

Jackson, Lesley. *The Sixties: Decade of Design Revolution*. London: Phaidon Press Limited, 1998. Reprinted 1999. Paperbound. Monochrome and color photographs and illustrations throughout. Covers all areas of design including ceramics, fashion, architecture, furniture, interior design, and graphics.

Lehnartz, Klaus. *New York in the Sixties*. New York: Dover Publications, Inc., 1978. Monochrome photographs of New York life.

Sann, Paul. *The Angry Decade: The Sixties.* New York: Crown Publishers, Inc., 1979. Monochrome photographs of people, places, and events.

Time-Life Books. *Our American Century: Turbulent Years: The 60s.* Alexandria, VA: Time-Life Books, 1998. Monochrome and color illustrations and photographs. Useful source for fashions, events and personalities of the decade. Includes arts and entertainment, sports and lifestyles, etc.

Yapp, Nick. *The Hulton Getty Picture Collection: 1960s.* Cologne, Germany: Konemann, 1998. Small paperback. Monochrome photographs with captions in English, French, and German. Useful source.

Hennessey, Val. *In the Gutter.* London, Melbourne, and New York: Quartet Books, 1978. Monochrome and color photographs of contemporary 1970s punk styles and "primitive peoples resplendent in their ritual adorments" as comparison.

Herald, Jaqueline. *Fashions of a Decade: The 1970s.* London: B. T. Batsford Ltd., 1992. Part of a series covering each decade from 1920s–1990s.

Yapp, Nick. *The Hulton Getty Picture Collection: 1970s.* Cologne, Germany: Konemann, 1998. Small paperback. Monochrome photographs with captions in English, French, and German. Useful source.

Time-Life Books. *Our American Century: Time of Transition: The 70s.* Alexandria, VA: Time-Life Books, 1999. Monochrome and color illustrations and photographs. Useful source for people and major events of the century.

Carnegy, Vicky. *Fashions of a Decade: The 1980s.* London: B. T. Batsford, 1990. Part of a series covering each decade from 1920s–1990s.

McDermott, Catherine. *Street Style: British Design in the 80s.* New York: Rizzoli International Publications, Inc., 1987. Monochrome and color photographs of clothes, accessories, furniture, posters, etc.

Time-Life Books. *Our American Century: Pride and Prosperity: The 80s.* Alexandria, VA: Time-Life Books, 1999. Monochrome and color illustrations. Useful source for people and major events of the century.

Specific Countries and Cultures

Aguet, Isabelle. Trans. Bonnie Christen. *A Pictorial History of the Slave Trade.* Geneva, Switzerland: Minerva, 1971. Monochrome illustrations and photographs throughout. Useful source.

van den Beukel, Dorine. *A Pictorial History of Costume.* A Pepin Press Design Book. New York: Costume and Fashion Press. An Imprint of Quite Specific Media Group Ltd. Paperbound reprint. 500 color plates illustrating costume from antiquity to nineteenth century. Includes ethnic, religious, military, and civilian costume from all over the world at various periods throughout history.

Jonas, Susan, ed. *Ellis Island: Echoes from a Nation's Past. A Celebration of the Gateway to America.* New York: Aperture Inc., 1989. Published by Aperture in association with the National Park Service, U.S. Department of the Interior, and Montclair State College. Monochrome and color photographs with text.

Kennett, Frances. *Ethnic Dress: A Comprehensive Guide to the Folk Costume of the World.* New York: Facts On File Inc., 1995. Color photographs of contemporary ethnic clothing and headgear from around the world.

Scarce, Jennifer, *Women's Costume of the Near and Middle East.* London: Unwin, Hyman Ltd., 1987. Monochrome illustrations of primary sources. Some not-to-scale patterns.

THE AMERICAN WEST

Beard, Tyler. *100 Years of Western Wear.* Salt Lake City, UT: Gibbs-Smith, 1993. Paperbound.

Lists of museums and western wear sources. Excellent color and monochrome illustrations throughout with brief text. 1890–1990s.

Hamley & Co. *Cowboy Clothing and Gear: The Complete Hamley Catalog of 1942.* New York: Dover Publications, Inc., 1995. Paperbound. Monochrome illustrations.

Kauffman, Dandra. *The Cowboy Catalog.* New York: Clarkson N. Potter, Inc., distributed by Crown Publishers, 1980. Monochrome and color plates.

Reedstrom, Ernest Lisle. *Historic Dress of the Old West.* Poole, Dorset, England; New York; and Sydney: Blandford Press, 1986. Nineteenth century Plains Indians, gamblers, soldiers, cowboys, lawmen, etc. Color illustrations by the author, line drawings, and monochrome photographs.

Sayers, Isabelle S. *Annie Oakley and Buffalo Bill's Wild West.* New York: Dover Publications, Inc., 1981. Monochrome photographs.

Time-Life. *The American West.* 26 vols. and master index. New York: Time-Life Books, 1973–76. Monochrome and color illustrations, many from primary sources.

Visalia Stock Saddle Co. *Saddle and Western Gear Catalog, 1938.* New York: Dover Publications, Inc. Paperbound reprint.

NATIVE AMERICANS

Mather, Christine. *Native American Arts: Traditions & Celebrations.* New York: Clarkson N. Potter Inc., 1990. Lavishly illustrated with color and monochrome photographs.

AUSTRALIA

Flower, Cedric. *Duck and Cabbage Tree: A Pictorial History of Clothes in Australia 1788–1914.* Sydney, Melbourne, Singapore, and London: Angus and Robertson, Ltd., 1968. Monochrome illustrations and photographs.

CHINA

Beers, Burton F. *China in Old Photographs 1860–1910.* New York: Dorset Press, 1981. Monochrome photographs.

Scott, A. C. *Chinese Costumes in Transition.* Singapore, Kuala Lumpur, Hong Kong, and Tokyo: Donald Moore, 1958. Distributed by Theatre Arts Books, New York. Line drawings. Mid-nineteenth to mid-twentieth century.

Spence, Jonathan D., and Annping Chin. *The Chinese Century: A Photographic History of the Last Hundred Years.* New York: Random House, 1996. Monochrome photographs (some very gruesome, showing decapitations), etc. An excellent source nevertheless!

Worswick, Clark, and Jonathan Spencer. *Imperial China: Photographs 1950–1912.* New York: A Pennwick/Crown Book, 1978. Sepia photographs.

INDIA

Lynton, Linda. *The Sari: Styles, Patterns, History, Techniques.* New York: Harry N. Abrams, Inc., 1995. Monochrome and color illustrations. Comprehensive work and invaluable source of information.

JAPAN

Liddell, Jill. *The Story of the Kimono.* New York: E. P. Dutton, 1989. Beautifully illustrated. Includes comprehensive history and instructions on how to wear the kimono. Very useful.

Noma, Seiroku. *Japanese Costume and Textile Arts.* New York and Tokyo: John Weatherhill, Inc., 1974. Monochrome and color illustrations and photographs of textiles and clothing.

Shima, Yukiko, trans. *A Step to Kimono and Kumihimo.* Los Angeles: Kyoto Kimono Academy, Inc., 1979. History of Japanese clothing, kimono assemblage, and accessories. Includes a section on Japanese braided cord (kumihimo). Line drawings and color photographs.

Sichel, Marion. *Japan.* London: B. T. Batsford, Ltd., 1987. Monochrome and some color drawings.

Yang, Sunny, and Rochelle M. Narasin. *Textile Art of Japan.* Tokyo: Shufunotomo Co., Ltd., 1989. Many color photographs of techniques, details, and garments.

RUSSIA

Allshouse, Robert H., ed. *Photographs for the Tsar: The Pioneering Color Photography of Sergei Mikhailovich Prokudin-Gorskii.* New York: The Dial Press, 1980. Color and some monochrome photographs of Russia and its people. Good for peasant and ethnic costume.

FitzLyon, Kyril, and Tatania Browning. *Before the Revolution: A View of Russia Under the Last Tsar.* Woodstock, NY: The Overlook Press, 1978. Monochrome photographs of Russian life from the end of the nineteenth century to 1917. Includes hospital, military, domestic, fashionable, and lots of good peasant clothing.

Korshunova, Tamata. Trans. Inna Sorokina. *The Art of Costume in Russia: 18th to Early 20th Century.* Leningrad, Russia: Aurora Art Publishers, 1979. Revised edition 1983. Monochrome and color photographs of men's and women's fashionable clothing (including French couture) from the collection of costume at the Hermitage. Includes paintings and accessories with close-up views showing construction, embroidery, and trim details.

Lyons, Marvin. *Russia in Original Photographs 1860–1920.* New York: Charles Scribner's Sons, 1977. Monochrome photographs of all walks of Russian life, many showing good clothing detail.

Massie, Robert K. *The Romanov Family Album.* New York: The Vendome Press, 1982. Monochrome photographs of the good life in old Russia in the late nineteenth and early twentieth century from the family albums of the last tsar.

Moynahan, Brian. *The Russian Century: A Photographic History of Russia's 100 Years,* New York: Random House, 1994. Monochrome photographs with accompanying text. Rare photographs collected from archives, museums, and private collections by Annabel Merullo and Sarah Jackson. Excellent source.

Obolensky, Chloe. *The Russian Empire: A Portrait in Photographs.* New York: Random House, Inc., 1979. Monochrome photographs, 1850s–1915, show clothing from all walks of life.

Onassis, Jacqueline, ed. *In the Russian Style.* New York: A Studio Book, The Viking Press, 1976. Published in conjunction with an exhibit of Russian costume at the Metropolitan Museum of Art. Illustrations from contemporary sources, monochrome and some color photographs of clothing. Seventeenth to early twentieth century.

Salisbury, Harrison E. *Russia in Revolution 1900–1930.* New York: Holt, Rinehart and Winston, 1978. Monochrome and color photographs and illustrations, some of which are useful for clothing.

Sichel, Marion. *USSR.* London: B. T. Batsford, Ltd., 1986. Monochrome and color line drawings.

State Hermitage Museum and the State Archive of the Russian Federation. *Nicholas and Alexandra: The Last Imperial Family of Tsarist Russia.* New York: Harry N. Abrams, Inc., 1998. Paperbound. Catalogue of an exhibit in Wilmington, DE, USA in 1998. Monochrome and color illustrations and photographs of clothing, artifacts, furniture.

Zaletova, Lidya, Fabio Ciofi degli Atti, Franco Panzini, et al. *Revolutionary Costume: Soviet Clothing and Textiles of the 1920s.* New York: Rizzoli International Publications, Inc., 1989. Drawings and photographs of garments and textile designs in monochrome and some color.

SAUDIA ARABIA

Ross, Heather Colyer. *The Art of Arabian Costume: A Saudi Arabian Profile*. Fribourg, Switzerland: Arabesque Commercial SA, 1981. Color photographs and illustrations, line drawings, and patterns (not to scale). Covers history and development of clothing, jewelry, and accessories. Useful.

————. *The Art of Bedouin Jewelry: A Saudi Arabian Profile*. Fribourg, Switzerland: Arabesque Commercial SA, 1981. Color photographs of jewelry. Glossary of Arabic words and lists of technical terms.

SCOTLAND

Dunbar, John Telfer. *The Costume of Scotland*. London: B. T. Batsford Ltd., 1981. Paperbound edition, 1989. Informative history with primary source illustrations and photographs in monochrome and color.

————. *The History of Highland Dress*. London: B. T. Batsford Ltd., 1979. Originally published in 1962. Scholarly study with monochrome and color illustrations and photographs from primary sources.

Munro, R. W. *Highland Clans and Tartans*. New York: Crescent Books, 1977. From beginning to present day with over 150 monochrome and color photographs. Informative.

Thompson, J. Charles. *So You're Going to Wear the Kilt: A Handy Guide to Wearing Scottish National Dress*. Edinburgh, Scotland: Paul Harris Publishing, 1979, 1981. Everything you wanted to know about wearing the kilt, including the answer to the age-old question!

SOUTH AFRICA

Telford, A. A. *Yesterday's Dress: A History of Costume in South Africa*. Cape Town, South Africa: Purnell and Sons, Ltd., 1972. Sepia and color line drawings by the author. 1488 to the end of the nineteenth century.

SPAIN

Anderson, Ruth Matilda. *Hispanic Costume 1480–1530*. New York: The Hispanic Society of America, 1979. Comprehensive, well-documented work on the costume of the Iberian peninsula, with monochrome and color illustrations.

SWEDEN

Larkin, David, ed. *The Paintings of Carl Larsson*. New York: A Peacock Press/Bantam Book, 1976. Color plates of the artist's work, showing family life in Sweden 1892–1914, useful for clothing.

Accessories

Bags and Purses

Foster, Vanda. *Bags and Purses*. The Costume Accessories Series. New York: Drama Book Publishers, 1982.

Wilcox, Claire. *Bags*. Victoria and Albert Museum: Fashion Accessories Series. London: V & A Publications, 1999. Beautiful color illustrations from primary sources. Fourteenth century to 1990s.

Eye Wear

Acerenza, Franca. *Eyewear. (Gli Occhiali)*. Bella Cosa Library Series. San Francisco, CA: Chronicle Books, 1997. Paperbound. Original Italian version published in Italy, 1988. Fourteenth to twentieth century. Beautiful color illustrations from primary sources with explanatory captions. Very brief text at end of book.

Corson, Richard. *Fashions in Eyeglasses from the 14th Century to the Present Day*. London: Peter Owen, 1980 (second impression with supplement). Comprehensive and well illustrated with plates and line drawings.

Davidson, D. C. *Spectacles, Lorgnettes and Monocles.* Shire Album 227. Princes Risborough, Aylesbury, Bucks, England: Shire Publications, Ltd., 1989. Small paperbound book with monochrome photographs.

Marly, Pierre. *Spectacles and Spyglasses.* France: Editions Hoebeke, 1988. Beautifully illustrated history of eye wear from thirteenth to twentieth centuries.

Winkler, Wolf, ed. *A Spectacle of Spectacles.* Leipzig, Germany: Edition Leipzig, 1988. Beautifully illustrated. History of eye wear from fourteenth to early twentieth century.

Fans

Alexander, Helen. *Fans.* The Costume Accessories Series. New York: Drama Book Publishers, 1985.

Armstrong, Nancy. *The Book of Fans.* New York: Mayflower, 1978. All color illustrations.

Gostelow, Mary. *The Fan.* Dublin: Gill and Macmillan, Ltd., 1976. Illustrated with photographs.

Hart, Avril, and Emma Taylor. *Fans.* New York: Costume and Fashion Press. An Imprint of Quite Specific Media Group Ltd. Seventeenth century to present day.

Footwear

Atkinson, Jeremy. *Clogs and Clogmaking.* Shire Album 113. Princes Risborough, Aylesbury, Bucks, England: Shire Publications, Ltd., 1984. History and use of clogs. Small, well-illustrated, and informative paperback.

Baynes, Ken, and Kate Baynes. *The Shoe Show: British Shoes Since 1790.* London: The Crafts Council, 1979. Useful, informative, and well illustrated with monochrome and color photographs.

Dobson, Bob. *Concerning Clogs.* Clapham, N. Yorkshire, England: Dalesman Books, 1979. Paperbound book on the use and history of clogs in England with line drawings and photographs.

Girotti, Eugenia. *Footwear: Fifty Years History 1945–1995 (La Calzatura: Un Cammino Lungo 50 Anni).* Milano: Itinerari d'Immag-

ini, Magnum. BE-MA editrice, 1995. Paperbound. Text in Italian and English. Monochrome and color illustrations and photographs throughout.

Heyraud, Bertrard. *5000 Ans de Chaussures.* Bournemouth, England: Parkstone Press, 1994 (Editions Parkstone). French text. Beautifully illustrated with monochrome and color plates and photographs.

McDowell, Colin. *Shoes: Fashion and Fantasy.* London: Thames and Hudson, 1989. New York: Thames and Hudson, 1994. Paperbound. Monochrome and color illustrations.

O'Keeffe, Linda. *Shoes: A Celebration of Pumps, Sandals, Slippers & More.* New York: Workman Publishing, 1996. Paperbound. Over 1,000 color photographs of shoes.

Pratt, Lucy, and Linda Woolley. *Shoes.* Victoria and Albert Museum: Fashion Accessories Series. London: V & A Publications, 1999. Color illustrations from primary sources. Medieval to 1990s.

Probert, Christina, comp. *Shoes in Vogue Since 1910.* In Vogue Series. New York: Abbeville Press, 1981. Monochrome and color illustrations from *Vogue.*

Swann, June. *Shoes.* The Costume Accessories Series. New York: Drama Book Publishers, 1982.

———. *Shoemaking.* Shire Album 155. Princes Risborough, Aylesbury, Bucks, England: Shire Publications, Ltd., 1986. Roman times to twentieth century.

Wilcox, R. Turner. *The Mode in Footwear.* New York: Charles Scribner's Sons, Ltd., 1948. Line drawings.

Wilson, Eunice. *A History of Shoe Fashion.* New York: Theatre Arts Books, 1974. Line drawings and some photographs from primary sources.

HANDKERCHIEFS

Braun-Ronsdorf, Dr. M. *The History of the Handkerchief.* Leigh-on-Sea, England: F. Lewis Publishers, Ltd., 1967. Plates of actual handkerchiefs and paintings showing them in use.

Peri, Paolo. *The Handkerchief.* The Twentieth Century Histories of Fashion Series. New York: Costume and Fashion Press. An Imprint of Quite Specific Media Ltd. World history of the handkerchief from 1000 B.C. to 1990.

HATS—See Hats, Hair, Wigs, and Make-up

JEWELRY

Bayer, Patricia, Vivienne Becker, Helen Craven, Peter Hinks, Ronald Lightbrown, Jack Ogden, and Dina Scaresbrick. *The Jewelry Design Source Book. A Visual Reference for All Jewelry Collectors & Enthusiasts.* New York: Van Nostrand Reinhold, 1989. Beautiful large color photographs with excellent detail.

Black, J. Anderson. *A History of Jewels.* London: Orbis Publishing, 1974. Prehistory to twentieth century.

Coles, Janet, and Robert Budwig. *The Book of Beads.* New York: Simon and Schuster, 1990. Beautiful color photographs of every bead imaginable.

Evans, Joan. *A History of Jewellery 1100–1870.* New York: Dover Publications, Inc. 1990. Paperbound.

Frank, Larry, and Millard J. Holbrook II. *Indian Silver Jewelry of the Southwest 1868–1930.* Westchester, PA: Schiffer Publishing, Ltd., 1990. Monochrome and color illustrations with good detail.

Hart, Harold H. *Jewelry: A Pictorial Archive of Woodcuts & Engravings.* New York: Dover Publications, Inc., 1981. Paperbound.

Hornung, Clarence P. *A Sourcebook of Antiques and Jewelry Designs.* New York: Da Capo Press, Inc., 1977.

Scarisbrick, Diana. *Jewelry.* The Costume Accessories Series. New York: Drama Book Publishers, 1985.

Weiner, Louis. *Handmade Jewelry: A Manual of Techniques.* New York: Van Nostrand Reinhold Co., 1981. Line drawings and monochrome photographs. Good process sequences.

NECK WEAR

Colle, Doriece. *Collars, Stocks, Cravats: A History and Costume Dating Guide to Civilian Men's Neckpieces 1655–1900.* Emmaus, PA: Rodale Press, Inc., 1972. Good information. Plates and line drawings (line drawings are not always clear).

Gibbings, Sarah. *Ties: Trends and Traditions.* New York and Toronto: Barron's Educational Series, Inc., 1990. Misleading title as it covers the history of neckwear from the seventeenth to twentieth century. Well illustrated and informative.

Hart, Avril. *Ties.* New York: Costume and Fashion Press. An Imprint of Quite Specific Media Group Ltd. 1670s to present. Illustrated with photographs of ties from the collection at the Victoria and Albert Museum.

Laver, James. *The Book of Public School Old Boys, University, Navy, Army, Air Force and Club Ties.* London: Seely Service and Co., Ltd., 1968. Many color plates.

Mosconi, Davide, and Riccardo Villarosa. *Getting Knotted: 188 Knots for Necks: The History, Techniques and Photographs.* Milan, Italy: Rajti, 1985.

SOCKS AND STOCKINGS—See Underwear

UMBRELLAS AND PARASOLS

Crawford, T. S. *A History of the Umbrella.* Newton Abbot and London, England: David and Charles, 1970. Informative and well illustrated.

Les Accessoires du Temps. *Ombrelles Parapluies.* Paris: Paris-Musees, 1989. From an exhibit at the Musée de la Mode et du Costume. Beautiful color and monochrome photographs.

Mackrell, Jeremy. *Umbrellas and Parasols.* The Costume Accessories Series. New York: Drama Book Publishers, 1986.

MISCELLANEOUS

Cumming, Valerie. *Gloves.* The Costume Accessories Series. New York: Drama Book Publishers, 1982. Informative and beautifully illustrated.

————. *The Visual History of Costume Accessories. From Hats to Shoes: 400 Years of Costume Accessories.* London: B. T. Batsford Ltd., 1998. Paperbound edition distributed in the U.S. by Costume and Fashion Press. An Imprint of Quite Specific Media Group Ltd. Monochrome and some color illustrations. Brief, well-illustrated survey including gloves, parasols, legwear, jewelry, fans, etc.

Eckstein, E., J. Eckstein, and G. Firkins. *Gentleman's Dress Accessories.* Shire Album 205. Princes Risborough, Aylesbury, Bucks, England: Shire Publications, Ltd., 1987. Small paperbound book with monochrome illustrations.

Farrell, Jeremy. *Scarves, Stoles and Shawls.* The Costume Accessories Series. New York: Drama Book Publishers, 1986.

Hague, Norma. *Combs and Hair Accessories.* Cincinnati, OH: Seven Hills Books, 1985. Small paperback with monochrome photographs, 1760–1940.

Grafton, Carol Belanger. *Shoes, Hats and Fashion Accessories: A Pictorial Archive 1850–1940.* New York: Dover Publications, Inc., 1998. Paperbound. Black-and-white illustrations from contemporary periodicals including *Harper's Bazaar, London Illustrated News, La Mode Illustrée, The Delineator,* and *Life* as well as assorted fashion catalogs.

Johnson, Eleanor. *Fashion Accessories.* Shire Album 58. Princes Risborough, Aylesbury, Bucks, England: Shire Publications, Ltd., 1982. Small paperbound book with monochrome illustrations.

Lester, Katherine Morris, and Bess Viola Oerke. *Accessories of Dress: An Illustrated History of the Frills and Furbelows of Fashion.* Peoria, IL: The Manual Arts Press, 1940. Monochrome plates, photographs, and line drawings. Covers accessories worn at the neck, head, shoulder, waist, feet, legs, arms, and wrist, and those carried.

Ceremonial, Academic, and Religious Dress

Arch, Nigel, and Joanna Marschner. *Splendour at Court: Dressing for Royal Occasions Since 1700.* New York, London and Sydney: Unwin Hyman, 1987. Monochrome and color illustrations from primary sources. Includes court dress, debutantes, and formal attire for reigning monarchs.

Clare, Rev. Wallace. *Historic Dress of the English Schoolboy.* London: The Society for the Preservation of Ancient Customs, n.d. (c. 1939).

Cumming, Valerie. *Royal Dress: The Image and the Reality 1580 to Present Day.* London: B. T. Batsford, Ltd., 1989.

Davidson, Alexander. *Blazers, Badges and Boaters: A Pictorial History of School Uniform.* Horndean, Hants, England: Scope Books Ltd., 1990. History of British school uniforms with monochrome illustrations and photographs from primary sources.

Dearmer, Rev. Percy. *The Arts of the Church: The Ornaments of the Ministers.* London: A. R. Mowbray and Co., Ltd., 1908. History and origins with illustrations.

Campbell, Una. *Robes of the Realm: 300 Years of Ceremonial Dress.* London: Ede and Ravenscroft Ltd./Michael O'Mara Books Ltd., 1989. Published to mark the tercentenary of the London robemaking firm of Ede and Ravenscroft. History of the firm includes legal, clerical, and academic robes; orders of chivalry; court dress; and royal attire. Useful reference.

Gummere, Amelia Mott. *The Quaker: A Study in Costume.* New York and London: Benjamin Blom, Inc., 1968. 1901 reprint. Quaker dress in Britain and America, seventeenth to nineteenth century.

Haycroft, Frank W. *The Degrees and Hood of the World's Universities and Colleges.* London: The Cheshunt Press, 1923.

Jenkins, Graham. *The Making of Church Vestments.* Westminster, MD: The Newman Press, 1957. Historical information, shapes and sizes of garments with patterns (not to scale).

Macalister, R. A. S. *Ecclesiastical Vestments: Their Development and History.* London: Elliot Stock, 1896. Monochrome illustrations and line drawings from primary sources.

Mansfield, Alan. *Ceremonial Costume.* London: Adam and Charles Black, 1980. Monochrome illustrations, photographs, and line drawings of parliamentary dress, coronation robes, court uniforms, etc.

Mayer-Thurman, Christa C. *Raiment for The Lord's Service: A Thousand Years of Western Vestments.* Chicago: The Art Institute of Chicago, 1975. Monochrome photographs of textiles and garments in the exhibit.

Mayo, Janet. *A History of Ecclesiastical Dress.* New York: Drama Book Publishers, 1984. London: B. T. Batsford Ltd., 1984. Monochrome and some color illustrations from primary sources. Useful reference.

Norris, Herbert. *Church Vestments: Their Origin and Development.* London: J. M. Dent and Sons, Ltd., 1949. Includes patterns, monochrome plates, and line drawings redrawn from original sources.

Rubens, Alfred. *A History of Jewish Costume.* London: Valentine, Mitchell and Co., Ltd., 1967. Monochrome illustrations from primary sources, spanning antiquity to mid-nineteenth century, by country.

Shaw, G. W. *Academic Dress of British Universities.* Cambridge, England: W. Heffer and Sons, 1966. Information on all major universities, with diagrams of the various hood and gown shapes.

Smith, Hugh. *Academic Dress and Insignia of the World.* Cape Town: A. A. Balkema, 1970. A definitive work in 3 volumes with line illustrations.

Tyack, Rev. Geo. S. *The Historic Dress of the Clergy.* London: William Andrews and Co., 1897. Engravings and line illustrations.

Children's Costume

Cunnington, Phillis, and Anne Buck. *Children's Costume in England 1300–1900.* London: Adam and Charles Black, 1965. Contemporary quotations, primary source illustration, and line drawings.

Ewing, Elizabeth. *History of Children's Costume.* London: B. T. Batsford, Ltd., 1977. Primary source illustrations.

Grafton, Carol Belanger. *Children: A Pictorial Archive from Nineteenth-Century Sources.* New York: Dover Publications, Inc., 1978.

Harris, Kristina. *The Child in Fashion 1750–1920.* With price guide. Atglen, PA: Schiffer Publishing Ltd., 1999. Paperbound. Monochrome and color illustrations and photographs showing extant clothing, some modeled by children as well as illustrations from primary sources. Brief text.

Mager, Alison, ed. *Children of the Past in Photographic Portraits.* New York: Dover Publications, Inc., 1978.

Martin, Linda. *The Way We Wore: Fashion Illustration of Children's Wear 1870–1970.* New York: Charles Scribner's Sons, 1978.

Olian, JoAnne. *Children's Fashions 1860–1912: 1,065 Costume Designs from "La Mode Illustrée."* New York: Dover Publications, Inc., 1994. Paperbound. 128pp. 1,065 costumes in 362 black-and-white illustrations.

Pierce, A. J., and D. K. Pierce. *Victorian and Edwardian Children from Old Photographs.* London: B. T. Batsford, Ltd., 1980. Monochrome photographs of children form all walks of life.

Rose, Claire. *Children's Clothes.* New York: Drama Book Publishers, 1990. Seventeenth to twentieth century.

Hats, Hair, Wigs, and Make-up

Albrizio, Ann, and Osnat Lustig. *Classic Millinery Techniques: A Complete Guide to Making & Designing Today's Hats.* New York: Lark Books. A Division of Sterling Publishing Co., Inc., 1998. Paperbound. A how-to book by the millinery instructor at the Fashion Institute of Technology, New York.

Amphlett, Hilda. *Hats: A History of Fashion in Headwear.* Chalfont St. Giles, Bucks., England: Richard Sadler Ltd., 1974. Line illustrations redrawn from original sources, covering 2,000 years. Mainly Western European civil and military—men, women, and children. Small chapters on crowns, ecclesiastical headwear and non-European hats.

Anlezark, Mildred. *Hats on Heads: The Art of Creative Millinery.* Kenthurst, NSW, Australia: Kangaroo Press Pty Ltd., 1965. Revised edition 1991. Paperbound. Distributed in United States by Lacis, Berkeley, CA. Many of the hats have a distinctively 60s look. It covers millinery techniques, flowers, and trimmings in a wide variety of materials.

Arnold, Janet. *Perukes and Periwigs.* London: Her Majesty's Stationery Office, 1970. c. 1660 to 1740.

Arthur, Jane L., ed. *Yesterday's Headlines: The Hat Collection of the Stoke-on-Trent City Museum and Art Gallery.* Stoke-on-Trent, England: Stoke-on-Trent City Museum and Art Gallery, n.d. (c. 1986). Slim paperbound catalogue of hats in the museum collection, published in conjunction with an exhibition. It includes a brief description of each acquisition, and small monochrome photographs of the majority of mostly women's hats.

Asser, Joyce. *Historic Hairdressing.* London: Sir Isaac Pitman & Sons Ltd., 1966. New York: Hippocrene Books, 1975. Comprehensive survey of hairdressing from ancient Egypt to the 1970s. Illustrated with line drawings.

Bawden, Juliet. *The Hat Book: Creating Hats for Every Occasion.* Asheville, NC: Lark Books, 1993. Paperbound. Basic how-to book for making and trimming contemporary hats (without the need of a block). Line drawings and color photographs throughout.

Ben-Yusef, Mme. Anna. *Edwardian Hats: The Art of Millinery (1909).* Mendocino, CA: R.L. Shep, 1992. Paperbound reprint with additional illustrations. Monochrome photographs and line drawings. Includes instructions for making hats with wire frames and buckram shapes, sewing techniques, and trimmings.

Blum, Dilys E. Philadelphia Museum of Art Bulletin. *Ahead of Fashion: Hats of the 20th Century.* Philadelphia, PA: Philadelphia Museum of Art, 1993. Paperbound catalogue of an exhibition held at the museum. Explanatory text, monochrome and color photographs.

Botham, Mary, and L. Sharrad. *Manual of Wigmaking.* London: Heinemann, 1964. Distributed in the U.S. by David and Charles, Inc., North Pomfret, VT. 3rd edition, 1982. Paperbound. Clear line drawings and informative text on the art of wigmaking.

Broe, Bert. *Theatrical Makeup.* London: Pelham Books Ltd.; New York: Beaufort Books, 1984. Basic techniques, well illustrated with color photographs throughout.

Bryer, Robin. *The History of Hair: Fashion and Fantasy Down the Ages.* Philip Wilson Publishers, Ltd., 2000. Beautifully illustrated in monochrome and color.

Buchet, Martine, and Laziz Hamani. *Panama: A Legendary Hat*. Paris: Editions Assouline, n.d. Beautiful monochrome and color photographs throughout. Informative text—all you could ever want to know about Panama hats!

Campione, Adele. *Women's Hats (Il Cappello da Donna)*. San Francisco: Chronicle Books, 1994. Small paperbound book. Translation from the Italian version published in 1989. Color photographs of millinery from 1880 to 1969 with explanatory captions in Italian and English.

———. *Men's Hats (Il Cappello da Uomo)*. San Francisco: Chronicle Books, 1995. Small paperbound book. Translation from the Italian version published in 1988. Color photographs of men's hats from fourteenth to present century with explanatory captions in Italian and English. Includes traditional headgear from several countries and a brief history of men's hats.

Charles, Anne, and Roger DeAnfrasio. *The History of Hair: An Illustrated Review of Hair Fashions for Men Throughout the Ages*. New York: Bonanza Books, 1970. Line drawings, engravings, photographs, and paintings.

Clarke, Fiona. *Hats*. The Costume Accessories Series. New York: Drama Book Publishers, 1982. Brief but well illustrated with men's and women's hats from 1600–present day.

Corey, Irene. *The Face Is a Canvas: The Design & Technique of Theatrical Make-up*. New Orleans, LA: Anchorage Press, 1990. Beautifully illustrated, color and monochrome, with transparent overlays.

Corson, Richard. *Fashions in Hair: The First Five Thousand Years*. London: Peter Owen, 1965. Rev. 1971, 2nd rev. ed. 2001. Line drawings and engravings.

———. *Fashions in Makeup*. New York: Universe Books, 1972. Photographs, engravings, and line drawings.

Corson, Richard, and James Glaven. *Stage Makeup*. (9th ed.). Boston, MA: Allyn & Bacon, 2000.

Updated version of the "makeup bible" with monochrome and color illustrations and photographs.

Couldridge, Alan. *The Hat Book*. Englewood Cliffs, NJ: Prentice-Hall, Inc., 1980. Paperbound. Line drawings and photographs. Patterns and construction for c. 1980 women's hats.

de Courtais, Georgine. *Women's Headdresses and Hairstyles in England from A.D. 600 to the Present Day*. London: B. T. Batsford Ltd., 1973. Line drawings.

Dial, Tim. *Basic Millinery for the Stage*. Portsmouth, NH: Heinemann, 2002. Paperbound.

Dreher, Denise. *From the Neck Up: An Illustrated Guide to Hatmaking*. Minneapolis, MN: Madhatter Press, 1981. Paperbound. Instructions for making theatrical millinery, illustrated with line drawings, scaled patterns, engravings, and photographs.

Folledore, Giuliano. *Men's Hats*. The Twentieth Century Histories of Fashion Series. Modena, Italy: Zanfi Editori, 1989. Distributed in the U.S. by Costume and Fashion Press. An Imprint of Quite Specific Media Group Ltd., New York. Monochrome and color illustrations, line drawings, photographs, engravings, and fashion plates, all from primary sources. Antiquity–1980s. An excellent resource.

Freeman, Charles. *Luton and the Hat Industry*. Luton, Bedfordshire, England: The Corporation of Luton Museum and Art Gallery, 1953. Small paperbound book with monochrome photographs and line drawings of period hats, equipment, and machinery.

de Garsault, Mons. *The Art of the Wigmaker*. London: The Hairdresser's Registration Council, 1961. Reprint from 1767.

Ginsburg, Madeleine. *The Hat: Trends and Traditions*. New York and Toronto: Barron's Educational Series, Inc., 1990. Monochrome and color illustrations from primary sources. History of men's and women's headwear from medieval times to twentieth century.

Hopkins, Susie. *The Century of Hats: Headturning Style of the Twentieth Century*. Edison, NJ: Chartwell Books, Inc. A Quintet Book, 1999. Distributed by Harry N. Abrams, Inc. Beautiful black-and-white and color illustrations throughout of primary source material. Chapters by decade include some men's but mostly women's hats.

Huggett, Renee. *Hair-Styles and Head-Dresses*. North Pomfret, VT: David and Charles, 1982. Line drawings, engravings, photographs, and paintings from primary sources. A very brief history from ancient times to 1980s.

Jones, Dylan. Haircults: *Fifty Years of Styles and Cuts*. London: Thames and Hudson, Ltd., 1990. Monochrome and some color photographs, 1940s to 1980s.

Kaye, Georgina Kerr. *Millinery for Every Woman*. Berkeley, CA: Lacis Publications, 1992. Reprint of 1926 edition. Paperbound. Line illustrations and monochrome photographs throughout. Full of useful information, especially good for wire frame hats without a block, trimmings, and making a variety of flowers.

Kliot, Jules, and Kaethe Kliot, eds. *Millinery, Feathers, Fruit, Flowers*. Berkeley, CA: Lacis Publications, 2000. Monochrome illustrations throughout. Paperbound. Reprint of *Millinery Materials*, originally published by the Women's Institute, 1927, and *The Art of Ostrich Plume Making*, by Melvin and Murgotten, Inc., published in 1912.

Langley, Susan. *Vintage Hats and Bonnets 1770–1970 Identification & Values*. Paducah, KY: Collector Books, 1988. Well illustrated with primary source material including fashion plates, old photographs, clothing catalogs, and advertisements as well as photographs of extant hats. An excellent source.

Lax, Roger, and Maria Carvainis. *Moustache*. New York, London, and Tokyo: Quick Fox, 1979. Illustrations and photographs of a large variety of moustaches.

Lens, Bernard. *The Exact Dress of the Head*. London, England: The Costume Society, 1970. Small paperbound book. Reproduction of original line drawings by Bernard Lens (1725) from the Victoria and Albert Museum with additional explanatory text. Women's caps and headdresses, men's wigs, bows, and bags.

McClellan, Mary Elizabeth. *Felt, Silk & Straw Handmade Hats: Tools and Processes*. Tools of the Nation Maker Series, Vol. 111. Doylestown, PA: The Bucks County Historical Society, 1977. Slim paperbound book with line drawings and photographs and information on historical American processes and equipment.

McDowell, Colin. *Hats: Status, Style and Glamour*. New York: Rizzoli International Publications, Inc., 1992. Monochrome and color photographs, line illustrations and engravings from primary sources. Men's and women's hats and hatmakers throughout history. Interesting and informative.

Nardi, Vincent, and Fred Nardi. *How to Do Your Hair Like a Pro*. New York: Perigee Books, 1977.

Pepin Press. *Hats*. A Pepin Press Design Book. New York: Costume and Fashion Press. An Imprint of Quite Specific Media Group Ltd., 1998. Paperbound. A collection of monochrome and color illustrations of hats for men, women, and children. Middle Ages–1920s. No text, and dates and descriptions are inconveniently listed in the back, but loads of good and useful stuff.

Probert, Christina, comp. *Hats in Vogue Since 1910*. In Vogue Series. New York: Abbeville Press, 1981. Paperbound. Monochrome and color photographs and fashion illustrations of women's hats from *Vogue*.

Reilly, Maureen, and Mary Beth Detrich. *Women's Hats of the 20th Century for Designers & Collectors with Price Guide*. Atglen, PA: Schiffer Publishing Ltd., 1997. Color illustrations and photographs throughout. Chapters by era, each spanning about 15 years.

Values put on all hats, but no actual dates given for many of the hats within these groupings.

Reynolds, William, and Ritch Rand. *The Cowboy Hat Book*. Salt Lake City, UT: Gibbs-Smith, Publisher, 1995. Paperbound. Monochrome and color photographs. All you ever wanted to know about cowboy hats and more.

Severn, Bill. *The Long and the Short of It: Five Thousand Years of Fun and Fury over Hair*. New York: David McKay Company, Inc., 1971. Photographs, line drawings, and engravings.

Shep, R. L., ed. *The Ladies' Self Instructor in Millinery & Mantua Making, Embroidery & Applique (1853)*. Mendocino, CA: R. L. Shep, 1988. Reprint. Paperbound. Revised edition with additional illustrations from *Godey's Lady's Book*. Small section on millinery.

Shields, Jody. *Hats: A stylish history and collector's guide*. New York: Clarkson N. Potter Inc., 1991. Monochrome and color photographs. 1920s to 1960s women's hats.

Smith, Desire. *Hats: with Values*. Atglen, PA: Schiffer Publishing Ltd., 1996. Color photographs of women's fashion hats from early nineteenth century to present day with price reference list.

Snyder, Jeffrey B. *Stetson Hats and the John B. Stetson Company 1865–1970*. Atglen, PA: Schiffer Publishing Ltd., 1997. Over 500 mostly color illustrations of men's and women's hats, hat boxes, and other items. Extensive history of the Philadelphia-based company whose name, although synonymous with western hats, also produced a large range of both men's and women's hat in numerous other styles.

Stevens, Angela. *How to Set and Style Your Own Wig*. New York: Arco Publishing Co., Inc., 1972.

Stevens Cox, James. *An Illustrated Dictionary of Hairdressing and Wigmaking*. New York: Drama Book Publishers, 1984. Line drawings, engravings and photographs.

Swinfield, Rosemarie. *Stage Makeup Step by Step*. The complete guide to: basic makeup, planning and designing makeup, adding and reducing age, ethnic makeup, special effects, make-up for film and television. Color illustrations and photographs throughout. Cincinnati, OH: Betterway Books, 1994.

Turudich, Daniela. *1940s Hairstyles*. Long Beach, CA: Streamline Press, 2001. Paperbound. Monochrome photographs and line drawings of hairstyles with "how-to" instructions. Useful.

Wilcox, R. Turner. *The Mode in Hats and Headdress: Including Hairstyles, Cosmetics and Jewelry*. New York: Charles Scribner's Sons, 1945, updated 1959. Line drawings of men's, women's, and children's hairstyles and headgear from antiquity–1959.

Woodforde, John. *The Strange Story of False Hair*. London: Routledge and Keegan Paul, 1971. Paintings, engravings and line drawings.

Men's Costume

Brander, Michael. *The Victorian Gentleman*. London: Gordon Cremonesi, 1975. "The manner, morals (and immorals) of our fathers and grandfathers." Not specifically on costume, but useful.

de Buzzaccarini, Vittoria. *Men's Coats*. The Twentieth Century Fashion Series. Modena, Italy: Zanfi Editori, 1994. Distributed in the U.S. by Costume and Fashion Press. An Imprint of Quite Specific Media Group Ltd., New York. Primary source illustrations in monochrome and color. Useful source.

Byrde, Penelope. *The Male Image: Men's Fashion in England 1300–1970*. London: B. T. Batsford Ltd., 1979. Monochrome illustrations from primary sources.

Chenoune, Farid. *A History of Men's Fashion*. Paris: Flammarion, 1993. Beautifully illustrated with monochrome and color illustrations and photographs from primary sources spanning eighteenth century to 1990. Excellent source.

Costantino, Maria. *Men's Fashion in the Twentieth Century: From Frock Coats to Intelligent Fibres.* London: B. T. Batsford Ltd., 1997. Distributed in the U.S. by Costume and Fashion Press. An Imprint of Quite Specific Media Group Ltd., New York. Illustrated throughout with monochrome photographs and illustrations of men's fashions and accessories.

Davis, R. I. *Men's 17th & 18th Century Costume, Cut & Fashion: Patterns for Men's Costumes.* Additional material by William-Alan Landes. Studio City, CA: Players Press, Inc., 2000. Scaled pattern drafts of period clothing. Profusely illustrated in monochrome and color. Line drawings, costume sketches, and photographs of actual costumes and extant garments. Very useful.

———. *Men's Garments 1830–1900: A Guide to Pattern Cutting.* London: B. T. Batsford Ltd., 1989. Rev. 2nd edition published by Players Press, Studio City, CA. n.d. Tailor's pattern drafts with instructions and line illustrations. Includes frock and morning coats, vests, trousers, top coats, and jackets.

Ettinger, Roseann. *Men's Clothing and Fabrics in the 1890s.* A Schiffer Book for Collectors. Atglen, PA: Schiffer Publishing Ltd., 1998. Paperbound. Monochrome and color illustrations throughout of men's tailored clothing and fabric samples. Includes sports clothes, uniforms, overcoats, vests, suits, smoking jackets, etc.

Halls, Zillah. *Men's Costume 1580–1750.* London: Her Majesty's Stationery Office, 1970. Catalogue with photographs of costumes from the London Museum.

———. *Men's Costume 1750–1800.* London: Her Majesty's Stationery Office, 1973. More costumes from the London Museum.

Harter, Jim. *Men: A Pictorial Archive from Nineteenth-Century Sources.* New York: Dover Publications, Inc., 1980.

Keers, Paul. *A Gentleman's Wardrobe: Classic Clothes and the Modern Man.* New York: Harmony Books, 1987. Informative text with contemporary and period illustrations.

de Marly, Diana. *Fashions for Men: An Illustrated History.* New York: Holmes and Meier Publishers, 1985. Illustrations from primary sources.

Martin, Richard, and Harold Koda. *Jocks and Nerds: Men's Style in the Twentieth Century.* New York: Rizzoli, 1989. Beautiful illustrations of men from a cross-section of society.

McDowell, Colin. *The Man of Fashion: Peacock Males and Perfect Gentlemen.* London: Thames and Hudson Ltd., 1997. Illustrated with men's fashions throughout the centuries.

Jno. J. Mitchell Co. *Jno. J. Mitchell Co. Men's Fashion Illustrations from the Turn of the Century.* New York: Dover Publications, Inc., 1990. Paperbound. Monochrome illustrations of men's formal and informal fashions from 1900–1910 from *The Sartorial Art Journal.*

Peacock, John. *Men's Fashon: The Complete Sourcebook.* London and New York: Thames and Hudson Ltd., 1996. Line drawings with color similar to his other books. Could be useful, if only because it covers men's clothing from late eighteenth century to 1994.

Schoeffler, O. E., and William Gale. *Esquire's Encyclopedia of 20th Century Men's Fashions.* New York: McGraw-Hill, 1973. Invaluable reference 1900–1970.

Shep, R. L., ed & comp. *Early Victorian Men.* Mendocino, CA: R. L. Shep, 2001. Paperbound. Includes *The Tailor's Masterpiece: All Kinds of Coats.* Rev. ed. 1838 by George Walker, supplemented by text of *Hints on Etiquette and the Uses of Society, 1836,* with additional fashion plates from *Modes de Paris 1836–1838.*

Shep, R. L., and Gail Cariou. *Shirts & Men's Haberdashery 1840s to 1920s.* Mendocino, CA: R. L. Shep, 1999. Paperbound. Includes patterns for men's shirts, underwear, nightwear, robes, and work clothing; and additional illustrations all taken from contemporary sources. An invaluable source.

Vincent, W. D. F. *Tailoring of the Belle Époque: Vincent's Garments (1903)*. Revised edition. Five parts in one volume. Reprint with additional illustrations. Mendocino, CA: R. L. Shep, 1991.

Walker, Richard. *Savile Row: An Illustrated History*. New York: Rizzoli International Publishers, Inc., 1989. Color and monochrome photographs of primary sources. Interesting book.

Waller, Jane. *A Man's Book: Fashion in the Man's World in the 20s and 30s*. London: Gerald Duckworth and Co., Ltd., 1977. Monochrome illustrations. Articles, interviews, formal and informal clothing and knitting patterns.

Occupational and Regional Costume

Barsis, Max. *The Common Man Through the Centuries: A Book of Costume Drawings*. New York: Frederick Ungar Publishing Co., 1973. Line drawings, not directly from original sources.

Braun and Schneider. *Historic Costume in Pictures*. New York: Dover Publications, Inc., 1975. Reprint of a 1907 German publication. 125 monochrome plates. Countries of the world from ancient times to late nineteenth century.

Copeland, Peter F. *Working Dress in Colonial and Revolutionary America*. Westport, CT: Greenwood Press, 1977. Monochrome illustrations and line drawings redrawn from original sources.

Cunnington, Phillis. *Costume of Household Servants: From the Middle Ages to 1900*. New York: Barnes and Noble; London: Adam & Charles Black, 1974. Line drawings, engravings, photographs, and paintings from primary sources covering the British domestic scene.

Cunnington, Phillis, and Catherine Lucas. *Occupational Costume in England: From the 11th Century to 1914*. London: Adam & Charles Black, 1967. Revised edition 1976. Line drawings, engravings, paintings, prints, and photographs.

———. *Charity Costumes of Children, Scholars, Almsfolk, Pensioners*. London: Adam and Charles Black, 1978. Line drawings, engravings, paintings, prints, and photographs.

Ewing, Elizabeth. *Everyday Dress 1650–1900*. London: B. T. Batsford, Ltd., 1984. Includes lots of occupational clothing for men and women from all walks of life. Monochrome illustrations and photographs from contemporary sources.

Grafton, Carol Berlanger. *Trades and Occupations: A Pictorial Archive from Early Sources*. New York: Dover Publications, Inc., 1990. Paperbound. Over 1,100 black-and-white illustrations.

Hiley, Michael. *Victorian Working Women: Portraits from Life*. London: Gordon Fraser, 1979. Photographs of women miners, milkmaids, gymnasts, maids, etc.

Hine, Lewis W. *Women at Work: 153 photographs by Lewis W Hine*. New York: Dover Publications, Inc., 1981. Working women 1907–1938.

———. *Men at Work: Photographic Studies of Modern Men and Machines*. New York: Dover Publications, Inc., 1977. Originally published in 1932.

Kennett, Frances. *Ethnic Dress*. Facts on File. An Infobase Holdings Company. New York: Reed International Books Limited, 1995. Great Britain: Mitchell Beazley, an imprint of Reed Consumer Books Limited, 1994. Color photographs showing contemporary folk costume from around the world.

Lansdell, Avril. *The Clothes of the Cut: A History of Canal Costume*. London: British Waterways Board, n.d. Monochrome illustrations and photographs.

———. *Occupational Costume and Working Clothes, 1776–1976*. Shire Album 27. Princes Risborough, Aylesbury, Bucks., England: Shire Publications, Ltd., 1977. Monochrome plates and photographs.

Lister, Margot. *Costumes of Everyday Life: An Illustrated History of Working Clothes.* Boston: Plays Inc., 1972. Line drawings.

de Marly, Diana. *Working Dress: A History of Occupational Clothing.* New York: Holmes & Meir Publishers, Inc., 1986. Monochrome illustrations and photographs with color insert. British men's and women's work clothes from seventeenth to mid-twentieth century.

Masson, Madeleine. *A Pictorial History of Nursing.* Twickenham, Middlesex, England: Hamlyn Publishing, 1985. Early times to 1980s, mostly British sources.

May, Trevor. *The Victorian Domestic Servant.* A Shire Album. Princes Risborough, Bucks., England: Shire Publications Ltd., 1998. Paperbound. Monochrome illustrations— engravings and photographs. Mostly female servants. A useful source.

———. *The Victorian Undertaker.* Shire Album 330. Princes Risborough, Bucks., England: Shire Publications Ltd., 1996, Paperbound. Black-and-white photographs and illustrations throughout.

McGowan, Alan. *Sailor: A Pictorial History.* New York: David McKay Company, Inc., 1977.

Oakes, Alma, and Margot Hamilton Hill. *Rural Costume: Its Origin and Development in Western Europe and the British Isles.* New York: Van Nostrand Reinhold, 1970. Line drawings.

De Pauw, Linda Grant, and Conover Hunt. *Remember the Ladies: Women in America 1750–1815.* New York: The Viking Press, 1976. Monochrome and color plates throughout.

Pyne, William H. *Rustic Vignettes for Artists and Craftsmen.* New York: Dover Publications, Inc., 1977. Early nineteenth century.

———. *Pyne's British Costumes.* Ware, Hertfordshire, England: Wordsworth Editions, Ltd., 1989. Reprint from 1805 with color drawings of occupational clothing.

Smart, J. E. *Clothes for the Job.* London: Her Majesty's Stationery Office, 1985. Paperbound. Catalogue of the Science Museum Collection. Work clothes for extreme heat or cold, flying, handling hazardous materials, industrial and protective clothing, sportswear, etc. Mostly twentieth century, some earlier examples. Useful and unique source of information.

Snowdon, James. *The Folk Dress of Europe.* New York: Mayflower Books, Inc., 1979. Monochrome and color illustrations, primary source plates, and photographs.

White, William Johnstone. *Working Class Costume 1818.* Reprint. London: The Costume Society, 1971. Eighteen plates of English rural life.

Williams-Mitchell, *Christobel. Dressed for the Job: The Story of Occupational Costume.* New York: Sterling Publishing Co., Inc., 1982. Color illustrations, engravings, prints, and photographs.

Sports Clothes

Cunnington, Phillis, and Alan Mansfield. *English Costume for Sports and Outdoor Recreation from the 16th to the 19th Centuries.* London: Adam and Charles Black, 1969. Line drawings, engravings, paintings, prints, and photographs.

Durant, John, and Otto Bettmann. *Pictorial History of American Sports: From Colonial Times to the Present.* Cranbury, NJ: A. S. Barnes and Company; London: Thomas Yoseloff Ltd., 1952, 1965, 3rd rev. ed. 1973. Monochrome illustrations and photographs throughout.

Fashion Institute of Technology. *All American: A Sportswear Tradition.* New York: Fashion Institute of Technology, 1985. Published in conjunction with an exhibit at FIT. Monochrome and color illustrations from primary sources and of clothing in the exhibit.

The Gallery of English Costume. Picture Book Number Eight: *Costume for Sport.* Manchester, England: Art Galleries Committee of the

Corporation of Manchester, 1963. Monochrome photographs of clothing and accessories in the Gallery of English Costume.

Green, Stephen. *Cricketing Bygones.* Shire Album 90. Princes Risborough, Aylesbury, Bucks., England: Shire Publications, Ltd., 1982.

Gurney, Gerald N. *Tennis, Squash and Badminton Bygones.* Shire Album 121. Princes Risborough, Aylesbury, Bucks., England: Shire Publications, Ltd., 1984.

Lane, Andrew. *Motoring Costume.* Shire Album 197. Princes Risborough, Aylesbury, Bucks., England: Shire Publications, Ltd., 1987.

Lansdell, Avril. *Seaside Fashions 1860–1939.* History in Camera Series. Princes Risborough, Aylesbury, Bucks., England: Shire Publications, Ltd., 1990. Tradespeople and holidaymakers at the English seaside. Paperbound with monochrome photographs and line illustrations throughout.

Lee-Potter, Charles. *Sportswear in Vogue Since 1910.* London: Thames and Hudson, 1984.

Lencek, Lena, and Gideon Bosker. *Making Waves: Swimsuits and the Undressing of America.* San Francisco: Chronicle Books, 1989. History of swimwear in the twentieth century.

Martin, Richard, and Harold Koda. *Splash: A History of Swimwear.* New York: Rizzoli International Publications, Inc., 1990. paperbound. Monochrome and color photographs. Published in conjunction with an exhibit at the Fashion Institute of Technology, New York.

The Metropolitan Museum of Art. *Man and the Horse.* New York: Simon and Schuster/The Metropolitan Museum of Art, 1984. Published in conjunction with an exhibit at the Museum. Monochrome and color illustrations and photographs from primary sources. Early times to twentieth century.

Okkonen, Marc. *Baseball Uniforms of the 20th Century: The Official Major League Baseball Guide.* New York: Sterling Publishing Co., Inc., 1991. The title says it all!

Pilley, Phil, ed. *Golfing Art.* Topsfield, MA: Salem House Publishers, 1988. Artists' work depicting various aspects of the sport, seventeenth to twentieth century.

Poli, Doretta Davanzo. *Beachwear and Bathing-Costume.* The Twentieth Century Fashion Series. Modena, Italy: Zanfi Editori, 1995. Distributed in the U.S. by Costume and Fashion Press. An Imprint of Quite Specific Media Group Ltd., New York. Monochrome and color illustrations.

Time-Life Books. Our American Century: A Century of Sports. Alexandria, VA: Time-Life Books, 2000. Monochrome and color illustrations and photographs.

Probert, Christina. *Swimwear in Vogue Since 1910.* In Vogue Series. New York: Abbeville Press, 1981. Illustrations from the fashion magazine.

Vandervell, Anthony and Charles Coles. *Games and the English Landscape: The Influence of the Chase on Sporting Art & Scenery.* New York: A Studio Book/The Viking Press, 1980. Engravings, paintings, prints, and photographs. Fifteenth to twentieth century, not specifically on costume but a useful source.

Underwear

Caldwell, Doreen. *And All Was Revealed: Ladies' Underwear 1907–1980.* New York: St. Martin's Press, 1981. Amusing and informative, illustrated with color line illustrations.

Carter, Alison. *Underwear: The Fashion History.* London: B. T. Batsford Ltd., 1992. Paperbound. Monochrome and color photographs and illustrations. 1490–1990. Emphasis on twentieth century with an odd man or two here and there but mainly women.

Chenoune, Farid. *Beneath It All: A Century of French Lingerie.* New York: Rizzoli International Publications, 2000.

Colmer, Michael. *Whalebone to See Through: A History of Body Packaging.* London and Edinburgh: Johnston and Bacon, 1979. Monochrome and color illustrations from primary sources.

Cunnington, C. Willett, and Phillis Cunnington. *A History of Underclothes.* With revisions by A. D. and Valerie Mansfield. London and Boston: Faber and Faber Ltd., 1981. Originally published in 1951. Men and women from fifteenth century to 1950. Line drawings and primary source illustrations.

———. *A History of Underclothes.* New York: Dover Publications, Inc., 1992. Paperbound reprint of the above.

Doyle, Robert. *Waisted Efforts: An Illustrated Guide to Corset Making.* Halifax, Nova Scotia, Canada: Sartorial Press Publications, 1997. Paperbound. Monochrome photographs, fashion illustrations, and corset patterns.

Ewing, Elizabeth. *Dress and Undress: A History of Women's Underwear.* New York: Drama Book Publishers, 1989. Partially based on *Underwear, a History.* Line drawings and monochrome illustrations from primary sources.

———. *Underwear, a History.* New York: Theatre Arts Books, 1972. Line drawings.

Farrell, Jeremy. *Socks and Stockings.* The Costume Accessories Series. London: B. T. Batsford Ltd., 1992. Monochrome and some color illustrations and photographs 1600–1990.

Fashion Institute of Technology. *The Undercover Story.* New York: Fashion Institute of Technology, 1982. Published in conjunction with an exhibit at F.I.T. Illustrations and photographs of nineteenth and twentieth century underwear in the exhibit.

Fontanel, Beatrice. *Support and Seduction: A History of Corsets and Bras.* New York: Harry N. Abrams, Inc., Publishers, 1997. First published in French in 1992 by Editions de la Martiniere. Beautifully illustrated.

Gottwald, Laura, and Janusz Gottwald, eds. *Frederick's of Hollywood 1947–1973: 26 Years of Mail Order Seduction.* New York: Castle/Drake Publishers, Inc., 1973. A collection of monochrome illustrations from the catalogs. No text.

Morel, Juliet. *Lingerie Parisienne.* New York: St. Martin's Press, 1976. Fashion illustrations and photographs of 1920s lingerie.

Neret, Gilles. *1000 Dessous: A History of Lingerie.* Koln, Germany: Taschen, 1998. Paperbound. Monochrome and color photographs and illustrations of underwear of all descriptions throughout the centuries—much of it might be classified as pornographic! No text but useful.

Page, Christopher. *Foundations of Fashion: The Symington Collection. Corsetry from 1856 to the Present Day.* Leicester, England: Leicester Museums, 1981.

Probert. *Lingerie in Vogue Since 1910.* In Vogue Series. New York: Abbeville Press, 1981. Illustrations from the fashion magazine.

Reyburn, Wallace. *Bust-Up: The Uplifting Tale of Otto Titzling and the Development of the Bra.* Englewood Cliffs, NJ: Prentice-Hall, Inc., 1972. Amusing account with line drawings and photographs.

Rothacker, Nanette. *The Undies Book.* New York: Charles Scribner's Sons, 1976. Scale patterns, line drawings, and construction instructions for 1970s-era underwear including bras, slips, camisoles, panties, and girdles.

Saint-Laurent, Cecil. *The History of Ladies' Underwear.* London: Michael Joseph, 1968. Early times to 1960s. Monochrome and color illustrations from primary sources.

———. *The Great Book of Lingerie.* New York: The Vendome Press, 1986. Distributed in the U.S. by Rizzoli International Publications, New York. Beautiful monochrome and color illustrations and photographs spanning antiquity to 1980s. Similar to above but enlarged and expanded.

Shep, R. L., comp. *Corsets: A Visual History*. Mendocino, CA: R. L. Shep, 1993. A compilation of black-and-white illustrations from various sources including advertisements, clothing catalogues, and magazines pre-1870 to 1930s.

Steele, Valerie. *The Corset: A Cultural History*. New Haven, CT and London: Yale University Press, 2001. Beautifully illustrated with monochrome and color photographs.

Warren, Philip. *Foundations of Fashion: The Symington Corsetry Collection 1860–1990*. Leicester, England: Leicestershire County Council Museums, Arts and Records Service, 2001. Monochrome and color illustrations and photographs of extant garments, fashion plates, advertisements, and memorabilia.

Waugh, Nora. *Corsets and Crinolines*. New York: Theatre Arts Books, 1954. Paperbound. Scale patterns, line drawings, monochrome illustrations, and pertinent commentary from primary sources. An invaluable reference.

Uniforms, Arms, and Armor

Ashdown, Charles Henry. *British and Continental Arms and Armour*. New York: Dover Publications, Inc., 1970. Reprint from 1909. Ancient times to seventeenth century.

Barthorp, Michael. *British Infantry Uniforms Since 1660*. Poole, Dorset, England: Blandford Press, 1982. Distributed in the U.S. by Sterling Publishing Co., Inc., New York. Beautiful color plates, primary source illustrations, and photographs.

Blaire, Claude. *European Armour circa 1066 to circa 1700*. New York: Crane, Russak and Co., Inc., 1972. Reprint from 1958. Line drawings and photographs from primary sources.

Blakeslee, Fred Gilbert. *Uniforms of the World*. New York: E. P. Dutton and Co., Inc., 1929. Useful source for police, army, navy, and civilian uniforms for most countries to circa 1929.

Detailed descriptions, monochrome photographs.

Cassin-Scott, Jack, and John Fabb. *Ceremonial Uniforms of the World*. New York: Arco Publishing Co., Inc., 1977. Color illustrations redrawn from primary sources.

Cochrane, Peter. *Scottish Military Dress*. London: Blandford Press, 1977. Color plates redrawn from primary sources.

Davis, Brian. *British Army Uniforms and Insignia of World War Two*. London; Melbourne; Harrisburg, PA; Cape Town: Arms and Armour Press, 1983. Monochrome photographs and line drawings. Comprehensive.

———. *German Army Uniforms and Insignia 1933–1945*. New York: Arco Publishing Co., Inc., 1977. Line drawings and many monochrome photographs.

———. *German Combat Uniforms of World War Two*. Vol. 1. Poole, Dorset, England: Arms and Armour Press, 1985.

———. *German Combat Uniforms of World War Two*. Vol. 11. London; Melbourne; Harrisburg, PA; Cape Town: Arms and Armour Press, 1985. Monochrome and some color photographs.

Davis, Brian Leigh, and Pierre Turner. *German Uniforms of the Third Reich 1933–1945*. New York: Arco Publishing Co., Inc., 1980. Detailed color illustrations redrawn from primary sources.

Elting, John R., ed. *Military Uniforms in America: The Era of the American Revolution, 1755–1795*. San Rafael, CA: Presidio Press, 1974. Detailed color illustrations redrawn from primary sources.

———. *Military Uniforms in America: Long Endure: The Civil War Period 1852–1867*. Novato, CA: Presidio Press, 1982. Sixty-four color illustrations, each accompanied by explanatory text.

Ewing, Elizabeth. *Women in Uniform Through the Centuries*. London: B. T. Batsford, Ltd.,

1975. Monochrome illustrations and photographs from primary sources.

Fitzsimons, Bernard. *Heraldry and Regalia of War*. New York: Beekman House, 1973. World Wars I and II.

Fox-Davis, Arthur Charles. *A Complete Guide to Heraldry*. New York: Bonanza Books, 1978. Reprint from 1909. Monochrome and some color illustrations. Comprehensive.

Harwell, Richard. *Uniforms and Dress of the Army and Navy of the Confederate States*. New York: St. Martin's Press, Inc., 1960. First published as *Uniforms and Dress of the Army of the Confederate States* in 1861 by Charles A. Wynne, Printer, Richmond, VA.

Haythornthwaite, Philip, and Michael Chappell. *Uniforms of 1812: Napoleon's Retreat from Moscow*. Poole, Dorset, England: Blandford Press, 1982. Color and some monochrome illustrations.

Hoffschmidt, E. J., and W. H. Tantum IV, eds. *German Army, Navy Uniforms and Insignia 1871–1918*. Old Greenwich, CT: WE, Inc., 1968. Monochrome illustrations and photographs.

Ingleton, Roy. *Police of the World*. New York: Scribner's Sons, 1979. Monochrome photographs throughout with descriptive text. Useful source.

Jarrett, Dudley. *British Naval Dress*. London: J. M. Dent and Sons, Ltd., 1960. Men's and women's uniforms, seventeenth to twentieth century.

Katcher, Philip. *Armies of the American Wars 1753–1815*. New York: Hastings House, Publishers, 1975. Color illustrations, monochrome plates and photographs from primary sources.

———. *Uniforms of the Continental Army*. York, PA: George Shumway Publisher, 1981. Photographs of extant garments and accessories, primary source illustrations, and a few patterns, some to scale. Comprehensive work.

Kelly, Francis M. *A Short History of Arms and Armour 1066–1800*. Newton Abbot, Devon, England: David and Charles, 1972. Reprint from 1931. Monochrome engravings and plates from primary sources.

Knotel, Herbert Jr., and Herbert Steig. *Uniforms of the World: A Compendium of Army, Navy and Air Force Uniforms 1700–1937*. New York: Charles Scribner's Sons, 1980. Reprint of 1937. Line drawings. Excellent source of information.

Koch, H. W. *Medieval Warfare*. London: A Bison Book. Dorset Press, 1982. Excellent monochrome and color illustrations from primary sources.

Lord, Francis. *Uniforms of the Civil War*. Cranbury, NJ: Thomas Yoseloff, 1970. Monochrome illustrations and photographs from primary sources.

Martin, Paul. *Arms and Armour: From the 9th to the 17th Century*. Rutland, VT: Charles E. Tuttle Company, Inc., 1967. Survey. Good monochrome and some color illustrations from primary sources.

———. *European Military Uniforms: A Short History*. London: Spring Books, 1967. Originally published as *Der Bunte Rock* in 1963. Color plates and line drawings.

May, Commander W. E. *The Dress of Naval Officers*. London: Her Majesty's Stationery Office, 1966. Paperbound. Monochrome photographs and illustrations from the National Maritime Museum and information on uniforms since inception in 1748—not much information on uniforms after the turn of the twentieth century.

McGowan, Alan. *Sailor: A Pictorial History: Life aboard the world's fighting ships from the beginnings of photography to the present day*. New York: David McKay Company, Inc., 1977. Monochrome photographs.

Men-At-Arms Series. London, Osprey Publishing Co. An extensive series of small books. Each book has 40 pages and includes 8 pages of color illustrations redrawn from primary sources dealing with a specific military event. Includes many countries and periods. Very useful.

Mollo, Andrew. *The British Armed Forces of WWII: Uniforms, Insignia and Organization.* New York: Crown Publishers, Inc., 1981. Beautifully illustrated.

Mollo, Boris. *The British Army from Old Photographs.* London: J. M. Dent and Sons Ltd., 1975. Numerous monochrome photographs from the National Army Museum.

———. *The Indian Army.* Poole, Dorset, England; New York; Sydney: New Orchard Editions/Blandford Press Ltd., 1981. Monochrome and color illustrations from primary sources. 1660–1947.

Mollo, Boris, and John Mollo. *Uniforms of the Imperial Russian Army.* Poole, Dorset, England: Blandford Press, 1979. Color illustrations covering Peter the Great to 1917.

Mollo, John, and Malcolm McGregor. *Uniforms of the Seven Years War 1756–63.* Poole, Dorset, England: Blandford Press, 1977. Color illustrations.

———. *Uniforms of the American Revolution.* New York: Macmillan Publishing Co., Inc., 1975. Color illustrations.

———. *Army Uniforms of World War 2.* London: Blandford Press, 1973. Detailed color illustrations redrawn from primary sources.

Mollo, Andrew, and Pierre Turner. *Army Uniforms of World War I.* New York: Arco Publishing Company, Inc., 1978. Detailed color illustrations redrawn from primary sources.

North, Anthony. *An Introduction to European Swords.* Owing Mills, MD: Stemmer House Publishers, Inc., 1982. Fourteenth to nineteenth century. Monochrome and color photographs.

North, Rene. *Military Uniforms.* London: Hamlyn, 1970. Brief but useful.

Ogden, H. A. *Uniforms of the United States Army, 1774–1889, In Full Color.* New York: Dover Publications, Inc., 1998. Paperbound reprint with 44 color plates.

Pimlott, Dr. John, and Adrian Gilbert. *Military Uniforms of the World: Uniforms and Equipment Since World War II.* New York: Crescent Books, 1986. Many color illustrations, monochrome and color photographs. Excellent source.

Robinson, H. Russell. *The Armour of Imperial Rome.* New York: Charles Scribner's Sons, 1975. First century B.C. to third century A.D. Numerous illustrations. Comprehensive.

———. *Oriental Armour.* Mineola, New York: Dover Publications, Inc., 2002. Paperback republication of 1967 edition. Line illustrations and monochrome photographs showing armor of the nineteenth and early twentieth centuries.

Risignoli, Guido. *The Illustrated Encyclopedia of Military Insignia of the 20th Century. A Comprehensive A-Z guide to the badges, patches and embellishments of the world's armed forces.* Secaucus, NJ: Chartwell Books, Inc., 1986.

Sachse, L., & Co. *Full-Color Uniforms of the Prussian Army: 72 Plates from the Year 1830.* New York: Dover Publications, Inc., 1981.

Saxtorph, Niels M. *Warriors and Weapons of Early Times in Color.* New York: The Macmillan Company, 1972. Illustrations based on research but not directly from primary sources.

Schick, I. T., ed. *Battledress: The Uniforms of the World's Great Armies 1700 to the Present.* London: Peerage Books, 1983. Line drawings in color, monochrome photographs, and primary source illustrations. Comprehensive.

Sietsema, Robert. *Weapons and Armor.* New York: Hart Publishing Company, Inc., 1978. Collection of monochrome pictures from public domain, shown by category.

Smith, Digby, and Michael Chappell. *Army Uniforms Since 1945.* Poole, Dorset, England: Blandford Press, 1980. Monochrome and color illustrations redrawn from original sources. Includes Korea, Vietnam, Israel, etc.

Stibbert, Frederick. *European Civil and Military Clothing: From the First to the Eighteenth Century*. New York: Dover Publications, Inc., 2001. Paperbound reprint. 217 plates of wonderful line engravings with captions but no text.

Stone, George Cameron. *A Glossary of the Construction, Decoration and Use of Arms and Armor in All Countries and in All Times, Together With Some Closely Related Subjects*. New York: Jack Brussel, 1961. Black-and-white illustrations with the text of alphabetical entries.

Sweeting, C. G. *Combat Flying Clothing. Army Air Forces Clothing During World War II*. Washington, DC: Smithsonian Institution Press, 1984. Over 150 detailed monochrome photographs. Very complete.

Tincey, John. *Soldiers of the English Civil War (2): Cavalry*. London: Osprey Publishing, 1990. Detailed information. Monochrome illustrations and photographs, with twelve color plates.

Unwin, Gregory J. W. *The United States Infantry: An Illustrated History, 1775–1918*. London, New York, Sydney: Blandford Press, 1988. Color plates, monochrome prints, maps, and photographs.

———. *The United States Cavalry: An Illustrated History*. Poole, Dorset, England; New York; and Sydney: Blandford Press, 1983. Monochrome photographs and thirty-two color plates covering 1776–1944.

War Office. *Dress Regulations for the Army 1900*. Reprint of 1900 official edition from Her Majesty's Stationery Office. London, Rutland, VT: Charles E. Tuttle Company, 1970. Monochrome plates of photographs of uniforms, trimmings, and equipment of the British Army.

WE. *German Military Uniforms and Insignia 1933–1945*. Old Greenwich, CT: WE, Inc., 1967. Line drawings and (not very clear) monochrome photographs.

Windrow, Martin, and Gerry Embleton. *Military Dress of North America 1665–1970*. New York: Charles Scribner's Sons, 1973. Color plates, monochrome illustrations and photographs.

Wise, Arthur, *Weapons in the Theatre*. New York: Barnes and Noble, Inc., 1968. Stage combat.

Zaloga, Steven J. *Soviet Army Uniforms in World War Two*. London: Arms and Armour Press, 1985. One hundred twenty-nine monochrome photographs of soldiers in action.

———. *Soviet Army Uniforms Today*. London, Melbourne, Harrisburg, PA; and Cape Town: Arms and Armour Press, 1985. Ninety-nine monochrome photographs of soldiers in action.

Weddings and Funerals

Baker, Margaret. *Wedding Customs & Folklore*. Totowa, NJ: Rowman and Littlefield, 1977.

Clark, Rowena. *Hatches, Matches and Dispatches: Christening, Bridal & Mourning Fashions*. Victoria, Australia: National Gallery of Victoria, 1987. Paperbound. Published in conjunction with a costume exhibit of the same name. Illustrated with monochrome and color photographs of clothing and accessories spanning sixteenth to twentieth centuries.

Cunnington, Phillis, and Catherine Lucas. *Costume for Births, Marriages & Deaths*. London: Adam and Charles Black, 1972. Medieval times to 1900. Line drawings, engravings, illustrations, and photographs from primary sources.

Felger, Donna H., comp. *Bridal Fashions: Victorian Era*. Cumberland, MD: Hobby House Press, Inc., 1986. Reprinted from fashion magazines of the period. Primarily for antique dolls, but useful.

Ginsburg, Madeleine. *Wedding Dress 1740–1970*. London: Her Majesty's Stationery Office, 1981. Sepia fashion drawings and photographs.

Lansdell, Avril. *Wedding Fashions 1860–1980*. History in Camera Series. Princes Risborough, Aylesbury, Bucks., England: Shire Publications, Ltd., 1983. Monochrome photographs.

McBride-Mellinger, Maria. *The Wedding Dress*. New York: Random House 1993. In 3 parts—1. The wedding dress in history. 2. The modern wedding dress. 3. Your wedding dress. Monochrome and color photographs.

Monsarrat, Ann. *And the Bride Wore. . .: The Story of the White Wedding*. New York: Dodd, Mead and Company, 1973. Comprehensive text but no illustrations.

Morley, John. *Death, Heaven and the Victorians*. London: Studio Vista, 1971. Monochrome and color illustrations, engravings and photographs.

O'Hara, Georgina. *The Bride's Book: A Celebration of Weddings*. London: Michael Joseph Ltd., 1991. Brides and weddings through the ages beautifully illustrated with paintings and engravings in monochrome and color.

Olian, JoAnne. *Wedding Fashions 1862–1912: 380 Costume Designs from "La Mode Illustrée."* New York: Dover Publications, Inc., 1994. Paperbound. Monochrome illustrations originally published in *La Mode Illustrée*, Paris, 1862–1912.

Probert, Christina. *Brides in Vogue Since 1910*. New York: Abbeville Press, Inc., 1984.

Stevenson, Pauline. *Bridal Fashions*. London: Ian Allen, Ltd., 1978. 1800–1970s with small section covering years prior to 1800. Monochrome and some color engravings, illustrations, and photographs.

Taylor, Lou. *Mourning Dress: A Costume and Social History*. London: George Allen and Unwin, 1983. Monochrome engravings, illustrations, and photographs.

Zimmerman, Catherine S. *The Bride's Book: A Pictorial History of American Bridal Gowns*. New York: Arbor House, 1985.

Costume Design, Theatre, and Film

Anderson, Cletis, and Barbara Anderson. *Costume Design*. New York: CBS College Publishing/Holt, Rinehart and Winston, 1984. Black-and-white photographs, line drawings, and color illustrations throughout. Covers design, construction, history, color etc. Comprehensive textbook.

Appelbaum, Stanley, ed. *The New York Stage: Famous Productions in Photographs*. New York: Dover Publications, Inc., 1976. 148 photographs 1883–1939, from the Theatre and Music Collection of the Museum of the City of New York.

Bailey, Margaret J. *Those Glorious Glamour Years: Classic Hollywood Costume Design of the 1930s*. London: Columbus Books, 1982. Paperbound edition, 1988. Black-and-white photographs throughout the text.

Bakst, Leon. *The Decorative Art of Leon Bakst*. New York: Dover Publications, Inc., 1981. Seventy-seven full-page illustrations, 44 in color.

Barton, Lucy. *Historic Costume for the Stage*. Boston: Walter H. Baker Company, 1935. New material added 1961. Line drawings.

Brooke, Iris. *Costume in Greek Classic Drama*. Reprint from 1962. Westport CT: Greenwood Press Inc., 1973. Line drawings.

———. *Medieval Theatre Costume: A Practical Guide to the Construction of Garments*. New York: Theatre Arts Books, 1967. Basic scale patterns and line drawings.

Chierichetti, David. *Hollywood Costume Design*. New York: Crown Publishers, 1976. Sketches and photographs.

Duchatre, Pierre Louis. *The Italian Comedy*. Reprint from 1929. New York: Dover Publications, Inc., 1966. Drawings, engravings and prints from primary sources.

Engelmeier, Regine, and Peter Engelmeier, eds. *Fashion in Film*. Munich, Germany: Prestel-

Verlag, 1990. Paperbound. Published in conjunction with an exhibition *Film und Mode—Mode im Film* held in Frankfurt am Main in 1990. Monochrome photographs throughout covering 7 decades.

Green, Ruth M. *The Wearing of Costume.* London: Sir Isaac Pitman and Sons Ltd., 1966. Line drawings. Movement for actors wearing period costume.

Gutner, Howard. *Gowns by Adrian: The MGM Years 1928–1941.* New York: Harry N. Abrams, Inc., 2001. Black-and-white movie stills, color inserts, and costume sketches.

Hartnoll, Phyllis. *The Theatre: A Concise History.* London: Thames and Hudson, 1985. Revised edition. First published in 1968 as *A Concise History of the Theatre.* Good quick reference with excellent monochrome and color photographs, many of costumes.

Hunt, Marsha. *The Way We Wore: Styles of the 1930s and 40s and Our World Since Then. Shown and Recalled by Hollywood's Star of the Golden Age of Movies.* Fallbrook, CA: Fallbrook Publishing, Ltd., 1993. Monochrome photographs throughout—movie stills, publicity shots, etc., all featuring the author!

Kelly, F. M. *Shakespearean Costume for Stage and Screen.* Reprint of 1938 edition with corrections and revisions by Alan Mansfield. New York: Theatre Arts Books, 1976. Line drawings and plates.

Laver, James. *Costume in the Theatre.* New York: Hill and Wang, 1964. Early times to twentieth century. Sketches, engravings, prints, and photographs from primary sources.

Leese, Elizabeth. *Costume Design in the Movies.* New York: Frederick Ungar Publishing Co., 1977. Sketches and photographs of costumes by selected designers.

Lewis, Jac, and Miriam Streizheff. *Costume: The Performing Partner.* Colorado Springs, CO: Meriwether Publishing Ltd., 1990. A book for actors about costumes.

Maeder, Edward. *Hollywood and History: Costume Design in Film.* Los Angeles, CA: Los Angeles County Museum/Thames and Hudson, 1987. Published in conjunction with an exhibit at the museum. Well documented and informative.

de Marly, Diana. *Costume on Stage 1600–1940.* Totowa, NJ: Barnes and Noble Books, 1982. Engravings, prints, and photographs from primary sources.

McConathy, Dale, and Diana Vreeland. *Hollywood Costume: Glamour! Glitter! Romance!* New York: Harry N. Abrams, Inc., 1976. Monochrome and color photographs. Published in conjunction with an exhibit at the Metropolitan Museum of Art.

Molinari, Cesare. *Theatre Through the Ages.* New York: McGraw-Hill Book Company, 1975. Ancient times to twentieth century. Monochrome and color illustrations from primary sources. Useful for costume.

Motley. *Designing and Making Stage Costumes.* New York: Watson-Guptill Publications, 1965. Plates of monochrome and color sketches and line drawings.

Newton, Stella Mary. *Renaissance Theatre Costume and the Sense of the Historic Past.* New York: Theatre Arts Books, 1975. Monochrome illustrations form primary sources. A scholarly work.

Russell, Douglas A. *Costume History and Style.* Boston: Allyn and Bacon, Inc., 1983. Monochrome photographs and line drawings.

———. *Period Style for the Theatre.* Boston: Allyn and Bacon, Inc., 1980. Monochrome photographs and illustrations of costumes, furniture, architecture, etc.

———. *Stage Costume Design: Theory, Techniques and Style.* Englewood Cliffs, NJ: Prentice-Hall, Inc., 1973.

———. *Theatrical Style: A Visual Approach to the Theatre.* Palo Alto, CA: Mayfield Publishing Company, 1976. Monochrome illustrations and photographs.

Strong, Roy. *Festival Designs by Inigo Jones: Drawings for Scenery and Costumes.* International Exhibits Foundation, 1967–8. Catalogue of a touring exhibit of drawings from the Devonshire Collection, Chatsworth, England. Monochrome and some color plates.

Time-Life Books. *Our American Century: 100 Years of Hollywood.* Alexandria, VA: Time-Life Books, 1999. Monochrome and color illustrations and photographs.

Toshio, Kawatake. *Kabuki: Eighteen Traditional Dramas.* San Francisco, CA: Chronicle Books, 1985. Beautiful color illustrations and photographs of the Danjuro Kabuki Dramas.

Van Witsen, Leo. *Costuming for Opera.* Bloomington, IN: Indiana University Press, 1981. Line drawings and photographs.

Decorative Design

Audsley, W., & G. *Designs and Patterns from Historic Ornament.* New York: Dover Publications, Inc., 1968. Paperbound. An unabridged republication of *Outlines of Ornament in the Leading Styles (1882).* A wide variety from ancient times, Oriental, medieval, etc. Paperbound.

Baldaukski, Karen, and François Gos. *Alpine Flower Designs for Artists and Craftsmen.* New York: Dover Publications, Inc., 1980. Paperbound.

Christie, Archibald H. *Pattern Design: An Introduction to the Study of Formal Ornament.* New York: Dover Publications, Inc., 1969. Paperbound.

D'Addetta, Joseph. *Treasury of Chinese Motifs.* New York: Dover Publications, Inc., 1981. Paperbound.

D'Avennes, Prisse, ed. *Arabic Art in Color.* New York: Dover Publications, Inc., 1972. Paperbound.

Meyer, Franz Sales. *Handbook of Ornament.* New York: Dover Publications, Inc., 1957. Paperbound.

Mucha, Alphonse, Maurice Verneuil, and Georges Auriol. *Art Nouveau Designs in Color.* New York: Dover Publications, Inc., 1974. Paperbound.

Proctor, Richard M., and Jennifer F. Lew. *Surface Design for Fabric.* Seattle, WA, and London: University of Washington Press, 1984. Dyeing, printing and needlework techniques. Monochrome process photographs, line drawings and surface design examples. Some color. Paperbound.

Rhodes, Zandra, and Anne Knight. *The Art of Zandra Rhodes.* London: Jonathan Cape Ltd., 1984. Drawings, design details, and photographs of garments, mostly in color.

Suguy, E. A. *Seguy's Decorative Butterflies and Insects in Full Color.* New York: Dover Publications, Inc., 1977. Paperbound.

———. *Full-Color Floral Design in the Art Nouveau Style.* New York: Dover Publications, Inc., 1977. Paperbound.

Speltz, Alexander. *The Styles of Ornament.* New York: Dover Publications, Inc., 1959. Paperbound.

Verneuil, M. P. *Floral Patterns.* New York: Dover Publications, Inc., 1981. Paperbound.

———. *Art Nouveau Floral Ornament in Color.* New York: Dover Publications, Inc., 1976. Paperbound.

Drawing and Color Studies

Birren, Faber. *Creative Color: A Dynamic Approach for Artists and Designers.* New York: Van Nostrand Reinhold Co., 1961.

Edwards, Betty. *Drawing on the Artist Within.* New York: Simon and Schuster, Inc., 1986. All about new ways of seeing.

———. *Drawing on the Right Side of the Brain.* Los Angeles, CA: Jeremy P. Tarcher, Inc., 1986. Revised edition. Readily accessible text that relates how we see to what we draw.

Eisman, Leatrice, and Lawrence Herbert. *The Pantone Book of Color.* New York: Harry N.

Abrams, Inc., 1990. Brief discussion of color theory and over 1,000 color standards.

Gerstner, Karl. *The Forms of Color: The Interaction of Visual Elements*. Cambridge, MA, and London: The MIT Press, 1986. Interesting discussion of color and design.

Itten, Johannes. *The Art of Color*. New York: Reinhold Publishing Corp., 1961. Good theory.

———. *The Elements of Color: A Treatise on the Color System of Johannes Itten based on His Book* The Art of Color. New York: Van Nostrand Reinhold Co., 1970. Simplified, condensed version of the above.

Kumagai, Kojiro. *Fashion Illustration*. Tokyo, Japan: Graphic-sha Publishing Co. Ltd., 1984. All aspects of fashion drawing, figures, garments, and details.

Loomis, Andrew. *Figure Drawing for All It's Worth*. Cleveland, Ohio: The World Publishing Co., 1943. Clear presentation, good illustrations.

Mugnaini, Joseph. *The Hidden Elements of Drawing*. New York: Van Nostrand Reinhold Co., 1974. Interesting investigation of figure drawing.

Penders, Mary Coyne. *Color and Cloth. The Quiltmaker's Ultimate Workbook*. San Francisco: The Quilt Digest Press, 1989. Hands-on exercises with color photographs and monochrome line drawings.

A Quarto Book. *Mix and Match Designer Colors*. New York: Van Nostrand Reinhold, 1990. Over 600 color swatches, each shown as halftone and with black-and-white type.

Raynes, John. *Human Anatomy for the Artist*. New York: Crescent Books, 1979. Male and female anatomy clearly presented; illustrated with photographs and drawings.

Scanlon, Rory. *Costume Design Graphics: A Workbook in Figure Drawing and Clothing Techniques*. New York and Hollywood: Costume and Fashion Press, 2000. Paperbound. A 'draw along workbook.' Useful for anyone who has difficulty drawing and clothing the human figure.

Sheppard, Joseph. *Drawing the Living Figure*. New York: Watson-Guptill Publications, 1984. Comparison of surface anatomy with underlying bone and muscle structure.

Sloan, Eunice Moore. *Illustrating Fashion*. New York: Harper and Row, 1968. Full of techniques useful for costume rendering.

Walters, Margaret. *The Nude Male: A New Perspective*. New York: Penguin Books, 1979. A study of the male figure from artist's work over the centuries includes some useful illustrations.

Yajima, Isao. *Mode Drawing—Costume*. Tokyo, Japan: Graphic-sha Publishing Company Ltd., 1987. Costume sketching to capture mood, movement, and activity. Includes photographs and the drawings they inspired.

Dyeing, Painting, Textiles, and Crafts

Baines, Patricia. *Flax and Linen*. Shire Album 133. Princes Risborough, Aylesbury, Bucks., England: Shire Publications, Ltd., 1985. Paperbound. Linen process from plant to woven cloth with monochrome illustrations.

Dryden, Deborah M. *Fabric Painting and Dyeing for the Theatre*. Portsmouth, NH: Heinemann, 1993. Paperbound. An indispensable book full of detailed instructions for various techniques for dyeing, painting, and aging costumes for theatre.

Finch, Karen, and Greta Putnam. *Care and Preservation of Textiles*. New York: Drama Book Publishers, 1972.

Green, David. *Fabric Printing and Dyeing*. Newton Center, MA: Charles T. Branford Co., 1972.

Grey, Robin. *Robin Grey's Batiker's Guide*. San Raphael, CA: DTC Publications, 1976.

James, Thurston. *The Prop Builder's Mask-Making Handbook*. White Hall, VA: Betterway Publications, Inc., 1990. Monochrome photographs and line drawings illustrate the process.

Johnson, Meda Parker, and Glen Kaufman. *Design on Fabrics.* New York: Reingold, 1967.

Joseph, Marjory L. *Essentials of Textiles.* Fort Worth, Chicago, San Francisco, Philadelphia, Montreal, Toronto, London, Sydney, Tokyo: Holt, Rinehart and Winston, Inc., 1876. 4th edition, 1988.

Kleeberg, Irene Cumming, ed. *The Butterick Fabric Handbook.* New York: Butterick Publishing, 1975.

Miller, Edward. *Textiles: Properties and Behaviour in Clothing Use.* London: B. T. Batsford, Ltd., 1984. Distributed in the U.S. by David and Charles, Inc., North Pomfret, VT. Useful reference.

Motley, P. *Theatre Props.* New York: Drama Book Specialists (Publishers), 1975.

Neumann, Robert von. *Design and Creation of Jewelry.* Revised edition. Radnor, PA: Chilton Book Co., 1972.

Pizzuto, Joseph. *Fabric Science.* New York: Fairchild Publications, 1999. Revised 7th ed. Monochrome photographs, line drawings, charts. Extensive and useful.

———. *Fabric Science Swatch Kit, 7th Edition.* New York: Fairchild Publications, 2001. Designed to accompany the above publication in both student and teacher versions.

Queen, Sally A. *Textiles for Colonial Clothing: A Workbook of Swatches and Information.* Arlington, VA: Q Graphics Production Company, 2000. Small spiral-bound book of fabric swatches with explanatory text. Swatches approximate as closely as possible to those used for clothing in eighteenth-century colonial America. Great historical reference.

Ribbon Art Publishing Company. *Old-Fashioned Ribbon Art: Ideas and Designs for Accessories and Decorations.* New York: Dover Publications, Inc., 1986. Abridged version of the 1920s original. Line drawings and monochrome photographs.

Rutt, Richard, Bishop of Leicester. *A History of Hand Knitting.* London: B. T. Batsford, Ltd., 1987. Monochrome and color photographs, diagrams and charts. 1500 to 1980s.

Story, Joyce. *The Thames and Hudson Manual of Dyes and Fabrics.* New York: Thames and Hudson, Inc., 1978.

Tortora, Phyllis G. *Fairchild's Dictionary of Textiles.* New York: Fairchild Publications, 1996. Revised, expanded edition. Useful reference.

Weiner, Louis. *Handmade Jewelry: A Manual of Techniques.* New York: Van Nostrand Reinhold, Co., 1981. Good process sequences illustrated with line drawings and monochrome photographs.

Patterns and Construction

de Alcega, Juan. *Tailor's Pattern Book 1589.* Trans. Jean Pain and Cecilia Bainton. New York: Costume and Fashion Press. An Imprint of Quite Specific Media Group Ltd. Paperbound. 135 tailoring patterns originally published in 1589 as *Libro de Geometria, Practica y Traca.*

Amaden-Crawford, Connie. *The Art of Fashion Draping.* New York: Fairchild Publications, 1996. Paperbound. 2nd edition. Excellent instructions for draping women's clothing.

Arnold, Janet. *Patterns of Fashion: The Cut and Construction of Clothes for Men and Women c. 1560–1620.* New York: Costume and Fashion Press. An Imprint of Quite Specific Media Group Ltd., 1985. Paperbound. Detailed drawings of Elizabethan clothing with scaled patterns. Photographs of actual garments and close-up details, paintings and engravings. Invaluable.

———. *Patterns of Fashion 1 c. 1660–1860: Englishwomen's Dresses and Their Construction.* New York: Costume and Fashion Press. An Imprint of Quite Specific Media Group Ltd., 1977. Paperbound. Drawings of extant period garments showing their construction with detailed scale patterns. Invaluable.

———. *Patterns of Fashion 2 c. 1860–1940: English-women's Dresses and Their Construction*. New York: Costume and Fashion Press. An Imprint of Quite Specific Media Group Ltd., 1977. Paperbound. Drawings of extant period garments showing their construction with detailed scale patterns. Invaluable.

Baumgarten, Linda, and John Watson with Florin Carr. *Costume Close-up: Clothing Construction and Pattern 1750–1790*. Williamsburg, VA: The Colonial Williamsburg Foundation in Association with Costume and Fashion Press. An Imprint of Quite Specific Media Group Ltd., New York, 1999. Paperbound. Patterns for eighteenth-century clothing taken from extant garments. Beautifully illustrated with monochrome and color photographs. Detailed and informative text.

Bradfield, Nancy. *Costume in Detail: Women's Dress 1730–1930*. New York: Costume and Fashion Press. An Imprint of Quite Specific Media Group Ltd., 1980. Paperbound. Line drawings and photographs of extant garments with construction details.

Brown, P. Clement. *Art in Dress (1922)*. Mendocino, CA: R. L. Shep, 1993. Paperbound reprint with additional material. Line illustrations, patterns, and instructions for women's clothing.

Burnham, Dorothy K. *Cut My Cote*. Toronto, Ontario: Royal Ontario Museum, 1973. Small paperbound book. Line drawings with metric scale patterns for shirts, chemises, smocks, surplices, and cotes.

Cabrera, Roberto, and Patricia Flaherty Meyers. *Classic Tailoring Techniques: A Construction Guide for Men's Wear*. New York: Fairchild Publications, 1983.

———. *Classic Tailoring Techniques: A Construction Guide for Women's Wear*. New York: Fairchild Publications, 1984. Both these books include excellent pattern adjustment information for many body types.

Collard, Eileen. *The Cut and Construction of Women's Dress in the 1930s*. Burlington, Ontario: Eileen Collard, 1983. Paperbound with monochrome illustrations, line drawings and patterns.

Croonborg, Frederick T. *The Blue Book of Men's Tailoring: Theatrical Costumemaker's Pattern Book for Edwardian Men's Costumes*. New York: Van Nostrand Reinhold, 1977. Reprint from 1907. Line drawings and patterns.

Davis, R. I. *Men's 17th & 18th Century Costume, Cut & Fashion: Patterns for Men's Costumes*. Additional material by William-Alan Landes. Studio City, CA: Players Press, Inc., 2000. Scaled pattern drafts of period clothing. Profusely illustrated in monochrome and color with line drawings, costume sketches and photographs of extant garments. Very useful.

———. *Men's Garments 1830–1900: A Guide to Pattern Cutting*. London: B. T. Batsford Ltd., 1989. Rev. 2nd edition published by Players Press, Studio City, CA. Tailor's pattern drafts with instructions and line illustrations. Includes frock and morning coats, vests, trousers, top coats, and jackets.

Devere, Louis. *The Handbook of Practical Cutting on the Centre Point System (1866). Illustrated with Nearly 350 Model Patterns or Diagrams*. Lopez Island, WA: R. L. Shep, 1986. Revised, enlarged reprint of original edition. Paperbound. Pattern drafts for men's tailored garments.

Edson, Doris, and Lucy Barton. *Period Patterns*. Boston: Walter H. Baker Co., 1942. Paperbound supplement to *Historic Costuming for the Stage*. Patterns taken from extant garments and period pattern sources and adapted to modern sizes.

Ericson, Sandra, ed. *Draping & Designing with Scissors and Cloth 1930s*. St. Helena, CA: Retro-Prints, 1992. Line drawings throughout. Paperbound reprint from the Women's Institute of Domestic Arts and Sciences.

Gehret, Ellen J. *Rural Pennsylvania Clothing: Being a Study of the Wearing Apparel of the German and English Inhabitants both Men and Women in the Late Eighteenth and Early Nineteenth Century.* York: PA: Liberty Cap Books/George Shumway Publisher, 1976. Scale patterns, construction instructions, line drawings, and photographs of extant clothing and accessories.

Gibbs, Patricia. *U.S. Pattern Book: Patterns for the U.S. Fatigue Uniform, 1861–1865.* Fredericksburg, VA: Historians Unlimited, 1980. Scale patterns, construction directions, and drawings of completed items.

Giles, Edward B. *The Art of Cutting and History of English Costume.* Lopez Island, WA: R. L. Shep, 1987. Paperbound reprint of original edition published in 1887.

Gordon, S. S. *Turn-of-the-Century Fashion Patterns and Tailoring Techniques.* New York: Dover Publications, Inc., 2000. Paperbound republication of *The "Standard" Work on Cutting Ladies' Tailor-Made Garments*, 1901.

———. Jules Kliot and Kaethe Kliot, eds. *Ladies' Tailor-Made Garments 1908.* Berkeley, CA: Lacis Publications, 1993. Monochrome illustrations and patterns throughout. Paperbound reprint of *The "Standard" Work on Cutting Ladies' Tailor-Made Garments* originally published by the Jno. J. Mitchell Co. with additional illustrations.

Grimble, Frances, ed. *The Voice of Fashion. 79 Turn-of-the Century Patterns with Instructions and Fashion Plates.* San Francisco: Lavolta Press, 1998. Paperbound. Pattern drafts and monochrome fashion illustrations from 1900–1906 with additional material.

———. *The Edwardian Modiste: 85 Authentic Patterns with Instructions, Fashion Plates, and Period Sewing Techniques.* San Francisco: Lavolta Press, 1997. Paperbound. Patterns and fashion plates reproduced from the *1905 American Garment Cutter Instruction and Diagram Book* and 1907–1909 issues of the quarterly *American Modiste* with additional material.

Hansen, James A. *The Frontier Scout & Buffalo Hunter's Sketchbook.* Chadron, NE: The Fur Press, 1980. Paperbound. Line drawings and patterns from extant garments (not to scale) of shirts, leather coats, jackets, trousers, etc.

Hansen, James Austin, and Kathryn J. Wilson. *Feminine Fur Trade Fashions.* Chadron, NE: The Fur Press, 1976. Paperbound. Line drawings and patterns as above. Mainly Native American tools, accessories and clothing.

———. *The Mountain Man's Sketchbook.* Chadron, NE: The Fur Press, 1976. Paperbound. More patterns and drawings.

Harris, Kristina. *59 Authentic Turn-of-the Century Fashion Patterns.* New York: Dover Publications, Inc., 1994. Paperbound. Over 575 black-and-white line illustrations. Women's and children's dressmaker's patterns reproduced from *The Voice of Fashion*, originally published in the 1890s.

Harris, Kristina, ed. *Authentic Victorian Fashion Patterns: A Complete Lady's Wardrobe.* New York: Dover Publications, Inc., 1999. Paperbound. Black-and-white fashion illustrations and scaled dressmaker's patterns reproduced from *The Voice of Fashion*, originally published in the 1890s.

———. *Authentic Victorian Dressmaking Techniques.* New York: Dover Publications, Inc., 1999. Paperbound replication of *Dressmaking Up to Date* published by the Butterick Publishing Company in 1905.

Hecklinger, Charles. *Dress and Cloak Cutter: Women's Costume 1877–1882.* Lopez Island, WA: R. L. Shep, 1987. Paperbound revised edition of the original with additional material by R. L. Shep.

Hill, Margot Hamilton, and Peter A. Bucknell. *The Evolution of Fashion: Pattern and Cut from 1066–1930.* New York: Costume and Fashion Press. An Imprint of Quite Specific Media Group Ltd., London: B. T. Batsford, 1967. Paperbound with line illustrations and patterns adapted to modern sizes.

Holding, T. H. *Late Victorian Women's Tailoring: The Direct System of Ladies' Cutting (1897)*. Third ed. enlarged and edited by R. L. Shep. Mendocino, CA: R. L. Shep, 1997. Paperbound.

Holkeboer, Katherine Strand. *Costume Construction*. Englewood Cliffs, NJ: Prentice-Hall, Inc., 1989. Patterns, draping, sewing techniques, crafts, and accessories.

Hollen, Norma R., and Carolyn J. Kundel. *Pattern Making by the Flat-Pattern Method*. New York: Macmillan Publishing Company, 1987. 6th ed.

Hopkins, J. C. *Edwardian Ladies' Tailoring: The Twentieth Century System of Ladies Garment Cutting (1910)*. Reprint. Mendocino, CA: R. L. Shep, 1991.

Hopper, Elizabeth, and Ruth Countryman. *Women's Wear of the 1920s*. Studio City, CA: Player's Press. Patterns to scale, period drawings, and photographs.

———. *Women's Wear of the 1930s*. Studio City, CA: Player's Press. Second book in the series.

Hunnisett, Jean. *Period Costume for Stage & Screen: Medieval–1500*. Studio City, CA: Player's Press, Inc. 1996. Monochrome illustrations, and patterns to scale.

———. *Period Costume for Stage & Screen 1500–1800*. Studio City, CA: Player's Press, Inc. Period patterns to scale, many based on original garments. Excellent source.

———. *Period Costume for Stage & Screen 1800–1909*. Studio City, CA: Player's Press, Inc. Continuation of above.

———. *Period Costume for Stage & Screen: Outer Garments, Book 1 (Cloaks, Capes, Stoles and Wadded Mantles)*. Studio City, CA: Player's Press, Inc. The first in a series of a two-book set.

Kawashima, Masaaki. *Fundamentals of Men's Fashion Design: A Guide to Tailored Clothes*. New York: Fairchild Publications, 1980.

Kidwell, Claudia. *Cutting a Fashionable Fit: Dressmakers' Drafting Systems in the United States.* Washington, D.C.: Smithsonian Institution Press, 1979. Scholarly work on women's nineteenth and early twentieth century drafting systems.

Kirke, Betty. *Madeleine Vionnet*. San Francisco: Chronicle Books, 1998. Monochrome and color photographs and illustrations throughout with patterns taken from actual garments. Covers teens to 1930s. Beautifully illustrated account of the French couturier's life and work. A true labor of love on the author's part.

Klinger, Robert L. *Sketch Book 76: The American Soldier 1775–1781*. Union City, TN: Pioneer Press, 1967. Paperbound with sketches, notes, and patterns.

———. *Distaff Sketch Book: A Collection of Notes and Sketches on Women's Dress in America 1774–1783*. Union City, TN: Pioneer Press, 1974. Paperbound, includes patterns.

Kliot, Jules, and Kaethe Kliot, eds. *Garment Patterns: 1889 with Instructions*. Berkeley, CA: Lacis Publications, 1996. Paperbound with monochrome illustrations and patterns throughout. Reprinted material taken from *The National Garment Cutter Instruction Book* and *The National Garment Cutter Book of Diagrams* published in 1899. Women's and children's clothing.

Kopp, Ernestine, Vittorina Rolfo, Beatrice Zelin, and Lee Gross. *Designing Apparel Through the Flat Pattern*. New York: Fairchild Publications, 1960. Revised 6th edition, 1992. Pattern drafting for women's clothing using basic slopers.

Lawson, Joan, and Petr Revitt. *Dressing for the Ballet*. London: Adam & Charles Black, 1958. Line drawings, scale patterns and construction instructions. Includes knitting patterns.

Levine, Arnold, and Robin McGee. *Patterns for Costume Accessories*. New York: Costume and Fashion Press. An Imprint of Quite Specific Media Group Ltd., 2002. Paperbound.

Patterns for period and contemporary accessories including hats, neckwear, reticules, gauntlets, etc. with illustrations and instructions.

Liechty, Elizabeth L., Della N. Pottberg, and Judith A. Rasband. *Fitting and Pattern Alteration: A Multi-Method Approach.* New York: Fairchild Publications, 1992. Paperbound.

Marshall, Beverley. *Smocks and Smocking.* Sherbourne, Dorset, England: Alphabooks, 1980. Scale patterns and construction instructions for modern and period smocks, beautifully illustrated.

Minister, Edward, and Son. *The Complete Guide to Practical Cutting (1853).* Second ed., Revised—2 volumes in 1. Paperbound reprint. Enlarged and edited by R. L. Shep with additional garments and notes from other contemporary sources. Mendocino, CA: R. L. Shep, 1993. Paperbound. Men's and some women's tailoring patterns as well as uniforms, liveries, etc.

Mitchell, Jno. J. *"Standard" Work on Cutting. (Men's Garments): A Complete Treatise on the Art and Science of Garment Cutting.* Berkeley, CA: Lacis Publications, 1990. Paperbound reprint of the 1886 edition.

Moulton, Bertha. *Garment-cutting and Tailoring for Students.* New York: Theatre Arts Books, 1967. Scale patterns for women's garments, line drawings, and tailoring techniques.

Ralston, Margaret C. Jules and Kaethe Kliot, eds. *Fashion Outlines: Dress Cutting by the Block Pattern System. A system of scientific dressmaking explored through the classical styles of the late 1920s and early 1930s.* Berkeley, CA: Lacis Publications, 1990. Paperbound reprint of original.

Reader's Digest. *Complete Sewing Guide.* Pleasantville, NY, and Montreal: The Reader's Digest Association, Inc., 1976.

Shaeffer, Claire. *Fabric Sewing Guide, Updated Edition.* New York: Fairchild Publications, 1994. Paperbound. General guide to fiber content, with particular emphasis on the sewing and care of the various types of fabrics.

Shep, R. L. *The Great War: Styles and Patterns of the 1910s.* Mendocino, CA: R. L. Shep, 1998. Paperbound. More than 80 patterns with drafting instructions with some additional illustrations reprinted from contemporary sources, both American and British. Includes skirts, men's and women's outdoor wear, sportswear, and British military uniforms.

Thomas, Michael R. *A Confederate Sketchbook.* Highlands, NJ: M. R. Thomas, 1980. Drawings of garments with measurements and construction notes, but no actual patterns.

Thompson, Mrs. F. E. *Garment Patterns for the Edwardian Lady.* Berkeley, CA: Lacis Publications, 1991. Paperbound, originally published as *La Mode Universelle no. 22, A Book of Pattern Designs,* 1905.

Thursfield, Sarah. *The Medieval Tailor's Assistant: Making Common Garments 1200–1500.* Carlton, Bedford, England: Ruth Bean Publishers, 2001. Distributed in the U.S. by Costume and Fashion Press. An Imprint of Quite Specific Media Group Ltd., New York. Paperbound. Black-and-white and some color illustrations. Patterns for reproducing historical clothing.

Tilke, Max. *Costume Patterns and Designs: A Survey of Costume Patterns and Designs of All Periods and Nations from Antiquity to Modern Times.* New York: Hastings House, 1974. Garments illustrated flat and in color. Excellent source for ethnic costumes based on geometric shapes.

———. *Folk Costumes from East Europe, Africa and Asia.* London: A. Zwemmer, Ltd., 1978. Similar to the above.

Trautman, Patricia A. *Clothing America: A Bibliography and Location Index of Nineteenth-Century America Pattern Drafting Systems.* New York: The Costume Society of America, 1987.

Tyrrell, Anne V. *Changing Trends in Fashion: Patterns of the Twentieth Century.* London: B. T.

Batsford, Ltd., 1986. Men's and women's patterns to scale, 1900–1970. Formal and informal clothing, including British military uniforms of the two World Wars.

Vincent, W. D. F. *Tailoring of the Belle Époque: Vincent's Systems of Cutting All Kinds of Tailor-Made Garments (1903)*. Mendocino, CA: R. L. Shep, 1991. 5 parts in 1 volume: men and women, military, clergy, civil servants, court and academic, servants. Paperbound reprint.

———. *The Tailor and Cutter Academy Systems of Cutting All Kinds of Tailor-Made Garments*. In 5 parts. London: The John Williamson Co., Ltd., 1908–1912. Tailor's patterns.

Waugh, Norah. *The Cut of Men's Clothes 1600–1900*. London: Faber and Faber Limited; New York: Theatre Arts Books, 1964. Scale patterns, monochrome photographs of primary sources, and excellent commentary.

———. *The Cut of Women's Clothes 1600–1930*. New York: Theatre Arts Books, 1968, 1994. Women's version of the above. Both are costume shop staples.

Womans Institute of Domestic Arts and Sciences. *Drafting and Pattern Designing (1924)*. Berkeley, CA: Lacis Publications, 1994. Paperbound republication of the original.

———. *Draping and Designing with Scissors and Cloth: Details and Instructions for the Creating and Developing of Garments from Cloth Without Patterns*. Scranton, PA: Woman's Institute of Domestic Arts and Sciences, Inc., 1924.

Wright, Meredeth. *Put on Thy Beautiful Garments: Rural New England Clothing 1783–1800*. East Montpelier, VT: The Clothes Press, 1990. Paperbound with scale patterns, drawings, and instructions as well as historical information.

———. *Everyday Dress of Rural America, 1783–1800: With Instructions and Patterns*. New York: Dover Publications, Inc., 1992. Paperbound unabridged republication of the above.

Zamkoff, Bernard, and Jeanne Price. *Basic Pattern Skills for Fashion Design*. New York: Fairchild Publications, 1987. Paperbound.

Theory and Psychology of Dress

Baines, Barbara Burman. *Fashion Revivals from the Elizabethan Age to the Present Day*. London: B. T. Batsford Ltd.; New York: Drama Book Publishers, 1981. Survey of revived styles from all walks of life in England, covering sixteenth to twentieth centuries. Monochrome and some color illustrations from primary sources.

Bell, Quentin. *On Human Finery*. New York: Schocken Books, 1976. 2nd revised edition, first published in 1947. Theories on fashion and clothing with monochrome illustrations and line drawings.

Cremers-van der Does, Eline Canter. Leo Van Witson, trans. *The Agony of Fashion*. Poole, Dorset, England: Blandford Press, 1980. The pain and discomfort incurred by the fashion-conscious through the ages. Primary source illustrations, some color.

Gattey, Charles Nielsen. *The Bloomer Girls*. London: A Femina Book. Macdonald and Co., Ltd., 1967. Clothing reform. Monochrome illustrations.

Glynn, Prudence. *Skin to Skin: Eroticism in Dress*. London, Boston, and Sydney: George Allen and Unwin, 1982. Monochrome and color illustrations and photographs from primary sources of all ages and cultures.

Hollander, Anne. *Seeing Through Clothes*. New York: The Viking Press, 1978. Study of the connection between clothing in the visual arts and real life through the ages. Monochrome illustrations from primary sources.

Hollander, Anne. *Sex and Suits: The Evolution of Modern Dress*. New York: Alfred Knopf, 1994. Monochrome illustrations from primary sources.

Kaplan, Joel H., and Sheila Stowell. *Theatre and Fashion: Oscar Wilde to the Suffragettes*. New

York: Cambridge University Press, 1994. Monochrome illustrations and photographs. Explores relationship between theatre, fashion, and society in late Victorian and early twentieth-century England.

Lurie, Alison. *The Language of Clothes.* New York: Random House, 1981. Psychology of dress illustrated in monochrome and color.

Newton, Stella Mary. *Health, Art and Reason: Dress Reformers of the 19th Century.* London: John Murray, 1974. The movement toward less restricting, more comfortable clothing. Monochrome illustrations from primary sources.

Ribeiro, Aileen. *Dress and Morality.* London: B. T. Batsford, Ltd., 1986. Morality in dress from antiquity to 1980s. Monochrome illustrations from primary sources.

Rudofsky, Rudolph. *The Unfashionable Human Body.* New York: Doubleday and Co., Inc., 1971. An amusing look at fads and fashions and the changing shape of the human body through the ages. Monochrome illustrations from primary sources.

Steele, Valerie. *Fashion and Eroticism: Ideas of Feminine Beauty from the Victorian Era to the Jazz Age.* New York and Oxford: Oxford University Press, 1985. Monochrome illustrations.

Dictionaries, Bibliographies, Encyclopedias, and Reference

Anthony, Pegaret, and Janet Arnold. *Costume: A Bibliography of Costume Books.* London: The Victoria and Albert Museum in association with the Costume Society, 1966. Revised edition, 1974.

Arnold, Janet. *A Handbook of Costume.* London and New York: Macmillan, 1974. A guide to primary sources for costume research.

Baclawski, Karen. *The Guide to Historic Costume.* New York: Drama Book Publishers, 1995.

Alphabetical dictionary/directory of period clothing and accessories. Descriptions, black-and-white photographs and list of museum sources in the U.K.

The Costume Society of America. *A Bibliography of Recent Books Relating to Costume.* New York: The Costume Society of America, 1975.

Cunnington, C. Willett, Phillis Cunnington, and Charles Beard. *A Dictionary of English Costume.* London: Adam and Charles Black, 1960.

Filene, Adele B. *Bibliography.* New York: The Costume Society of America, 1975. Listing of recently published books at that time.

Grun, Bernard. *The Timetables of History: A Horizontal Linkage of People and Events.* New York: A Touchstone Book, Simon and Schuster, 1975. New third revised ed. 1991.

Huenefeld, Irene Pennington. *International Dictionary of Historical Clothing.* Metuchen, NJ: The Scarecrow Press, Inc., 1967. Information on garments in museums and private collections.

Jowers, Sydney Jackson, and John Cavanaugh. *Theatrical Costume, Masks, Make-up and Wigs: A Bibliography and Iconography.* Brighton, England and New York: Brunner-Routledge, 2000. Covers publications through 1996, with some updates to 1998. A comprehensive reference.

Kesler, Jackson. *Theatrical Costume: A Guide to Information Sources.* Vol. 6 in the Performing Arts Information Guide Series. Detroit, MI: Gale Research Company, 1979. Extensive bibliography of costume books in all categories.

Kybalova, Ludmila, Olga Herbenova, and Milena Lamarova. *The Pictorial Encyclopedia of Fashion.* New York: Crown Publishers, 1968.

National Geographic Society. *National Geographic Index 1888–1988.* Washington, D.C.: National Geographic, 1989. Listings by subject and author.

———. *National Geographic Index 1989–1993.* Washington, D.C.: National Geographic, 1994. Listings by subject and author.

———. *National Geographic Index 1994.* Washington, D.C.: National Geographic, 1995. Supplements to main index published annually from 1994.

O'Hara, Georgina. *The Encyclopaedia of Fashion: From 1840 to the 1980s.* London: Thames and Hudson Ltd., 1986. Monochrome illustrations, some color plates.

Picken, Mary Brooks. *A Dictionary of Costume and Fashion: Historic and Modern.* New York: Dover Publications, Inc. Paperbound reprint with illustrations.

Snowden, James. *European Folk Dress: A Bibliography.* London: The Costume Society, 1973.

Trautman, Patricia A. *Clothing America: A Bibliography and Location Index of Nineteenth-Century American Pattern Drafting Systems.* Published by the Costume Society of America, Region II, 1987.

Whalon, Marion K. *Performing Arts Research: A Guide to Information Sources.* Vol. 1 in The Performing Arts Information Guide Series. Detroit, MI: Gale Research Company, 1976. Extensive bibliography covering all aspects of the performing arts.

Wilcox, R. Turner. *The Dictionary of Costume.* New York: Charles Scribner's Sons, 1969.

Wilman, Polly. *Bibliography 1983.* New York: The Costume Society of America, 1983. Lists publications issued between 1979 and 1983.

Yarwood, Doreen. *The Encyclopaedia of World Costume.* New York: Hippocrene Books, 1978.

Miscellaneous

Ackroyd, Peter. *Dressing up. Transvestism and Drag: The History of an Obsession.* London: Thames and Hudson, 1979. Paperbound. With monochrome illustrations. Interesting, informative text.

Forty, George, and Anne Forty. *They Also Served: A Pictorial Anthology of Camp Followers Through the Ages.* Speldhurst, Kent, England: Midas Books, 1979. Pictorial record of entertainers, pets, tradespeople, tailors, correspondents, etc., who traveled with armies over the centuries.

History of Private Life. 4 vols. Cambridge, MA: Harvard University press. Vol. 1: Phillippe Aries, et al., ed. *From Pagan Rome to Byzantium*, 1987; Vol. 2: Georges Duby, ed. *Revelations of the Medieval World*, 1988; Vol. 3: Roger Chartier, et al., ed. *Passions of the Renaissance*, 1989; Vol. 4: Michelle Perrot, et al., ed. *From the Fires of the Revolution to the Great War*, 1990. All translated by Arthur Goldhammer. Excellent, well-illustrated texts.

Hodge, Francis. *Play Directing Analysis Communication and Style.* Englewood Cliffs, NJ: Prentice-Hall, Inc., 1971.

Holroyd, Michael. *The Genius of Shaw.* New York: Holt, Rinehart and Winston, 1979. Monochrome and color illustrations and photographs of Shaw, his life, stage productions, etc.

Hornby, Richard. *Script into Performance: A Structuralist View of Play Production.* Austin, TX, and London: University of Texas Press, 1977.

Ingham, Rosemary. *From Page to Stage: How Theatre Designers Make Connections Between Scripts and Images.* Portsmouth, NH: Heinemann, 1998. Paperbound. Monochrome illustrations and photographs.

Stevenson, Sara, and Helen Bennet. *Van Dyck in Check Trousers: Fancy Dress in Art and Life. 1700–1900.* Edinburgh, Scotland: Scottish National Portrait Gallery, 1978. Catalogue of an exhibition at the gallery. Monochrome and some color illustrations and photographs of fancy dress.

Speaight, George. *The Book of Clowns.* New York: Macmillan Publishing Co., Inc., 1980. Color and some monochrome illustrations and photographs tracing the history of clowning from its early development to present-day circus.

Health and Safety

McCann, Michael. *Artist Beware.* New York: Watson-Guptil Publications, 1979. The hazards and precautions in working with art and craft materials.

Rossol, Monona. *The Artist's Complete Health and Safety Guide. Everything you need to know about art materials to make your workplace safe and comply with United States and Canadian right-to-know laws.* New York: Allworth Press, 1990. 1994, 2nd ed. Covers all categories of artist's materials. Deals with toxicity, precautions, ventilation, protective equipment, chemical and physical hazards, and their control. A comprehensive and invaluable reference.

———. *Stage Fright: Health and Safety in the Theater. A Practical Guide for Everyone in the Performing Arts. The essential Information you need on stage, in the shop, or in the front office to ensure health, safety, and compliance with occupational hazard laws.* New York: Allworth Press, 1986, updated 1991. Covers protective equipment, ventilation, make-up, and hazardous materials; lists information sources.

———. *The Health and Safety Guide for Film, TV, & Theater.* New York: Allworth Press, 2001. The most up-to-date publication for people who work in all areas of the entertainment industry. An essential reference.

Website Information

Look for the regularly updated Shopping Guide/Source list for *The Costume Technician's Handbook* on our website:
http://www.heinemanndrama.com/ingham-covey

Index

About the Authors

Rosemary Ingham is a costume designer and writer. During the past four decades her design work has been seen at the Long Wharf Theatre, the Alley Theatre, the Dallas and Illinois Shakespeare Festivals, the Utah Shakespearean Festival, the Milwaukee Repertory Theater, Arena Stage, Woolly Mammoth Theatre, American Players Theatre, and others. She has served on the theatre faculties of Southern Methodist University and Mary Washington College. She is the author of *From Page to Stage: How Theatre Designers Make Connections Between Texts and Images* and, with Liz Covey, *The Costumer's Handbook, The Costume Technician's Handbook,* and *The Costume Designer's Handbook.* She received her formal education at the University of Montana, the Yale Drama School and St. John's College. Ms. Ingham lives in Fredericksburg, Virginia.

Liz Covey is a freelance costume designer whose work has been seen at America's leading theatres from coast to coast. Born and educated in England, she received her training at the Leicester College of Art and worked at many of the most prestigious theatres in London and the UK before moving to the United States. She has been a member of the faculties of Barnard College/Columbia University, Marymount Manhattan and Bennington College, Vermont and currently lives in Manhattan.

Also by Rosemary Ingham and Elizabeth Covey

THE COSTUME DESIGNER'S HANDBOOK
A Complete Guide for Amateur and Professional Costume Designers

Every craft and trade has its bible, and *The Costume Designer's Handbook* is exactly that. Anyone seriously interested in the practice of costume design should have this book.

In this new and expanded edition the authors take us from the designer's first reading of the play through pre-production to dress rehearsals to opening night. Their discussion of the business of costume design is coherent and comprehensive, including discussions of entering the job market, portfolios and resumes, freelancing and working in-house, and much more. Features of this new edition include:

- reading and analyzing a play
- establishing a costume plot
- working with directors and other designers
- research
- sketching, drawing, and drafting techniques
- the designer's workplace and selection of media for the final sketches
- art supplies and what to look for when shopping for them
- what the designer's responsibilities are during the pre-production and production periods
- the business of costume design
- 141 black and white photographs, drawings, and charts
- 8-page color insert
- complete, up to date reference section including a bibliography as well as a source list for art supplies, books, materials, and fabrics.

The Costume Designer's Handbook remains the most practical and complete book in its field. No professional or aspiring amateur can do without it.

0-435-08607-3   294 pages   illustrated   paperback

For more information or to save 10%, order your copy of
The Costume Designer's Handbook online at www.heinemanndrama.com.